Morton's Potteries: 99 Years

Volume II

1877-1976

By Doris and Burdell Hall

A historical sketch, product identification
and value guide for the Morton Potteries.

ISBN# 0-89538-028-5

Published by: L-W Book Sales
PO Box 69
Gas City, IN 46933

Please write for our free catalog.

Attention Collectors . . . if you would like to contribute photographs or information of your collection (possibly for profit), please call L-W Books (toll free) at 1-800-777-6450 Tuesday thru Friday 9am to 3pm EST.

BACK COVER INFORMATION: Rock gardens with fish ponds and lily pools were popular during the 1930's. Morton Pottery Company created this fish to use as a fountain. It is 8" tall and is hollow in order to fit over the pump.
Value Range: $15-20

FRONT COVER INFORMATION: Listed inside this book.

Table of Contents

Title Page . . . 1
Table of Contents . . . 3-5
Biographical information about the authors . . . 6
Dedication . . . 6
Acknowledgments & Pricing Note . . . 7

Part I
Rapp Brothers Brick and Tile Company . . . 8-11
Morton Brick and Tile Company . . . 11
Morton Pottery Works . . . 12
Morton Earthenware Company . . . 10
Introduction . . . 10-11
Marks . . . 8-9
Historic photographs . . . 10-13
Invoice/balance sheet . . . 13
Glaze formulas . . . 14

Chapter 1
Historical Sketch . . . 15-18

Chapter 2
Catalog No. 9 reprint with values . . . 19-27
Assortment #1 reprint with values . . . 28
Agate Rockingham reprint with values . . . 29
Dealer opportunity reprint with values . . . 27

Chapter 3
Photographs with values
Kitchenware . . . 30-33
Novelties . . . 34-36
Utility Ware . . . 37

Part II
Cliftwood Art Potteries, Incorporated
Introduction . . . 38
Marks . . . 38-39
Historic photographs . . . 40-42
Advertising samples . . . 43-45

Chapter 4
Historical Sketch . . . 46-50

Chapter 5
Catalog reprints with values . . . 51-94
Portfolio of lamp shapes . . . 95-97

Chapter 6
Photographs with values
Beverage service . . . 98-99
Candle sticks and clocks . . . 100
Dinnerware/Kitchenware . . . 101-103
Figurines . . . 104-109
Flower bowls and inserts . . . 110-111
Lamps . . . 112-114

Radio speakers . . . 115
Tree Trunk Line . . . 116-117
Vases . . . 118-124

Part III Midwest Potteries, Incorporated
Introduction . . . 124
Marks . . . 124
Historic photographs . . . 125, 127
Legal papers . . . 126-127
W-2 Form . . . 125

Chapter 7 Historical Sketch . . . 128-130
Chapter 8 Photographs with values
Figurines . . . 131-140
Kron Line TV Lamps . . . 141
Masks . . . 142
Miniatures . . . 143
Novelties . . . 144-145
Planters . . . 146-148
Shadow lamp . . . 149

Part IV American Art Potteries
Introduction . . . 150
Marks . . . 150
Historic photographs . . . 150-151
W2 statement . . . 151

Chapter 9 Historical Sketch . . . 152-153

Chapter 10 Photographs with values
Dolls . . . 154
Figurines . . . 155-156
Flower bowls and Flower frogs . . . 157
Lamps . . . 158
Novelties . . . 159
Planters . . . 160-162
Vases . . . 163
Wall pockets . . . 164

Part V Morton Pottery Company
Introduction . . . 165
Historic photographs . . . 166-167
Service pin . . . 167
Manufacturing flow sheet . . . 168
Marks . . . 169-172
Chapter 11 Historical Sketch . . . 173-182

Chapter 12 Rapp Artcraft Catalog reprint with values 183-188
Lamp portfolio with values 189-191
Mailers with values 192-194
Mailer Map with freight information 195
Sales Leaflet reprints with values
Flower holders and Book Ends 196
Holiday Novelties 197-198
Mother Earth Fruit and Vegetable Plant Growers 199-200
Novelty Planters 201-204
Novelty Plant Holders 205-207
Novelty Spoon Holders 208
Pitcher and Bowl sets 209
Vases 210-211

Chapter 13 Pilgrim ware price list with values 212-213
Amish pottery catalog reprint with values 214-217
Amish pottery sales leaflets with values 218-221
Decorated Amish pottery with values 222-223

Chapter 14 Photographs with values
Animals 224-226
Banks 227-228
Birds 229-230
Children's Miniatures 231
Cookie Jars 232-233
Holiday Novelties, Christmas 234-235
Holiday Novelties, Easter. 236-237
Flower Holders and Vases 238-240
Functional Items 241
Grass Growers 242-247
Kitchenware 248-249
Lamps 250-251
Lamps, Planter Bases 252
Lamps, TV 253
Vincent Price - Sears National Treasurers Collection 254-255
Novelties 256
Pie Vents 257
Political Memorabilia 258-259
Wall Hangers 260
Western Americana 261-263
Woodland Pottery 264-267
Woodland Pottery variations 268-269
Unclassified Miscellaneous 270-271
Epilogue 272

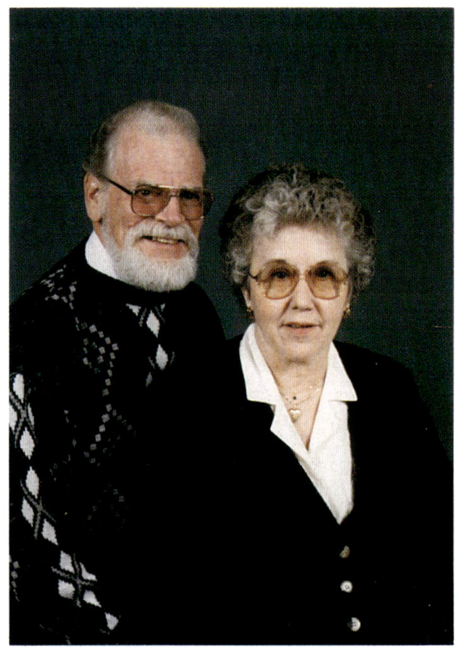

Burdell and Doris Hall

ABOUT THE AUTHORS

Burdell and Doris have collected "Morton Pottery" since their marriage, August 20, 1948. Burdell had worked at the Cliftwood Art Pottery before serving in World War II, so he had a few prized items at the time they were wed. During the past forty-six years, their collection has grown to include examples from all of the potteries that operated in Morton.

The Halls published Morton's Potteries: 99 Years in 1980. They have contributed numerous articles to pottery oriented journals and publications, and serve as advisors for three popular price guides.

Burdell was a high school social studies teacher, and Doris worked for many years as a bookkeeper/cashier. Today, they are antiques and collectibles dealers at the Pleasant Hill Antique Mall and Tea Room in East Peoria, Illinois. In their retirement, they divide their time between Morton, Illinois and Fairfield Bay, Arkansas. They have two sons, a loving daughter-in-law, two grandchildren, and Li'l Pepper, a Schnauzer that doesn't know he is a dog.

DEDICATION

Our family of pottery friends and associates is so vast that it is impossible to name them all in this dedication, but you know who you are. We dedicate this second volume of Morton's Potteries: 99 Years to you since you are the motivating force that has made our years of research both rewarding and worthwhile. We consider you family because we all have glaze in our veins, and an insatiable desire to become more knowledgeable about the American pottery industry.

ACKNOWLEDGMENTS

It would be impossible for us to mention all of the people who have encouraged us to expand our research and write a second volume relating to the pottery industry in Morton. We are indeed indebted to each of you who have asked, "When are you going to do another book on Morton?" We have responded to your many queries, and to each of you we say thanks.

We need to thank Neil and Scott Wood of L-W Book Sales for accepting our book proposal, and giving us the opportunity to complete this work.

Our heartfelt thanks must go to the following editors for allowing us the opportunity to serve on their advisory boards and thus force us to continually study and be aware of the fluctuating values in the collectibles market of "Morton Pottery":

Harvey Duke. Official Identification and Price Guide to Pottery and Porcelain.

Bob and Sharon Huxford. Schroeder's Antiques Price Guide.

Harry Rinker. Warman's Americana & Collectibles.

Jo Cunningham has been our mentor from the time that writing about Morton's potteries was just a figment of our imagination. She encouraged us to go for it, gave us help with the first book, and has continued to encourage us to this point. How can we thank you enough, Jo?

Susan Cox, editor of The American Clay Exchange, gave us an opportunity to write for her publication early on. When we asked to use some of her copyrighted articles to enhance our material on Vincent Price and his relationship with Sears Roebuck and Company, she was most gracious when granting permission.

The family of Samuel W. Rapp Jr., one of the owners of Morton Earthenware Company, and later, The Morton Pottery Company, gave us his files. From those files, we have been able to authenticate examples of Morton pottery from the catalogs and sales leaflets he had collected. Our gratitude to them is immeasurable.

We continue to get calls and letters from all parts of the country requesting information not found in our first book. To you we also are thankful for showing us that there is still a need for new information.

Last, but certainly not least, we want to acknowledge the many Morton pottery collectors who have made themselves known to us, and who have shared their precious treasures with us.

PRICING NOTE

The current values in this book should be used only as a guide. They are not intended to set prices, which vary from one section of the country to another. Auction prices as well as dealer prices vary greatly and are affected by condition as well as demand. Neither the author nor the publisher assumes responsibility for any losses that might be incurred as a result of consulting this guide.

*** ND – If ND is used as a value of any piece, this means that the price is not determined by the author.**

PART I

Rapp Brothers Brick and Tile Company 1877-1915

Morton Brick and Tile Company 1915-1936

Morton Pottery Works 1878-1915

Morton Earthenware Company 1915-1917

Each of these business entities were at the same location on Penn Street at the foot of Clifton Street, adjacent to the Penn-Central Railroad tracks on the south side of Morton. Name changes indicate management/ownership. Wares produced during those forty years of operation were common to all four of the companies.

The following are the only known marks used during that time span. It was very uncommon to mark products because they were primarily intended for local consumption. Little did the Rapps realize that a century later their products would be collectible.

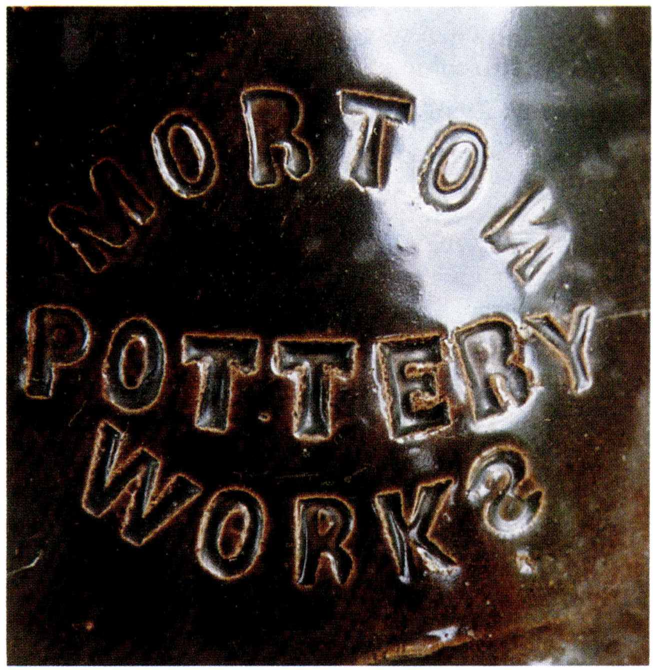

Mark #1 - This mark is usually found on the side of crocks, churns, and other food storage containers. The N and S are always reversed.

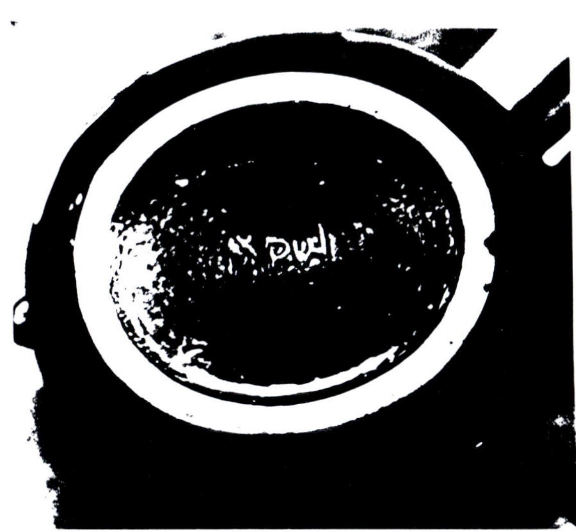

Mark #2 - The MPW mark is most frequently found on the bottom of large jugs. It is not molded, instead, it appears to be Albany slip that has been hand applied with a syringe, a method known as slip trailing.

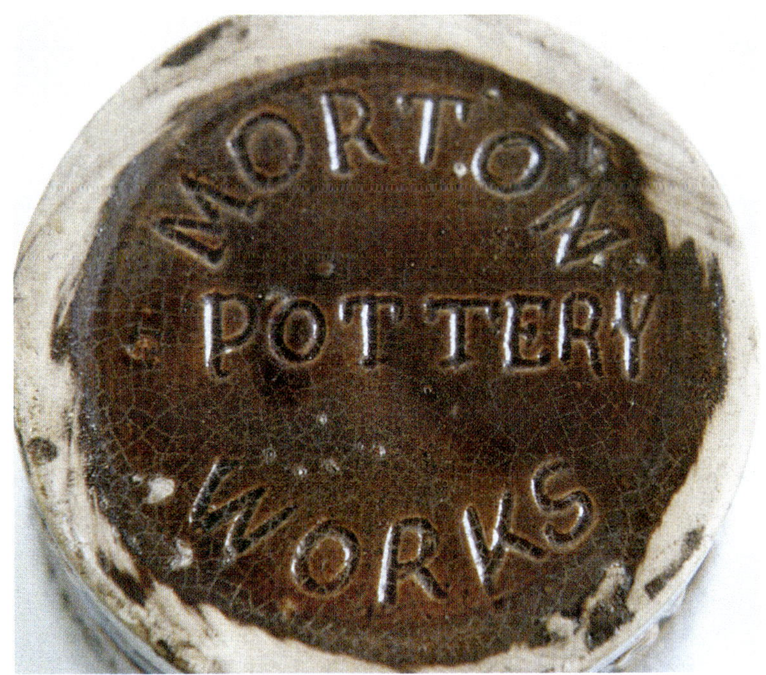

Mark #3 - This mark is more finely impressed than mark #1, and the N and S are never reversed. This mark infrequently appears on the bottom of the "Klar Ist" beer stein.

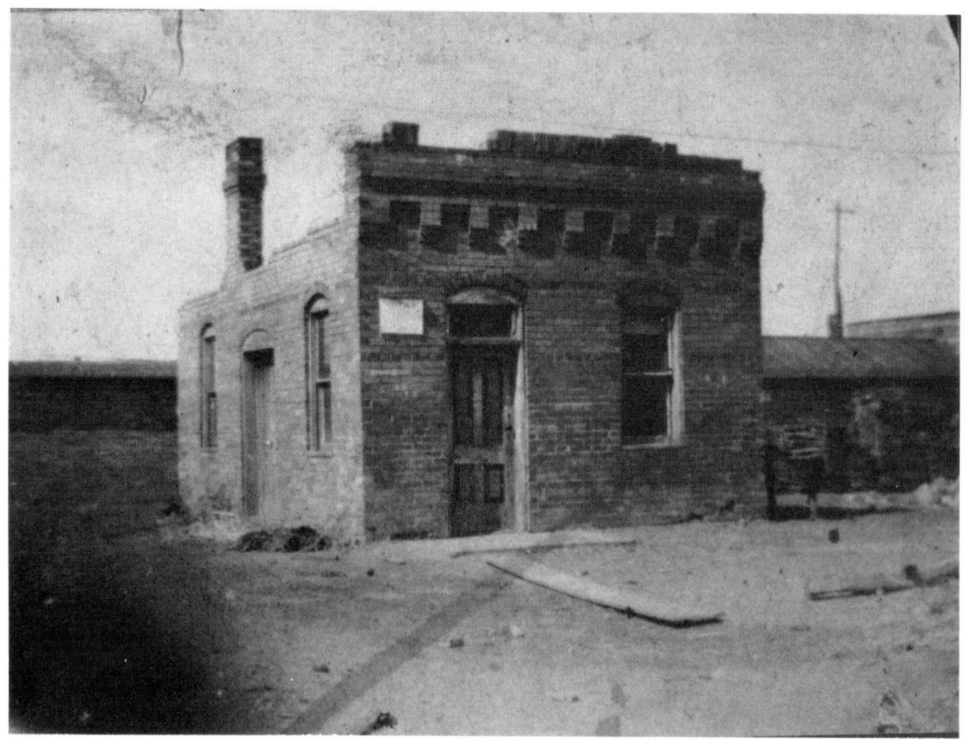

This is the office of the tile company and the pottery. It was later incorporated into the addition that was built to expand the pottery operation. Photograph courtesy of Geraldine Rapp Carius.

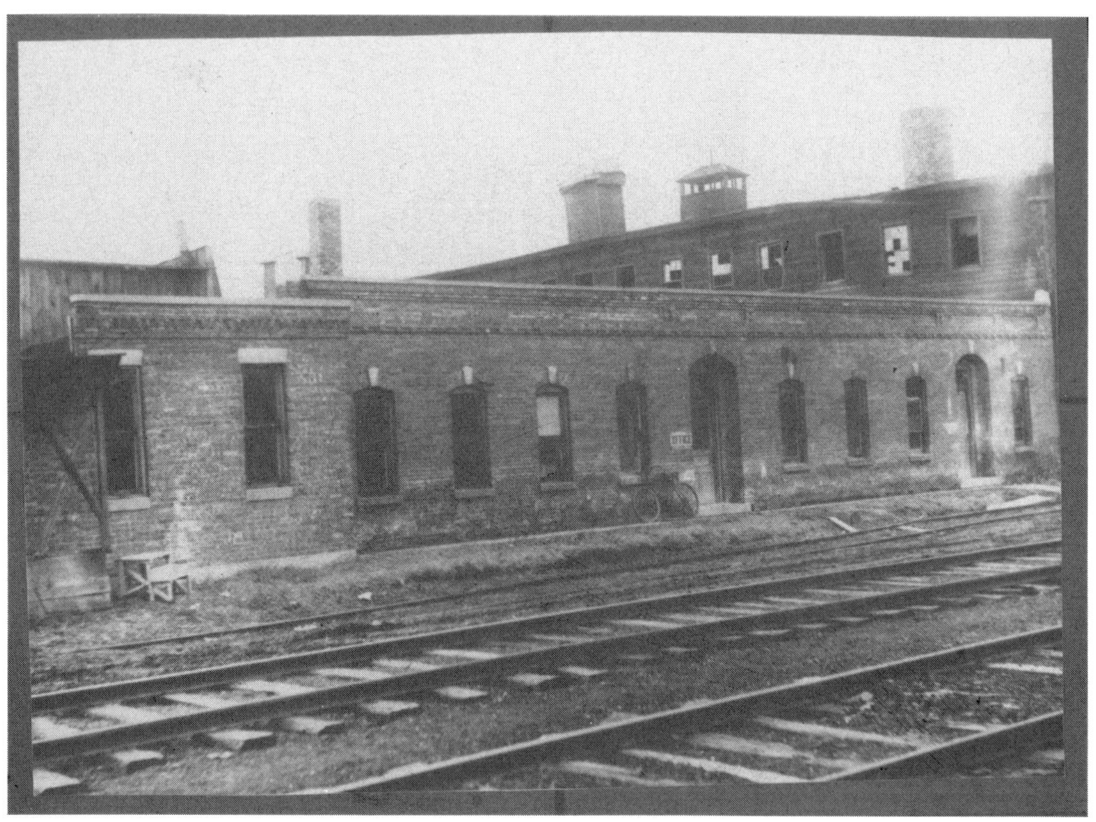

This photograph shows the office, on the left, protruding from the wing that was added to expand the pottery and tie it into the tile factory. This wing housed Rapp Brothers Pottery, the Morton Earthenware Company, and later, the Cliftwood Art Potteries, and the Midwest Potteries Incorporated, in that order. Photograph from the R.C. Conibear Collection, Morton Public Library.

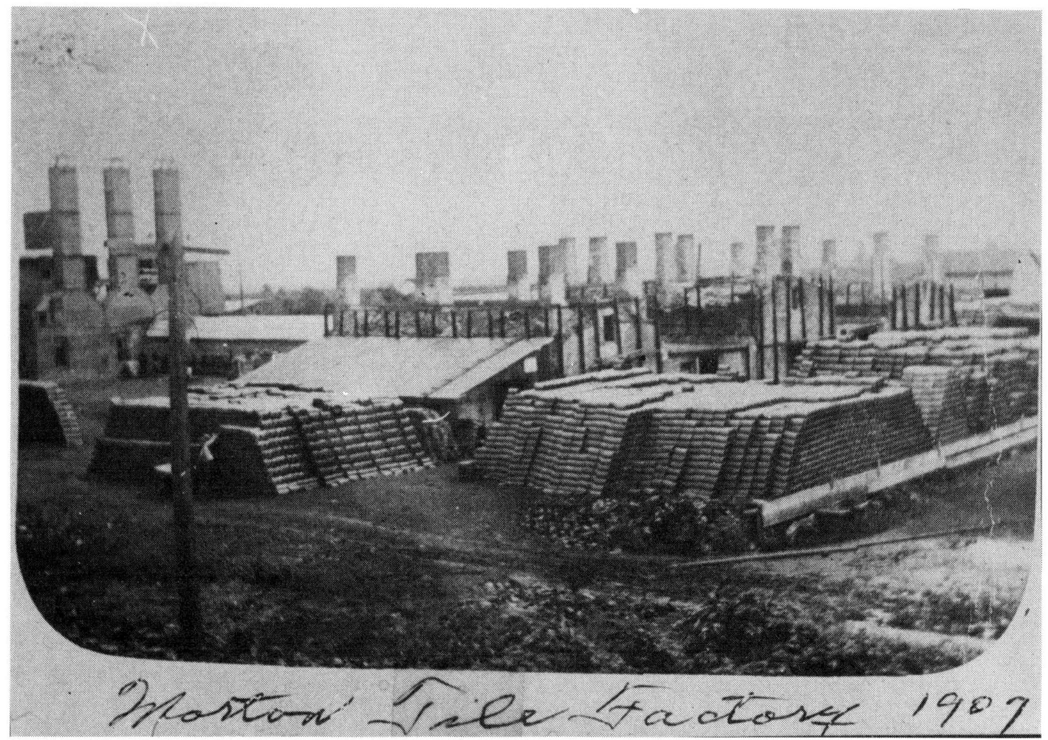

This is one of the earliest known photographs of the Rapp Brothers Brick and Tile Company. The pottery works can be seen to the far right, behind the stacks of tile. Photograph from the R.C. Conibear Collection, Morton Public Library.

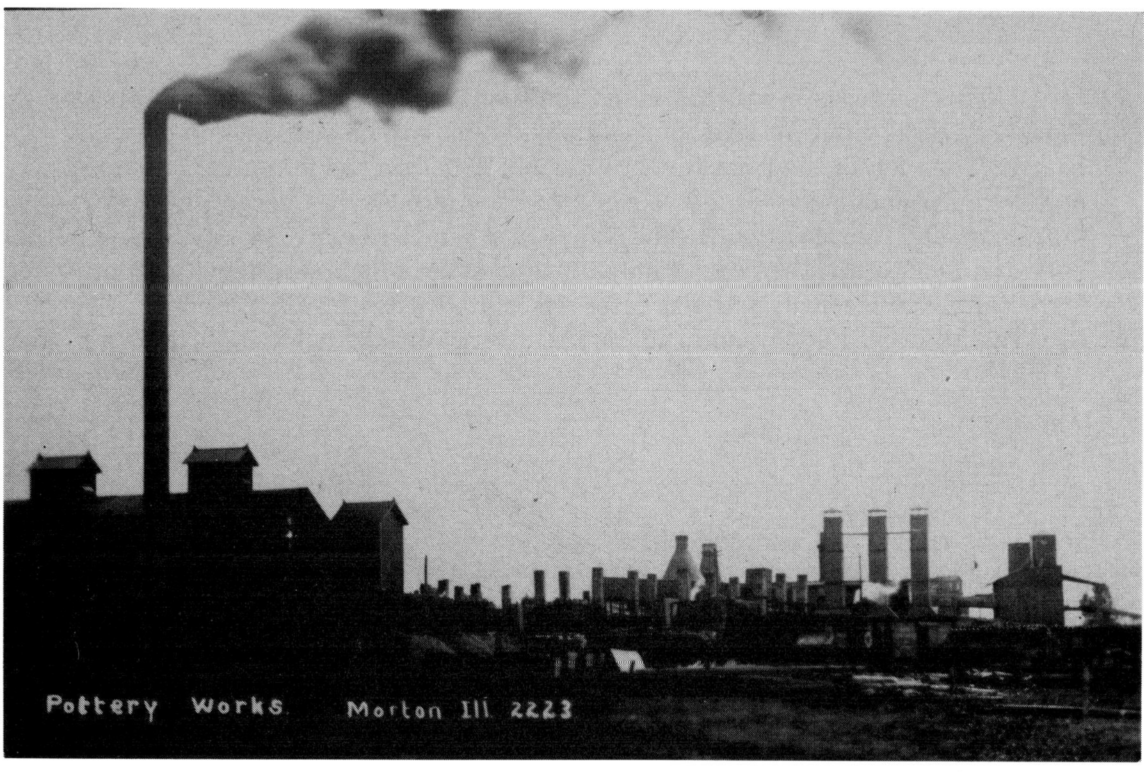

This photograph of the pottery dates to the turn of the century. The tile factory is on the right side of the photo, the pottery in the center, and the power plant is on the left. Note the piles of raw clay to the left, and the stack of field tile in the center. The two beehive kilns are visible in the center of the photograph directly beyond the tile. Two freight cars are at the dock ready to be loaded with tile for shipment. Photograph from the R.C. Conibear Collection, Morton Public Library.

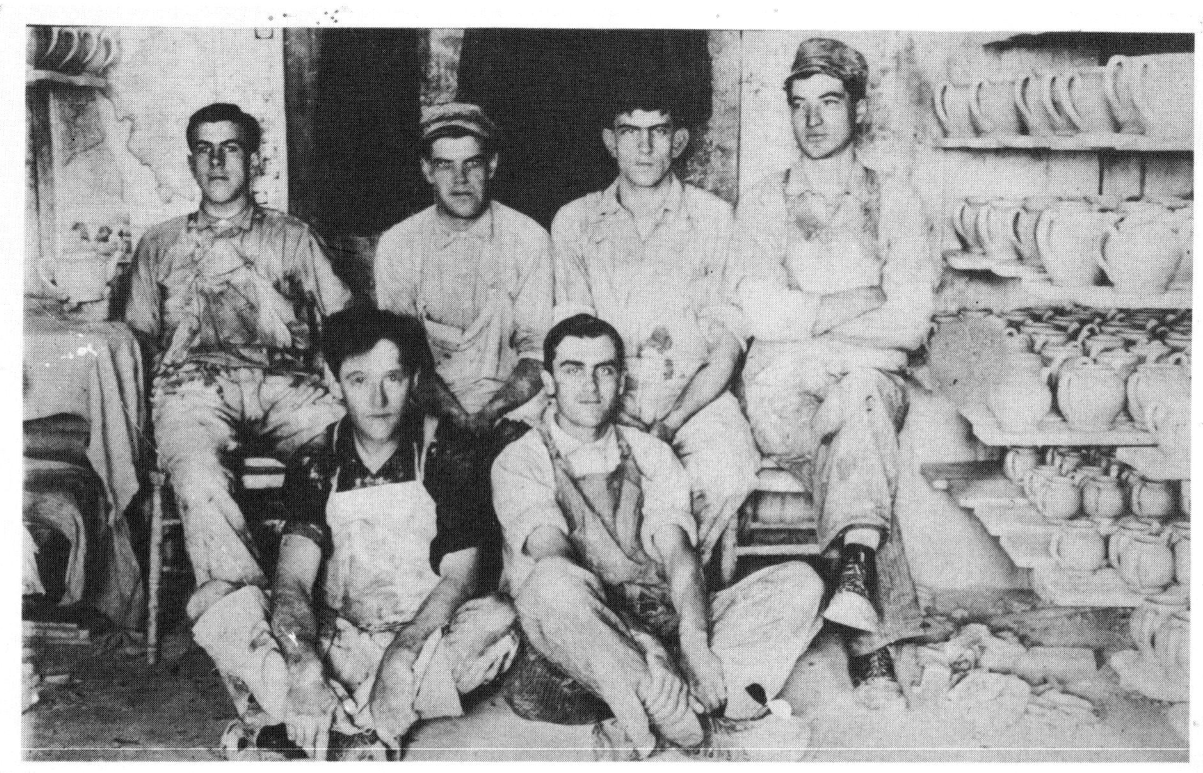

This photograph was taken in the finishing room at the Morton Pottery Works. Several different sizes of the globe teapot can be seen on the carrying boards. The men in the front row are Siebolt Kruse on the left, and Carl Rapp on the right. The back row, left to right, are Samuel Rapp, George Rapp, William Rapp, and George Binkele. The Rapps in the back row are the brothers who operated Morton Earthenware Company, and later, Morton Pottery Company. Carl Rapp was a cousin and was later associated with the Cliftwood Art Pottery, the Midwest Pottery, and the American Art Pottery.

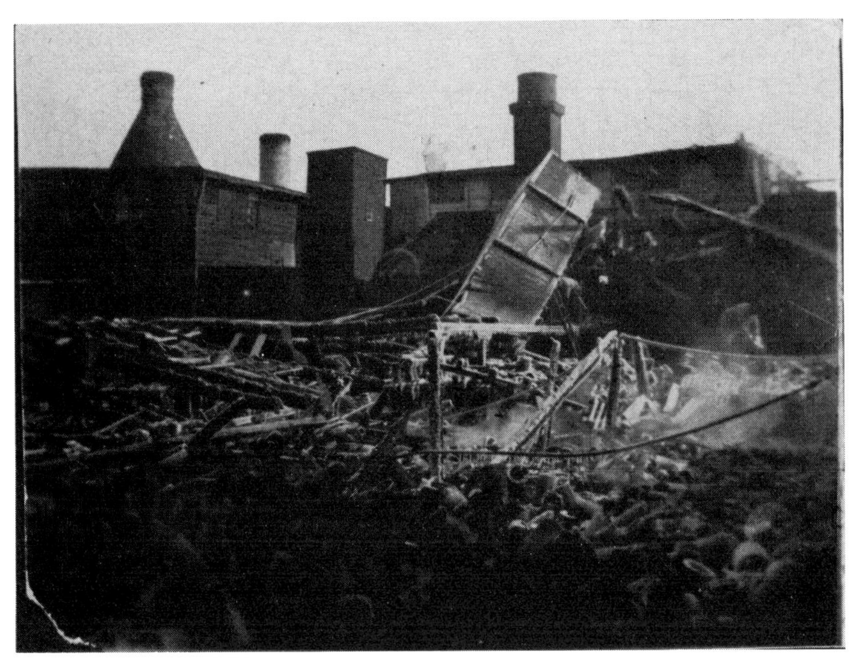

This photograph shows the tile factory the morning after the fire that destroyed it in January, 1910.

Rapp Brothers Morton, Ill. 19

Manufacturers of

Drain Tile and Brick

M...

....

Gentlemen: We enclose you herewith our check No. .... for $ .... in payment of following invoices:

Date		Description of Article	Invoice		Discount		Freight		Net	

Tile Factory

Power Plant	3000.
Office	250.
Bldg. Office, Mchy	100.
Machinery	1200.
Drier + Cars	7500.
Kilns (500)	1500.
Stock	1000.
Crusher + Motor	500.
Trestle Work + Cars	500.
Book accts.	500.
Real Estate (Plant)	3000.
do (Hale)	3000.
Raw Material	100.
	22,150.

Liabilities

Dist Notes	5000
[illegible]	600.54
	5600.54

Resources	22,150.
Liabilities	5600.54
	16549.46

The Rapp invoice above, is not dated. However, there is a crude, hand written balance sheet on the back showing tile factory assets of $22,150 and liabilities of $5600.54, leaving a balance of $16,549.46.

White Crystal Glaze
#1

Spar 32 Lbs.
Whiting 3 "
Zinc 4 " 20
E. Clay 6. "
Flint 3 " 14
Salt 1 "
Tin 3 "
Lead 16 "

White Bristol

Spar 55 1/4 #
Flint 2 #
Flordia China 50 1/3 #
English Ball 2 #
Whiting 2 1/2 #
Zinc oxide 5 1/4 #
Borax 1 3/4 "

#20

Old Rock Glaze

White Lead 50 #
Spar 14 #
Flint 15 #
Clay 5 #
Whiting 8 #
Maganese 10 #

With 5 Buckets Water.

Ivory Glaze

Spar 15 #
Flint 10 #
Kaolin 4 #
Whiting 3 #
Barytes 2 1/2 #

These glaze formulas are interesting. Only one indicates the amount of water to use with the basic ingredients. It does not state the size of bucket to be used, however.

CHAPTER 1

Historical Sketch
1877-1917

The Rapp Brothers Brick Company was the first clay operation to be established in Morton, Illinois. In 1877, when the plant opened, the primary emphasis was on brick manufacturing. Morton was booming at that time and there was a great demand for building brick which was in short supply.

Andrew, Barthol, and Christian, three of the six Rapp brothers, had emigrated to the United States from southern Germany in 1874 to escape military service. They settled on a farm near Forrest, Illinois. In 1975, the entire Rapp family, father, mother, three more brothers, and three sisters joined them at that rural Forrest location. Andrew and Barthol soon tired of farm work and left to become itinerant masons. Eventually they settled in Morton. Realizing the scarcity of building brick in central Illinois, the two brothers concluded that they could make more money manufacturing brick than they could laying them. They built a crude brick making machine and a kiln on land they acquired at the south side of town along the Penn-Central railroad tracks. They operated their business with a slim margin of profit, but they were providing a much needed service to Morton.

At the time that this new business began, Morton Township was situated on low, swampy land that could not be easily farmed. Andrew and Barthol conceived the idea that their business should be expanded to include the manufacturing of field drainage tile. They encouraged their brothers John, Christian, Samuel, and Matthew, who were still on the farm near Forrest, to join them in their business venture at Morton. A partnership was set up and would be known as Rapp Brothers Brick and Tile Company. All of the brothers had worked with clay as their trade in Germany. Perhaps that accounts for the success they met with from the beginning of their clay products operation in their new locale.

During the early years, the company manufactured its products with horse powered machinery invented by Barthol. Soon a second kiln was built in order to fire more brick and tile. As farmers and contractors came for brick and drainage tile, their wives and other towns-women would express their need for mixing bowls and other utility items that were not easily available to them. Heeding those demands, a second operation was set in motion at the brick and tile location. The true pottery business was brought to Morton and would be known as the Morton Pottery Works, or Rapp Brothers Pottery Works. Both names have been found on invoices and in advertising. This order sheet was set up so it could be used for either of the Rapp Brothers' operations. The two businesses operated as separate, but shared facilities.

As production increased, the brothers divided their work load so that each developed his own speciality. Andrew was in charge of the office and sales. Barthol was head of the brick and tile operation which he moved to East Peoria, Illinois in 1936. John managed the kilns and supervised the manufacture of sagger boxes. Christian was the fireman and engineer. His task was to maintain even firing temperatures in the kilns. Samuel supervised the glazing process at the pottery, and Matthew created the designs and made the plaster molds used to cast the greenware. Matthew also experimented with wheel thrown originals, but mass produced cast ware was far more profitable, so he seldom worked at the potter's wheel.

ORDER SHEET

RAPP BROTHERS

Manufacturers of Earthenware

MORTON, ILLINOIS

☞ We will send you more Order Sheets if wanted.

Ship to ....

Town and State: ....

Quantity	No.	Description.	Dol.	Cts.	Quantity	No.	Description.	Dol.	Cts.
							TOTAL:		

For which amount find enclosed { *Money Order* / *Bank Draft* } $ ....

Sign here: ....

Shown here is a reduced copy of an order sheet used by the Rapp Brothers. The original size of this sheet was 6 1/4" x 11 3/4".

In January, 1910, the tile works was destroyed by a fire that started in the drying room near the kilns. The fire rapidly spread to the side walls and the low rubberoid roof, then continued toward the pottery. It took nearly three hours to bring the fire under control and save the pottery from being destroyed. The firefighters remained at the scene all night long and occasionally hosed down new bursts of flames. The following morning the Rapp brothers and their employees set about cleaning up the debris so the tile works could be rebuilt immediately. In rebuilding, the wooden pillars and girders were replaced with steel, and a concrete roof was used rather than the rubberoid tile. Because so many of the iron dummy cars had been destroyed by the fire, the Rapps decided to use steel cars in the new operation. The local newspaper, in reporting the building progress, stated "this plan will give them proof against fire in the future and make it the best and most tile plant in the state if not in the entire west."

Though the pottery was not damaged, electrical lines were cut during the conflagaration and had to be repaired. Only one day of production was lost. The following expression of gratitude to those who had worked so hard fighting the fire was placed in the Morton News on January 13, 1910:

> "We feel in our hearts that the fire department, the town officials and the villagers in general have done us a great service in their successful efforts of saving our pottery from destruction by fire when the tile works was burning last Thursday night. We desire to publicly express our thanks, our gratitude, and great appreciation to you one and all for the timely and heroic assistance, and we assure you our feeling is deep seated and comes from the heart. To our farmer friends and others who cheerfully came Friday to aid us in cleaning up the ruins of the destroyed building, we tender our heartfelt thanks.
>
> Sincerely, Rapp Brothers."

Despite efforts to fireproof the new building, fires would continue to plague the tile works. On July 13, 1922, two fires broke out. At nine o'clock that evening, a fire was discovered in the roof that connected the two kilns. It was extinguished quickly with little damage to the roof. However, around midnight, the fire erupted a second time. In each case, the fire was on the roof between the first and second kiln. The roof was old and the lumber supporting it was beginning to decay. Its primary purpose was to provide shade for those who stoked the furnace in the kiln area when coal was used as fuel. After 1910 fire, natural gas was used to fire the kilns, so the roof was no longer a necessity and it was not replaced. As was the case in 1910, the pottery portion of the business was not damaged by the fire.

During the nineteen twenties, the tile works struggled to stay in business. The old buildings were torn down in December, 1922 after being sold to A. E. Gerber. Equipment that was serviceable was moved across town to the location of a new pottery (see Morton Pottery Company). Loss of the buildings did not stop the production of tile, but did slow it down considerably. At times, the operation was shut down completely. This account in the Morton News on August 10, 1923 alludes to the company's difficulties. "The Morton Brick and Tile Works has been operating during the last week with four persons being employed, and they will be ready to fill a kiln within the next few days. Samuel Rapp states that they plan to make tile until cold weather to fill the orders which he has."

After weathering the Great Depression, the destiny of the tile works was finalized at the end of June, 1936. It was destroyed by still another fire which was discovered about noon on Thursday, June 25th. The fire originated in a rubbish heap that had been left unattended at the rear of the factory. It ignited weeds, and spread rapidly to the buildings.

The fire was out of control by the time fire fighting equipment arrived. Flames were spreading toward the pottery building. Realizing that there was no hope of saving the tile factory, the fireman directed their attention to the pottery where flames were already burning the west side of the building. A stream of chemicals was played upon the wall and the flames were extinguished before causing any serious damage. The tile factory was completely destroyed except for a small storage warehouse and a small office building near the kilns. Though the loss was partially covered by insurance, the tile works was not rebuilt this time.

By the time the tile works was burned out for the last time, the pottery operation had undergone several changes in ownership and management. From its beginning as the Morton Pottery Works, or Rapp Brothers Pottery Works, the pottery had produced lines of yellow ware and Rockingham ware. As the pottery business grew, so did the Rapp Brothers' families. They trained their sons and daughters in the art of pottery making. As a result of that training, all pottery operations in Morton can be traced back to the original six Rapp brothers who brought the art to that community.

In 1915, a major reorganization took place. Andrew Rapp had died in 1911. The remaining five brothers tried to carry on both the tile and pottery business, but experienced numerous set backs. John retired because of poor health. Matthew left the pottery to design for a local farm machinery manufacturer. Barthol broke from the clan and established the Rapp Clay Products Company on Cole Street in East Peoria. That left Samuel and Christian with the responsibility for the Morton operation which they renamed Morton Brick and Tile Company. Four of Andrew's sons approached their uncles and offered to take over the pottery operation. An agreement was signed, and the four second generation Rapp brothers assumed operation of the pottery after renaming it the Morton Earthenware Company. They continued to use the name Rapp Brothers in their promotional materials, therefore, much confusion has developed in trying to separate the older wares from the newer ones produced by the nephews. Because they used the same molds and glaze formulas, establishing certainties is most difficult.

Morton Earthenware Company was in operation for only two years in 1915 and 1916. All production ceased from 1917-1920. During World War I, many employees were drafted or enlisted in the armed forces. Raw materials were nearly impossible to procure because of their diversion to the war effort. With shortages in both manpower and material the pottery closed down.

Three of John Rapp's sons used one of the buildings for experimental art pottery development during the war. They took their art pottery manufactory to Evanston, Illinois in 1920. There they were closer to raw material sources and it was near a more sophisticated market. That art pottery operation was short lived because the brothers took off to Oregon to pan for gold.

The Rapp Brothers Pottery did not reopen after the war. As it sat idle, Samuel and Christian struggled to keep the tile works, now known as Morton Tile Works, in operation. In 1920, Matthew decided to leave his work in farm machinery and return to the pottery. Matthew and his four sons, renovated the old structure and started their new business which they named Cliftwood Art Potteries.

CHAPTER 2

Catalog No. 9 is reproduced in its entirety on the following pages. Current **values** will be found at the bottom of each page.

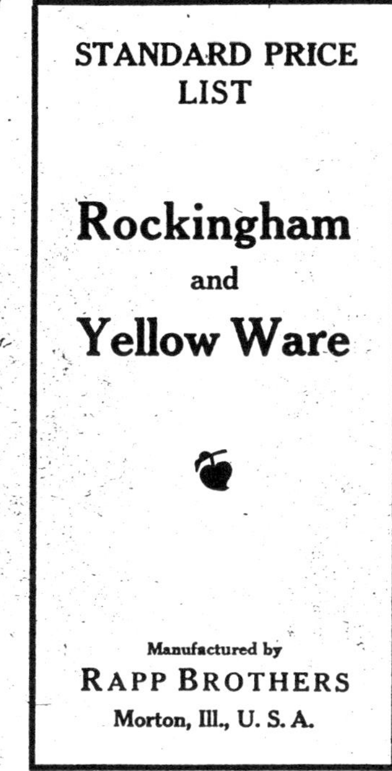

STANDARD PRICE LIST

Rockingham and Yellow Ware

Manufactured by
RAPP BROTHERS
Morton, Ill., U. S. A.

EARTHENWARE

Catalogue
No. 9

Manufactured by
RAPP BROTHERS
MORTON, ILL.

To the Trade

In compiling this catalogue we have tried to make it practical as a help in ordering.

Confusion and delay can be avoided by referring to sizes in left hand column – not to actual measurements.

We earnestly solicit your inquiries which will always have our best and prompt attention.

Yours respectfully,

RAPP BROTHERS,

Exclusive Manufacturers of Earthenware.

Terms of Sale

Net cash, by sight draft on Chicago, within thirty days from invoice dates. Accounts overdue will be liable to a draft at sight, with interest added and exchange on Chicago without further notice.

Goods delivered at the Vandalia Line or Atchison, Topeka & Santa Fe R. R. in this place, and receipts taken, after which our responsibility ceases and transporation companies become responsible for their safe carriage.

Our ware, being put up by experienced packers, in the most careful manner, we make no allowance for breakage, bills of lading being guarantee insured if desired. Packages charged for at net cost.

All orders, or parts of orders, good unless countermanded before shipment.

Packages

No. 0 Cask $2.00
No. 1 Cask 1.75
No. 2 Cask 1.60
No. 3 Cask 1.50
No. 4 Cask 1.40
No. 5 Cask 1.25
No. 6 Cask 1.10
No. 7 Cask 1.00
14 B Crates 2.25
12 B Crates 2.00
10 B Crates 1.75
8 B Crates 1.25
Large Barrels .... .40
Small Barrels .... .25

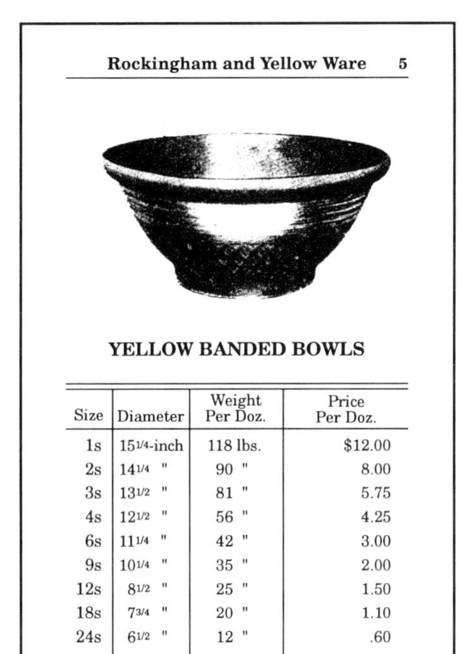

YELLOW BANDED BOWLS

Size	Diameter	Weight Per Doz.	Price Per Doz.
1s	15 1/4-inch	118 lbs.	$12.00
2s	14 1/4 "	90 "	8.00
3s	13 1/2 "	81 "	5.75
4s	12 1/2 "	56 "	4.25
6s	11 1/4 "	42 "	3.00
9s	10 1/4 "	35 "	2.00
12s	8 1/2 "	25 "	1.50
18s	7 3/4 "	20 "	1.10
24s	6 1/2 "	12 "	.60
30s	6 "	10 "	.50
36s	5 1/4 "	7 "	.40
42s	4 1/2 "	6 "	.35

Page 5
1s –**$125** 2s –**$100** 3s –**$90** 4s –**$80** 6s –**$70** 9s –**$60**
12s–**$55** 18s–**$50** 24s–**$45** 30s–**$40** 36s–**$35** 42s–**$30**

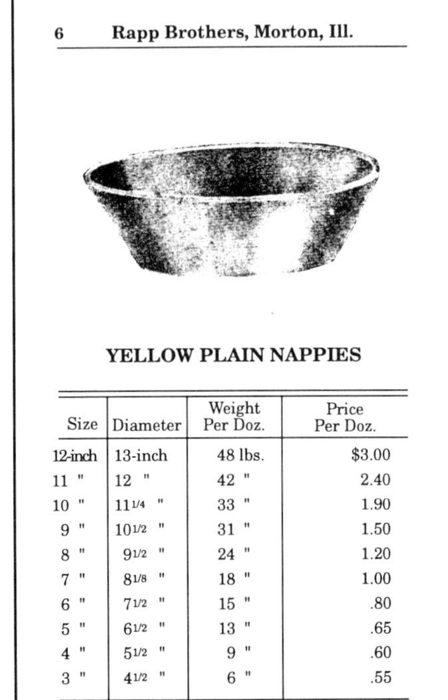

YELLOW PLAIN NAPPIES

Size	Diameter	Weight Per Doz.	Price Per Doz.
12-inch	13-inch	48 lbs.	$3.00
11 "	12 "	42 "	2.40
10 "	11 1/4 "	33 "	1.90
9 "	10 1/2 "	31 "	1.50
8 "	9 1/2 "	24 "	1.20
7 "	8 1/8 "	18 "	1.00
6 "	7 1/2 "	15 "	.80
5 "	6 1/2 "	13 "	.65
4 "	5 1/2 "	9 "	.60
3 "	4 1/2 "	6 "	.55

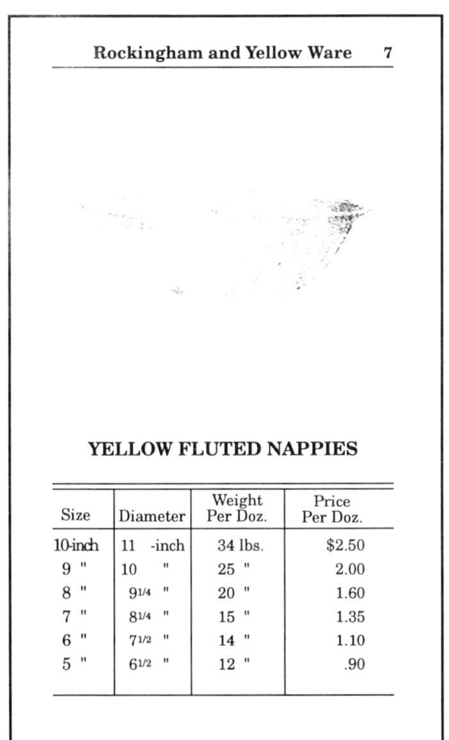

YELLOW FLUTED NAPPIES

Size	Diameter	Weight Per Doz.	Price Per Doz.
10-inch	11 -inch	34 lbs.	$2.50
9 "	10 "	25 "	2.00
8 "	9 1/4 "	20 "	1.60
7 "	8 1/4 "	15 "	1.35
6 "	7 1/2 "	14 "	1.10
5 "	6 1/2 "	12 "	.90

Page 6
12 inch-**$80** 11 inch-**$70** 10 inch-**$60**
9 inch-**$50** 8 inch-**$40** 7 inch-**$36**
6 inch-**$32** 5 inch-**$28** 4 inch-**$24**
3 inch-**$20**

Page 7
10 inch-**$75** 9 inch-**$65** 8 inch-**$55**
7 inch-**$50** 6 inch-**$45** 5 inch-**$40**

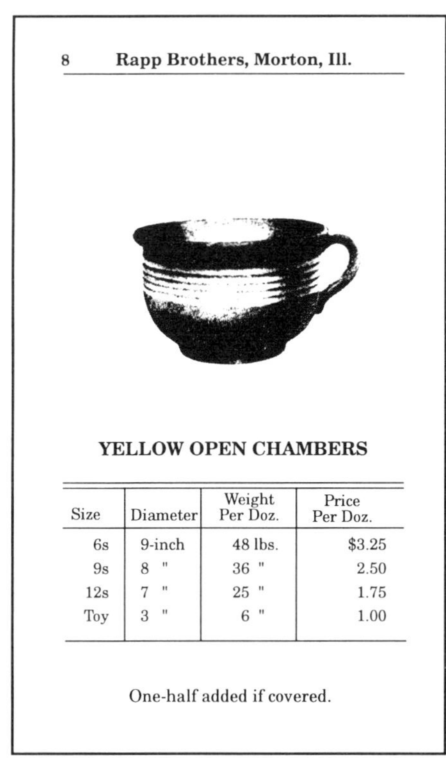
8 Rapp Brothers, Morton, Ill.

YELLOW OPEN CHAMBERS

Size	Diameter	Weight Per Doz.	Price Per Doz.
6s	9-inch	48 lbs.	$3.25
9s	8 "	36 "	2.50
12s	7 "	25 "	1.75
Toy	3 "	6 "	1.00

One-half added if covered.

Page 8

6s–**$60** 9s–**$55** 12s–**$50** Toy–**$75**

(Add 50% if covered)

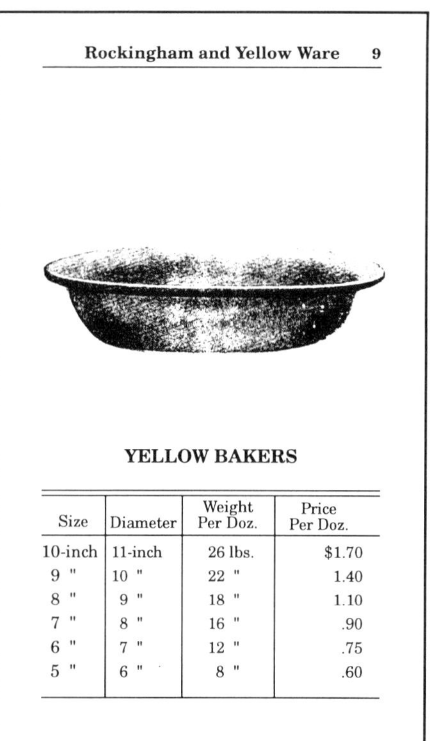
Rockingham and Yellow Ware 9

YELLOW BAKERS

Size	Diameter	Weight Per Doz.	Price Per Doz.
10-inch	11-inch	26 lbs.	$1.70
9 "	10 "	22 "	1.40
8 "	9 "	18 "	1.10
7 "	8 "	16 "	.90
6 "	7 "	12 "	.75
5 "	6 "	8 "	.60

Page 9

10 inch–**$65** 9 inch–**$55** 8 inch–**$50**

7 inch–**$45** 6 inch–**$40** 5 inch–**$35**

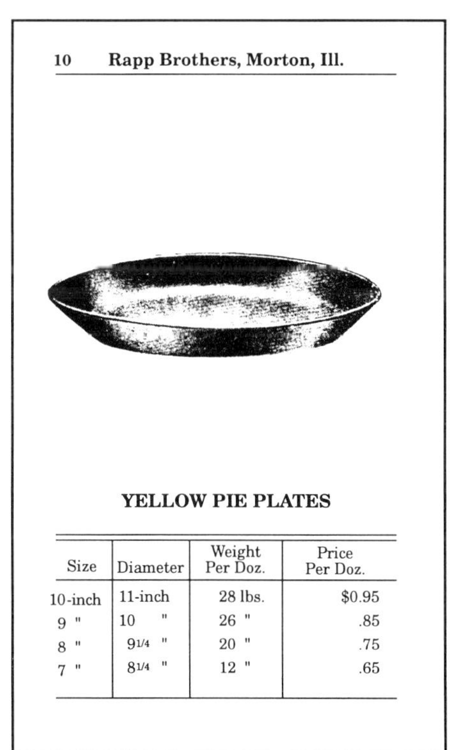
10 Rapp Brothers, Morton, Ill.

YELLOW PIE PLATES

Size	Diameter	Weight Per Doz.	Price Per Doz.
10-inch	11-inch	28 lbs.	$0.95
9 "	10 "	26 "	.85
8 "	9 1/4 "	20 "	.75
7 "	8 1/4 "	12 "	.65

Page 10

10 inch-**$100** 9 inch-**$90** 8 inch-**$80**

7 inch-**$70**

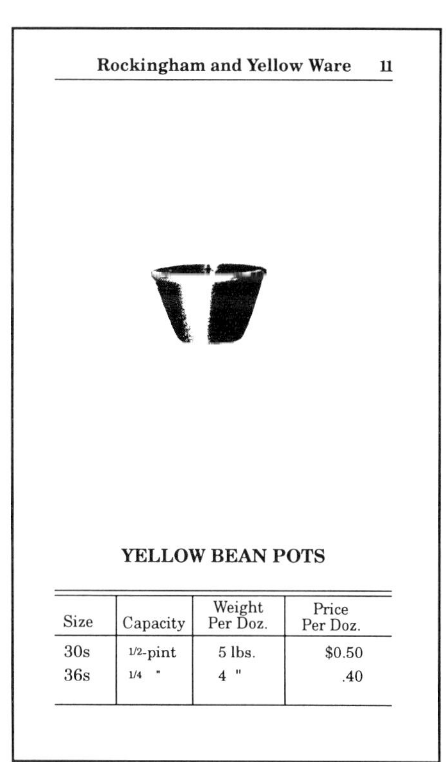
Rockingham and Yellow Ware 11

YELLOW BEAN POTS

Size	Capacity	Weight Per Doz.	Price Per Doz.
30s	1/2-pint	5 lbs.	$0.50
36s	1/4 "	4 "	.40

Page 11

30s – **$25** 36s–**$20**

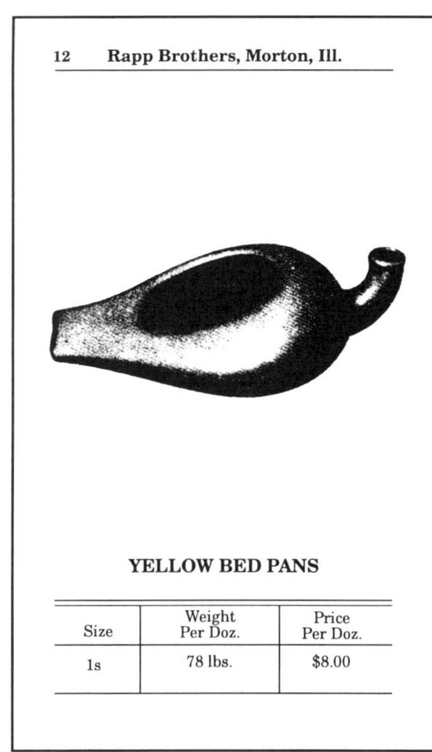
12 Rapp Brothers, Morton, Ill.

YELLOW BED PANS

Size	Weight Per Doz.	Price Per Doz.
1s	78 lbs.	$8.00

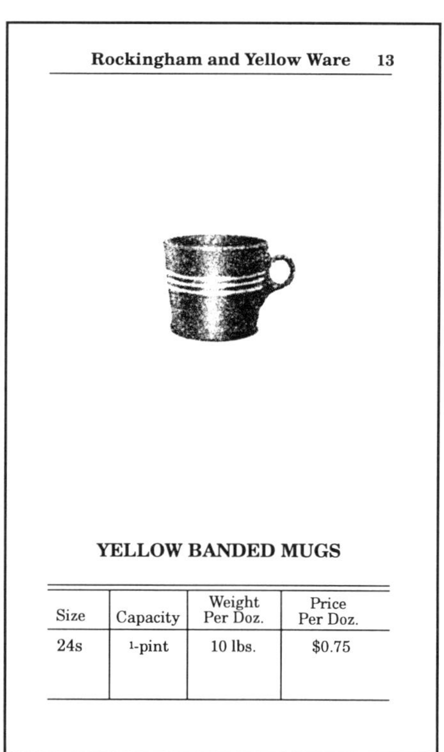
Rockingham and Yellow Ware 13

YELLOW BANDED MUGS

Size	Capacity	Weight Per Doz.	Price Per Doz.
24s	1-pint	10 lbs.	$0.75

Page 12
1s–**$50**
(brown Rockingham 10% less)

Page 13
24s – **$85**

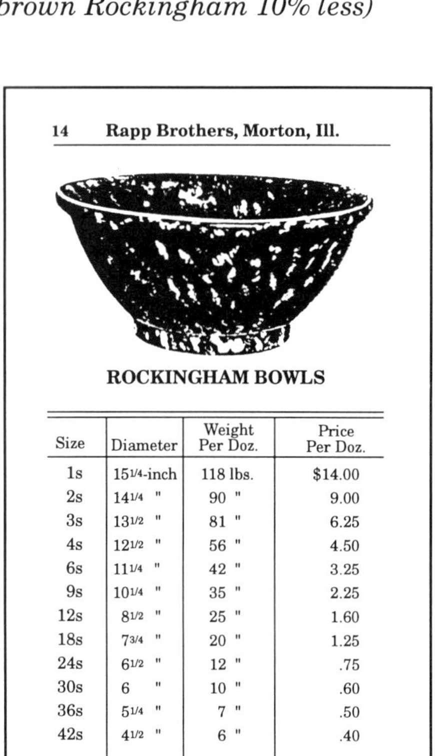
14 Rapp Brothers, Morton, Ill.

ROCKINGHAM BOWLS

Size	Diameter	Weight Per Doz.	Price Per Doz.
1s	15¼-inch	118 lbs.	$14.00
2s	14¼ "	90 "	9.00
3s	13½ "	81 "	6.25
4s	12½ "	56 "	4.50
6s	11¼ "	42 "	3.25
9s	10¼ "	35 "	2.25
12s	8½ "	25 "	1.60
18s	7¾ "	20 "	1.25
24s	6½ "	12 "	.75
30s	6 "	10 "	.60
36s	5¼ "	7 "	.50
42s	4½ "	6 "	.40

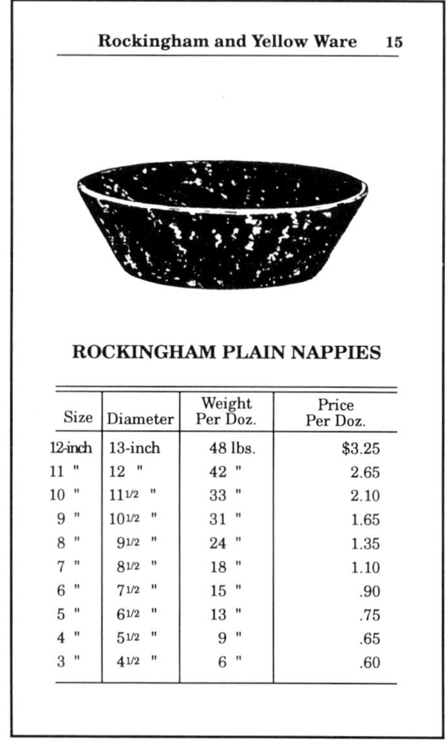
Rockingham and Yellow Ware 15

ROCKINGHAM PLAIN NAPPIES

Size	Diameter	Weight Per Doz.	Price Per Doz.
12-inch	13-inch	48 lbs.	$3.25
11 "	12 "	42 "	2.65
10 "	11½ "	33 "	2.10
9 "	10½ "	31 "	1.65
8 "	9½ "	24 "	1.35
7 "	8½ "	18 "	1.10
6 "	7½ "	15 "	.90
5 "	6½ "	13 "	.75
4 "	5½ "	9 "	.65
3 "	4½ "	6 "	.60

Page 14
1s–**$85** 2s–**$80** 3s–**$75** 4s–**$70**
6s–**$65** 9s–**$55** 12s–**$45** 18s–**$40**
24s–**$35** 30s–**$30** 36s–**$28** 42s–**$25**

Page 15
12 inch–**$60** 11 inch–**$55** 10 inch–**$50**
9 inch–**$45** 8 inch–**$40** 7 inch–**$36**
6 inch–**$32** 5 inch–**$28** 4 inch–**$24**
3 inch–**$20**

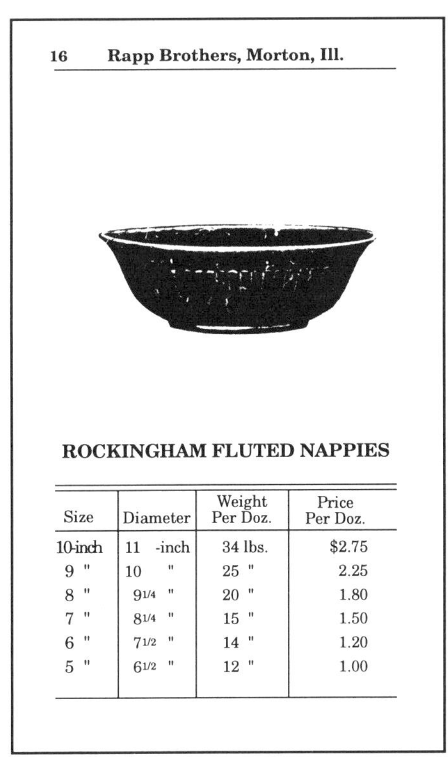

16 Rapp Brothers, Morton, Ill.

ROCKINGHAM FLUTED NAPPIES

Size	Diameter	Weight Per Doz.	Price Per Doz.
10-inch	11 -inch	34 lbs.	$2.75
9 "	10 "	25 "	2.25
8 "	9¼ "	20 "	1.80
7 "	8¼ "	15 "	1.50
6 "	7½ "	14 "	1.20
5 "	6½ "	12 "	1.00

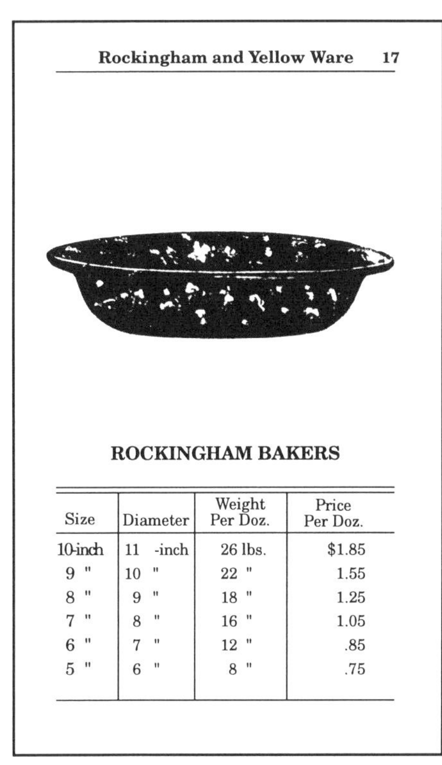

Rockingham and Yellow Ware 17

ROCKINGHAM BAKERS

Size	Diameter	Weight Per Doz.	Price Per Doz.
10-inch	11 -inch	26 lbs.	$1.85
9 "	10 "	22 "	1.55
8 "	9 "	18 "	1.25
7 "	8 "	16 "	1.05
6 "	7 "	12 "	.85
5 "	6 "	8 "	.75

Page 16
10 inch-**$60** 9 inch-**$50** 8 inch-**$45**
7 inch-**$40** 6 inch-**$35** 5 inch-**$30**

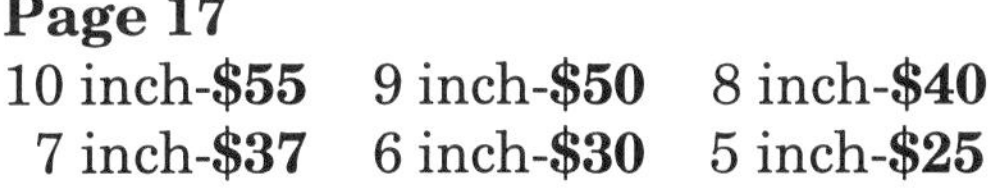

Page 17
10 inch-**$55** 9 inch-**$50** 8 inch-**$40**
7 inch-**$37** 6 inch-**$30** 5 inch-**$25**

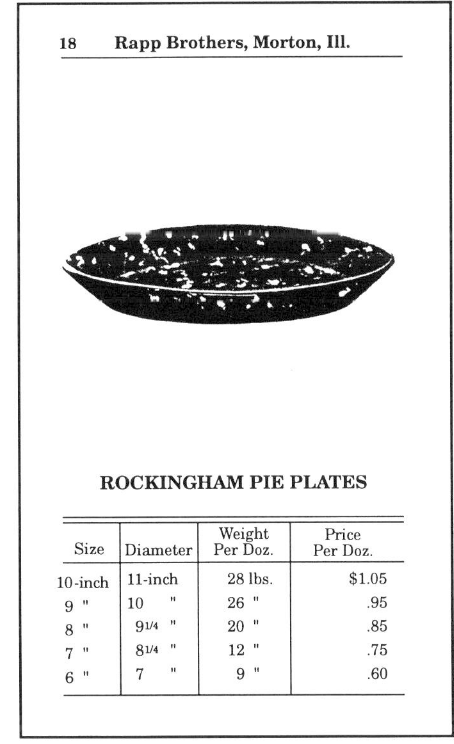

18 Rapp Brothers, Morton, Ill.

ROCKINGHAM PIE PLATES

Size	Diameter	Weight Per Doz.	Price Per Doz.
10-inch	11-inch	28 lbs.	$1.05
9 "	10 "	26 "	.95
8 "	9¼ "	20 "	.85
7 "	8¼ "	12 "	.75
6 "	7 "	9 "	.60

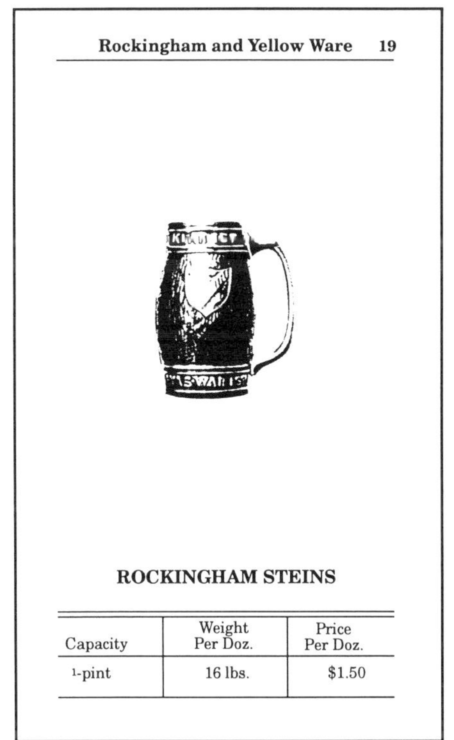

Rockingham and Yellow Ware 19

ROCKINGHAM STEINS

Capacity	Weight Per Doz.	Price Per Doz.
1-pint	16 lbs.	$1.50

Page 18
10 inch-**$100** 9 inch-**$90** 8 inch-**$80**
7 inch-**$70** 6 inch-**$60**

Page 19
1 pint – **$70**
(25% higher for green)

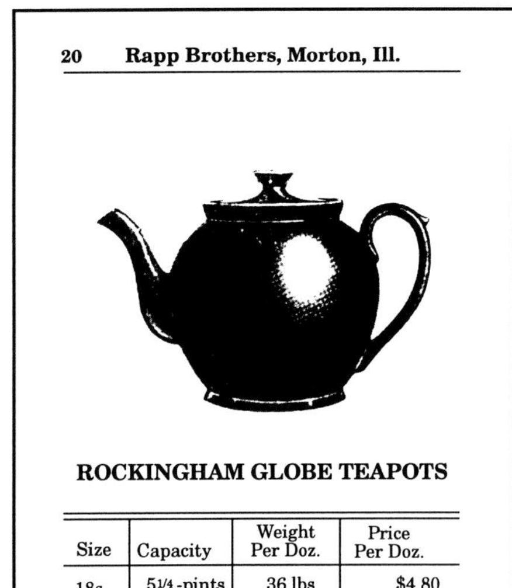

20 Rapp Brothers, Morton, Ill.

ROCKINGHAM GLOBE TEAPOTS

Size	Capacity	Weight Per Doz.	Price Per Doz.
18s	5 1/4 -pints	36 lbs.	$4.80
24s	4 "	30 "	4.00
30s	3 "	24 "	3.40
36s	2 1/2 "	21 "	2.85
42s	2 "	15 "	2.60
48s	1 1/4 "	14 "	2.40
54s	1 "	10 "	2.20
60s	3/4 "	9 "	2.00

Page 20

18s-**$60** 24s-**$55** 30s-**$50** 36s-**$45**
42s-**$40** 48s-**$30** 54s-**$30** 60s-**$25**

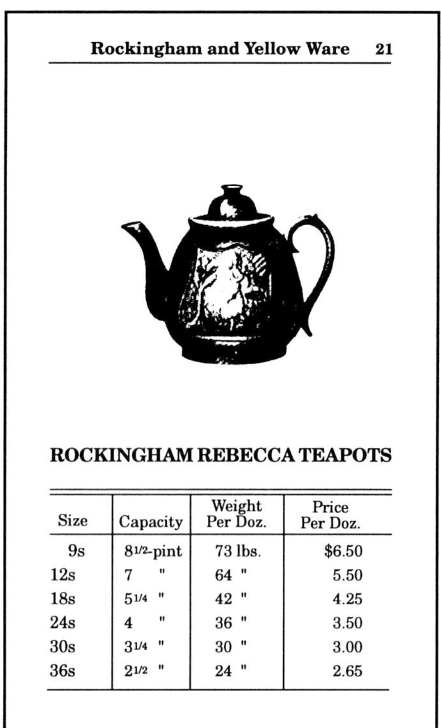

Rockingham and Yellow Ware 21

ROCKINGHAM REBECCA TEAPOTS

Size	Capacity	Weight Per Doz.	Price Per Doz.
9s	8 1/2-pint	73 lbs.	$6.50
12s	7 "	64 "	5.50
18s	5 1/4 "	42 "	4.25
24s	4 "	36 "	3.50
30s	3 1/4 "	30 "	3.00
36s	2 1/2 "	24 "	2.65

Page 21

9s-**$90** 12s-**$70** 18s-**$55** 24s-**$50**
30s-**$45** 36s-**$40**

22 Rapp Brothers, Morton, Ill.

RESTAURANT NESTING COVER TEAPOT

Size	Capacity	Weight Per Doz.	Price Per Doz.
54s	1 - pint	13 lbs.	$2.30
60s	3/4 "	9 "	2.10

Page 22

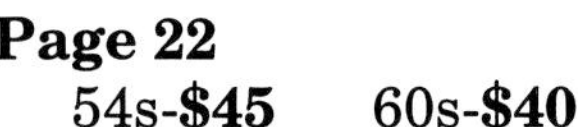

54s-**$45** 60s-**$40**

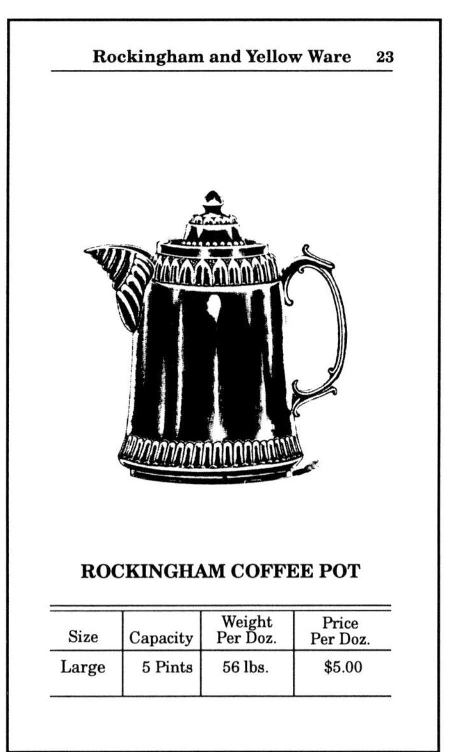

Rockingham and Yellow Ware 23

ROCKINGHAM COFFEE POT

Size	Capacity	Weight Per Doz.	Price Per Doz.
Large	5 Pints	56 lbs.	$5.00

Page 23

Large Pot is rare – **$125**

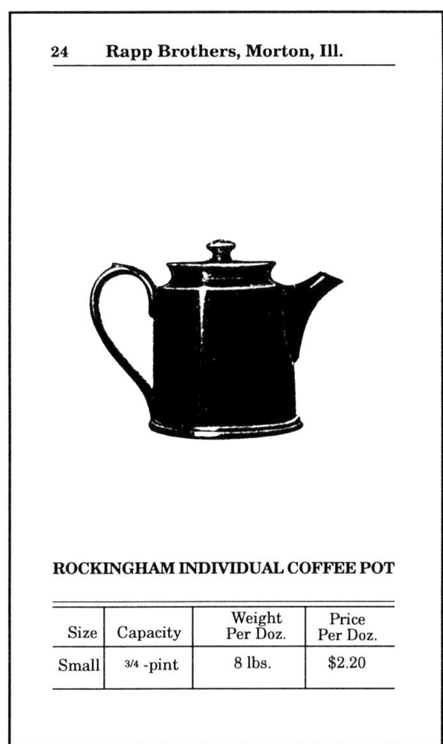

24 Rapp Brothers, Morton, Ill.

ROCKINGHAM INDIVIDUAL COFFEE POT

Size	Capacity	Weight Per Doz.	Price Per Doz.
Small	3/4 -pint	8 lbs.	$2.20

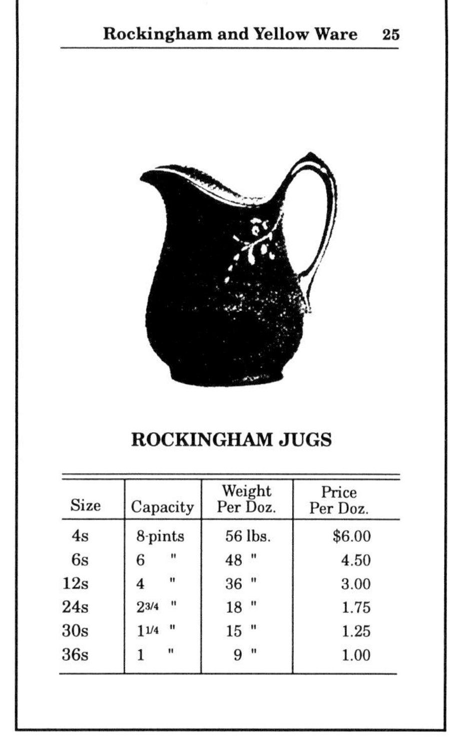

Rockingham and Yellow Ware 25

ROCKINGHAM JUGS

Size	Capacity	Weight Per Doz.	Price Per Doz.
4s	8-pints	56 lbs.	$6.00
6s	6 "	48 "	4.50
12s	4 "	36 "	3.00
24s	2 3/4 "	18 "	1.75
30s	1 1/4 "	15 "	1.25
36s	1 "	9 "	1.00

Page 24
Small pot – **$30**

Page 25
4s-**$110** 6s-**$100** 12s-**$90** 24s-**$75**
30s-**$55** 36s-**$50**

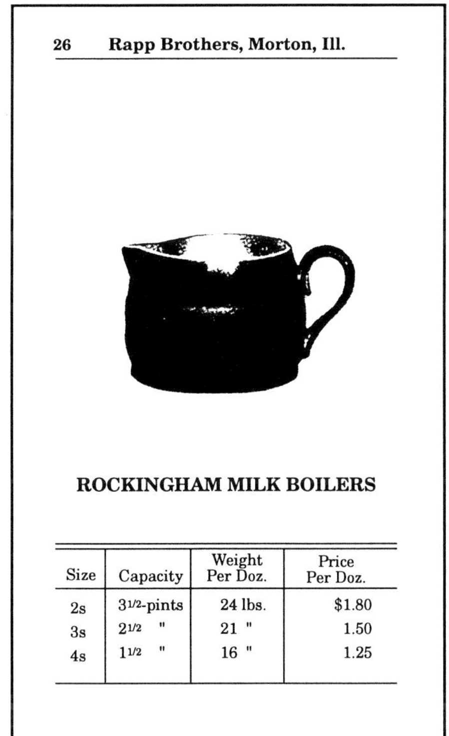

26 Rapp Brothers, Morton, Ill.

ROCKINGHAM MILK BOILERS

Size	Capacity	Weight Per Doz.	Price Per Doz.
2s	3 1/2-pints	24 lbs.	$1.80
3s	2 1/2 "	21 "	1.50
4s	1 1/2 "	16 "	1.25

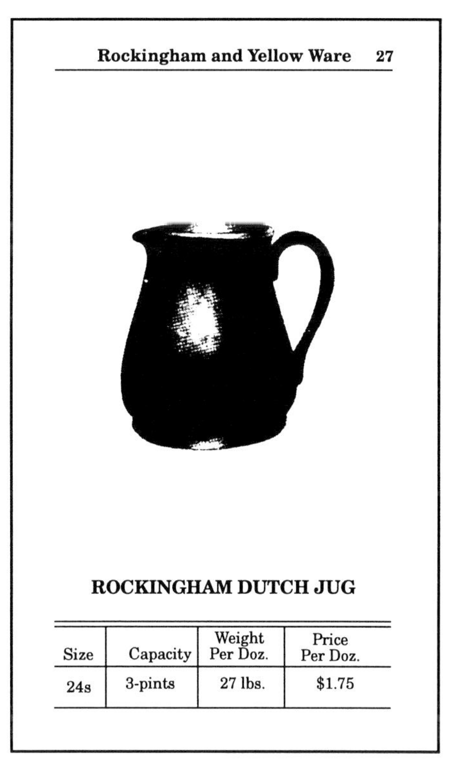

Rockingham and Yellow Ware 27

ROCKINGHAM DUTCH JUG

Size	Capacity	Weight Per Doz.	Price Per Doz.
24s	3-pints	27 lbs.	$1.75

Pagc 26
2s–**$55** 3s–**$50** 4s–**$45**

Page 27
24s – **$65**
(100% higher for cobalt)

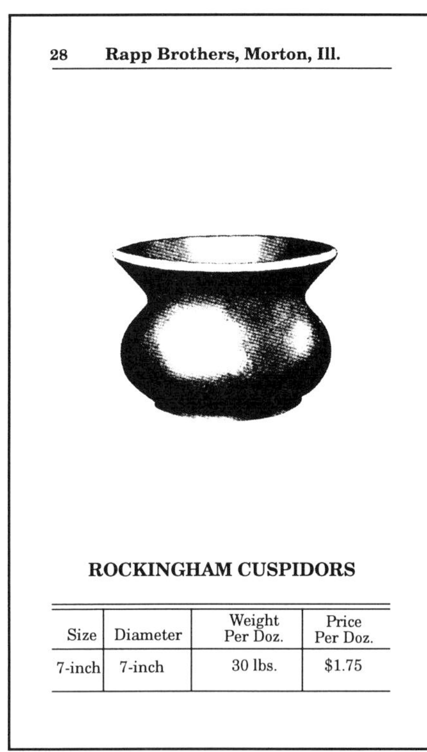
28 Rapp Brothers, Morton, Ill.

ROCKINGHAM CUSPIDORS

Size	Diameter	Weight Per Doz.	Price Per Doz.
7-inch	7-inch	30 lbs.	$1.75

Page 28

7 inch – **$50**

(25% higher for cobalt)

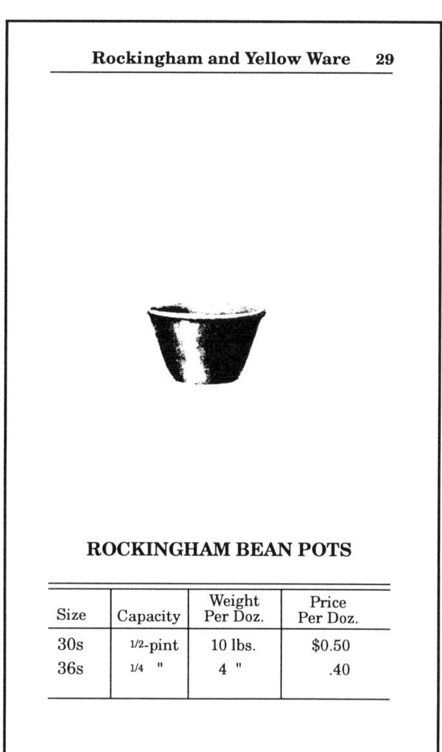
Rockingham and Yellow Ware 29

ROCKINGHAM BEAN POTS

Size	Capacity	Weight Per Doz.	Price Per Doz.
30s	1/2-pint	10 lbs.	$0.50
36s	1/4 "	4 "	.40

Page 29

30s – **$16** 36s – **$14**

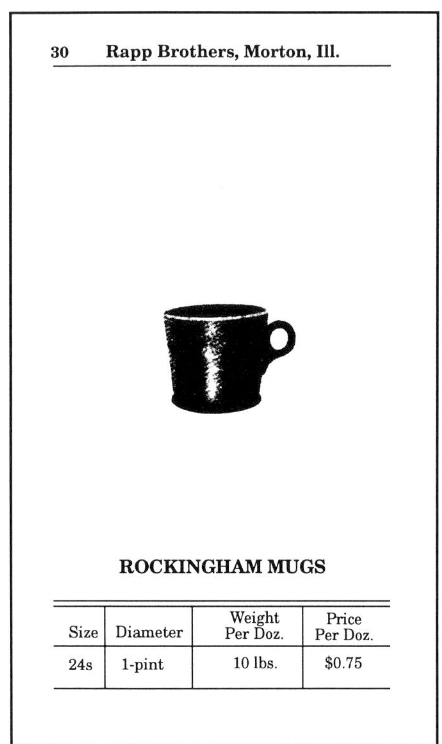
30 Rapp Brothers, Morton, Ill.

ROCKINGHAM MUGS

Size	Diameter	Weight Per Doz.	Price Per Doz.
24s	1-pint	10 lbs.	$0.75

Page 30

24s – **$60**

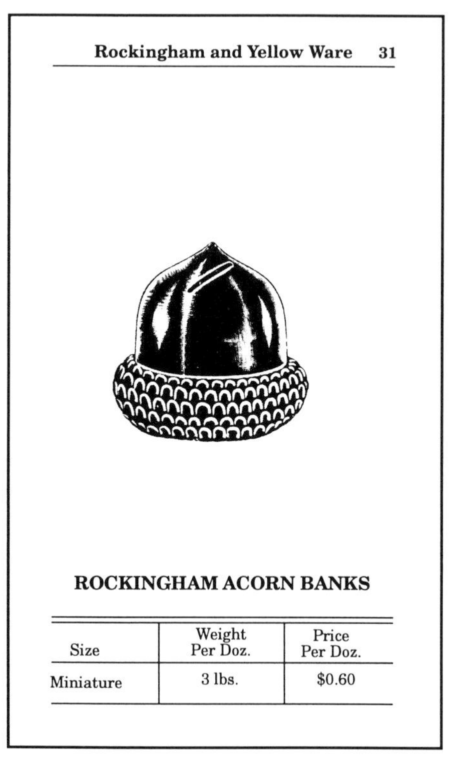
Rockingham and Yellow Ware 31

ROCKINGHAM ACORN BANKS

Size	Weight Per Doz.	Price Per Doz.
Miniature	3 lbs.	$0.60

Page 31

Miniature – **$50**

(25% higher for cobalt or green)

32 Rapp Brothers, Morton, Ill.

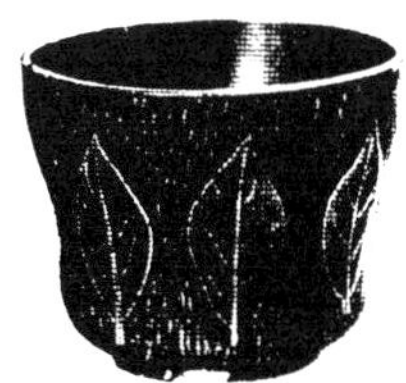

ROCKINGHAM JARDINIERS

Size	Diameter	Weight Per Doz.	Price Per Doz.
7-inch	7-inch	28 lbs.	$2.25

Page 32

7 inch – **$30**

(50% higher for green)

(100% higher for cobalt)

NO DEALER SHOULD OVERLOOK THIS OPPORTUNITY

BIG, EASY, QUICK, REPEATING PROFITS

BY SELLING

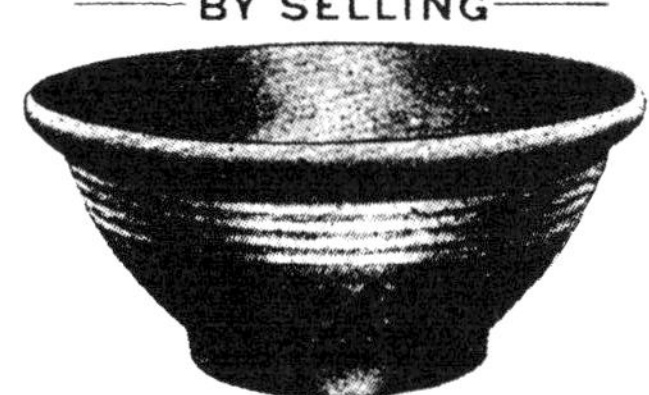

GENUINE EARTHEN YELLOW MIXING BOWLS

No Taste of Iron, Tin or Aluminum
Will Not Flake or Peel Off
Universally Adapted for all Mixing Purposes
Proven Welcome in Thousands of Homes

If you will act quick, now, we will ship you 36 pieces of fine quality, GENUINE EARTHEN, Yellow Mixing Bowls. Every piece is guaranteed GENUINE Earthenware, baked under 2,000 degrees F. of heat.

$2.85 is the exact amount for the entre assortment, no charge for package or packing. Dealer's profit ranges from 50 to 80 per cent. No dealer should overlook this big opportunity for profits. Be sure you don't. Buy from the manufacturer and save the jobber's profit. Mail in your order now. Tomorrow never comes.

THIS IS THE ASSORTMENT:
(No. 100)

1/4 dozen 4s, capacity 12 pints
1/4 dozen 6s, capacity 10 pints
1/4 dozen 9s, capacity 8 pints
1/4 dozen 12s, capacity 6 pints
1/4 dozen 18s, capacity 4 pints
1/4 dozen 24s, capacity 2 pints
1/4 dozen 30s, capacity 1 1/2 pints
1/4 dozen 36s, capacity 1 pint
1/4 dozen 42s, capacity 3/4 pint

F. O. B. Morton, Ill.
(Established 1877)

Morton Earthenware Co.
MORTON, ILLINOIS

(see catalog page 5 for values)

MONEY SAFES.

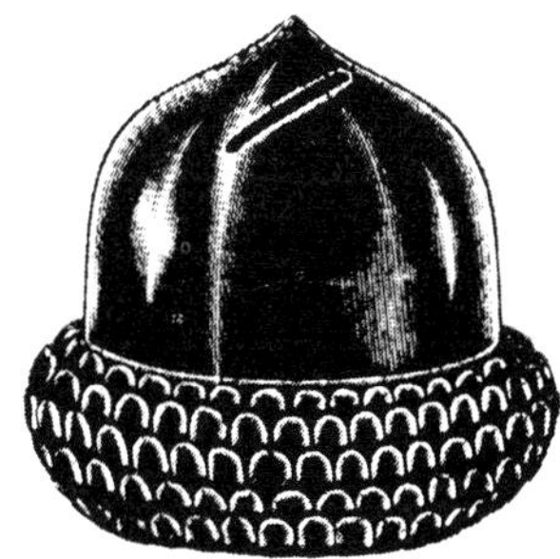

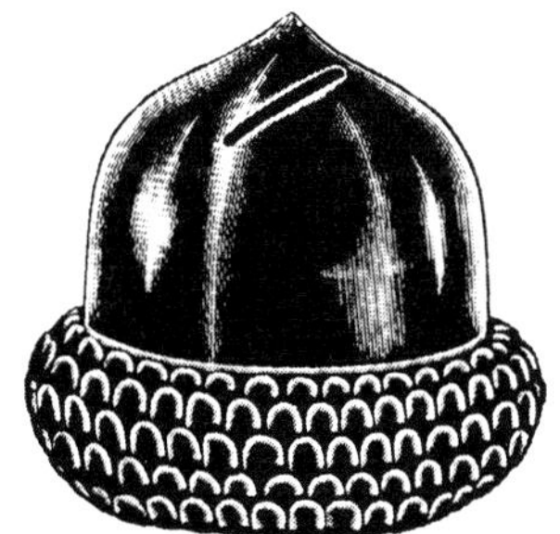

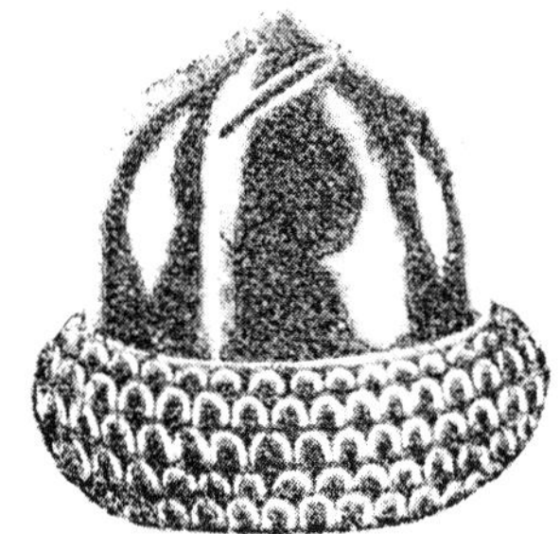

MANUFACTURED BY

RAPP BROS., - - MORTON, ILL.

(see catalog page 31 for values)

ASSORTMENT 1

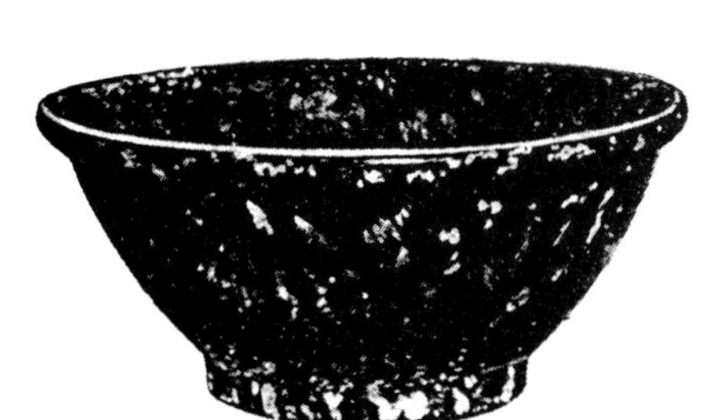

1 Doz. 18s Bowls

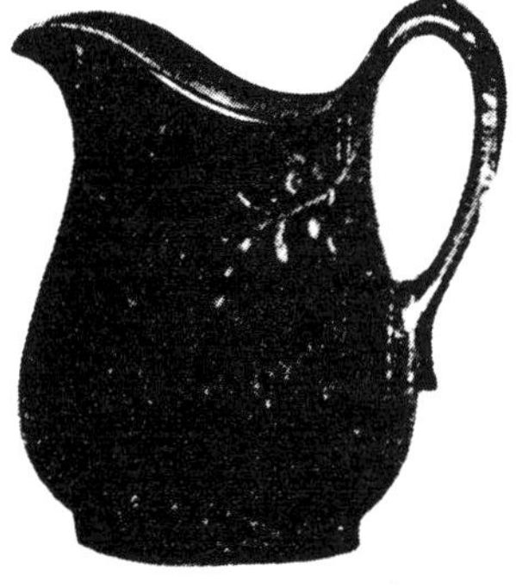

1 Doz. 30s Jugs

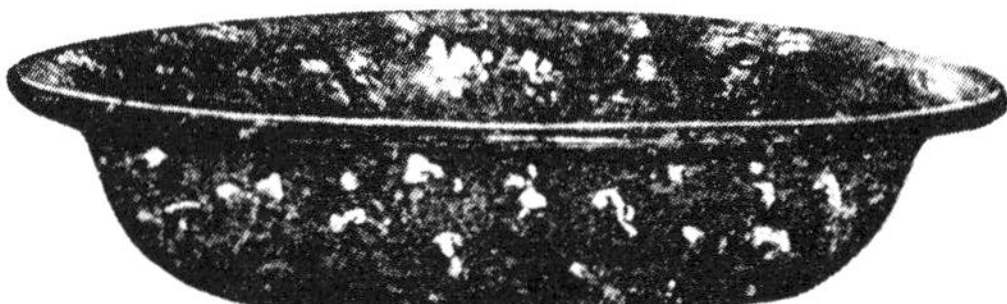

1 1/2 Doz. 8-inch Bakers

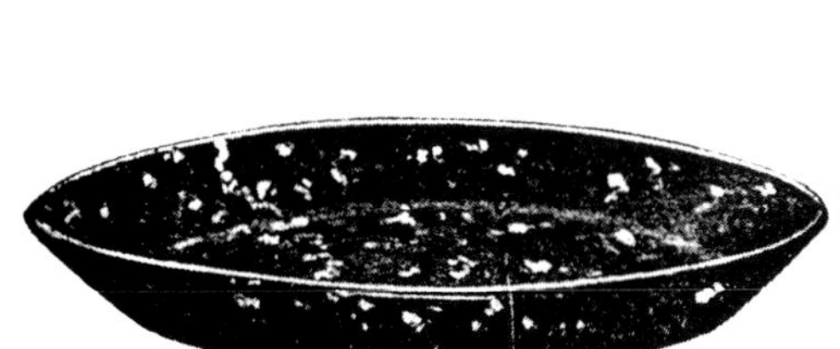

1 Doz. 9-inch Pie Plates

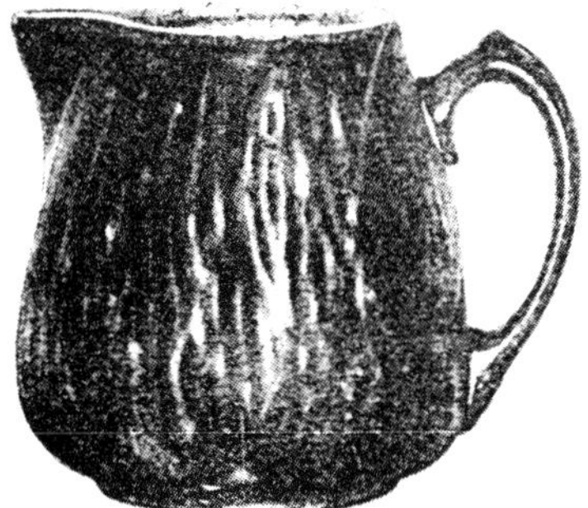

1 Doz. 24s Jugs

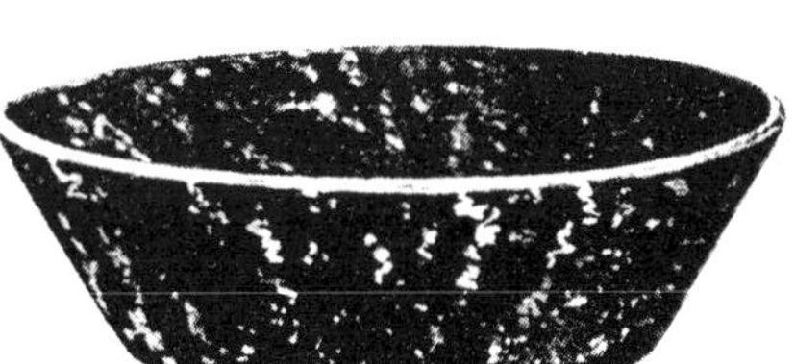

1 1/2 Doz. 8-inch Nappies

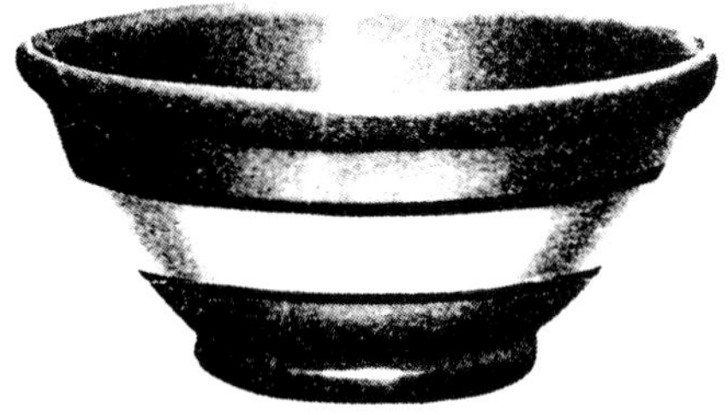

1 Doz. 18s Bowls

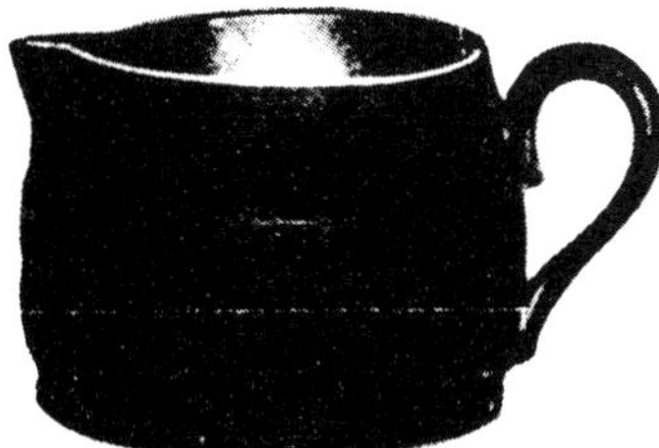

1 Doz. 4s Milk Boilers

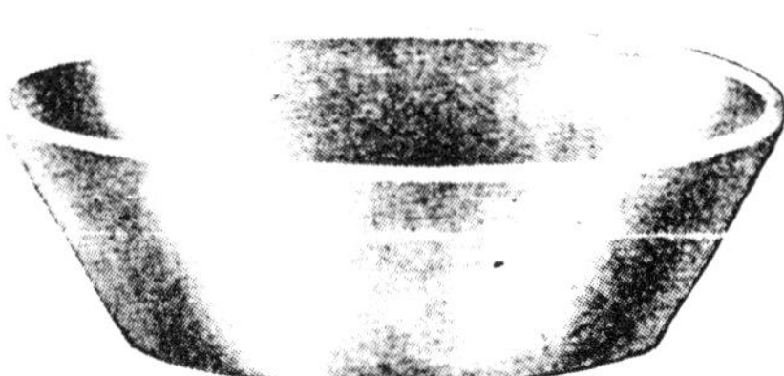

1 Doz. 8-inch Nappies

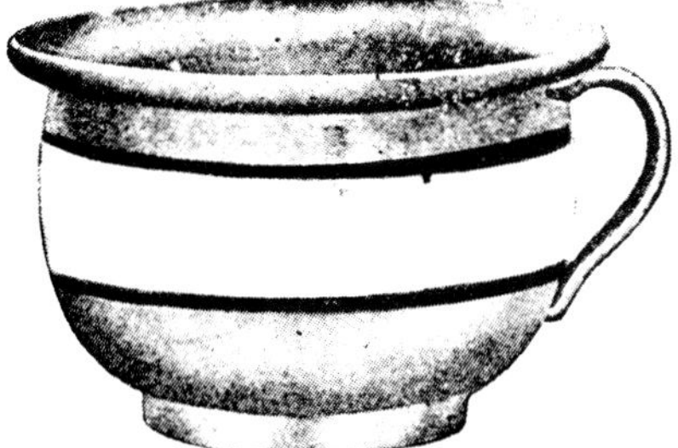

1 Doz. 12s Chambers

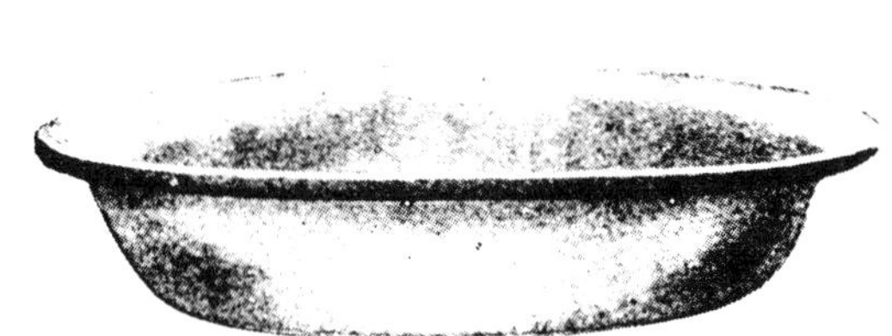

1 Doz. 8-inch Bakers

18s – **$40**
9s – **$90**
18s – **$40**
12s – **$40**

30s – **$55**
24s – **$75**
4s – **$45**

8 inch baker – **$45**
8 inch nappy – **$40**
8 inch nappy – **$55**
8 inch baker – **$60**

AGATE
ROCKINGHAM WARE
ASSORTMENT

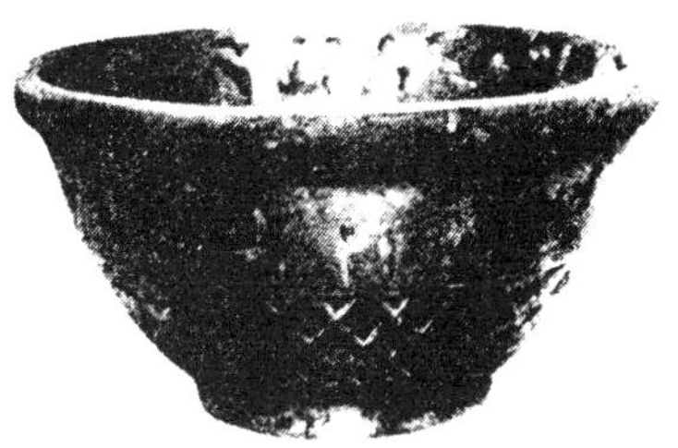

2 dozen 18s Mixing Bowls
Capacity 2 Quarts

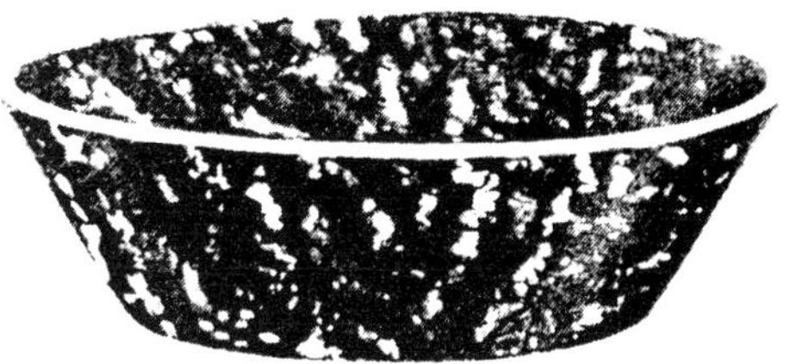

2 dozen 8 inch Nappies
Actual Measurement, 9 1/2 inches

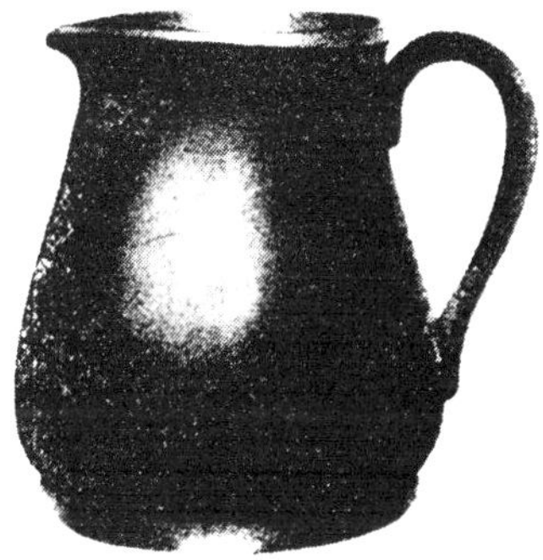

2 dozen Dutch Jugs
Capacity 3 Pints

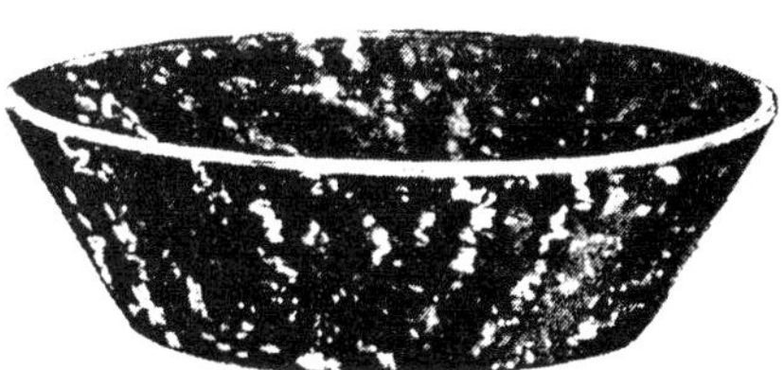

2 dozen 7 inch Nappies
Actual Measurement, 8 1/2 inches

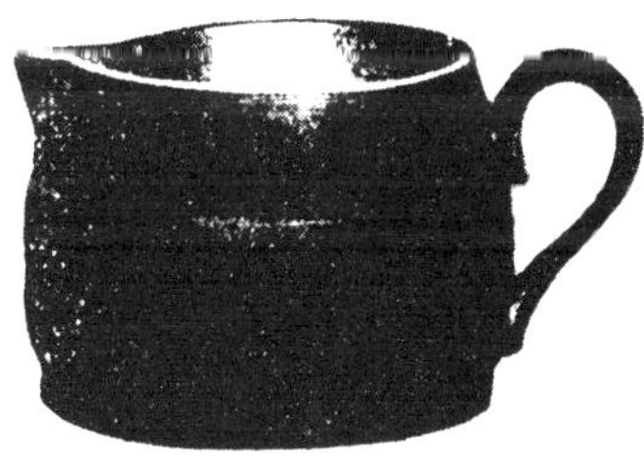

2 dozen 3s Milk Boilers
Capacity 3 Pints

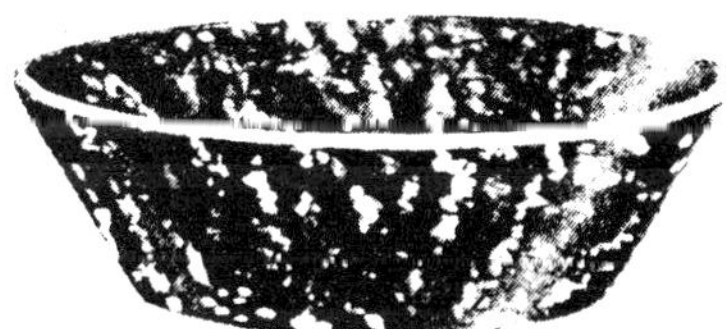

2 dozen 6 inch Nappies
Actual Measurement, 7 1/2 inches

This assortment is packed especially for

18s – **$50**
Dutch Jug – **$65**
3s – **$50**

8 inch – **$40**
7 inch – **$36**
6 inch – **$32**

CHAPTER 3

MORTON POTTERY WORKS / MORTON EARTHENWARE COMPANY

Kitchenware

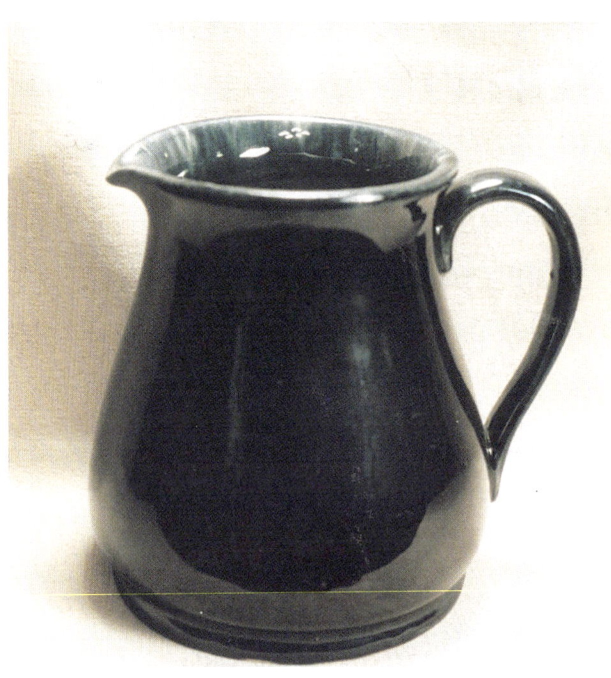

This milk jug was listed in catalogs as the Dutch jug. It has a capacity of 3 1/2 pints. In addition to the cobalt blue jug shown here, it was done in brown Rockingham.

Value Range: Cobalt blue: $75-80
Brown Rockingham: $45-50

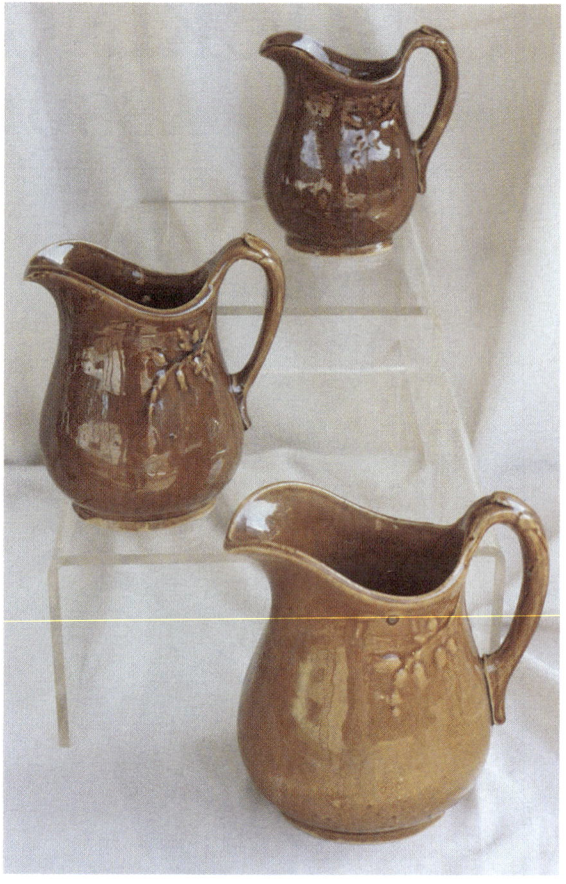

These three milk jugs are the smallest of the six sizes that were made. These are 1 pint, 1 1/4 pints, and 2 3/4 pints. Not pictured sizes are 4 pints, 6 pints, and 8 pints.

Value Range: $55 – $80

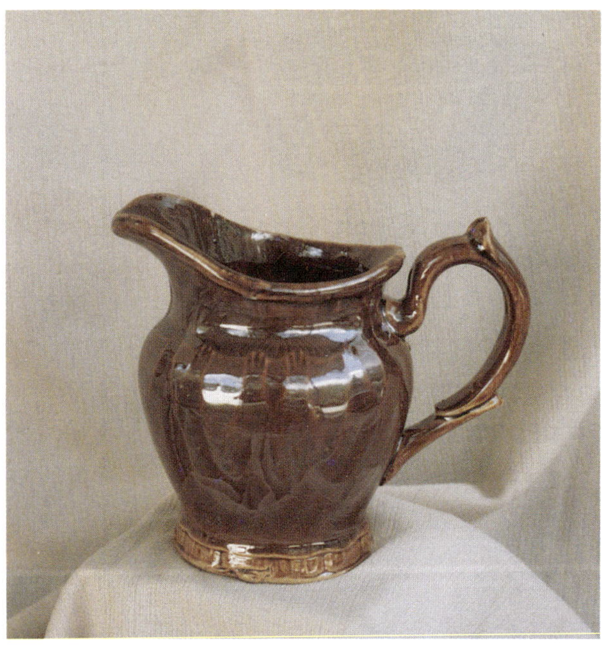

This milk jug is not as plain as others made at the pottery. It has interesting lines, making it more decorative.

Value Range: $45-55

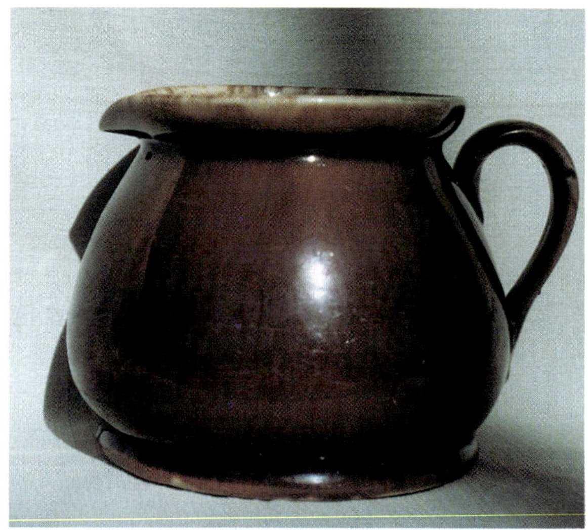

This is a smaller version of the Dutch jug. The top rim is more pronounced. It has a capacity of 3 pints.

Value Range: Cobalt blue: $65-70
Brown Rockingham: $40-45

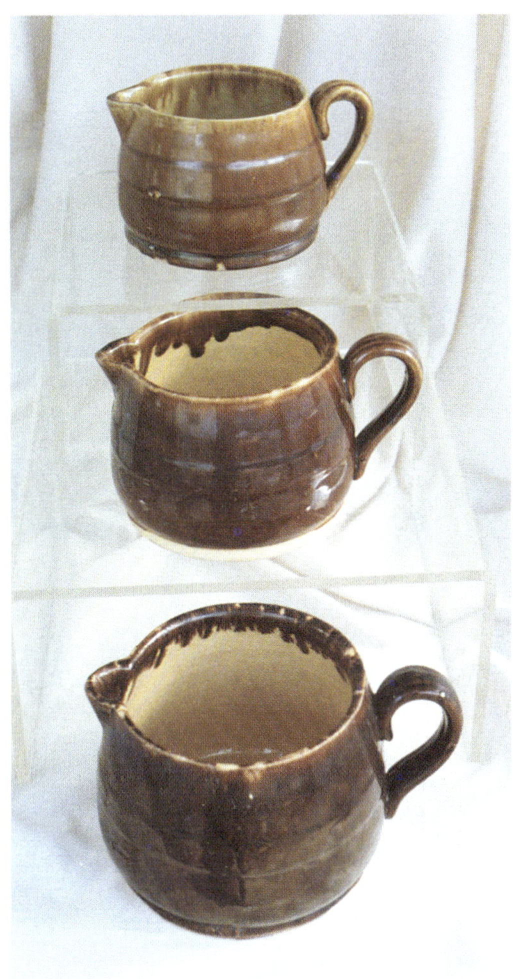

Milk boilers were made in only these three sizes. They were made for one basic purpose, to coagulate milk. When properly coagulated, curd could be removed from the whey for cheese making. **Value Range: $45-55**

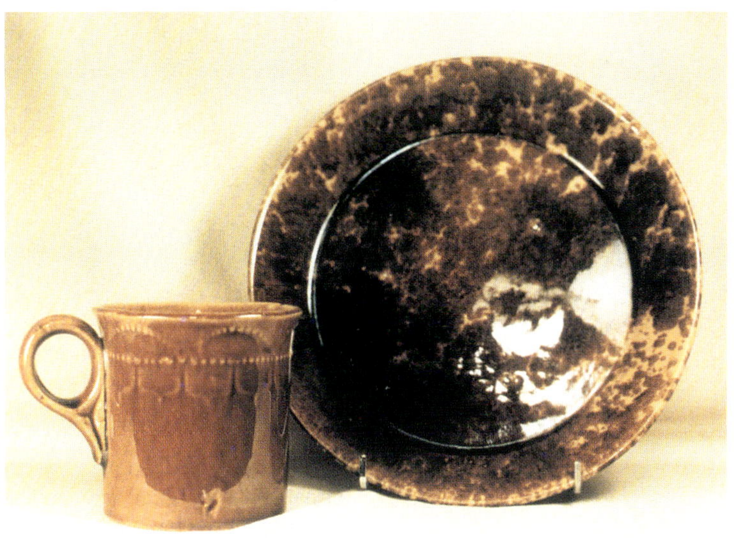

The Rockingham one pint mug has a shield and dot in mold decoration. The pie plate was described as Rockingham "Agate" in sales promotions. It was made in five sizes, from seven inches to eleven inches. **Value Range: Mug – $50-60 Pie Plate – $60-100**

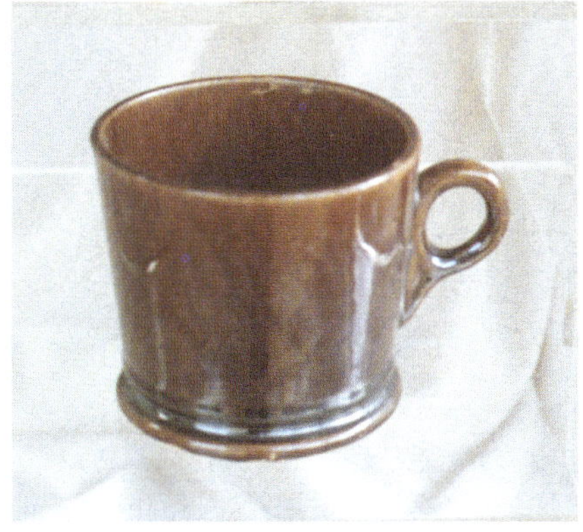

The plain Rockingham mug was made in two sizes.
Value Range: $40-50

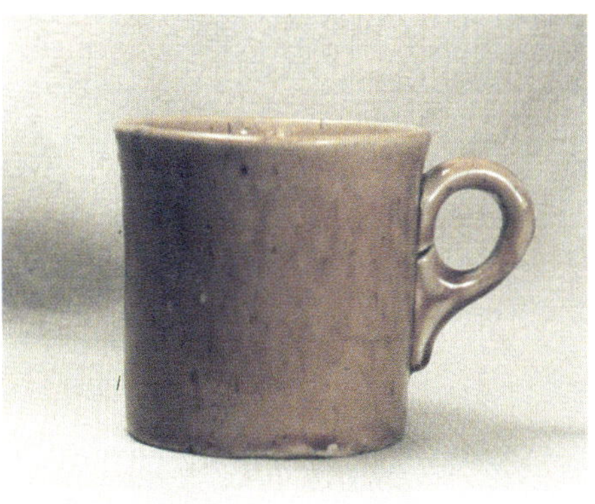

This is a vitereous yellow ware mug. It is rare. **Value Range: $60-70**

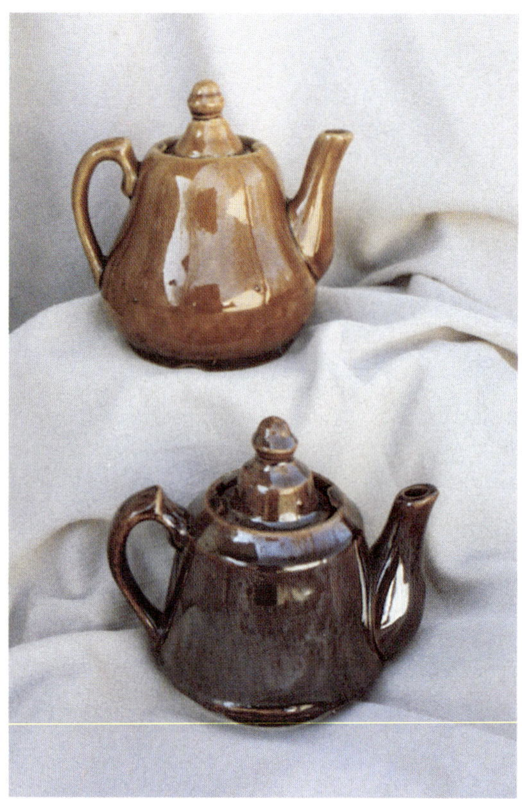

These individual tea pots have a capacity of $1\frac{1}{2}$ cups. Note the similarity in the finials, spouts, and handles. The pear shape pot is not as common as the standard pot.

Value Range: Pear shape: $35-40
Standard shape: $25-35

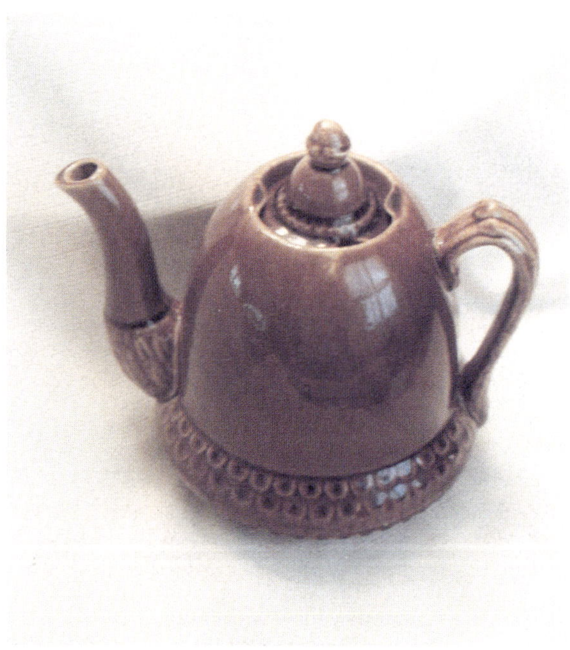

The acorn teapot has a capacity of $3\frac{3}{4}$ cups. The inverted acorn is very exact in its design.

Value Range: $70-80

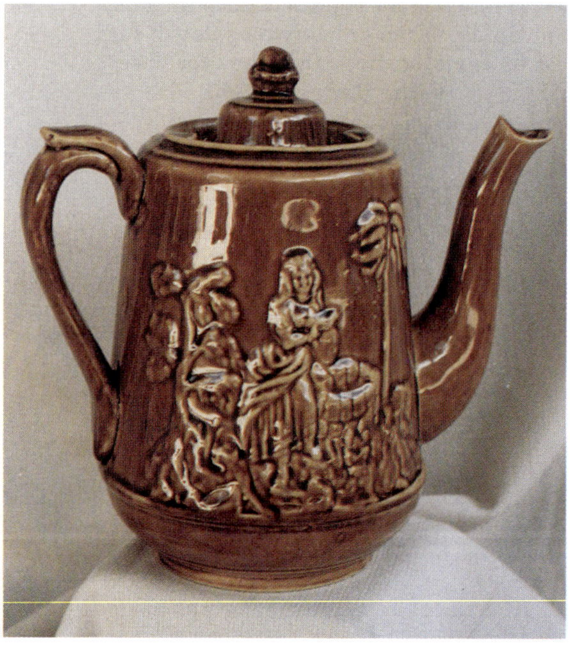

The Rebecca teapot was made in seven sizes, ranging from 2 pints to $8\frac{1}{2}$ pints.

Value Range: $50-130

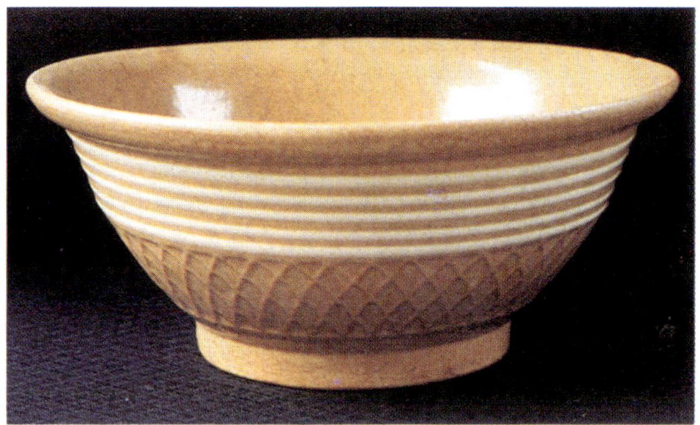

This yellow ware, slip lined, waffle base mixing bowl is #6s. It has a diameter of 11 1/4".

Value Range: $65-70

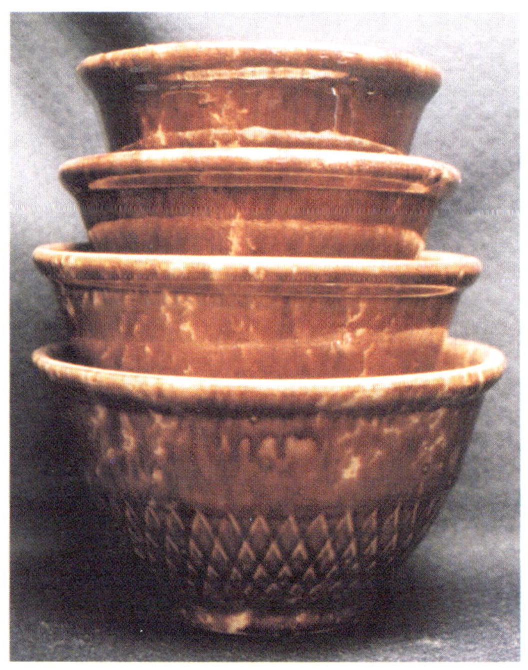

The Rockingham, waffle base mixing bowls were made in twelve sizes.

Value Range: (top to bottom)

1. $18-22
2. $24-28
3. $30-34
4. $36-40

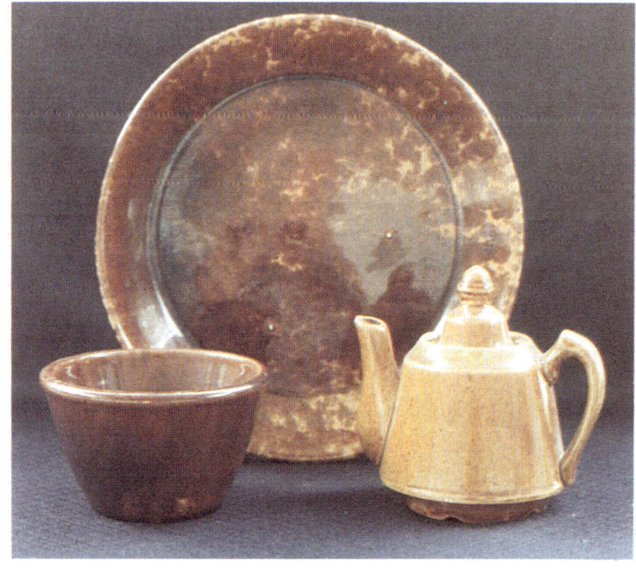

The Rockingham pie plate was made in five sizes. There were two different size bean pots, 1/2 pint, and 1/4 pint. The individual yellowware tea pot has a capacity of 1 1/2 cups.

Value Range: Pie Plate $60-100
Bean Pot $14-16
Tea Pot $40-50

NOVELTIES

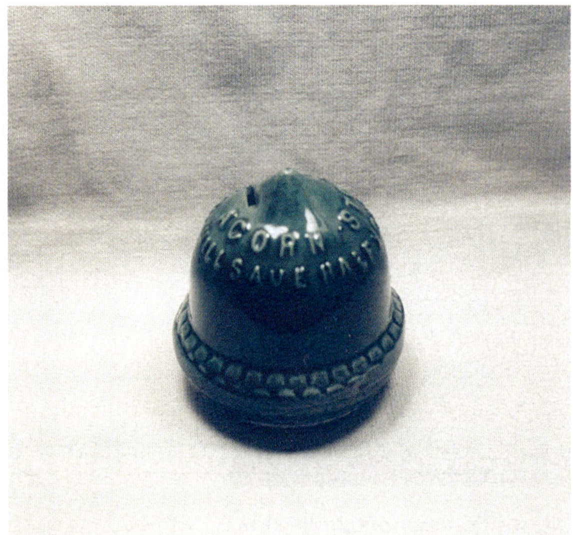

The acorn bank was made as an advertising give-away for the Acorn Stove Company. It was done in cobalt blue, green, and Rockingham brown. There is no opening on the bottom. The bank had to be broken in order to retrieve coins.

Value Range: Cobalt blue – $50-60
Green – $40-50
Brown – $30-40

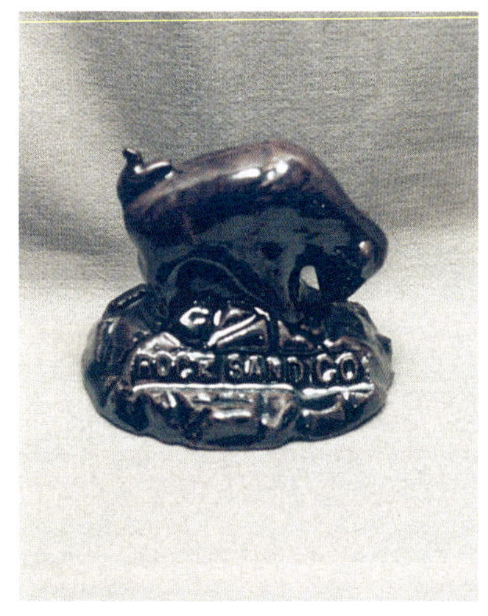

The buffalo paperweight was another advertising give-away made for the Rock Sand Company. It has been found only in Rockingham brown. The buffalo was copied from one done by Indiana Tumbler and Goblet Company, Greentown, Indiana in 1901.

Value Range: $30-40

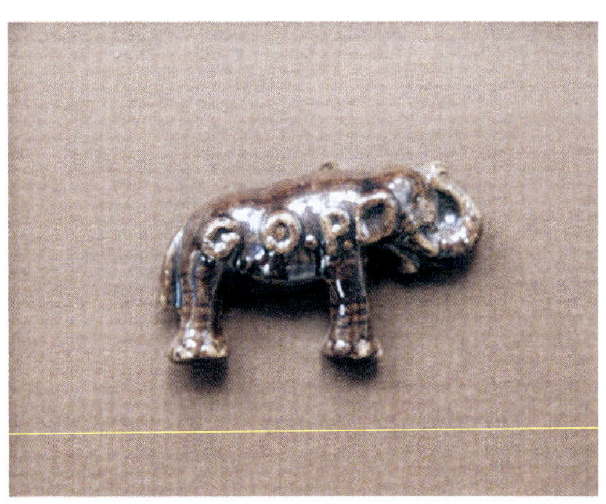

This elephant GOP campaign give-away is one of the earliest political items made at Morton. It has a flange on the reverse side so it can be attached to the button hole on the lapel of a man's coat. It is extremely rare.

Value Range: ND

Miniature pitchers were not commonly made at the potteries. That type of production was considered frivolous and not profit producing.

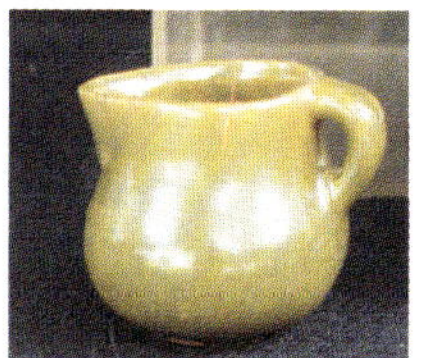

Green Pitcher
Value Range: $15-20

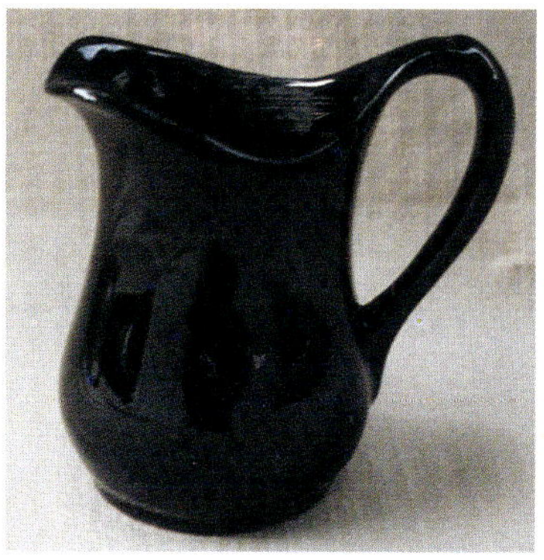

Cobalt blue Pitcher
Value Range: $50-60

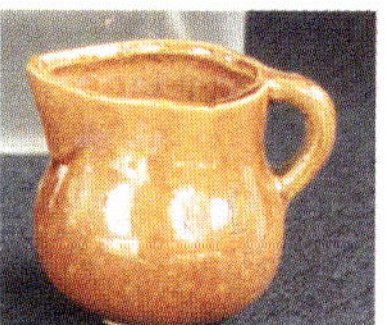

Brown Pitcher
Value Range: $15-20

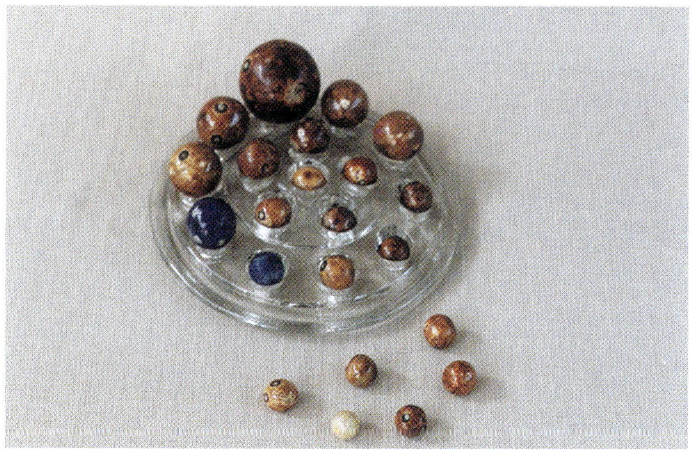

Marbles were made by Rapp children after school and on Saturdays. No proof of sale at the pottery has been found. Legend has it that when marbles were lost in games at school, new ones were quickly made for use in ensuing games.

Value Range: Large $6-8
Medium $4-6
Small $1-2

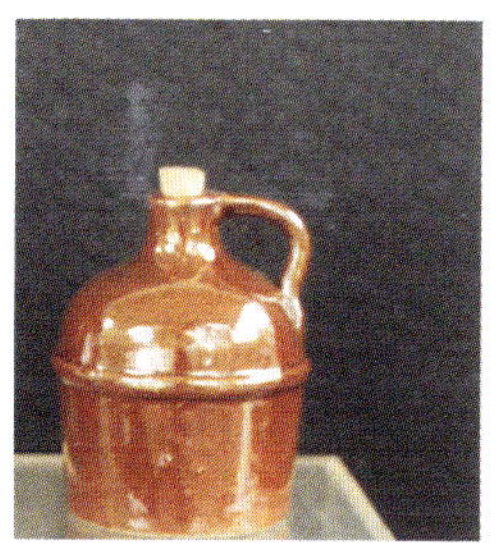

The little brown jug is a miniature, 1 1/2 inches tall. It was probably used as a sample by salesmen.
Value Range: $40-50

The miniature chamber pot was made as a joke. It has been found in both yellowware and brown, and always has a small residue in a contrasting color placed inside.
Value Range: $20-25

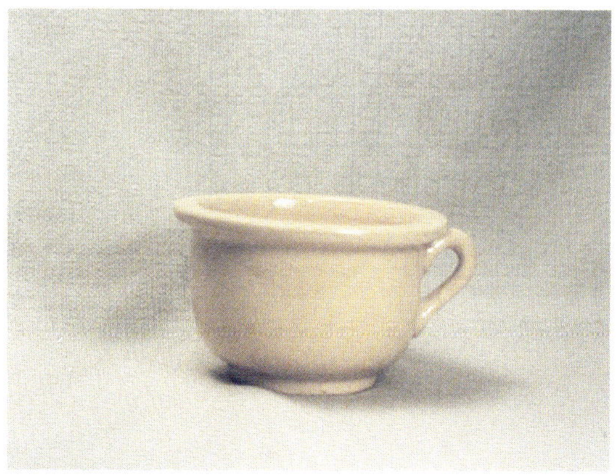

Toy kitchenware examples are not listed in any of the company catalogs or literature that has been found. Because these coffee pots are so accurate to those the pottery made, it is believed that they were made to be used as salesmen's samples.

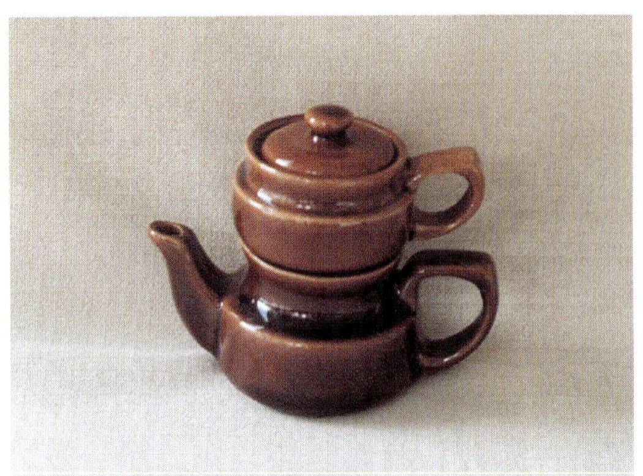

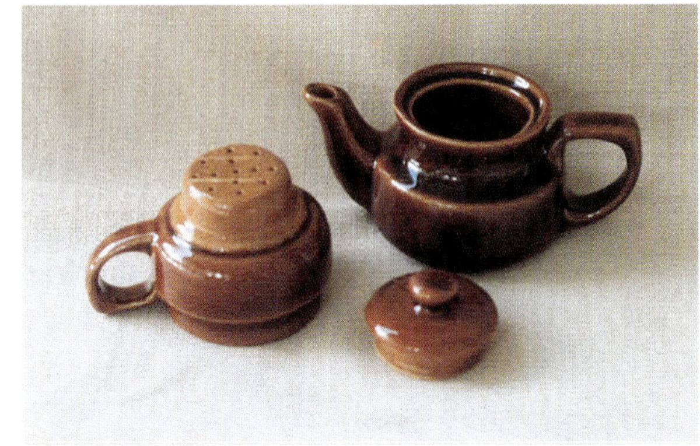

Three piece coffee pot
Value Range: $45-55

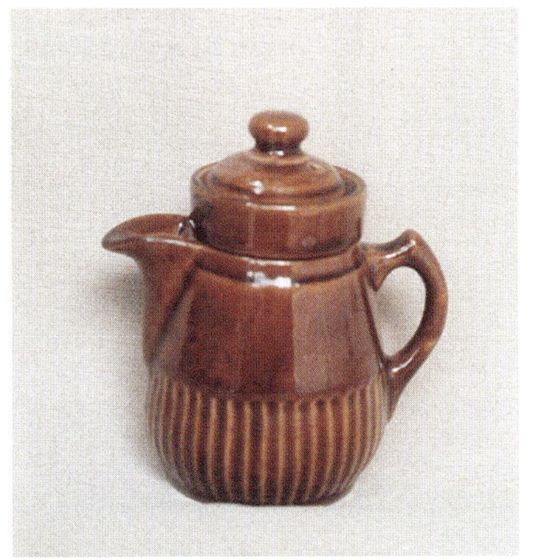

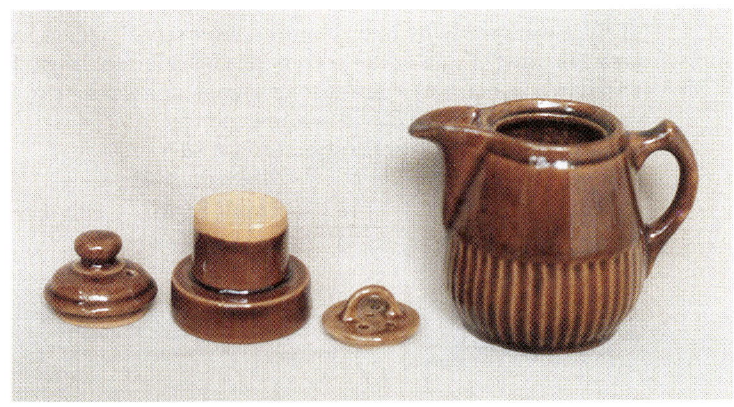

Four piece coffee pot
Value Range: $50-60

UTILITY WARES

The motto steins attest to the Rapp's Black Forest origins in Germany. The motto encircling the top and bottom reads: "Trinke was klar ist und rede was wahr ist." Translation: "Drink what is pure and speak what it true."
Value Range: Brown $60-70
Green (Rare) $75-85

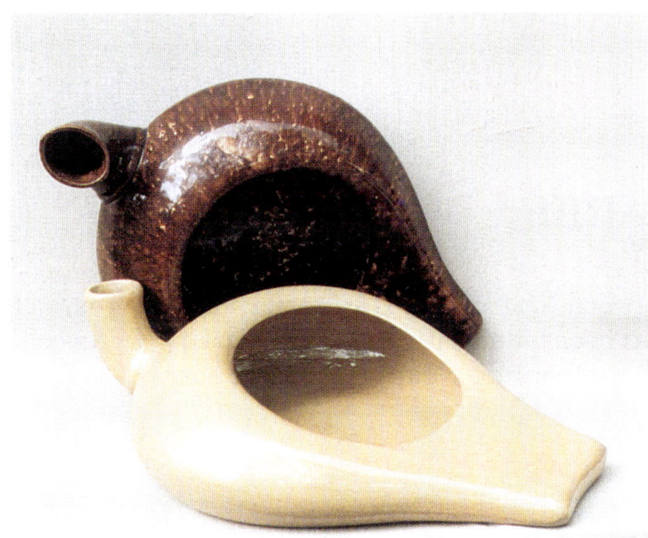

The Rapp Brothers catalog describes these urinals as "shovel shape."
Value Range: Rockingham $40-45
Yellow Ware $50-55

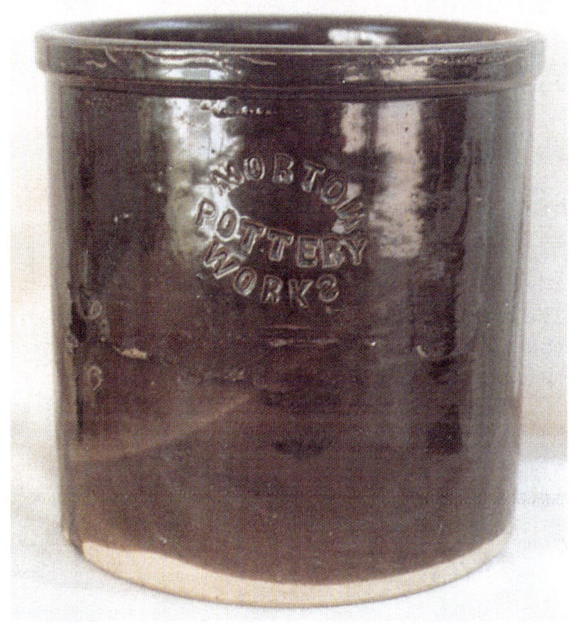

Crocks of this type were made in several sizes. They were used to store non perishable foods, to make pickles and sauerkraut, and to pack sausage in melted lard.
Value Range: $55-65

PART II

CLIFTWOOD ART POTTERIES, INCORPORATED

1920-1940

The Cliftwood Art Pottery was located at the same address, on Penn Street, where the Morton Pottery Works and the Morton Earthenware Company had been located from 1877 to 1917. It was familiar territory to Matthew Rapp who had helped found the pottery industry at that time and place. His reestablishment of the pottery industry in 1920 was welcomed by Mortonites.

MARKS

Marks are very uncommon for Cliftwood Art Pottery. During our forty-six years of collecting Morton's pottery, only one item has been found with an incised mark for Cliftwood. If any identification was used at all, it was a paper label. Paper labels are scarce.

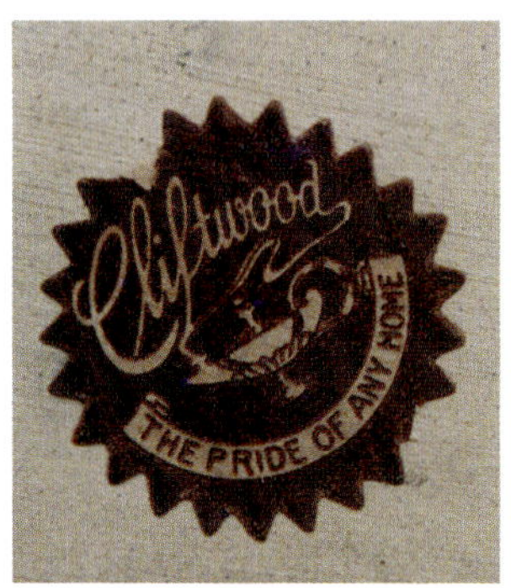

MARK #1:
The most common label to be found is this serrated paper seal used during the first eighteen years of operation.

MARK #2:
This paper label was used from 1938 until the pottery was sold in 1940.

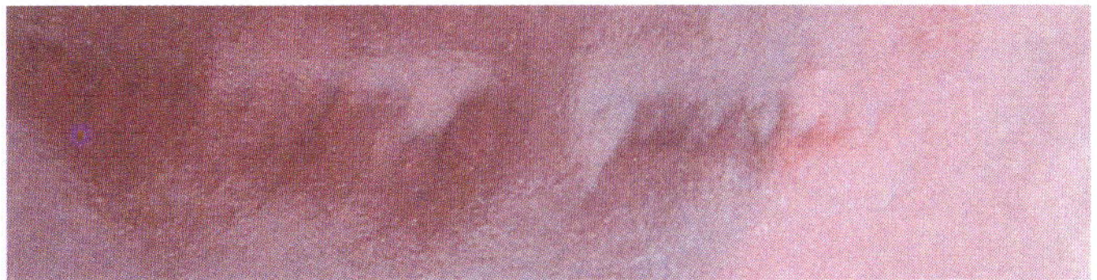

MARK #3A
Here is the rare incised mark. It is difficult to decipher.

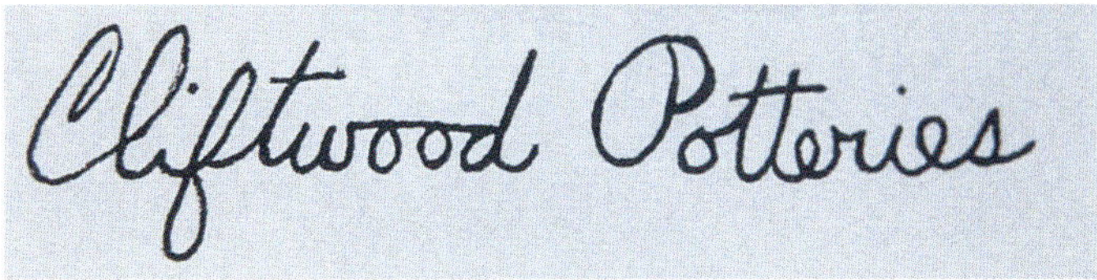

MARK #3B
This is a reproduced mark from a pencil rubbing of the original.

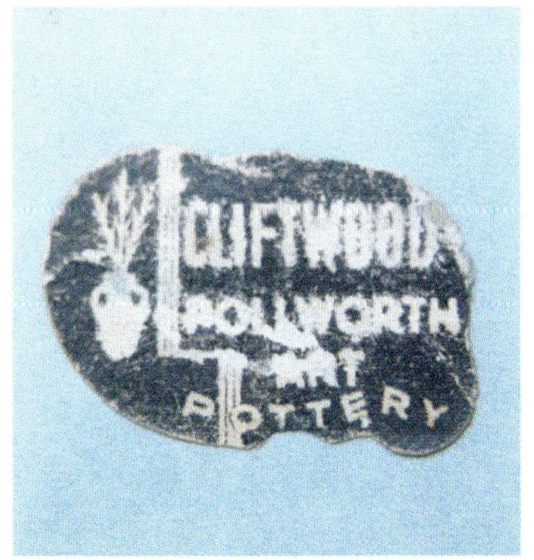

MARK #4:
This paper label is questionable because of the "Pollworth" inclusion. In all of our research, we have found no reference to it. The label is on the bottom of a Cliftwood vase that was being made at the time the pottery was sold in 1940. In all probability, the label is a forgery.

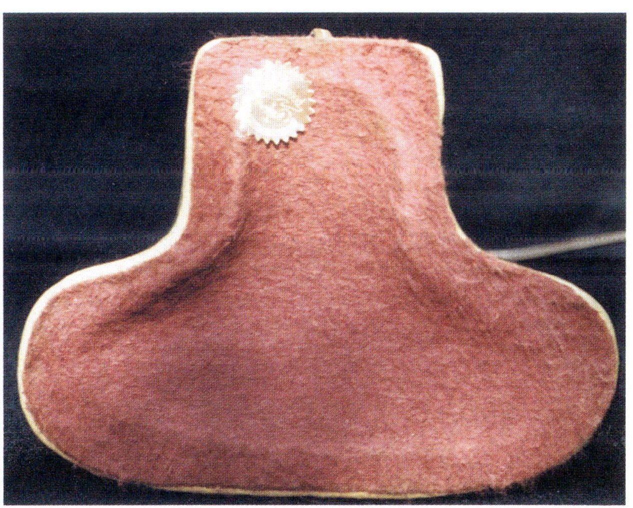

MARK #5:
Another rather certain method of identifying Cliftwood pottery is the maroon felt that was used on all items shipped from the pottery, or sold in the show room. Many examples are being found, still today, with the original felt intact.

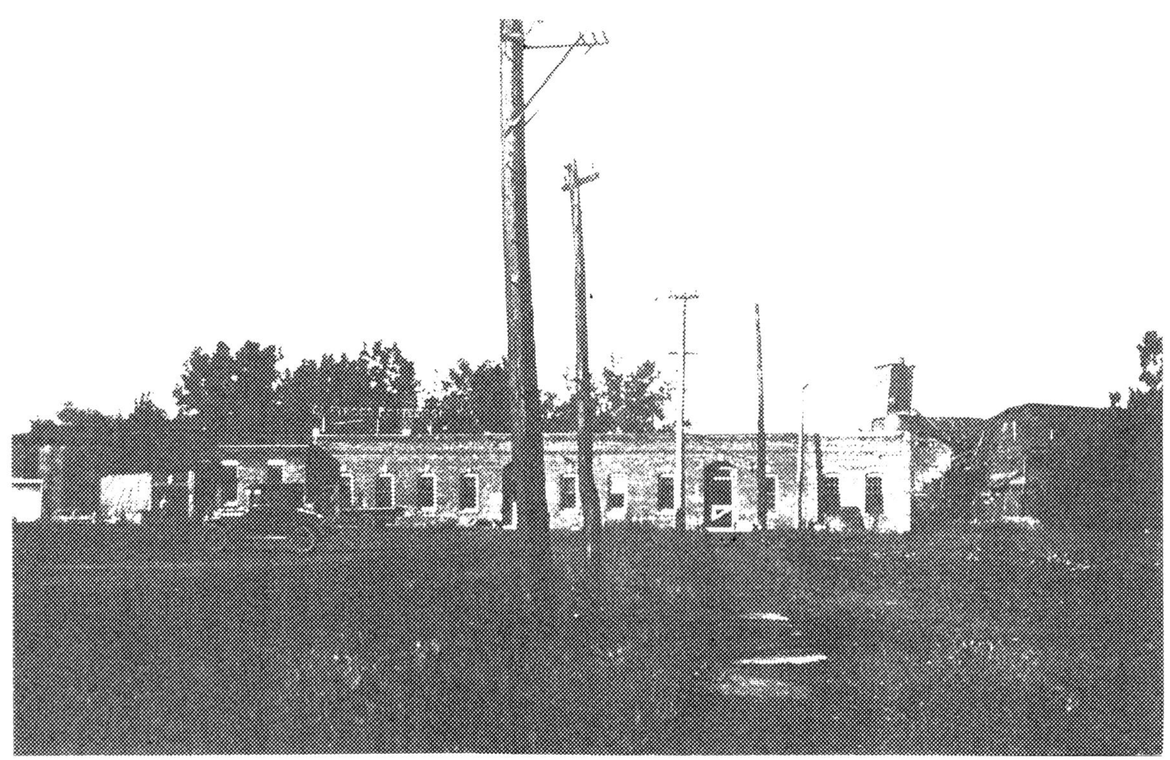

Photo #1: This photograph shows the Cliftwood Pottery shortly after it began production in the early 1920's. On the right side of the building is the remaining part of the old Morton Pottery Works. That structure was later removed to make way for a power plant.

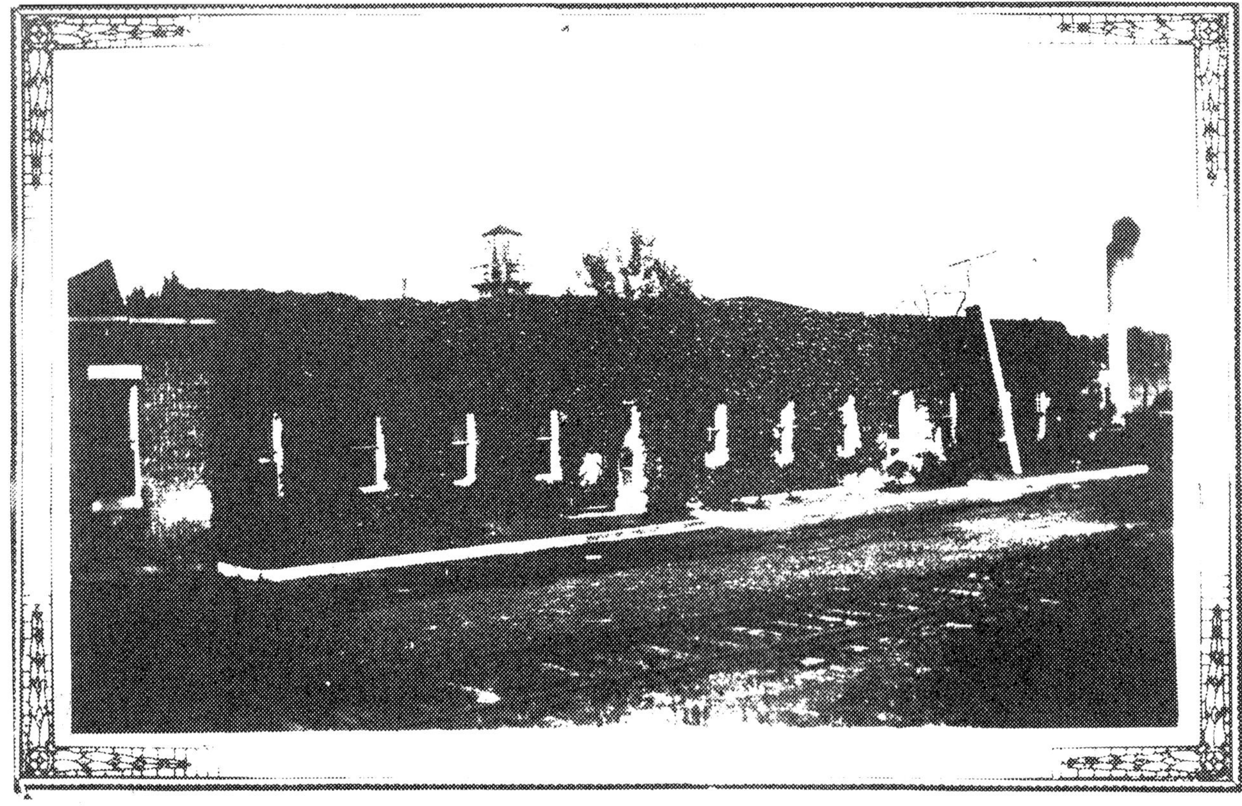

Photo #2 Here is the Cliftwood just before it was sold in 1940. The power plant is visible on the right. On the left is the original office used by the Morton Pottery Works. It continued to be used for that purpose by Cliftwood.

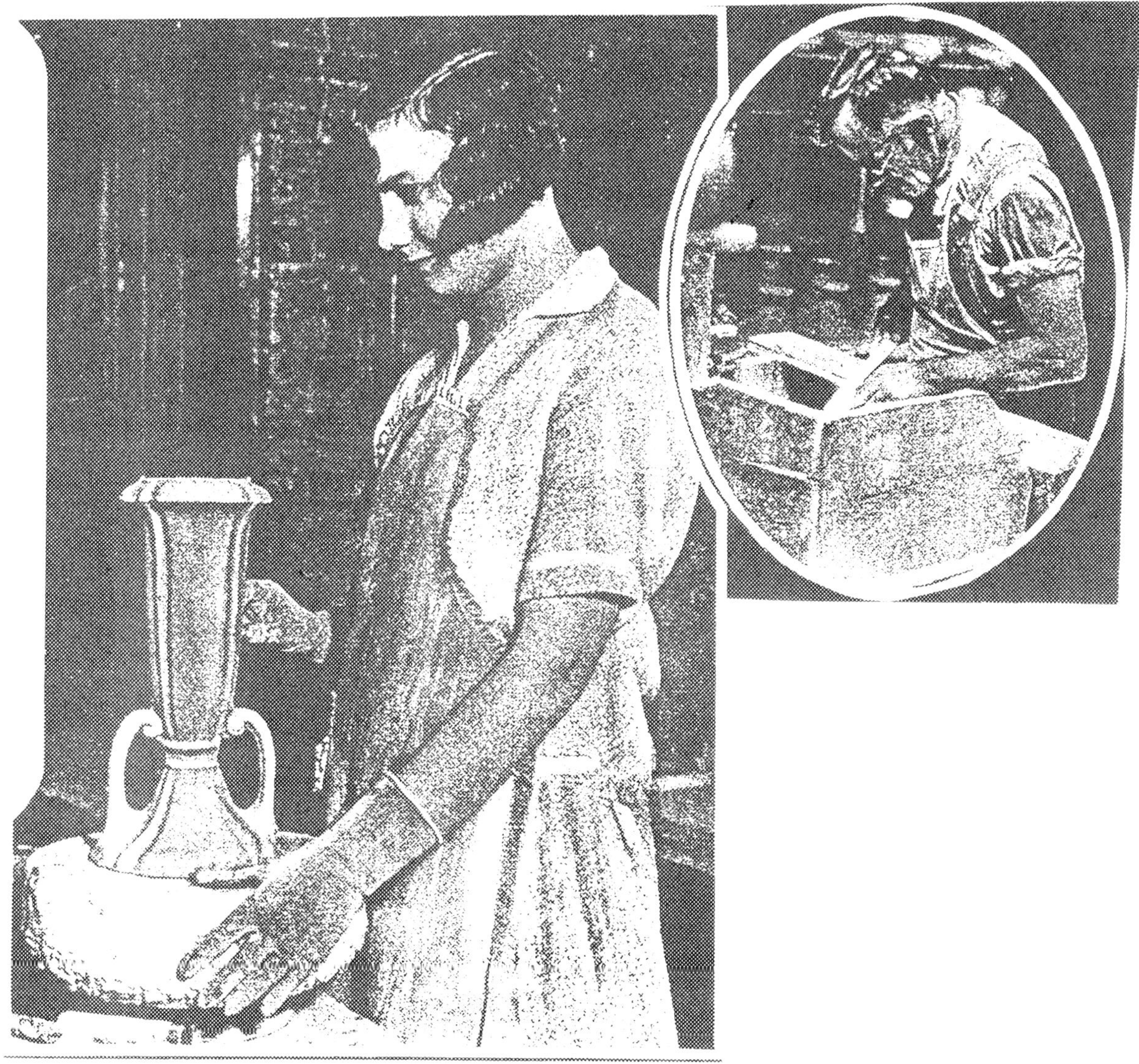

Above Dorothy Allenspach of the Cliftwood Potteries is seen working on what looks like a vase but it will be a lamp. At her right is Matthew Rapp, founder of the potteries, working in his shop.

This is a set of newspaper photographs found in a scrap book that was kept by a Morton Pottery Company employee in the 1930's. The girl appears to be trimming a piece of greenware. It was very unusual for a finisher to use the potter's wheel. It was probably used to add interest to the composition of the photograph. The inset photo of Matthew Rapp is very typical. He frequently worked at his wheel which was protected by the collapsible wooden barrier.

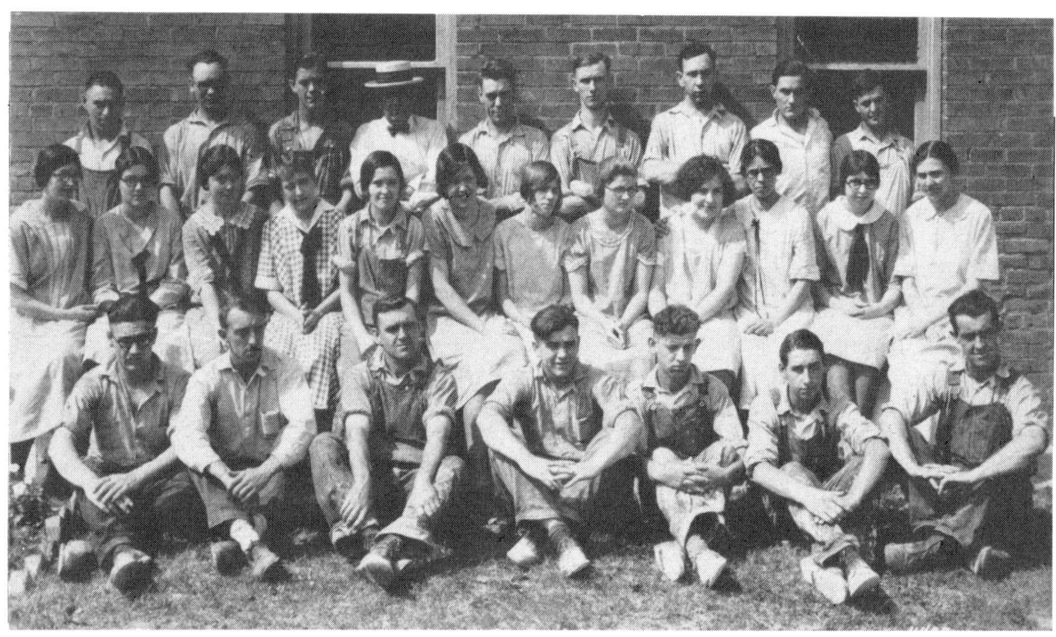

This picture shows the employees of the Cliftwood Pottery, Incorporated

Back Row (left to right): Al Wagler, Carl Spahr, Tedd Rapp, John Gerber, Walter "Girlie" Seidel, Bill Getz, Mike Krug, Ben Wagler, John Kipfer.

2nd Row (left to right): Katherine Moser, Mae Witzig, Olga Witzig, Ida Aupperle, Emily Musselman, Chester Dalby, Rose Slapinski, Esther Eigsti, Madeline Herman, Hannah Rapp, Verena Moser, Marie Kipfer.

1st Row (left to right): Joe Seidel, Lawrence Rapp, Carl Rapp, Ben Seidel, George Greiner, Reuben Wagler, John Rapp.

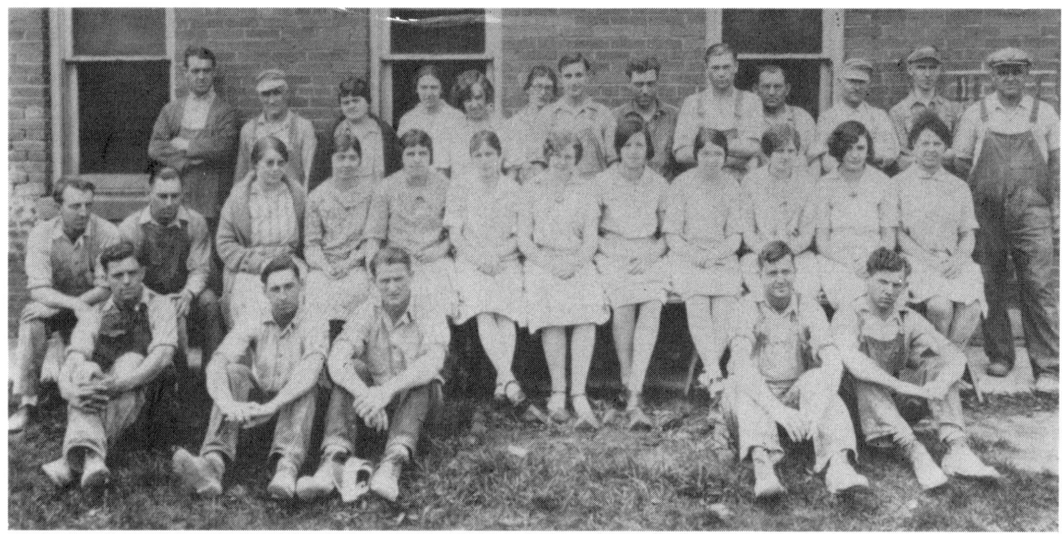

Cliftwood Art Potteries employees, circa 1929.

Back Row (left to right): John Rapp, Joe Getz, Ida Rapp, Marie Kipfer, Ruth Slapinski, Lillian Eigsti, Roy Moser, Walter Seidel, Les Ricketts, John Gerber, Sam Getz, Bill Getz.

Middle Row (left to right): Lawrence Rapp, Al Wagler, Fern Heiser, Olga Witzig, Sarah Rapp, Ida Aupperle, Ina Norquist, Esther Allenspach, Verena Moser, Esther Eigsti, Dorothy Allenspach, Elsie Kuntz, Carl Rapp.

Front Row (left to right): Ted Rapp, Reuben Wagler, Floy Aeschelman, John Kipfer, George Greiner.

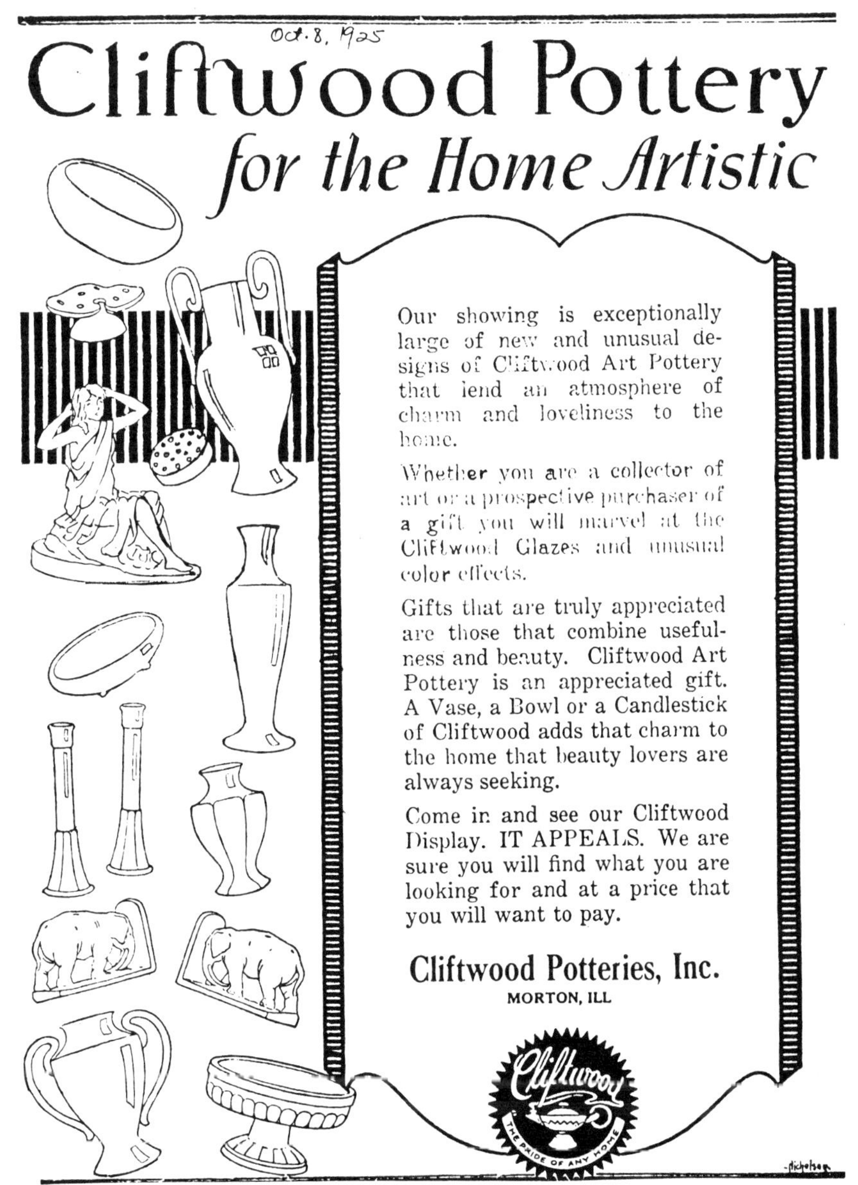

This ad, from the October 8, 1925 issue of the Morton News, pictures a collection of the more popular items in the Cliftwood Art ware line. The prices were very reasonable. The Lorilei flower holder was $3.00. The elephant book-ends were $4.50 a pair. The ten inch candle sticks, the bowl above them, and the lily paid flower holder near the top, sold for $8.00 for the four pieces.

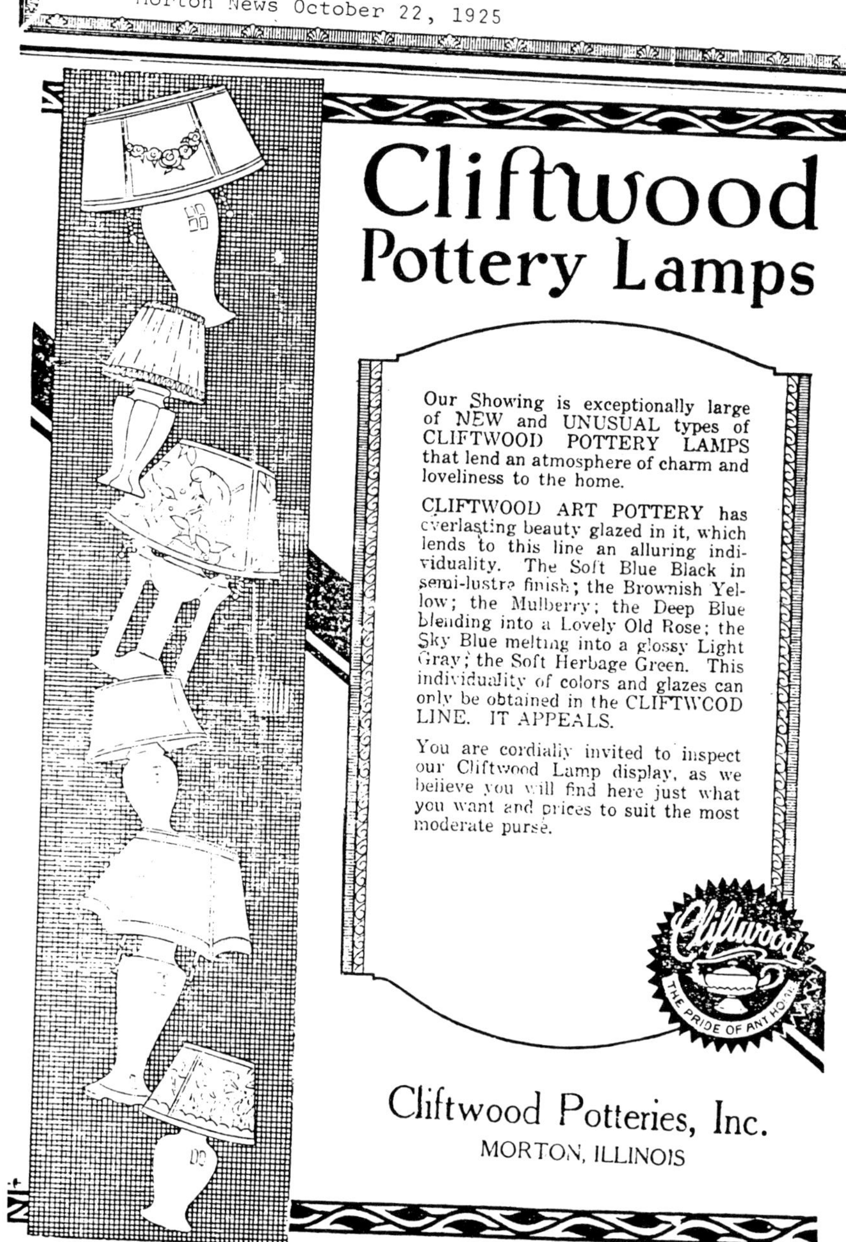
Morton News October 22, 1925

Cliftwood Pottery Lamps

Our Showing is exceptionally large of NEW and UNUSUAL types of CLIFTWOOD POTTERY LAMPS that lend an atmosphere of charm and loveliness to the home.

CLIFTWOOD ART POTTERY has everlasting beauty glazed in it, which lends to this line an alluring individuality. The Soft Blue Black in semi-lustre finish; the Brownish Yellow; the Mulberry; the Deep Blue blending into a Lovely Old Rose; the Sky Blue melting into a glossy Light Gray; the Soft Herbage Green. This individuality of colors and glazes can only be obtained in the CLIFTWOOD LINE. IT APPEALS.

You are cordially invited to inspect our Cliftwood Lamp display, as we believe you will find here just what you want and prices to suit the most moderate purse.

Cliftwood Potteries, Inc.
MORTON, ILLINOIS

The lamps pictured in this ad that ran in the Morton News in 1925 are six popular styles with shades made at The Cliftwood Studio. Table lamps and boudoir lamps are featured. Alternating from the top are table lamps. Number one is 25" tall, number three is 22 1/2" tall, and number five is 28" tall. The boudoir lamps are number two, 9" tall, and number four and number six are each 10 1/2" tall.

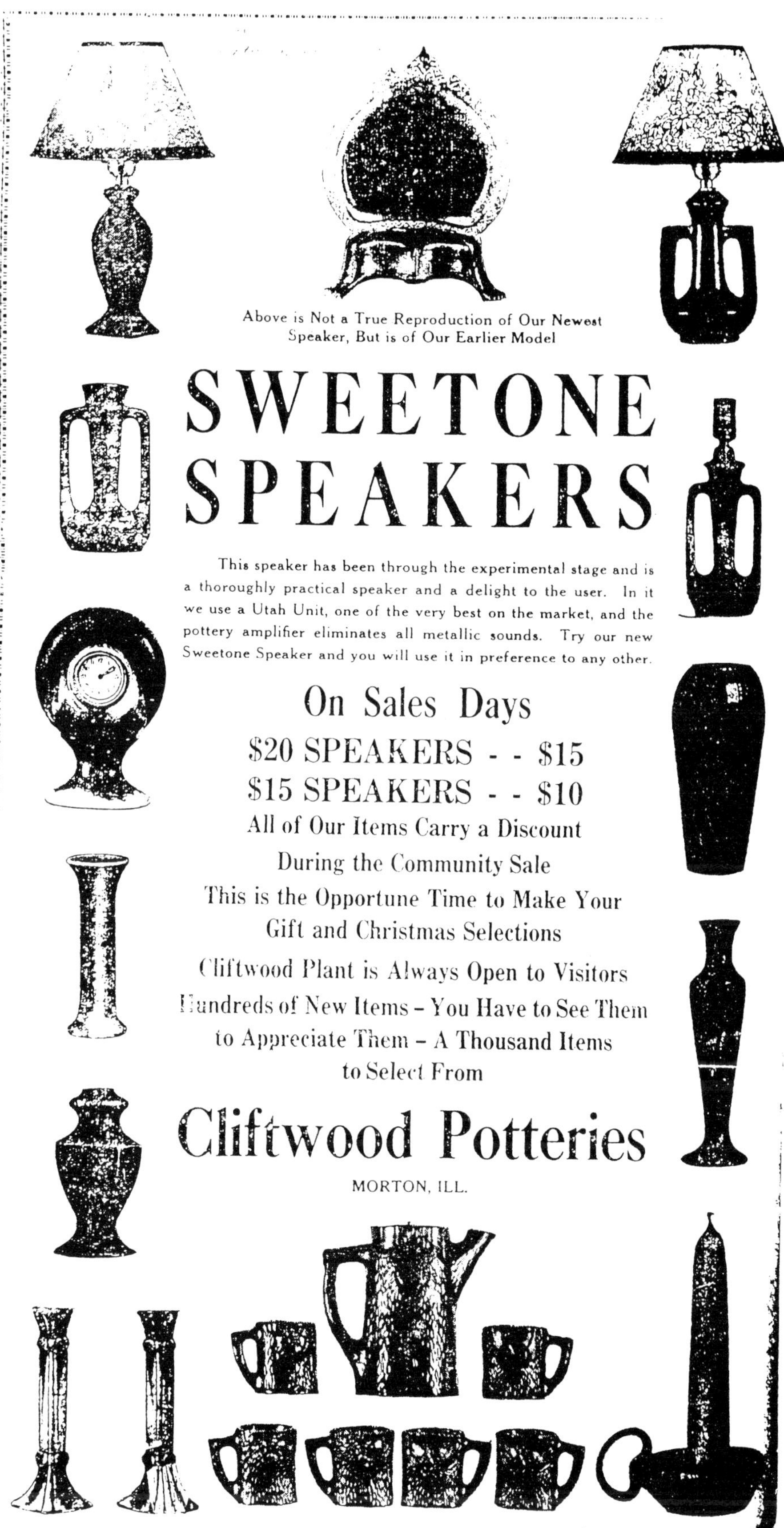

This was a sixteen inch, four column ad that ran in the <u>Morton News</u> on October 15, 1926. It was rather ostentatious for that period of time.

CHAPTER 4

Historical Sketch 1920-1940

Cliftwood Art Pottery owed its success to Matthew Rapp and his four sons, John, Carl, Lawrence, and Theodore. Matthew's experience with pottery making went back to the very first earthenware operation in Morton. He and his five brothers were founders of the Rapp Brothers Brick and Tile Company in 1877, and the Morton Pottery Works in 1878. Sons and daughters of all six brothers were apprenticed to the tile works and the pottery as soon as they were old enough to work. Therefore, the organizers of the Cliftwood Pottery were not novices. They had impressive credentials to carry along with them.

Production at the old pottery had stopped in 1917 when America entered World War I. Manpower shortages and the inability to procure some of the chemicals needed for production forced the closure of the pottery. Some limited experimental work was done during the war, but full production ceased.

By 1920, Matthew and his sons, eager to get back into the pottery business, began negotiating the takeover of the vacant pottery building where they had worked before the war. Extensive renovation work had to be done to the building. Machinery had to be inspected and repaired. New equipment had to be ordered. During the spring of 1920, the Rapps worked hard to put the pottery back into operation. Their activities were watched with interest by townspeople who were anxious for the return of pottery production to Morton.

From the very beginning of their new endeavor, the Rapps had a mission. That mission was to produce beautiful pottery that they and their community would be proud to acclaim. This foreword to one of their early catalogs makes a feeble attempt to explain that mission. Its extremely long sentence structure has many fragmented ideas loosley incorporated into the statement. That structure causes the reader to lose the message as he attempts to rearrange the effusive material while concentrating on the garbled message. However, the idea that they intend to improve upon the art forms of potteries before them, does filter out of that statement.

Foreword

DEEPLY ENGROSSED in the spirit, since 1877, over forty-five years ago, that glazed Art Pottery should everlastingly retain its beauty, depth, charm and loveliness — yea! even improved upon, we proudly announce to the collectors of art—no matter how critical—to those who appreciate unique, time-worn, distinctive shapes and colors, to those who have not yet found the joy in Art Pottery, in fact, to the great masses everywhere, an old Art carried down from ages unknown to mankind, but coated in new glazes, colors and combination of colors that only nature can explain in her mute, self-styled and most wonderful manner—called for your protection: CLIFTWOOD "The Pride of Any Home."

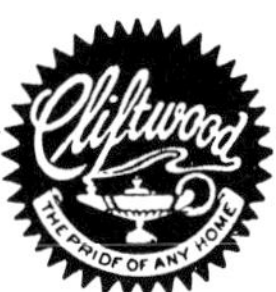

Matthew became the paragon of the art pottery activity that was to come from his newly organized pottery, M. Rapp and Sons. He was not a trained artist, but his inherent ability allowed him to re-direct the pottery industry from the drab, functional wares that he and his brothers had produced at the Morton Pottery Works, to a new color explosion and art deco forms that the 1920's ushered onto the American scene. He was constantly at work designing new pieces with beautiful lines. The effect of his designs was enhanced by new and colorful glazes that he and his son, John, developed. The drip glazes used at were different from any being used in the United States in the nineteen twenties. Operating as M. Rapp and Sons, the pottery was successful from its beginning.

Clay pits, located on the property, provided the primary ingredient for the miniature animals, toys, and novelties that were made. In addition to having an ample supply of clay on the property, the Rapps were also blessed with deep wells of natural gas on the site. That gas was used for firing the kilns. With an abundance of natural gas, the Cliftwood kilns could be regulated to exact temperatures. Those even temperatures limited the number of spoiled wares that often result from wide ranges of temperature during the firing process.

Three kilns were built at the Cliftwood. Each was specially adapted to a particular purpose. One was used to fire green ware which baked at 1500° f. At that temperature, the clay hardened, and the result was a medium beige colored bisque. The second kiln was used to fire glazed ware at 2100° f. The third kiln was smaller, and was used for gold and platinum decorated ware. That kiln fired at 1200° f. In order to set the liquefied finish that was hand applied by brush. Art ware, decorated in that manner, underwent three different kiln firings. All items that were made in solid gold or platinum, were glazed in a special white glaze before undergoing the decorator's brush. Pastel colors were also used for gold and platinum decorations. Only emphasis lines and high lighting effects were done on the colored items.

The gold room was an old building near the pottery that the employees referred to as the shack. It was so small that only two decorators had room to work. The output from that department was limited, and examples are not easily found today. When any are found, it is very unusual for them to be in mint condition. The thin covering of gold or platinum has succumbed to the harsh detergents that have been used to clean them over the years. They were sold with a warning that they should be cleaned with a soft cloth soaked in warm water, then dried and polished immediately. Those warnings, often lost early on, were not heeded. The result was worn or damaged decoration on the art object.

In June, 1922, M. Rapp and Sons incorporated and was named Cliftwood Art Potteries, Incorporated. At that time, twenty-one different shapes were being made. The Cliftwood line included vases, lamps, flower bowls, and single figurine designs. The figurines were animals, birds, and a limited number of human forms. Matthew was determined to bring beauty, charm, and loveliness out of Morton's clay pits, and put quality merchandise on his show room shelves.

In addition to the trendy designs, the Cliftwood glazes became a status symbol of the pottery. All glazes were developed by Matthew and John. One glaze, in particular, was met with much enthusiasm. It was Matthew's pride. He called it chocolate-brown drip, and it was the only glaze formula that he ever kept secret. He was the first potter, in America, to perfect that type of glaze, and he did not intend to share it. It was a combination of transparent glaze over the golden ochre clay that was processed from the pits on the pottery property. Brown glaze was air brushed on the object. That color flowed over the transparent glaze during kiln firing. That combination gave a pleasant brown and tan effect with traces of white highlights. The end result resembles chocolate syrup flowing over a dipper of vanilla ice cream. Frequently the rich brown glaze flowed in heavy drips that held the object to the sagger block. The remains of the sagger as well as the brown drip had to be ground on an abrasive power wheel. Today, the grinding marks on the base of an object is a real help in the identification of Cliftwood pottery.

Matthew kept the chocolate brown formula stored in his mind. He did not write it down, nor did he ever share it with John. The glaze was never produced again after Matthew's death in 1938. John experimented for many years in an effort to recreate the glaze. Though he produced a rather good brown glaze that flowed, he was never able to achieve the quality that his father had developed.

Hindsight has allowed us to analyze the problem for the glaze differences, and to offer a logical reason for John's dilemma. Matthew had used the local clay that was dug on site throughout his life time. By 1940, the supply of local clay was depleted. Commercial clay had to be shipped in from Indiana and South Carolina. The new clay fired out white, instead of the rich golden ochre color the pottery had produced since it's inception. The white clay base was a sharp deviation from the yellow clay that Matthew had used. Had John been able to experiment with the local clay, he might well have been able to duplicate his father's discovery, and continue with the production of the chocolate brown drip glaze.

John created an interesting new glaze that was added to Cliftwood's rainbow of color in 1926. It was called jade green. The local newspaper, The Morton News, credited John's achievement in its October 26th issue. ". . . jade green, a color which heretofore could not be used with the Cliftwood clay, has been developed and is meeting with great favor among pottery buyers. The color, the twentieth used by the company, has been produced by John Rapp, color and chemical man for the pottery." That glaze has never been reproduced either. The identifying secret of that beautiful jade green color is the iridescence that is noted when an object in that color is slowly turned in bright light. The glaze gives off a myriad of rainbow colors that are often found on rain drenched streets where gasoline and oil have been trapped in puddles.

Another color attributed to John was Cliftwood's cobalt blue. It is a high gloss glaze that appears to be black at first glance. Only in very bright sunlight can the deep blue color be detected. Another method of verifying the color is to examine the bottom of an object, or the inside, if there is an orifice. More pronounced tints of blue will be found in those places. The bottom of Cliftwood's products was not glazed, but paraffined. Lighter traces of the blue can be found where the waxed bottom was sponged before firing. Because cobalt was expensive, vases and other objects that could be glazed inside, were frequently hand submerged in the glaze barrel after the inside had been given a transparent glaze treatment. By submerging, only the outside was glazed in the cobalt blue with about an inch overrun on the lip. That overrun often flowed down into the transparent glaze, so traces of lighter blue can sometimes be detected on the inside of an object being examined.

Five years after the Cliftwood started production, the Rapps began producing their first examples of art pottery. J. E. Gerber was hired to head the sales division and promote the new line of art pottery. A contract was also signed with the newly organized Morton Pottery Company, whereby its sales representatives would also sell for Cliftwood. Sales reps carried large trunks full of samples, and a complete portfolio of photographs showing the art ware that was being produced in Morton. Those sales persons called on gift shops and floral supply companies throughout the entire United States. Records from the mid 1920's show orders coming from such diverse locations as Chicago, Illinois; Seattle, Washington; Rutland, Vermont; Waco, Texas; San Francisco, California; and Minneapolis, Minnesota, to name a few. Gerber also hired locals to work on a part time schedule. They went door to door in Morton and surrounding communities, and generated a good amount of business for the pottery. The very first piece of Cliftwood pottery in the authors' collection was purchased from a "door knocker."

To further expand the sales of Cliftwood Art Potteries, arrangements were made with the Fred C. Reimer Company at 49 West 23rd Street, New York City, to become a representative for the pottery. A show room was opened at that New York location, and Reimer advertised extensively in the Crockery and Glass Journal in the 1920's. Reimer's successful merchandising of Cliftwood Art Pottery led the company to consider Chicago as a mid-western location to display its pottery. A sample room was opened at 54 West Lake Street in December, 1929. In June, 1930, that show room was moved to the newly opened Merchandise Mart building on Wacker Drive. The pottery leased space for a year. At that time, the building had more floor space than any other building in the world. In room 15106, Cliftwood had a complete display of all products, showing every color and combination of colors done at the pottery. Business was flourishing. The pottery was receiving national recognition. The local newspaper reported it in this manner: "Matthew Rapp, who is the principal originator of all design, has been commended very highly by some of the large department store heads throughout the country."

Encouraged by the popularity of the art ware line and by the volume of orders that were coming to the pottery, two related businesses were begun by Matthew Rapp and his sons at two separate locations in Morton. On August 15, 1931, the Cliftwood Inn had its grand opening. Located on a busy highway at the west edge of Morton, it was a short order restaurant with a soda fountain, and a display area for the pottery. The Inn had evening and Sunday hours to allow time to man the operation after the day's work was done at the pottery. It was the wives of the Rapps who worked at the Cliftwood Inn, but the men helped out when time allowed. That venture was never a good money maker for the Rapps. At the end of two and a half years, it was sold. The new owners removed the pottery display in order to increase seating capacity in the restaurant. Since that first sale, there have been many others. Ironically, every new owner retained the name Cliftwood. The restaurant is still in operation at the original location on the west side of Morton. Though the pottery has long disappeared, the restaurant is viable evidence that it did exist.

Aug 6, 1931

Cliftwood Potteries, Inc.

Announce the Opening
of Their
New Show and Lunch Room
Known as

"CLIFTWOOD INN"

On Route 121

Watch for the Specials on the Date
of Our Grand Opening

SATURDAY, AUGUST 15

LAMPS SHADES VASES
KITCHENWARE NOVELTIES

Visitors Welcome

In January, 1932, the second satellite business, the Cliftwood Studio, was established by the Rapps in the two hundred block of south Main Street. That new decorating department occupied the Waldbeser Building which was razed in the 1950's to make space for a modern brick building that houses General Telephone Company. Maud Downes, from Chicago, was in charge of the studio. Two artists, Audrey York, from Texas, and Richard Betline from Chicago, assisted Mrs. Downes. Several local women were employed as apprentices at the studio.

By establishing the Cliftwood Studio, decorated lamps and made-to-order shades were added to Cliftwood's expanding line of pottery. The lamps and shades were decorated with birds, flowers, and geometric patterns. Special orders could be placed at the studio if more elaborate decoration was desired, or if a customer wanted to coordinate the lamps to a particular decorating scheme in the home. Local townspeople frequently referred to the studio as the lamp shade factory. To accommodate them, the pottery occasionally used that identity in its advertising. Thousands of the lamps were decorated and left the studio in the 1930's. Today, they are the most elusive of any of the art wares made by Cliftwood.

During the thirties, the pottery operated at full force, experiencing the general pitfalls of most potteries – kiln explosions, minor fires, and injuries – but 1938 was the most tragic year for the Cliftwood Art Potteries. After a short illness, Matthew Rapp died on January 8. His obituary honored him for the respect and appreciation he had in his community. It also recognized his skill as an artist. The spark that had made Cliftwood a leader in the art pottery world was gone.

As young men, Matthew's sons had been good apprentices. They were very competent to continue the business after his death, but Matthew's enthusiasm and drive was no longer there to propel the operation. Each of the sons were specialists in their own right. John had worked closely with his father to learn the intricacies of glazing. Not only had he been trained in the art of glaze chemistry, he had also been taught glazing and firing techniques. Lawrence emerged as the designer-artist and mold maker. Theodore, or "Ted", as everyone knew him, was responsible for clay preparation and for the molding and finishing departments at the pottery. Carl had always supervised the sales force and was responsible for packing and shipping orders as they came into the factory. Despite their expertise, not one of them was interested in the business transactions that were needed to keep the pottery financially sound. None of them were willing to assume the presidency and manage the overall operation of the pottery.

A business manager was brought in, but the magnetism of Matthew was no longer their guiding force. Within the year following Matthew's death, it was apparent that radical change was needed if the pottery was to continue a profitable operation. The brothers investigated several options, but finally made the difficult decision to sell the Cliftwood Art Pottery. The sale was finalized in early February, 1940. The glory that had been Cliftwood was gone.

CHAPTER 5
Original Cliftwood Catalog

CLIFTWOOD ∻ ART ∻ POTTERY

LIST PRICES

EFFECTIVE JANUARY 1, 1923

THE MORTON POTTERY COMPANY

MORTON, ILL.

Stock No.	Article	Illustrated on Page	Dimensions	List Price per dozen	List Price each
100	Vase	8	Height 8 -in.	$16.80	$1.40
101	Vase	8	Height 9½-in.	22.80	1.90
102	Vase	8	Height 8 -in.	19.20	1.60
103	Vase	5	Height 9½-in.	26.40	2.20
104	Vase	7	Height 7½-in.	21.60	1.80
105	Vase	4	Height 9¼-in.	30.00	2.50
106	Vase	6	Height 6½-in.	9.60	.80
107	Vase	5	Height 8 -in.	19.20	1.60
108	Vase	7	Height 5½-in.	12.00	1.00
109	Vase	6	Height 10½-in.	39.60	3.30
110	Vase	5	Height 10½-in.	43.20	3.60
111	Vase	6	Height 13½-in.	86.40	7.20
112	Vase	8	Height 6 -in.	13.20	1.10
113	Vase	7	Height 15 -in.	64.80	5.40
114	Vase	4	Height 16 -in.	108.00	9.00
115	Vase	5	Height 5¾-in.	13.20	1.10
116	Vase	4	Height 7 -in.	16.80	1.40
117	Vase	9	Height 4½-in.	8.40	.70
118	Vase	6	Height 5½-in.	14.40	1.20
119	Vase	7	Height 6 -in.	13.20	1.10
120	Vase	9	Height 18 -in.	120.00	10.00
121	Vase	9	Height 14 -in.	78.00	6.50
122	Bud Vase	8	Height 6 -in.	9.60	.80
123	Wall Vase	7	Height 6 -in.	14.40	1.20
1	Lamp Mount (with fixture)	8	Height 11 -in.	69.60	5.80
1	Lamp Mount (without fixt.)	8	Height 7½-in.	27.60	2.30
2	Lamp Mount (with fixture)	6	Height 11 -in.	69.60	5.80
2	Lamp Mount (without fixt.)	6	Height 7¼-in.	27.60	2.30
3	Lamp Mount (with fixture)	7	Height 23 -in.	150.00	12.50
3	Lamp Mount (without fixt.)	7	Height 11¾-in.	86.40	7.20
4	Lamp Mount (with fixture)	6	Height 23½-in.	172.80	14.40
4	Lamp Mount (without fixt.)	6	Height 13 -in.	108.00	9.00
6	Lamp Mount (with fixture)	4	Height 16½-in.	194.40	16.20
6	Lamp Mount (without fixt.)	4	Height 5 -in.	130.00	10.83
7	Lamp Mount (with fixture)	4	Height 11 -in.	37.60	3.13
7	Lamp Mount (without fixt.)	4	Height 7 -in.	16.80	1.40
200	Candlestick	9	Height 10½-in.	25.20	2.10
201	Candlestick	~~9~~ 5	Height 7 -in.	10.80	.90
225	Fruit Bowl	9	Height 5½-in., Dia. 6-in.	20.40	1.70
4 -in.	Shallow Flower Bowl	10	Diameter 4 -in.	4.80	.40
5 -in.	Shallow Flower Bowl	10	Diameter 5 -in.	7.20	.60
5½-in.	Shallow Flower Bowl	10	Diameter 5½-in.	8.40	.70
6½-in.	Shallow Flower Bowl	10	Diameter 6½-in.	10.80	.90
7 -in.	Shallow Flower Bowl	10	Diameter 7 -in.	14.40	1.20
8 -in.	Shallow Flower Bowl	10	Diameter 8 -in.	20.40	1.70
9 -in.	Shallow Flower Bowl	10	Diameter 9 -in.	25.20	2.10
10 -in.	Shallow Flower Bowl	10	Diameter 10 -in.	32.40	2.70

Stock No.	Article	Illustrated on Page	Dimensions	List Price per dozen	List Price each
5½-in.	Deep Flower Bowl	10	Diameter 5½-in.	9.60	.80
6½-in.	Deep Flower Bowl	10	Diameter 6½-in.	12.00	1.00
7 -in.	Deep Flower Bowl	10	Diameter 7 -in.	16.80	1.40
5 -in.	Deep Bulb Bowl	10	Diameter 5 -in.	10.80	.90
6 -in.	Deep Bulb Bowl	10	Diameter 6 -in.	14.40	1.20
1	Disk Insert*	11		1.80	.15
2	Disk Insert*	11		2.70	.23
3	Disk Insert*	11		5.40	.45
4	Disk Insert*	11		8.10	.68
1	Lily Insert*	11		5.40	.45
2	Lily Insert*	11		10.80	.90
1	Turtle Insert*	11		3.00	.25
2	Turtle Insert*	11		6.00	.50
1	Frog Insert*	11		10.80	.90
	Tiger	12		72.00	6.00
	Lion	12		72.00	6.00
	Elephant	12		72.00	6.00

*For proper use of Inserts see page 11 of our catalog.

READ CAREFULLY

HOW TO ORDER: Order by stock number and name of article (dimensions are not necessary). Specify quantity and letter of each color desired (see alphabetical color chart below or on page 3 of our catalog). If selection of colors is to be left to our taste, simply state "assorted colors". To illustrate:

½ dozen No. 105 Vases, 2-A, 2-B, 2-C
½ dozen 7-inch Shallow Bowls, Assorted Colors

TERMS: 30 days net or 2% for cash in 10 days. All quotations f.o.b. Morton, Illinois. Moderate charges for packages are made.

CLIFTWOOD COLOR CHART

Color Letter	Color	Description of Colors and Glazes
A	Black	A deep blue-black in semi-lustre finish.
B	Yellow	A rich creamy yellow of velvet finish.
C	Old Rose	A soft toned, velvety pink.
D	Blue	A clear sky blue.
E	Brown	A brownish yellow.
F	Mulberry	Similar to the spectrum between blue and brown.
G	Blue-Pink	A dark blue which appears to melt unevenly and gradually blends into a brilliant pink.
H	Blue-White	A clear sky blue which has the effect of melting over a light gray.
I	Sunset	A combination of several colors blending naturally into one another and which can be described only by referring to a beautiful sunset.
J	Ivory	True to the color ivory itself.
K	Green	Similar to the color of growing plants.
L	Blue-Mulberry	A rich blue which appears to melt unevenly and gradually blends into a beautiful mulberry.

Cliftwood
ART POTTERY

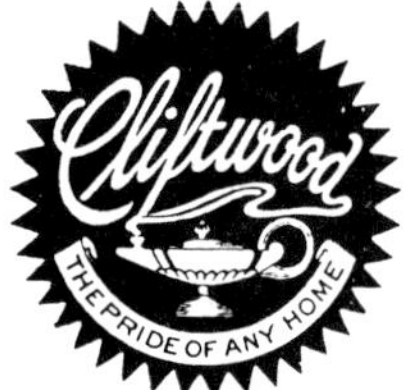

This emblem protects you

THE MORTON POTTERY CO.

Established 1877

HOME OFFICES AND SHOPS
MORTON, ILLINOIS

Foreword

DEEPLY ENGROSSED in the spirit, since 1877, over forty-five years ago, that glazed Art Pottery should everlastingly retain its beauty, depth, charm and loveliness — yea! even improved upon, we proudly announce to the collectors of art—no matter how critical—to those who appreciate unique, time-worn, distinctive shapes and colors, to those who have not yet found the joy in Art Pottery, in fact, to the great masses everywhere, an old Art carried down from ages unknown to mankind, but coated in new glazes, colors and combination of colors that only nature can explain in her mute, self-styled and most wonderful manner—called for your protection: CLIFTWOOD "The Pride of Any Home."

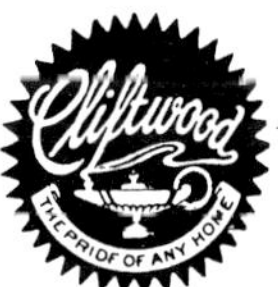

CLIFTWOOD Glazes and Colors

THE BEAUTIFUL EFFECTS obtained only in CLIFTWOOD glazes cannot be justifiably described in words. Any attempt to do so would not only give the reader a faint idea of their beautiful effects, but would be unfair to them.

The above, is also true of CLIFTWOOD colors, and for these reasons we have reproduced a few of our colors and combination of colors on our various shapes, as near as is humanly possible, in the following pages of this catalog. While CLIFTWOOD Art Pottery carries with it the unique distinction that no two pieces are exactly alike in color, we do not want our readers to interpret the illustrations shown in this catalog as being the limit of our colors and combinations of colors. Almost daily, in fact, upon drawing each kiln, new color effects are brought to light. Our ceramists unceasingly devote their labors day and night not only to develop new glazes, but to give CLIFTWOOD collectors a variety of Art Pottery that is both new and beautiful. These new creations will be announced in the order of their development.

For the convenience of our customers we have prepared an alphabetical color chart as follows:

Color Letter	Color	Description of Colors and Glazes
A	Black..........	A deep blue-black in semi-lustre finish.
B	Yellow.........	A rich, creamy yellow of velvet tone.
C	Old Rose......	A soft-toned velvety pink.
D	Blue...........	A clear sky-blue.
E	Brown.........	A tawny brown or brownish yellow.
F	Mulberry......	Similar to the spectrum between blue and brown.
G	Blue-Pink......	A dark blue which droops unevenly and gradually blends into a brilliant pink.
H	Blue-White...	A clear sky-blue which has the effect of melting over a glossy light gray.
I	Sunset......	A combination of several colors, each blending naturally with the others.
J	Ivory..........	True to the color of ivory itself.
K	Green.........	The color of herbage and growing plants.
L	Blue Mulberry.	A rich blue which appears to melt unevenly and gradually blends into a beautiful mulberry.

NOTE: When ordering, specify color by letter.

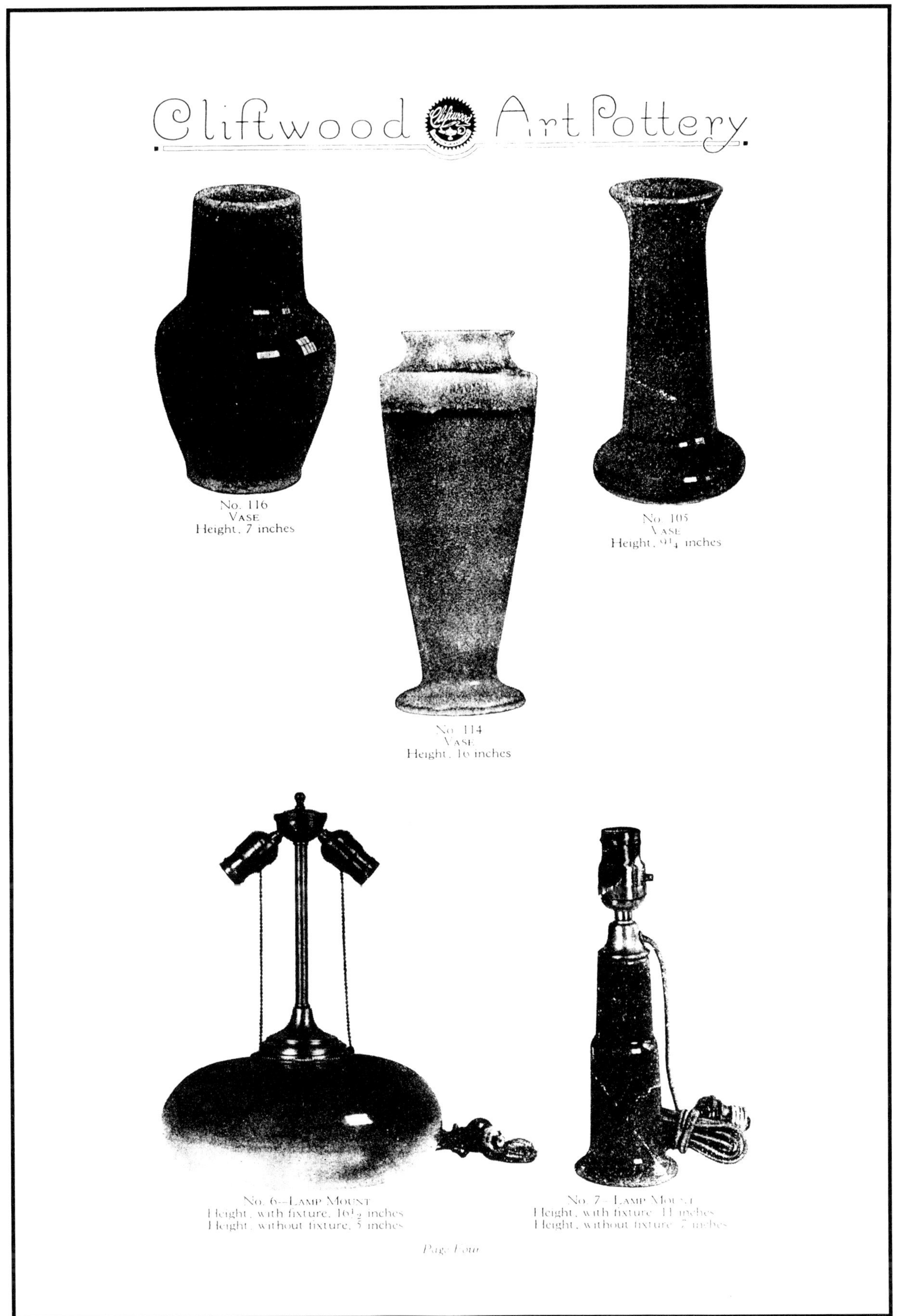

Cliftwood Art Pottery

No. 116
Vase
Height, 7 inches

No. 105
Vase
Height, $9\frac{1}{4}$ inches

No. 114
Vase
Height, 10 inches

No. 6—Lamp Mount
Height, with fixture, $16\frac{1}{2}$ inches
Height, without fixture, 5 inches

No. 7—Lamp Mount
Height, with fixture, 11 inches
Height, without fixture, 7 inches

Page Four

Note: The low end of the value range should be for solid colors. The upper end should be for drip glazes or color combinations.

Page 4 #116 – **$18-22** #114 – **$65-75** #105 – **$25-30** #6 – **$70-80** #7 – **$30-40**

Cliftwood Art Pottery

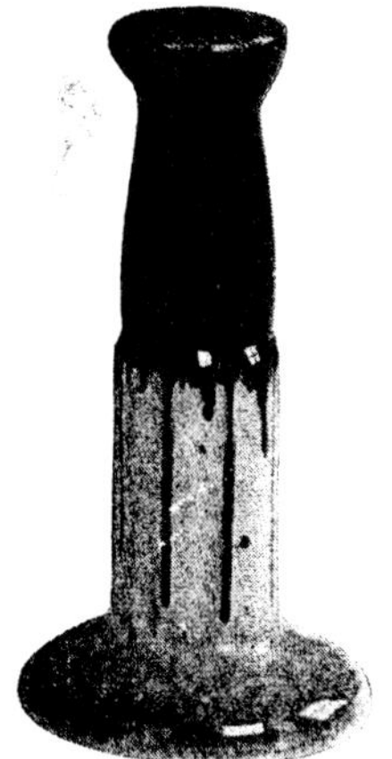

No. 201
CANDLESTICK
Height, 7 inches

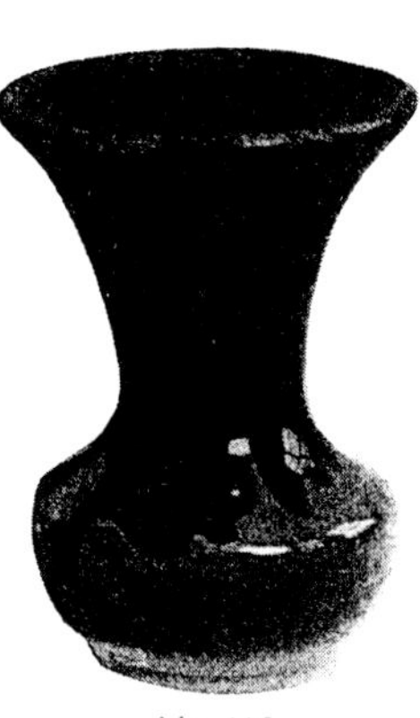

No. 115
VASE
Height, 5¾ inches

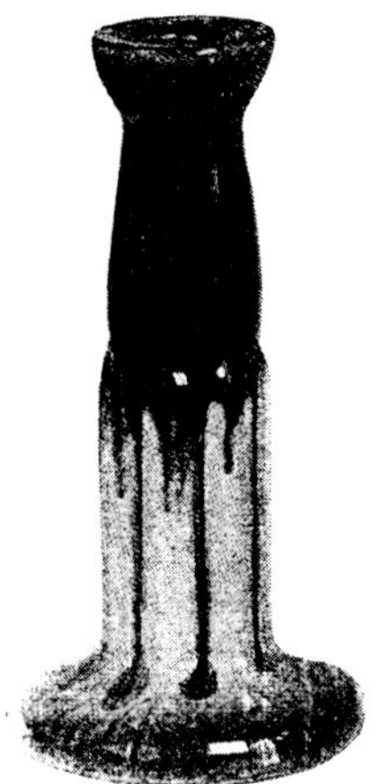

No. 201
CANDLESTICK
Height, 7 inches

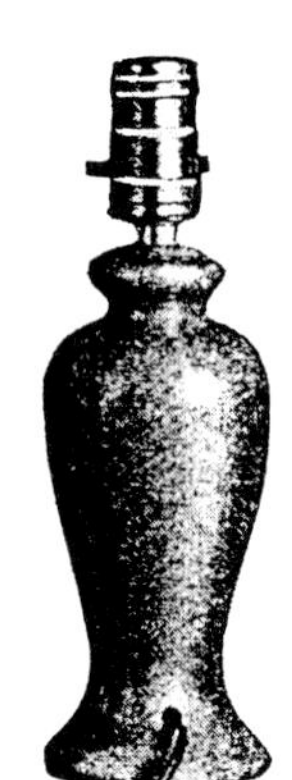

LAMP MOUNT
No. 2

Complete with fixture
Height, 10 inches
Price, each, $5.50

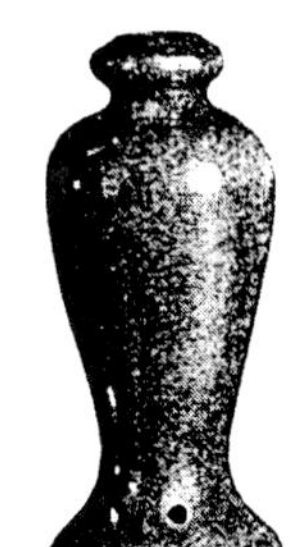

LAMP MOUNT
No. 2 N. F.

Without fixture
Height, 7½ inches
Price per doz., $24.00

Our No. 2 Boudoir Lamp with its delicate lines, has been approved by the most critical buyers.

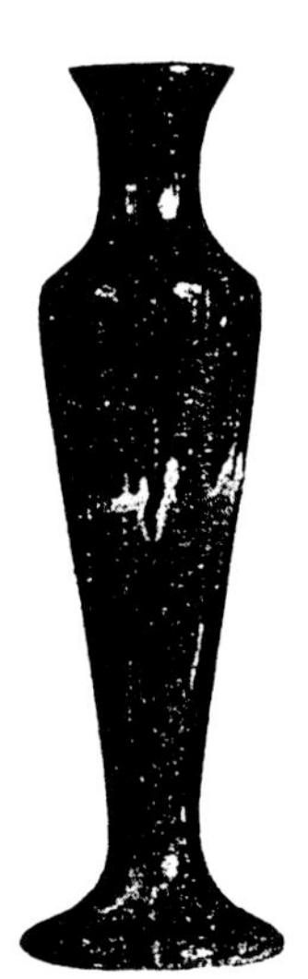

LAMP MOUNT
No. 4 N. F.

Without Fixture
Height, 15 inches
Price, each, $5.40

Page 5

#201 – **$40-50 pair** #115 – **$18-22** #110 – **$30-40** #103 – **$25-30** #107 – **$25-30**

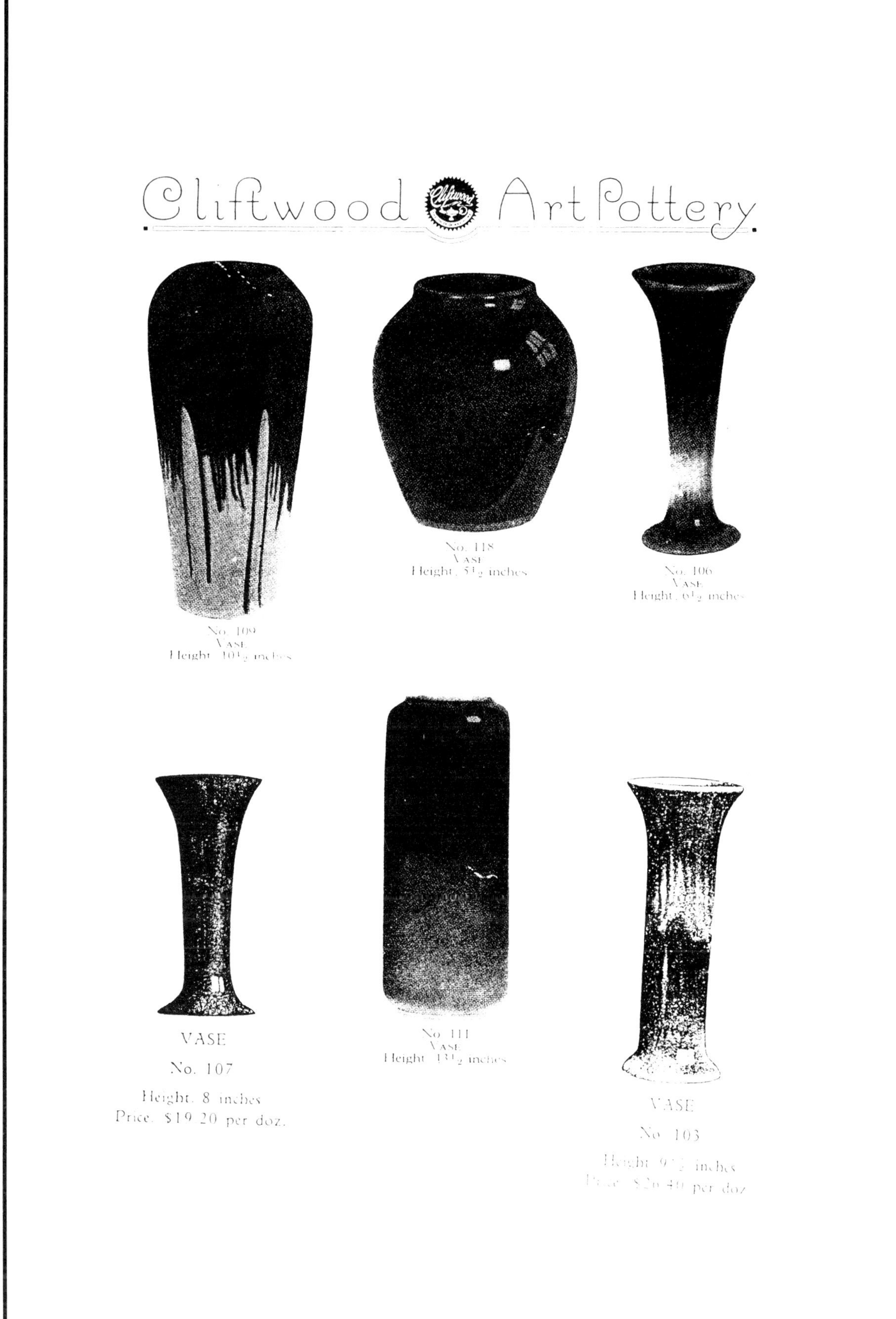

Page 6

#109 – **$30-40 pair** #118 – **$18-22** #106 – **$20-24** #111 – **$40-50**
#4 – **$50-60** #4NF – **$40-50** #2 – **#30-40** #2NF – **$20-24**

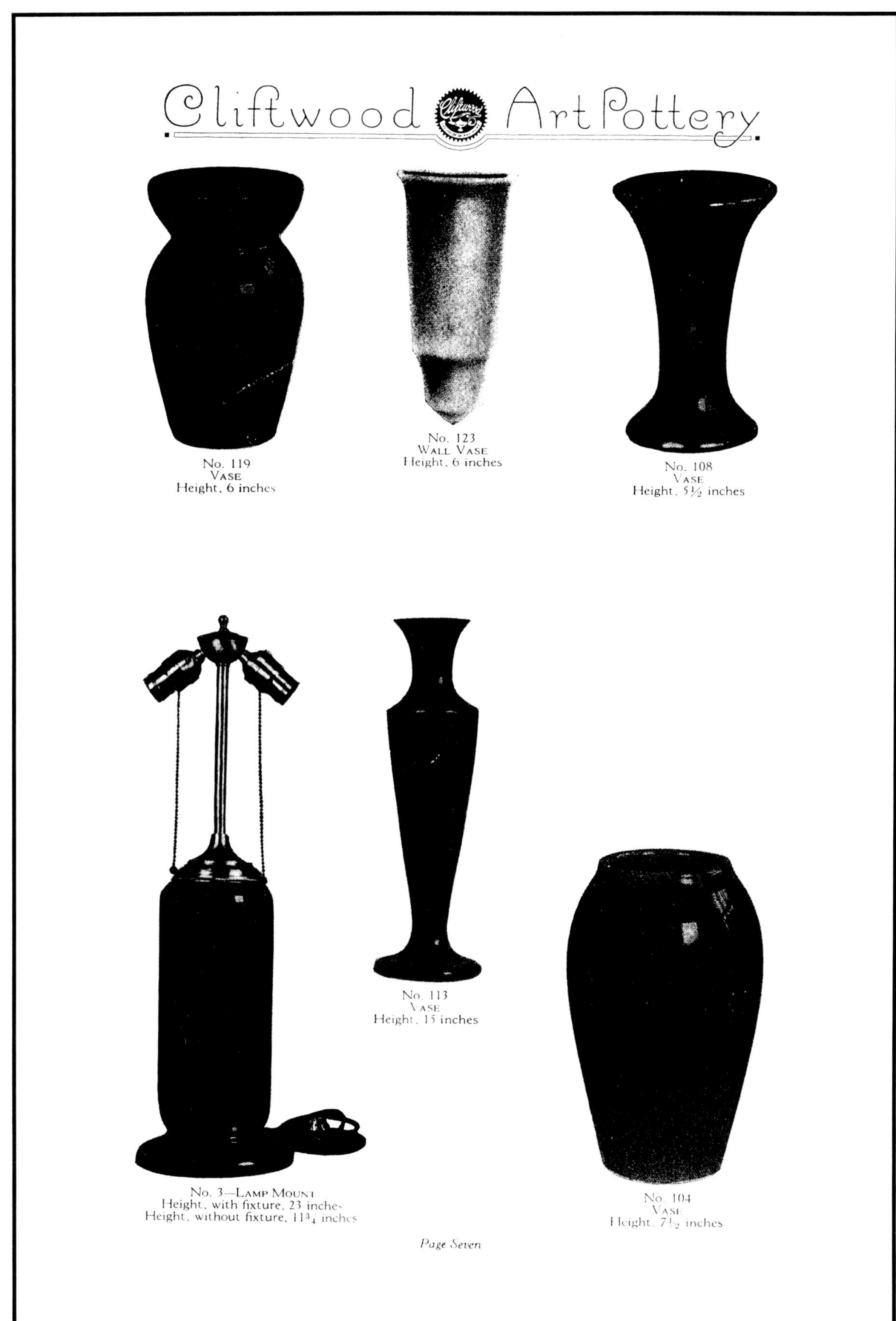

Cliftwood Art Pottery

No. 119
Vase
Height, 6 inches

No. 123
Wall Vase
Height, 6 inches

No. 108
Vase
Height, 5½ inches

No. 3—Lamp Mount
Height, with fixture, 23 inches
Height, without fixture, 11¾ inches

No. 113
Vase
Height, 15 inches

No. 104
Vase
Height, 7½ inches

Page Seven

Page 7

#119 – **$18-22** #123 – **$30-40** #108 – **$18-22** #113 – **$40-50** #3 – **$60-70** #104 – **$20-24**

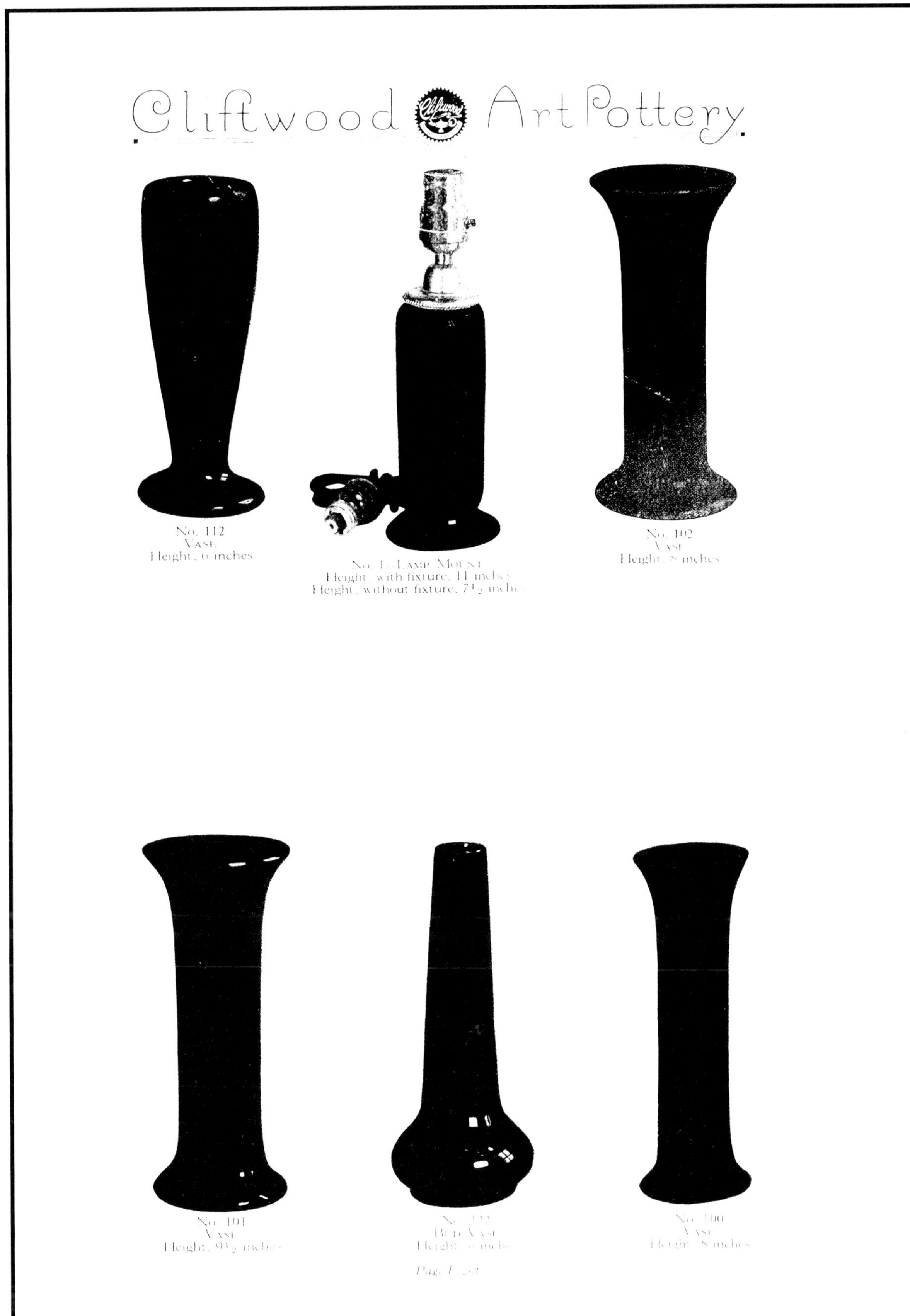

Page 8

#112 – **$18-22** #1 – **$40-50** #102 – **$20-24** #101 – **$25-30**
#122 – **$15-20** #100 – **$20-24**

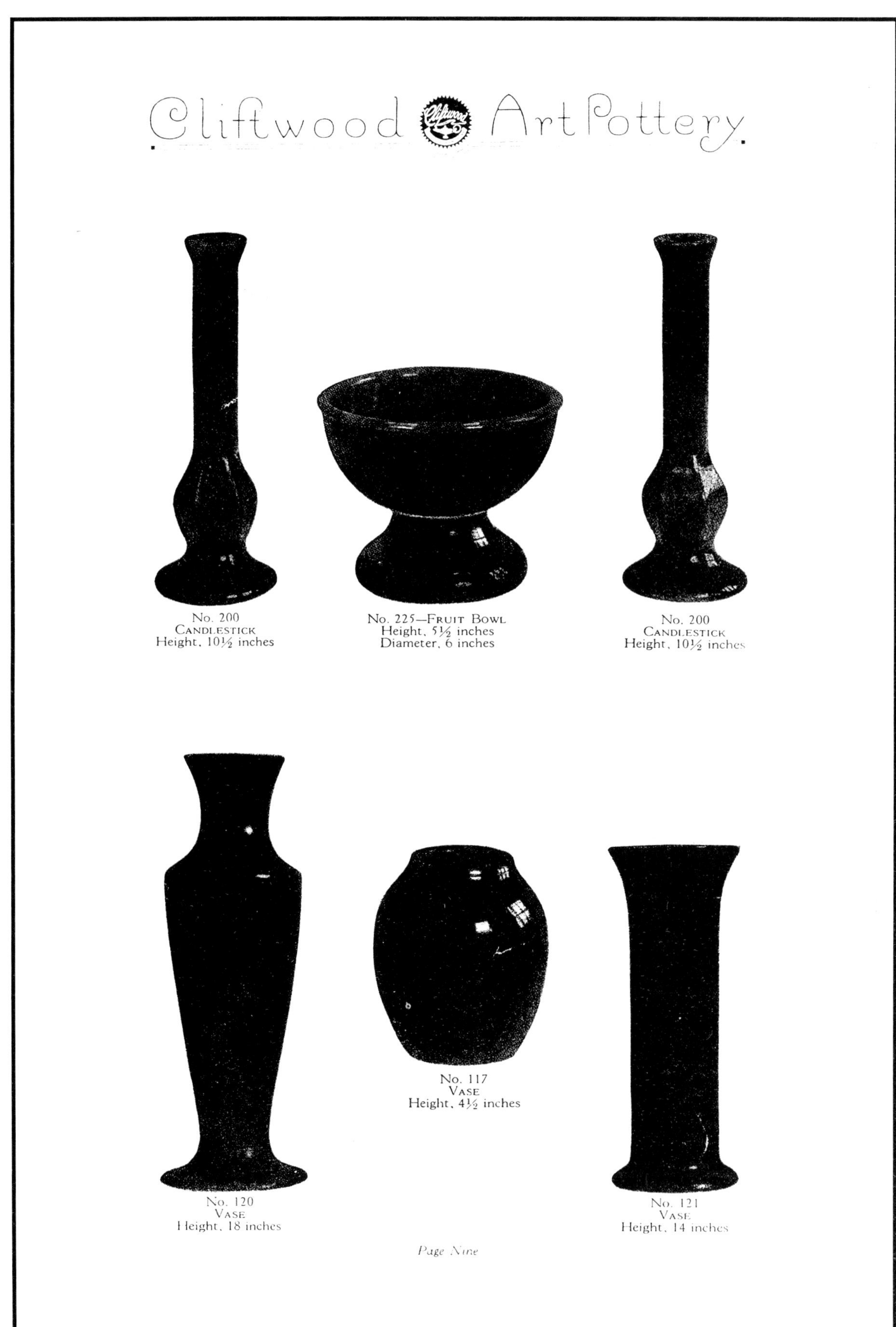
Cliftwood Art Pottery

No. 200
Candlestick
Height, 10½ inches

No. 225—Fruit Bowl
Height, 5½ inches
Diameter, 6 inches

No. 200
Candlestick
Height, 10½ inches

No. 117
Vase
Height, 4½ inches

No. 120
Vase
Height, 18 inches

No. 121
Vase
Height, 14 inches

Page Nine

Page 9

#200 – **$50-60 pair** #225 – **$40-50** #120 – **$55-60** #117 – **$16-18** #121 – **$40-50**

Cliftwood Art Pottery.

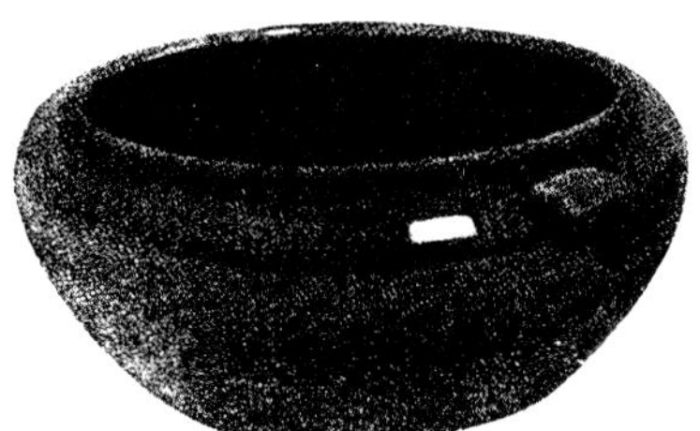

Deep Bulb Bowls
Diameter, 5 inches
Diameter, 6 inches

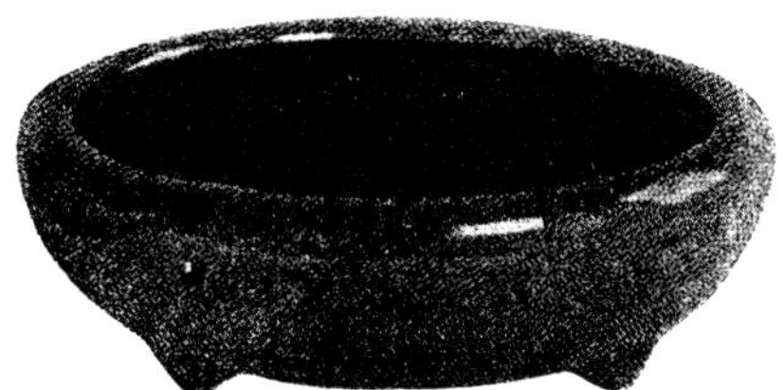

Deep Flower or Bulb Bowls
Diameter, 5½ inches
Diameter, 6½ inches
Diameter, 7 inches

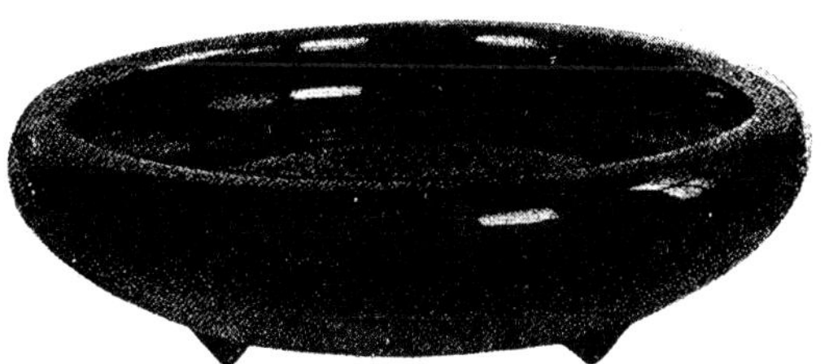

Shallow Flower Bowls
Diameter, 4 inches
Diameter, 5 inches
Diameter, 5½ inches
Diameter, 6½ inches
Diameter, 7 inches
Diameter, 8 inches
Diameter, 9 inches
Diameter, 10 inches

Page Ten

Page 10 Deep Bulb Bowls 5" - **$8-12** 6" – **$12-16**
Deep Flower of Bulb Bowl 5½" – **$12-16** 6½" – **$15-20** 7" – **$18-24**
Shallow Flower Bowls 4" – **$8-10** 5" – **$10-12** 5½" – **$12-14** 6½" – $15-20
7" – **$20-25** 8" – **$25-30** 9" – **$30-35** 10" – **$35-40**

Cliftwood Art Pottery

LILY INSERTS
No. 1—Use with 6½, 7 and 8-inch bowls
No. 2—Use with 9 and 10-inch bowls

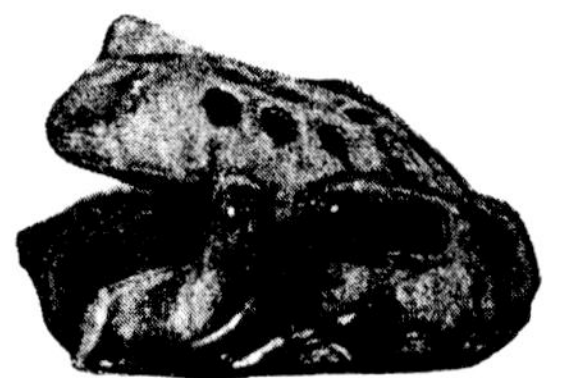

FROG INSERTS
No. 1—Use with 9 and 10-inch bowls

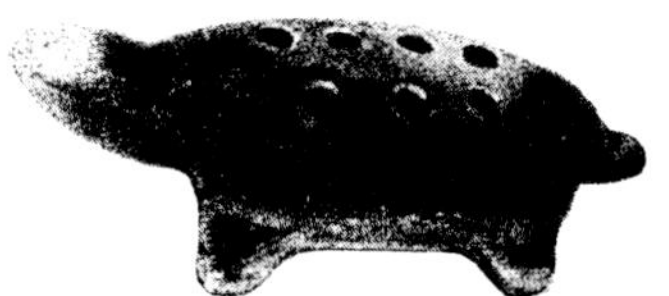

TURTLE INSERTS
No. 1—Use with 5, 5½, 6½ and 7-inch bowls
No. 2—Use with 8, 9 and 10-inch bowls

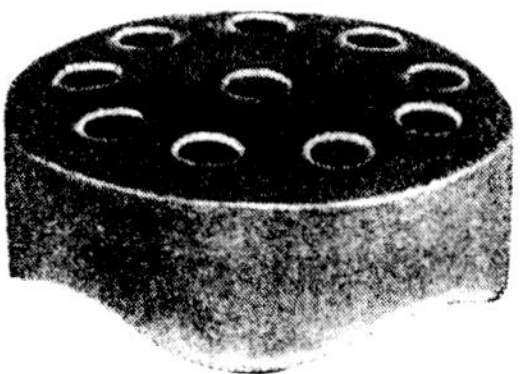

DISK INSERTS
No. 1—Use with 4-inch bowls
No. 2—Use with 5-inch bowls
No. 3—Use with 5½, 6½, 7 and 8-inch bowls
No. 4—Use with 9 and 10-inch bowls

Page 11

Lily Insert #1 – **$18-24** #2 – **$25-35** Frog Insert #1 – **$20-25**
Turtle Inserts #1 – **$12-20** #2 – **$16-24** Disk Inserts #1 – **$6-8** #2 – **$8-10**
#3 – **$10-12** #4 – **$12-14**

Cliftwood Art Pottery

Lion
Length, 16 inches
Height, 9¼ inches
Color, natural

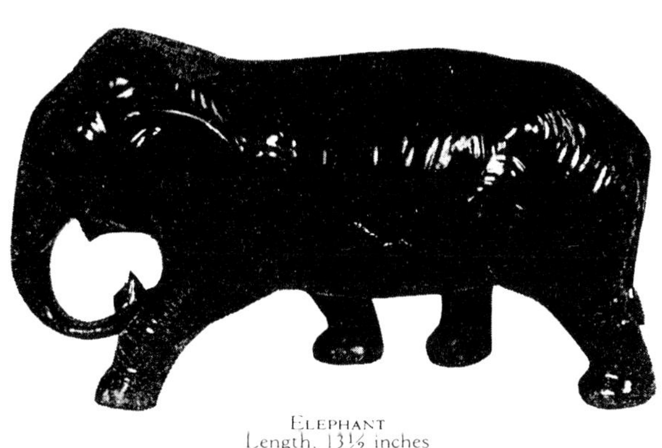

Elephant
Length, 13½ inches
Height, 7¼ inches
Color, natural

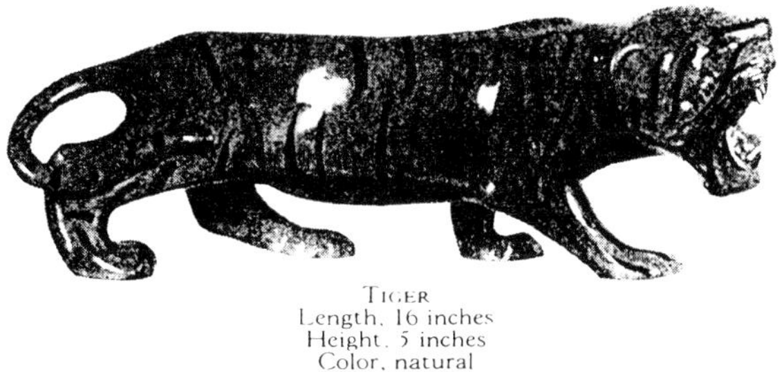

Tiger
Length, 16 inches
Height, 5 inches
Color, natural

Page Twelve

THE FAITHORN COMPANY
CHICAGO

Page 12

Lion – **$125-150** Elephant – **$75-100** Tiger – **$100-125**

CLIFTWOOD POTTERY

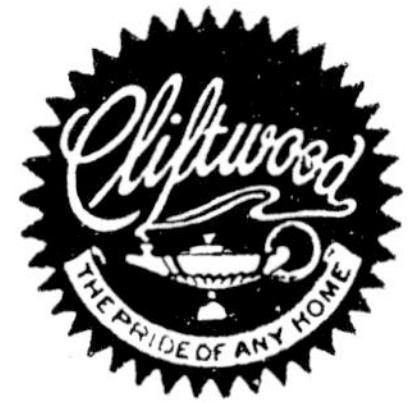

THE CLIFTWOOD POTTERIES
MORTON, ILLINOIS

CLIFTWOOD ART POTTERY

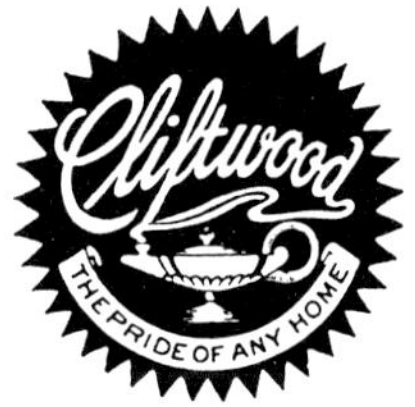

Cliftwood Potteries

Established 1877

MORTON, ILLINOIS

A Suburb of Peoria

Foreword

DEEPLY ENGROSSED in the spirit, since 1877, over forty-five years ago, that glazed Art Pottery should everlastingly retain its beauty, depth, charm and loveliness—yea! even improved upon, we proudly announce to the collectors of art—no matter how critical—to those who appreciate unique, time-worn, distinctive shapes and colors, to those who have not yet found the joy in Art Pottery, in fact, to the great masses everywhere, an old Art carried down from ages unknown to mankind, but coated in new glazes, colors and combination of colors that only nature can explain in her mute, self-styled and most wonderful manner — called for your protection: CLIFTWOOD

"The Pride of Any Home."

How to Order

When ordering give us the quantity desired of each number, then the catalog number of each item, specifying what colors you desire.

When you specify certain colors it will ordinarily take two to three weeks to complete your order.

Most of our customers when ordering specify shipment in assorted colors, in doing this we can ordinarily make deliveries in two to three days and give you an assortment of our very best colors.

Package Charges

There is no package charge on orders amounting to $50.00 at the net prices or over. Any orders that total less than $50.00 net, there is a package charge of 5 per cent or a minimum of 25c.

All goods F. O. B. cars, Morton, Illinois.

Cliftwood Pottery is made in the following items, and new numbers being made every month.

Vases	Candle Sticks
Lamps (mounted)	Fruit Bowls
Lamps (unmounted)	Compotes
Bulb Bowls	Book Ends
Flower Bowls	Pottery Stands, etc.
Flower Inserts	

The above are illustrated in the following pages.

CLIFTWOOD Glazes and Colors

THE BEAUTIFUL EFFECTS obtained only in CLIFTWOOD glazes cannot be described in words. Any attempt to do so would only give the reader a faint idea of their beautiful effects.

The above is also true of CLIFTWOOD colors. CLIFTWOOD Art Pottery carries with it the unique distinction that no two pieces are exactly alike in color, where more than one color is blended on pottery. Almost daily, in fact, upon drawing each kiln, new color effects are brought to light. Our ceramists unceasingly devote their labors day and night not only to develop new glazes, but to give CLIFTWOOD collectors a variety of Art Pottery that is both new and beautiful. These new creations will be announced in the order of their development.

For the convenience of our customers we have prepared an alphabetical color chart as follows:

Color Letter	Color	Description of Colors and Glazes
A	Black	A deep blue-black in semi-lustre finish.
B	Yellow	A rich, creamy yellow of velvet tone.
C	Old Rose	A soft-toned velvety pink.
D	Blue	A clear sky-blue.
E	Brown	A tawny brown or brownish yellow.
F	Mulberry	Similar to the spectrum between blue and brown.
G	Blue-Pink . . .	A dark blue which droops unevenly and gradually blends into a brilliant pink.
H	Blue-White . .	A clear sky-blue which has the effect of melting over a glossy light gray.
K	Green	The color of herbage and growing plants.
L	Blue Mulberry	A rich blue which appears to melt unevenly and gradually blends into a beautiful mulberry.

NOTE: When ordering specify color by letter.

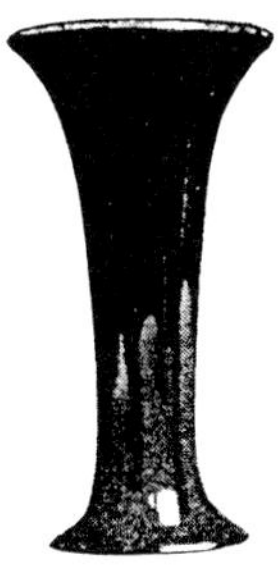

VASE
No. 106
Height, 6¼ inches
Price, $9.60 per doz.

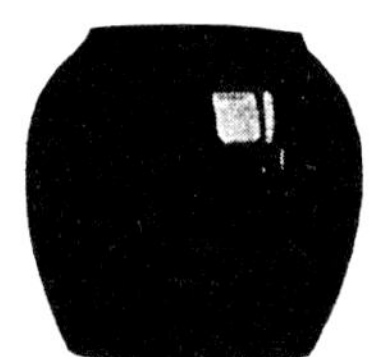

VASE
No. 117
Height 4¼ inches
Price, $8.40 per doz.

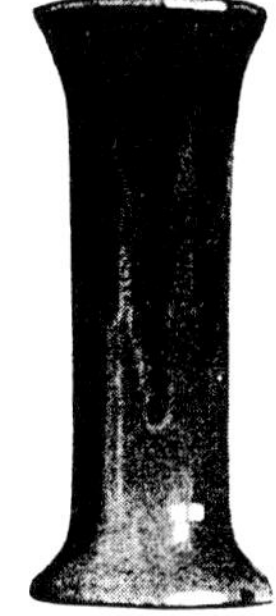

VASE
No. 100
Height, 7½ inches
Price, $16.80 per doz.

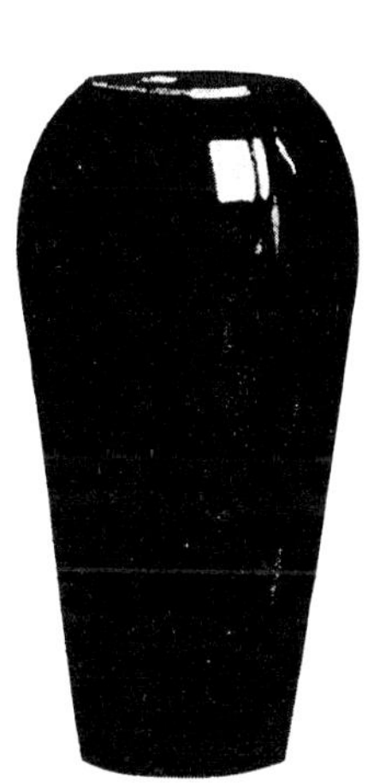

VASE
No. 110
Height, 10 inches
Price, $36.00 per doz.

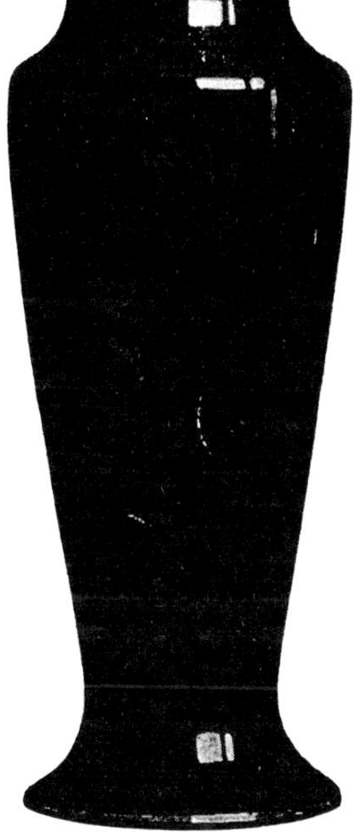

No. 114
VASE
Height, 16 inches
Price, each, $10.00

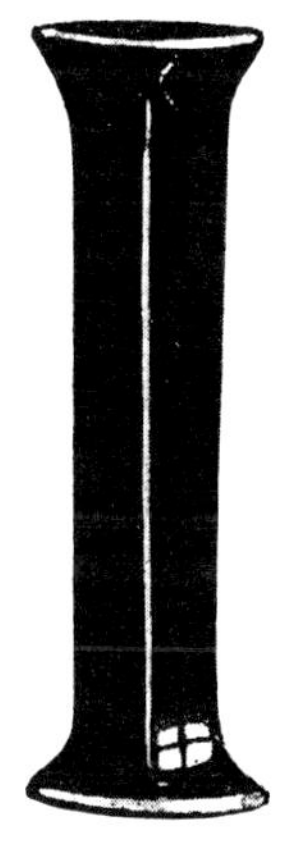

VASE
No. 101
Height, 9½ inches
Hexagon shape.
Price, $22.80 per doz.

Made up attractively in all Cliftwood colors.

(See Alphabetical Color Chart on Page 4)

Page 5 #106 – **$20-24** #117 – **$16-18** #100 – **$20-24** #110 – **$30-40** #114 – **$65-75** #101 – **$25-30**

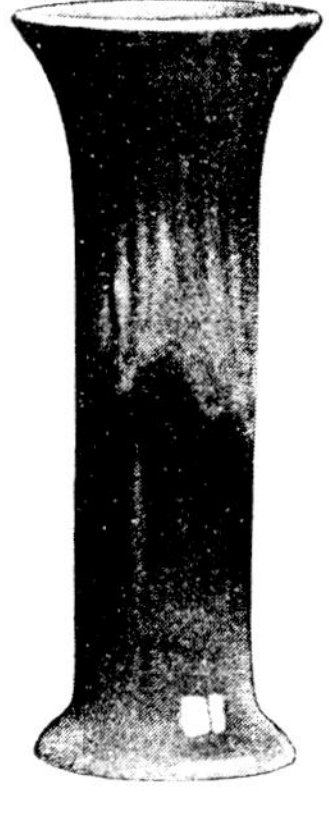

VASE
No. 103
Height 9½ inches
Price, $26.40 per doz.

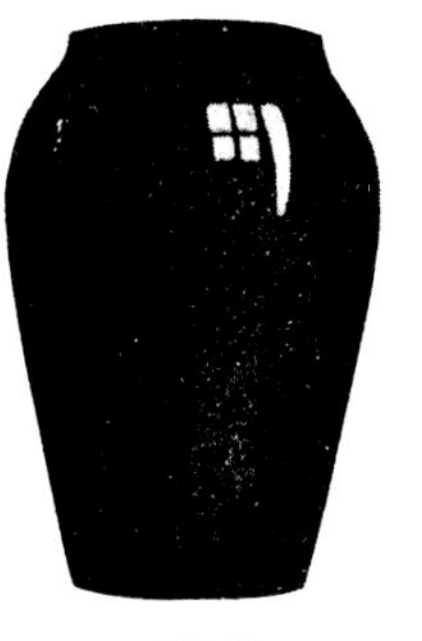

VASE
No. 104
Height 7½ inches
Price, $21.60 per doz.

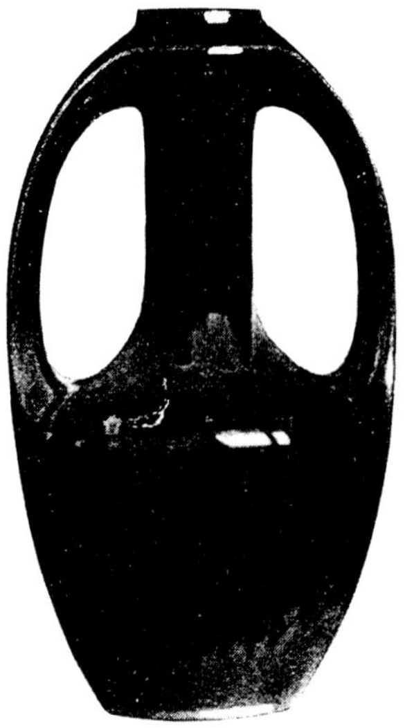

VASE
No. 127
Height, 12½ inches
Width, handle to handle, 7½ inches. Grecian Design.
Price, each, $8.00

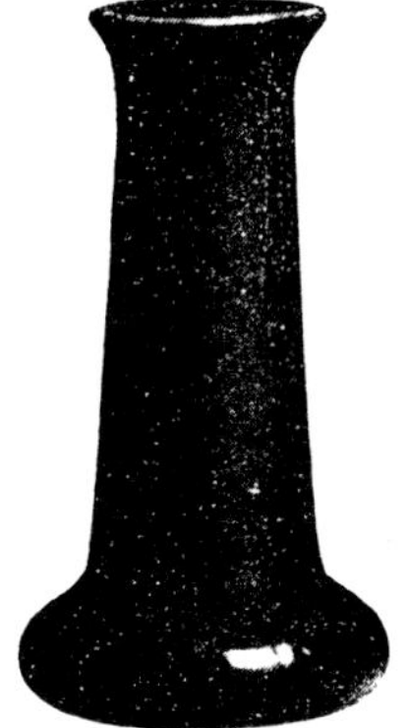

VASE
No. 105
Height 9¼ inches
Price, $30.00 per doz.

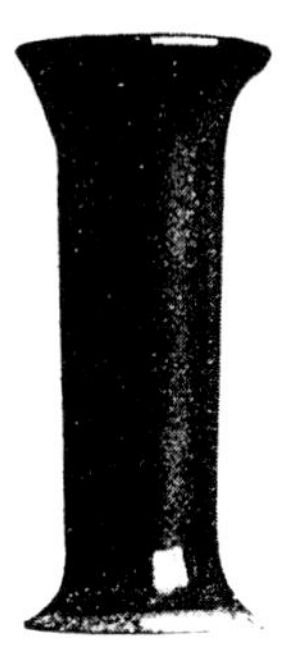

VASE
No. 102
Height, 7½ inches
Price, $19.20 per doz.

Made up attractively in all Cliftwood colors.

(See Alphabetical Color Chart on Page 4)

Page 6
#103 – **$25-30** #104 – **$20-24** #127 – **$50-60** #105 – **$25-30** #102 – **$20-24**

CLIFTWOOD ART POTTERY

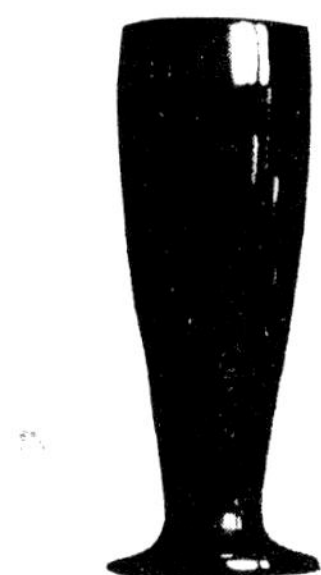

VASE

No. 112

Height, 7 inches
Price, $13.20 per doz.

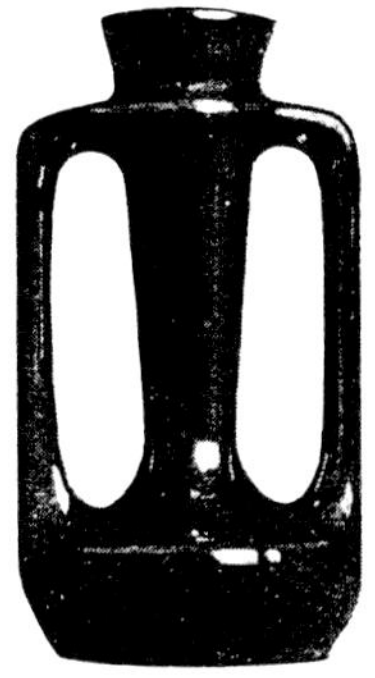

VASE

No. 126

Height, 8¼ inches
Egyptian design.
Price, $36.00 per doz.

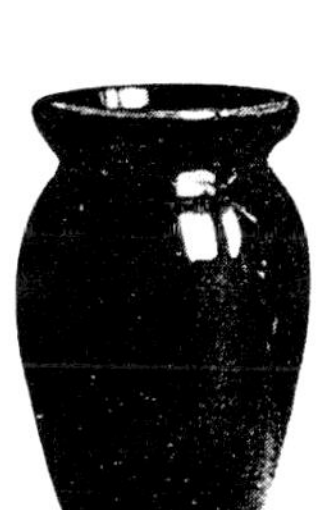

VASE

No. 119

Height, 5½ inches
Price, $13.20 per doz.

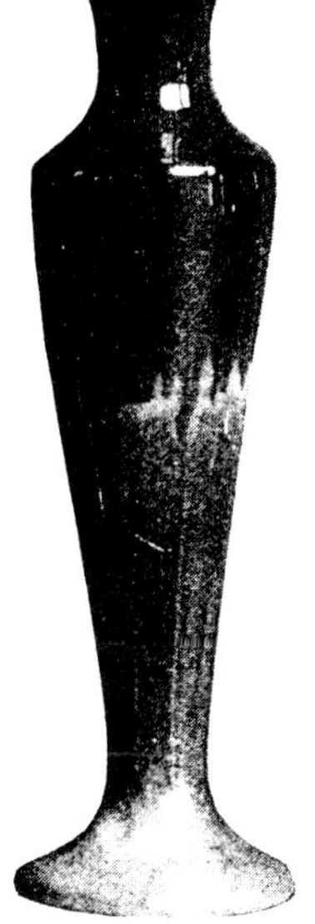

VASE

No. 113

Height, 14½ inches
Very graceful lines.
Price each $5.40

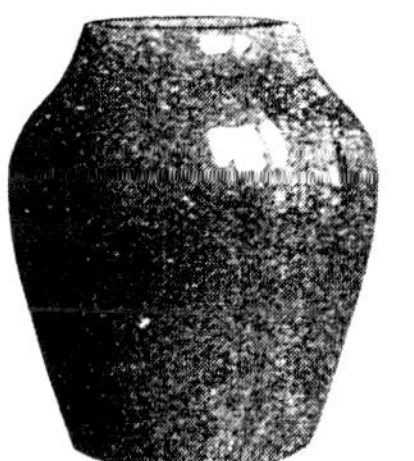

VASE

No. 118

Height, 5½ inches
Price, $14.40 per doz.

Made up attractively in all Cliftwood colors.

(See Alphabetical Color Chart on Page 4)

Page 7

#112 – **$18-22** #126 – **$35-40** #119 – **$18-22** #113 – **$40-50** #118 – **$18-22**

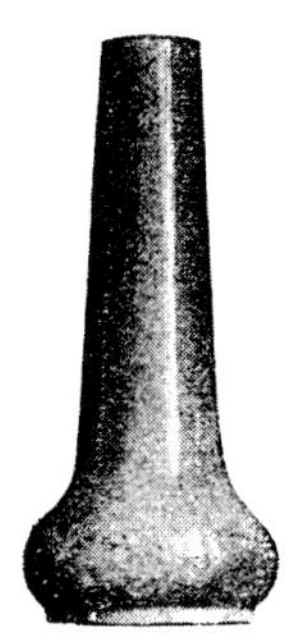

BUD VASE
No. 122
Height, 7¾ inches
Price, $9.60 per doz.

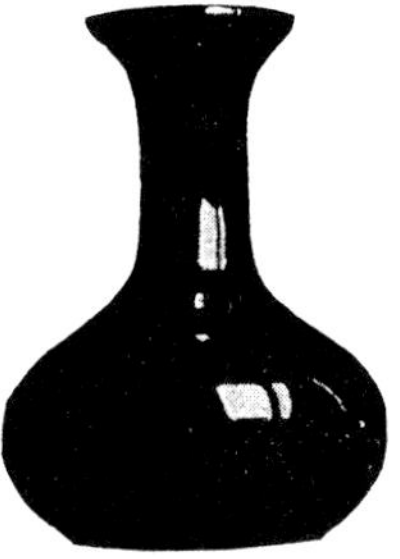

VASE
No. 130
Height, 6¾ inches
Price, $28.80 per doz.

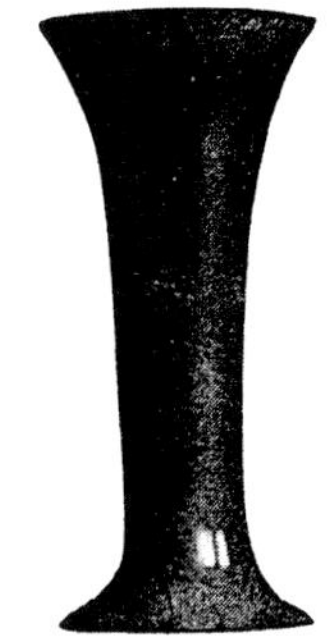

VASE
No. 107
Height, 8 inches
Price, $19.20 per doz.

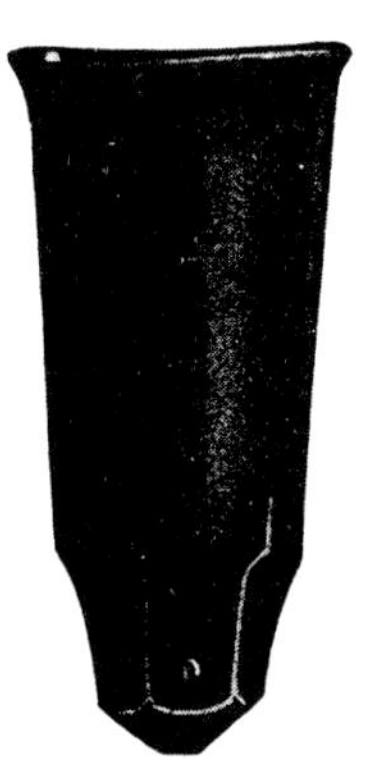

WALL VASE
No. 123
Height, 8¾ inches
Price, $14.40 per doz.

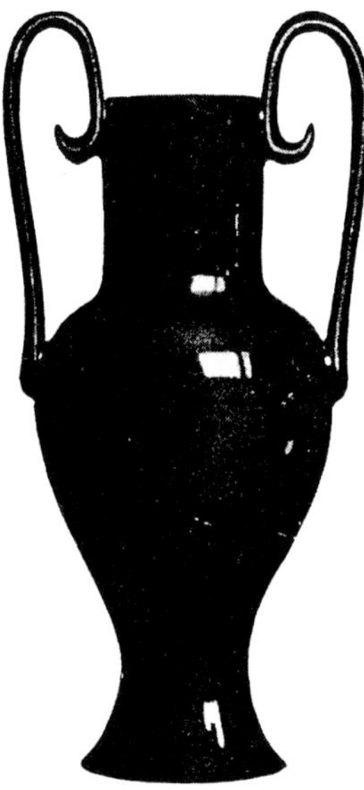

VASE
No. 128
Italian Design
Height, 13 inches over all
Width, handle to handle,
7 inches.
Price, each, $7.00

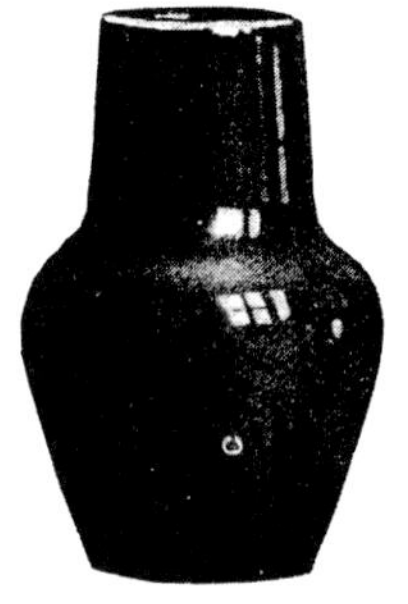

VASE
No. 116
Height, 7 inches
Price, $16.80 per doz.

Made up attractively in all Cliftwood colors.

(See Alphabetical Color Chart on Page 4)

Page 8
#122 – **$15-20** #130 – **$20-25** #107 – **$25-30** #123 – **$30-40** #128 – **$60-70** #116 – **$18-22**

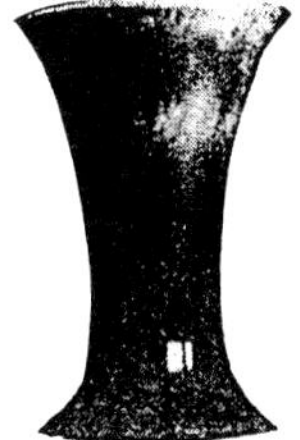

VASE

No. 108

Height. 5½ inches
Price. $12.00 per doz.

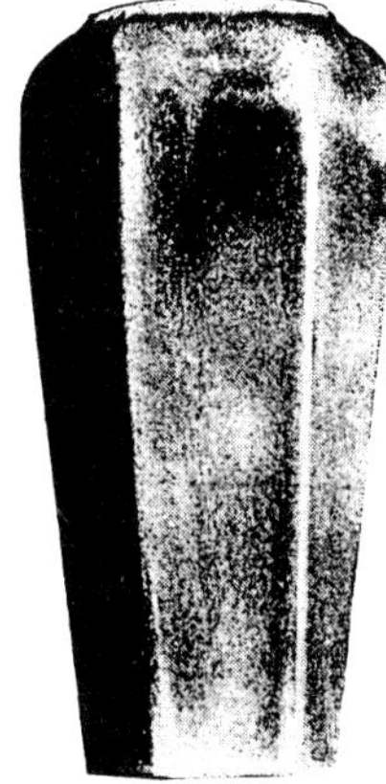

VASE

No. 109

Height. 10 inches
The shape is Hexagon
Spanish design
Price. $36.00 per doz.

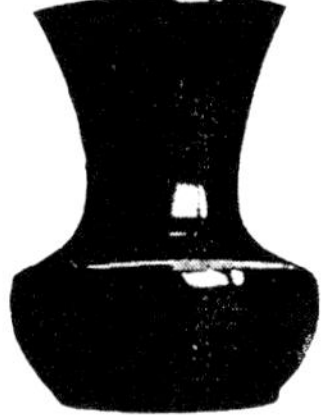

VASE

No. 115

Height. 5½ inches
Price. $13.20 per doz.

VASE

No. 111

Height. 13½ inches
Price each. $6.00

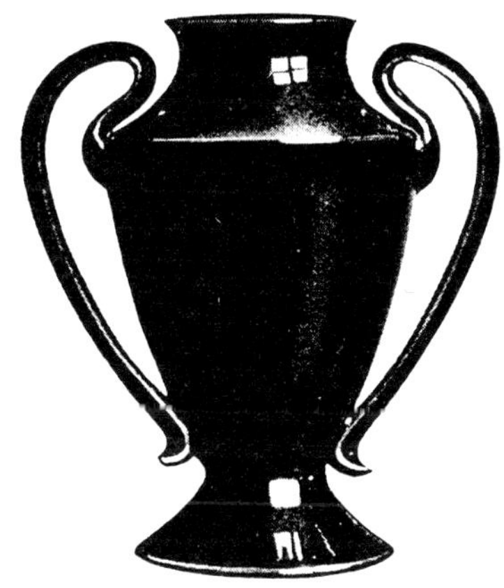

VASE

No. 129

Italian design
Very new.
Height. 10 inches
Width. handle to handle. 9 inches
Price. each $7.00

Made up attractively in all Cliftwood colors.

(See Alphabetical Color Chart on Page 4)

Page 9

#108 – **$18-22** #109 – **$30-40** #115 – **$18-22** #111 – **$40-50** #129 – **$50-60**

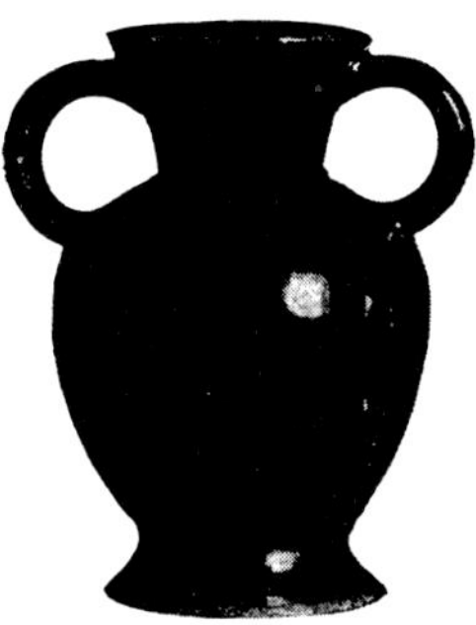

VASE
No. 133
Height 7 ½ inches
Price, $36.00 per doz.

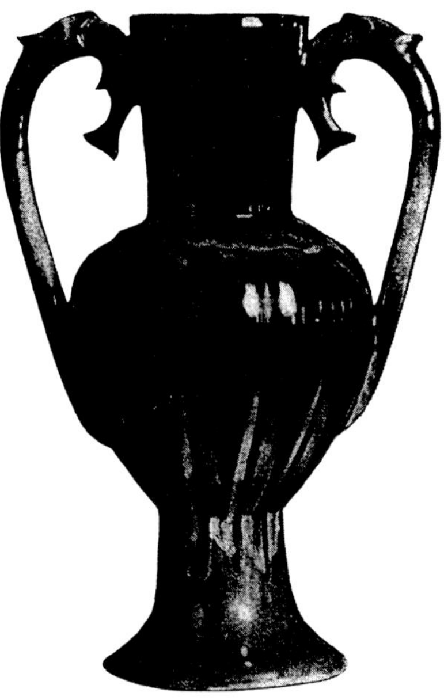

VASE
No. 132
Height, 18¼ inches
Width, handle to handle, 12 inches
A real Egyptian design
Massive appearance and very suitable for interior decoration.
Price, each, $20.00

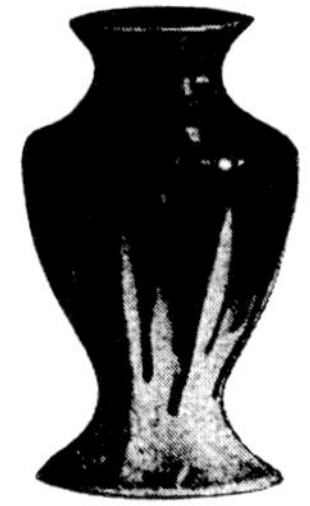

VASE
No. 131
Height, 6 inches
Price, $12.00 per doz.
The shape is Octagon

Made up attractively in all Cliftwood colors and glazes.

(See Alphabetical Color Chart on Page 4)

Page 10 #133 – **$30-35** #132 – **$80-90** #131 – **$20-25**

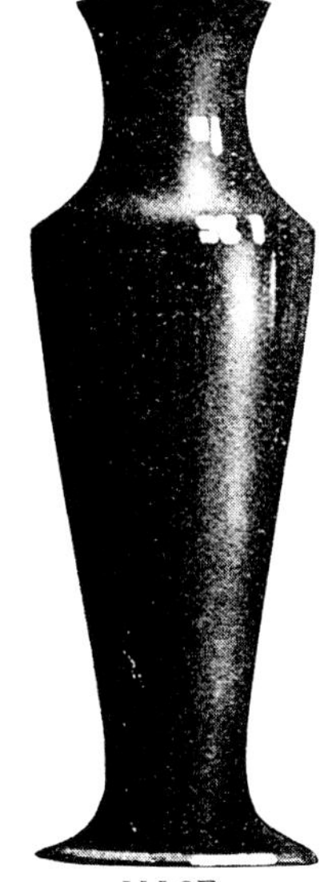

VASE
No. 120
Height, 18 inches
Price, each, $10.00

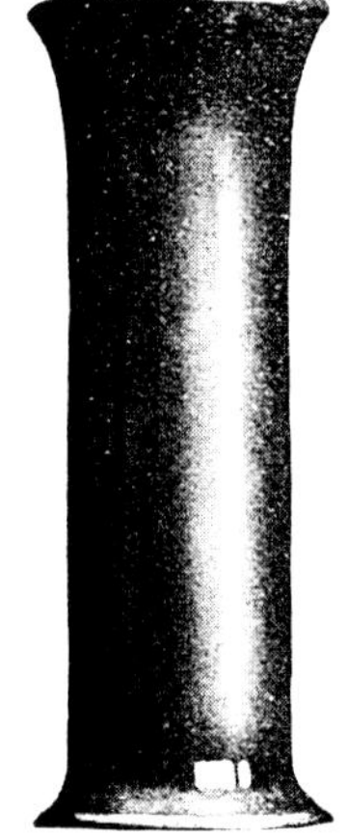

VASE
No. 121
Height, 14 inches
Price, each, $6.00

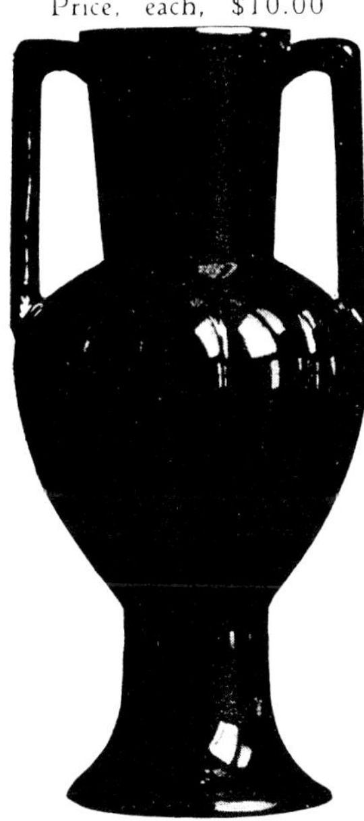

VASE
No. 124
Height, 18¼ inches
Egyptian Design
Price, each, $15.00

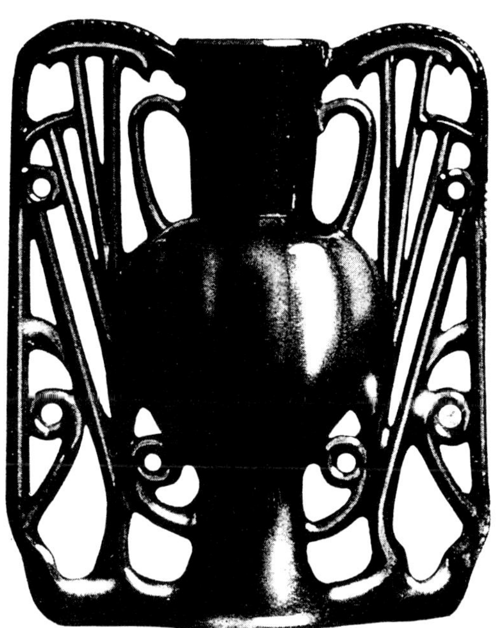

VASE No. 125
Height, 18¼ inches. Width, 15 inches
A real show piece for interior decoration. A repleca of original vase taken from Egyptian tomb.
Price, each, $50.00

Made up attractively in all Cliftwood colors.

(See Alphabetical Color Chart on Page 4)

Page 11 #120 – **$55-60** #121 – **$40-50** #124 – **$65-75** #125 – ND

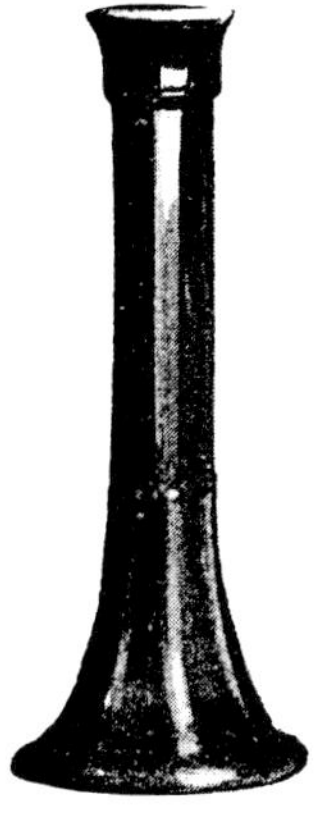
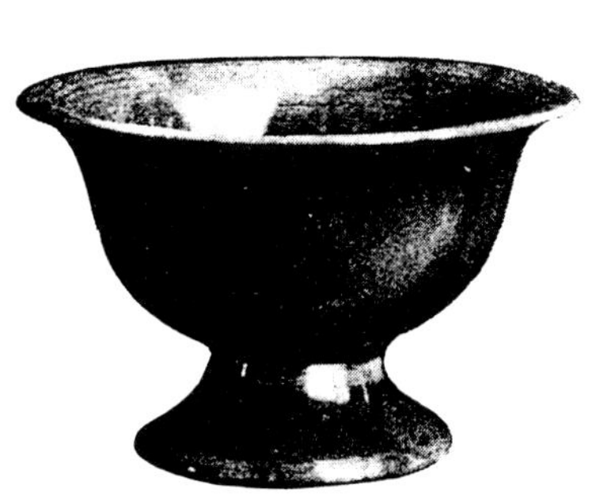
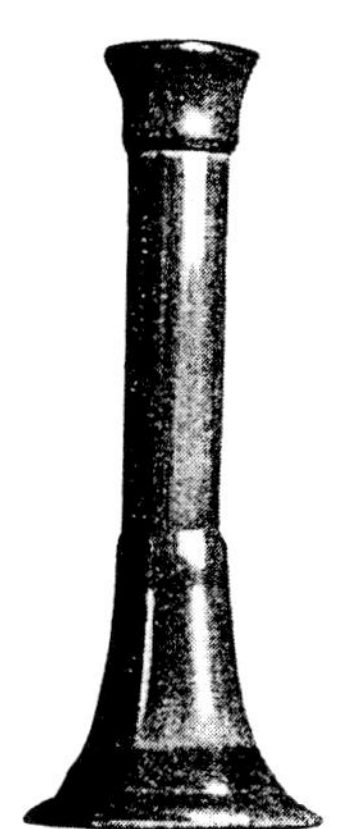

COMPOTE SET

No. 226

One Fruit Bowl, Height, 6 inches
Width, 9 inches
Two Candle Sticks, Height, 10 inches
Price per set, 3 pieces, $8.00

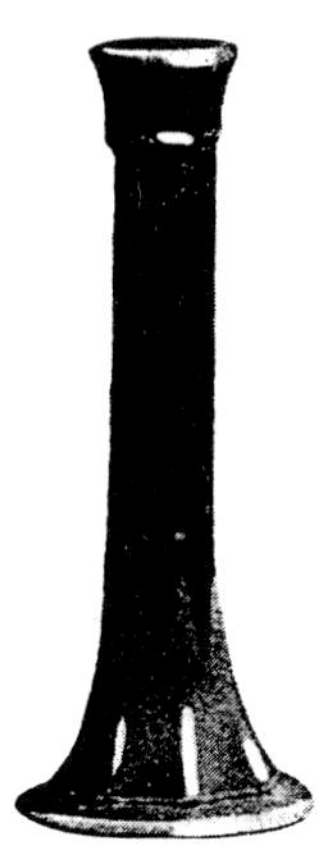
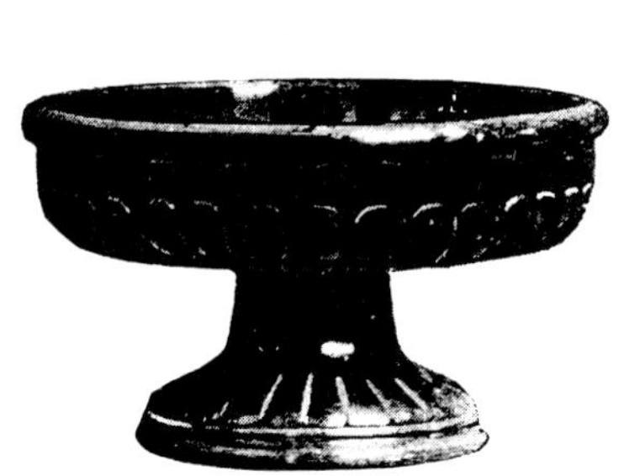
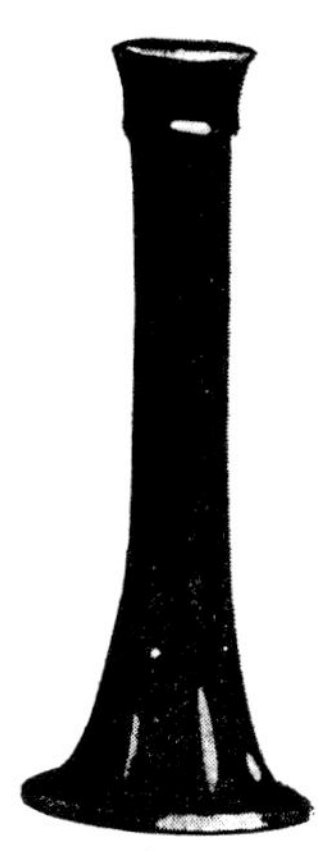

COMPOTE SET

No. 227

One Fruit Bowl, Height, 5 inches
Width, 8½ inches
Two Candle Sticks, Height, 10 inches
Price per set, 3 pieces, $8.00

Made up attractively in the following Cliftwood colors—Yellow, Black, Old Rose, Mulberry, Blue, Brown, Blue-Pink, Green and Blue-White.

Page 12

#226 – **$80-100 set** Candle Sticks – **$40-50 pair** Compote – **$40-50**
#227 – **$80-100 set** Candle Sticks – **$40-50 pair** Compote – **$40-50**

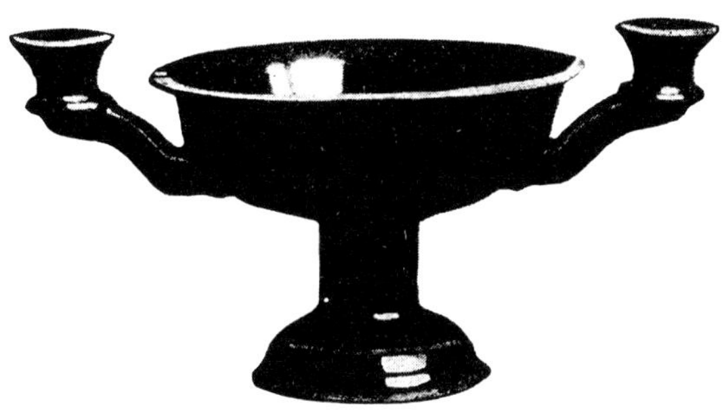

COMPOTE

No. 229

A Venetian Design
Here is a new departure in a Compote. Absolutely new and original.
Height, 6 inches
Width of Bowl, 8 inches
Width of Candle Stick to Stick, 13 inches.
Price, each, $7.00

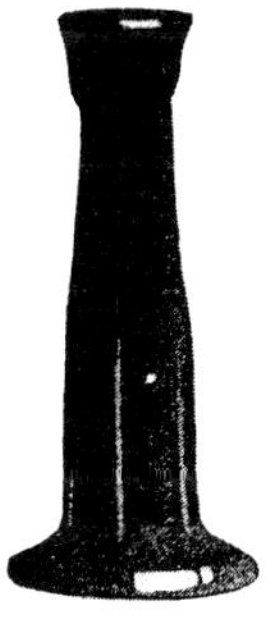

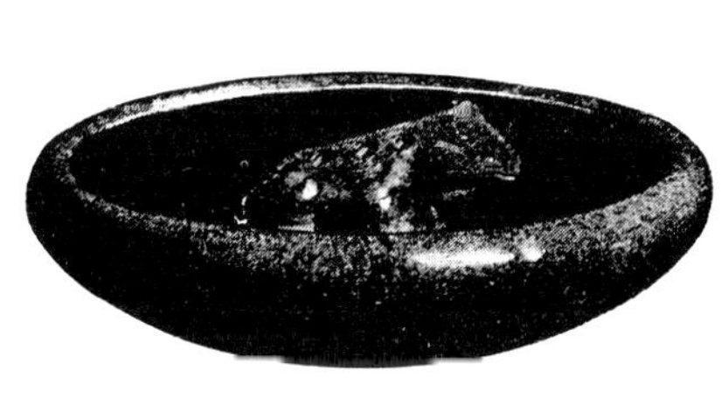

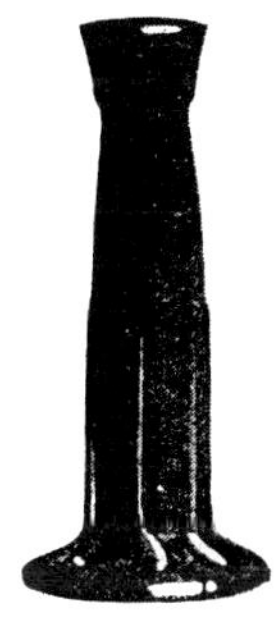

COMPOTE SET

No. 228

One 9 inch Footed Bowl
Two 7 inch Candle Sticks
One 5½ inch Frog Insert
Set complete, 4 pieces, $5.50

Made up attractively in the following Cliftwood colors—Yellow, Black, Old Rose, Mulberry, Blue, Brown, Blue-Pink, Green and Blue-White.

Page 13
#228 – **$80-100 set** Candle Sticks – **$30-40 pair** Bowl – **$30-35** Frog – **$20-25**

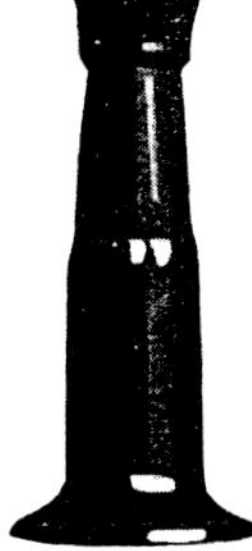
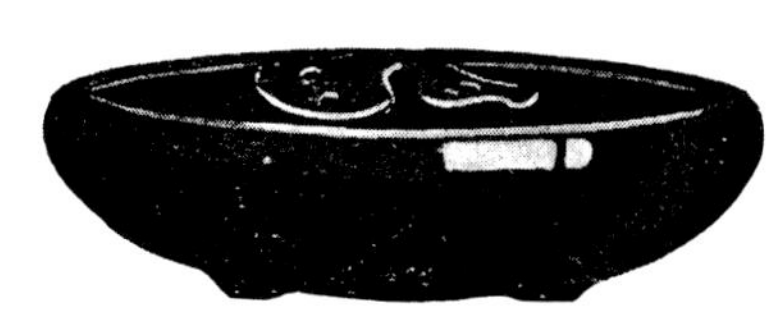
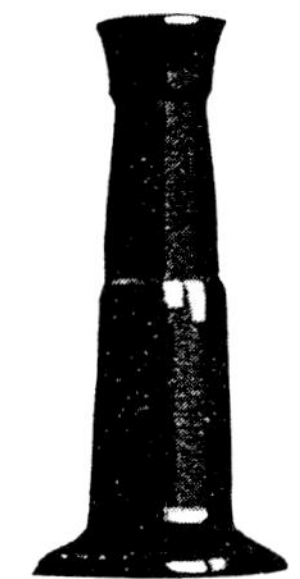

COMPOTE SET

No. 230

One 8 inch Footed Bowl
Two 7 inch Candle Sticks
One 4 inch Lilly Insert
Set complete, 4 pieces, $4.50

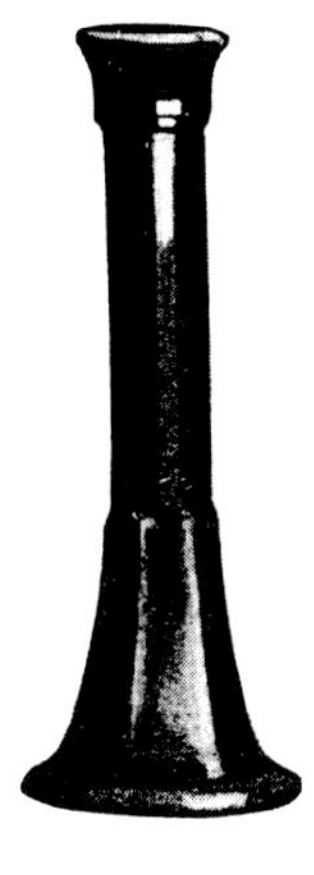
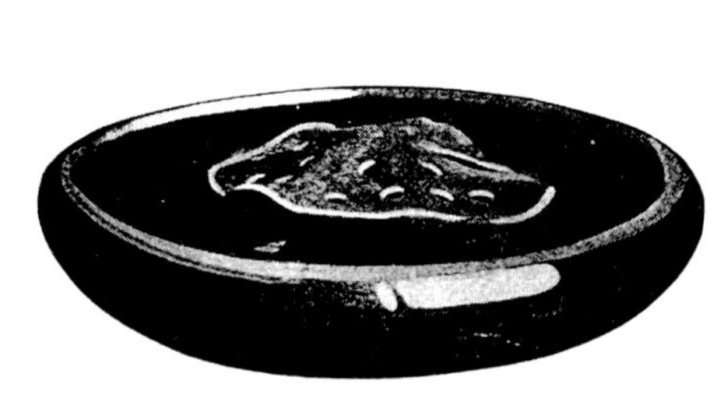
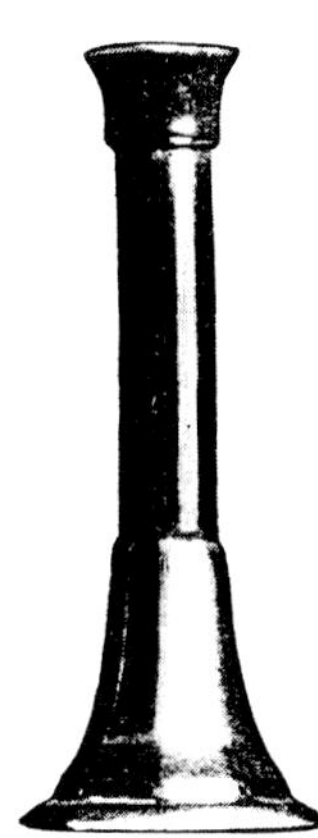

COMPOTE SET

No. 231

One 10 inch Footed Bowl
Two 10 inch Candle Sticks
One 6 inch Lilly Insert
Set complete, 4 pieces, $8.00

Made up attractively in the following Cliftwood colors—Yellow, Black, Old Rose, Mulberry, Blue, Brown, Blue-Pink, Green and Blue-White.

Page 14

#230 – **$75-95 set** Candle Sticks – **$30-40 pair** Bowl – **$25-35** Lily Insert – **$18-24**

#231 – **$100-125 set** Candle Sticks – **$40-50 pair** Bowl – **$35-40** Lily Insert – **$25-35**

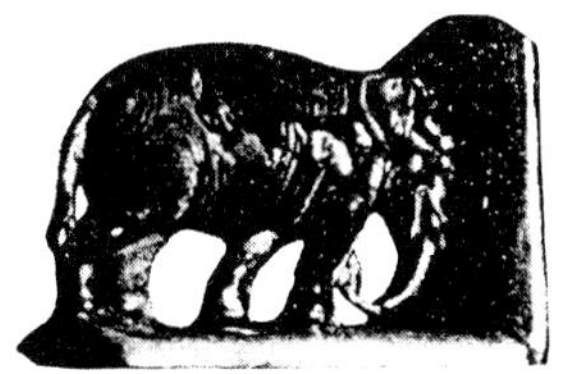

ELEPHANT BOOK ENDS

Height, 4¼ inches. Length, 6 inches.
Neatly felted on bottom
Price, per pair, $4.50

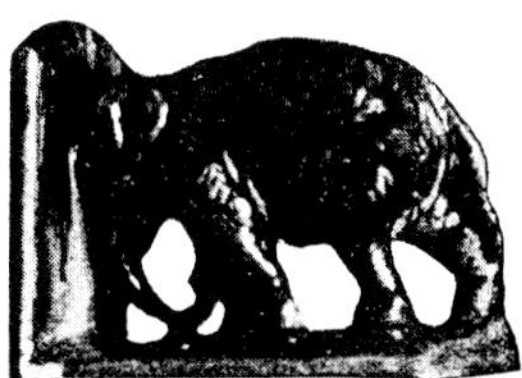

THE LORILEI FLOWER INSERT

Height, 6½ inches. Width, 4½ inches

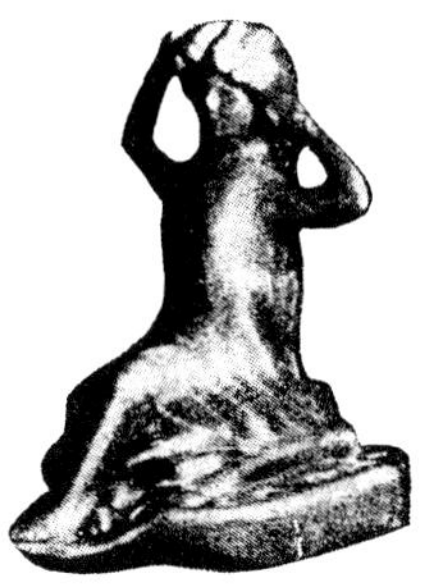

Price, each, $3.00

The fairest Virgin sitting
Upon the rock so bare,
Her precious jewels are sparkling;
She combs her golden hair.

She combs with a golden comb,
And sings a song thereby;
Which has a wonderful tune,
It's called the Lorilei.

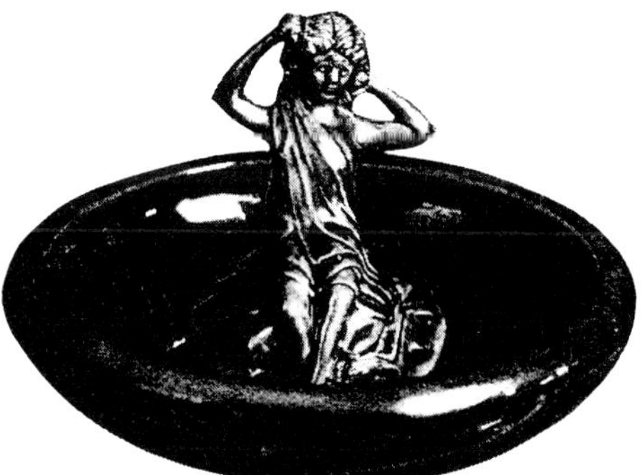

No. XL
Our 10 inch Bowl which is deep, complete
with The Lorilei Flower Insert
Price, each, $6.00

All numbers on this page made up attractively in the following Cliftwood colors and glazes: Black, Blue, Yellow, Brown, Rose, Mulberry, Blue-White, Green and Blue-Pink.

Page 15

Elephant book ends – **$100-125 set** Lorilei Flower Insert – **$50-60**
#XL – **$85-95 set**

DEEP FLOWER
BOWLS

Footed

10 inch

Price, $36.00 per doz.

DEEP FLOWER
BOWLS

Footed

9 inch

Price, $30.00 per doz.

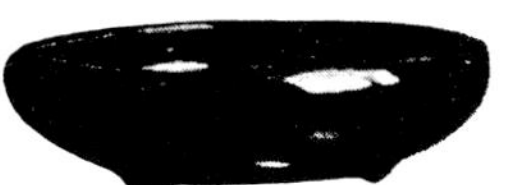

DEEP FLOWER
BOWLS

Footed

8 inch

Price, $24.00 per doz.

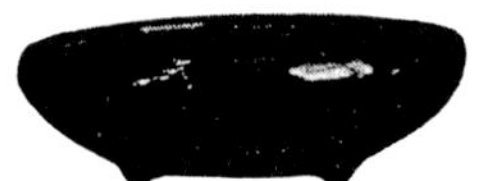

DEEP FLOWER
BOWLS

Footed

7 inch

Price, $18.00 per doz.

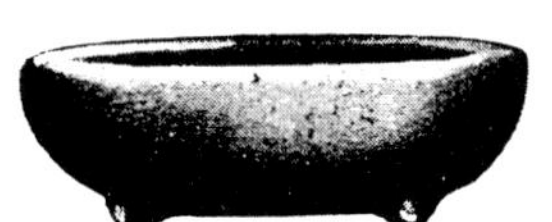

DEEP FLOWER
BOWLS

Footed

6½ inch

Price, $14.40 per doz.

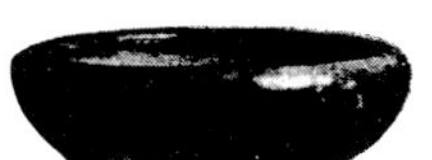

DEEP FLOWER
BOWLS

Footed

5½ inch

Price, $9.60 per doz.

4 inch Footed

SHALLOW FLOWER
BOWL

$4.80 per doz.

All Flower Bowls made up attractively in the following Cliftwood colors: Black, Rose, Blue, Brown, Mulberry, Yellow, Blue-Pink, Green and Blue-White.

Page 16 Deep Flower Bowl 10" – **$35-40** 9" – **$30-35** 8" – **$25-35** 7" – **$20-25** 6½" – **$15-20** 5½" – **$12-14** Shallow Flower Bowl 4" – **$8-10**

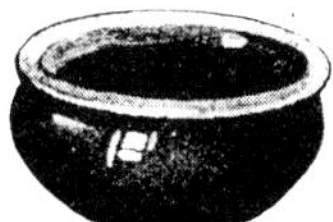

3 inch deep
BOWL
Suitable for individual bulbs.
$4.80 per doz.

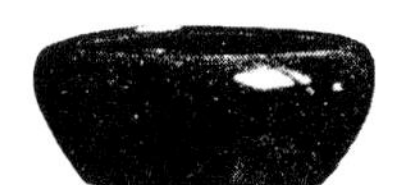

DEEP BULB BOWL
4 in., $6.00 per doz.
5 in., $9.60 per doz.

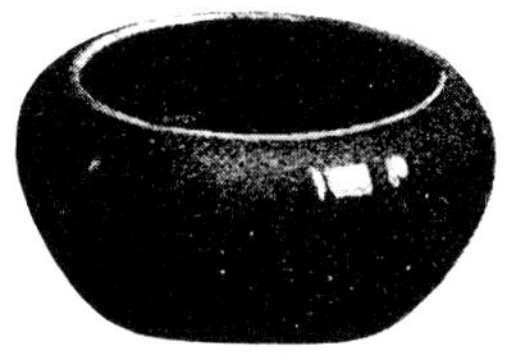

6 inch
BULB BOWL
$12.00 per doz.

DISCS

No. 1 DISC

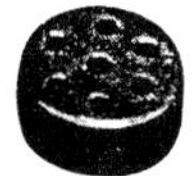

2 inch
Suitable for 4 inch Bowl.
$2.00 per doz.

No. 2 DISC

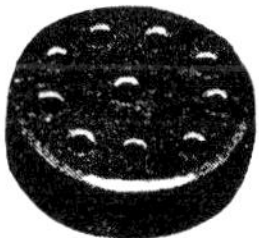

3 inch
Suitable for 5, 5½, 6½, and 7 inch Bowls.
$3.00 per doz.

No. 3 DISC

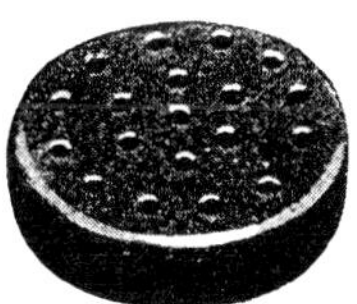

4 inch
Suitable for 5½, 6½, 7 and 8 inch Bowls.
$6.00 per doz.

No. 4 DISC

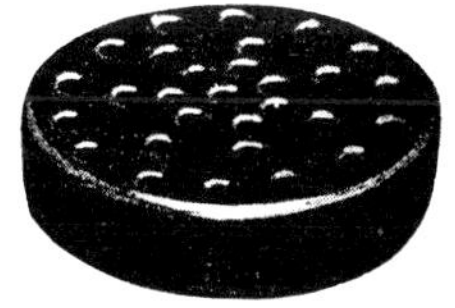

5 inch
Suitable for 9 and 10 inch Bowls.
$8.50 per doz.

Made up attractively in the following Cliftwood colors—Yellow, Black, Old Rose, Mulberry, Blue, Brown, Blue-Pink, Green and Blue-White.

Page 17 Bowl 3" – **$5-7** Bulb Bowl 4"– **$6-8** 5" – **$8-12** 6" – **$12-16**
Discs #1 – **$6-8** #2 – **$8-10** #3 – **$10-12** #4 – **$12-14**

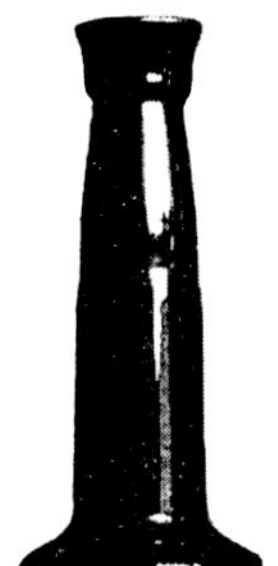
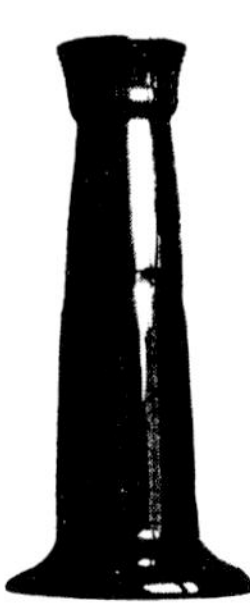
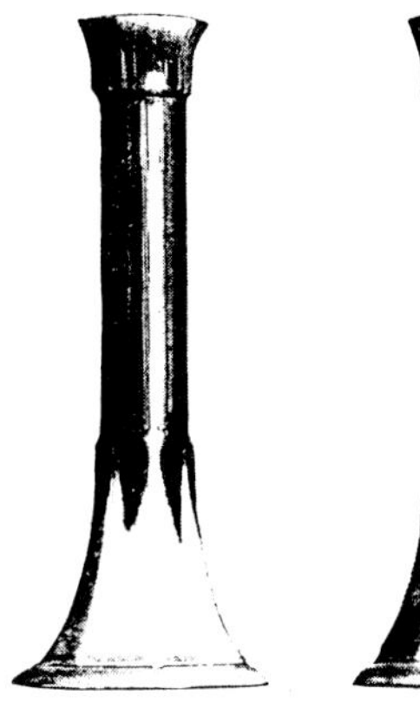
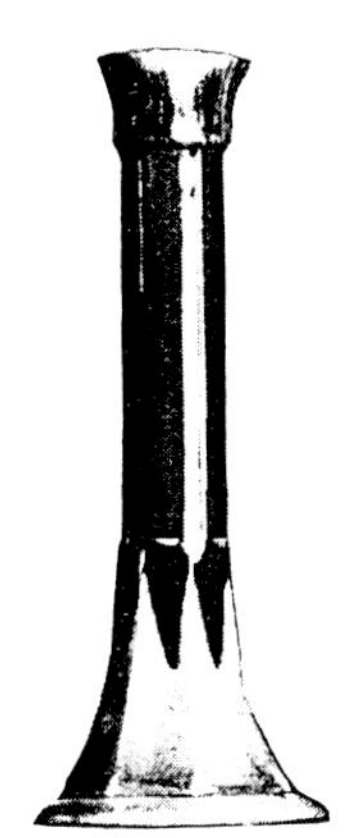

CANDLE STICKS
No. 201
Height, 7 inches
Price, per pair, $2.00

CANDLE STICKS
No. 200
Height, 10 inches
Price, per pair, $4.00

Candle Sticks made up attractively in all Cliftwood colors.
(See Alphabetical Color Chart on Page 4)

FLOWER INSERTS

TURTLE INSERT
No. 1

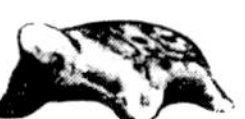

4 inches
Suitable for 5, 5½, 6½ and 7 inch Bowls.
$3.00 per doz.

TURTLE INSERT
No. 2

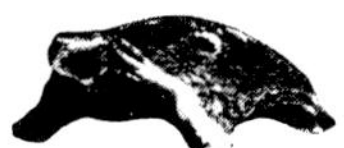

5½ inches
Suitable for 8, 9 and 10 inch Bowls.
$6.00 per doz.

LILLY INSERT
No. 1

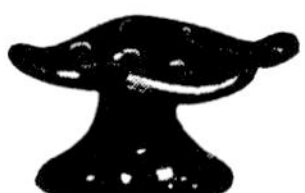

4 inches
Suitable for 6½, 7 and 8 inch Bowls.
$6.00 per doz.

LILLY INSERT
No. 2

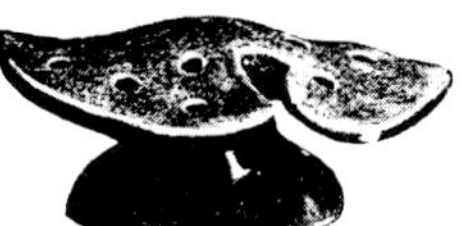

6 inches
Suitable for 9 and 10 inch Bowls.
$12.00 per doz.

FROG INSERT
No. 1

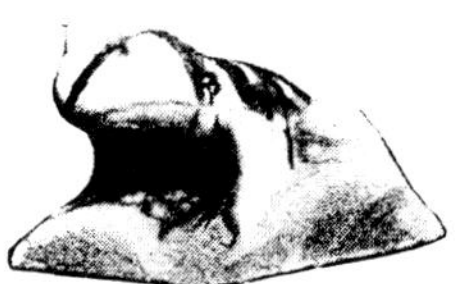

5½ inches
Suitable for 9 and 10 inch Bowls.
$12.00 per doz.

Flower Insert smade up attractively to match all Cliftwood Bowls, or may be ordered separately in the following colors—Yellow, Black, Old Rose, Mulberry, Blue, Brown, Blue-Pink, Green and Blue-White.

Eighteen

Page 18 #201 – **$30-40 pair** #200 – **$40-50 pair** Turtle Insert #1 – **$12-20** #2 – **$16-24** Lilly Insert #1 – **$18-24** #2 – **$25-35** Frog #1 – **$20-25**

Cliftwood Pottery Lamps

COMPLETE WITH FIXTURES

WE have prepared a line of the most exclusive Table and Boudoir Lamps which will enable you to make your selections so as to meet every requirement of your customers.

All Table Lamps equipped with a high class two light Adjustable Fixture in a handsome Golden Satin finish, with about six feet of silk cord ready to connect to electric fixture.

Cliftwood Pottery Lamps are distinctive and original in designs.

Illustrated on following pages.

WITHOUT FIXTURES

FOR the trade that desires to mount their own lamps, using your own idea of a fixture, we have for your convenience a very complete line. made up especially for the purpose, all drilled ready for you to equip with fixtures. Illustrations and descriptions in full on the following pages.

For lamps, the low end of the value range is for lamp mount with no fixture. The upper end of the value range is for completely wired lamps.

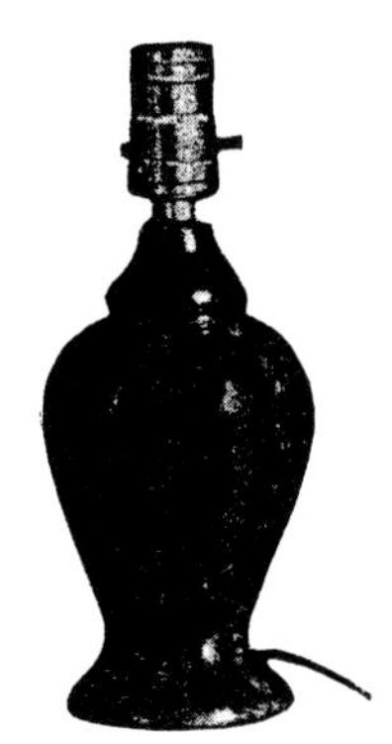

LAMP MOUNT
No. 12
Complete with fixture
Height, 9½ inches
Price, each, $4.00

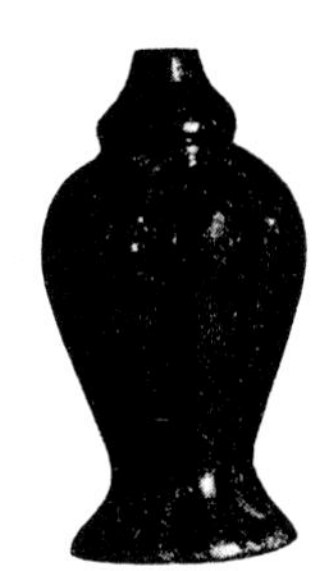

LAMP MOUNT
No. 12 N. F.
Without fixture
Height, 7¼ inches
Price per doz., $24.00

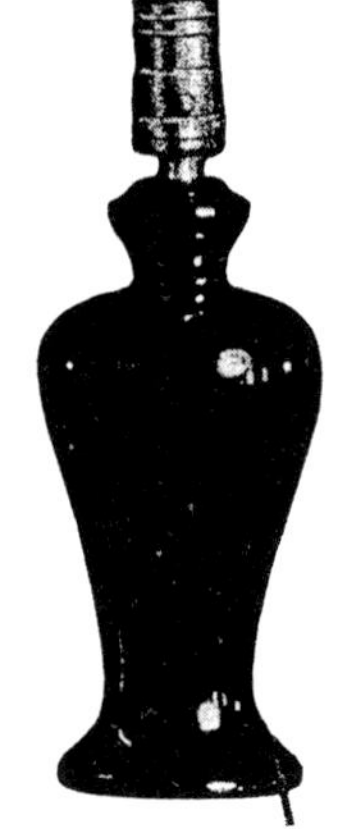

LAMP MOUNT
No. 3
Complete with fixture
Height, 11½ inches
Price, each, $6.50

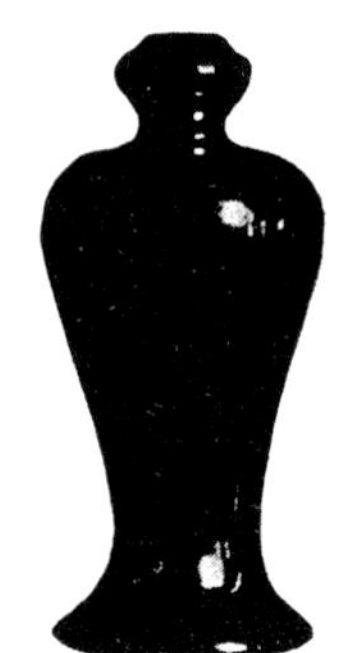

LAMP MOUNT
No. 3 N. F.
Without fixture
Height, 9 inches
Price per doz., $36.00

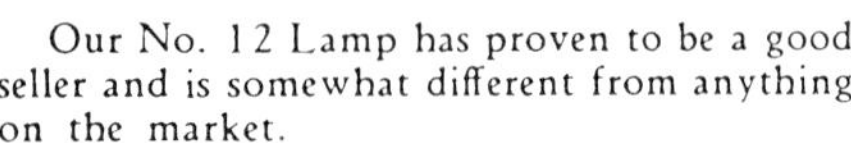

Our No. 12 Lamp has proven to be a good seller and is somewhat different from anything on the market.

Our No. 3 Lamp is a Boudoir Lamp, a shape that is very unique and chosen by many buyers.

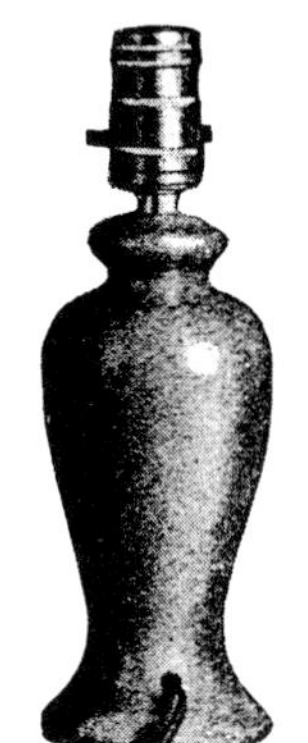

LAMP MOUNT
No. 2
Complete with fixture
Height, 10 inches
Price, each, $5.50

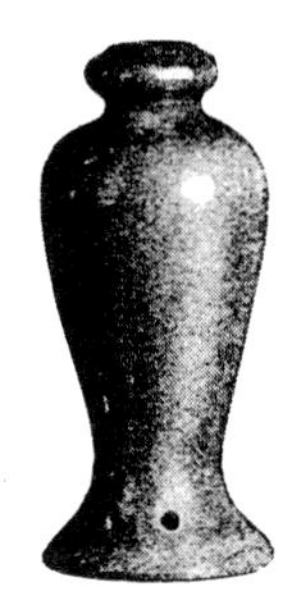

LAMP MOUNT
No. 2 N. F.
Without fixture
Height, 7½ inches
Price per doz., $24.00

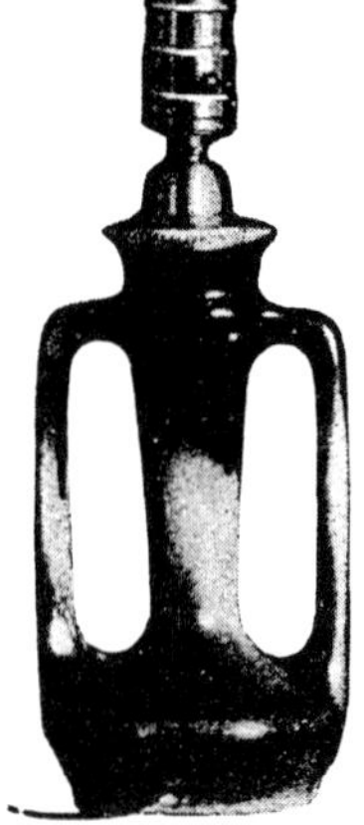

LAMP MOUNT
No. 11
Complete with fixture
Height, 12 inches
Price, each, $7.00

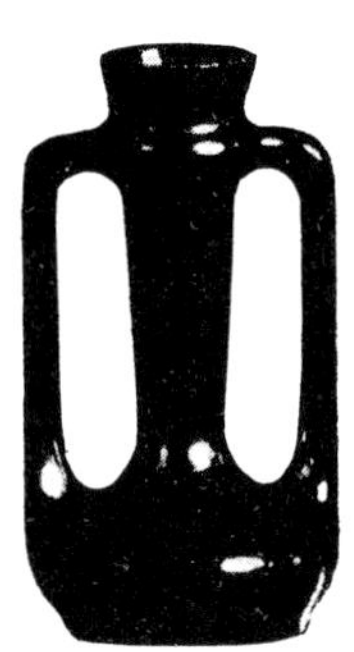

LAMP MOUNT
No. 11 N. F.
Without fixture
Height, 8¼ inches
Price per doz., $36.00

Our No. 2 Boudoir Lamp with its delicate lines, has been approved by the most critical buyers.

Our No. 11 Lamp Mount is strictly Egyptian design, a lamp that has individuality and is different.

Made up attractively in all Cliftwood colors and glazes. These lamps with fixtures are all neatly felted on bottoms.

(See Alphabetical Color Chart on Page 4)

Page 20

#12 – **$20-40** #3 – **$30-50** #2 – **$20-40** #11 – **$40-60**

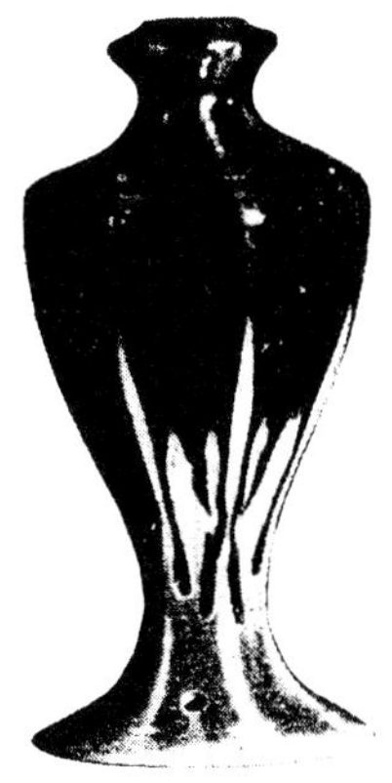

LAMP MOUNT

No. 15 N. F.

Without Fixture
Height, 10 inches
The shape is Hexagon
Price per doz., $48.00

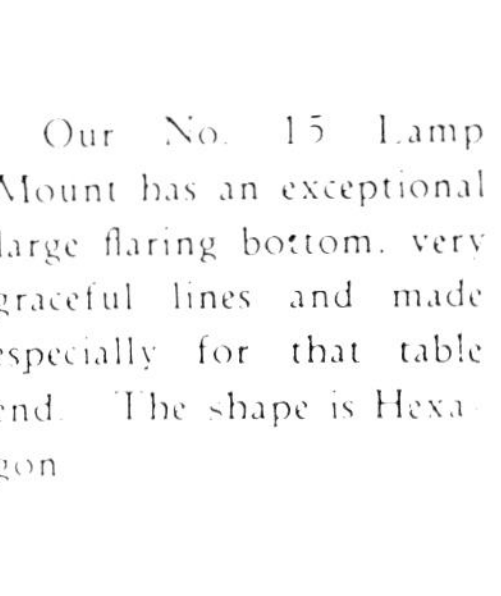

Our No. 15 Lamp Mount has an exceptional large flaring bottom, very graceful lines and made especially for that table end. The shape is Hexagon.

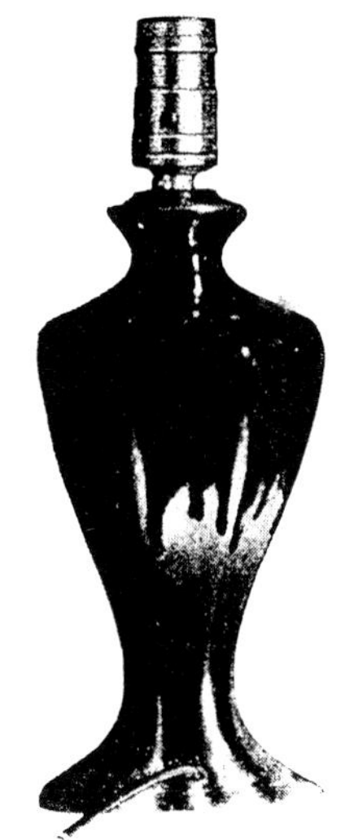

LAMP MOUNT

No. 15

Complete with Fixture
Height, 12 inches
The shape is Hexagon
Price each $7.50

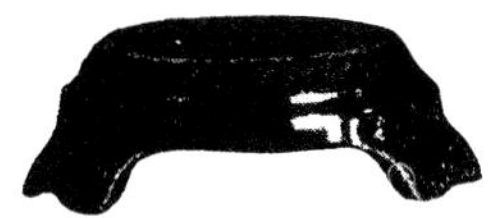

POTTERY STANDS

Size, 3½ inch top

Our No. 2, 5, 11, 12, 16 Lamps will set nicely on this stand.

Made in plain colors only

Price per doz., $9.60

LAMP MOUNT

No. 5 N. F.

Without Fixture
Height, 7 inches
Price per doz., $24.00

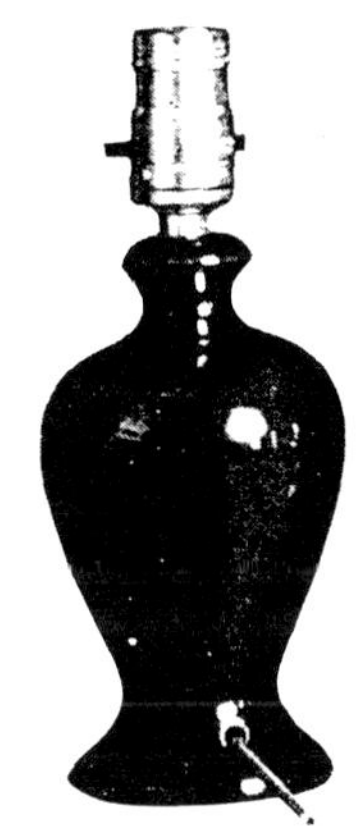

LAMP MOUNT

No. 5

Complete with fixture
Height 10½ inches
Price each $5.00

The above Lamps made up attractively in all Cliftwood colors and glazes. These Lamps with fixtures are all neatly felted on bottoms.

(See Alphabetical Color Chart on Page 4)

Page 21
#15 – **$30-40** Pottery Stand ND (usually fused to mount when fired) #5 – **$20-30**

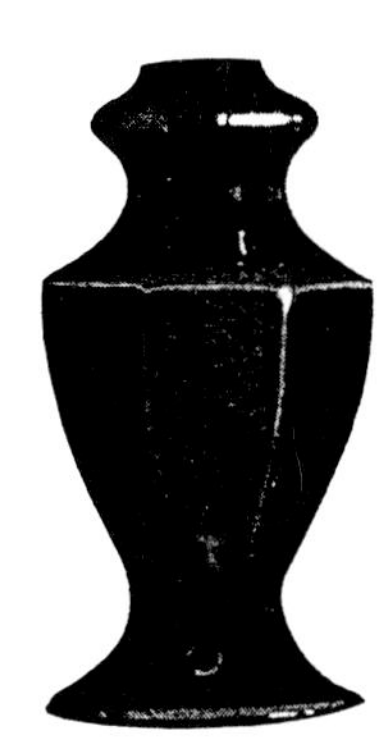

NO. 16 N. F. LAMP MOUNT
Without Fixture
Height, 6½ inches
Price, each, $1.60

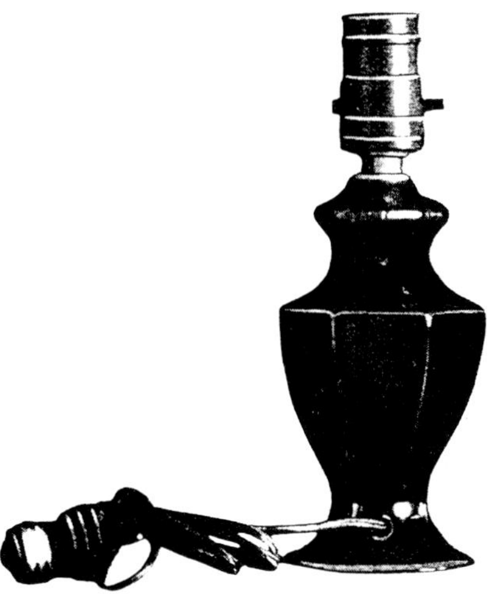

NO. 16 LAMP MOUNT
Complete with Fixture
Height, 9 inches
Price, each, $3.50

This Lamp we are making for a special trade which demands a somewhat smaller lamp at a moderate price.

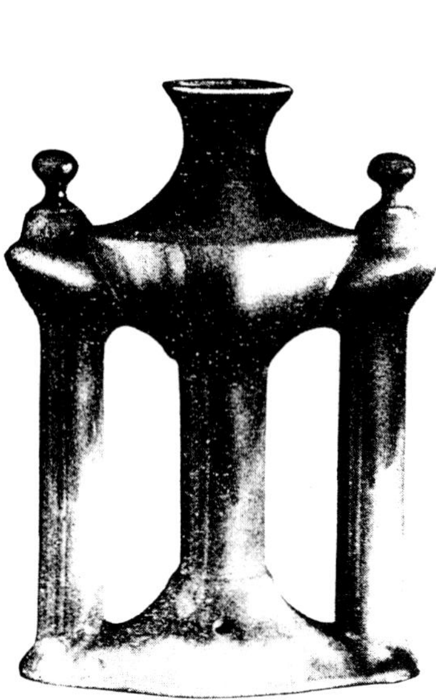

NO. 17 N. F. LAMP MOUNT
Without Fixture
Height, 10¼ inches
Width, handle to handle, 7½ inches
Price, each, $7.00

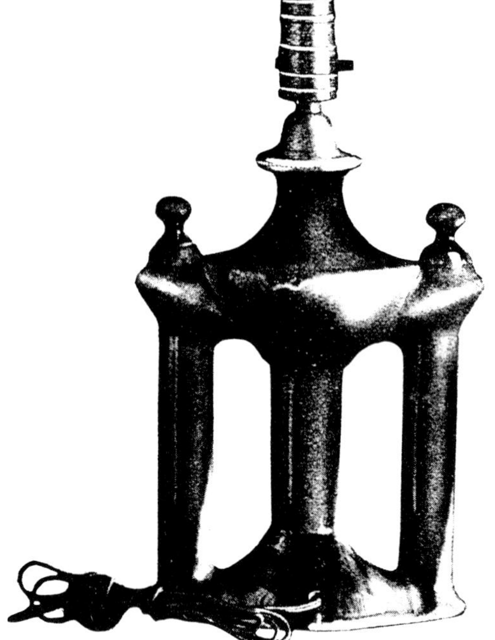

NO. 17 LAMP MOUNT
Complete with Fixture
Height, 14¼ inches
Width, handle to handle, 7½ inches
Price, each, $11.00

This Colonial Lamp is an entirely new pattern and we believe it will meet with favor among the critical buyers. Made up attractively in all Cliftwood Colors.

(See Alphabetical Color Chart on Page 4)

#16 – **$18-24** #17 – **ND**

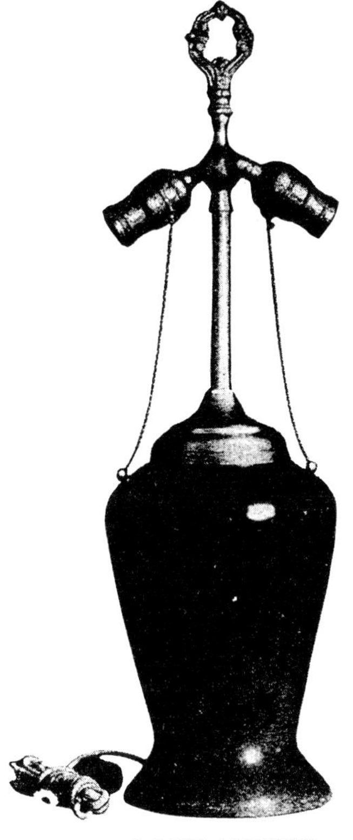

LAMP MOUNT

No. 10

Complete with Fixture
Height, 23 inches
Price, each, $12.00
LAMP MOUNT

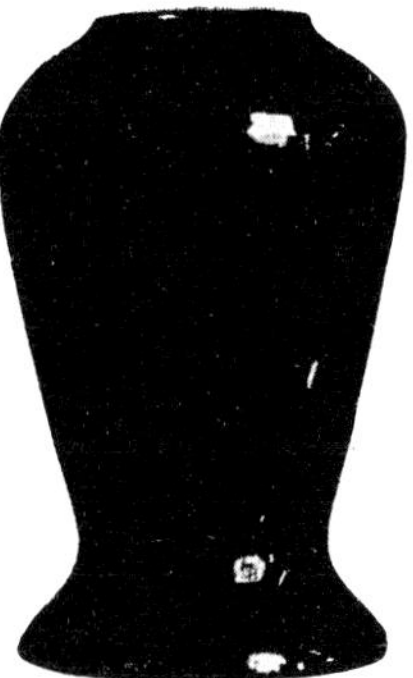

No. 10 N. F.

Without Fixture
Height, 10½ inches
Price, each, $7.00

Our No. 10 Lamp Mount is just the right size to be used as a Table End Lamp.

Made up attractively in all Cliftwood colors and glazes. This Lamp with fixture neatly felted on bottom.

(See Alphabetical Color Chart on Page 4)

Page 23 #10 – **$65-75**

Our Leader for a Library Lamp

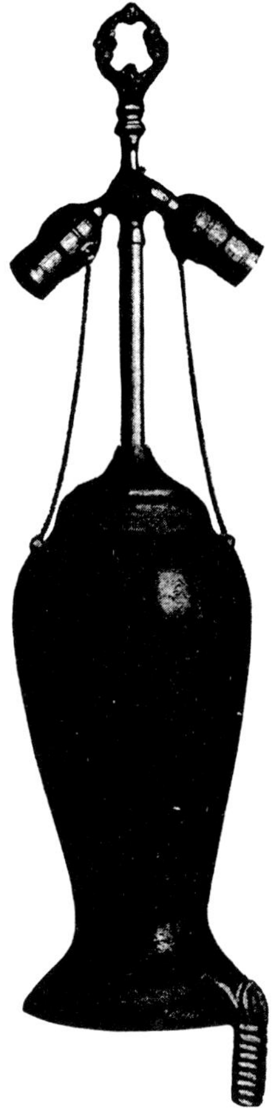

LAMP MOUNT
No. 8
Complete with Fixture
Height, 25 inches
Price, each, $15.00

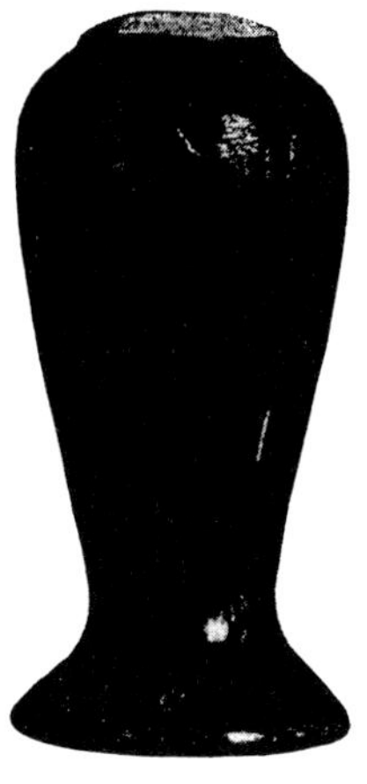

LAMP MOUNT
No. 8 N. F.
Without Fixture
Height, 12½ inches
Price, each, $10.00

Made up attractively in all Cliftwood colors and glazes. This Lamp with fixture neatly felted on bottom.

(See Alphabetical Color Chart on Page 4)

#8 – **$60-70**

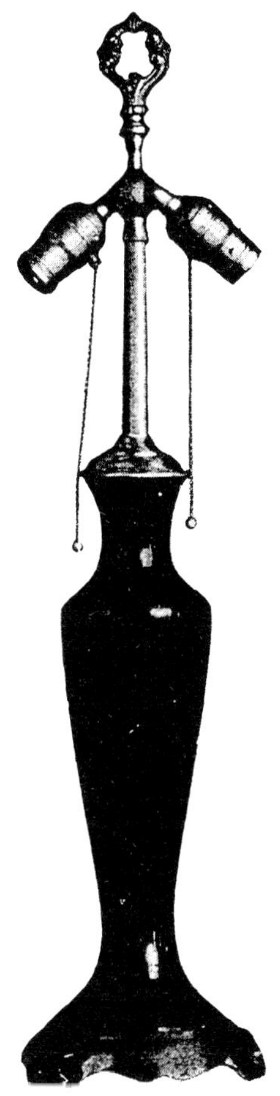

LAMP MOUNT

No. 4

Complete with Fixture
Height, 27 inches
Complete with beautiful golden satin finish metal stand.
Price, each $17.00

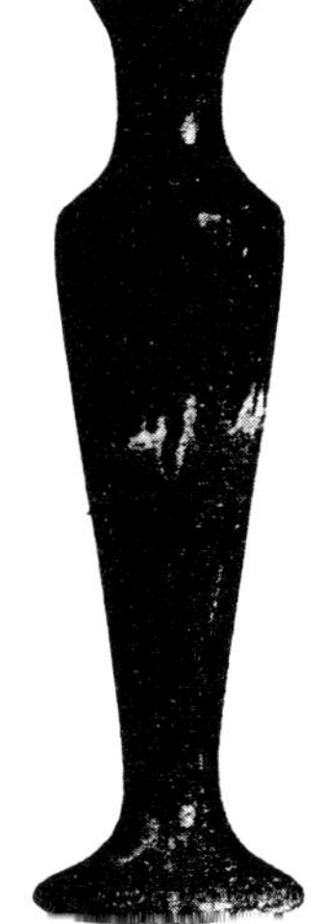

LAMP MOUNT

No. 4 N. F.

Without Fixture
Height, 15 inches
Price, each, $5.40

Drilled with 3/8 inch hole at bottom. Can supply with 1/4 inch hole at side also for cord if so ordered.

Our No. 4 Lamp Mount with its tall slender lines is a wonder.

Made up attractively in all Cliftwood colors and glazes.

(See Alphabetical Color Chart on Page 4)

Page 25 #4 – **$85-95**

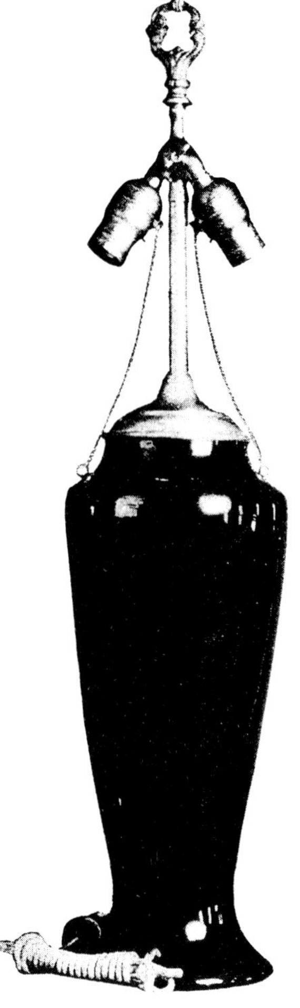

LAMP MOUNT
No. 13
Complete with Fixture
Height, 28 inches
Price, each, $20.00

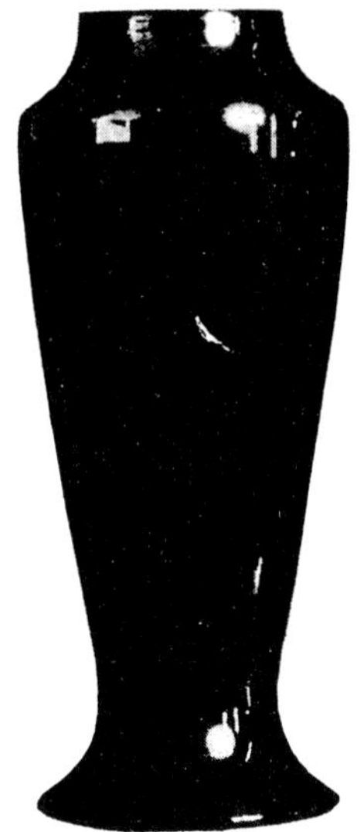

LAMP MOUNT
No. 13 N. F.
Without Fixture
Height, 16 inches
Price, each, $10.00

Our No. 13 Lamp Mount is just right in size for that large spacious living room or library.

Made up attractively in all Cliftwood colors and glazes. This Lamp with fixture neatly felted on bottom.

(See Alphabetical Color Chart on Page 4)

 #13 – **$90-100**

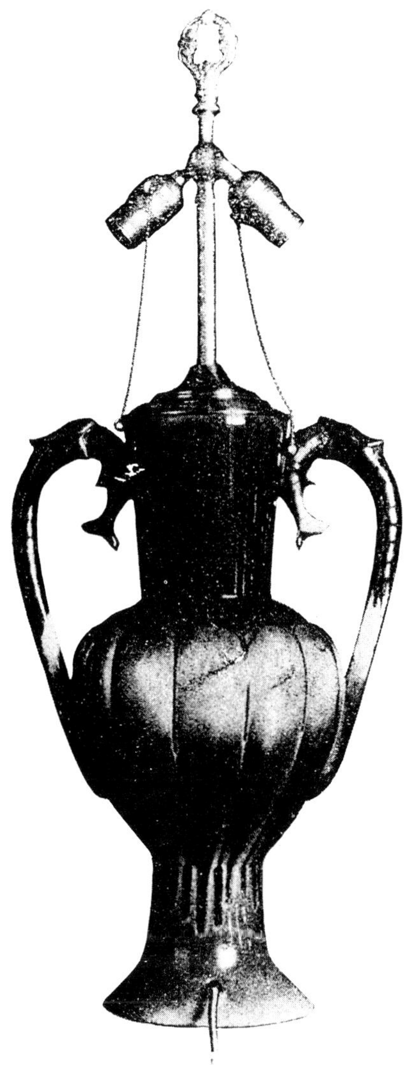

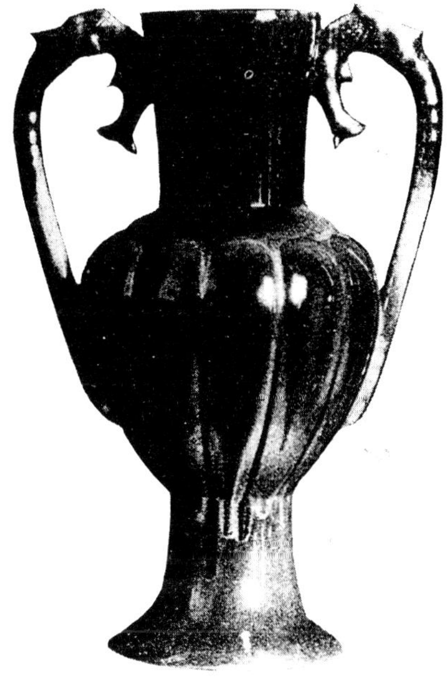

No. 9 LAMP MOUNT
Complete with Fixture
Height, 30 inches
Width, handle to handle, 12 inches
Price, each, $30.00

No. 9 N. F. LAMP MOUNT
Without Fixture
Height, 18 inches
Width, handle to handle, 12 inches
Price, each, $20.00

Here is the wonder Lamp, massive in construction with very graceful lines.

Made up attractively in all Cliftwood colors and glazes. This lamp with fixture neatly felted on bottom.

(See Alphabetical Color Chart on Page 4)

Page 27 **#9 – $100-125**

LAMP MOUNT
No. 15
Complete with fixtures and Harp
Height, 21-inches overall
Width, 4¾-inches
The Shape is Hexagon
Price, each, $8.50

No. 17 LAMP MOUNT
Complete with fixtures and harp
Height, 22½-inches
Width, handle to handle, 7½ inches
Price, each, $12.00

Made up attractively in all Cliftwood colors.
See Alphabetical color chart on Page 4.

#15 – **$45-55** #17 – **ND**

A COLLECTION OF CLIFTWOOD LAMP SHAPES

These line drawings are of lamp shapes that were in production at the Cliftwood Art Potteries in 1922. The drawings were made by an employee, Verena Moser, for the salesmen to carry in their sales portfolios. The salesmen carried only one or two samples with them, so the drawings allowed them to show their customers all of the designs that were currently available at the pottery.

Though somewhat crude, the drawings show a considerable amount of detail. They are most helpful for identification purposes.

Value Range: ND

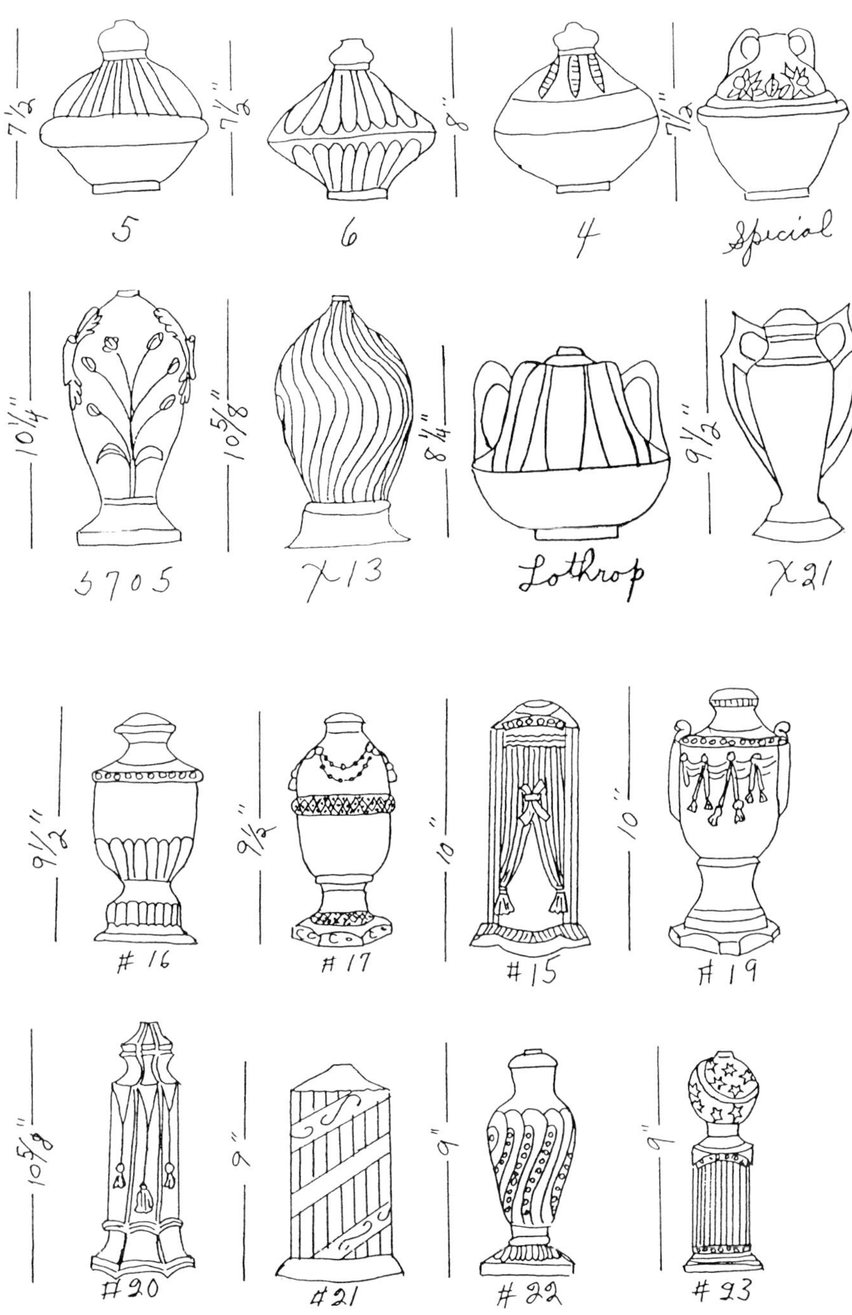

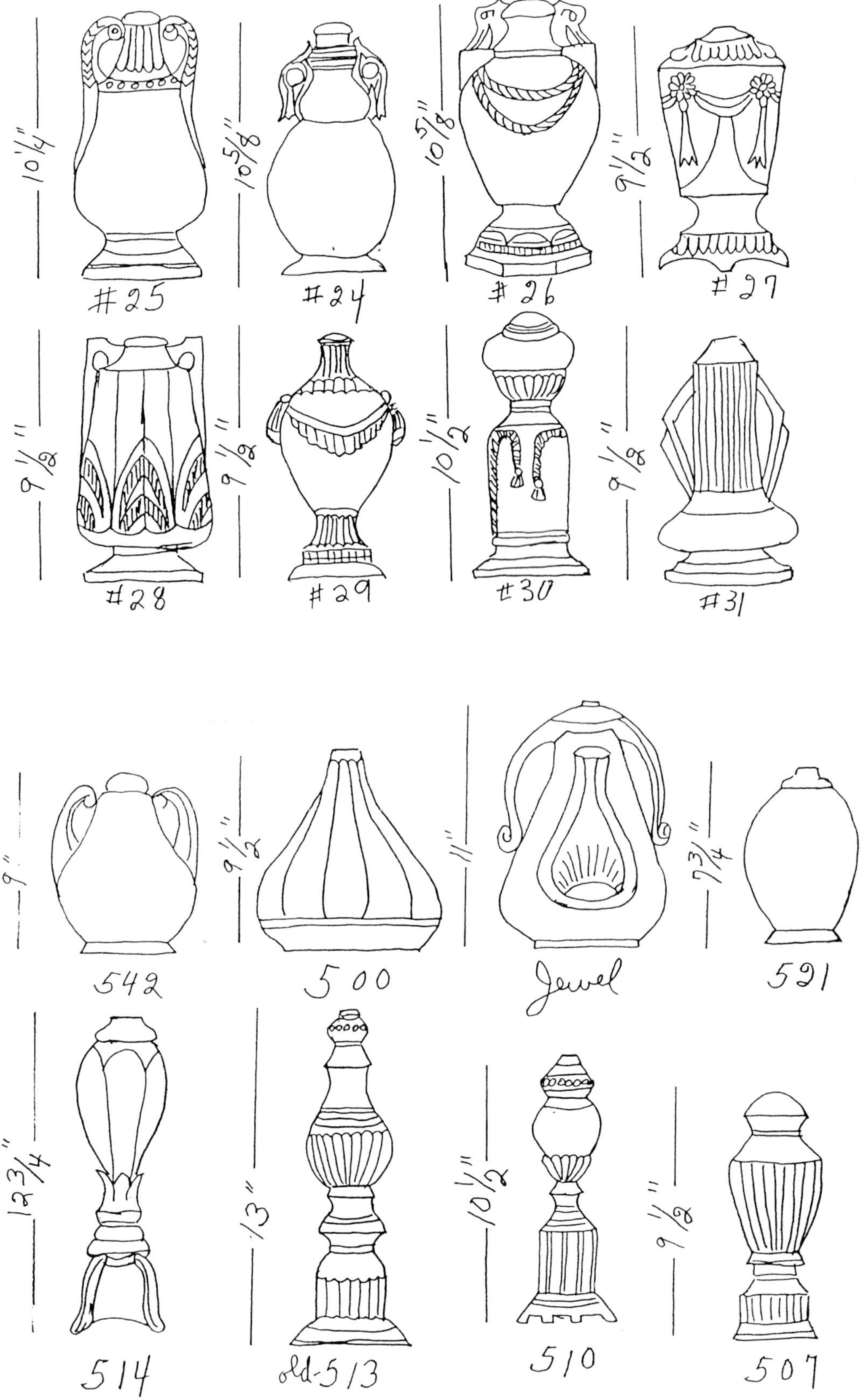
10¼"
#25
10⅝"
#24
10⅝"
#26
9½"
#27
9½"
#28
9½"
#29
10½"
#30
9½"
#31
9"
542
9½"
500
11"
Jewel
7¾"
521
12¾"
514
13"
old-513
10½"
510
9½"
507

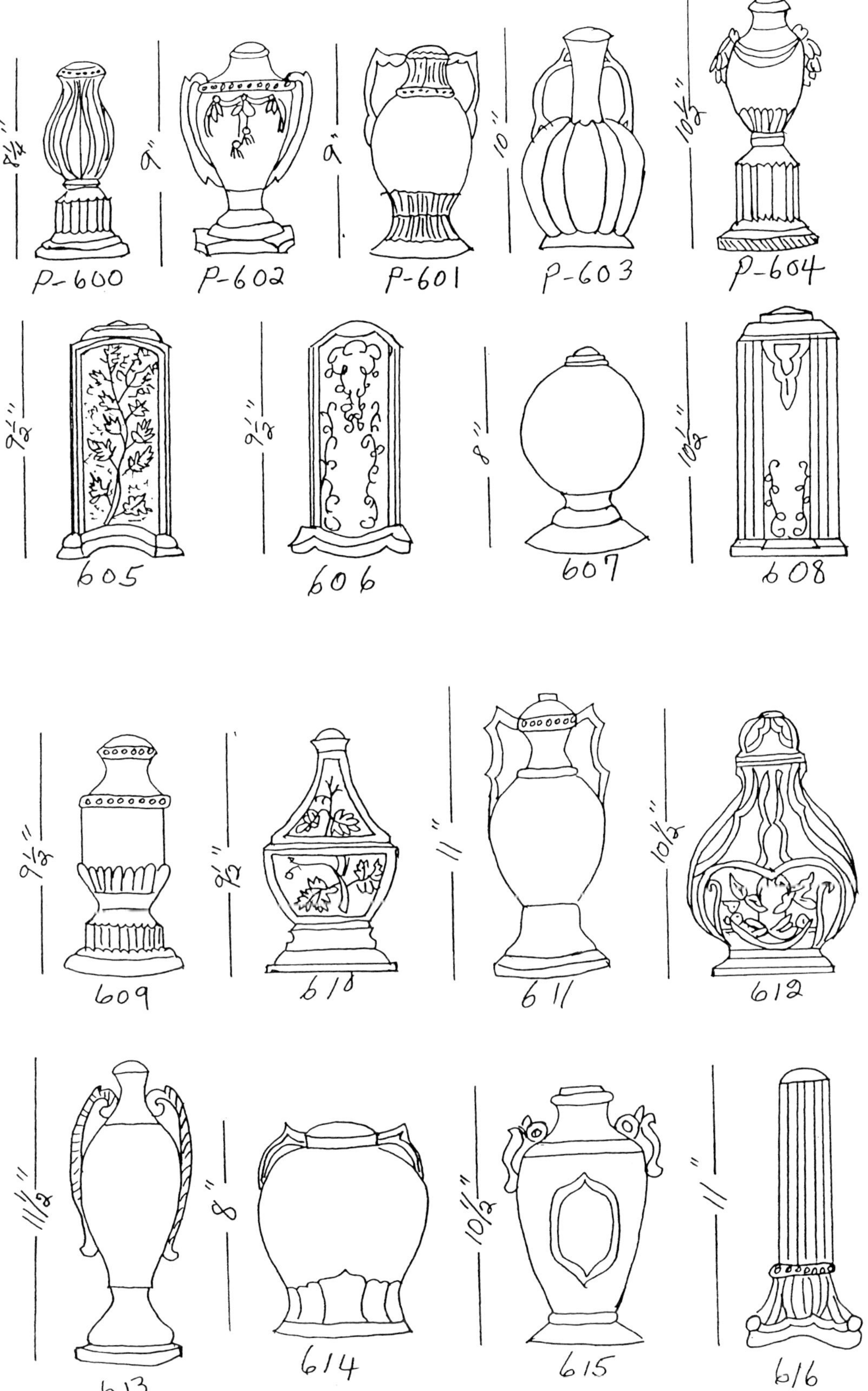
P-600
P-602
P-601
P-603
P-604
605
606
607
608
609
610
611
612
613
614
615
616

CHAPTER 6
CLIFTWOOD ART POTTERIES, INC.
BEVERAGE SERVICE

The Rapp family traced its roots back to the Black Forest region of south Germany. It was only natural that one of the early items to be put into production at Cliftwood was the beer set. The set consisted of a pitcher and six steins. The set was advertised for lemonade and ice tea, as well as beer.

Five glaze styles are pictured. The tankard stein is a larger alternative to the barrel steins. Miniature steins were made in all Cliftwood colors. They are rare.

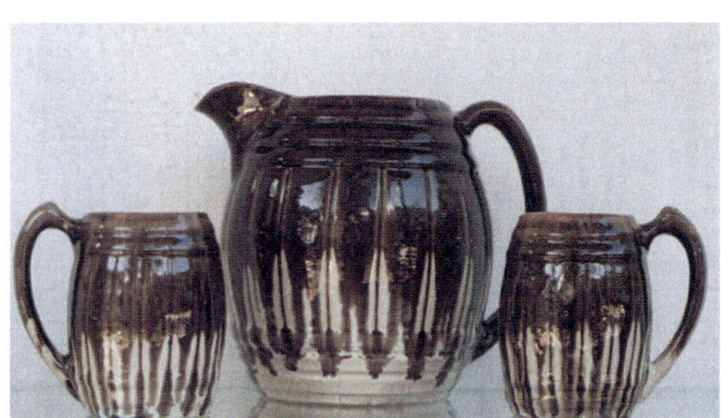

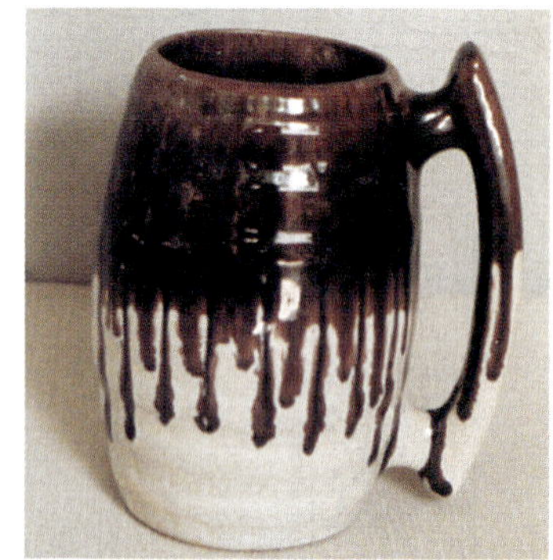

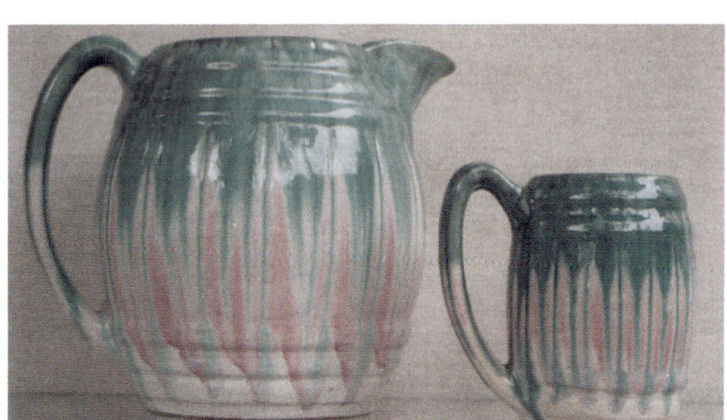

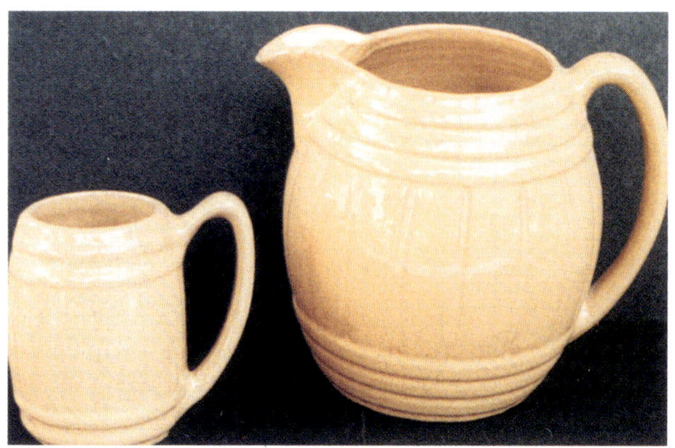

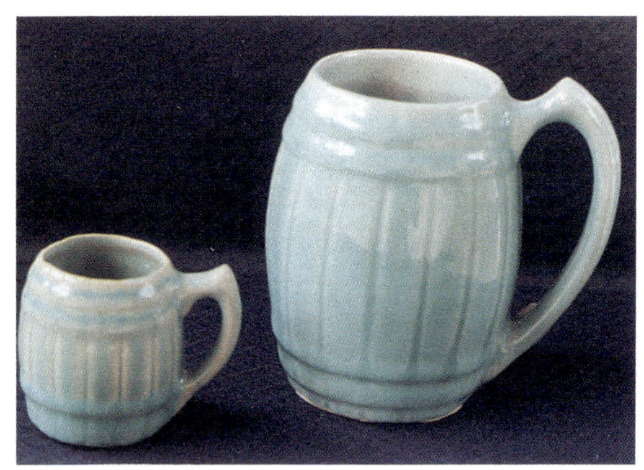

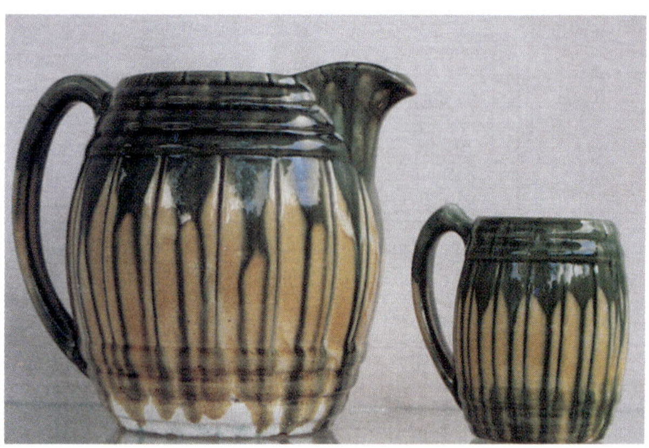

Value Range:
Set – **$140-180** Pitcher – **$30-60** Stein – **$15-20**
Tankard Stein – **$18-24** Mini Stein – **$20-25**

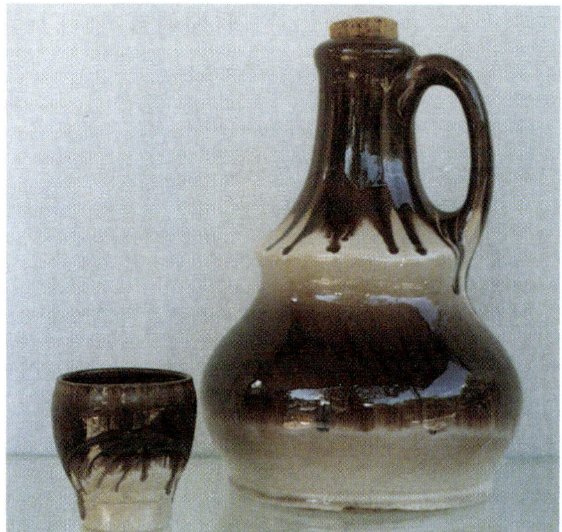

The wine jug is very unusual. It has a music box set into the bottom that plays a polka when the jug is lifted. The on/off switch retracts when setting on a smooth surface, shutting the music box off. It plays each time the jug is lifted.

Value Range: Jug – $100-125
Wine Glass – $6-10

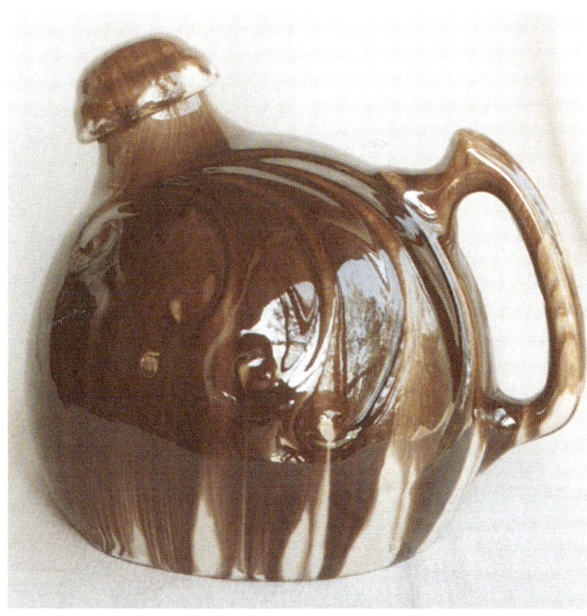

This style wine jug is very similar to jugs made by Rumrill, Camark, Niloak, and other contemporary potteries.

Value Range: $40-50

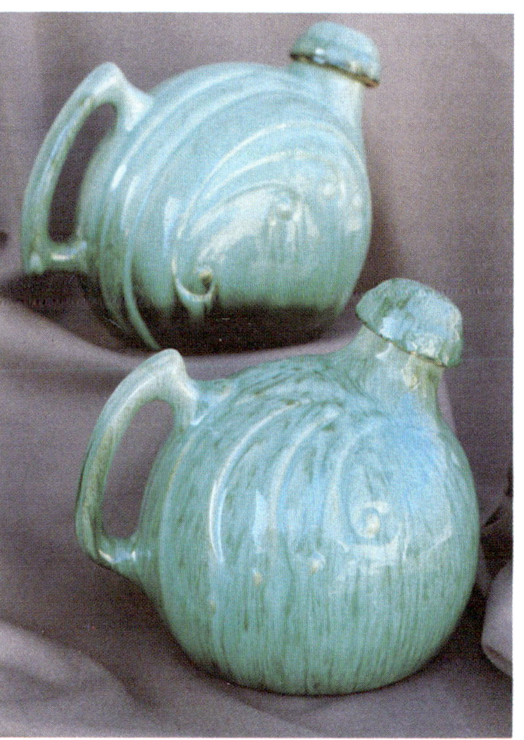

Similar in appearance, these jugs have different style necks, and the embossed design has been reversed.

Value Range: $40-50

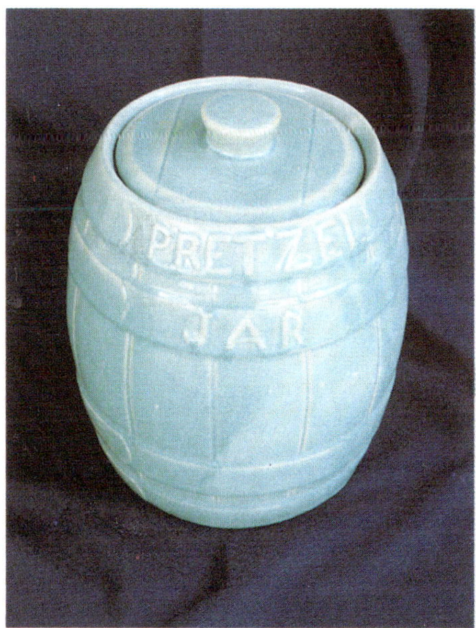

Pretzel jars are elusive. They were designed as a companion piece to the beer sets. The barrel shape was very popular in the 1930's.

Value Range: $50-60

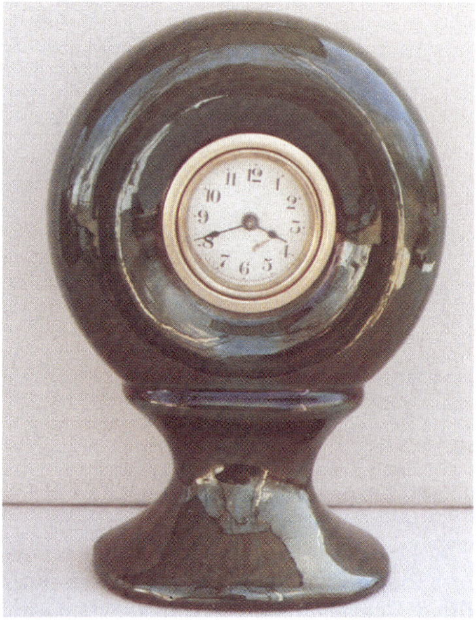

The 8 1/2" donut shape clock case is an example of John Rapp's herbage green glaze. The clock is by Lux Clock Works, Waterbury, Connecticut.

Value Range: $70-90

This console set is in Cliftwood's cobalt blue glaze. The compote is from set #227, but the candlesticks were made to go with dinnerware that was produced for just a short period of time.

Value Range:
Set – $90-110
Compote – $40-50
Candlesticks – $45-55 set

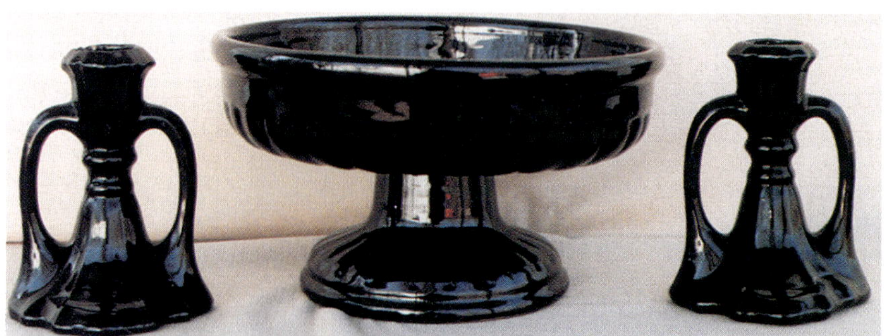

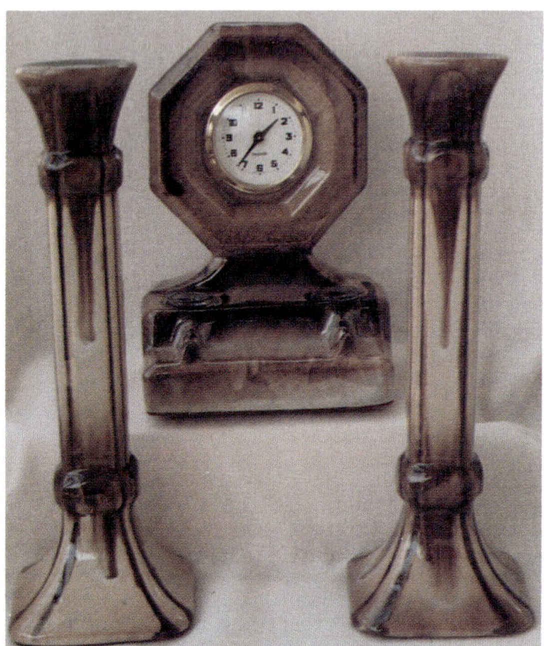

This unit was sold as a desk set at the pottery. This octagonal clock case has two glass inkwell inserts on the top step, and a pen rack across the first step. The glaze is Matthew Rapp's secret chocolate brown drip.
Value Range: Set – $190-225 Clock – $150-170
Candlesticks – $45-55 set

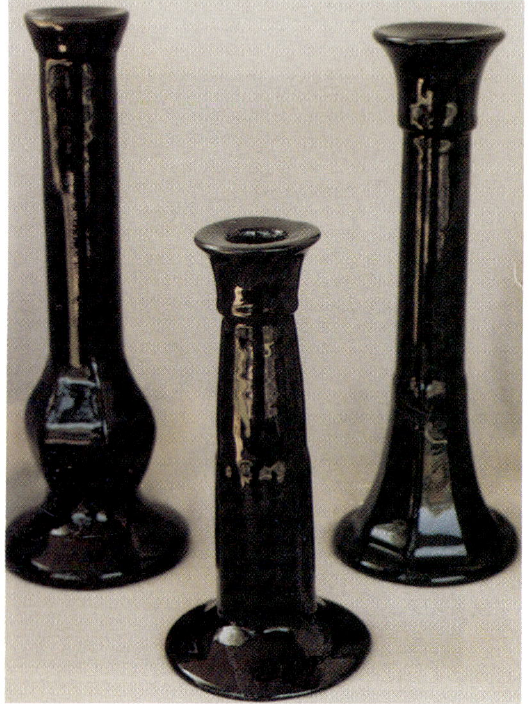

Here are three different style candlesticks in cobalt blue glaze. The one on the left is 10 1/2" tall. The center one measures 7" tall, and on the left is a 10" candlestick.
Value Range: Left – $25-30 Center – $15-20
Right – $20-25

DINNERWARE AND KITCHENWARE

Cliftwood Art Potteries did not design a complete set of dinnerware. Plates, cups and saucers, pitchers, and a sugar and creamer were made in the late 1920's, but were never really good sellers. All items from that line are scarce today. Utilitarian kitchenware was made all through the twenties and thirties, however. Examples of those utility items, though not common, are still being located by collectors.

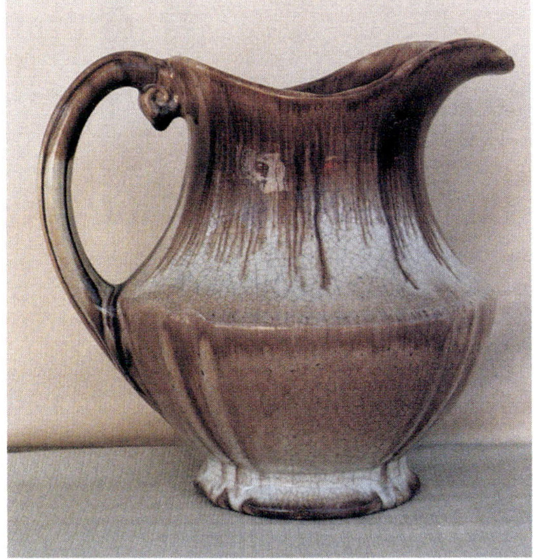

The water pitcher is 7 3/4" tall. It was designed to be part of the dinnerware line. It is done in the chocolate brown drip glaze. The water pitcher is elusive.

Value Range: $50-70

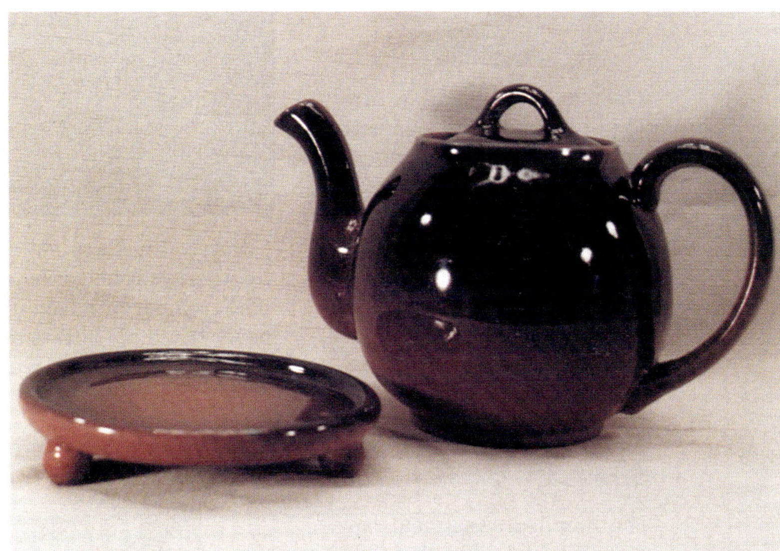

The 8 cup globe teapot was a standard item during the pottery's twenty years of operation. The footed trivet is quite rare. This set is in blue mulberry glaze, color coded as letter L in the catalogs.

Value Range: $60-80 set Teapot: $20-30 Trivet : $40-50

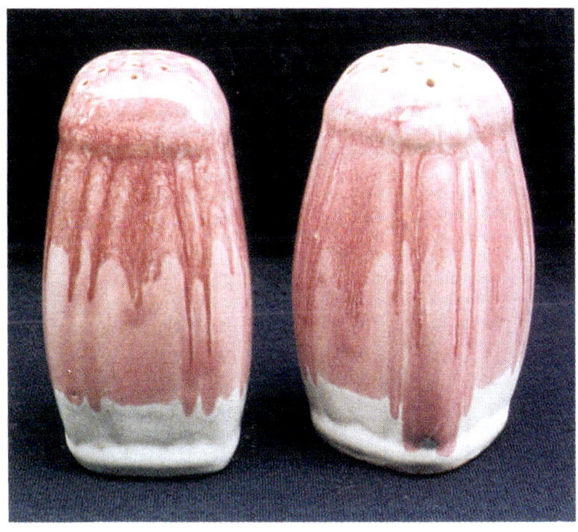

Stove top / counter top salt and pepper shakers were made in every color and combination of colors that Cliftwood did. These are old rose over pink, over white.

Value Range: $20-30 set

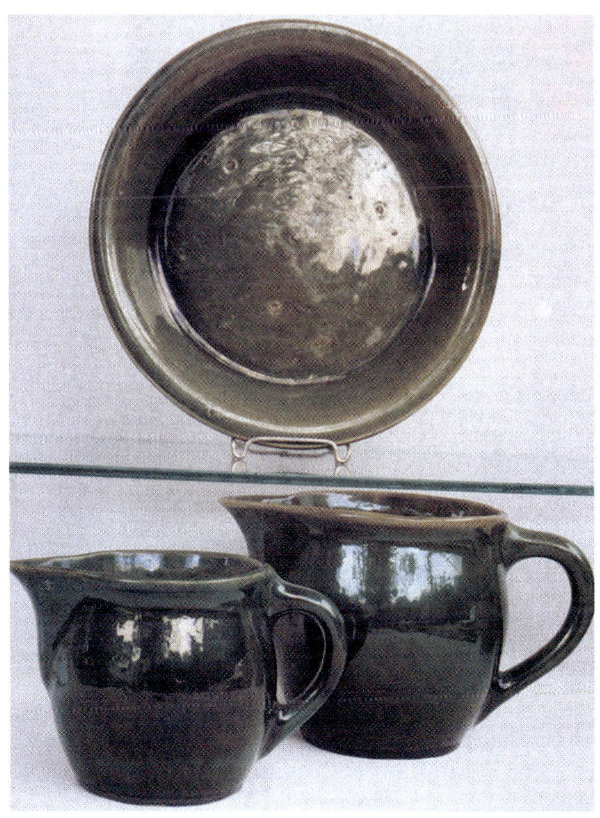

The 9" pie plate is jade green, as are both of the milk jugs. The milk jugs were made in three different sizes. The smallest is not shown here.

Value Range: Pie Plate – $40-50
Large Jug – $35-40 Small Jug – $25-30

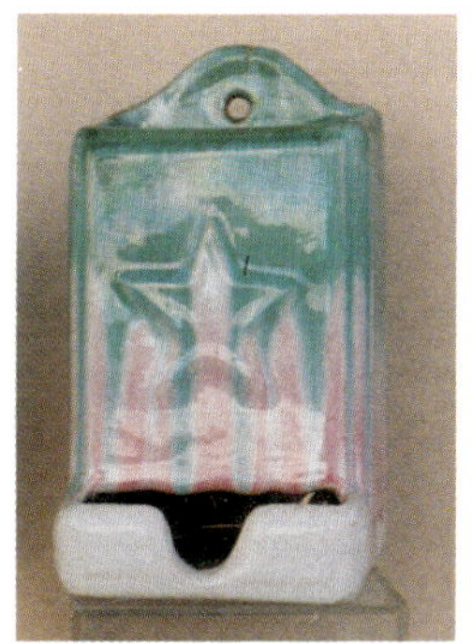

The match box holder is rare. This one is spray glazed with turquoise and pink over white.

Value Range: $30-50

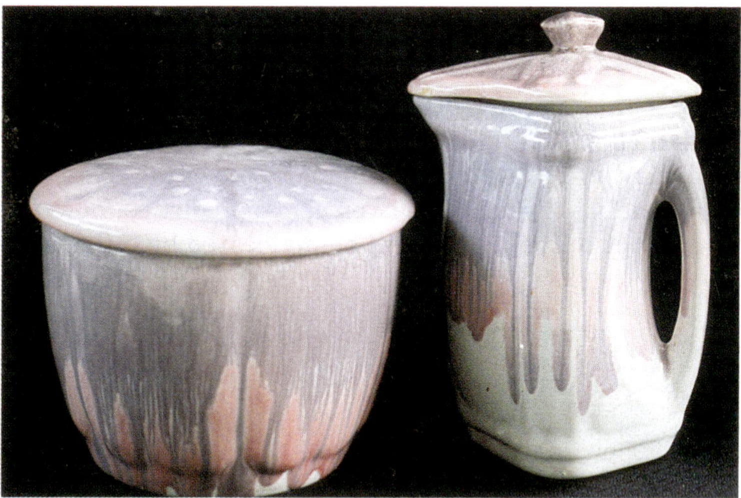

Covered items are not common. Because of daily use, the lids were frequently broken or badly damaged. The ice box storage bowl and the pint creamer are done in orchid and pink over white. This glaze was never listed in Cliftwood catalogs.

Value Range: Ice Box Bowl – $25-35
Creamer – $30-40

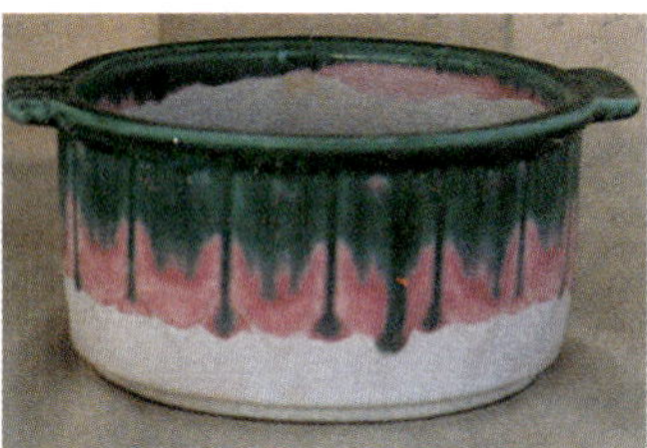

The handled sweetmeat bowl probably had a lid. It is also turquoise and pink drip over white.

Value Range: $20-25

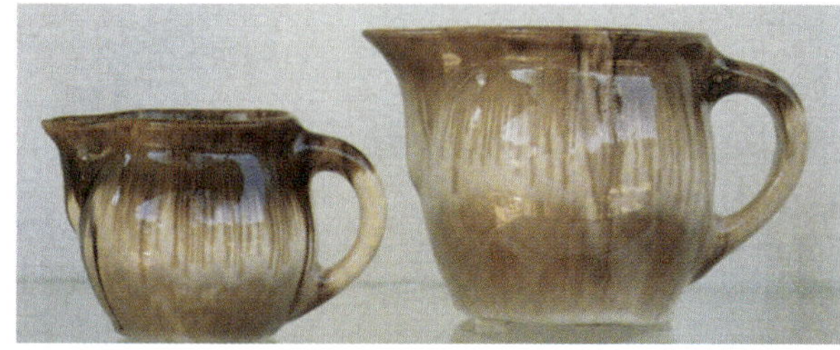

These are the small and medium size milk jugs in chocolate brown drip glaze.

Value Range: Small Jug – $35-45
Large Jug – $40-45

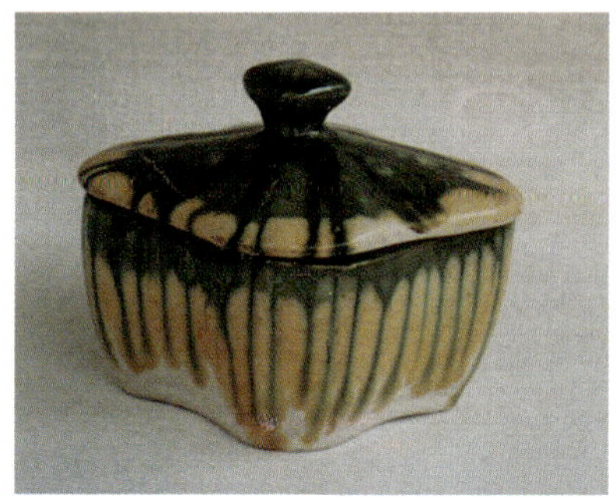

The square, covered sweetmeat bowl is not common, nor is the green and yellow drip glaze.

Value Range: $45-50

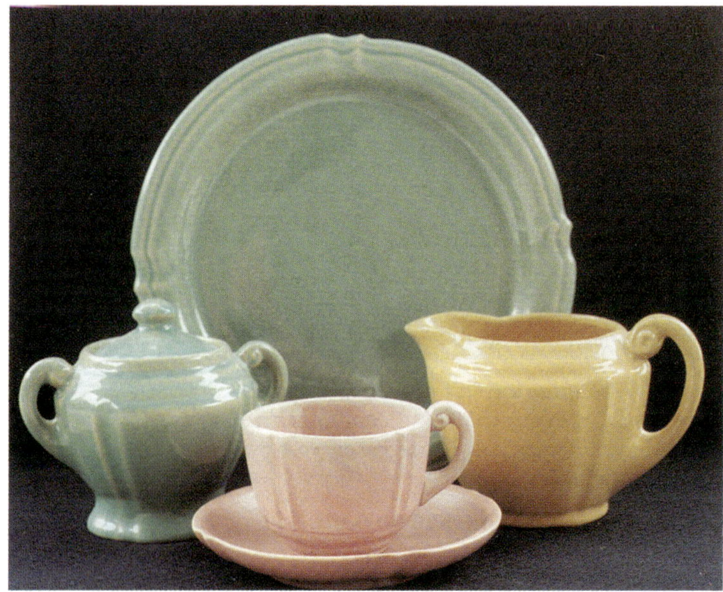

The 10" dinner plate is apple green, a color seldom used by Cliftwood. The cup and saucer are old rose matte glaze. The goldenrod yellow on the creamer is not a common Cliftwood color. The covered sugar is rare.

Value Range: Plate – $20-25
Cup & Saucer – ND Creamer – $15-20 Sugar – $20-25

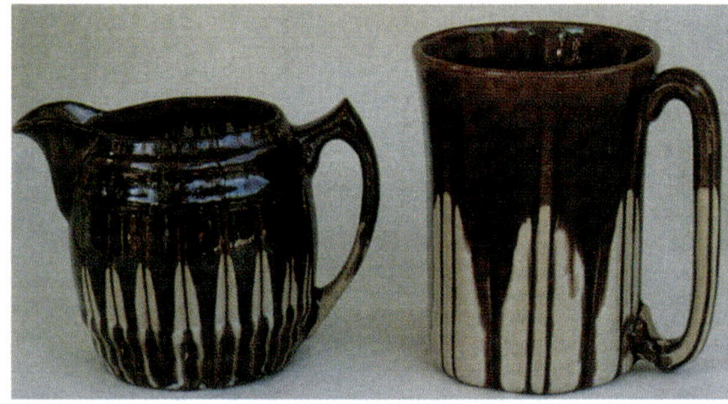

This creamer is barrel shape. The mug was listed in the sales literature.

Value Range: Creamer – $35-40
Mug – $30-35

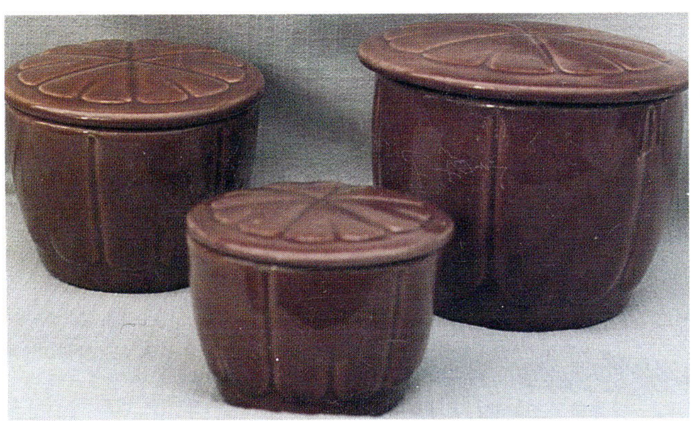

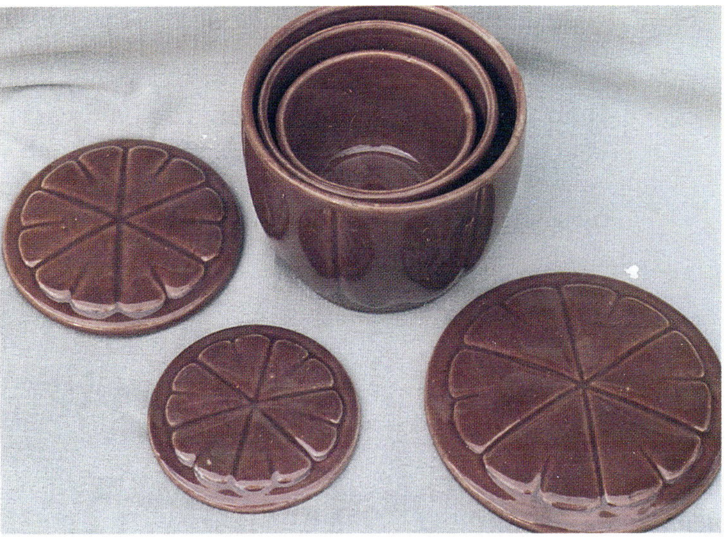

The nested set of ice box storage bowls is very difficult to locate complete and in mint condition. The individual bowls are rather common without the lid.

Value Range: $40-50 set (add 20% for drip glazes)

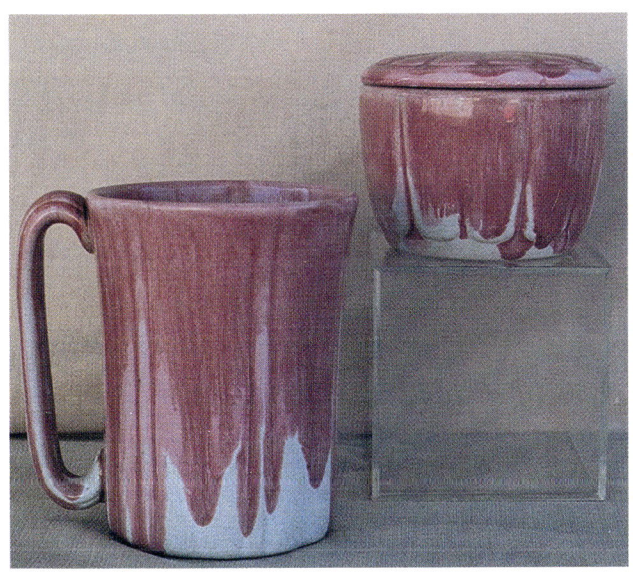

This is a buttermilk mug and a grease jar with cover. Both are done in old rose over white glaze.

Value Range: Mug – $30-35
Jar – $20-25

The batter bowl and grease jar are glazed with orchid and pink over white. Batter bowls are extremely rare.

Value Range: Batter Bowl – ND
Grease Jar – $20-25

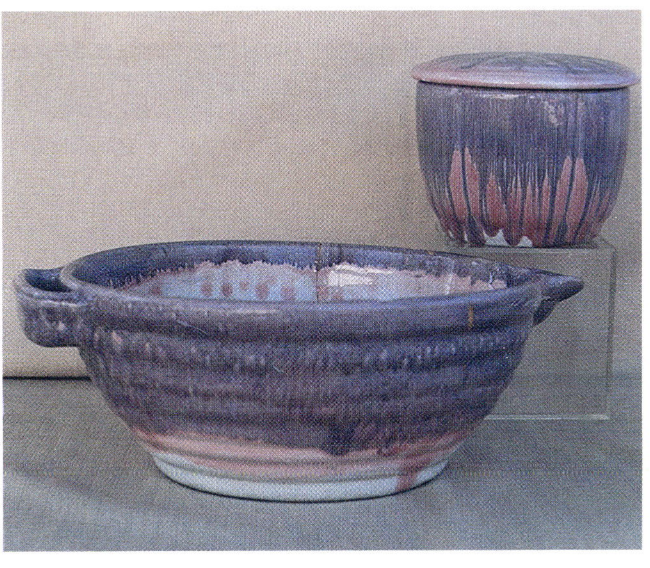

FIGURINES

Cliftwood Art Potteries, Inc. is not known to have done any human figurines other than the Lorilei flower holder. The bald eagle is the only bird figurine to be located up to this time. Four legged animals were the Rapp's forte. Some were well executed, others were somewhat primitive in design. All figurines can be classified as scarce. Figurines were frequently altered to be used as planters. The figural planters are elusive.

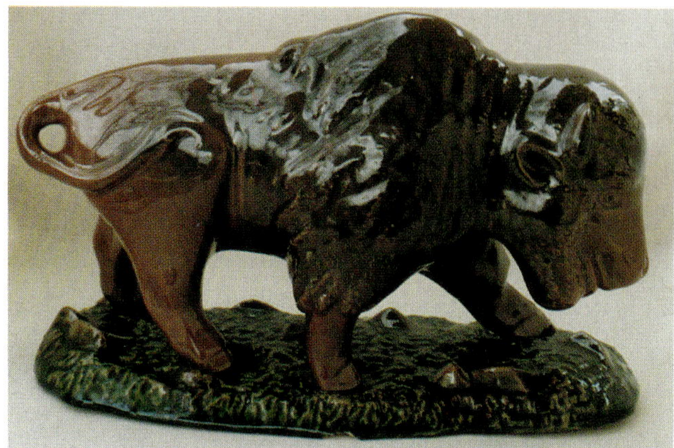

The buffalo is the rarest of all Cliftwood figurines. Glazed in natural colors, it is a fine example of the early air brushing (spray glazing) technique. The figure is 10" long and 6 1/4" tall.

Value Range: ND

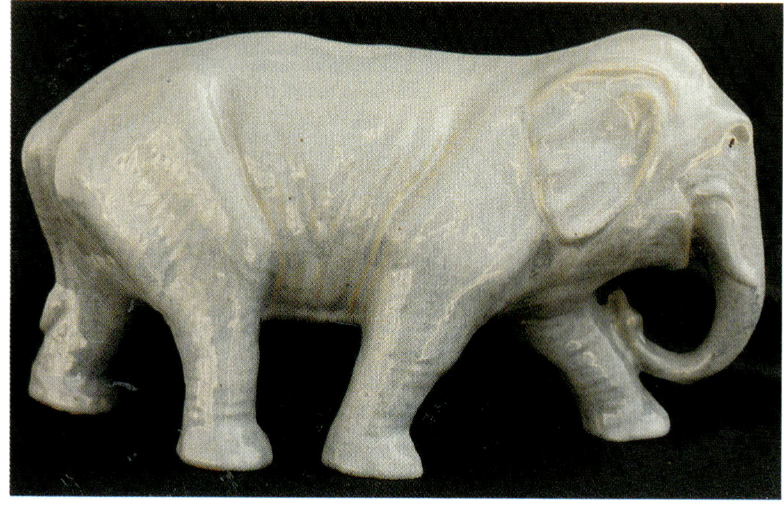

This elephant was once owned by Lawrence Rapp. Rapp's initials, LR are on a piece of adhesive tape on the elephant's stomach. This figure is 13 1/2" long and 7 1/4" tall.

Value Range: $75-100

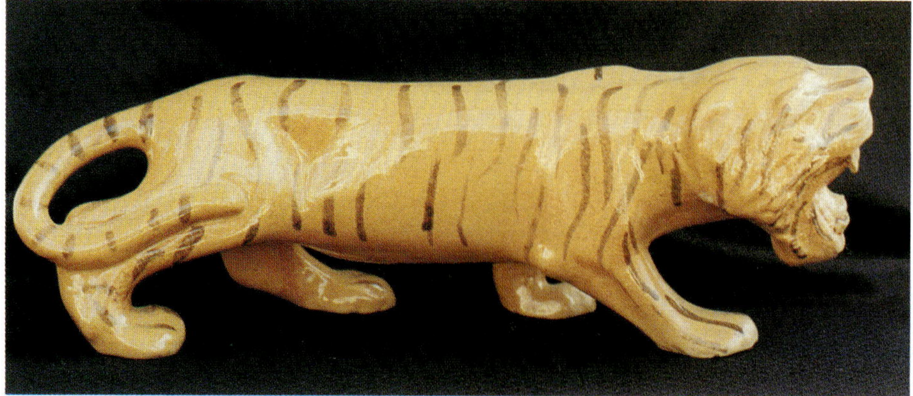

The tiger is one of the earliest figurines made at Cliftwood. It is solid cast, and appears to have been made from tile clay. It is 16" long and 5" tall.

Value Range: $100-125

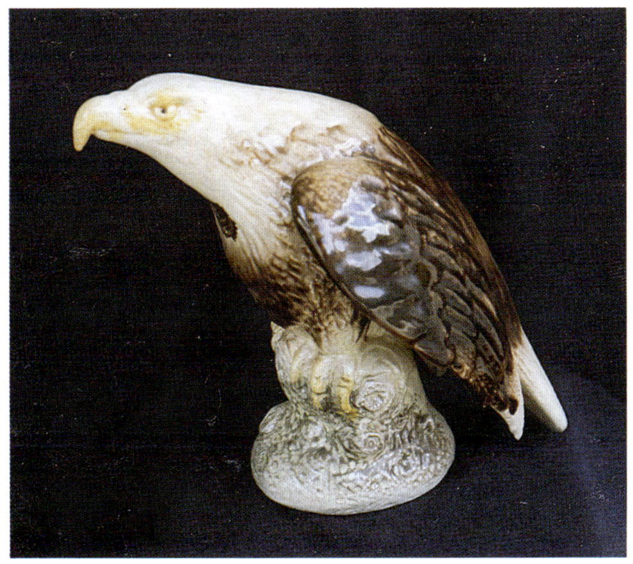

The bald eagle is a fine example of air brushing the glaze to achieve a natural look. The eagle is 81/2" tall. Note the Cliftwood paper label on the breast.

Value Range: $85-95

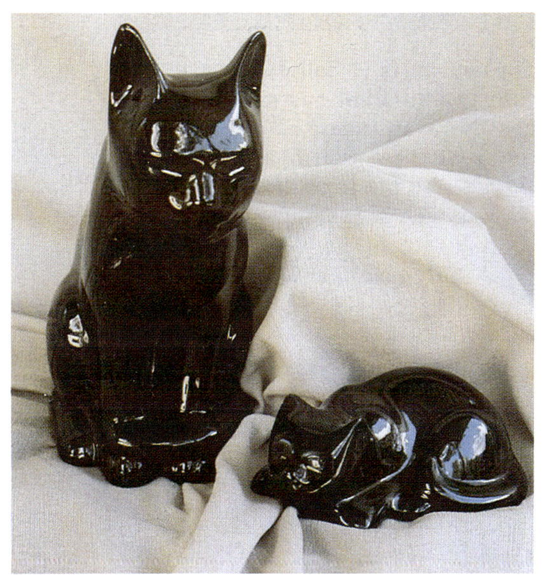

The black cats are really cobalt blue. Cliftwood very seldom used a black glaze. The large cat is 53/4" tall. The small one is 41/2" long.

Value Range: Large Cat – $30-40
Small Cat – $15-20

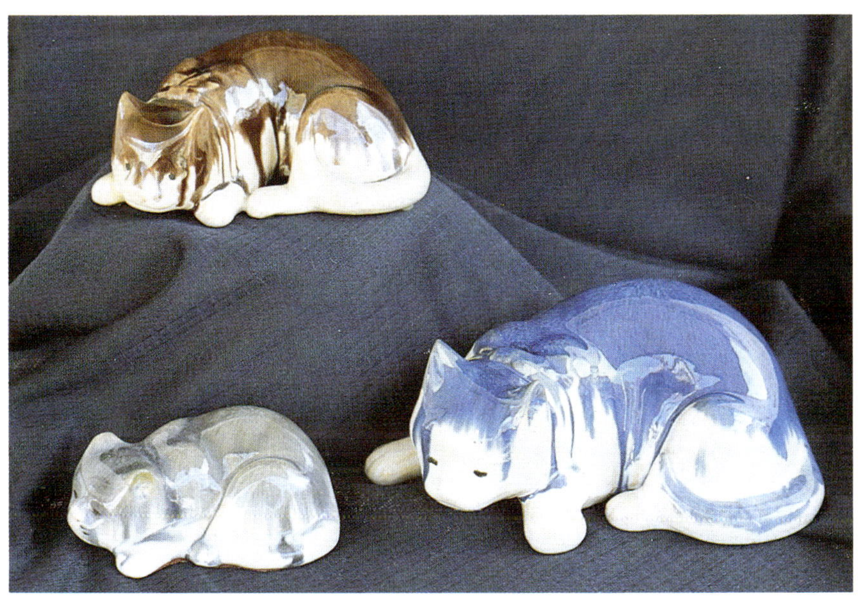

The three different size cats were very popular. The large cat is blue-white in the catalog color list. The small cat is grey drip, and the medium size is chocolate brown drip glaze.

Value Range: Small Cat – $20-25
Medium Cat – $25-35
Large Cat – $25-45
25% less in solid colors

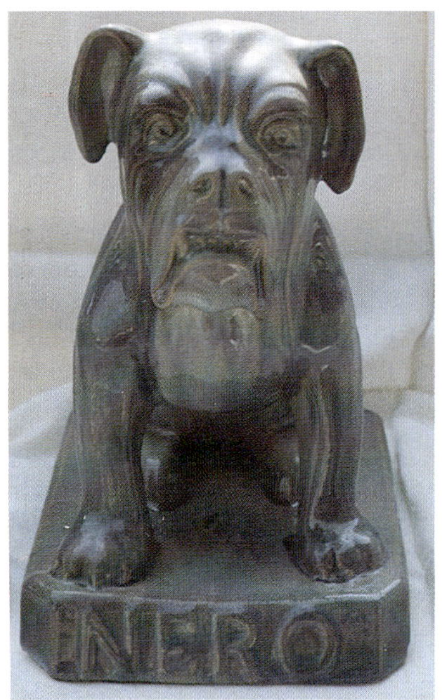

The bull dog is 11" tall. It was made with two different bases. This one has "Nero" in raised letters across the front. The other has "Barking Dog" across the front, but it is not barking. The dogs are identical.

Value Range: $75-95

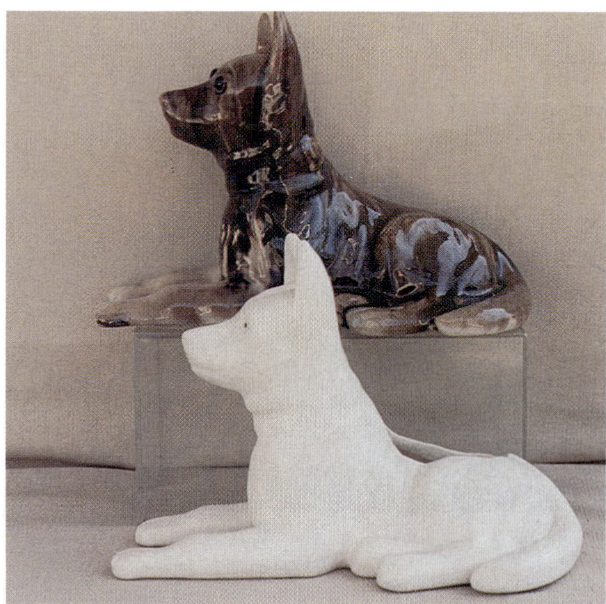

This police dog figurine is shown with the alteration that allows it to be used as a planter. The figurines have glass eyes that are wired into the eye sockets. The planter has painted eyes.

Value Range: Figurine $80-90
25% less for solid colors
Planter $20-30

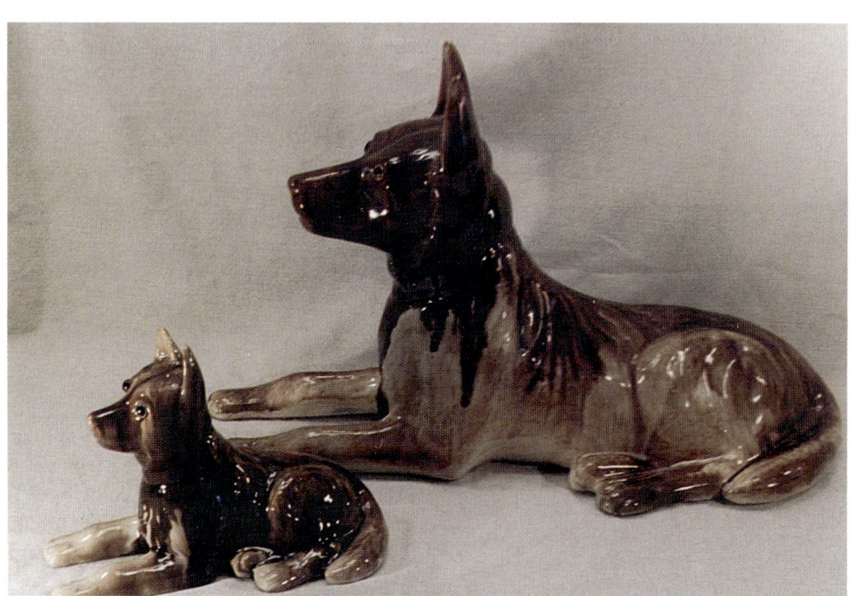

The police dog was made in three sizes. The one in the photograph above is 8" x 12". The large dog in this photograph is 11" x 18". The small dog is 5" x 81/2".

Value Range: Large Dog $100-150
Small Dog $55-75
25% less for solid colors

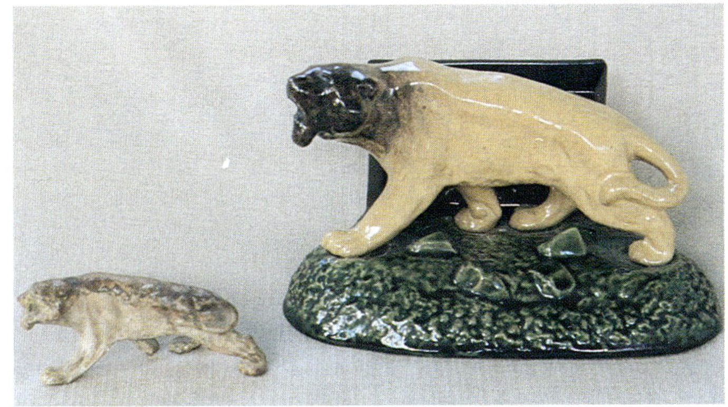

The lioness figurines pictured here date to the 1920's. The miniature is one of the toys that Cliftwood made during its first two years. Those miniatures are extremely rare. The large animal is a book end. She should have a male companion.

Value Range: Miniature – ND
Book End – $50-60
100% more for the pair

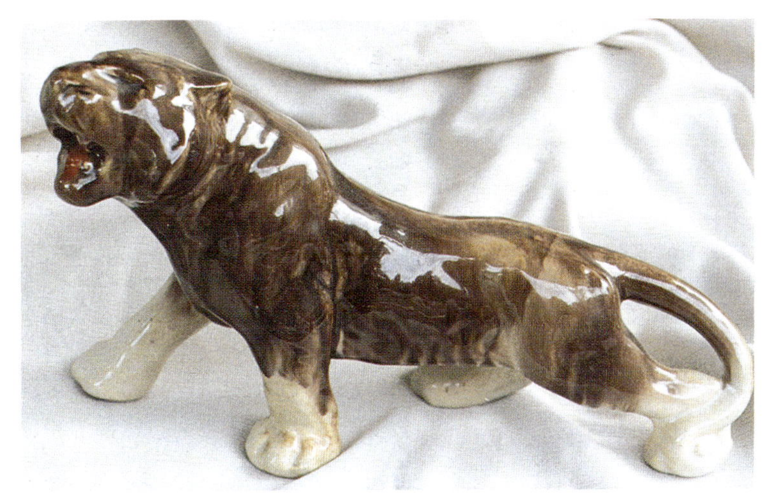

This lioness is not known to have ever had a male companion. She is 7" x 12".

Value Range: $70-80

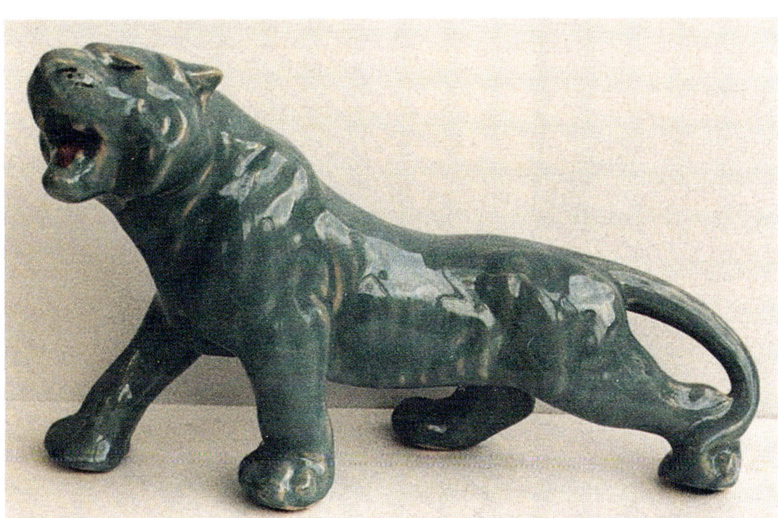

This is the same lioness, but in herbage green glaze. They are shown together for contrast.

Value Range: $50-60

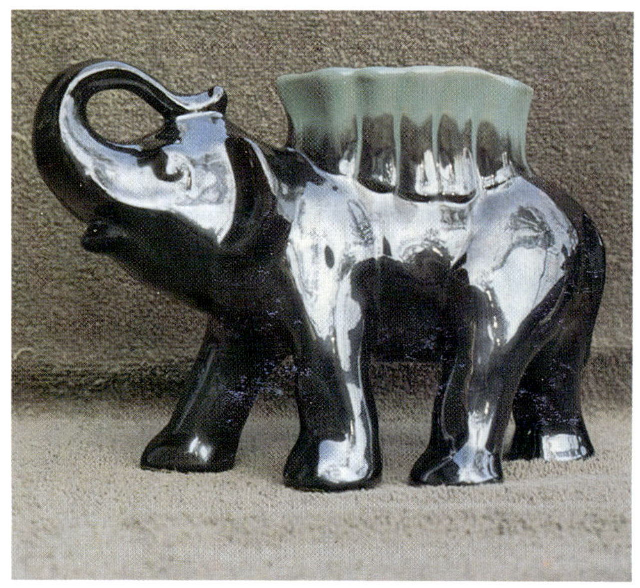

This elephant is cobalt blue with a green edged howdah platform. The platform is open so the figurine can be used as a planter.

Value Range: $25-30

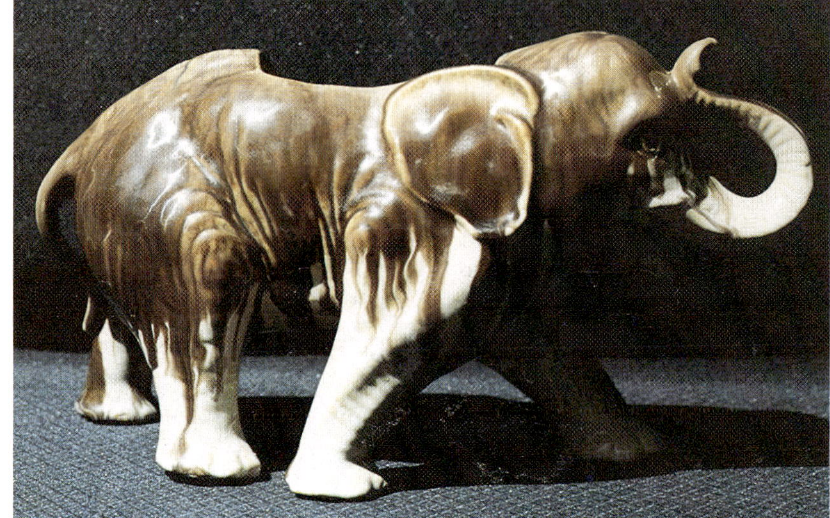

This figure has had the back removed and is a planter.

Value Range: $40-50

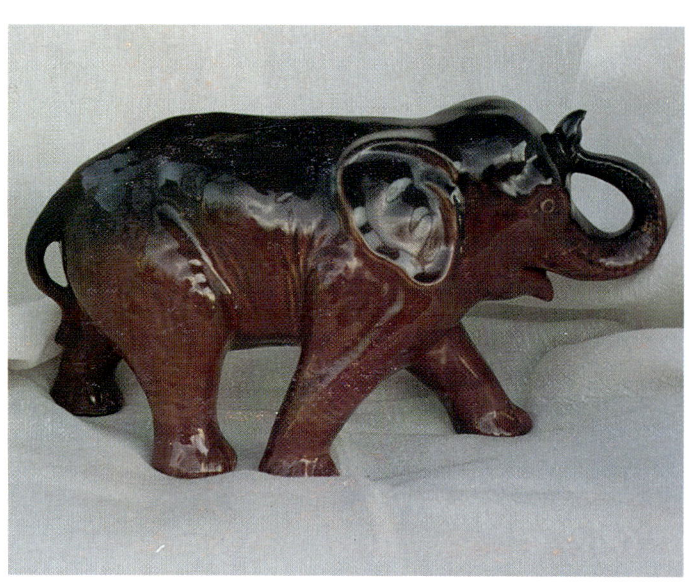

This figurine is the same elephant as No. 41. It is blue-mulberry glaze.

Value Range: $50-70

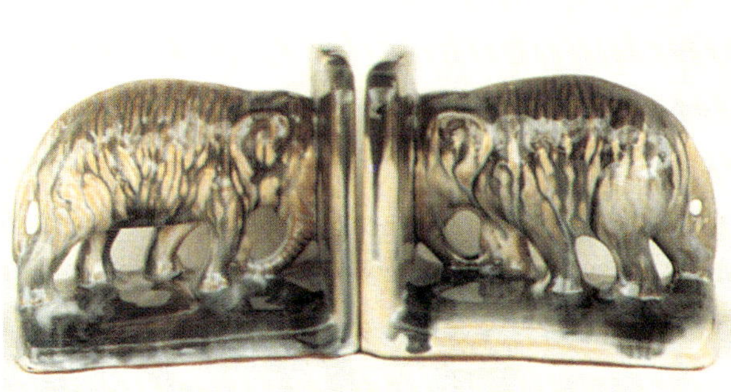

The elephant bookends are 41/4" tall and 6" long. The original red felt can be seen on the bottom.

Value Range: $100-125

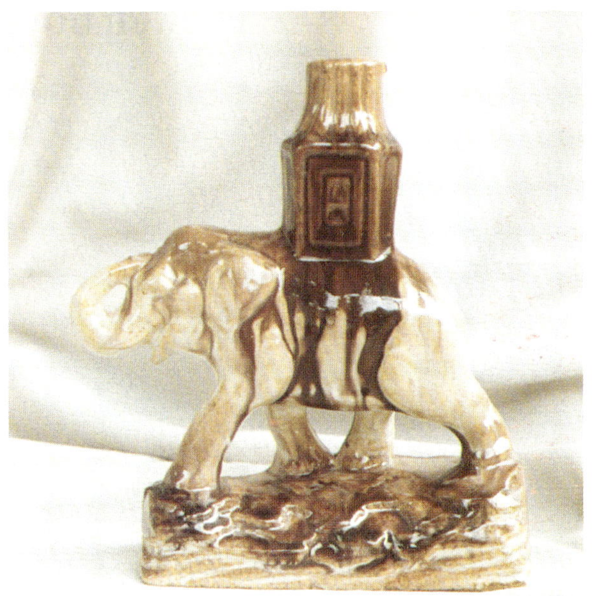

This elephant is a widget. Its purpose is not known. The jar has been drilled, but the opening is quite small. The log resembles items from the tree trunk line. The figure is 61/2" tall and 5" long.

Value Range: $40-60

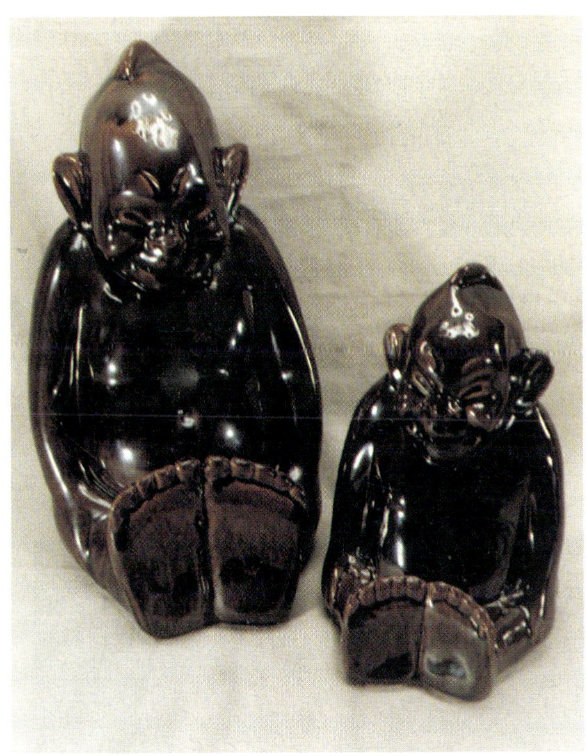

The billikin doll originally had a place for incense between the toes and the belly. It was enlarged and fattened upon suggestions from several Cliftwood salesmen. He can still be used as an incense burner. The billikin has only been found in Rockingham brown, shown here, and cobalt blue.

Value Range: Small doll (71/2") $55-75
Large doll (11") $85-100

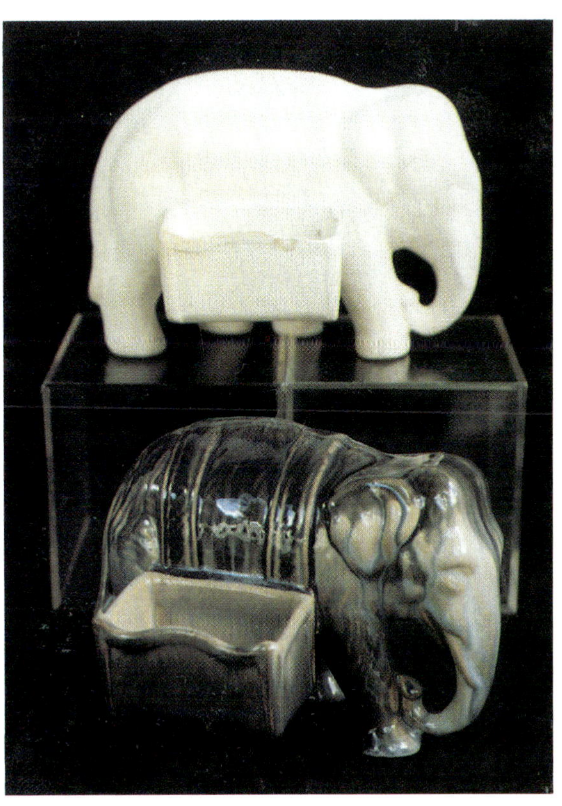

This elephant with the side packs was intended as a planter. It is frequently used as a business card holder. The figure is 51/2" tall and 8" long. The top figure is unfired clay that was found at the pottery's trash dump. It is a sharp contrast to the grey drip figure below.

Value Range: Clay Figure – ND
Glazed Figure – $60-80

FLOWER BOWLS AND INSERTS

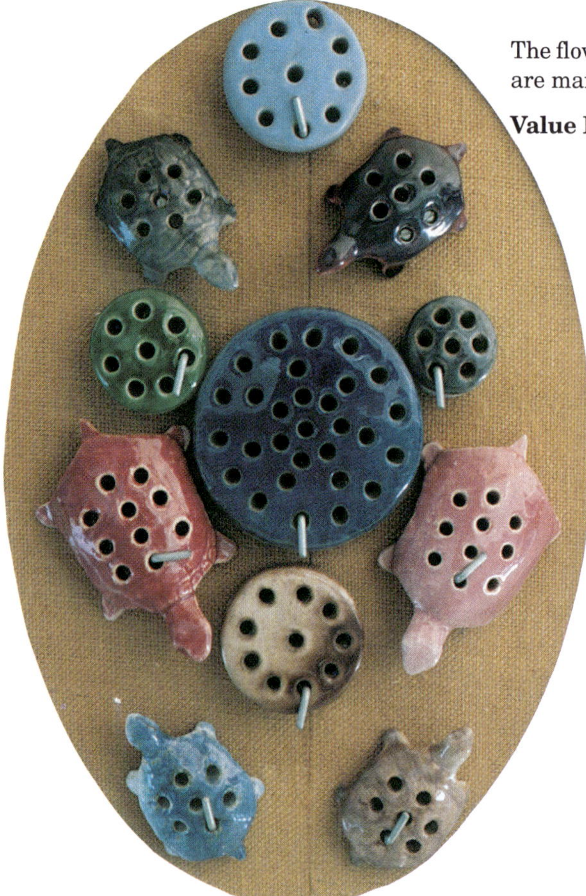

The flower discs are often mistaken for Weller. Most Weller discs are marked. Cliftwood's were never marked.

Value Range: **2" Disc $6-8** **3" Disc $8-10**
4" Disc $10-12 **5" Disc $12-14**
Small Turtle $12-20 **Large Turtle $16-24**

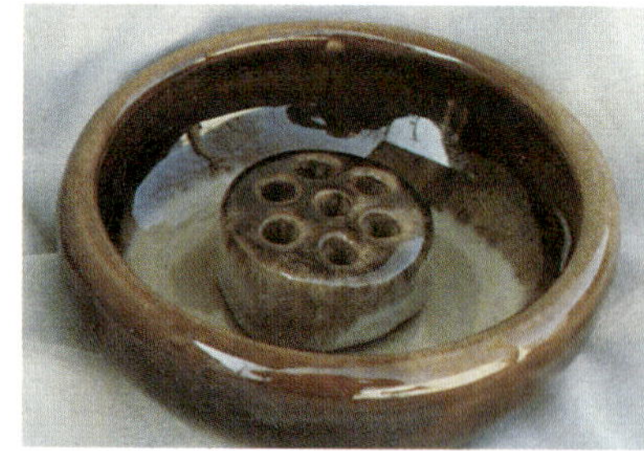

This is the 4 inch deep bulb bowl with a No. 1 flower disc.

Value Range: Bowl $6-8
Disc $6-8

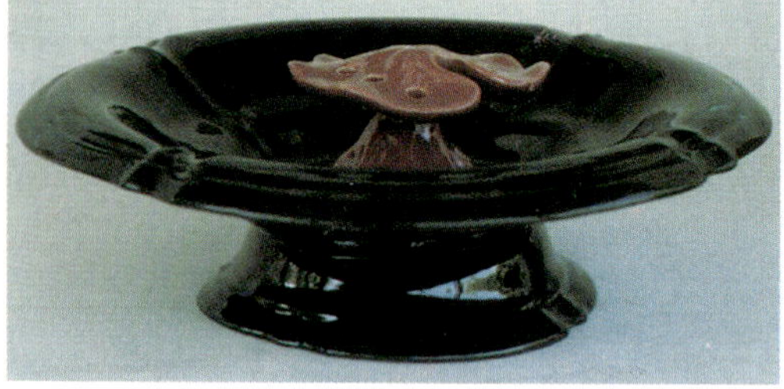

The cobalt blue footed flower bowl also doubled as a compote. The lily flower insert is the 4 inch size.

Value Range: Footed bowl $35-40
Lily Instert $18-24

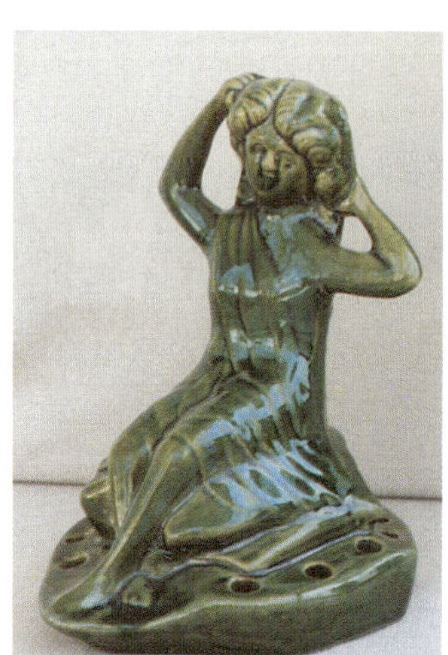

The Lorilei flower insert is 61/2" tall, and 41/2" wide. She is glazed in herbage green.

Value Range: $50-60

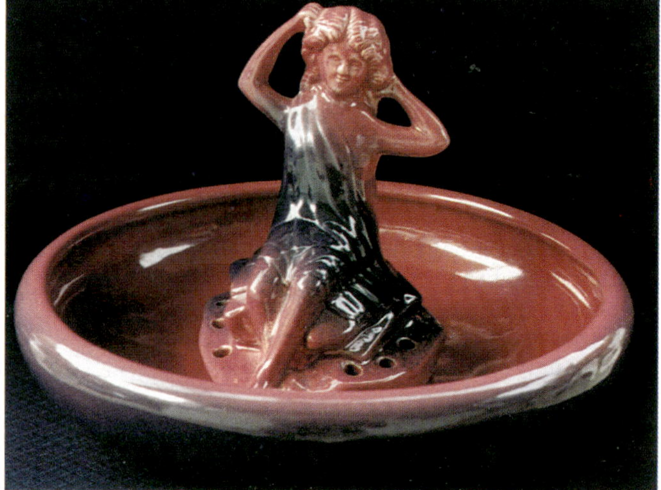

This is the Lorilei flower holder in the 10 inch shallow flower bowl. The color is blue-mulberry.

Value Range: $90-110 set

All dolphin base flower holders are extremely rare. They were time consuming to make. Fifteen individually molded pieces were hand assembled to create each item in this line. Each dolphin was three separate pieces. The center support, and the four dolphins surrounding it, frequently collapsed in the kiln during firing. All imperfect pieces were destroyed in the trash barrel.

The round bowl is a high glass glaze in old rose. It is 8 1/2" in diameter, and 6" tall.

Value Range: $70-90

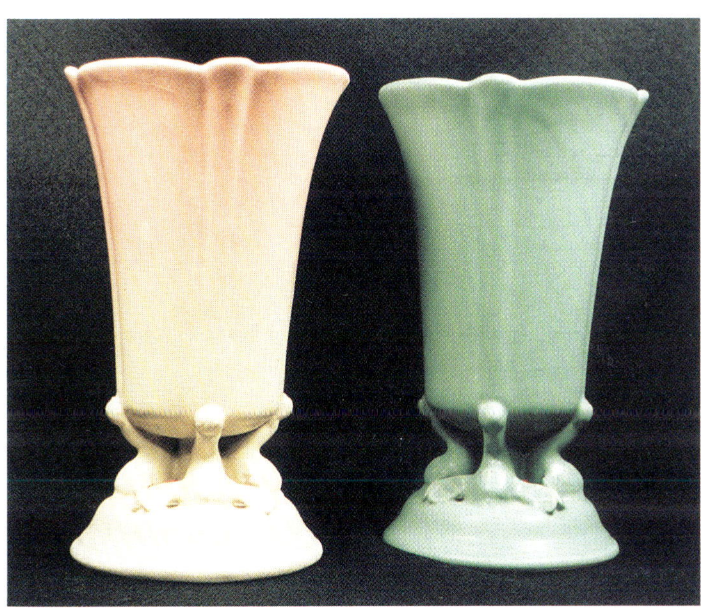

The pair of vases show two vastly different decorating styles. Both are matte glaze. They are 10" tall.

Value Range: $65-75 each

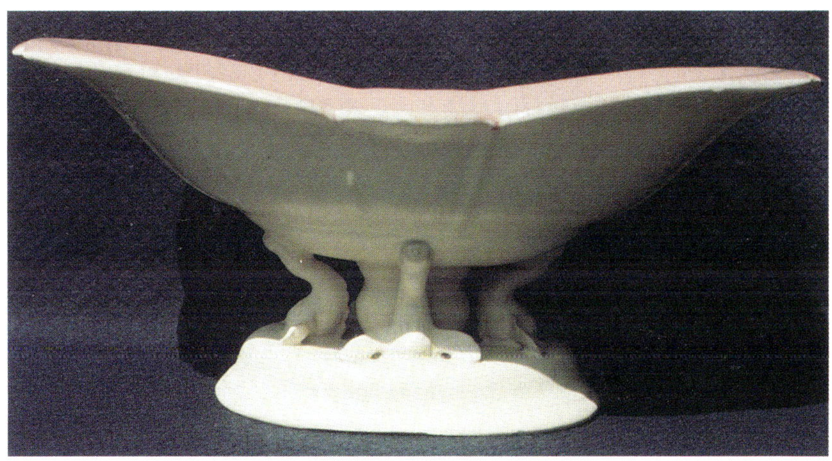

The console bowl is 12" x 6". It has a matt ivory exterior with a high gloss, old rose, interior. This bowl has a "Cowan look."

Value Range: $85-100

LAMPS

Cliftwood Art Pottery had a complete line of lamps. The lamps were sold completely wired, or the mounts could be purchased without fixtures. Lamps, complete with fixtures were priced individually. The lamp mounts were priced per dozen. The Cliftwood catalog states "Cliftwood Pottery Lamps are distinctive and original in design." The bottom of the lamps was always felted at the factory.

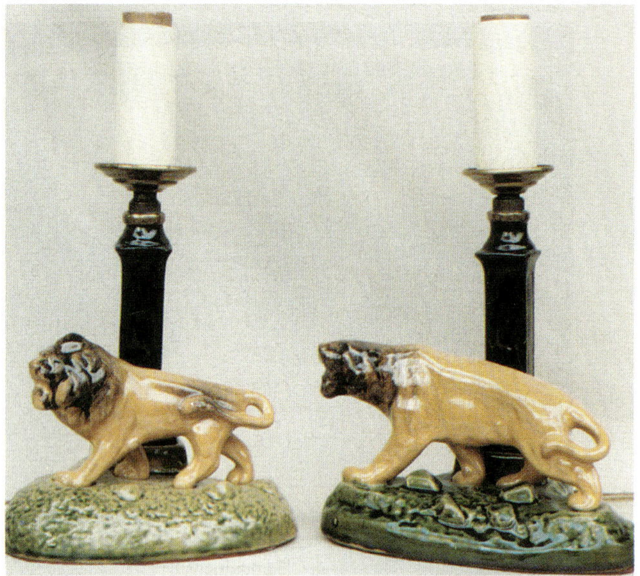

Photo A

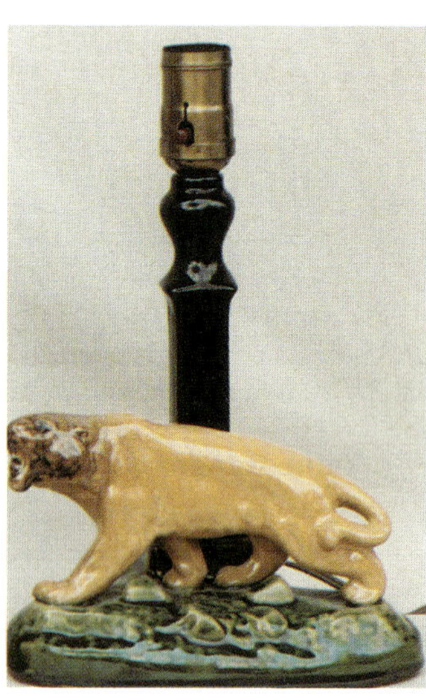

The lion desk lamps are extremely rare. They were always glazed in natural colors with a cobalt blue post. Photo A shows a completely different design for the post.

Value Range: $125-150
A $50-75

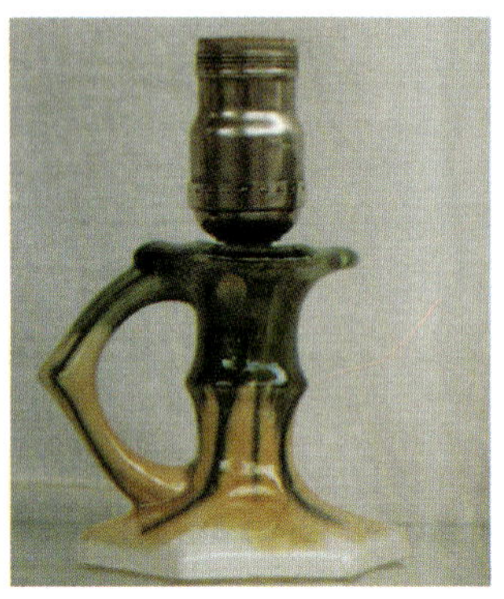

The finger lamp is unusual. It was originally designed as a candle holder, but was altered to be used as a boudoir lamp.

Value Range: $20-25

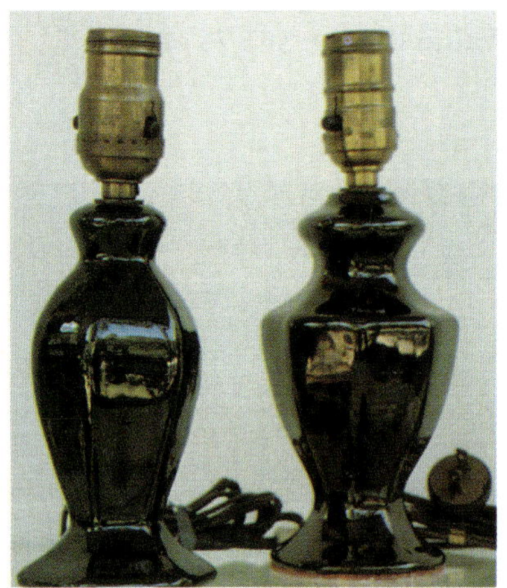

The cobalt blue boudoir lamps are 6 1/2" tall. On the left is a variation of lamp mount No. 12. On the right is lamp mount No. 16.

Value Range: $18-24 each

This lamp is an adaptation of the 7 1/2" special lamp that was made in 1922. The glaze is apple green.

Value Range: $40-50

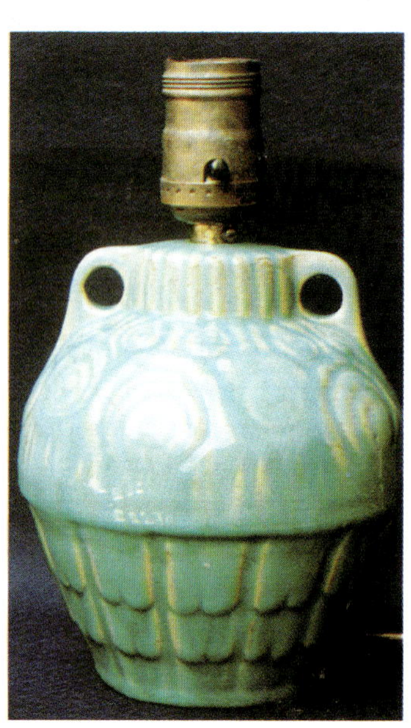

All of the lamps shown here are glazed in the chocolate brown drip glaze. Because of the inability to control the drip during kiln firing, these lamps were all one of a kind.

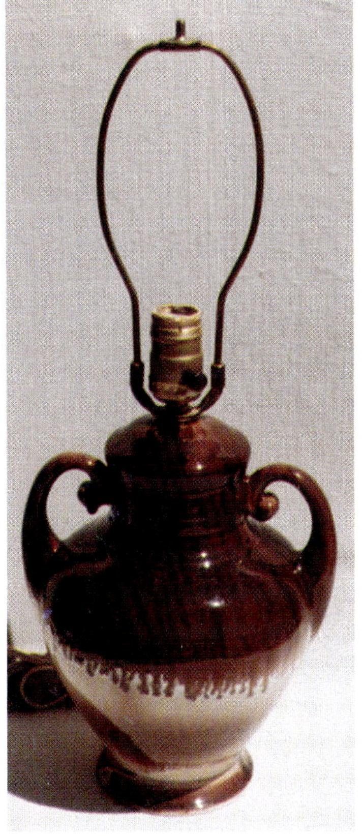

9" handled lamp mount.
Value Range: $50-60

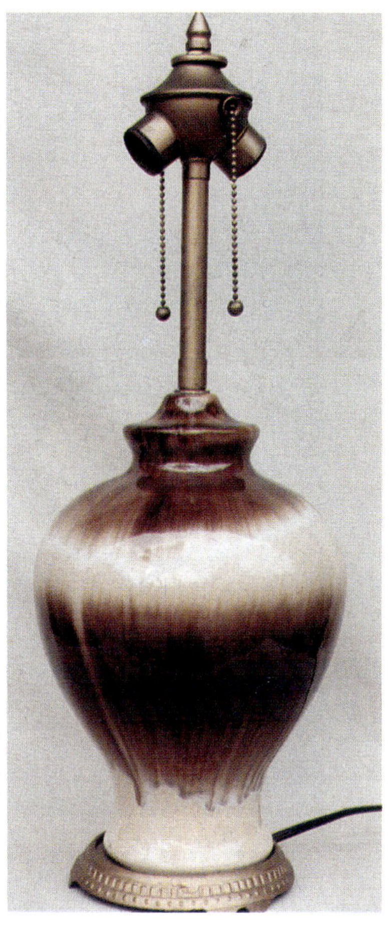

101/2" lamp mount with metal base

Value Range: $60-70

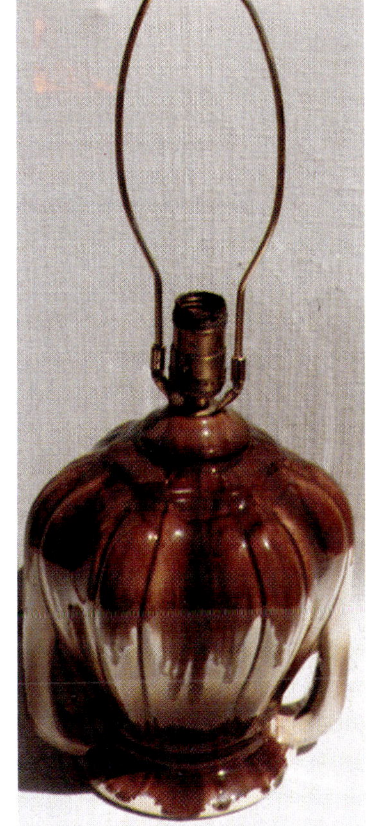

10" handled lamp mount.
Value Range: $60-70

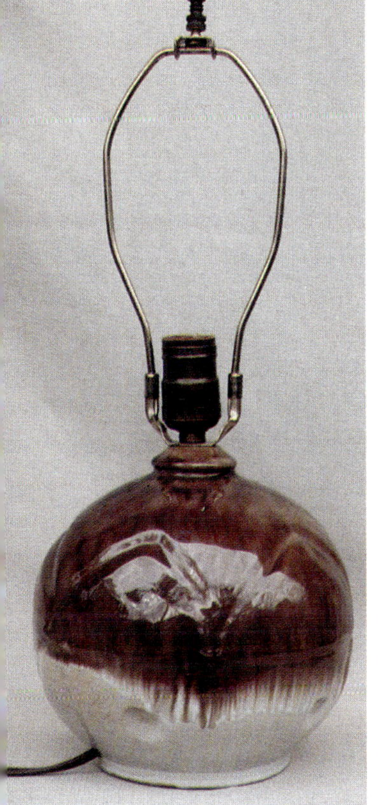

7" spherical lamp mount
Value Range: $40-50

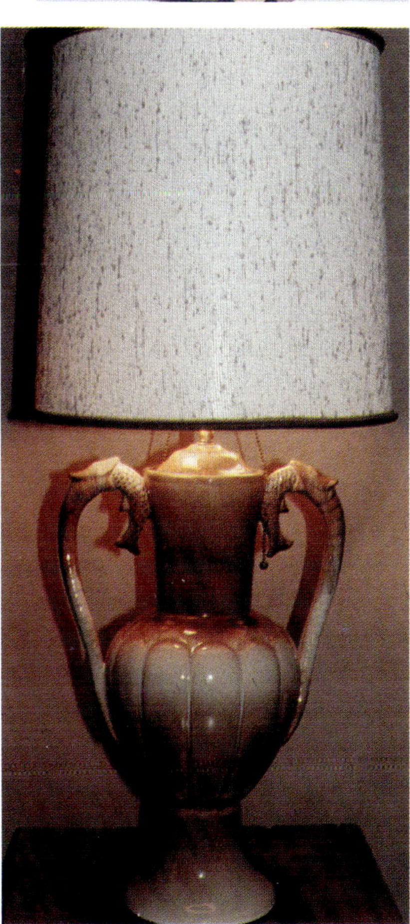

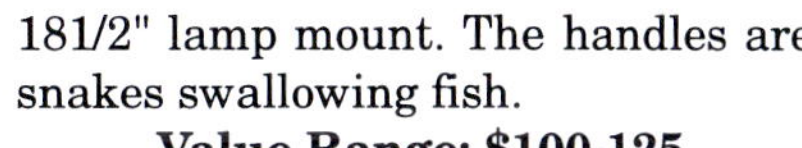

181/2" lamp mount. The handles are snakes swallowing fish.
Value Range: $100-125

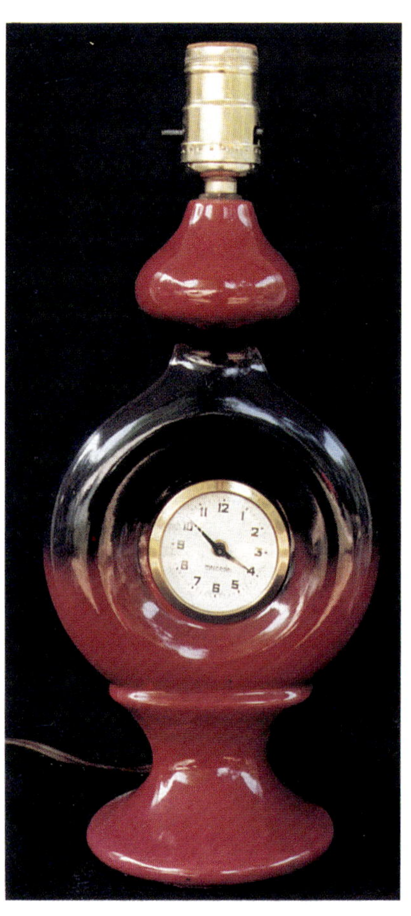

The donut shape clock lamp is rare. It is 8 1/2" tall. The glaze color is blue-mulberry.

Value Range: $125-150

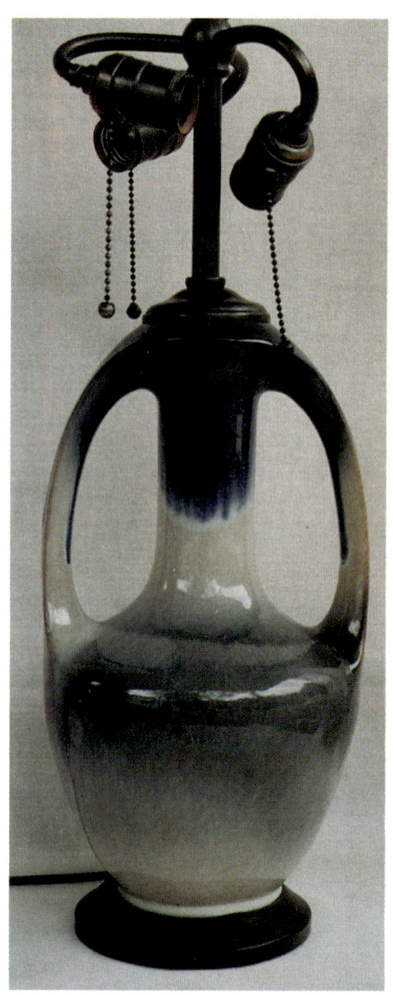

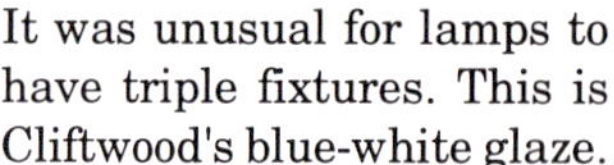

It was unusual for lamps to have triple fixtures. This is Cliftwood's blue-white glaze.

Value Range: $80-90

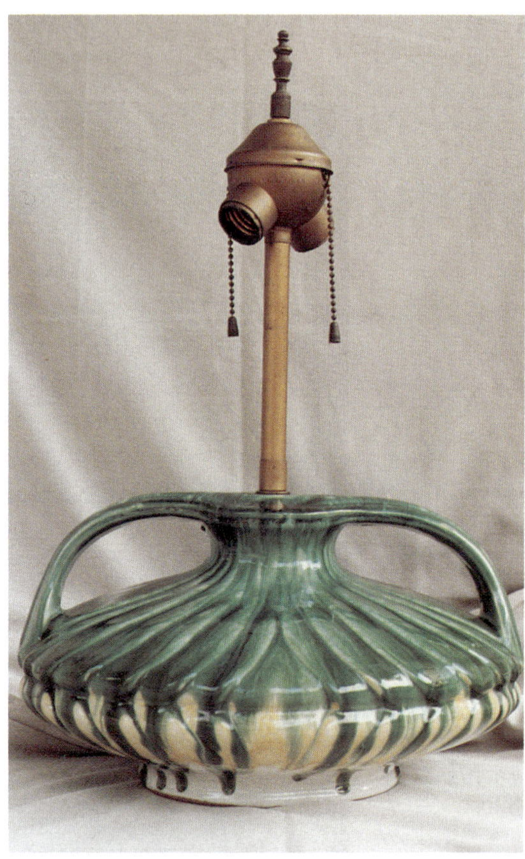

The lamp mount is 6 1/2" tall with a 12" diameter. It measures 11" to the top of the finial.

Value Range: $70-80

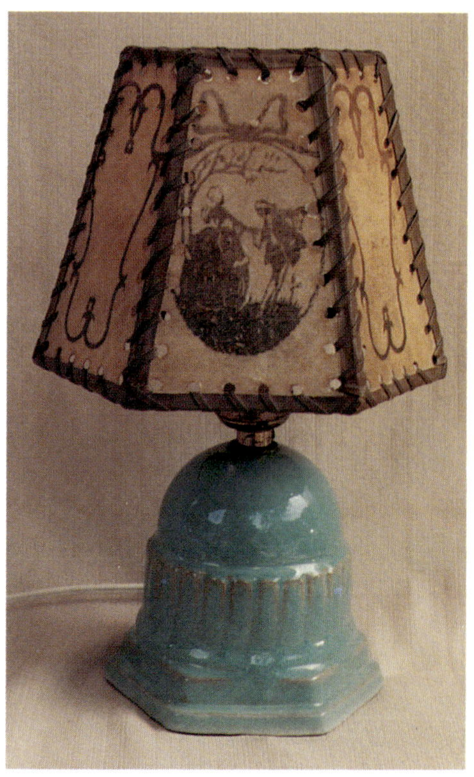

This lamp has an original shade made at The Cliftwood Studio in the early 1930's.

Value Range: $60-70

RADIO SPEAKERS

Only two types of radio speakers were made at the Cliftwood Art Pottery. They were designed to disguise the dry cell battery that sat on top of the radio to power it. The speakers have a hollow core that the battery fits into. Before the speakers, an electric lamp was made to fit over the battery. While researching the Cliftwood period, the authors found a pictorial ad in a 1926 newspaper that described the speakers. The speakers did not sell well. The ceramic sounding box was not effective. The Rapp's advertized that the amplifier eliminated metalic sounds, but it produced a harsh sound with a slight echo.

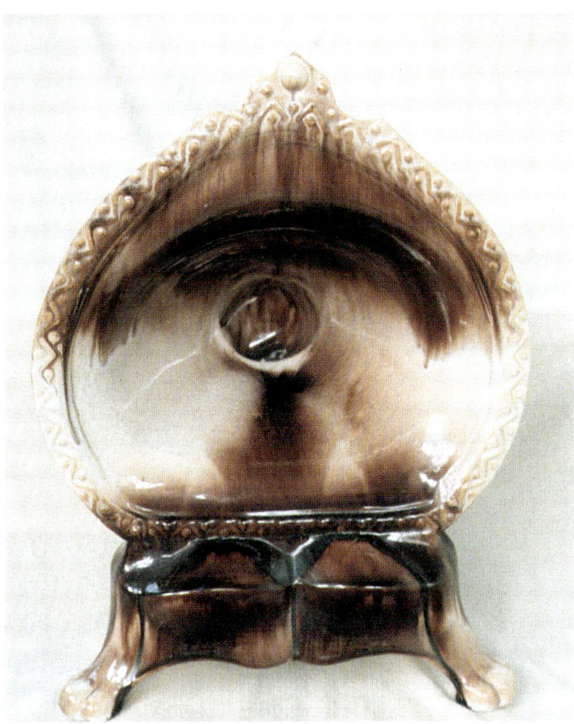

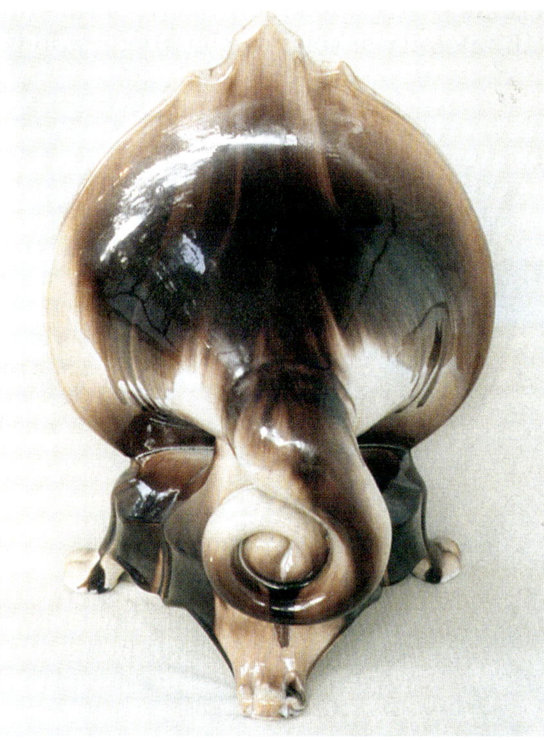

This is the early model speaker. It has animal paws for the three feet, and a large tail entwined down the back.
Value Range: $100-125

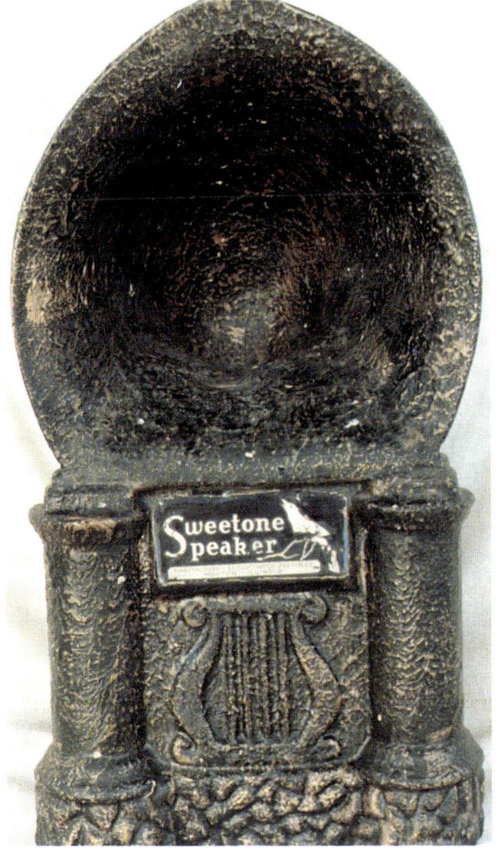

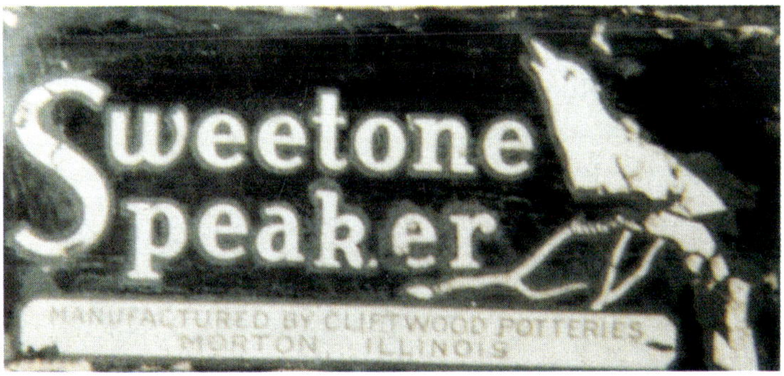

This is the later model that was changed to actually have the appearance of a radio speaker. It is glazed cobalt blue, then plastered with papier-mâché, and high lighted with gold leaf.

Value Range: $125-150

TREE TRUNK LINE

The tree trunk line was a distinctive line of art pottery produced by Cliftwood. The bark has a realistic leathery appearance. On some of the designs, the bark has been peeled away to expose the wood portion of the tree trunks and limbs. Handled items were made to resemble twigs and limbs. Most of this line was glazed in the chocolate brown drip glaze, but any color or color combination could be special ordered.

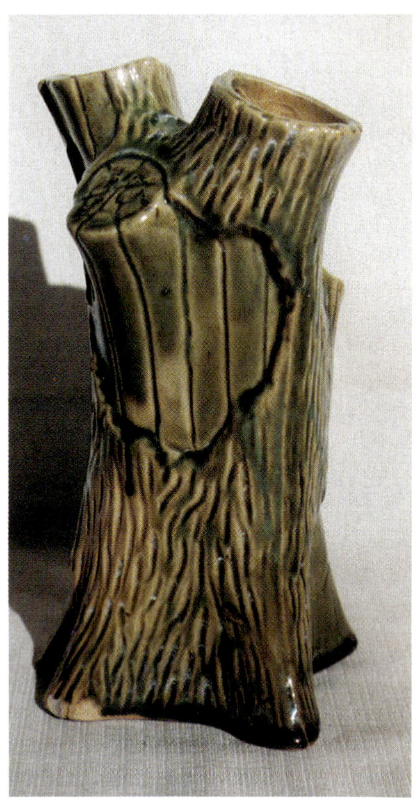

The tree trunk vase has three limbs open at the top for floral arrangement. It is 9" tall. It is glazed in herbage green.

Value Range: $60-70

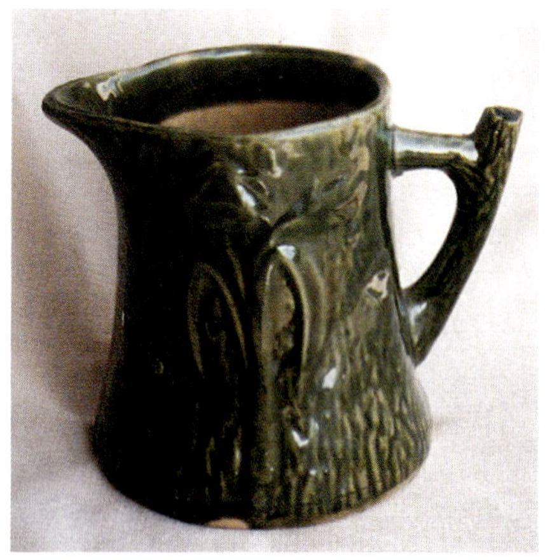

The creamer is unusual. It has a palmate leaf-stalk super imposed over the bark. It is also herbage green.

Value Range: $25-30

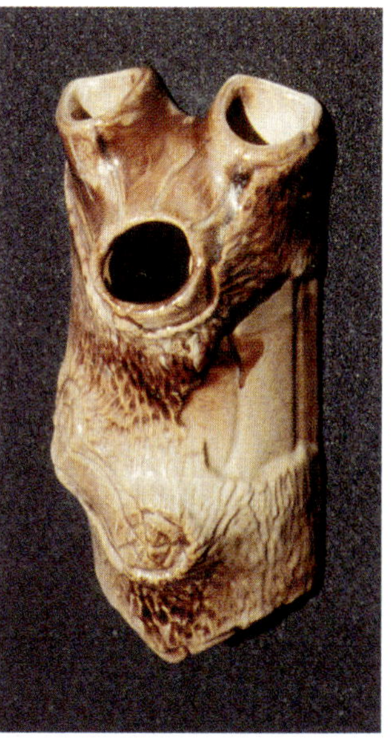

This wall pocket is extremely rare. Like the vase, it has open limbs to hold flowers. The wall pocket is 8" tall.

Value Range: $70-80

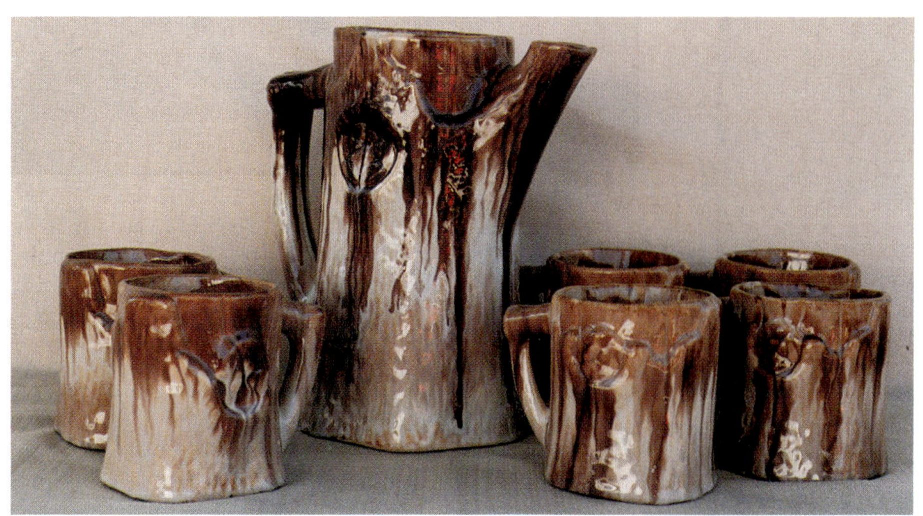

This is chocolate / lemonade set. Because the clay body is heavy, it holds heat and cold quite well.

Value Range:
$150-175 set
Pitcher $65-70
Mug $15-20

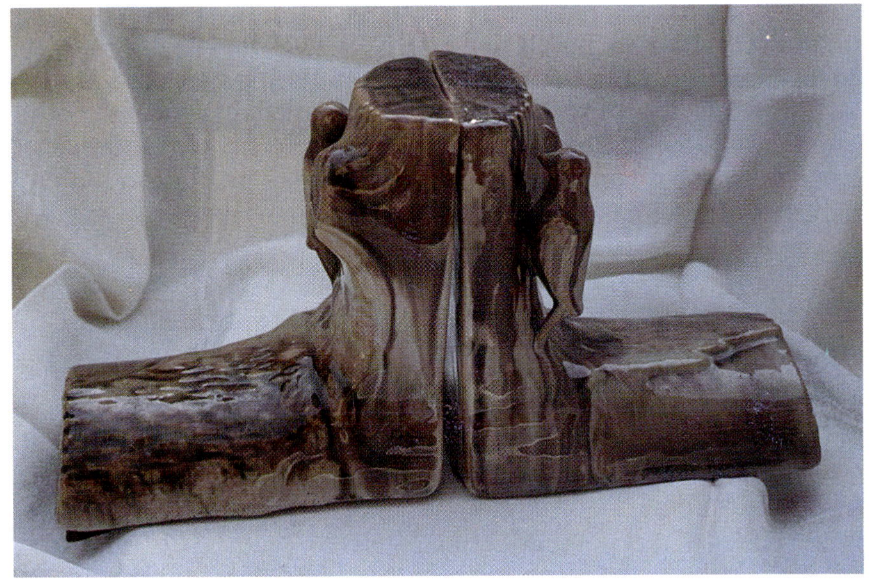

The book ends have birds attached to the trunks. These are from the same mold rather than being opposite designs. A small squirrel was sometimes used instead of the birds. Squirrels were seated on the horizontal log facing away from the trunk. One of each made an interesting pair of bookends.

Value Range: $90-100 pair

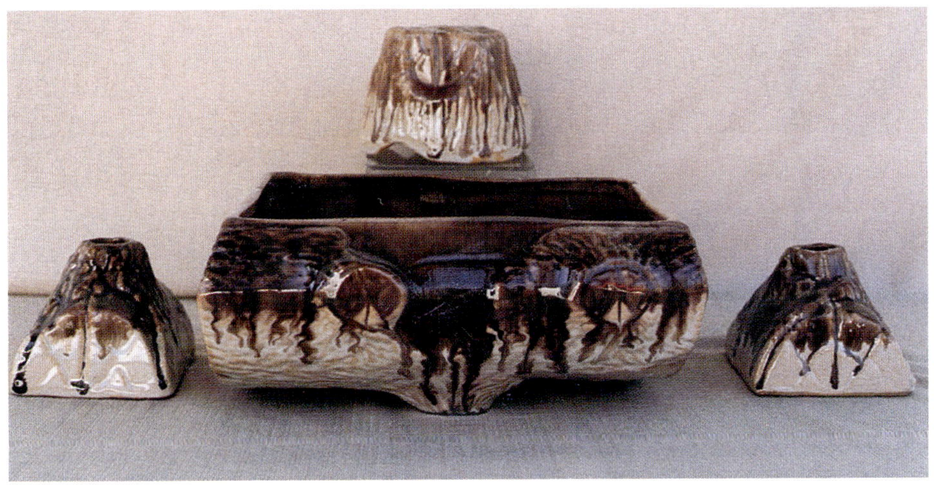

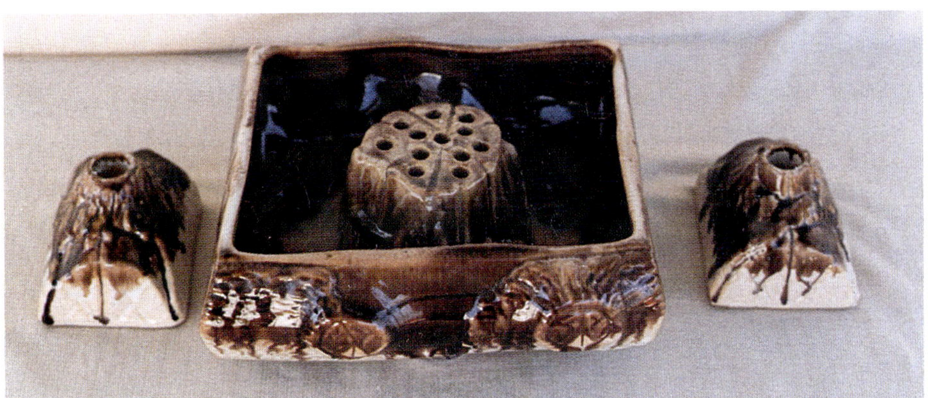

The console set is seldom found complete. This one went together one piece at a time. Both views are shown to enhance the top detail of the flower insert and the candle holders.

Value Range: $95-100 set Bowl $35-45 Flower Insert $25-30 Candle Sticks $18-24 each

VASES

Vases were the most prolific items to be produced at Cliftwood Art Potteries, Inc. New shapes, that have never been documented, continue to be found. The clay and the glazing style used at the pottery make it easier to authenticate a shape when no catalog identification is available. Both common, and unusual shapes are shown to give the collector an idea of the diversity of vase designs at Cliftwood. Many of the vases were adapted and made into lamps. It is not uncommon to find matching lamps and vases. This group of vases has been glazed in the chocolate brown drip glaze.

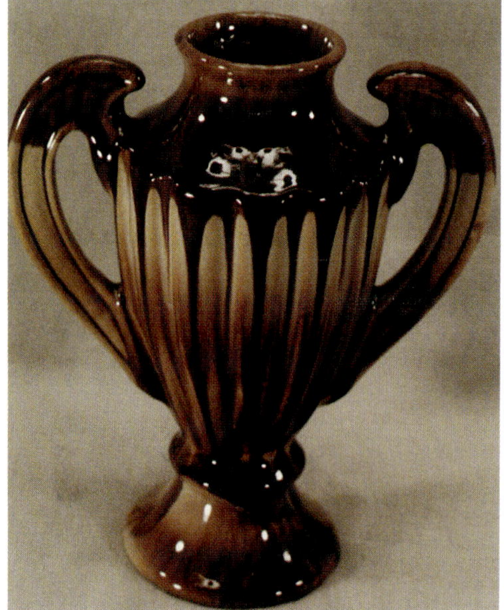

Not numbered, handled vase 81/2" tall.
Value Range: $45-50

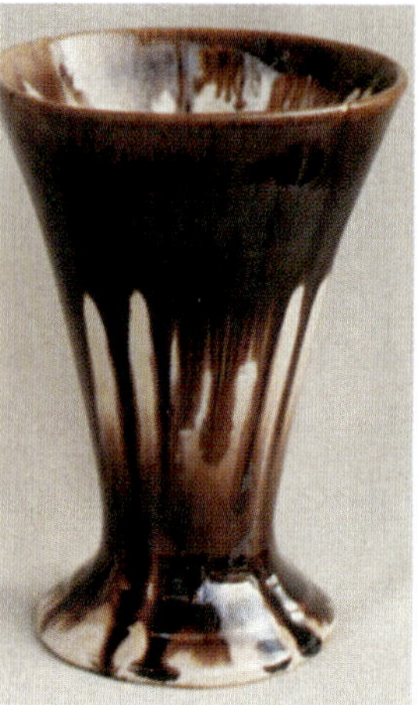

Not numbered, 51/2" tall.
Value Range: $25-30

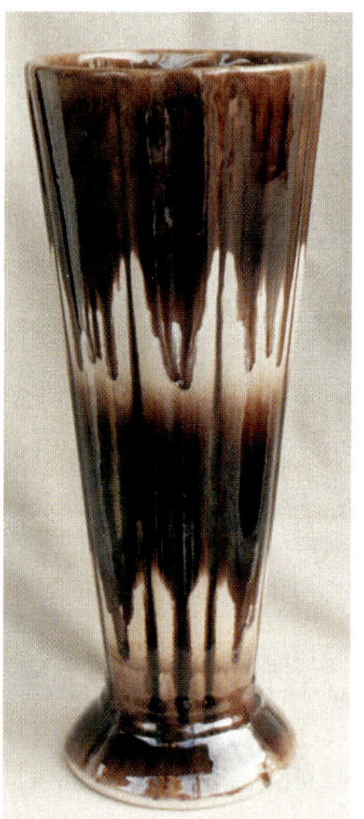

Not numbered, 141/2" tall.
Value Range: $45-50

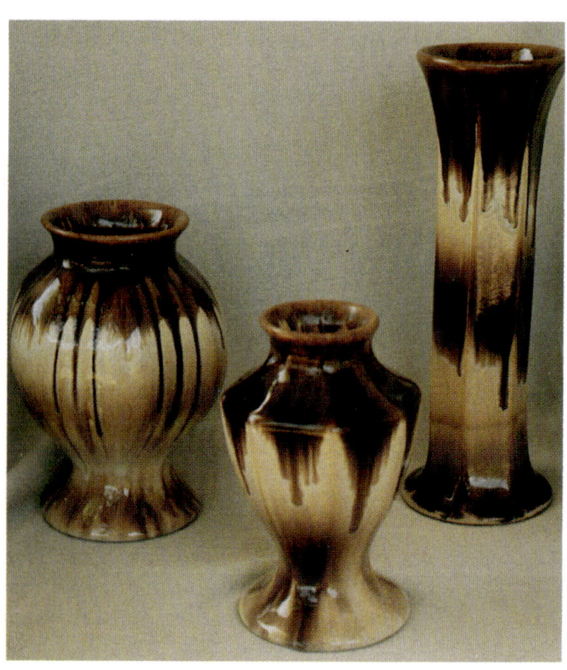

Not numbered, 61/2" tall. – **Value Range: $35-40**
No. 131, 6" Tall – **Value Range: $20-25**
No. 101, 91/2" tall – **Value Range: $25-35**

VASES

This group of vases is finished in matte glaze colors. Matte glazes achieved their greatest popularity in the later years of production, 1938 and 1939. None of these were given numbers in the line of vases.

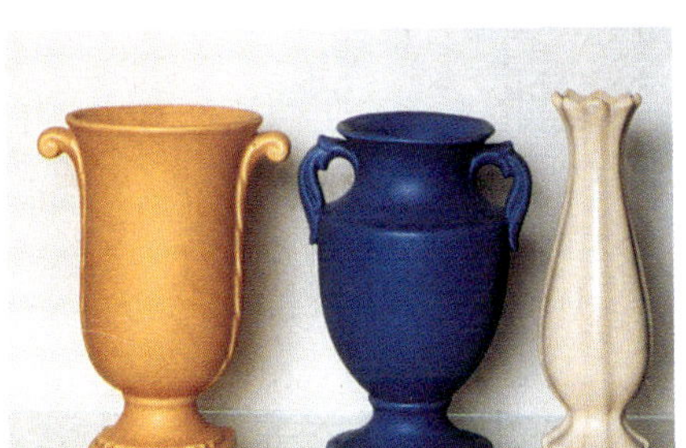

The yellow and blue vases are each 9" tall. The ivory bud vase is 10" tall.

Value Range: Yellow $20-25
Blue $20-25
Ivory $15-20

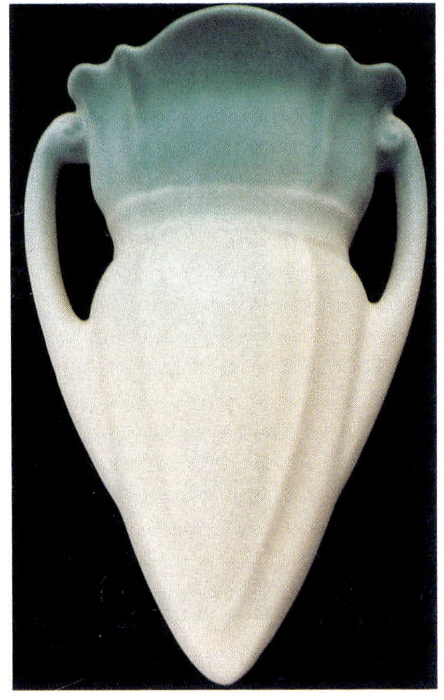

The wall pocket is 7 1/2" tall.

Value Range: $25-30

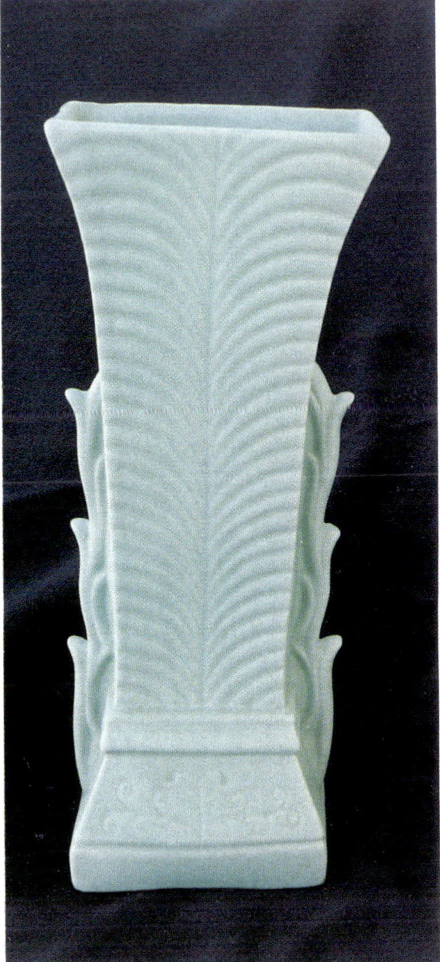

The turquoise peacock feather vase is 15 1/2" tall.

Value Range: $30-40

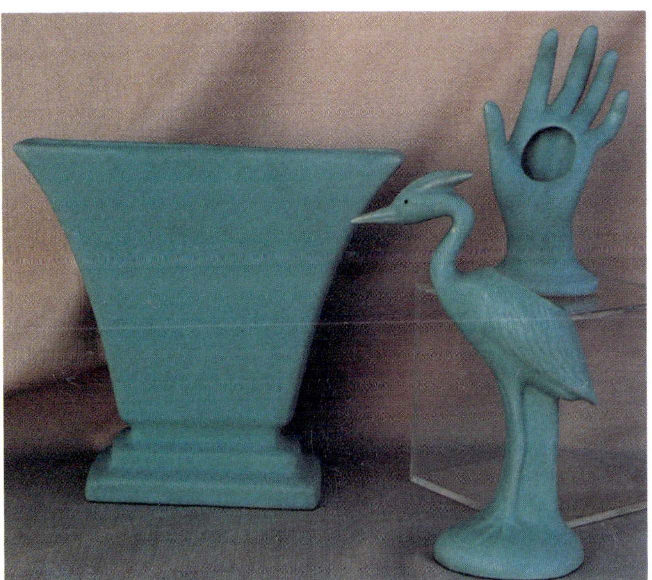

All three of these items were continued in production after the pottery sold in 1940.

Flat fan vase, 6 1/4" tall. – **Value Range: $20-25**

The heron is not a figurine. The back is opent to be used as a vase. It is 6" tall.

Value Range: $14-18

The hand bud vase is 4 1/2" tall. It was made in two sizes.

Value Range: 4 1/2" hand – **$10-12**
6" hand – **$15-20**

The flared, diamond shape vase and the handled vase are a seldom used drip combination of burgundy red and blue over white. The ovoid and flared vases have had orchid substituted for the blue to give them an entirely different appearance. The two small vases on the following page are glazed in herbage green. The squatty, bulbous vase is blue-white drip, and the slender bulbous vase is chocolate brown drip, but the turquoise tints are a mistake. The decorator used a spray gun nozzle that had not been properly cleaned.

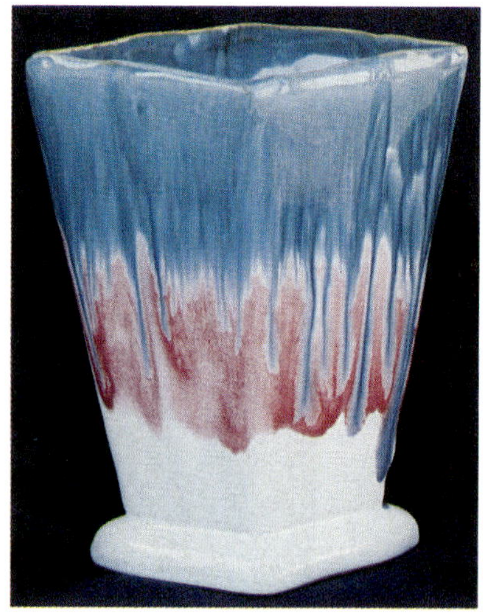

8" tall – **Value Range: $45-50**

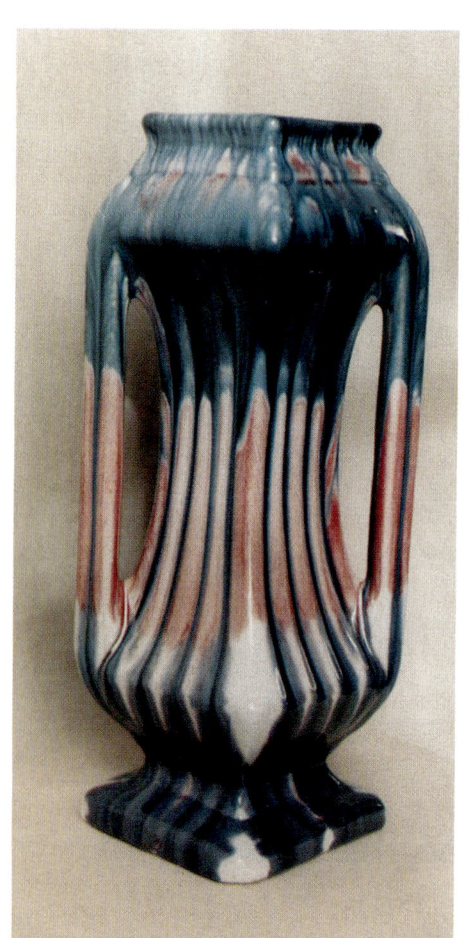

9" tall – **Value Range: $50-55**

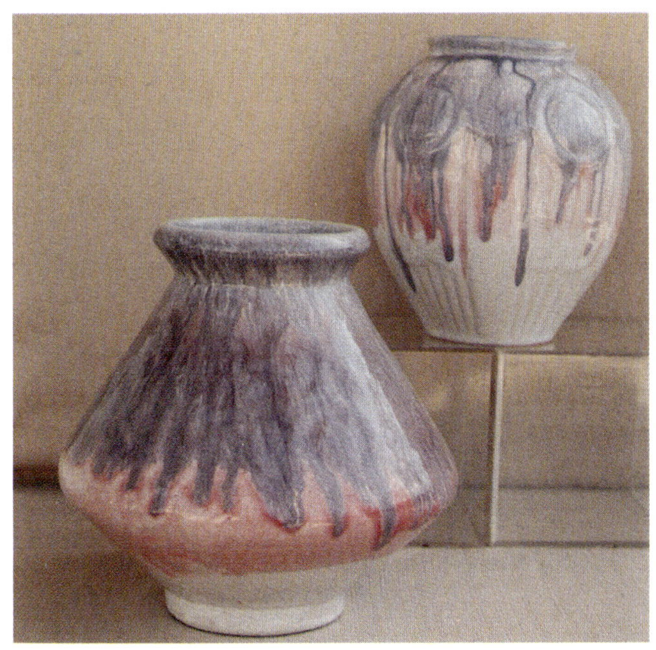

Left, $6^{1/2}$" tall. – **Value Range: $45-50**
Right, $5^{1/2}$" tall – **Value Range: $45-50**

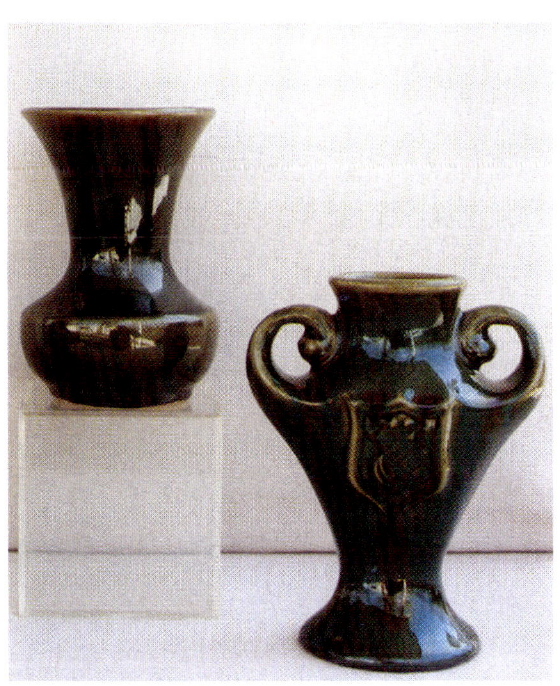

Left, No. 115, $5^{1/2}$" tall – **Value Range: $18-22**
Right, 11" tall – **Value Range: $25-30**

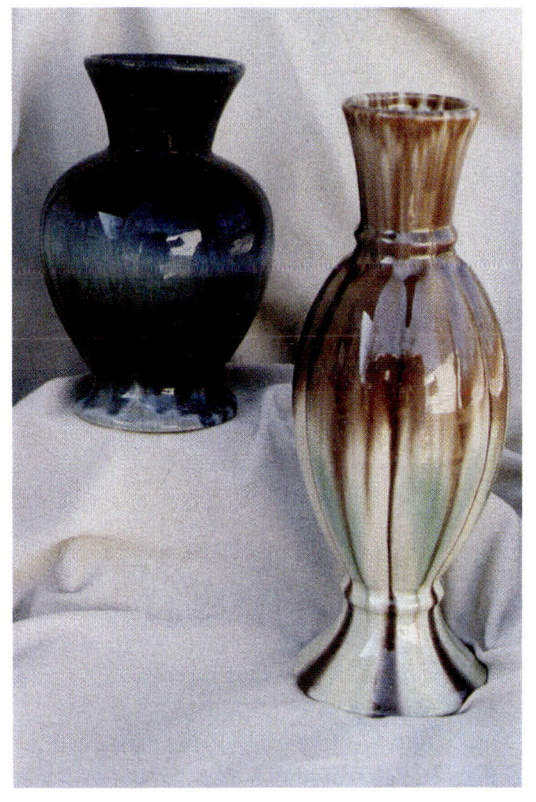

Left, $7^{1/2}$" tall – **Value Range: $30-35**
Right, 11" tall – **Value Range: $40-45**

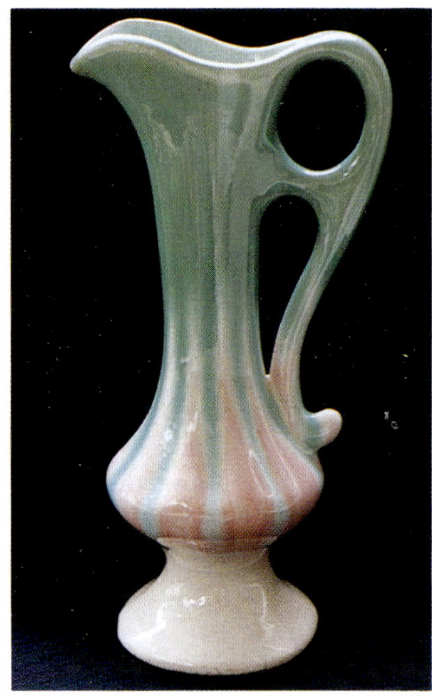

The ewer vase is glazed in green and pink drip over white. 9" tall, it is another vase that was continued in production after the pottery was sold in 1940.

Value Range: $20-25

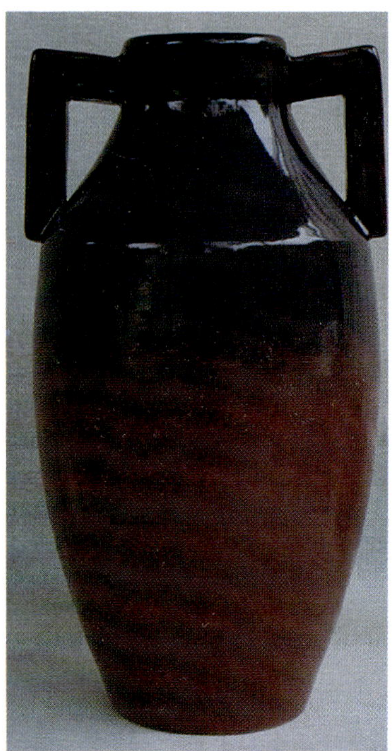

The 14" tall vase is an example of a blue mulberry drip glaze that did not flow. There are several reasons for the lack of dripping. The measure of flux may have been incorrect, the temperature of the kiln was too low, or the firing rate was too slow. A special skill was needed to fire flowing glazes.

Value Range: $60-65

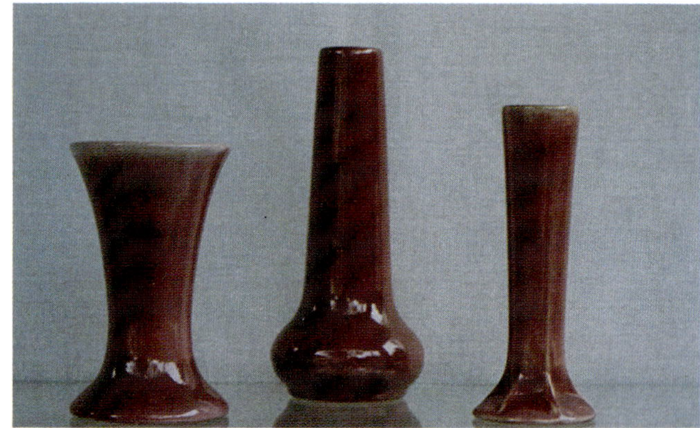

The vase on the left is No. 108, 5 1/2" tall. In the center is No. 122, 7 3/4" tall, and the bud vase on the right, 6" tall, is not numbered. All are in the old rose glaze, color C on the color chart.

Value Range: No. 108 $18-22 No. 122 $15-20
Bud Vase $18-22

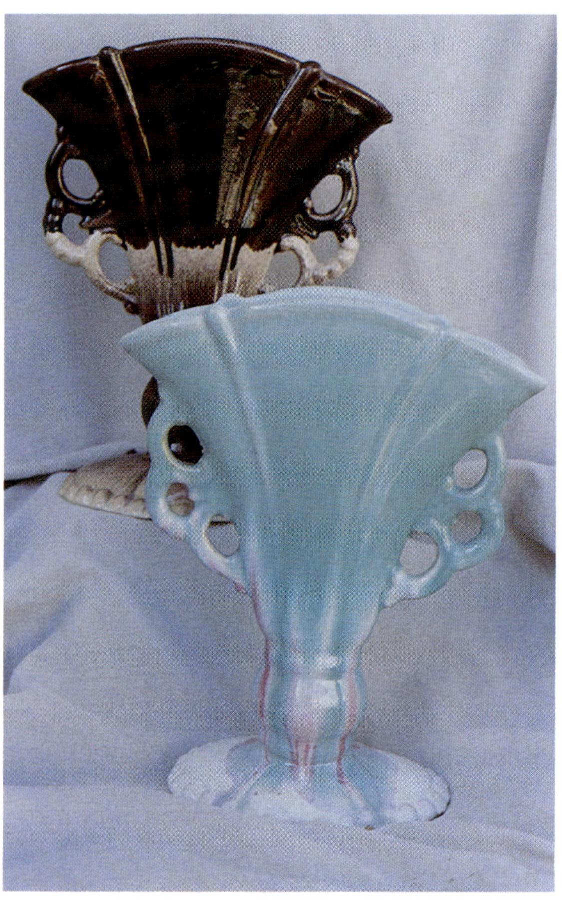

The handled fan shape vases are 9" tall. The handles resemble brass knuckles.

Value Range: $30-40 each

Except for the two vases in top right photo, all of this group are cobalt blue. For the yellow and blue drip over white, the amount of cobalt was altered to create a dark, navy blue.

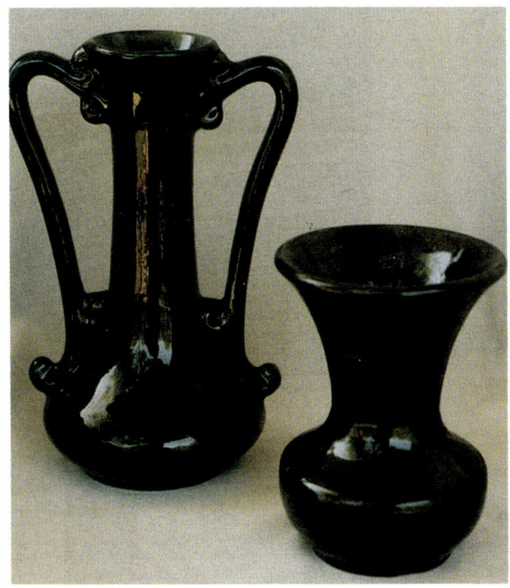

The taller, handled vase is 81/2" tall.
Value Range: $25-30
No. 115 is 51/2" tall. – **Value Range: $20-24**

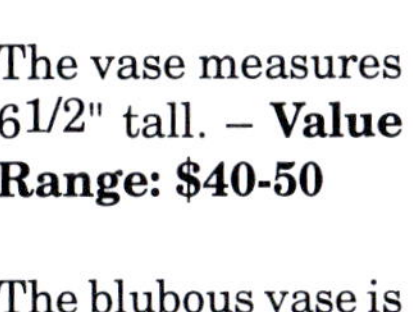
The vase measures 61/2" tall. – **Value Range: $40-50**

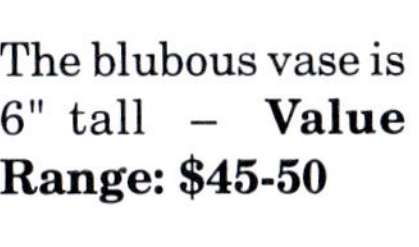
The blubous vase is 6" tall – **Value Range: $45-50**

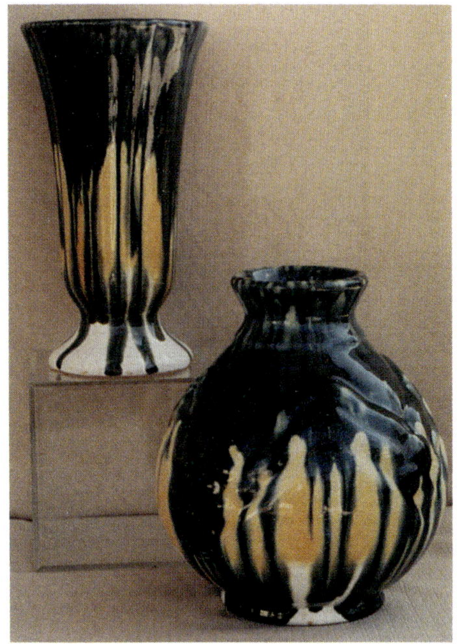

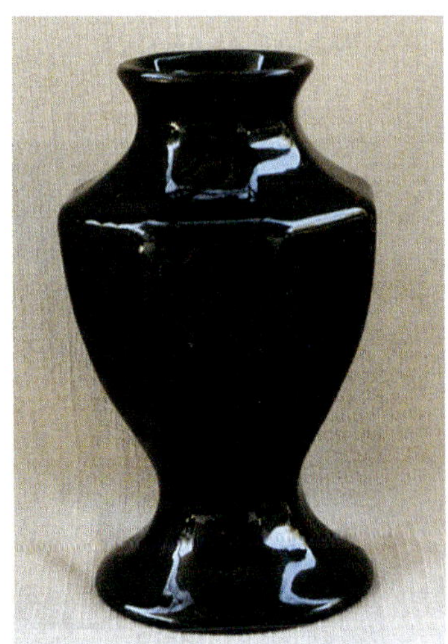

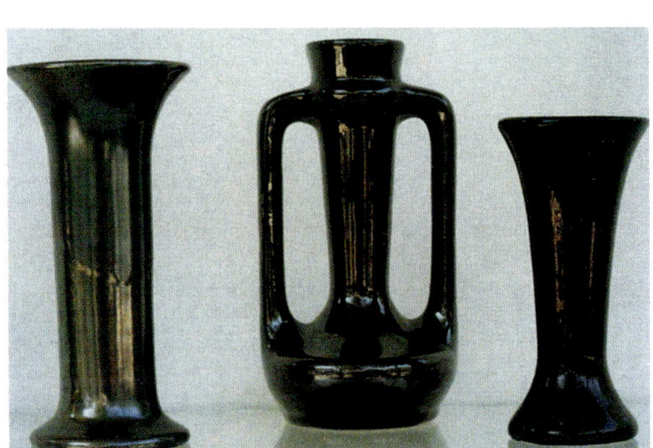

The vase on the left is No. 100, 71/2" tall. – **$20-24**
In the center is No. 126, 81/4" tall. – **$35-40**
On the right is No. 107, 8" tall. – **$25-30**

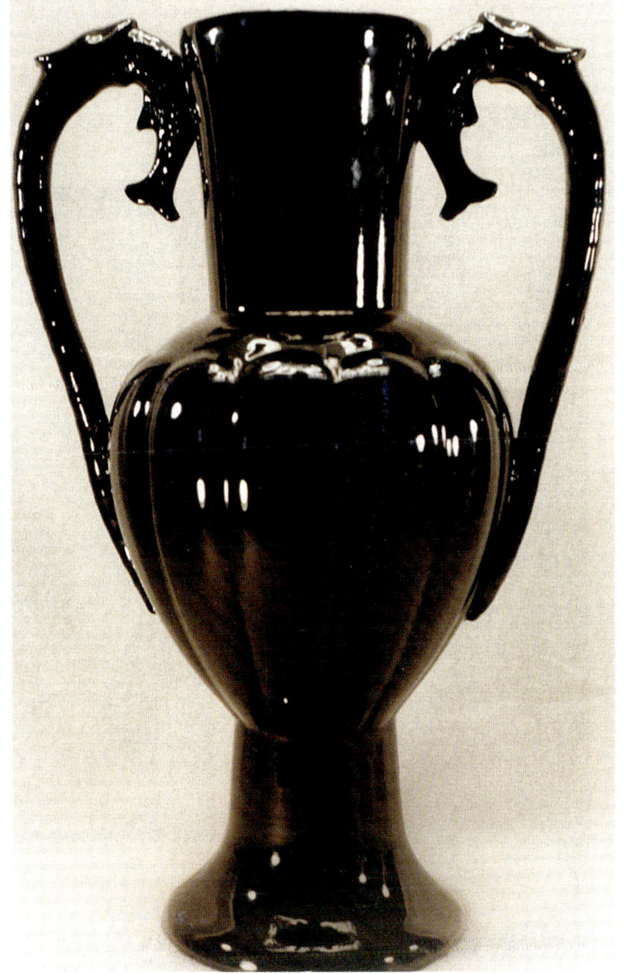

Vase No. 132 is 181/4" tall. Its width from handle to handle is 12".
Value Range: $80-90

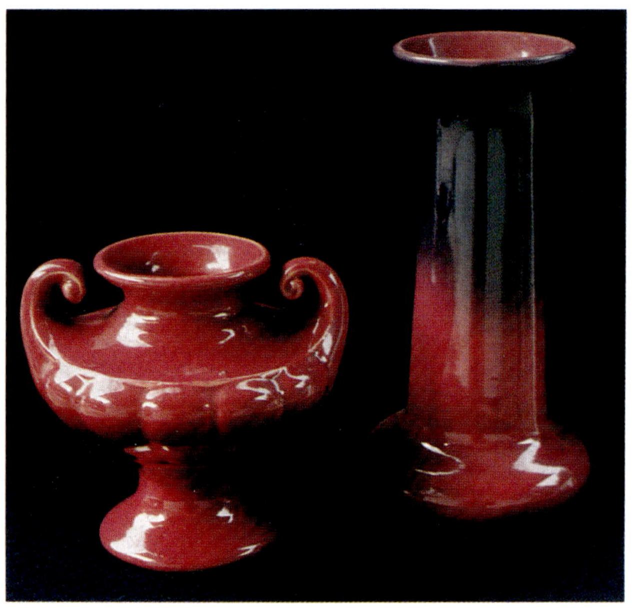

Grecian Urn, 6" tall, old rose glaze.
Value Range: $30-35
No. 105, 9 1/2" tall, blue mulberry glaze.
Value Range: $25-35

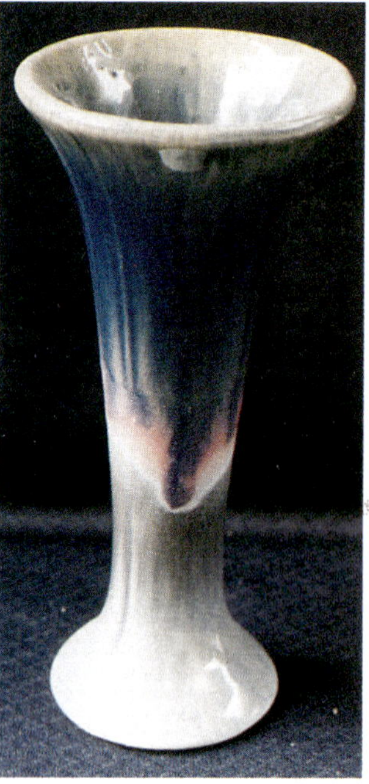

No. 107, 10" tall, an unusual blend of old rose with blue and grey drip.
Value Range: $25-30

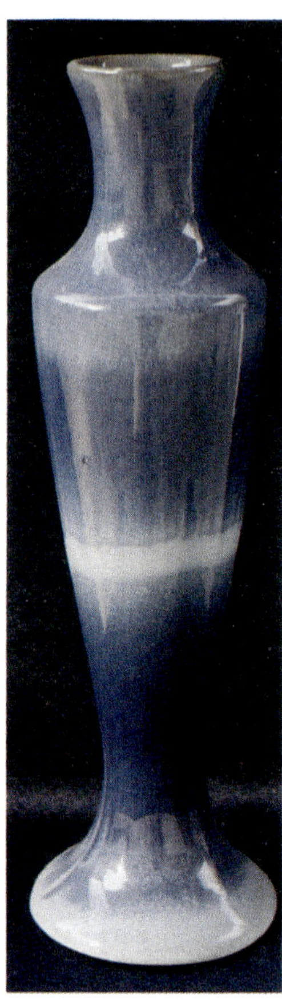

No. 113, 14 1/2" tall, blue white drip glaze.
Value Range: $40-50

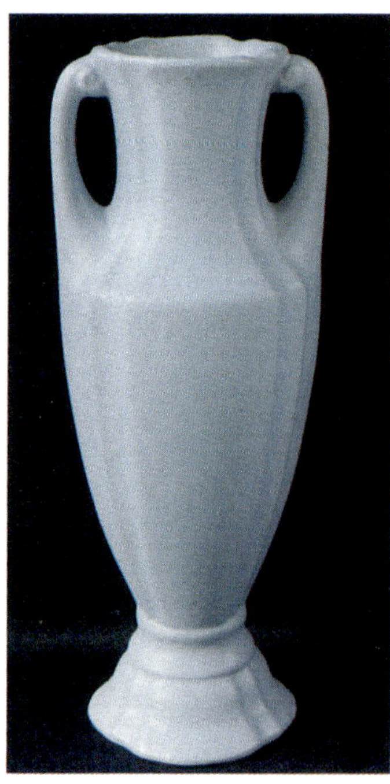

Not numbered, 12" tall, matte blue glaze.
Value Range: $35-45

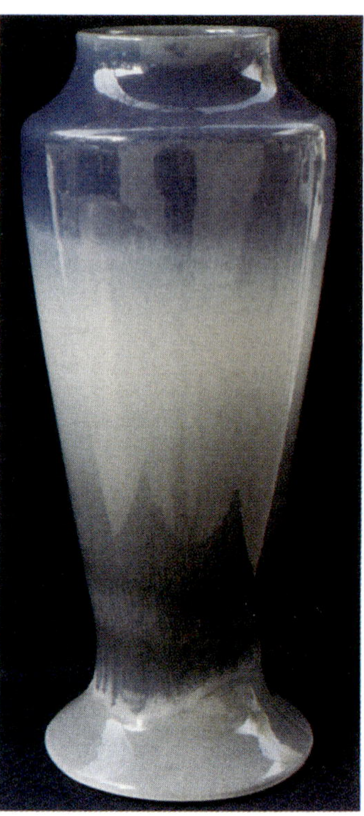

No. 114, 16" tall, blue white drip glaze.
Value Range: $65-75

PART III

MIDWEST POTTERIES, INCORPORATED 1940-1944

The Midwest pottery was the shortest lived of the six potteries that operated in Morton, Illinois from 1877 to 1976. Like all of Morton's potteries, the Midwest traced its origins back to the six Rapp brothers who came from Germany to start the pottery business in Morton. Midwest's foundation had been laid by Matthew Rapp, one of the original founding brothers, who with his four sons, established the Cliftwood Art Pottery in 1920. Those four sons were responsible for the transition that changed Cliftwood to Midwest.

Marks

#1 Foil Label

This foil label is the only known mark to ever have been used by Midwest Potteries, Inc. It is a definite allusion to the second generation Rapp brothers' association with the Cliftwood Art Pottery.

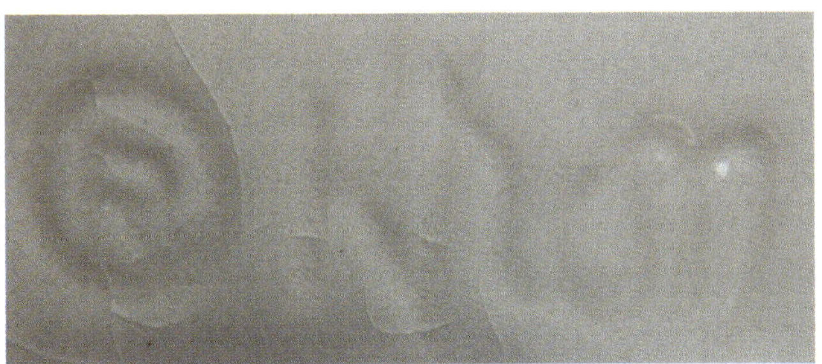

#2 Impressed Kron Mark

The registered Kron mark was never used at Morton. It was used on a line of TV lamps that were made at the South Milwaukee, Wisconsin Midwest Pottery. The pottery moved there after the disastrous fire at the Morton plant in 1944.

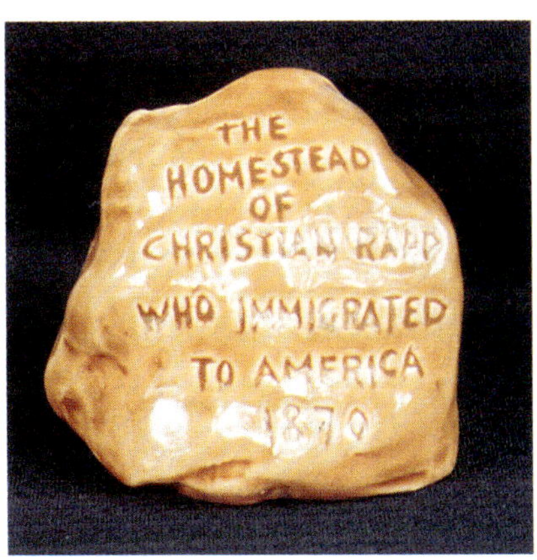

#3 Christian Rapp Planter

The Midwest Pottery made a limited number of memorial planters, like this simulated rock, for the families of each of the original Rapp brothers who settled in Morton to launch the pottery manufactory.

A copy of the corporation papers for Midwest Potteries, Inc. signed February 23rd, 1940.

Certificate Number 25101

1-2876

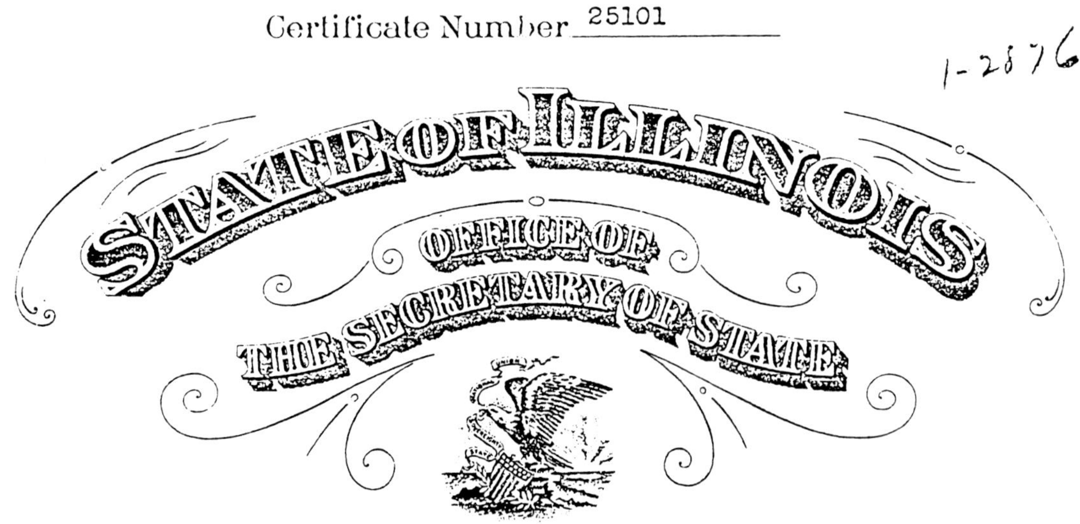

To all to whom these Presents Shall Come, Greeting:

Whereas, *Articles of Incorporation duly signed and verified of* MIDWEST POTTERIES, INC. *have been filed in the Office of the Secretary of State on the* 23rd *day of* February *A. D. 19*40, *as provided by* "THE BUSINESS CORPORATION ACT" *of Illinois, in force July 13, A. D. 1933.*

Now Therefore, I, EDWARD J. HUGHES, *Secretary of State of the State of Illinois, by virtue of the powers vested in me by law, do hereby issue this certificate of incorporation and attach thereto a copy of the Articles of Incorporation of the aforesaid corporation.*

In Testimony Whereof, *I hereto set my hand and cause to be affixed the Great Seal of the State of Illinois, Done at the City of Springfield this* 23rd *day of* February *A.D. 19*40 *and of the Independence of the United States the one hundred and* 64th.

Edward J. Hughes

SECRETARY OF STATE.

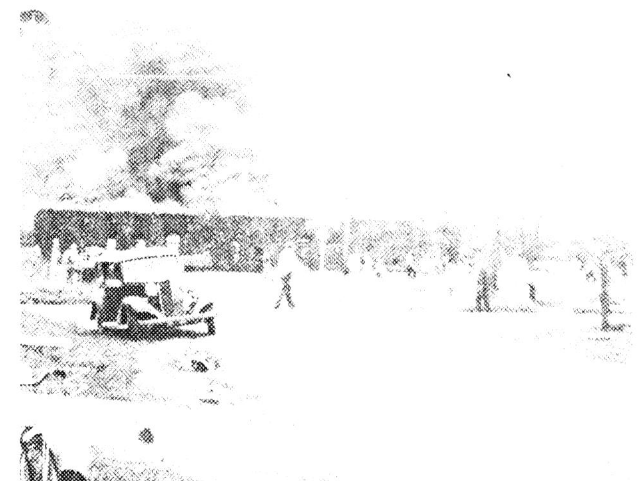

This photograph shows the Midwest Pottery burning on Sunday evening, March 19, 1944. That fire brought an end to the pottery manufacturing where it originated in 1878.

CERTIFICATE OF DISSOLUTION

STATE OF ILLINOIS, } ss.
Sangamon County,

In the Circuit Court

THE PEOPLE OF THE STATE OF ILLINOIS AT THE RELATION OF GEORGE F. BARRETT, ATTORNEY GENERAL,

vs.

MIDWEST POTTERIES, INC.

In Chancery
No. 86702

TO THE HONORABLE RICHARD YATES ROWE, SECRETARY OF STATE,
SPRINGFIELD, ILLINOIS

And to Any Other Official to Whom These Presents May Come:

I, ~~E. L. CRANE,~~ Clerk of the Circuit Court aforesaid, do hereby certify that a decree dissolving the above corporation was entered by the said circuit court on DEC 1 9 1944, and that the original decree is on file in my office, and that I am the lawful keeper thereof.

Witness my hand and official seal this DEC

Clerk of the Circuit Court of Sangamon County

14 (62336)

This is a copy of the certificate of dissolution for Midwest.

CHAPTER 7

Historical Sketch
1940-1944

When Matthew Rapp's sons made the decision to sell the Cliftwood Art Potteries in 1939, they searched for a buyer who would continue to use them in the positions they had held at Cliftwood. They were specialists. Carl was responsible for sales, packing, and shipping. John was the chemist and was responsible for glaze development. He supervised the glazing department and the kiln operation. Lawrence created designs and made the molds for them. Theodore was in charge of the clay operation. He supervised the slip casting room where the molds were poured, and the trimming and finishing department where green ware was made ready for bisque firing.

Early in 1940, three businessmen from the nearby city of Peoria agreed to purchase the pottery with a stipulation that the Rapp brothers remain in their respective positions in order to prevent any interruption in the output of the pottery. Based on verbal agreements from the Rapps to stay on, corporation papers were filed with the Secretary of State at Springfield, Illinois on February 23, 1940. With the official filing of those papers, Cliftwood Art Potteries, Incorporated was renamed Midwest Potteries, Incorporated. The Rapp brothers were now free to pursue their expertise in pottery creation and forget the worry of business management.

The new owners issued two thousand shares of common stock at $5.00 a share. None of those owners were knowledgeable about the pottery business, so they concentrated on the sale of stock and relied upon the Rapps to continue as the heartbeat of the pottery. Few changes were made in the operational procedures. The Cliftwood line of wares was continued, but the figurine production began to expand. A new line of figurines was designed exclusively for Midwest, reflective of the Art Deco movement that had begun with the advent of the Paris Exposition Internationale des Arts Decoratifs et Industriels Modernes in 1925. Though the Art Deco movement was slowing down in 1940, Lawrence continued to create new designs in the deco style.

Under the new ownership, the Rapps were able to expand their gold decoration department. Experimental work on applying liquid gold to glazed pottery items was begun in a small room at the front of the pottery when it was still the Cliftwood Art Potteries. Theodore Rapp's wife, Florence, was the first gold decorator at Midwest, and was probably responsible for getting the new owners interested in that novel style of decoration. The gold operation flourished and became a major department at Midwest.

The new owners were really not interested in the decorative arts. They wanted low cost items that could be mass produced and return huge profits. Their philosophy of mass production and volume sales forced the pottery to turn out planters, vases, and mediocre figurines. Within a year the directors had become disillusioned with their new venture. They were not satisfied with the sale of stock, nor with the profits they were realizing from their investment. They decided to sell the pottery.

Fortunately, a buyer was quickly located. A second set of corporation papers was filed on July 29, 1941. Those papers transferred ownership to Sherman Deutch, an entrepreneur from Canton, Illinois. The Rapps were retained in their positions so that work at the pottery could continue smoothly. At last there seemed to be a continuity that would allow the pottery to swing back and become the powerful entity it had been under Matthew Rapp's guidance.

By 1943, Midwest Potteries, Incorporated was back on a full production schedule. The future looked bright, but that new burst of activity was short lived. Sherman Deutch enlisted in the United States army. The Rapps were forced to endure one more transition. To ensure the pottery's continued output during his enlistment, Deutch hired Richard G. Dunn to manage the pottery. Dunn encouraged the continuation and expansion of the gold decorating department, giving the pottery the financial boost that it needed. A small building, across the railroad tracks, in front of the pottery was leased and enlarged. After the remodeling, the entire gold decorating department was moved there. That frame building, known locally as the shack, became the most prolific of all Midwest's operations. Orders came to the pottery with such frequency that it was impossible to keep production ahead of the orders. New designs were continually being introduced, and salesmen were dispatched to all parts of the United States, Mexico, and Canada.

R.G. Dunn was not a potter, but he was a high powered, overly zealous businessman. His temperament was quite different than any the Rapp brothers had ever experienced. Dunn's business philosophy was a sharp contrast to their father, Matthew's. The Rapps were soon disillusioned, as were the seventy-five employees at the pottery. All of the workers were forced into a bonus plan after intensive time studies at each level of production showed what effort was expected in order for them to earn a few additional pennies. The disgruntled workers complained to the Rapps. Some of them quit their jobs, and others threatened to unionize. Unable to endure those working conditions that were being inflamed, the four Rapp brothers severed their relationships with the Midwest Pottery early in 1943. For the first time in their lives, Morton's clay pits and their family business held no interest for them. Carl, John, and Lawrence left Morton to continue their skills elsewhere. Theodore stayed in the area and made an effort to sell insurance.

The Midwest Pottery was never able to regain the recognition that had come from Matthew Rapp's artistic and business astuteness. Faced with inadequate supervision in the various departments, and misdirected leadership at the top, the pottery was beset by labor problems and unrest. The future started to look bleak. All of those problems came to an end the evening of March 19, 1944. Midwest Pottery was destroyed by a devastating fire that raged for six hours. That fire brought an end to sixty-seven years of pottery production on the site where Morton's first pottery began in 1877.

The loss from the fire was set at $65,000. The building was valued at $40,000, and the contents at $25,000. The alarm was called in by a woman who lived across the tracks from the pottery. Ironically, Richard Dunn and several other employees were working in another part of the plant at the time the fire was detected. None of them knew of the fire until the alarm was sounded. The building was completely destroyed. Only the ivy covered front wall remained after the fire. It stood as a grim reminder of the fire until the spring of 1946 when the fire chief recommended that it be torn down to prevent any accidents.

Dunn immediately applied to the War Production Board for permission to rebuild the pottery. The loss was covered by insurance, and local speculation suggested that the pottery would quickly be rebuilt. It never was. Instead, a small pottery in South Milwaukee, Wisconsin was purchased and the operations of Midwest Potteries, Incorporated were transferred to that plant. R. G. Dunn went there to manage the plant for Sherman Deutch who was still in the army, and stationed in Hawaii. John Rapp eventually went to South Milwaukee where he produced the spray glazes that he had perfected at Morton.

Little is known about the South Milwaukee operation, but according to Lois Lehner's research, [1] that plant produced a Cliftwood line and a Kron line of art pottery. Examples of the Kron line are shown in the section of photographs that follows. So far, none from the Cliftwood line have been found. Lehner found no listings for Midwest Potteries, Incorporated in Milwaukee city directories after 1953.

[1] Lehner's Encyclopedia of U.S. Marks on Pottery, Porcelain, & Clay.

MIDWEST POTTERIES, INCORPORATED

This is the shack that was located across the railroad tracks from the pottery. It was leased in order to expand the gold decorating department that had outgrown its space in the pottery building.

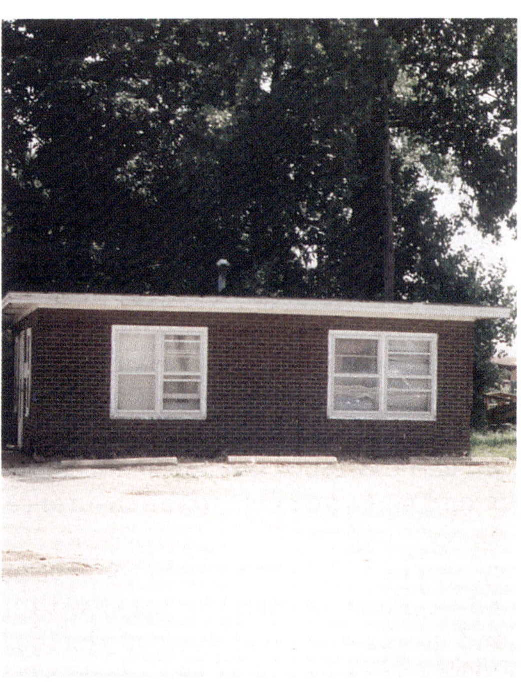

Form W-2
U. S. TREASURY DEPARTMENT
INTERNAL REVENUE SERVICE

STATEMENT OF INCOME TAX WITHHELD ON WAGES
By Employer
(EMPLOYEE'S RECEIPT)

Calendar Year 1943

INSTRUCTIONS TO EMPLOYER

Prepare this form in duplicate for each employee from whom a tax has been withheld. Furnish original to employee. Forward duplicate with Return of Income Tax Withheld on Wages, Form W-1, for the fourth quarter of the year (or with the employer's final return, if filed at an earlier date). (See Circular WT.)

INSTRUCTIONS TO EMPLOYEE

This is your receipt for Income Tax (including Victory Tax) withheld. You should keep it for use in preparing your Income and Victory Tax return for 1943, and as evidence of tax withheld.

EMPLOYEE TO WHOM PAID

(Print full name of employee, home address, and social security number, if any. If employee is a married woman, name of husband should also be furnished)

EMPLOYER BY WHOM PAID   Midwest Pottery
Morton, Illinois

(Name and address of employer)

STATEMENT OF INCOME TAX WITHHELD ON WAGES

Wages paid during the calendar year 1943 .... $ 1154.57

Amount of income tax withheld .... $ 95.00

(OVER)

16—34840-1

This W-2 form was issued in 1944, shortly before the pottery burned. It is both interesting and important. Interesting, because it mentions that part of the income tax paid at that time included a Victory Tax that went to the war effort. Important, because it shows the employee's total salary for 1943. That salary broke down to $22.50 per week, 27 2/4¢ an hour, or $96.21 per month. By today's standards, that was certainly a low rate of pay.

MIDWEST POTTERIES, INCORPORATED
Figurines, Animals

DEER

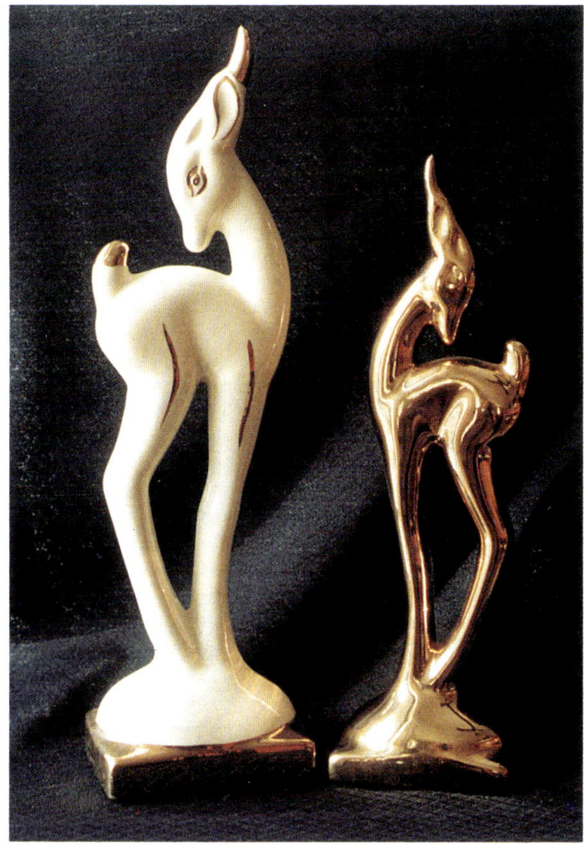

The stylized deer was made in two sizes, 12" tall and 10 1/2" tall. The shorter one is less common.

Value Range: 12" $20-25
10 1/2" $18-24

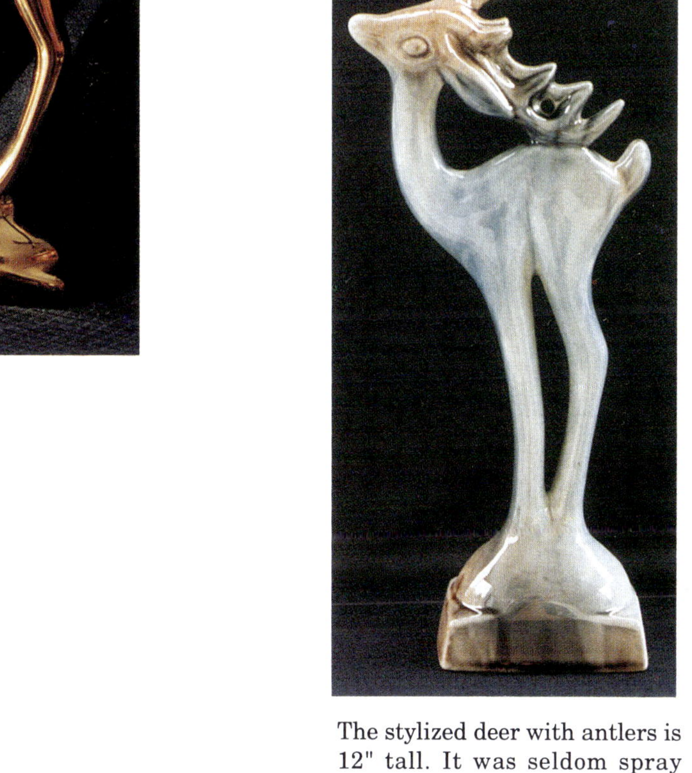

The stylized deer with antlers is 12" tall. It was seldom spray glazed in two colors. It is more commonly found in solid colors or white with gold decoration.

Value Range: $20-25

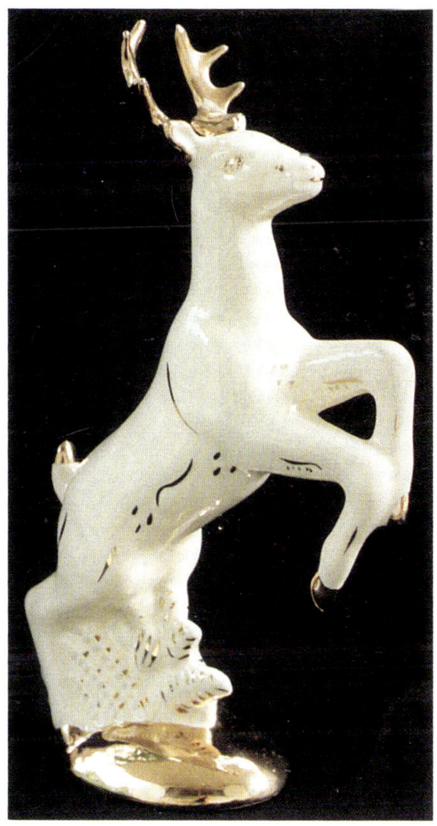

The deer with antlers is 12" tall.

Value Range: $35-40

DOGS

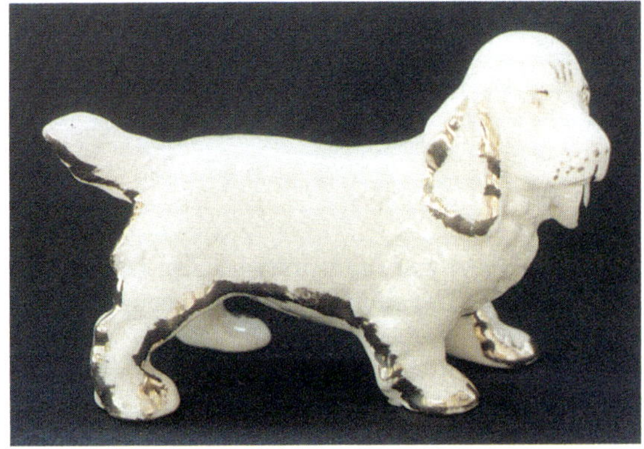

The spaniel with gold decoration is 4" tall and 6" long.

Value Range: $20-25

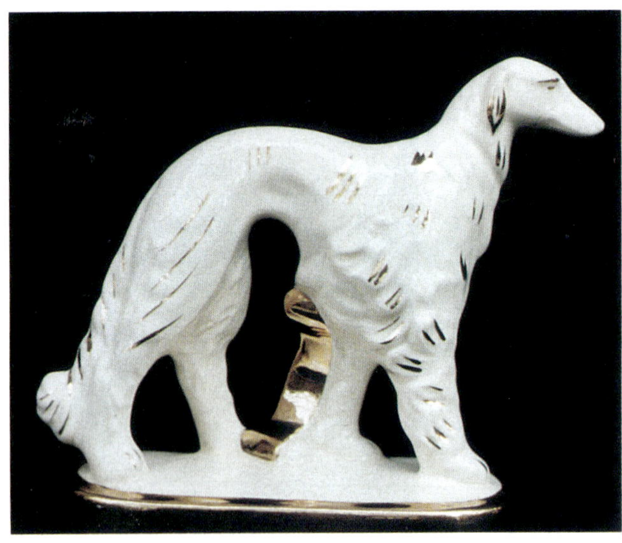

The Afghan hound with gold decoration is 7" tall and 81/2" long.

Value Range: $30-35

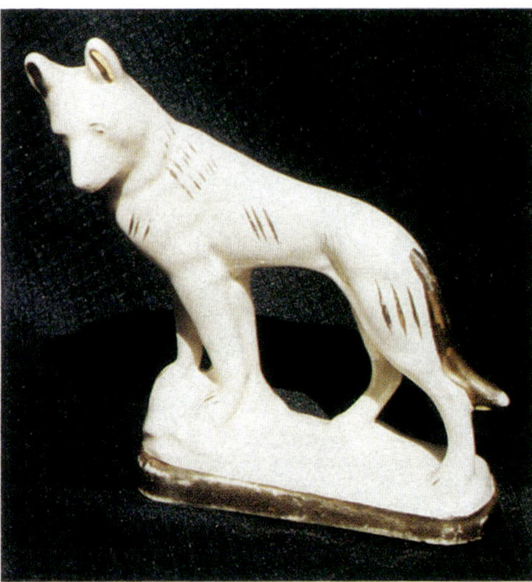

The German shepherd with gold decoration is 61/2" tall and 51/2" long.

Value Range: $20-25

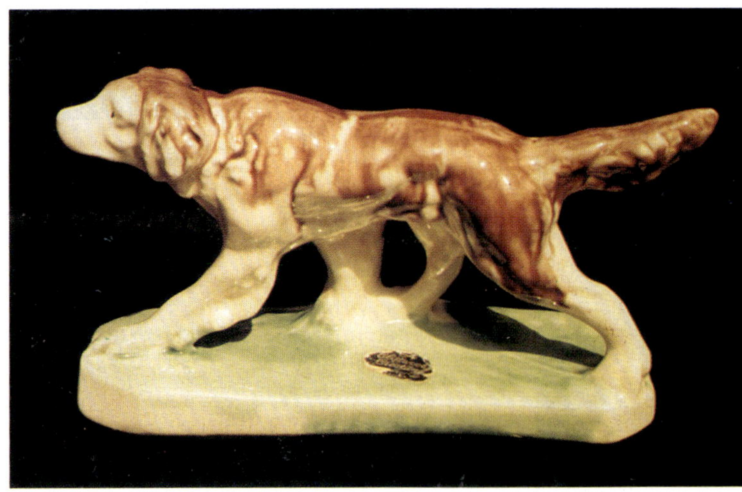

The Irish setter, in natural colors, is 4" tall and 8" long.

Value Range: $30-35

HORSES

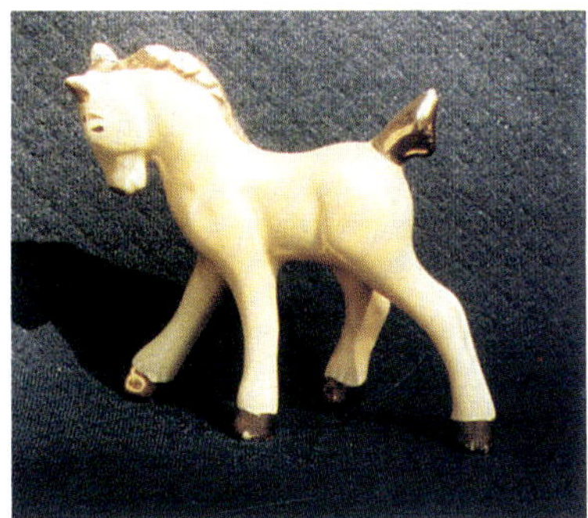

The yellow pony with gold decoration is 31/2" tall. Lawrence Rapp designed it for Camark pottery at Camden, Arkansas after the Midwest burned. A similar pony is claimed by Camark.

Value Range: $12-18

The race horse was a two piece mold. The figure was placed on the base to be fused when fired. Few of the race horses were made. The figure frequently fell over in the kiln, or came out with one or more cracked legs. The figure is 71/2" tall x 61/2" long.

Value Range: $75-100

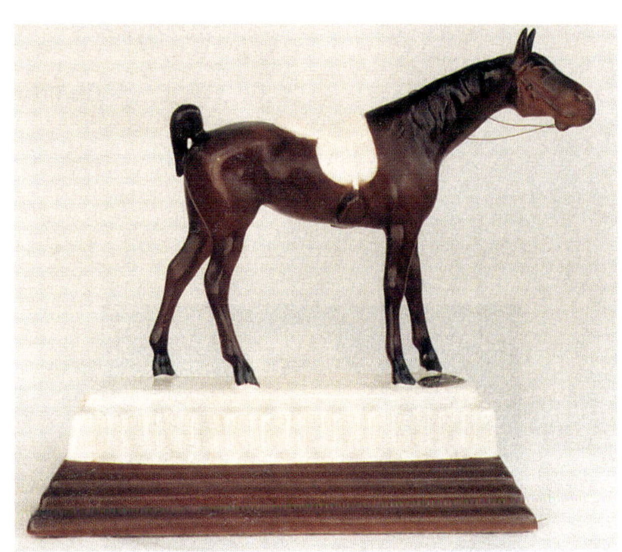

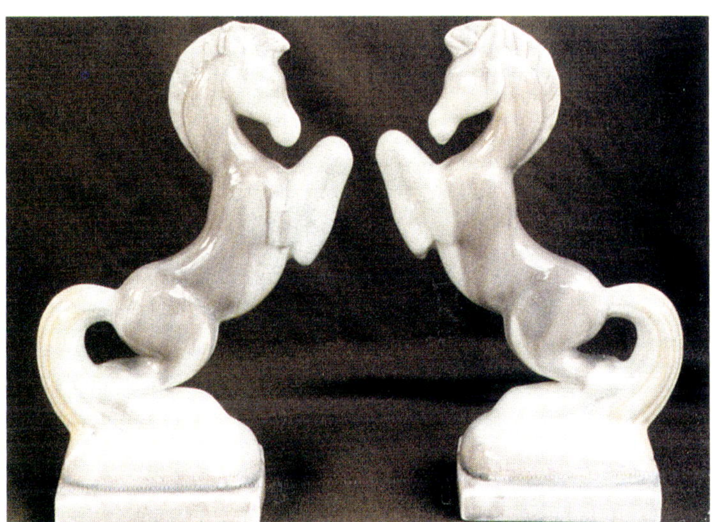

The rearing horses are 103/4" tall. Filled with sand, they make ideal bookends. The Dutchess of Windsor bought a pair of these horses decorated in 14K gold at a Miami, Florida gift shop in 1941.

Value Range: $25-35

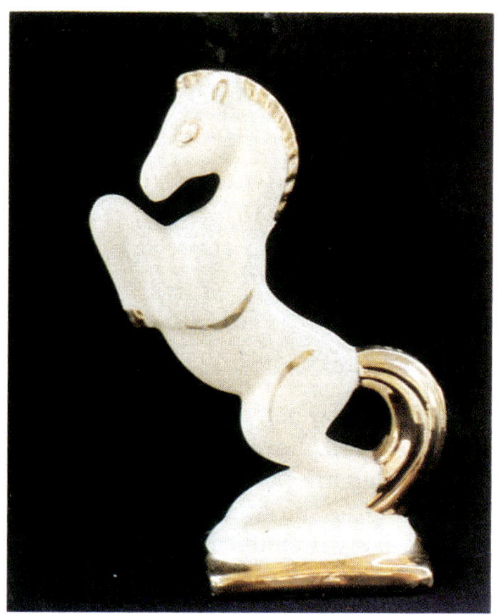

This small rearing horse is a miniature of those in photo #8. It is 71/2" tall x 61/2" long.

Value Range: $15-20

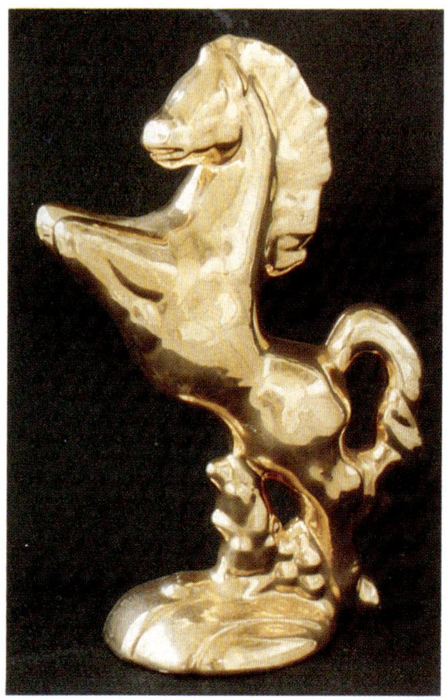

The rearing stallion is 103/4" tall. It was listed as a wild horse.

Value Range: $25-30

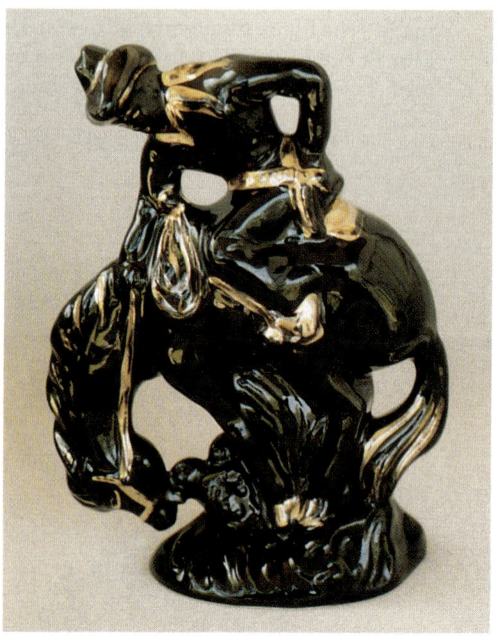

The cowboy on the bucking bronco is 71/2" tall. This figure is black glaze, not Cliftwood's cobalt.

Value Range: $25-30

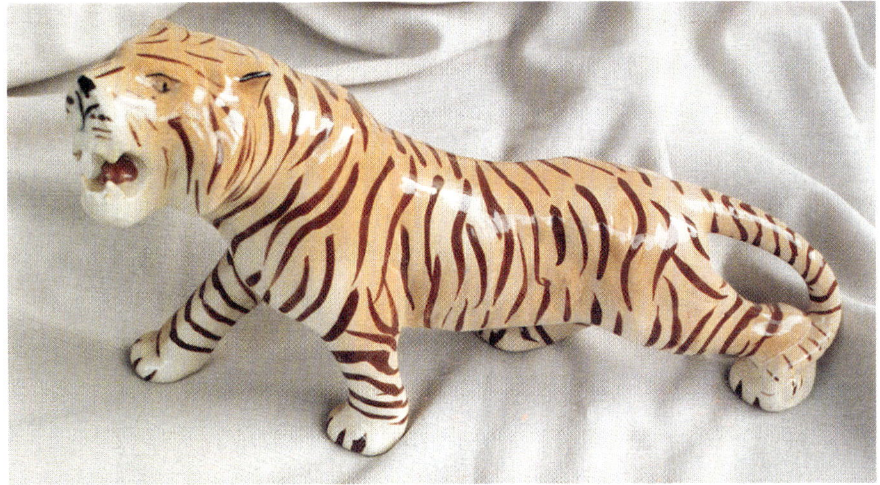

The tiger is a copy of the Cliftwood lioness. It is 7" x 12". This figure was also made in yellow with black hand painted underglaze stripes.

Value Range: $35-40

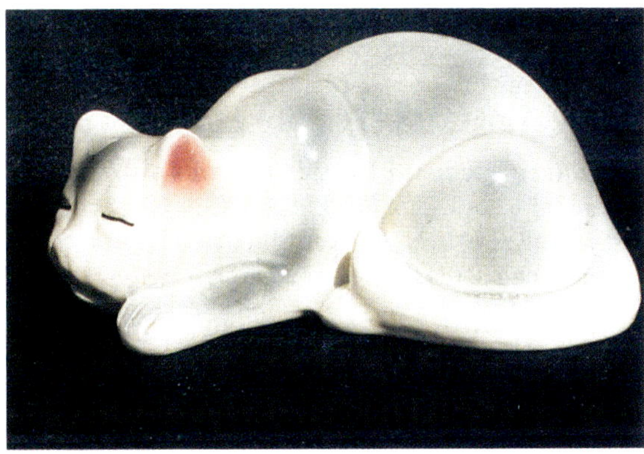

The cat is similar to the Cliftwood cats, but is larger. It is 4" tall x 9" long. Cliftwood's largest cat was 3" tall x 8" long.

Value Range: $30-40

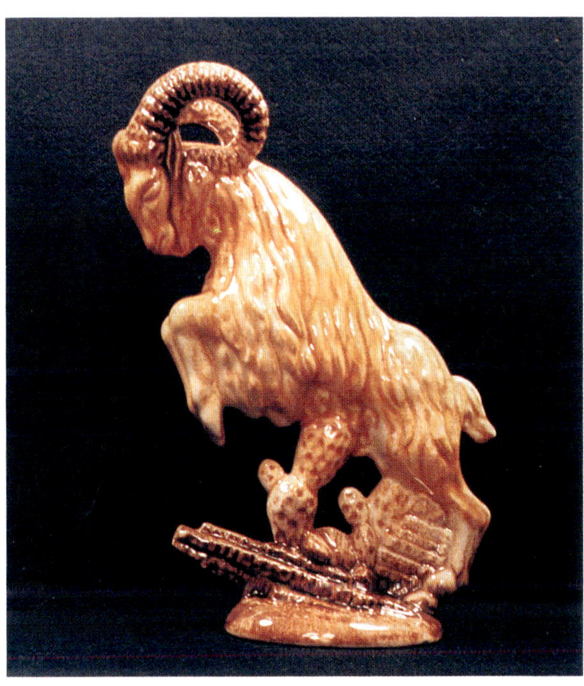

The mountain goat is spray glazed in natural colors. It is 91/2" tall.

Value Range: $25-30

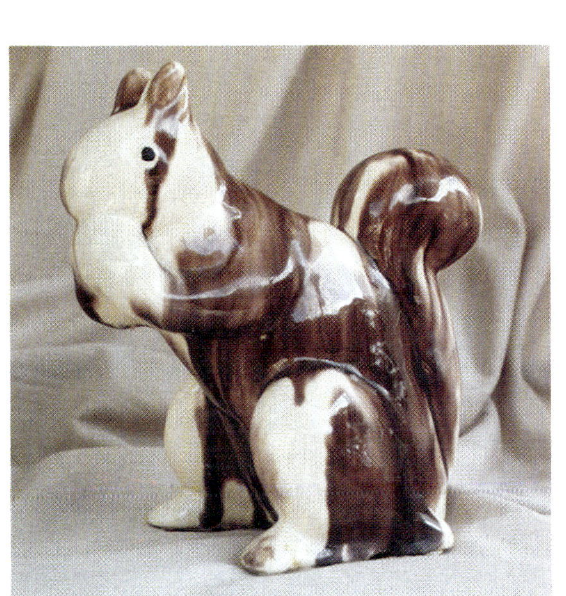

The squirrel, done in brown drip glaze, is 9" tall. This is John Rapp's best effort in trying to reproduce his father's chocolate brown drip glaze.

Value Range: $35-40

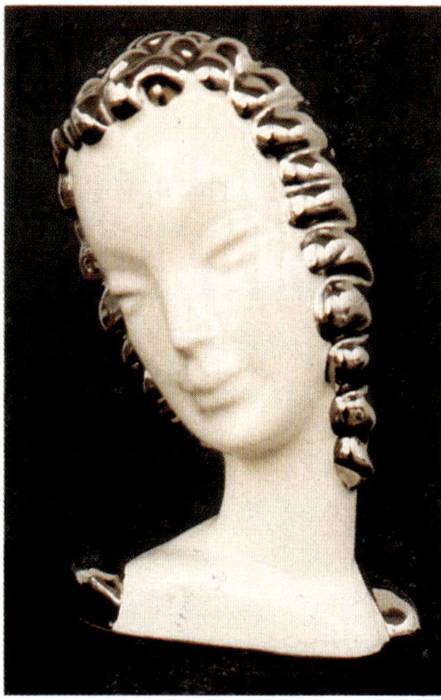

This bust was designed from the high school graduation photo of John Rapp's daughter, Peggy. It is 8 1/2" tall. The figure can be found with either platinum or gold decoration. It was also made in a variety of pastel colors.

Value Range: $40-80

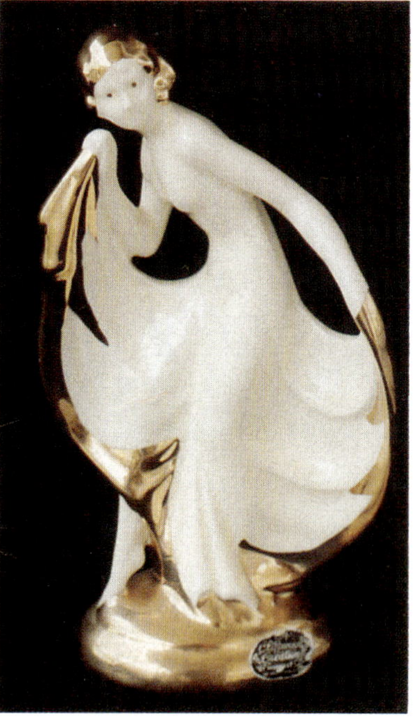

The dancing lady is 8 1/2" tall. She was also done in pastel colors. Morton Pottery Company copied this figure, but enlarged the dress behind so it could be used as a flower holder.

Value Range: $20-30

(See Morton Pottery Company for the flower holder).

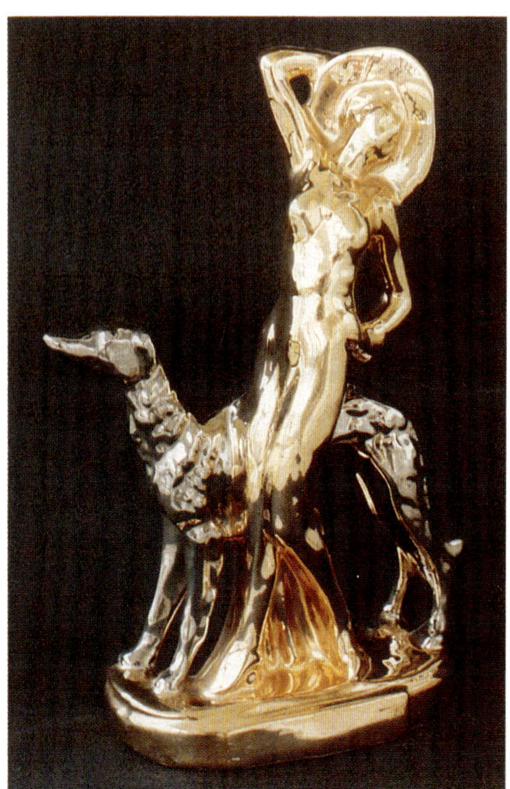

The woman with the Russian wolfhound is 11" tall. The platinum and gold decoration is very unusual for this figurine. Ordinarily the dog was brown and the lady's dress and hat were in pastel colors. This figure belonged to Lawrence Rapp, Midwest's designer.

Value Range: $65-125

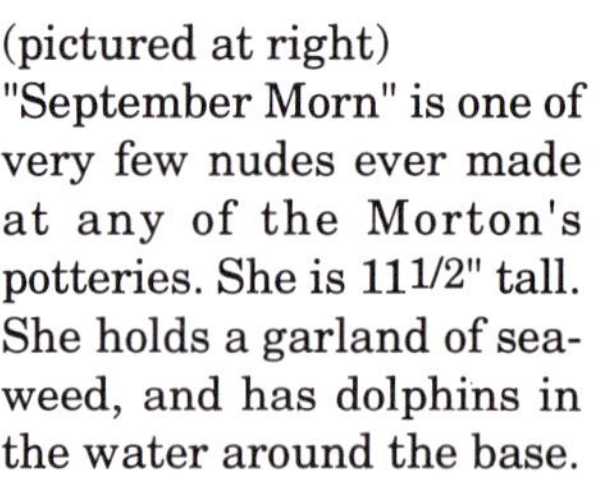

(pictured at right)
"September Morn" is one of very few nudes ever made at any of the Morton's potteries. She is 11 1/2" tall. She holds a garland of seaweed, and has dolphins in the water around the base.

Value Range: $50-100

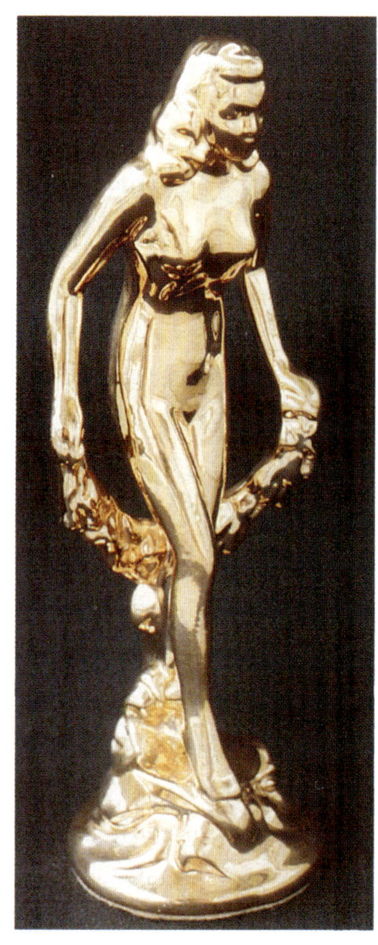

BIRDS

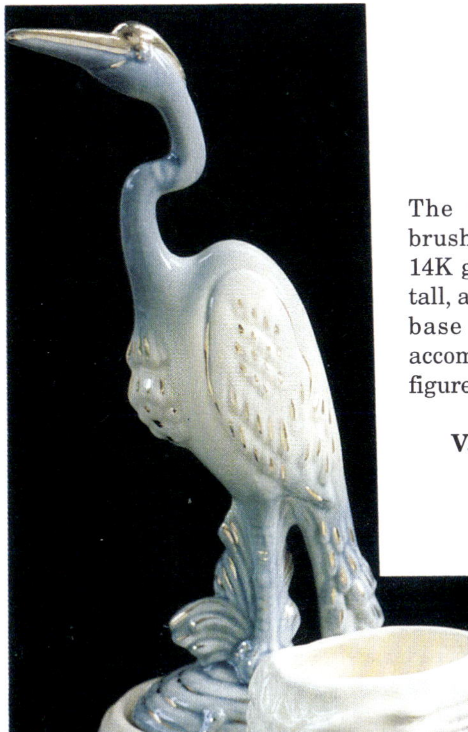

The heron has been air brushed with blue, and has 14K gold decoration. It is 11" tall, and is placed on a planter base that was made to accomodate several different figures.

Value Range: $25-35

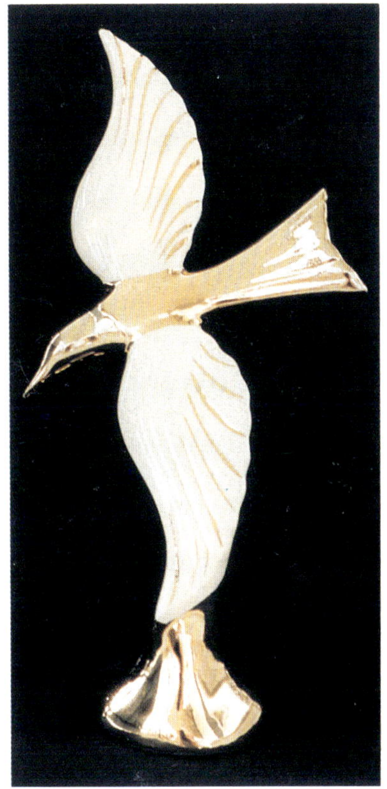

The sea gull in flight is 12" tall. It is a copy of Cambridge Glass Company's sea gull flower holder No. 1138.

Value Range: $30-35

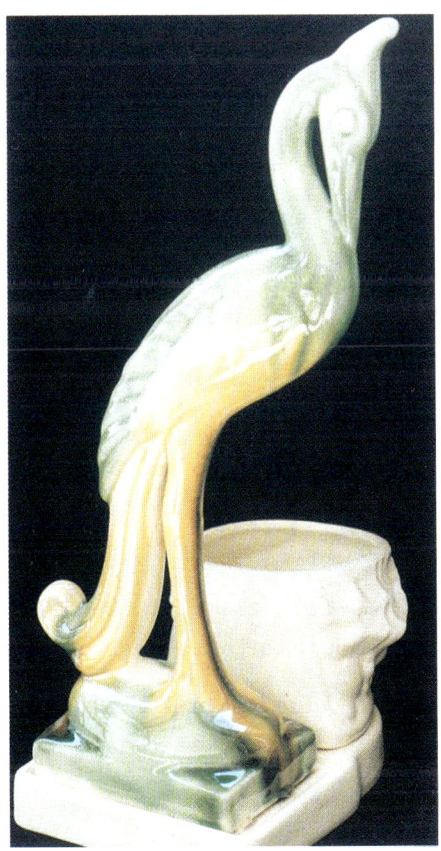

The crane is 11" tall and is attached to another style planter base.

Value Range: $20-35

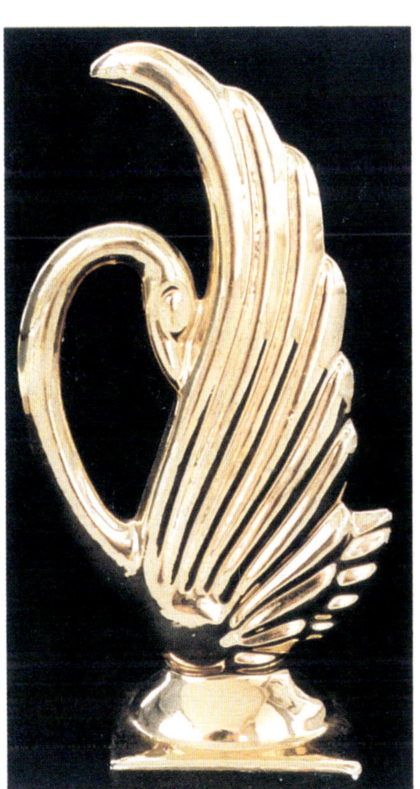

The swan is 12" tall.
Value Range: $20-25

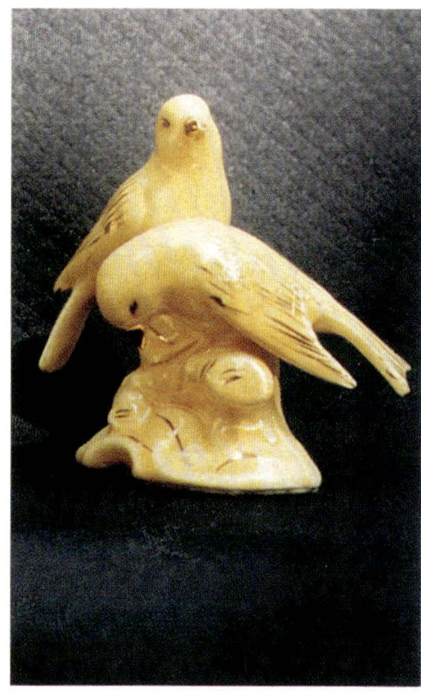

The canaries on the stump are 41/2" tall. The bird with its head bent was molded separately and hand applied to the stump. Seldom were they applied in exactly the same manner.

Value Range: $20-30

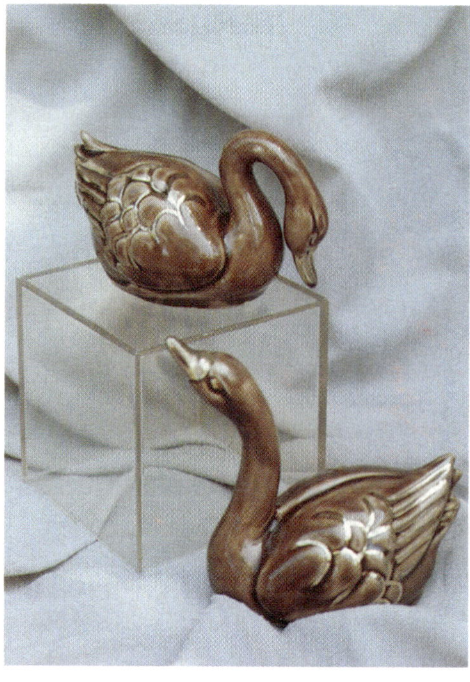

Most swans were white with gold decoration. Brown figures are most uncommon. The top swan is 3" tall, the other is 41/2" tall.

Value Range: $18-24 each

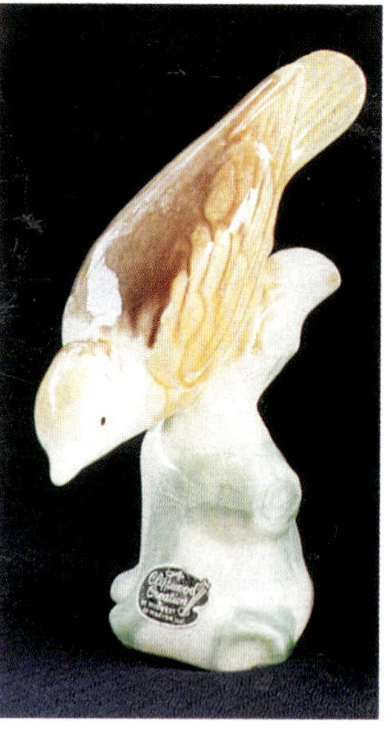

This is a generic bird, 61/2" tall. Glazed in this manner, it resembles a thrush. It was also done in blue, and resembles a jay.

Value Range: $16-20

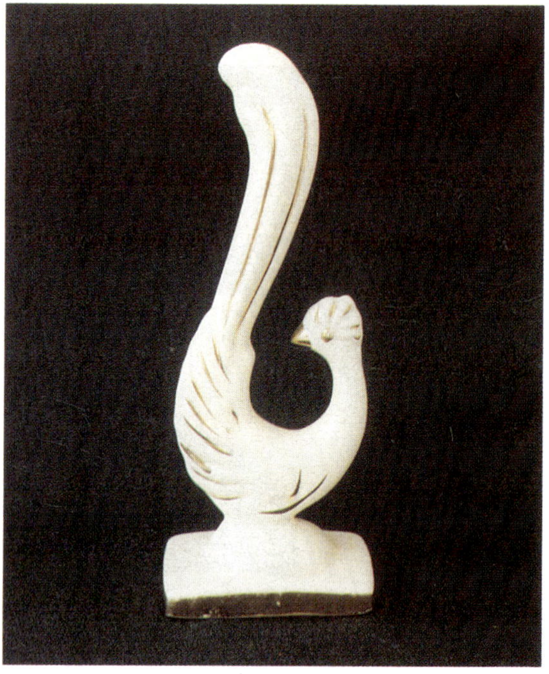

This is a smaller model of the roadrunner. It is 8" tall.

Value Range: $12-18

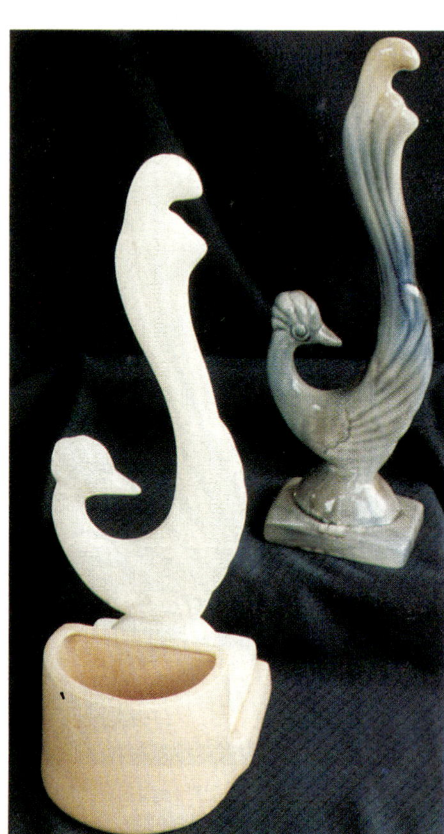

This appears to be a roadrummer, highly stylized. It is 12" tall and is shown with another style planter base.

Value Range: Figurine $20-25
Planter $18-20

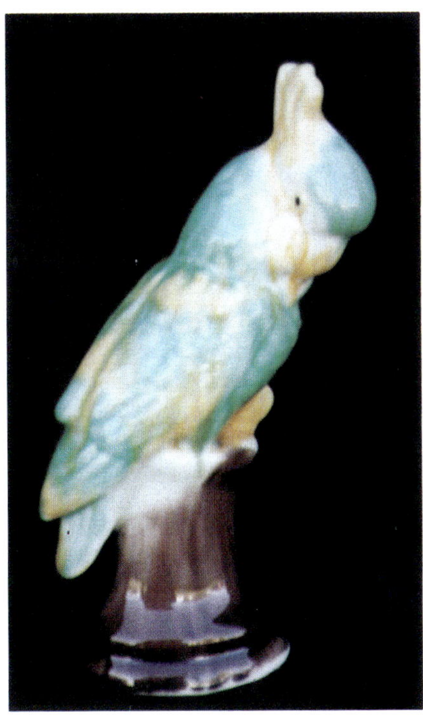

The cockatoo is 8 1/2" tall. It was made in blue as well as the green shown here.

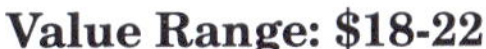

Value Range: $18-22

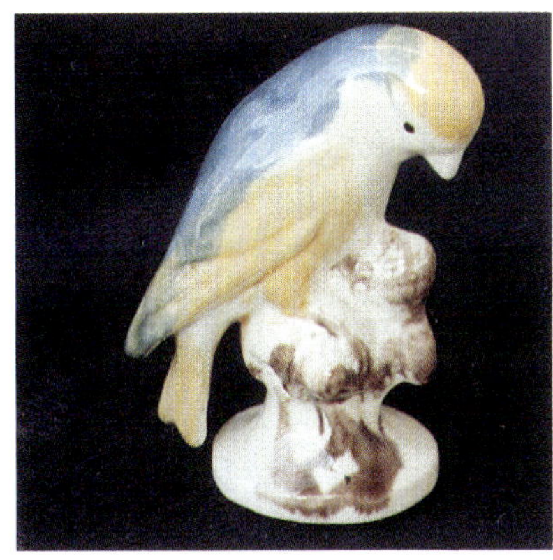

The parrot is 4 1/2" tall. It was made in green as well as the blue shown here.

Value Range: $10-15

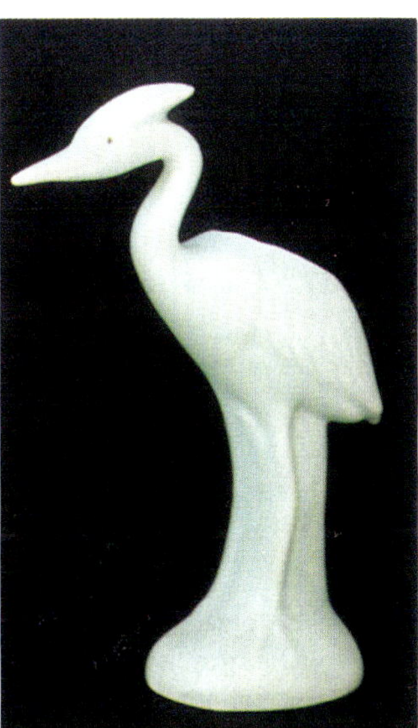

The 6" heron is matte turquoise glaze. It is very similar to one made by the Metlox Manufacturing Company at Manhattan Beach, California. The Metlox bird is usually ink stamped. Midwest used only a paper label.

Value Range: $12-16

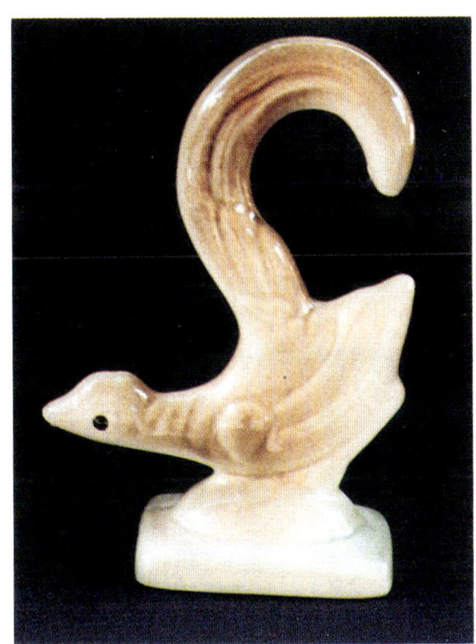

This stylized fighting cock is 6" tall.

Value Range: $12-16

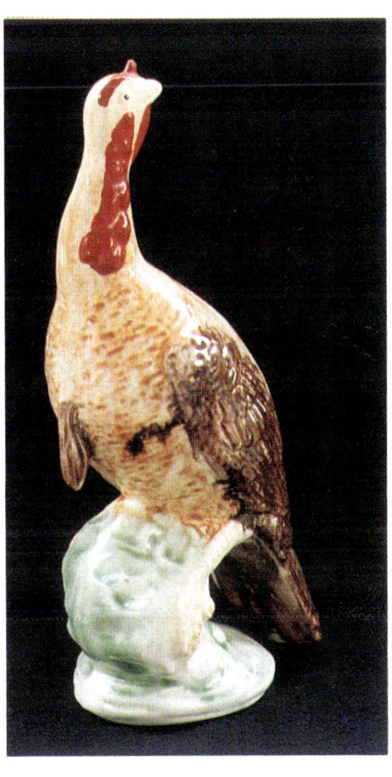

The turkey is 12" tall. It was usually decorated in this manner. The wattle and comb were always cold painted red.

Value Range: $25-30

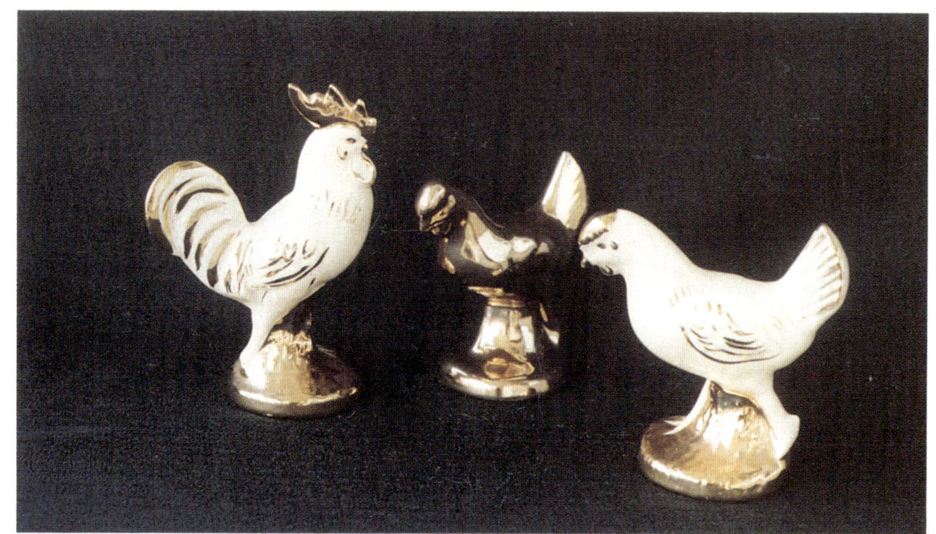

The rooster is 5" tall, the hens are 3 3/4" tall. All have been decorated in 14Kgold. The center figure is solid gold.

Value Range: Rooster $18-20
Hens $12-18 each

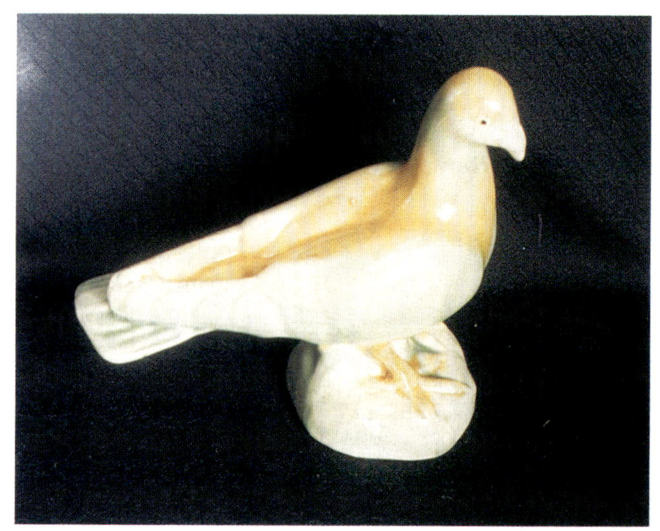

The pigeon is 8" tall. It was decorated with either green or blue wings, tail, and neck with the yellow body.

Value Range: $16-20

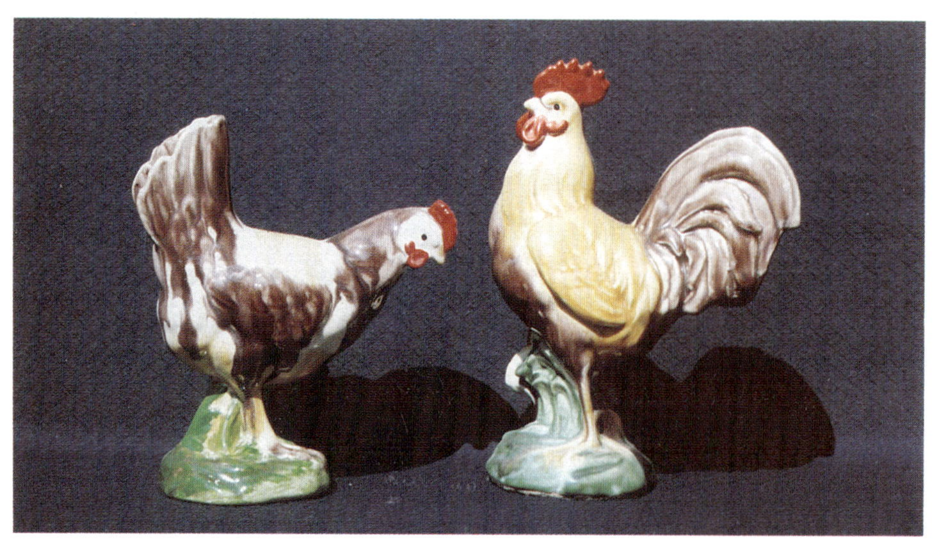

The hen is 7" tall, the rooster is 8" tall. They were made in several color combinations as well as white. All figures had combs and wattles painted with red cold paint.

Value Range: $20-25 each

KRON LINE TV LAMPS

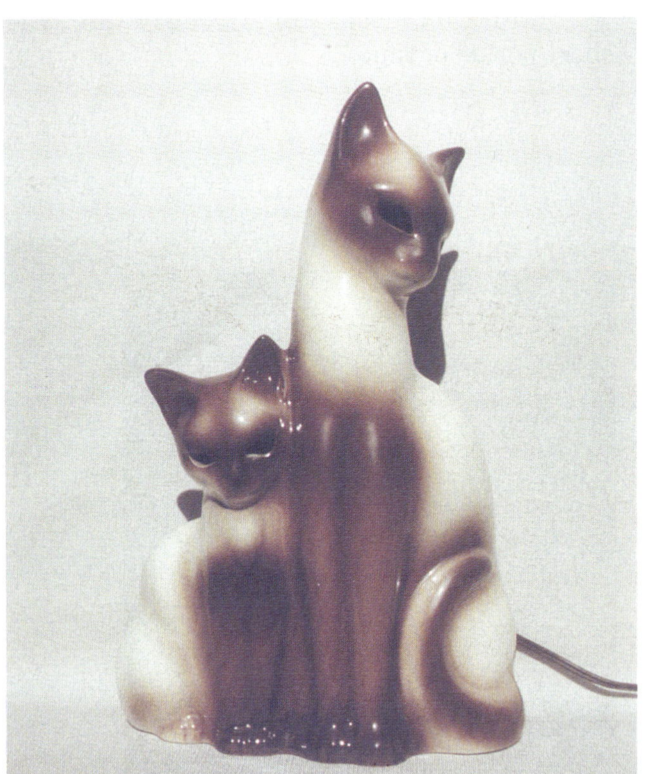

This pair of Siamese cats is the more common of the TV lamps. The tallest cat is 13¼" tall, the smaller one is 8".

Value Range: $30-50

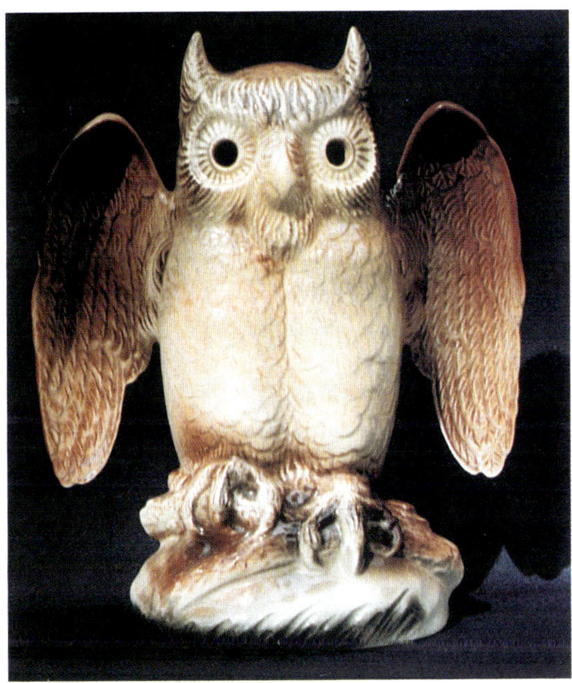

The owl is 12" tall. It has excellent detail. The air brushing is well done.

Value Range: $40-60

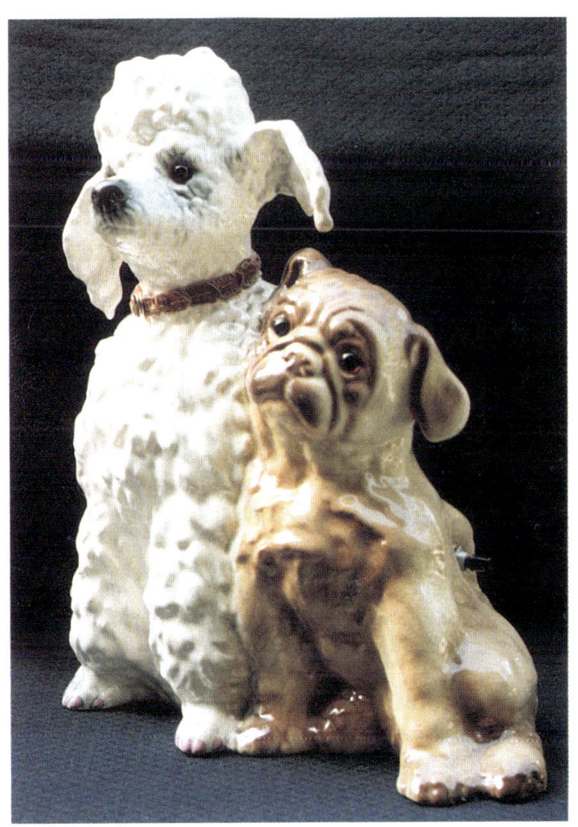

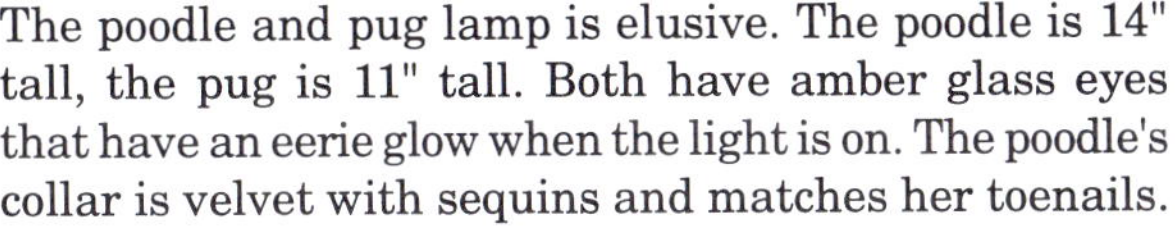

The poodle and pug lamp is elusive. The poodle is 14" tall, the pug is 11" tall. Both have amber glass eyes that have an eerie glow when the light is on. The poodle's collar is velvet with sequins and matches her toenails.

Value Range: $40-60

MASKS

All wall masks are extremely rare. They did not sell well, so were made for only a short period of time.

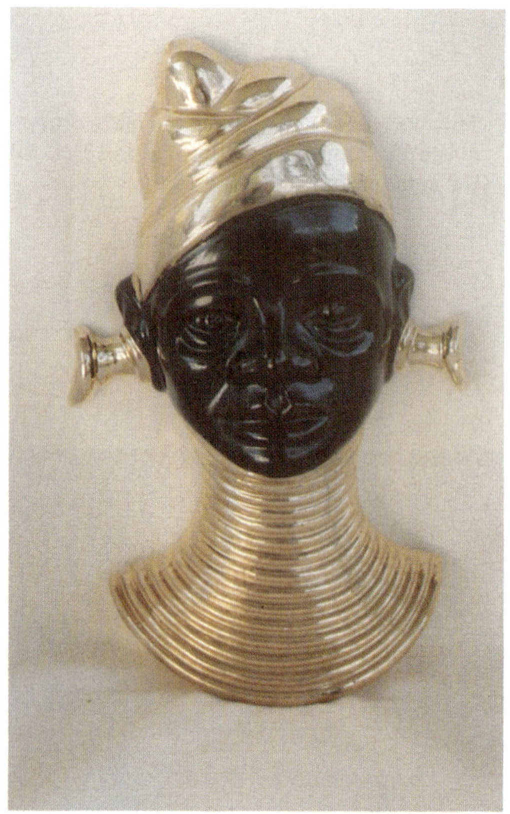

This is the African female wall mask done in high gloss black glaze with heavy gold decoration.

Value Range: $40-50

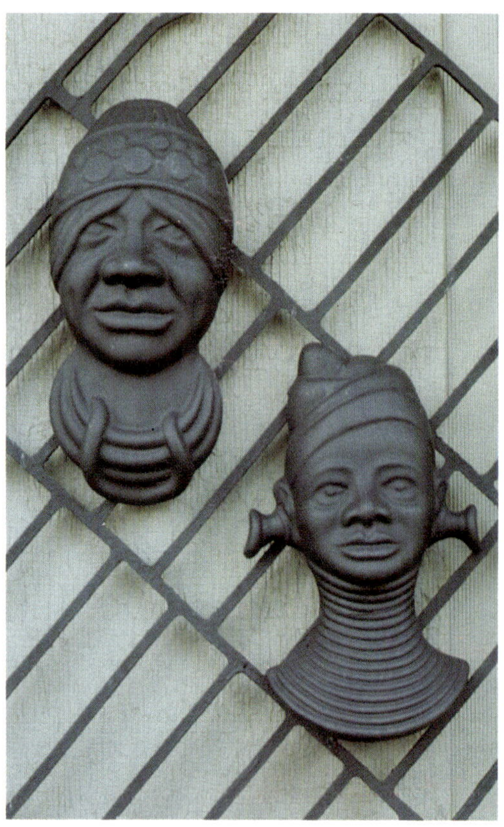

The African male and female wall masks are 9" tall and 4" wide. These are matte black glaze.

Value Range: $30-40

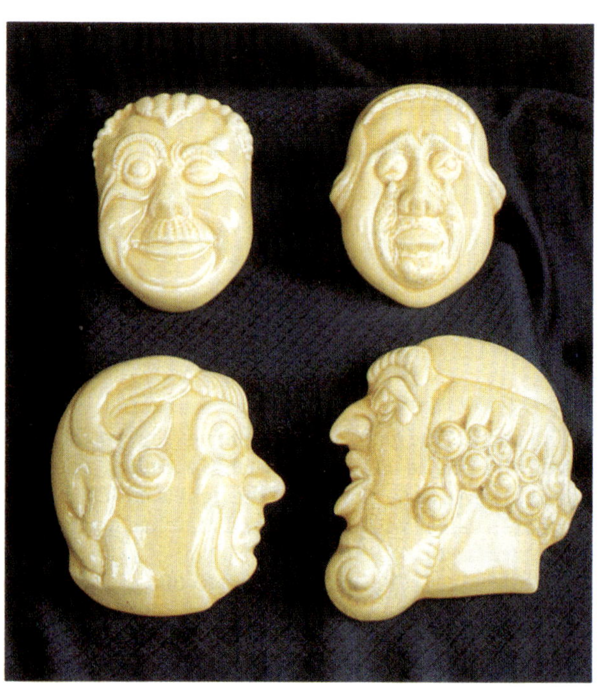

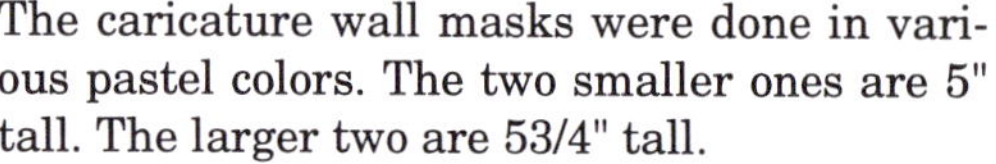

The caricature wall masks were done in various pastel colors. The two smaller ones are 5" tall. The larger two are 53/4" tall.

Value Ranges: Winking Mask $20-30
Pouting Mask $20-30
Classical Greek Mask $25-35
18th Century English Mask $35-40

MINIATURES

Midwest miniatures were usually dip glazed in solid colors. Special orders were hand decorated using a large artist's brush. Predominant colors were yellow, brown, blue, and green.

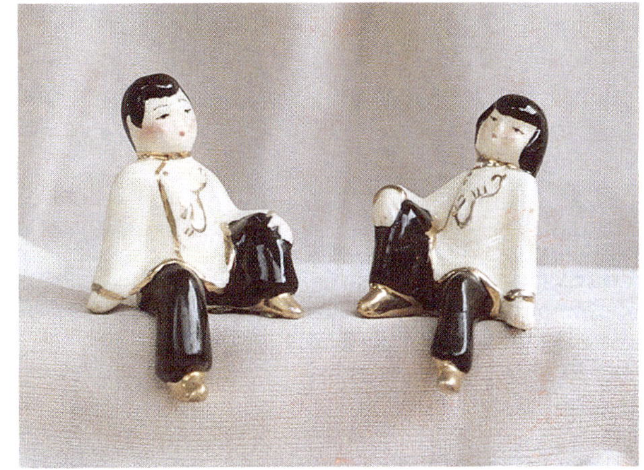

The shelf sitters are similar to a pair made by Ceramic Art Studio at Madison, Wisconsin. The dragons and facial features are less well defined on these made by Midwest.

Value Range: $20-25 pair

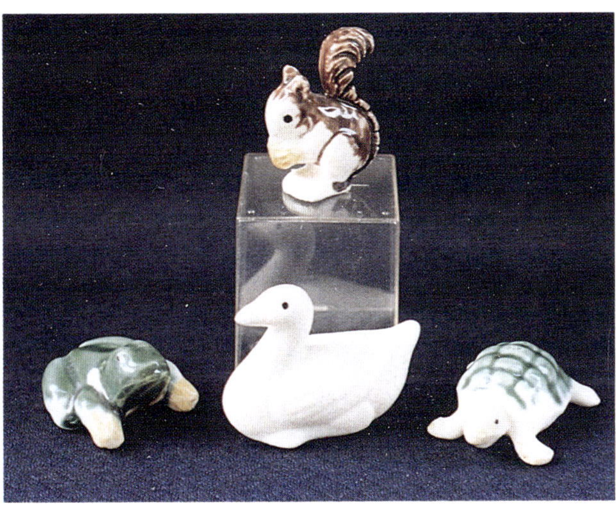

Squirrel, 2" tall – **Value Range: $10-12**
Frog, 1" tall – **Value Range: $8-10**
Swan, 2" tall– **Value Range: $10-12**
Turtle, 1" tall – **Value Range: $8-10**

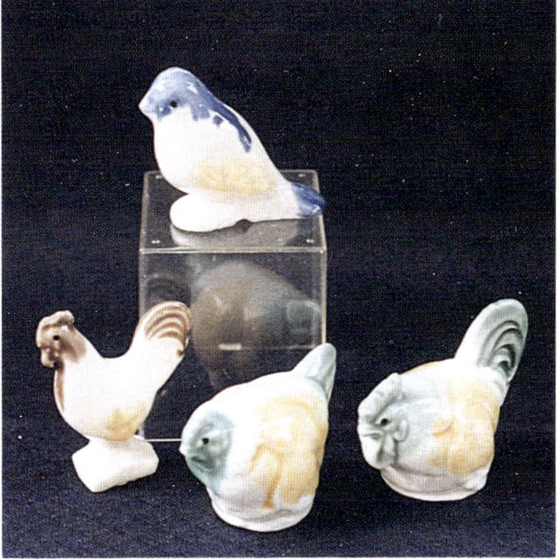

Bird, 1 1/2" tall – **Value Range: $8-10**
Rooster, 2" tall – **Value Range: $8-10**
Hen, 1 1/4" tall – **Value Range: $8-10**
Rooster, 1 1/2" tall – **Value Range: $8-10**

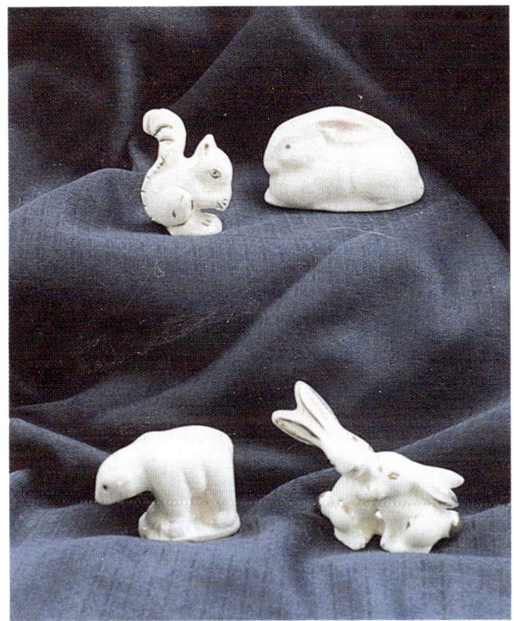

Squirrel, 2" tall – **Value Range: $10-12**
Rabbit, 1 1/2" tall – **Value Range: $10-12**
Polar bear, 1 3/4" tall – **Value Range: $10-12**
Kissing Rabits, 2 1/2" tall – **Value Range: $20-25**

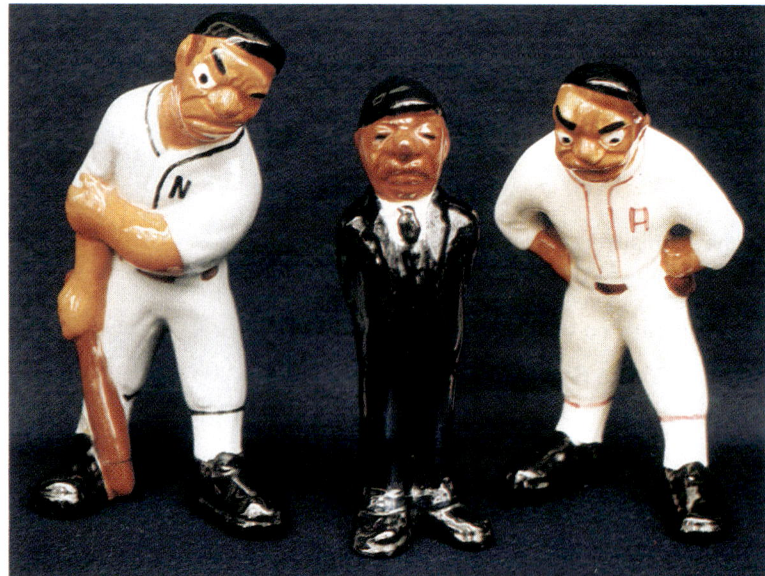

"Kill the umpire." These figurines were always sold as a set of three. The stoic umpire is 61/4" tall. The irate batter is 71/4" tall, and the livid pitcher is 63/4" tall. This set is extremely rare.

Value Range: ND

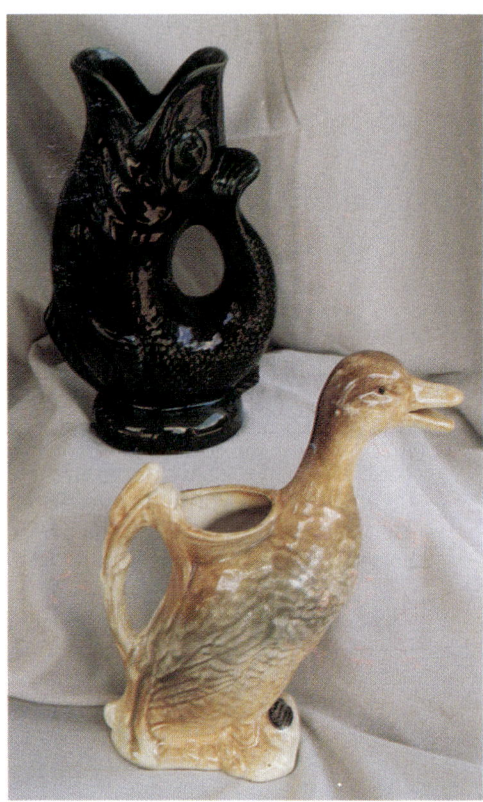

The fish pitcher is 91/2" tall. If slip was removed from the mold soon enough, an air hole formed between the tail and the head. Those pitchers make a gurgling sound when poured.

Value Range: $25-35

The duck is 10" tall and has a cattail handle. It is very similar to a duck pitcher made by the Camark pottery in Arkansas. Seldom was this pitcher air brushed. Instead, it was hand decorated with one and two inch paint brushes.

Value Range: $30-40

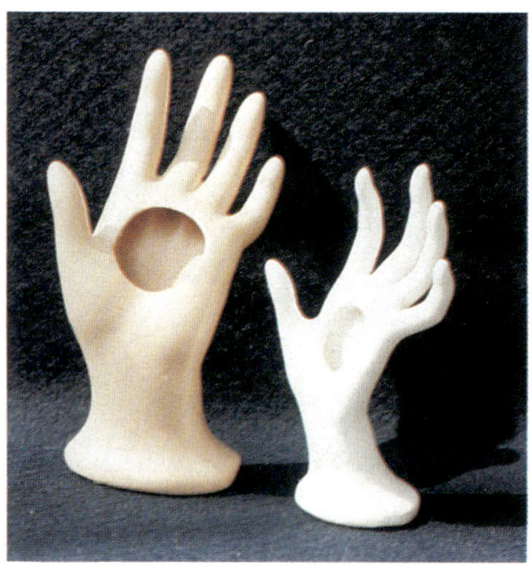

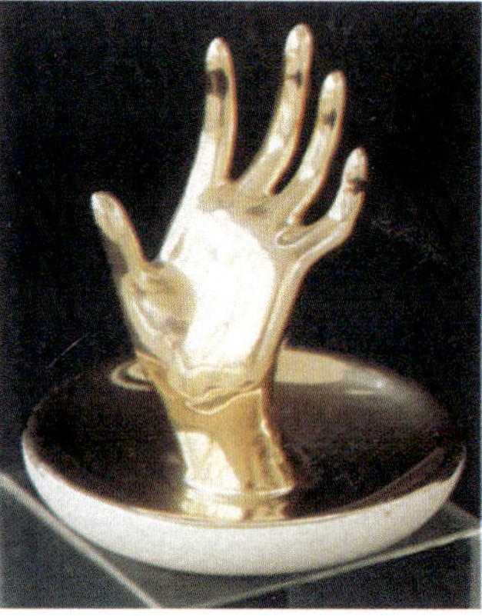

Hand bud vases were good sellers to floral supply companies. The large hand is 61/2" tall. The smaller hand is 41/2" tall. The small hand was also solid cast and placed in a saucer to form a jewelry holder or an ashtray.

Value Range:
Large Hand $15-20
Small Hand $10-15
Jewelry Holder/Ashtray $20-25

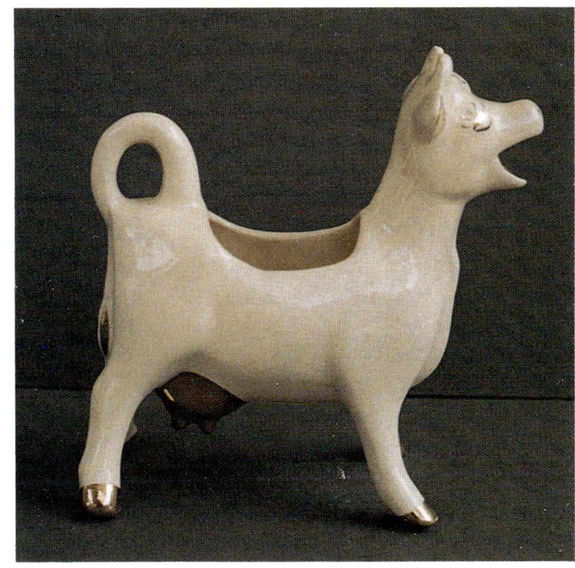

The cow creamer is 5" tall. It was commonly glazed in pastel colors. To have gold decoration is somewhat unusual.

Value Range: $15-20

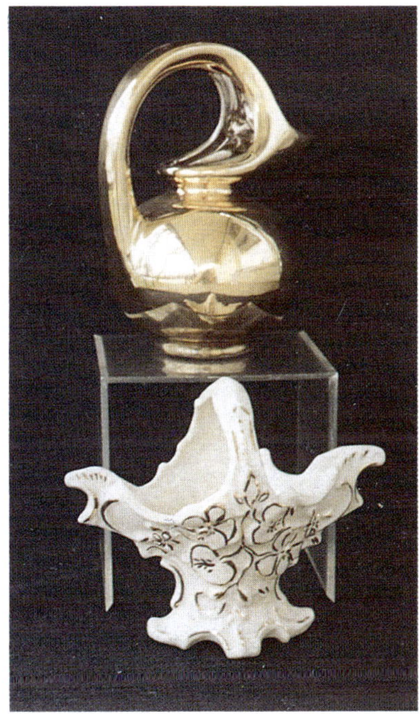

The honey jug is 5" tall. It is 14K gold with platinum interior. This jug was normally glazed one color, inside and out.

Value Range: $20-25

The violet basket, 4" tall, has the flowers and leaves outlined in gold.

Value Range: $15-20

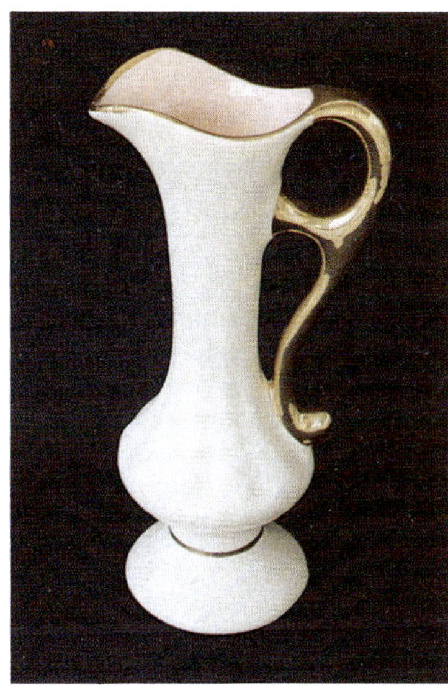

The ewer is 8 1/4" tall. It was usually done in white with a variety of pastel interiors.

Value Range: $20-25

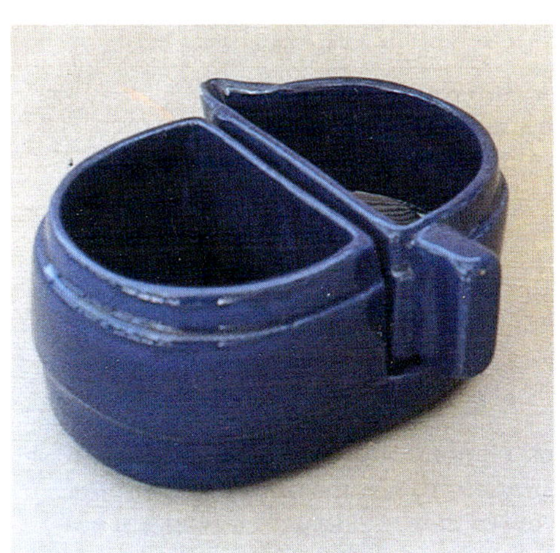

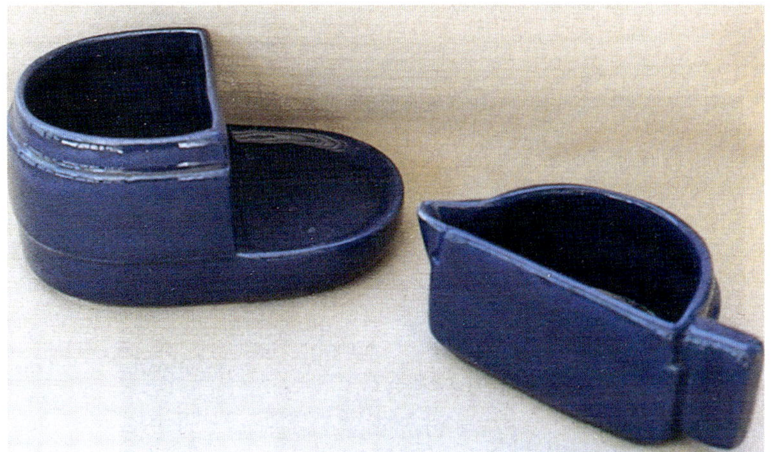

This sugar and creamer is similar to one that was made by the Camark pottery in Camden, Arkansas.

Value Range: $10-15

PLANTERS

The gringham dog and the calico cat were not decorated to fit their genre. They were dappled by the decorators using one inch paint brushes to apply overglaze colors of blue and yellow, brown and yellow, or green and yellow. The planters were also glazed in solid colors. The dog is more commonly found than is the cat.

Value Range: $14-18 each

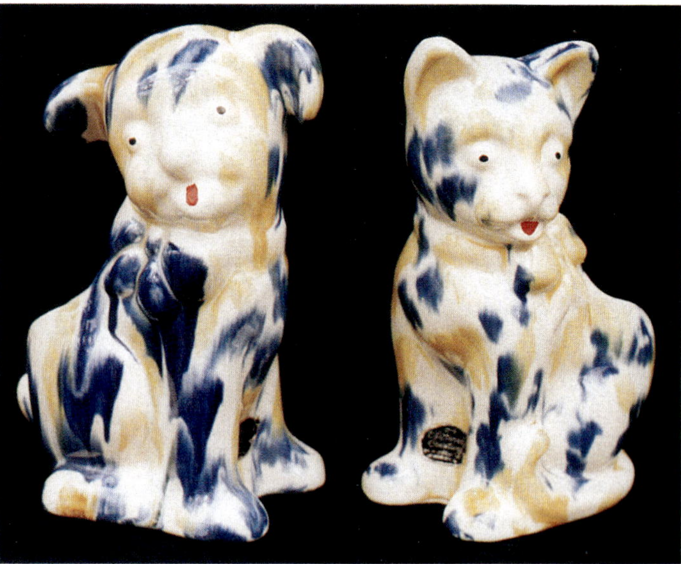

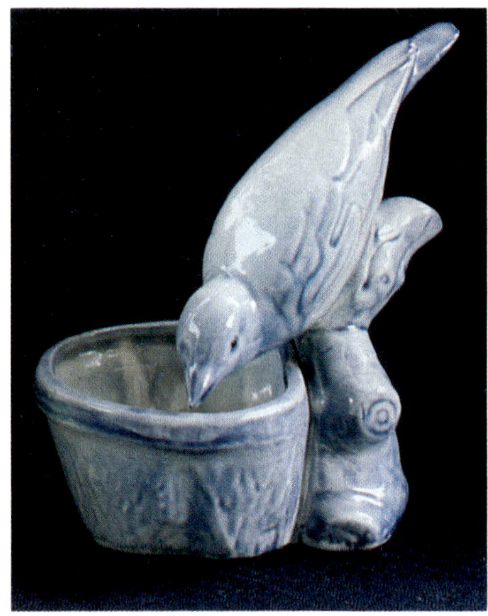

The bird and nest planter is 61/2" tall. The nest opening is 31/2".

Value Range: $12-18

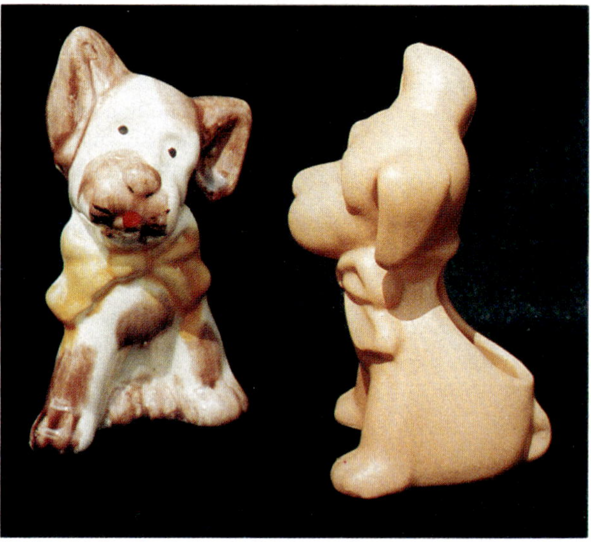

The dog with the bow tie is 51/4" tall. The brush painted overglaze is the common decorating style. Matte glaze planters are elusive.

Value Range: $8-12
Add 10% more for matte finish.

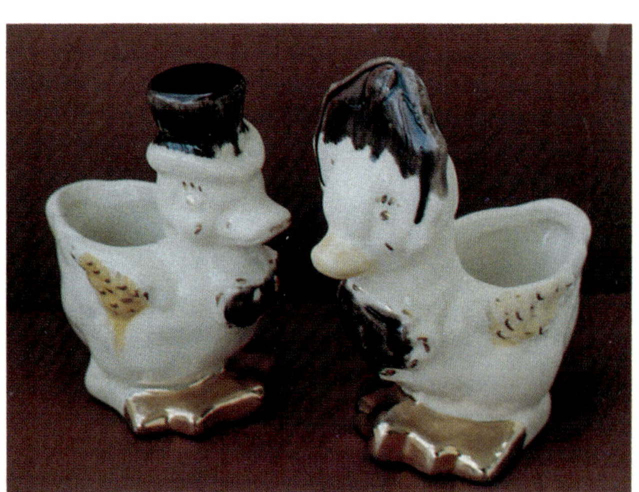

The duck planters are very uncommon with gold decoration. They can be found with brown, blue, or green hats and ties. The planters are 53/4" tall.

Value Range: $10-15 each
Add 25% for gold decoration

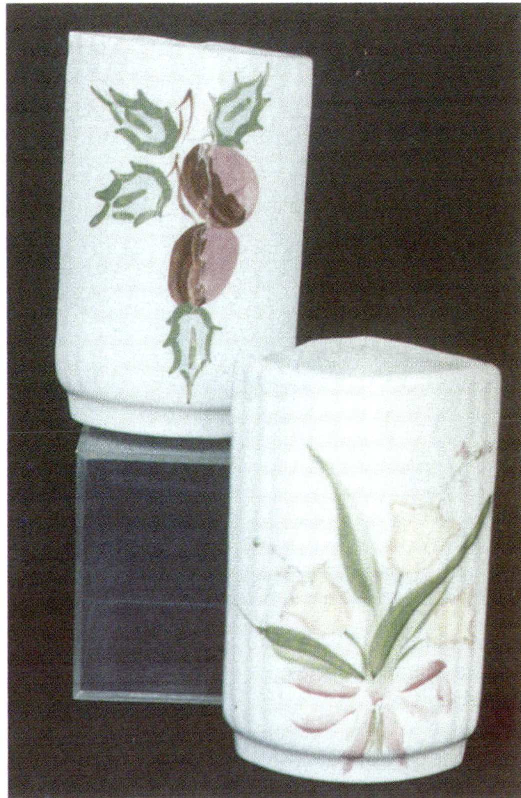

The wall pockets are examples of Midwest's hand painted underglaze. They are 51/2" tall. Fruit and flowers were standard decorating styles.

Value Range: $15-20

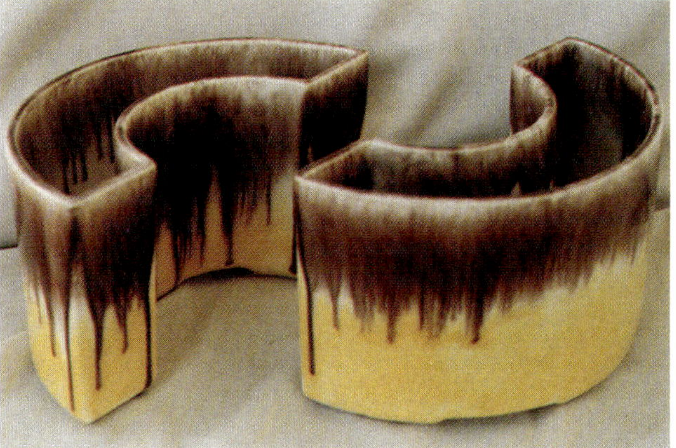

This two piece planter is 41/2" tall with an 83/4" diameter when placed together. Intended as a centerpiece, it has several combinations for use from round to serpentine.

Value Range: $25-30

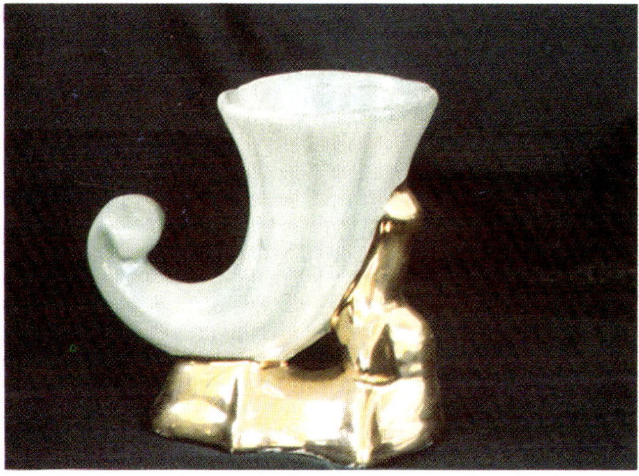

This 61/2" tall cornucopia planter is supported by a dolphin at the front which is very similar to the dolphins used by the Cliftwood Art pottery.

Value Range: $20-25

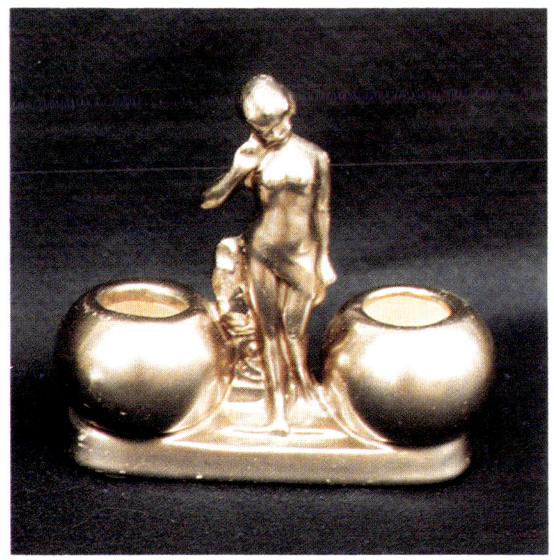

The semi-draped nude figure with the globe planters was difficult to fire. It frequently warped or exploded in the kiln. The planter was copied by the Japanese, so be wary of this one. The copy is much lighter weight. The planter is 51/2" x 53/4".

Value Range: $30-35

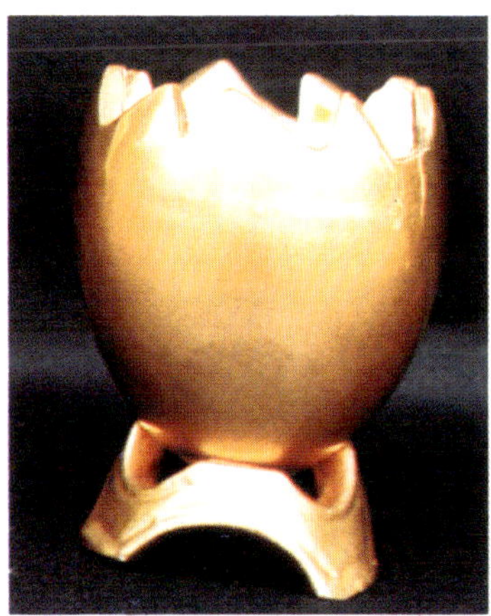

The broken egg planter is 33/4" tall. It was a popular Easter item. The planter was made as two separate pieces, and the egg was not always placed squarely on the tripod. It is frequently found askew. Eggs were done in pastel colors of blue, yellow, green, and pink with contrasting colors for the tripod. 14K and platinum eggs are rare.

Value Range: $15-20

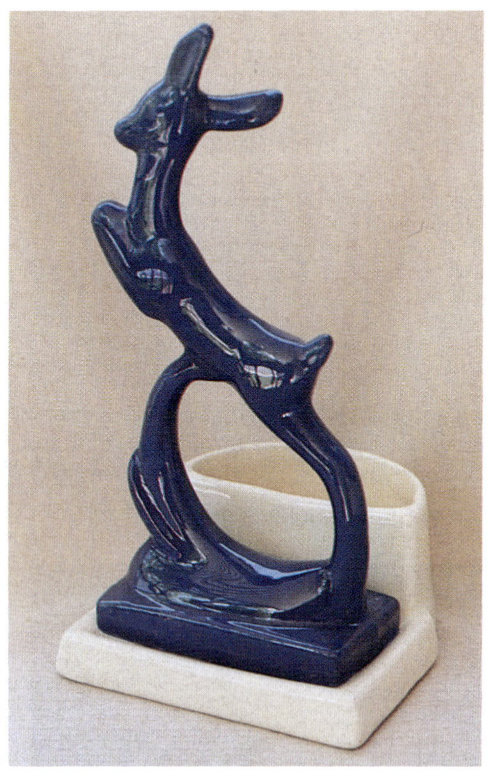

The leaping fawn planter is 8" tall.
Value Range: $12-18

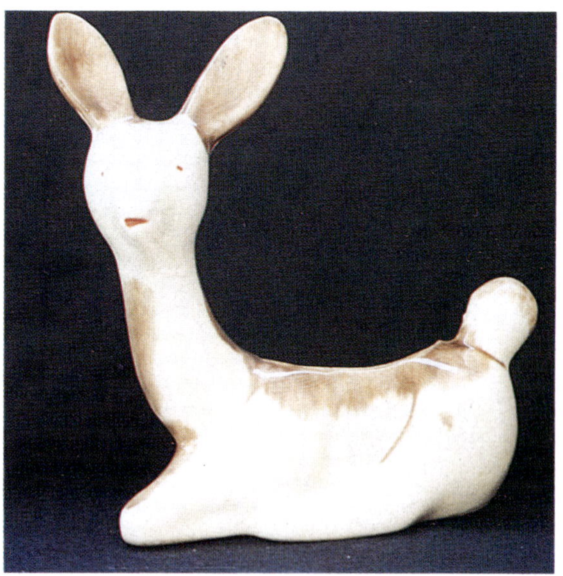

The deer planter is 6 1/2" tall x 5 1/2" long. It was made as a standing figure as well as this one in a reclining position.

Value Range: $12-18

The cat was made as a cactus planter. The cactus formed the cat's tail.

Value Range: $8-10

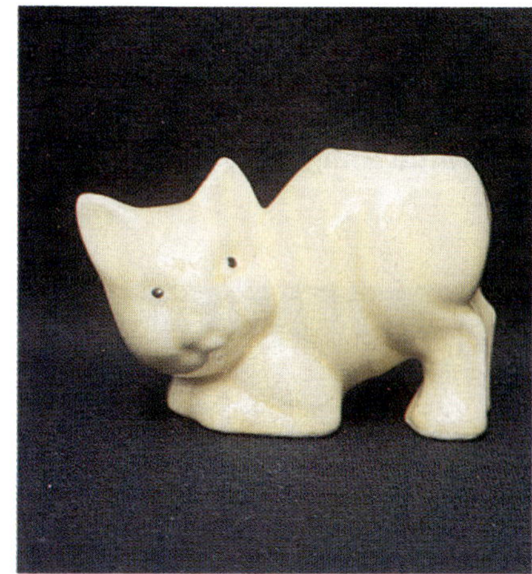

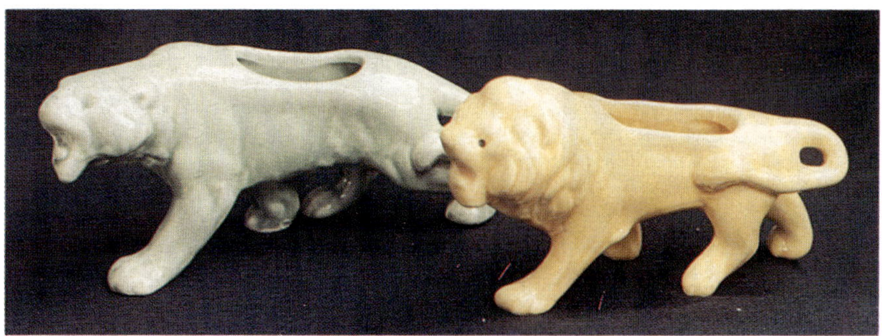

The lioness and lion were copied from the Cliftwood line that was made in the early 1920's. They are 3 1/4" x 6 1/2".

Value Range: $8-12 each

SHADOW LAMP FOR FIGURALS

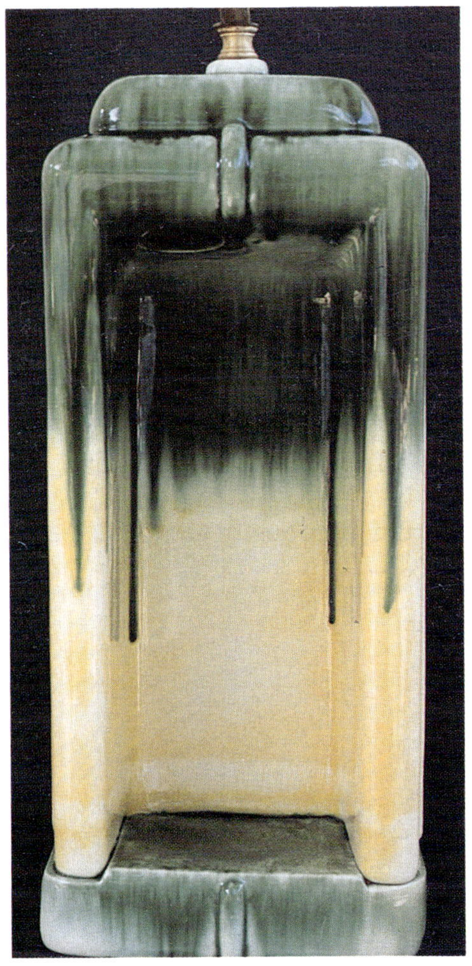

This lamp was made to hold a variety of the figurines made by Midwest. It has a three way electrical unit that allows a night light to shine through a round hole above the figurine, giving the figure a backlighted effect. The lamp is 17 1/2" x 7 1/2" x 5 1/2". The opening for the figurine is 12 3/4" x 5" x 3 3/4". This lamp style is rare.

Value Range: $50-60

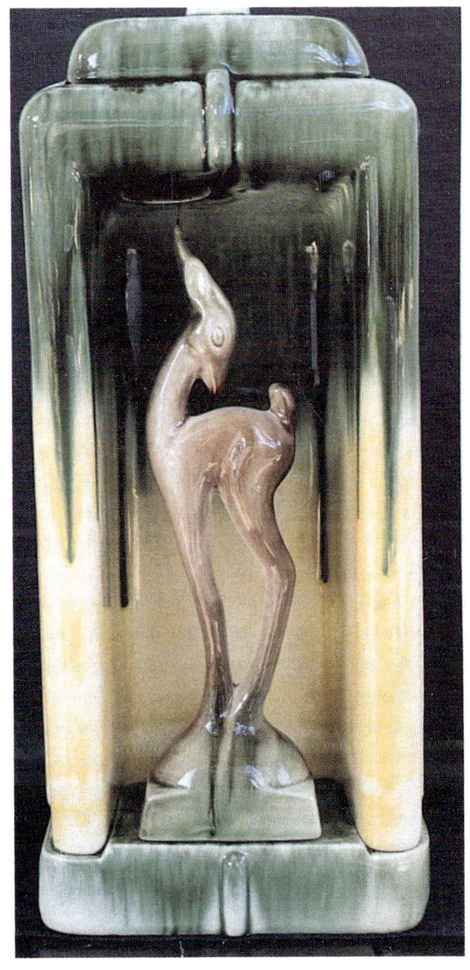

The lamp, complete with figurine, is very Art Deco.

Value Range: $70-90 complete

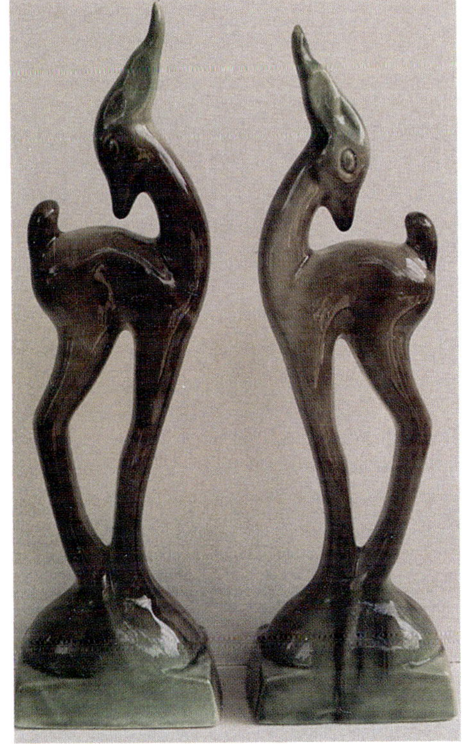

The figurines are 12" tall and are air brushed in brown and green.

Value Range: $20-25

PART IV

AMERICAN ART POTTERIES 1947-1963

After the four Rapp brothers severed relationship with the Midwest Pottery in 1943, they found themselves pursuing independent careers for the very first time in their lives. Carl went to California to work in a pottery in Hollywood. John went to South Milwaukee, Wisconsin to work at a pottery purchased by Midwest Pottery after the Morton fire. Theodore stayed in Morton and sold insurance. Lawrence became an itinerant mold maker. He moved between potteries at Bellville and White Hall, Illinois, and at Little Rock and Camden, Arkansas. That was no easy life, so he eventually went to work at a pottery at Clinton, Illinois. Theodore soon joined him. They commuted daily from Morton to Clinton.

By 1946, the four brothers were all back in Morton, anxious to establish their own pottery once again.

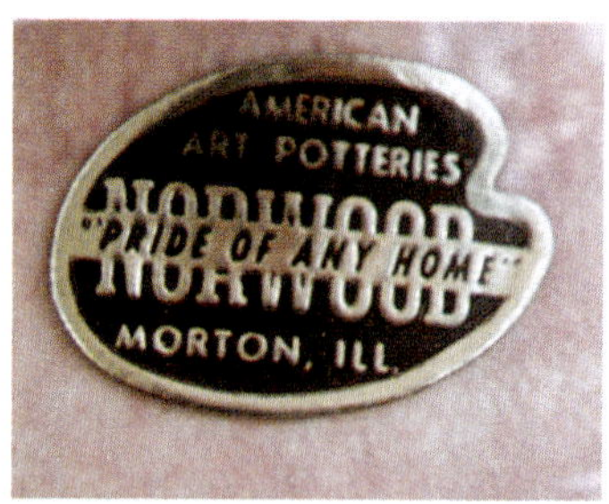

This is the only mark, a foil label, used by the American Art Potteries. It was much the same shape as the one the Rapps used at Midwest. This label, however, has the slogan "Pride of Any Home" from the old Cliftwood paper label that they had used when the pottery began in 1920.

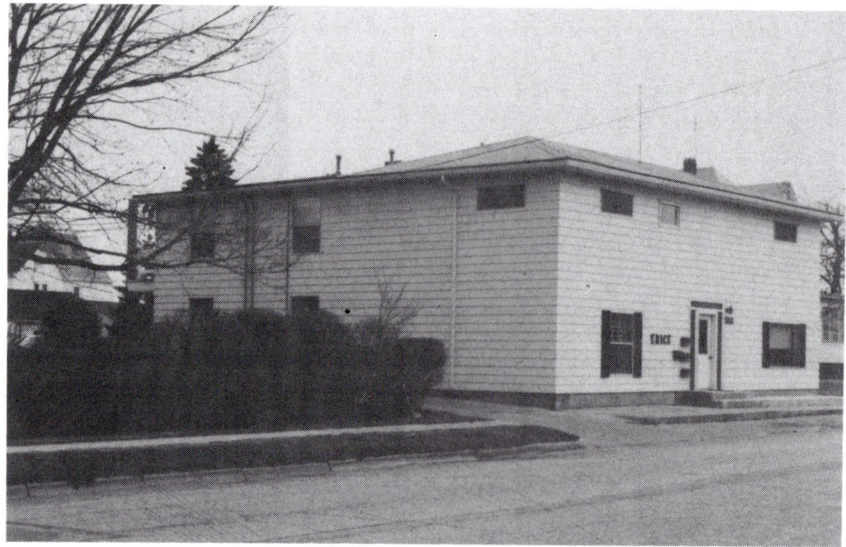

This building was the location of the Rapp brothers' new pottery at 503 West Jefferson Street. It had been an automobile dealership and service garage. After extensive renovation and remodeling, the pottery opened here in 1947.

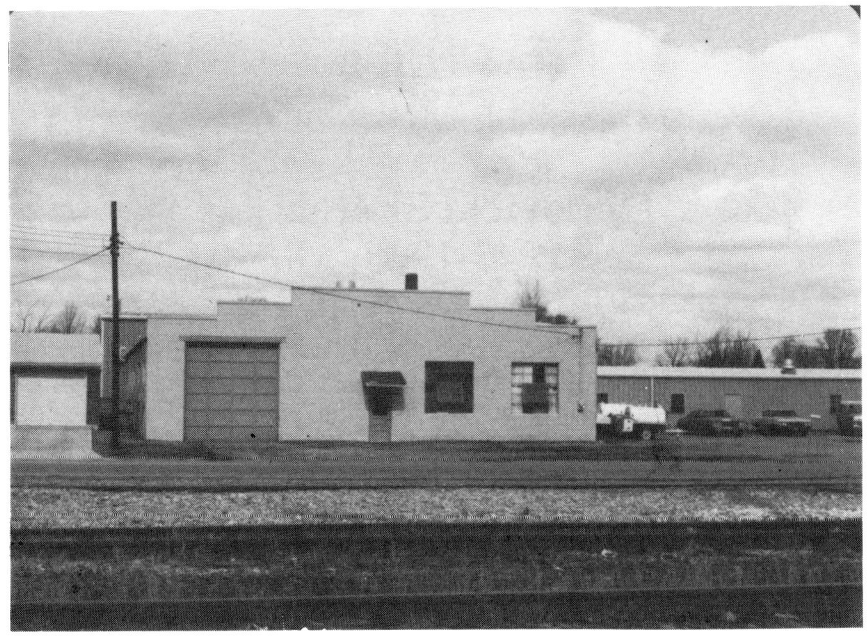

This is the Custenborder Manufacturing building on Morton Avenue that was purchased in 1950 to house a new tunnel kiln and to provide much needed space for the mold making department.

Form W-2
(Revised July 1948)
U. S. Treasury Department
Internal Revenue Service

WITHHOLDING STATEMENT—1948
Wages Paid and Income Tax Withheld

EMPLOYEE'S COPY (DUPLICATE)

EMPLOYEE TO WHOM PAID (Print name, full address, and Social Security Number)

Total wages (before pay-roll deductions) paid in 1948	Federal income tax withheld, if any
$ 933.80	$ 62.42

EMPLOYER BY WHOM PAID (Name, address, and Social Security Identification Number)

American Art Potteries 37 0627643
503 West Jefferson Street
Morton, Illinois

KEEP THIS COPY FOR YOUR OWN RECORD

This W-2 form for 1948 gives an idea of the wage scale at that time. The withholding statement was issued in the second year of American Art Pottery's operation. That was several years prior to the difficulties with the IRS.

CHAPTER 9

Historical Sketch 1947-1963

The products manufactured at the American Art Potteries were very similar to those the Rapps had produced during the Cliftwood and Midwest years. The brothers assumed the same specialty areas they had been responsible for at the earlier potteries. Lawrence designed and made the new molds. Theodore supervised the casting and trimming department. John was responsible for glazing, decorating, and kiln operation. Carl reestablished himself in sales and shipping.

Few designs that had been used during the Cliftwood and Midwest years were made at the new pottery. Many fresh designs went into production. Television lamps, ceramic doll parts, new figurines, and a new line of novelty planters were introduced by American Arts. None of the items produced at the pottery were marked. The foil labels were used exclusively. All wares produced at this location were marketed under the trade name "Norwood Pottery."

John Rapp's unique glazing techniques help to identify the wares produced by American Art Potteries. The colors were all hand painted or spray painted over a white or opaque glaze base. Though some solid colors were produced, the majority of the work done during this period of operation has a mottled appearance, or a sharply defined color separation that came from the hand application of the glaze. Another help in identifying American Art products is the pattern of glaze crazing. Older pottery has a closely woven basket type of crazing rather than the sharp, long lines of crazing that are found on American Art examples. Crazing often appeared soon after the ware was taken from the kiln. The Rapps were never able to determine what the problem really was. It is certain that they had not intended to create the well known crackle glazes. In all probability, the glaze contracted at a greater rate than the clay body during the cooling process. That would account for the rapidity in crazing at the pottery.

When the pottery started operation at the west Jefferson Street location, there was not enough floor space for the mold making operations. Lawrence developed his designs and produced the mold for them in an old building known as the Mauriceau Building. That building, located near where the Midwest Potteries had burned in 1944, was unhandy. The molds had to be carried across town in an old panel truck and were frequently damaged during the trip. To eliminate that inconvenience, an addition was built across the front of the building in 1949. That addition extended the building to the sidewalk in front.

By the time the addition was completed, the volume of business had grown so fast that the new addition, instead of housing the mold making division, had to be used as a showroom and an expanded area for the packing and shipping departments. The pottery was outgrowing its facilities. It was obvious that there was a need to further increase the floor space of the pottery, but expansion at that location was not possible. It was also obvious that more capital was necessary to meet the increased demands for American Art pottery. In order to provide both needs, a Peoria businessman, William F. Shanemeyer, became a partner with the brothers.

As a result of that partnership, the American Art Potteries purchased the Custenborder building, a machinery manufacturing business, on Morton Avenue. That transaction took place in May, 1950. It provided the pottery an additional 6000 square feet of floor space just two blocks from the main pottery building. The design and mold department was moved from the Mariceau building to the new facility. Following that move, a new warehouse was built on the north side of the building adding another 3000 square feet of space. That addition made it possible to install a new pusher type automatic tunnel kiln. The kiln was operated with natural gas fuel, and had an automatic temperature indicator. It ran continuously, twenty-four hours a day. Depending on the speed of the automatic pusher, ware could be fired in ten to thirty hours.

The additional area allowed American Art Potteries to reassign production areas. The original building on west Jefferson street was used to house the business office, a sales and display room, and the shipping department. Three small kilns were left at that location to be used for gold decoration and overglazing air brushing. The casting, finishing, and glazing departments were kept there also.

The newly acquired floor space was used for badly needed storage. A pug mill and blunger were installed at the new location, and an underground system was built to pressure pump the slip clay from the blunger to the casting department where it was poured into molds.

The pottery kept as many as thirty employees on its payroll during the 1950's. From 1951 to 1961 the pottery operated at full production. During that time, William Shanemeyer assumed the management and control of the pottery so the Rapps could concentrate on the expansion and production, and not be restricted by the many problems of management. Production continued and increased. The Rapps were once again recouping the reputation they had established in the world of ceramic artisanship.

That recaptured glory did not last. Shanemeyer was not persistent in paying the Internal Revenue taxes for the business. Sometimes, the payments were late. Eventually, he faltered completely. Shanemeyer's problem escalated when on April 26, 1961, the pottery was seized for nonpayment of federal taxes. The business was closed, and the doors at both locations were padlocked. Signs placed on the doors read: "Warning. This property seized for nonpayment of internal revenue taxes by virtue of a levy issued by the District Director of Internal Revenue." The warning was signed by Stanley Decker, the IRS officer in charge of the seizure.

Within a month, Shanemeyer paid the federal liens against the pottery that totaled $11,529 for unpaid social security and unemployment taxes. The pottery was allowed to resume operations early in June, 1961. Despite that first encounter with the IRS, others would come during the next year and a half. On March 15, 1962, local newspapers released information that the pottery was to be sold by the federal government. Sealed bids were to be opened at the pottery business office at 10 a.m. on Friday, March 16th. Figures released at that time showed that the pottery owed a bit more than $5000 for withholding tax, social security, and unemployment compensation contributions. Again, it was stipulated that Shanemeyer could redeem the property by paying the back taxes up to the time that the sealed bids were opened. At 9:45 a.m., just fifteen minutes before the bids were to be opened, Shanemeyer paid tax claims of $5312 and the sale was cancelled. The pottery was again back in business but it was on very shaky ground. By November, 1963, Shanemeyer was having his third go about with the IRS. The pottery was again seized by T-Men and was placed at auction in order to retrieve the money owed to the federal government.

The auction was held at the Jefferson street facility on November 8th at 9:30 a.m. The equipment destined for the auction block was valued at $70,000. The list of items to be sold included office equipment, trucks, processing machinery, and kilns. The buildings were not included in the auction, but thousands of pieces of pottery were.

All of the processing machinery, some molds, and one of the kilns was purchased by the Morton Pottery Company. Though the two potteries had no business relationships, there was a family bond. Both potteries traced their origins back to the six Rapp brothers who originally established the pottery industry in Morton. The American Art Potteries was started by Matthew's sons. The sons of Andrew established the Morton Pottery Company.

Both finished and unfinished pottery sold briskly at the auction. For the most part, finished items were purchased by florists, nursery and garden people, and gift shop owners from as far away as Chicago. Unfinished items went to Cub Scout den mothers and amateur and studio potters. Two Catholic nuns from the Sisters of Alverno Novitiate, 3rd Order of St. Francis bought some of the molds and green ware to be used in ceramic classes at the Novitiate which is located north east of Peoria.

The buildings eventually sold devoid of IRS intervention. The Jefferson street building became a plumbing business for a number of years and has now been remodeled into apartments. The Morton avenue building was purchased by Libby-McNeil and Libby and is used as a machine shop directly across the street from the canning factory that is now a subsidiary of Nestlés.

The four Rapp brothers, Carl, John, Lawrence, and Theodore, have all passed on. Though they all had children, none of the third generation has made pottery production their vocation. However, they take pride in the art pottery their fathers and grandfathers created.

AMERICAN ART POTTERIES

DOLL PARTS

The doll heads, arms, and legs were reproductions of old German porcelain doll parts. They are not porcelain, but low fired ceramic of average quality. They show a strong resemblance to the old dolls from which they were copied.

The doll parts were made for a wholesaler in Indiana. They were packaged with instructions and material for making the cloth bodies. The facial features and hair are handpainted underglaze. Each part received two coats of spray glaze, one before decorating, then another after the decoration was completed. The second spray created the proper skin tone.

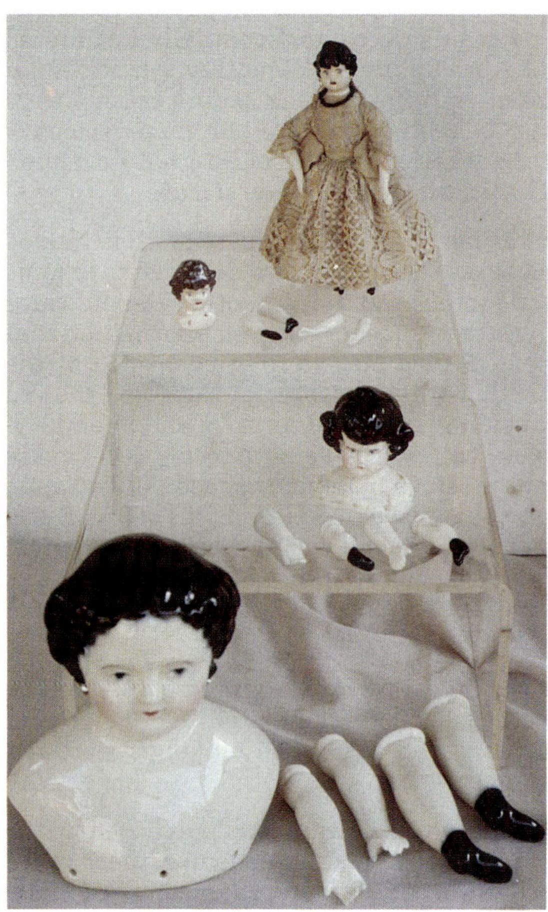

The doll heads measure 11/2" (top), 3" (middle), and 7 1/4" (bottom). The doll wears a dress fashioned from the wedding dress worn by Doris's mother.

The value ranges are for heads and appendages only. A doll with body and fully dressed should command 100% more.

11/2" head and appendages $60-70
3" head and appendages $50-60
71/4" head and appendages $80-90

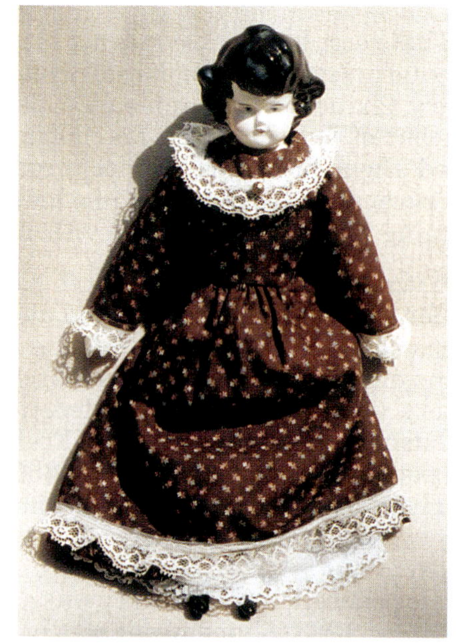

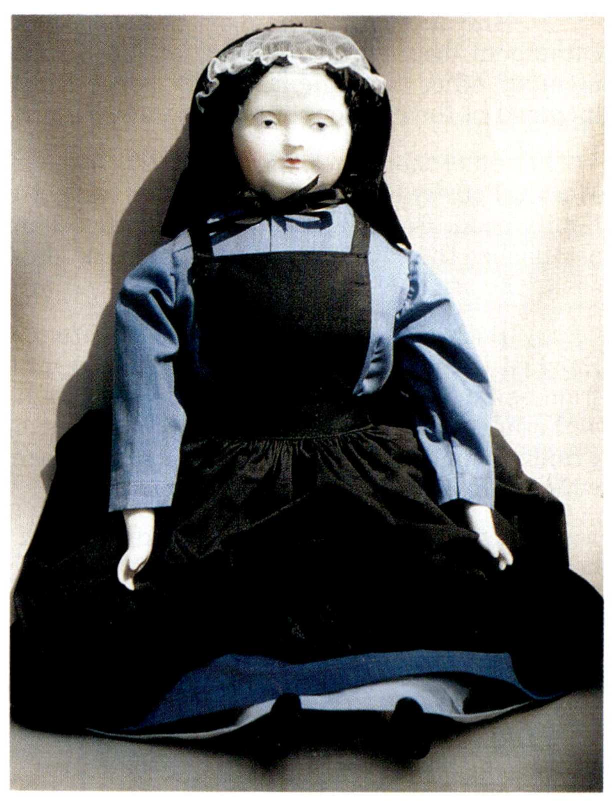

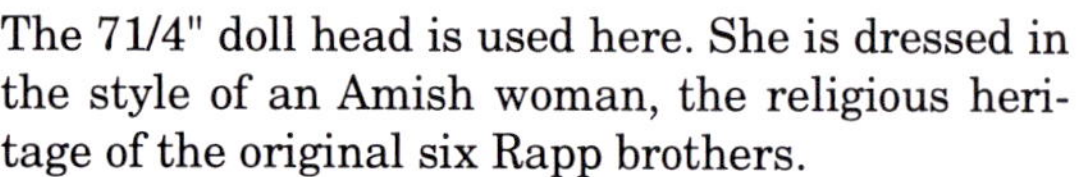

The 71/4" doll head is used here. She is dressed in the style of an Amish woman, the religious heritage of the original six Rapp brothers.

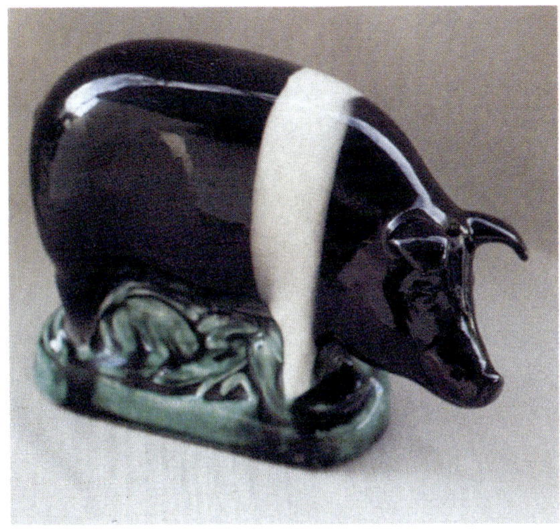

The hampshire hog was made as a planter as well as a figurine. The ears and tail were molded separately and applied by hand. The hog will also be found as a bank, but the bank was made by Morton Pottery Company from molds purchased at the American Art Potteries bankruptcy auction. The hog is 5 1/2" tall.

Value Range: $30-35

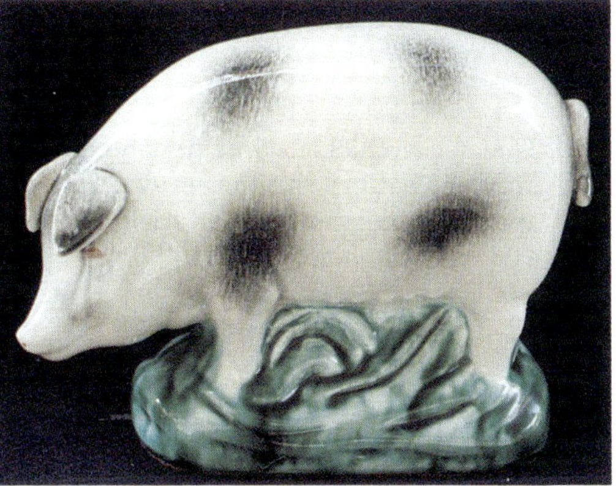

This is the same hog mold, but it has been decorated to resemble a Poland China hog.

Value Range: $35-40

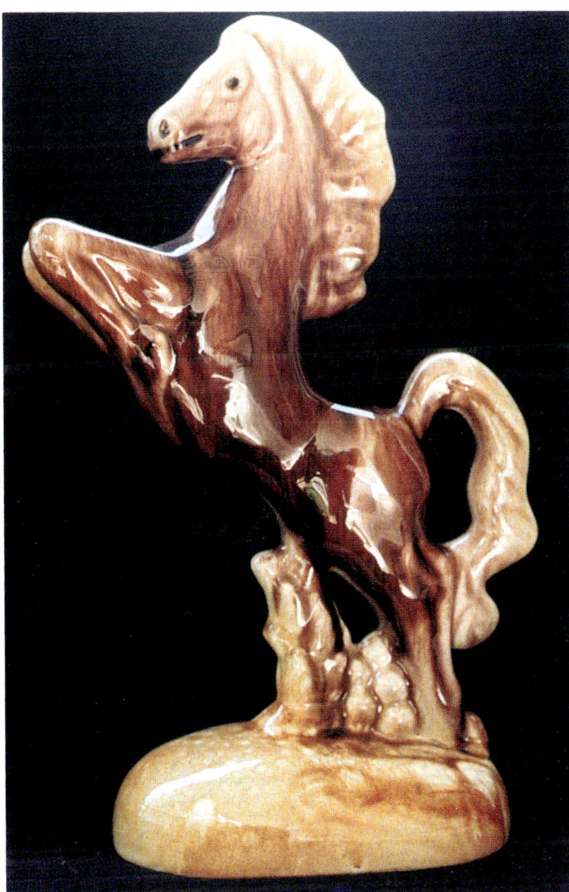

The wild horse is 11 1/2" tall. It is a carry over from the Midwest Pottery with slight changes.

Value Range: $30-35

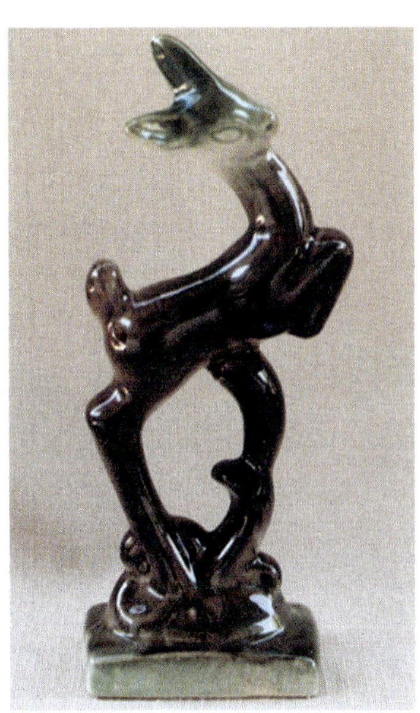

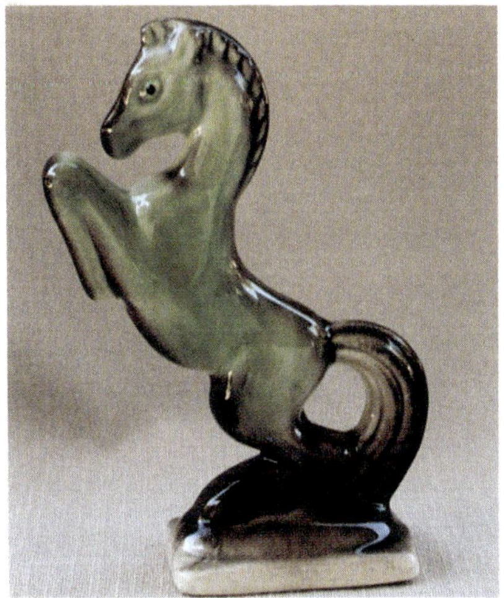

These are also carry overs from the Midwest pottery. The horse is an exact copy. The fawn has a slightly different base and front support. The air brushing (spray glazing) technique sets them apart from Midwest's.

Value Range: Fawn $14-18
Horse $12-16

This set of chickens was first produced at the Midwest Pottery, but the spray glaze sets them apart as American Art Potteries. The rooster is 4 1/2" tall, the hen is 3" tall.

Value Range: $18-22 set

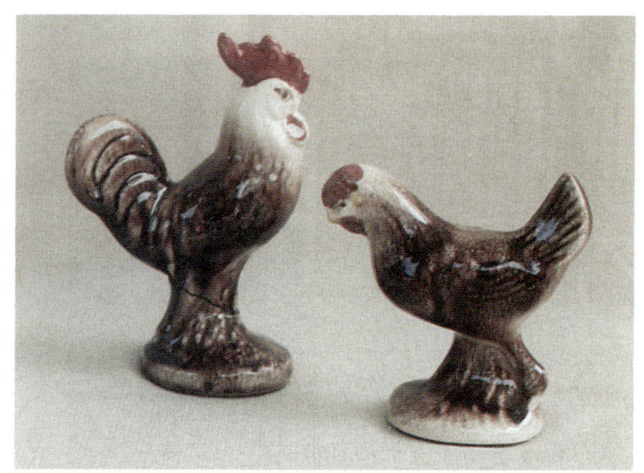

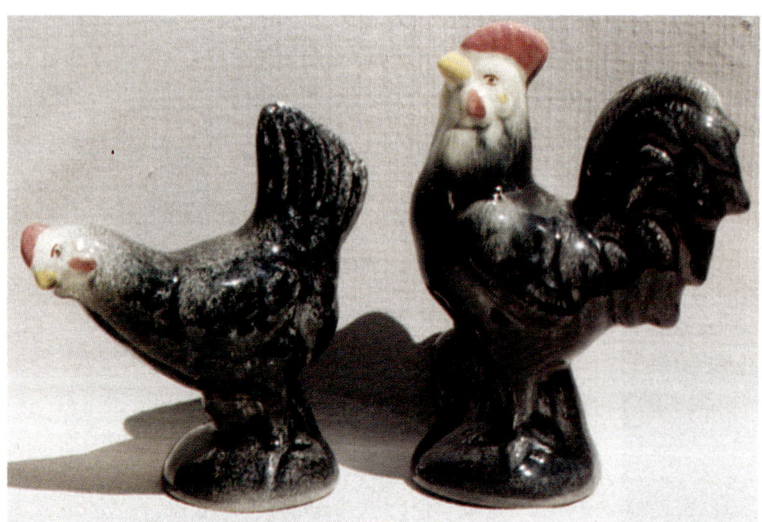

The larger set of chickens is similar to those made at the Midwest Pottery, but are not as well refined. The combs and beaks are hand applied underglaze. The rooster is 8" tall. The hen is 6 1/2" tall.

Value Range: $25-30 set

The squirrel is 5 1/2" tall. It was also made with a planter base.

Value Range: $15-20
Deduct 10% for the planter

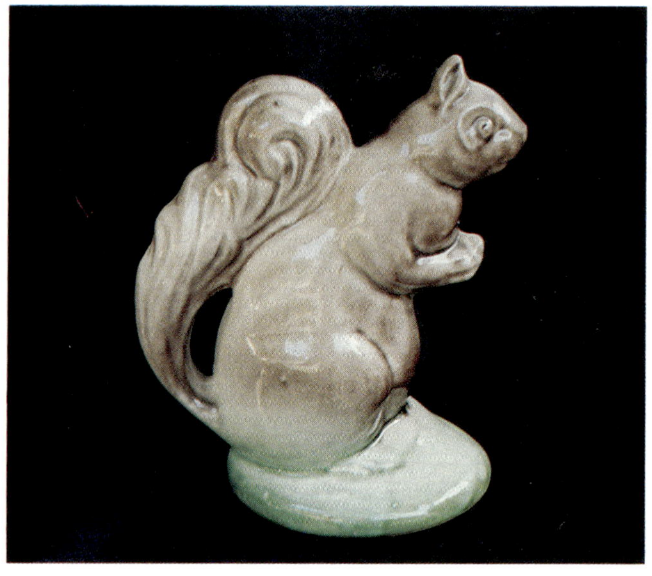

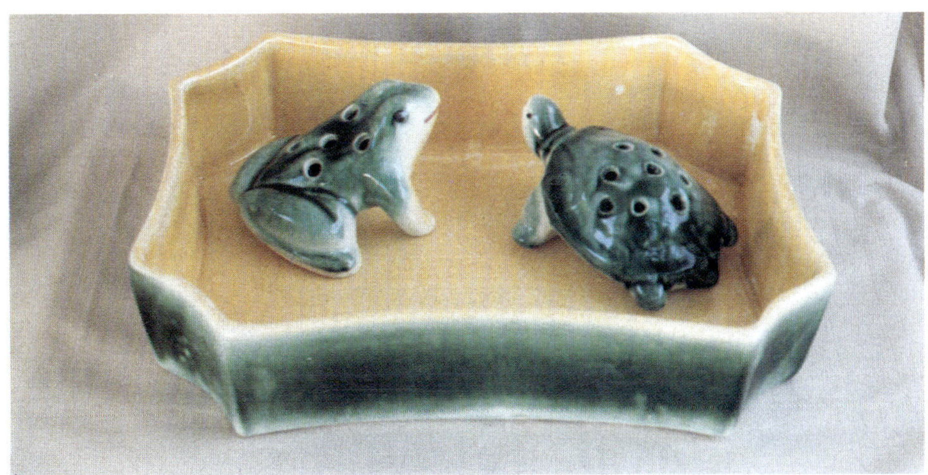

The rectangular flower bowl is 2" x 10" x 6". It is an unusual octagonal shape. The frog is 21/2" tall. The turtle is 2" tall.

Value Range:
Bowl $5-10
Turtle $10-12
Frog $10-12
Complete Set $25-35

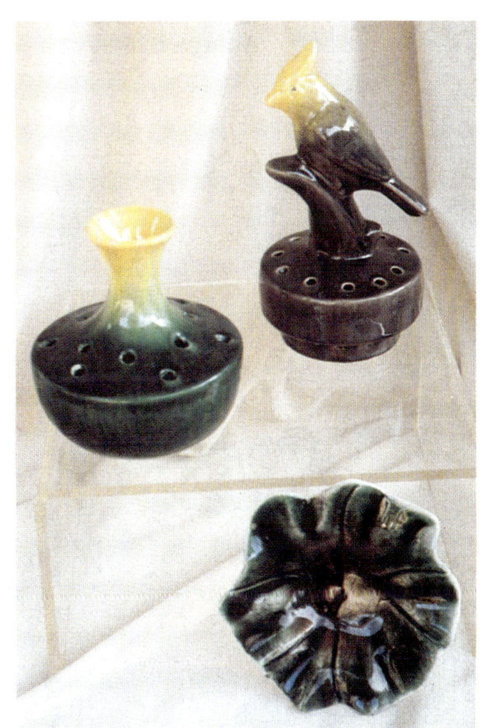

The vase with perforations for flower stems is 43/4" tall.
Value Range: $10-15

The tufted titmouse is 8" tall.
Value Range: $15-20

The bowl is 51/2" in diameter. It was made to float small, short stem flowers.
Value Range: $4-8

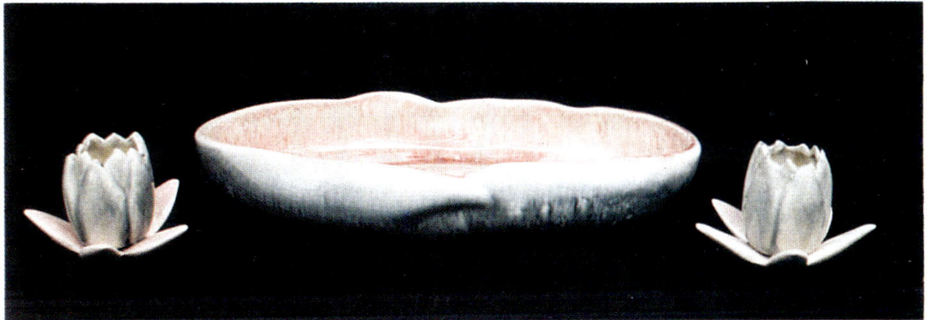

The console set has a stylized petal design. The bowl is 10" x 61/2" x 13/4". The candle holders are 13/4" tall.

Value Range: Bowl $5-10
Candle holder $8-12 each Complete set $20-25

LAMPS

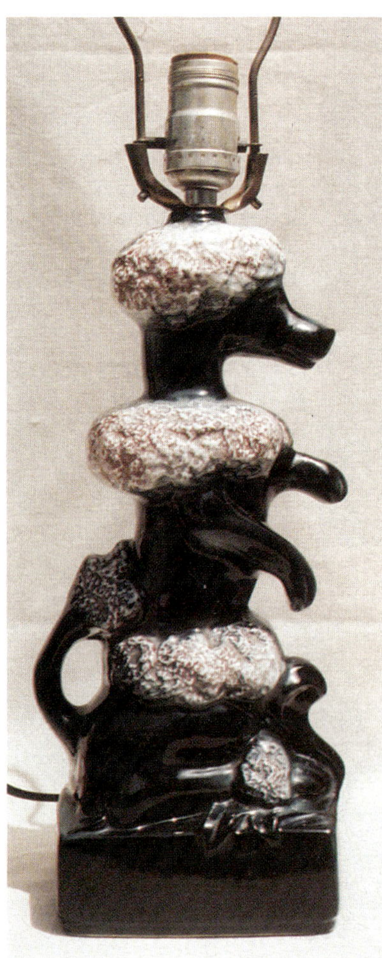

The poodle lamp is 15" tall. – **Value Range: $25-30**

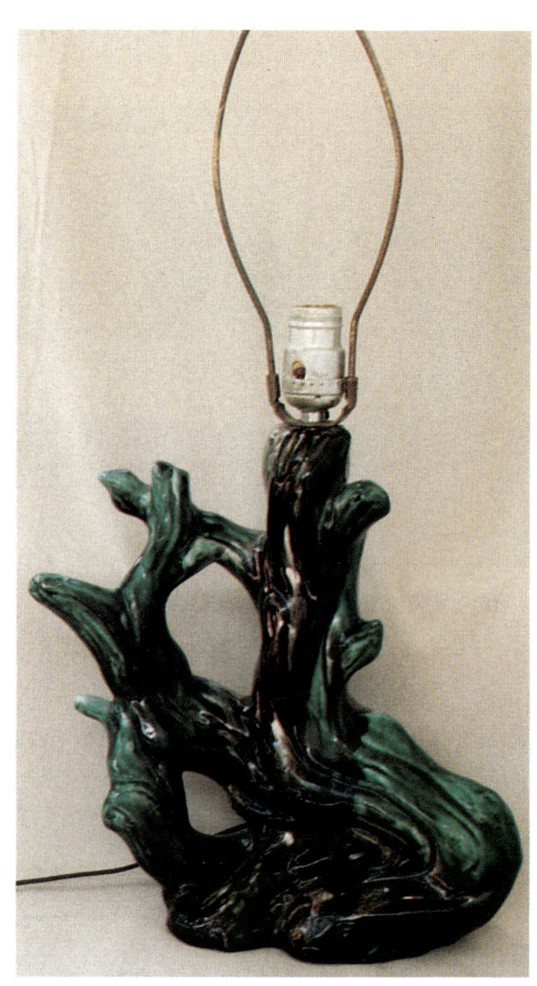

The gnarled tree trunk is 12" tall.
Value Range: $20-25

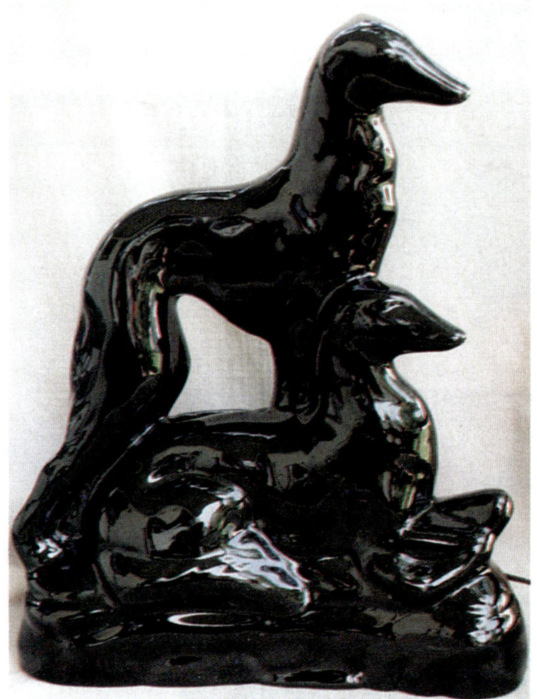

The pair of Afghan hounds is 15" tall. This one is a TV lamp. The lamp was also wired with a brass rod that supported a fixture and a large shade above the hounds.

Value Range: TV Lamp $45-55 Lamp $65-75

The fish TV lamp is 6" x 9" x 3 1/2". A tubular globe fits behind the rectangular base.

Value Range: $20-25

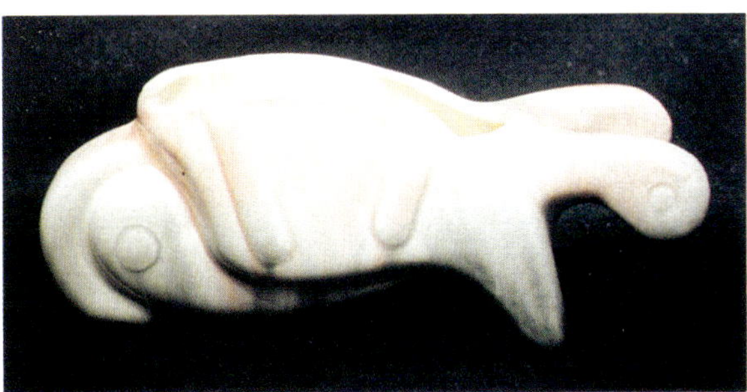

This wheelbarrow is 21/2" tall and 61/2" long. Upon close examination, the wheelbarrow has the appearance of a parrot.

Value Range: $8-12

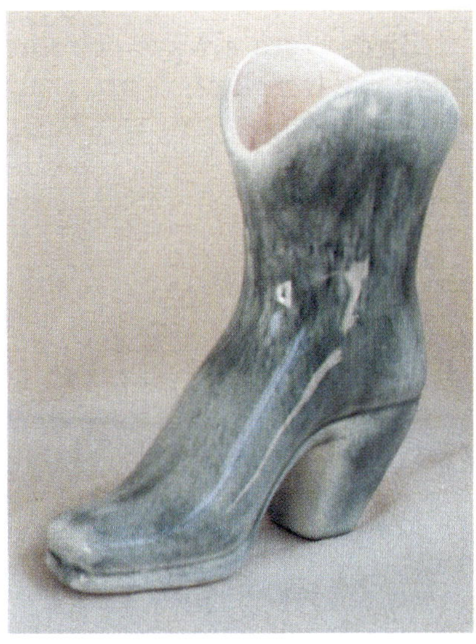

The cowboy boot is 5" tall.
Value Range: $10-15

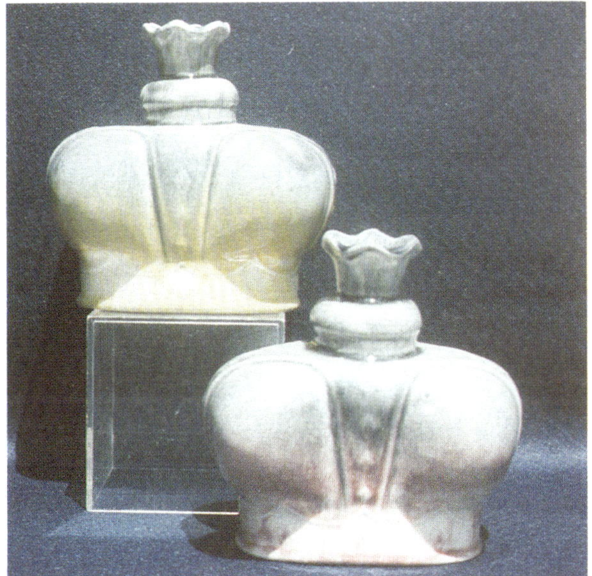

The crown bottles were made to hold after shave lotion. They are 6" tall.

Value Range: $12-18 each

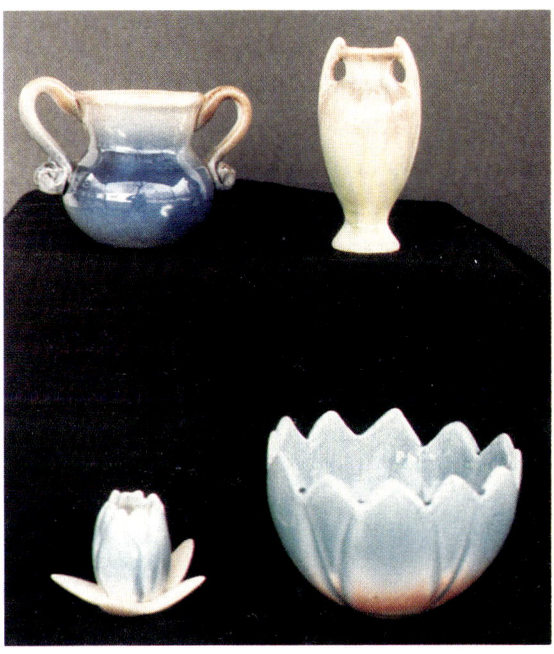

The handled, bulbous vase (top left) could easily be used as a sugar bowl. It is 3" tall.
Value Range: $8-10

The slender, handled vase is 4" tall.
Value Range: $6-10

The candle holder was also sold as a toothpick holder. It is 13/4" tall.
Value Range: $8-12

The petal bowl is 31/4" tall. It was referred to as the water lily bowl at the pottery.
Value Range: $10-15

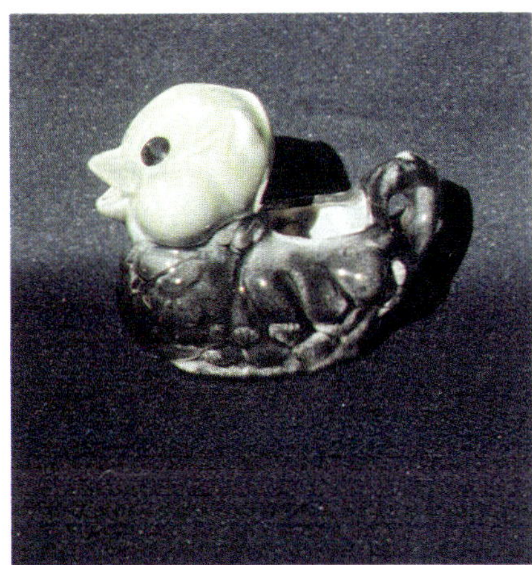

This bird creamer has an open beak for pouring. The tail is designed to be used as a handle.

Value Range: $10-15

PLANTERS

Birds were always popular designs by Lawrence Rapp. His birds were somewhat stylized. The log planters are reminiscent of the Cliftwood Pottery's tree trunk line.

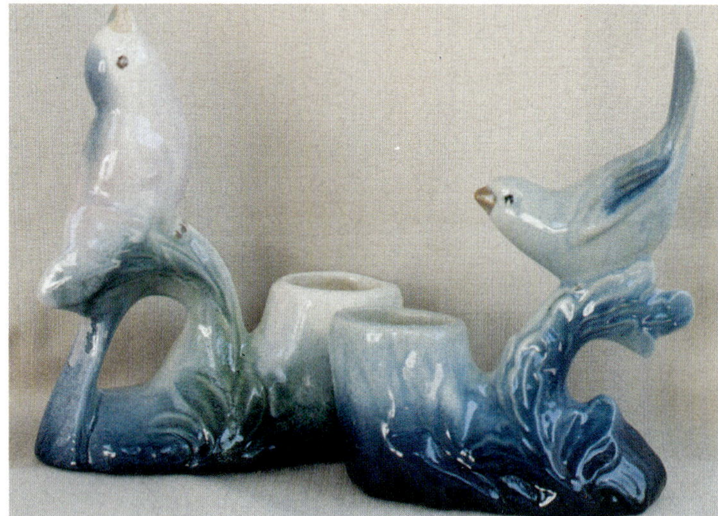

Value Range: $12-18 each

It was not unusual for birds to be separated from the planter base to be used as a figurine.

Value Range: Figurine $10-14
Planter $12-18

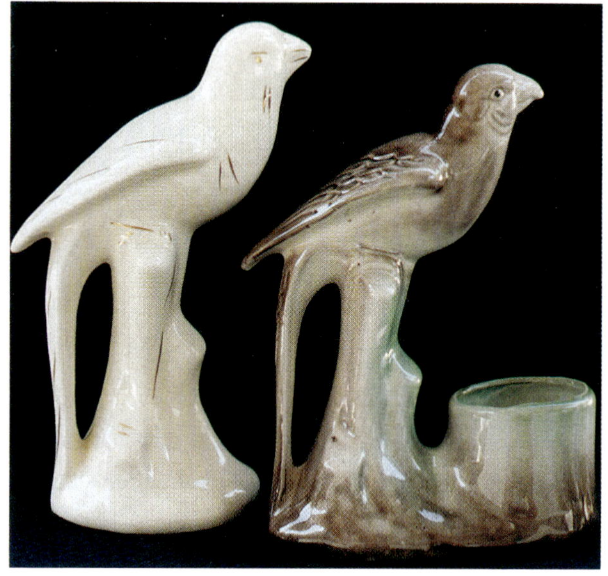

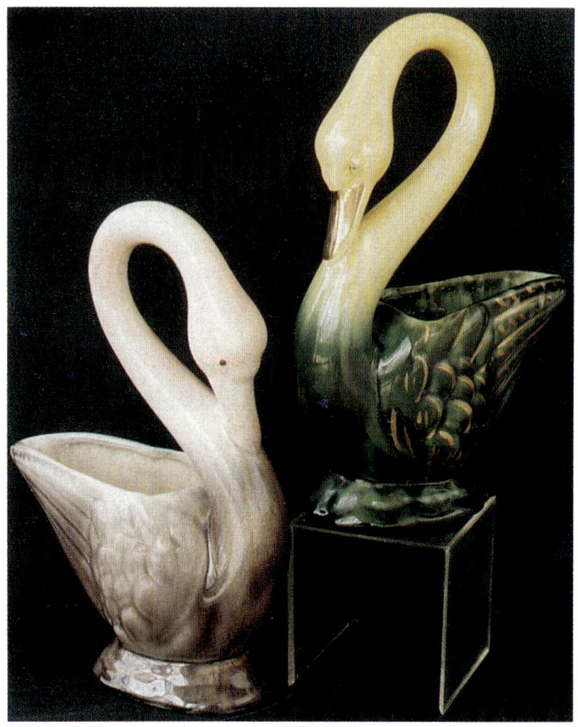

The swan planter is 10 1/4" tall.

Value Range: $20-25
Add 10% for gold decoration.

This grotesque duck planter is 5 1/2" tall. It was a popular item in the pottery showroom.

Value Range: $10-14

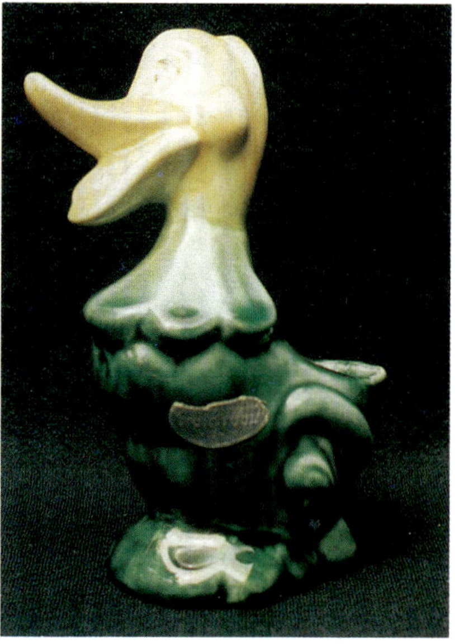

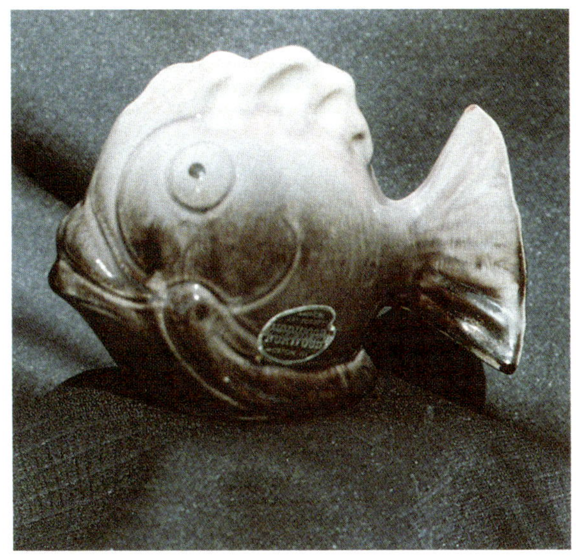

This fish planter is 41/2" tall. It is the fish that was used on the TV lamp.

Value Range: $12-14

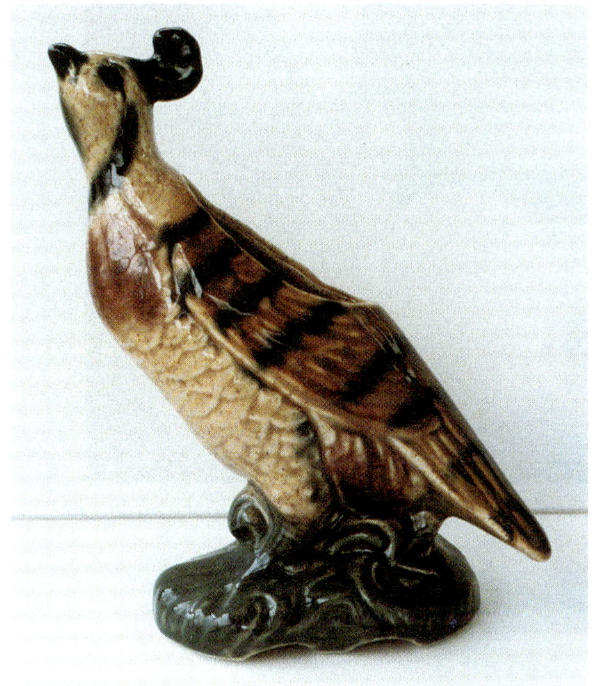

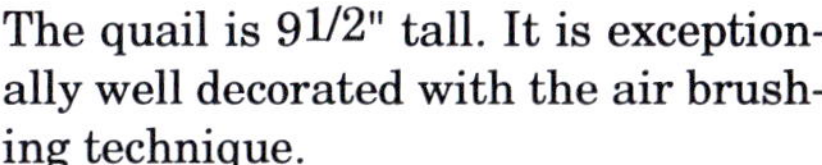

The quail is 91/2" tall. It is exceptionally well decorated with the air brushing technique.

Value Range: $25-30

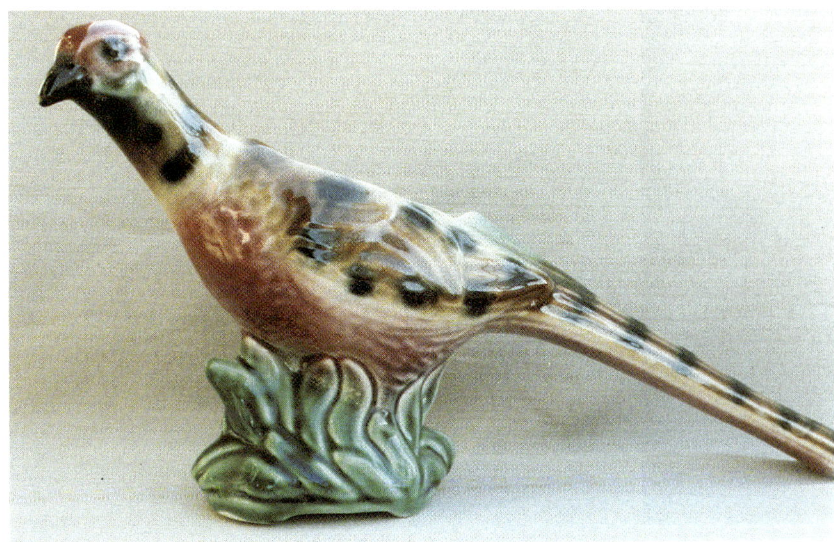

The pheasant is 81/2" tall, and is 18" long. The tail is fragile.

Value Range: $25-35

The teddy bear on three blocks was a favorite gift for newborn children. It is 12" x 4" x 4". The bear is 6" tall.

Value Range: $18-24

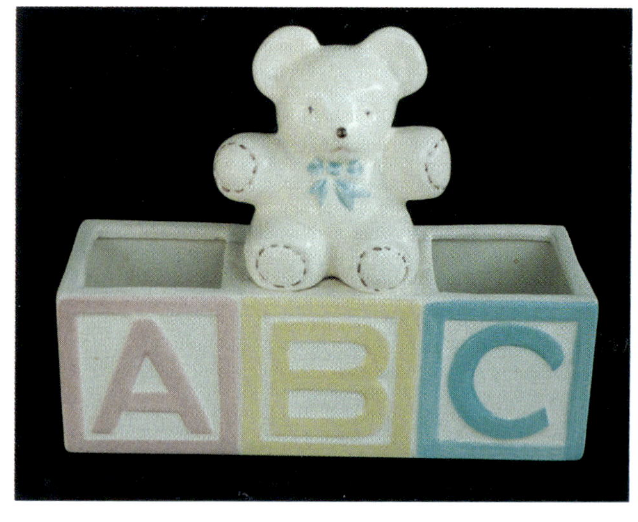

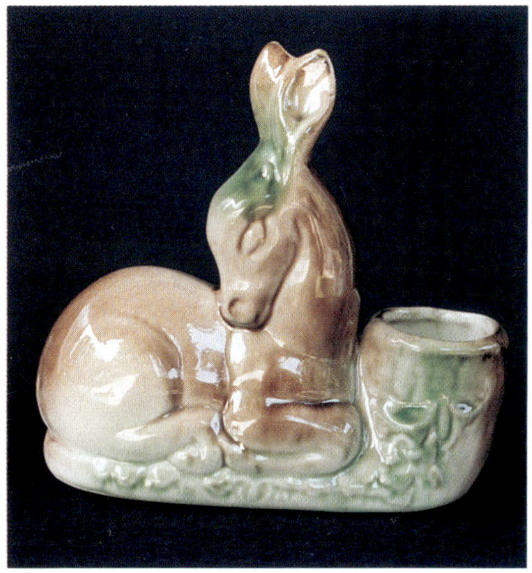

The deer has a planter base similar to the birds. It is 5" tall.

Value Range: $14-18

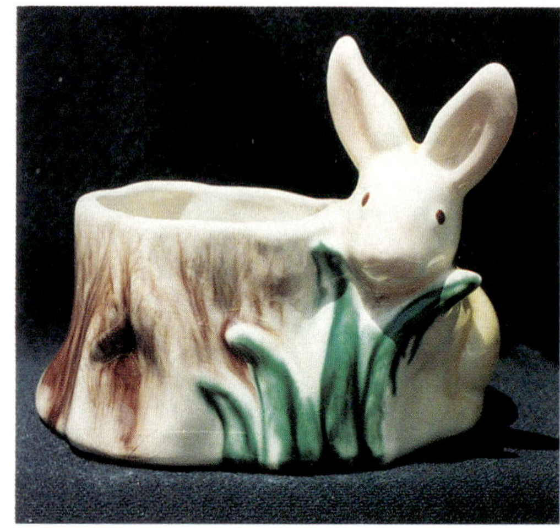

The bunny behind the log is $4\frac{3}{4}$" tall.

Value Range: $14-18

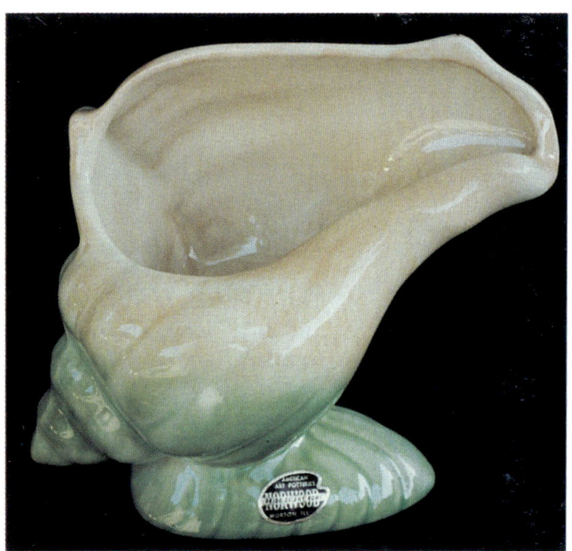

The conch shell is 6" tall. It was also drilled and wired to be used as a TV light.

Value Range: Planter $16-20
TV Lamp $25-30

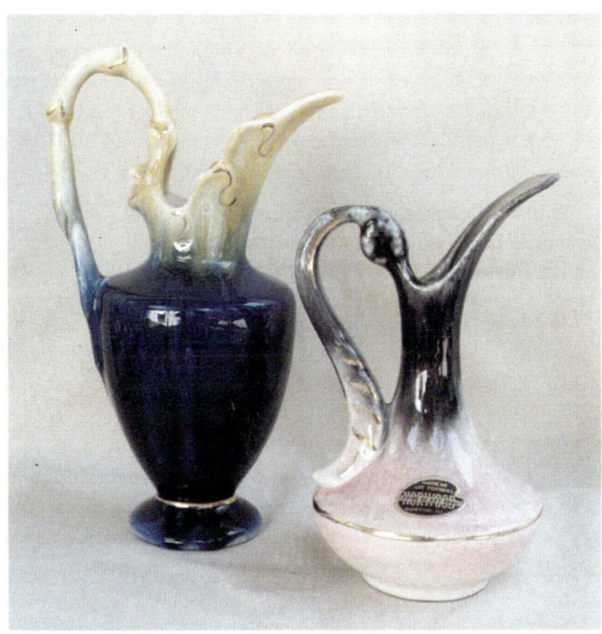

These are the two styles of ewer vases made by American Art Potteries. Both have 14K gold decoration. The vase on the left is 8 1/2" tall. The vase on the right is 6 3/4" tall.

Value Range: $22-24 (left) & $18-20 (right)

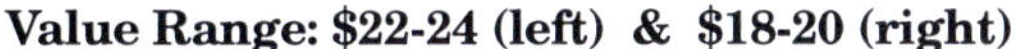

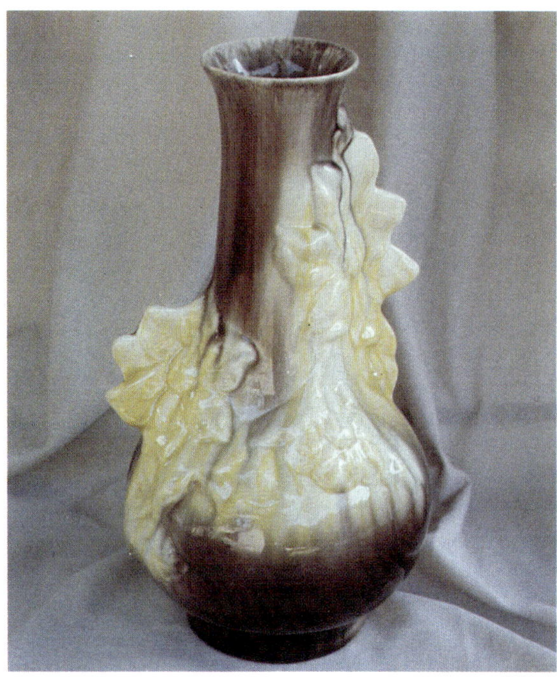

This bulbous vase has molded clusters of flowers on each side. It is 12 3/4" tall.

Value Range: $35-45

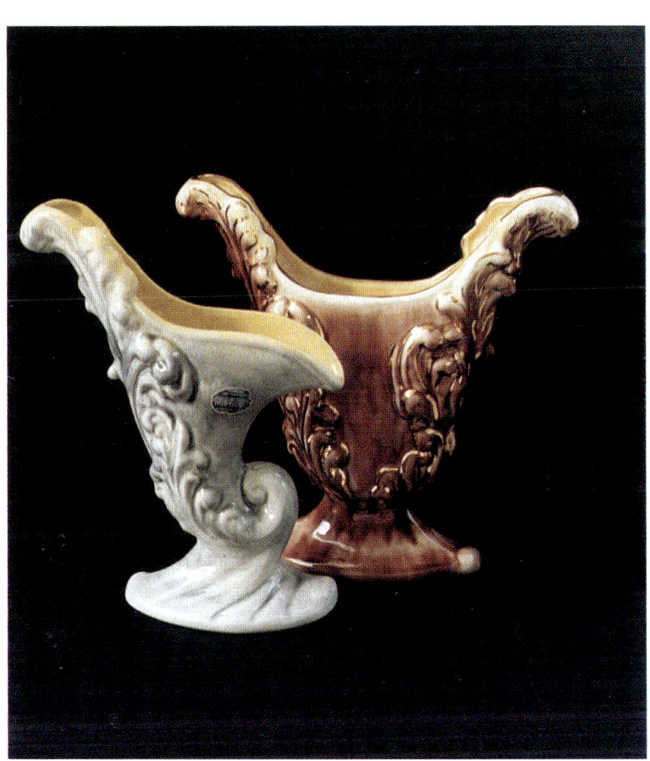

The feathered cornucopia vase is 10 1/2" tall.

Value Range: $25-30 Single
$35-45 Double

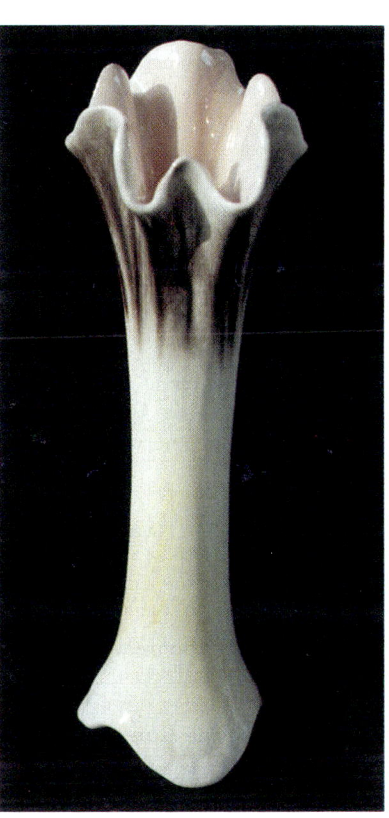

This ruffled tulip vase is 9" tall. It was copied from a glass vase that had belonged to Burdell's grandmother.

Value Range: $18-24

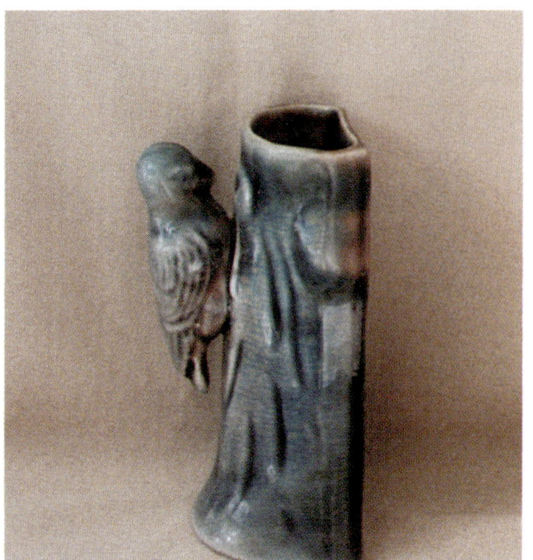

This wall pocket closely resembles the tree trunk line book ends made by Cliftwood Art Potteries. It is 5" tall.

Value Range: $14-18

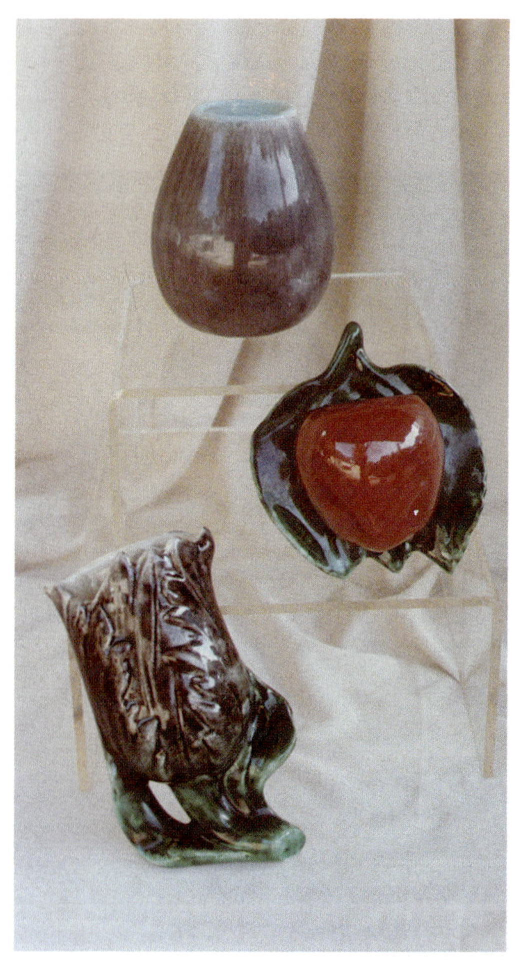

The pear shape wall pocket at the top of the photograph is 5 1/2" tall.

Value Range: $10-15

The apple is very similar to the wall pocket made by McCoy Pottery. The McCoy apple has two branches instead of one.

Value Range: $12-18

The chrysanthemum type flower wall pocket is 8" tall.

Value Range: $18-22

PART V

MORTON POTTERY COMPANY

1922-1976

Morton Pottery Company was cloned from the Morton Pottery Works and the Morton Earthenware Company. Molds for tea pots, pudding dishes, bean pots, coffee pots, mixing bowls, bakers, and storage jars from both of those potteries had been saved and were used for production in the early period of this new pottery.

Two of the incorporators, Daniel W. Rapp, and William Rapp, had been affiliated with the Morton Pottery Works and the Morton Earthenware Company. J.E. Gerber, the third incorporator, purchased the old pottery building and moved the serviceable equipment across town to the new pottery location.

According to incorporation papers filed with the Illinois Secretary of State, Louis L. Emmerson, on December 8, 1922, Gerber and two Rapps comprised the first board of directors.

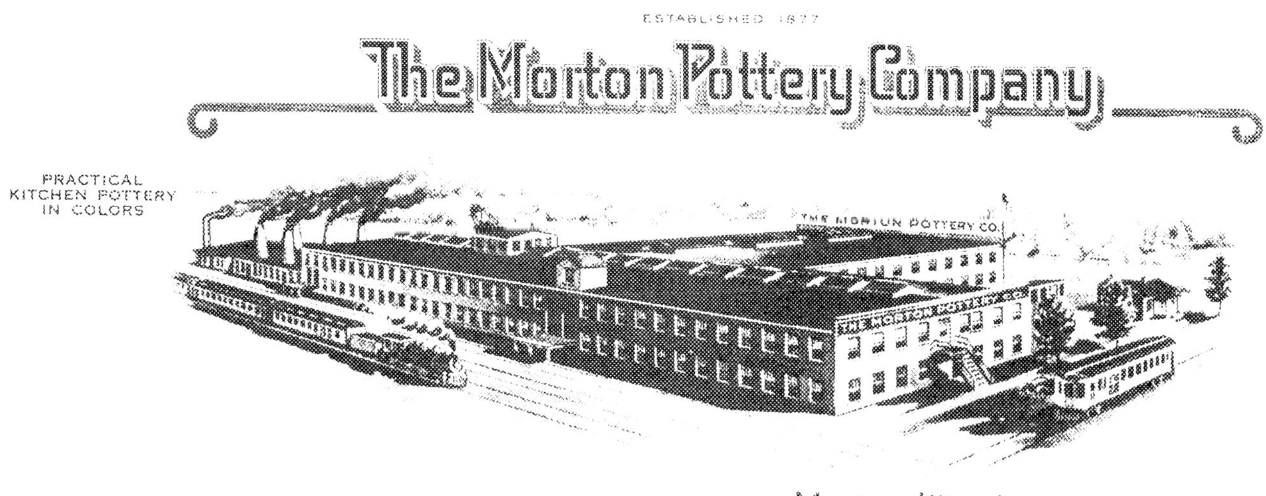

This letterhead, used by the pottery when it began production in 1923, was made from an architect's drawing. It clearly shows the five bottle kilns. The wing to the right of the midsection burned in October, 1923, and was not rebuilt. The date of establishment is erroneous. That date refers to the beginning of Morton Pottery Works, not Morton Pottery Company.

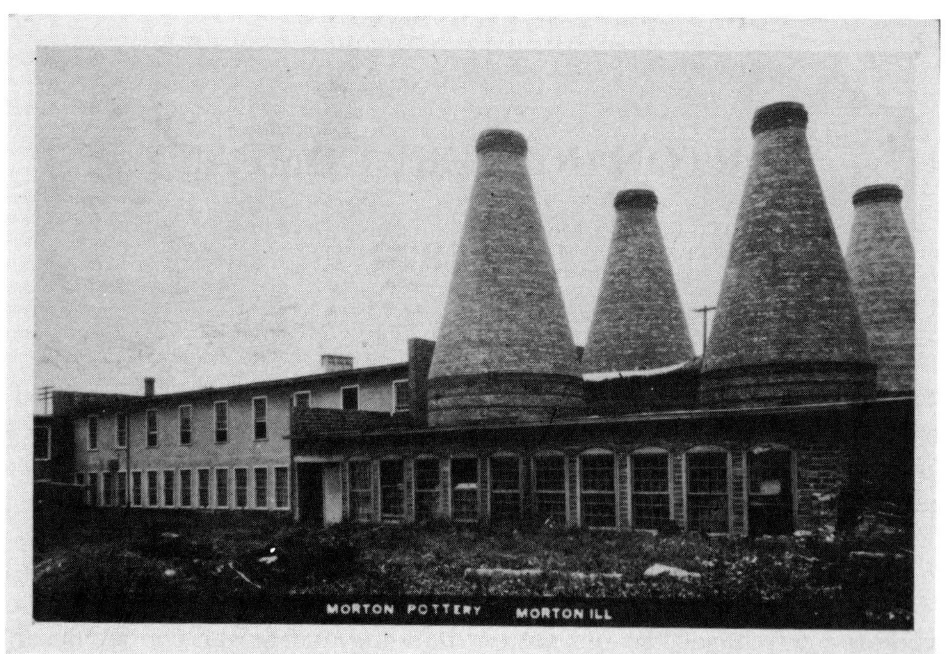

This photograph shows the back of the pottery around 1924. There were five updraft bottle kilns operating when the pottery began production in 1923. Only four can be seen here. Those kilns were replaced by a continuous firing Dressler tunnel kiln in 1934. An Allied circular muffle kiln was installed in 1940. When ceramic tile went into the line of products in 1958, a longer tunnel kiln was built in a specially constructed steel building that housed the new tile manufactory.

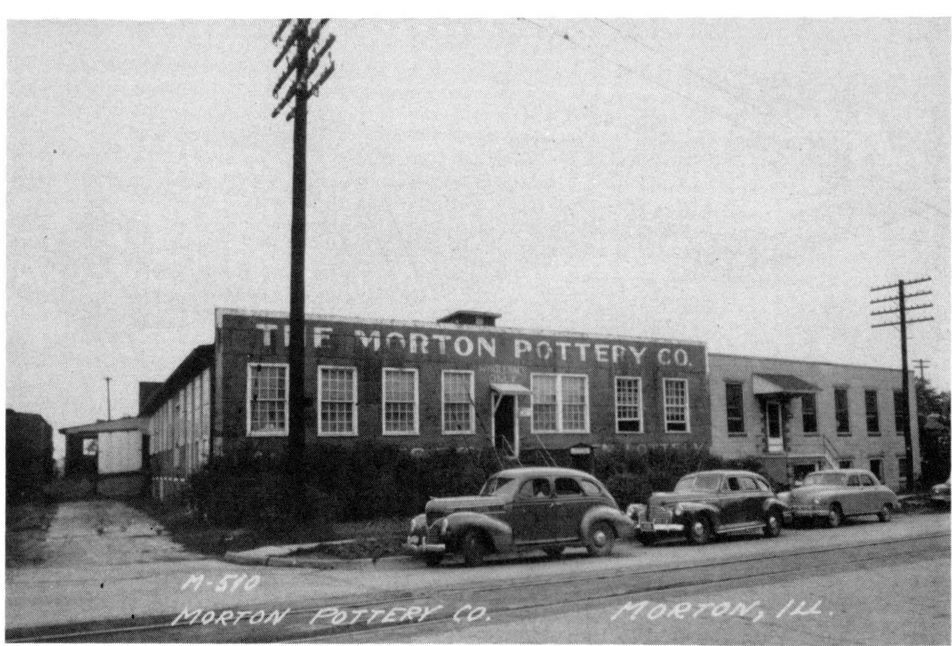

Here is a view of the pottery after the bottle kilns were removed. The new wing, on the right, was added to increase office space and to house the new circular kiln that was installed in 1940.

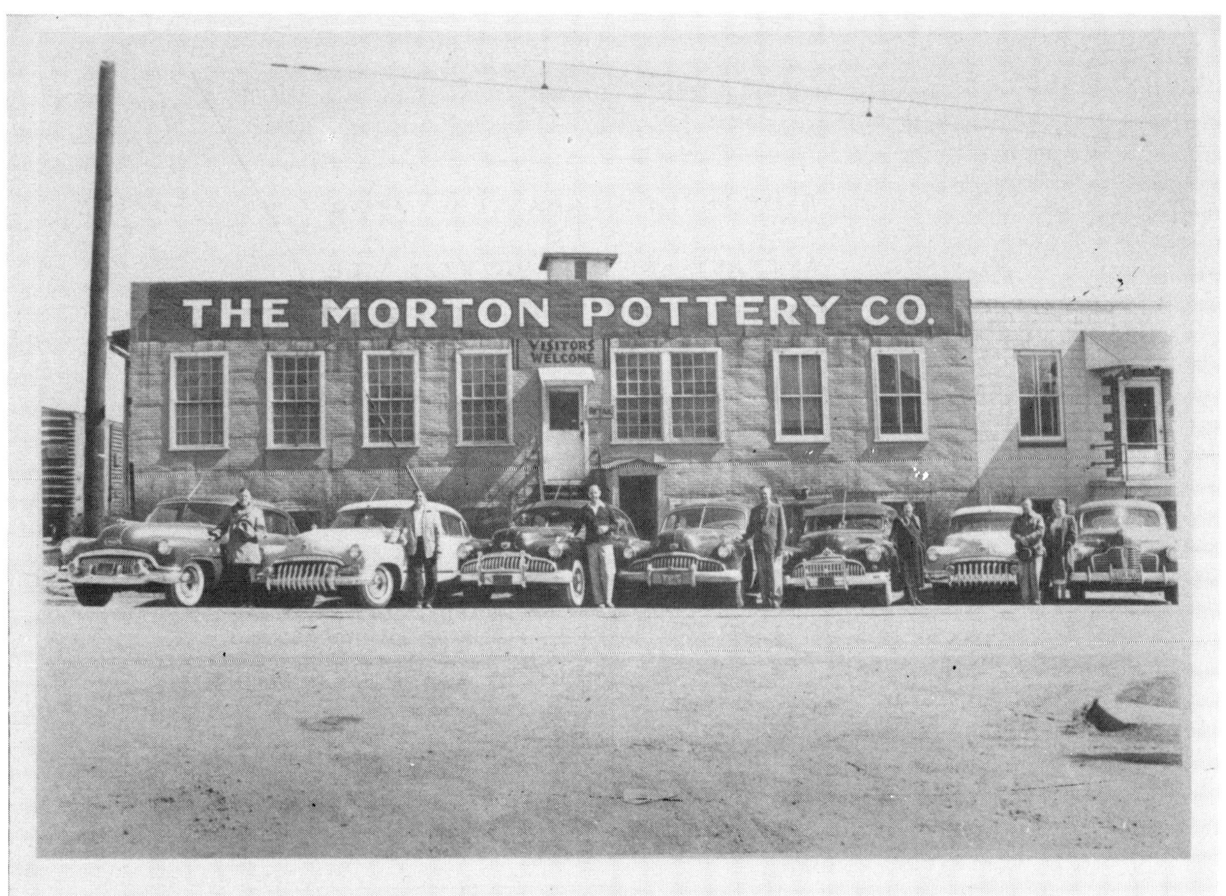

This photograph shows some of the Rapp brothers and sisters posing with their Buicks in front of the pottery. From left to right, they are Henry Rapp, Nathan Rapp, Solomon Rapp, Dan Rapp, Emma Rapp, Samuel Rapp, and Sally Rapp. The men all had responsibilities in the factory. Emma was a decorator, and Sally worked in the business office.

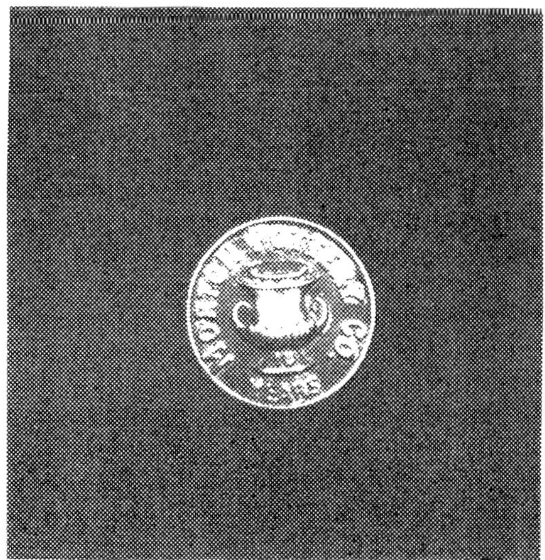

This is the type of bronze service pin that was given to the employees of Morton Pottery Company at annual recognition dinners. Pins were given for 5, 10, 15, and 20 years of service to the pottery.

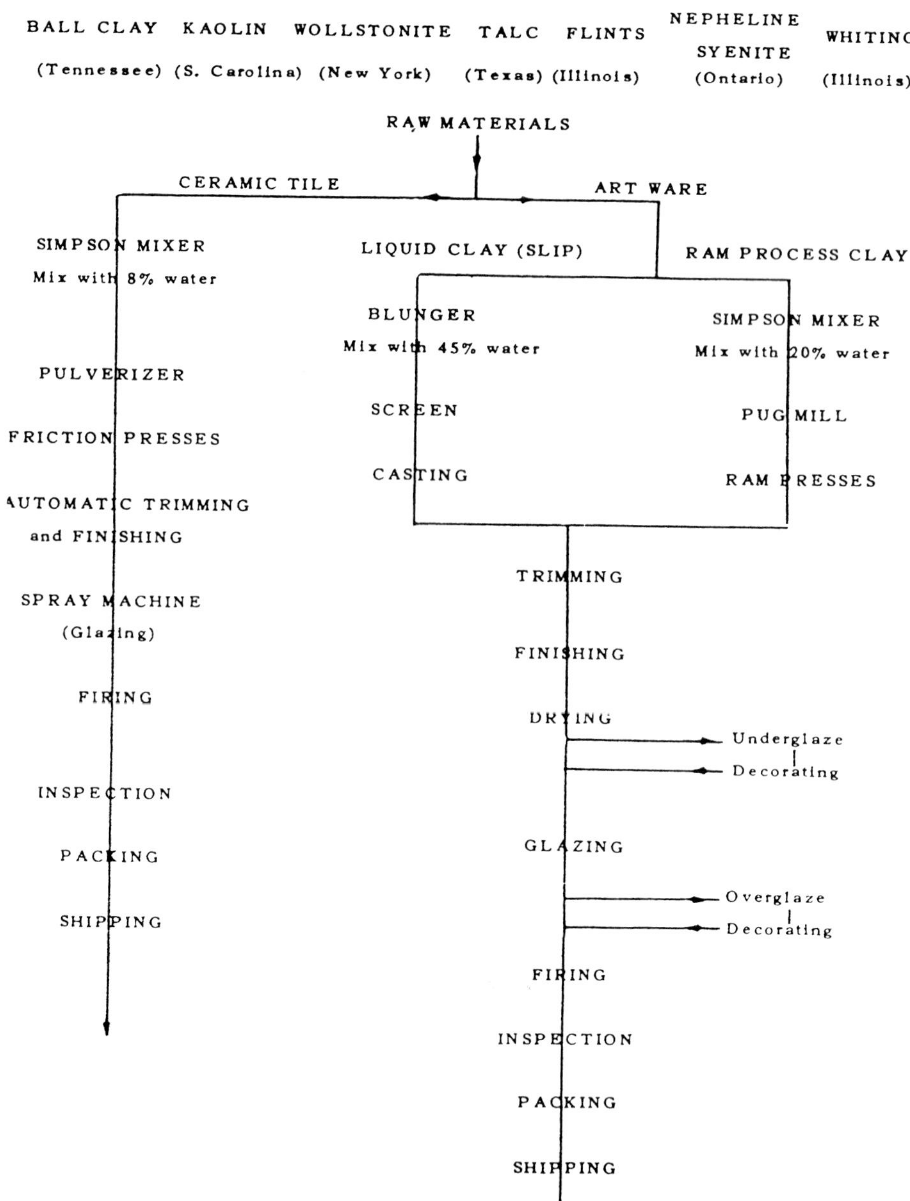

Here is an outline of the methods used to make pottery at Morton Pottery Company. Seldom is such a step by step explanation of production so simply and clearly stated. This is a page from a ten page booklet that sold in the pottery showroom for ten cents a copy. The booklet was very popular with tour groups.

MORTON POTTERY COMPANY MARKS

The following marks were used at various times during the fifty-four years of production at Morton Pottery Company.

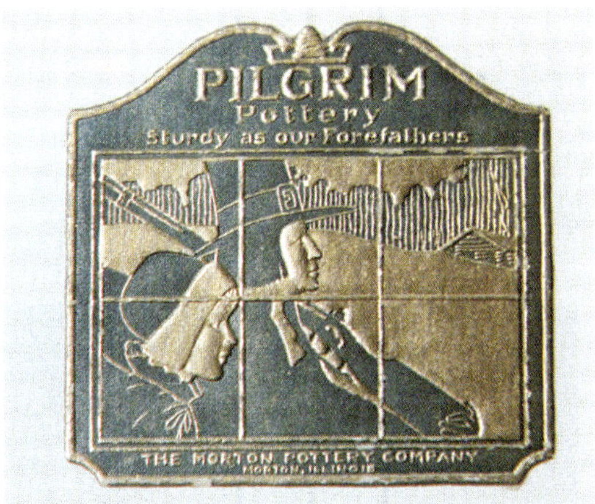

This foil seal was used in 1926 when the Pilgrim line of pottery was first introduced.

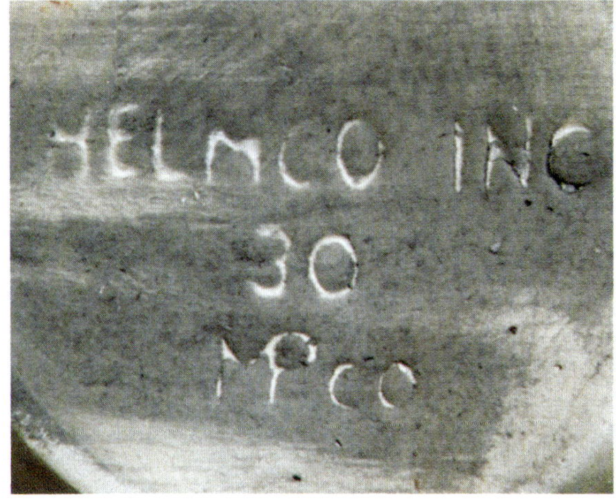

The Helmco mark is the only one found, to date, that uses the letters MP instead of the full name. Helmco was a wholesale grocer in Bloomington, Illinois. This mark is usually found on quart size stoneware lard jars.

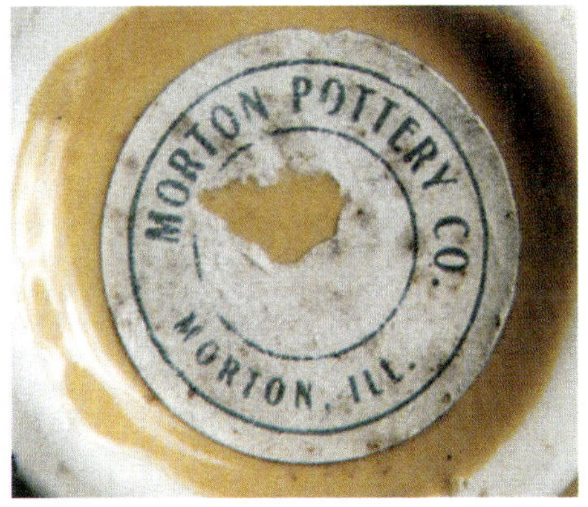

White paper labels were printed on inferior paper made from rag pulp. Few of them have survived.

Note the winged style of this mark. We refer to it as the "feather mark." The line number 3691 indicated that the piece of pottery is a chip and dip bowl.

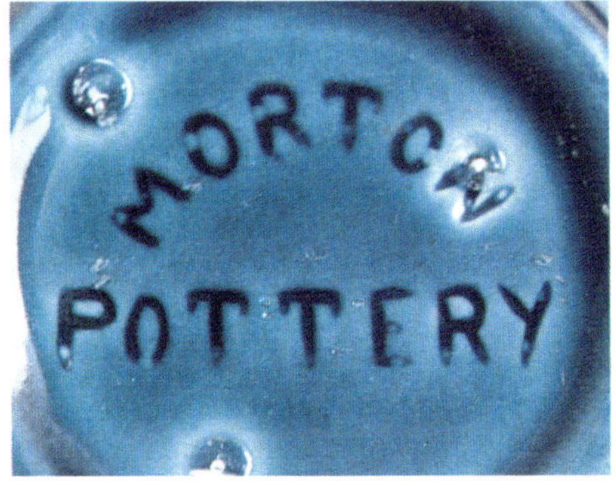

Here is one of the more common incised, in mold marks used at the pottery.

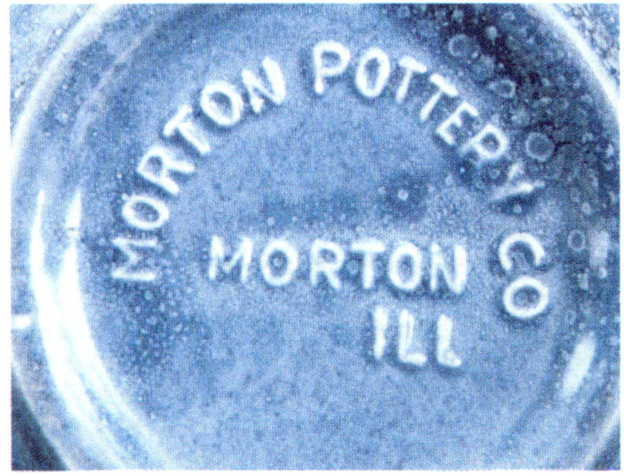

This mark is similar to #5, but it is a raised, in mold mark. It has the location of the pottery. This mark is very elusive.

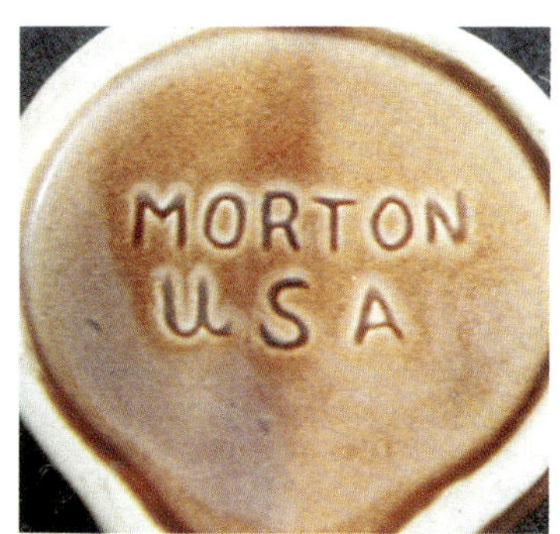

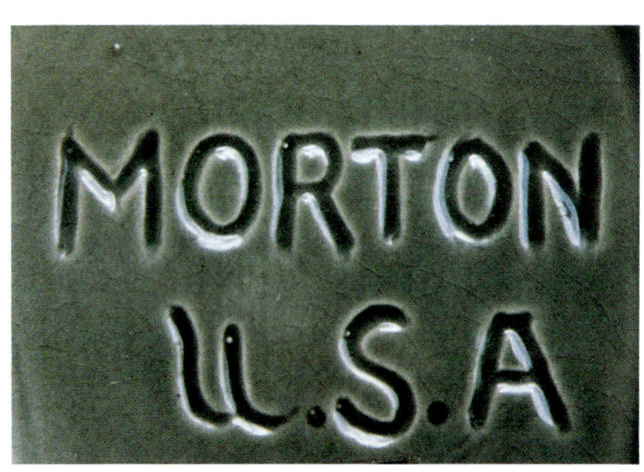

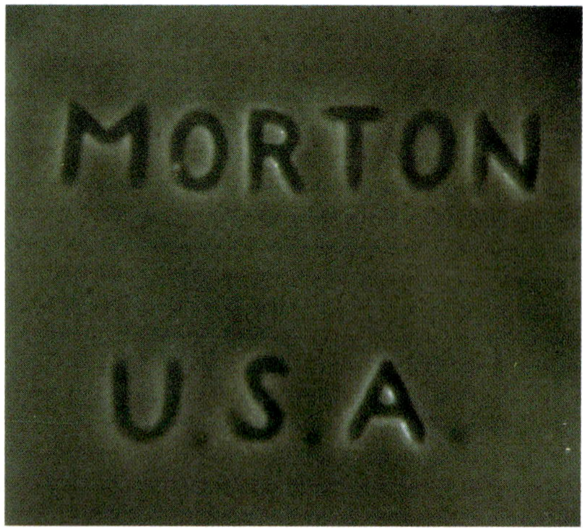

These are all incised, in mold marks that appear to be the same. Upon close examination, there are significant differences in the placement of the periods in "USA", and the style of the U.

This is an ink stamp found on the unglazed bottom of a picture frame. It was most likely made to stamp envelopes and invoices.

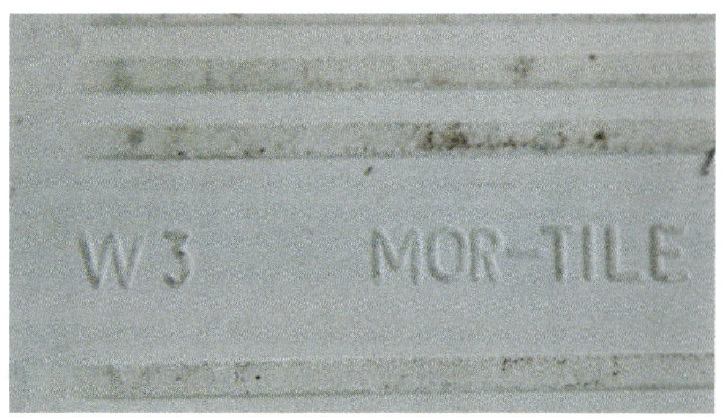

This mark is found only on ceramic tile that went on line in 1956. Letters and numbers were used to identify colors.

This mark is found only on the bottom of the no-spot pitcher. It was used while the patent was being processed.

Incised

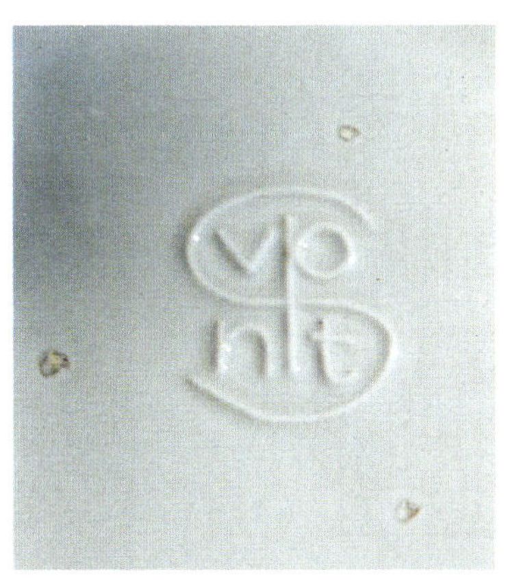

Raised

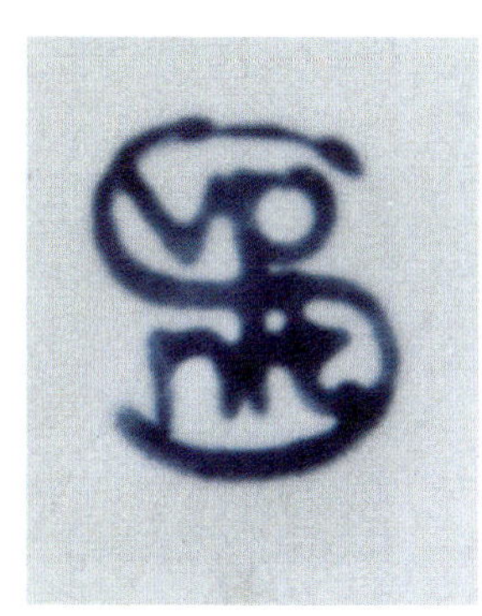

Ink Stamp

The incised and raised in mold marks, were placed on items made for Sears and Roebuck and Company in 1967 and 1968. Known as the Vincent Price mark, (see the historical sketch,) they are rare. This mark was also done as an ink stamp.

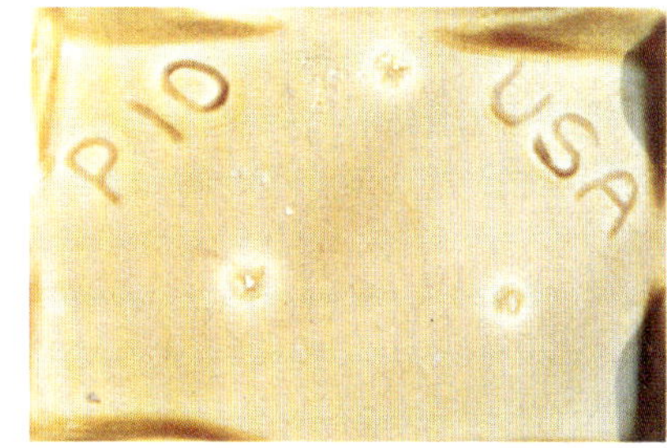

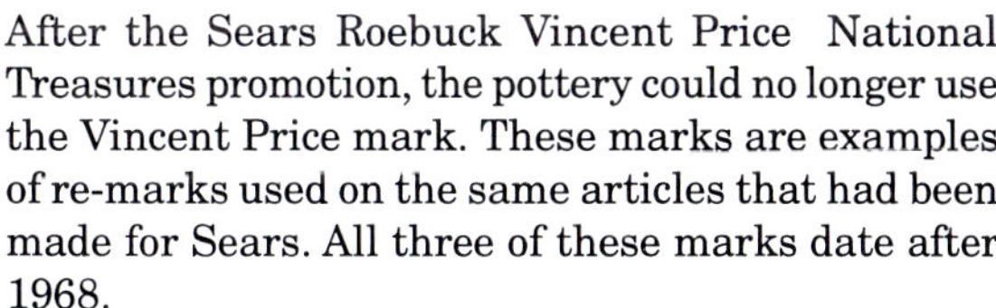

After the Sears Roebuck Vincent Price National Treasures promotion, the pottery could no longer use the Vincent Price mark. These marks are examples of re-marks used on the same articles that had been made for Sears. All three of these marks date after 1968.

This is the last known paper label to be used by the Rapps before they sold the pottery in 1969.

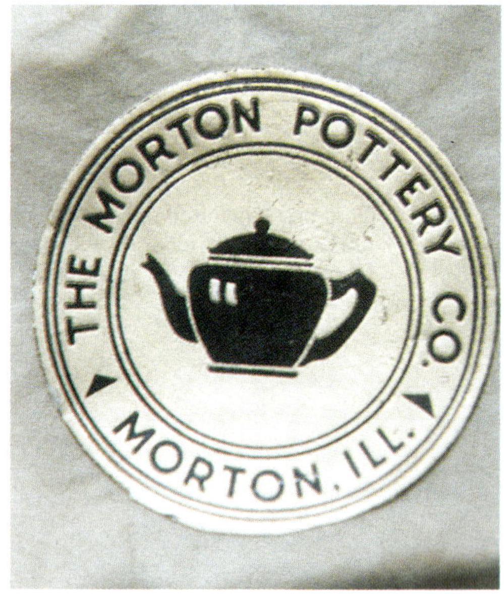

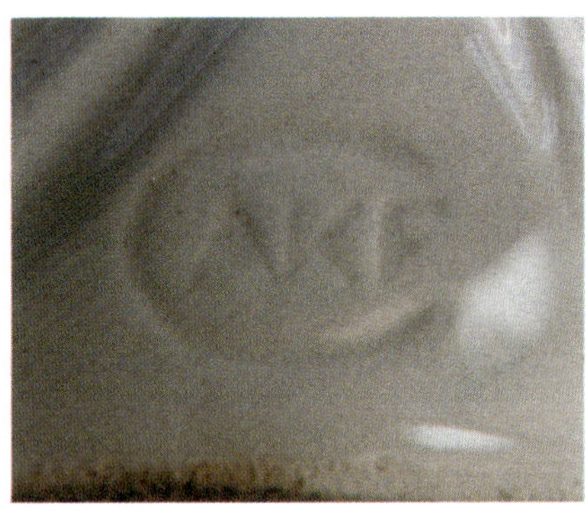

The AKF mark was in use only from March, 1971, until October, 1972. It is seldom found on any item other than the panda cookie jar.

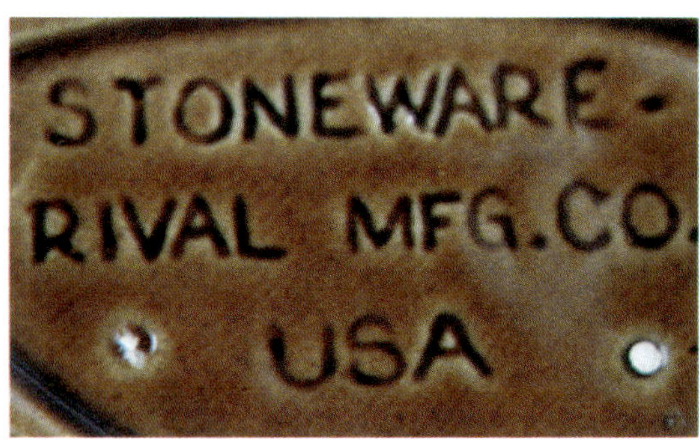

The Rival mark was the last to be used at the pottery. Morton Pottery Company was never incorporated into this mark that was used from 1972 to 1976.

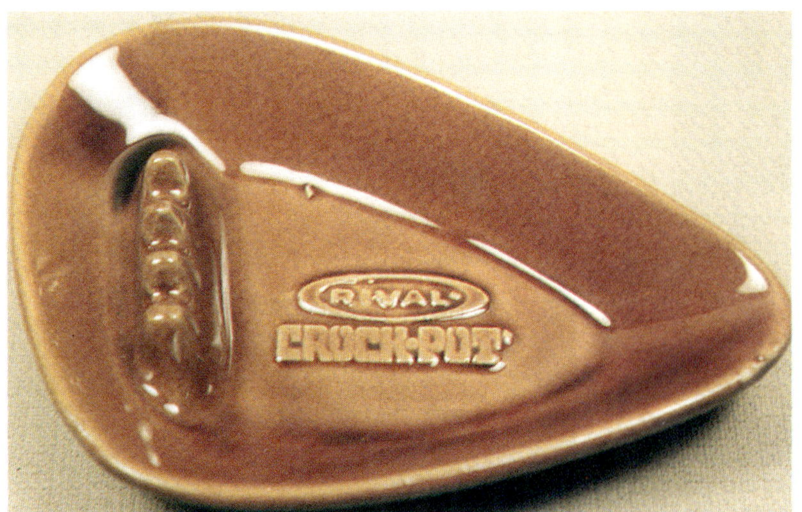

The ashtray was a give-away. It is scarce.

Value Range: ND

CHAPTER 11

Historical Sketch
1922-1976

In the summer of 1922, interest in a pottery similar to the old Morton Pottery Works was rekindled when the village of Morton's Commercial Club met to hear a proposal from Daniel W. Rapp. Rapp was the son of Andrew Rapp who had been one of the founders of Morton's first pottery. Supported by his brothers, with whom he had purchased that pottery in 1915, Daniel was well prepared for that meeting. He presented figures taken from the records of the old pottery, showing the cost of production in that plant, and the profits that were made there. He compared those costs and profits with those of Morton Earthenware Company when it ceased operation in 1917. He then projected his figures to the 1922 business climate to emphasize the feasibility of a new pottery.

After Rapp's presentation, the meeting was opened for discussion and questions from Commercial Club members. Out of that meeting a basic plan for a new, modern pottery was agreed upon. When finalized, the plan provided for a building and equipment values at $50,000. In addition to the building, the plan included state of the art machinery and equipment. Three kilns were proposed. New equipment would include clay disintegrators, mixers, pug mills, blungers for mixing slip clays and glazes, and jiggers for plate production. That type of modern facility would speed up production and reduce costs. It was enthusiastically supported by the Commercial Club.

The products to be made at the new pottery were to be the same as those made earlier, kitchen ware, food storage containers, bakers, and flower pots. Art pottery and ornamental pottery was not considered because the Cliftwood Art Pottery was making those wares. The proponents for the new pottery did not want to create an atmosphere of competition with their uncle and cousins.

From research done before the Commercial Club meeting, the Rapps were able to report a positive and receptive market for their products. Inquiries had been made to large crockery jobbers and distribution warehouses in major cities to verify the demand for the type of production that they planned. Not only was the demand there, the central location, the availability of experienced workers, and low freight rates were noted as further strengths for reestablishing the pottery business.

Before the meeting adjourned, a major concern was addressed. How would the new pottery be capitalized? A committee was appointed to canvass the community to determine the amount of stock that might be purchased by the local citizenry.

J. E. Gerber, president of the Morton Corporation, had been very supportive of this new business venture. He had worked very hard to bring it to fruition. By the time of the Commercial Club meeting in July, he had already obtained the assurance of $25,000 worth of stock purchases. A thermometer was placed at the post office to show the weekly increases. By August 16th, $38,000 had been raised. A headlined feature in the Morton News, on September 28th, stated "New Pottery is Assured: Gerber Raised the Funds." Actually, the project was $3,000 short at that time. Gerber was appointed to collect the subscriptions so the articles of incorporation could be applied for. By mid November, 1922, the entire $50,000 had been raised.

At the first stockholder's meeting on November 29th, Hiram Todd was chosen to preside. Todd was the attorney for the new pottery business. Daniel W. Rapp was made acting secretary for that all important meeting. J. E. Gerber, William Rapp, and Daniel W. Rapp were elected as the incorporators. They were also to serve as directors for the corporation until the annual stockholders meeting that was set for the third Tuesday in January, 1923. The incorporators immediately set to work to get the corporation papers in order and filed with the Secretary of

State. The papers were signed and sealed on December 8, 1922, making Morton Pottery Company a legal entity.

At the first annual meeting of stockholders, the following officers were elected: President, J. E. Gerber; Vice President, William Oelwin; Secretary, D. W. Rapp; and Treasurer, Charles Husted. Leonard Hillis was elected to serve with the officers as a director. William Rapp was named superintendent of the manufacturing department.

A large portion of Gerber's Morton Corporation became the location for the new pottery. Situated on Bloomington Street (now Jefferson Street) where the Santa Fe Railroad and the Illinois Terminal System Railroad intersected, it was an ideal location. An addition built during World War I housed the pottery. An eighty by one hundred foot extension was added to accommodate the three kilns and the heating plant. Two natural gas wells were drilled to supplement the fuel needed to operated the pottery. Six months prior to its first kiln firing, Morton Pottery Company had fifteen men working to install equipment and appliances, do carpenter work, and make molds and saggers.

By July 7th, when the first kiln load of wares was fired, the pottery had 270 molds and 3000 sagger boxes ready for used. Three regional sales managers had been named, and Morton Pottery Company entered into a contract with the Cliftwood Pottery that allowed the sales managers to also sell Cliftwood's art ware. Daniel W. Rapp went to Kansas City. From there he sold in the southwestern states. D. E. Mathis went to Chicago and was responsible for the central states. Frank Tichnor based his operations in Morton but sold in the eastern section of the country. Daniel Rapp eventually left the pottery and settled in Michigan City, Indiana where he gained a reputation for building fine, hand made furniture.

Realizing that the pottery would most certainly succeed, four of William Rapp's brothers, Andrew, Henry, Nathan, and Solomon went to work on Monday, July 9th. All had learned the pottery trade as youths when they worked for their father and uncles at the Morton Pottery Works. A fifth brother, Samuel, could not start at that time because he was operating a farm machinery production plant in Morton, and had interest in a Peoria bank. He eventually did join his brothers at the pottery and served as secretary of the corporation until its demise in 1969.

The summer of 1923 was a busy one for the Rapps. Attempting to get the pottery into full operation took concerted effort on all their parts. By fall, the business was operating smoothly, but on October 18th, disaster struck. Fire broke out in the portion of the building used by the Morton Corporation. The fire quickly engulfed that whole wing. The pottery was saved because of the fast action of J. E. Gerber who lived across the street from the building. After calling the fire department, Gerber entered the burning building through a window and closed a fire door that separated the pottery from the Morton Corporation. Though the pottery was not damaged, the office which was in the Morton Corporation wing, was destroyed. The Morton Corporation remained a mass of ruins for two years. In October, 1925, the Morton Pottery Company purchased the ruins and the real estate for the purpose of expanding the pottery. That expansion was completed and in operation by the summer of 1926.

New items were added to the regular line of stock after the expansion was completed. Most notable was the Pilgrim line that was introduced in the fall of 1926. Though it was produced for only one year, that line of ware was very popular. For the very first time, kitchen ware was being produced in decorator colors of blue, apple green, and yellow. Included in the line were custard cups, mixing bowls, a nested set of baking nappies, a beverage set, pitchers, an ice box jug, and a beater bowl set. Other items were a covered butter box, a wall mounted match box, and a salt box. There were also shakers, a four piece waffle set, pie bakers, casseroles, and a twin tea set. A special foil label was created to be used with that line (see marks.) Pilgrim ware was featured in the October 1, 1926 issue of The Crockery and Glass Journal. K. P. Lockitt Company handled the Pilgrim ware in its New York City store. Select items from the line were exhibited at the Metropolitan Museum in New York because that was one of the earliest attempts to introduce color to kitchenware in America.

A second fire, on August 15, 1927, prematurely halted the production of Pilgrim pottery. That fire totally destroyed the manufacturing building and the ware houses. The remainder of the pottery was saved due to William Rapp's heroism. He went into the smoke filled building to make sure the fire doors were closed. He then ran the elevator to the second floor in order to eliminate drafts that could feed the fire. The kilns were kept in operation during the fire, and ware in the kilns was not damaged. At the time of the fire, the pottery had unfilled orders for Pilgrim ware on hand. Most of those orders were filled after the fire, but the Pilgrim line never did go back into production.

Again, the pottery was in need of extensive repair and renovation. After the fire, the board of directors received offers to relocate the pottery from three Illinois cities, Joliet, Peoria, and Pekin. Attractive incentives accompanied each of the offers, but the board of directors decided to remain in Morton after several Mortonites offered to assist in financing the rebuilding of the pottery. That generosity, coupled with a sizeable insurance payment, kept the pottery in Morton.

Work on plans for a new pottery building with modern, new labor saving machinery was begun immediately. The new plant was built in about the same space the burned out portion had occupied. New equipment came from the Patterson Company at East Liverpool, Ohio. It was the most advanced on the market. With a much greater manufacturing capacity, the pottery resumed full production on October 17, 1927. A new feature that greatly enhanced productivity, was a monorail system that conveyed ware quickly and easily from one department to another.

Orders continued to come for Pilgrim ware, but they could not be filled. Plagued with that dilemma, the board of directors gave considerable time and study to the feasibility of bringing the line back. The final decision was negative, but those items that were most frequently requested would form the nucleus of a line that was to be known as the Amish Pottery (pantry ware) line. The carryovers from Pilgrim ware were the beater bowl, the match box holder, the salt box, one size custard cup, the shakers, the casseroles, and pie baker, the mixing bowls, the ice box jug, and the waffle set. Eight inch breakfast plates were added to the waffle set. New items designed for the Amish Pottery line were cooking and serving bowls, an ice tea set consisting of the pitcher, beakers, and coasters. Restyled pitchers, a restyled teapot with covered sugar and creamer, and cups and saucers were in the new line. Other new items were a covered ice box jar, a covered pudding dish, a covered, handled bean pot, a four piece canister set, and a porridge bowl with saucer. The new Amish Pottery (pantry ware) was announced on February 1, 1929 in Morton's local newspaper. While researching that period of the pottery's history, a copy of The Crockery and Glass Journal dated November 1928 was located. This full page ad, taken from the journal, refutes that announcement by the Morton News.

The six items identified as Amish Pottery are Pilgrim pottery items that were to be carried over to the new line of production. The authors believe that this was really a preview of the line because the next two issues of The Crockery and Glass Journal, December, 1928, and January, 1929, had ads using the same photographs. The December issue used the match holder, shakers, and ice box jug in a full page spread. In January the beater set and the nappies were used in the ad. From February through June, every item pictured in ads was a new creation for the Amish Pottery line. No item from the Pilgrim line was featured in any of the 1929 advertising in the journal. There is still confusion today as to when one line was discontinued and the other begun.

For a short period of time, the Amish Pottery (pantry ware) was available with hand painted decorations. The designs were applied with cold paints after the glazing process had been completed. Over the years that paint has deteriorated. Seldom is an example found in mint condition. Usually chips of paint are missing and there is noticeable scratching. Flowers, grape clusters, and snow berries were most frequently used for the decoration.

Shortly after introducing the new line of kitchenware, the pottery began to feel the effects of the Great Depression. As orders declined, efforts were made to create other lines that could be produced in great volume and that would be less costly to produce. Though most of the

INTRODUCING

AMISH POTTERY

(PANTRY WARE)

THE accompanying illustrations show a few of the newer numbers of Amish Pottery. The pleasing designs, beautiful colors, and popular prices cause this line to move quickly. Write today for circulars and prices.

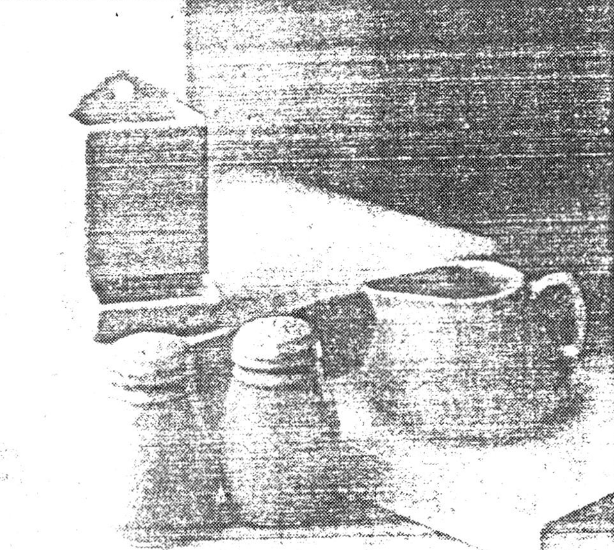

Three popular numbers, Match Box, Salt and Pepper, and Ice Box Jug.

This Beater Bowl Set and Nappy Nest are among the quickest moving numbers of Amish Pottery.

This pantry ware is being sold in assortments by dealers everywhere in the United States; the consumer being interested in more than just replacement purchases. Its colors, designs, variety of sizes and prices make it attractive to everyone. If you have never stocked Amish Pottery try a small assortment and see how quickly it moves from your shelves. We have many interesting numbers in custards, mixing bowls, pie plates, casseroles, tea pots and sets, beverage sets, pitchers and many other items. Write today for our descriptive literature and prices.

MORTON POTTERY CO.

MORTON, ILLINOIS

Tell our advertisers you saw it in THE CROCKERY AND GLASS JOURNAL

Rapps were dedicated Republicans, it was Franklin Roosevelt's Democratic campaign for the Presidency in 1933 that offered the pottery the opportunity to devise such a line. FDR's campaign promise to repeal the prohibition amendment was quickly endorsed by the Morton Pottery Company's board of directors. The pottery created two miniature beer steins that were used quite effectively in the campaign. The steins were designed with a flange opposite the handle so they could be worn in the lapel button hole of a man's suit coat. One stein had the traditional handle, the other had a handle in the shape of a donkey. Both had "We want beer" in raised letters on one side. On the opposite side was "Repeal the 18." The steins were glazed in Rockingham brown, and were produced by the thousands to be used as giveaways during the Presidential campaign.

After Roosevelt's victory in 1932, one of the first things the new Congress did was to propose the 21st Amendment passed on March 22nd. It was ratified very quickly, and went into effect December 5, 1933. During the ratification process, Congress passed the Beer-Wine Revenue Act as a means of quickly securing additional revenue for the federal treasury. The act legalized the sale of 3.2 beer. It went into effect on April 7th.

Pottery officials immediately began contacting breweries with the prospect of using steins for promotional advertising. A standard barrel shape stein could be quickly altered to carry the brewer's name or logo by using a small blank inserted into the mold. The result of those contacts was contracts that had the pottery turning out 4000 steins a day. Three shifts of employees worked twenty-four hours a day in order to satisfy the orders that flooded the plant. The April 20, 1933 issue of the Chicago Tribune carried a short news story with the headline, "Orders For Beer Steins Swamp Pottery Plant." In the article, it was noted that an order for 1,000,000 steins for Blatz Brewing Company of Milwaukee had been filled, and that contracts had been signed with other breweries.

Near the end of the 1930's, as beer stein production began to wane, the first of many novelties to be produced by the pottery was put on line. From the group of miniature animals that was being produced, the Rapps took the #606 elephant figure and put GOP on its side. By word of mouth, they were able to get contracts from local politicians whose names were placed on the opposite side. Those elephants made excellent campaign giveaways. They were very popular from the 1940's through the 1950's. Thousands were ordered by virtually every influential Republican candidate seeking office, even Richard M. Nixon.

Illinois Senator, Everett M. Dirksen, was one of the company's best customers. His campaign headquarters around the state handed out hundreds of the little elephants. When Dirksen campaigned for the House of Representatives in 1944, the pottery designed a special ashtray to be handed out to delegates at the Republican convention in Chicago. Octagonal in shape, and glazed Delft blue, the ashtray has this inscription across the top rim: "Everett McKinley Dirksen." Around the bottom rim is: "From Lincoln's Illinois." In the bottom of the ashtray is an elephant with "GOP" above its back. Twenty-five hundred ashtrays were distributed at that convention by Mortonites who were friends and political hackneys of Dirksen.

In 1950, during Dirksen's campaign for the United States Senate, he chose a special elephant to be produced as a ring holder. Number 608 in the line of miniature animals, it was a baby elephant in a diaper. The head was tilted back with the trunk extending upward in a trumpeting position to accommodate the rings. The last name, "Dirksen", is stamped across its back in brown ink.

When Dirksen made a bid for the Presidential nomination in 1956, he chose the earlier GOP miniature elephant with his name on the side. Most of the earlier campaign elephants had been glazed in Delft blue. To make his distinct from others in previous years, Dirksen's elephants were grey. During September and October, the pottery shipped one hundred twenty-one cartons of elephants to Dirksen who did not get the nomination, but his elephants continue to surface in the collectible market.

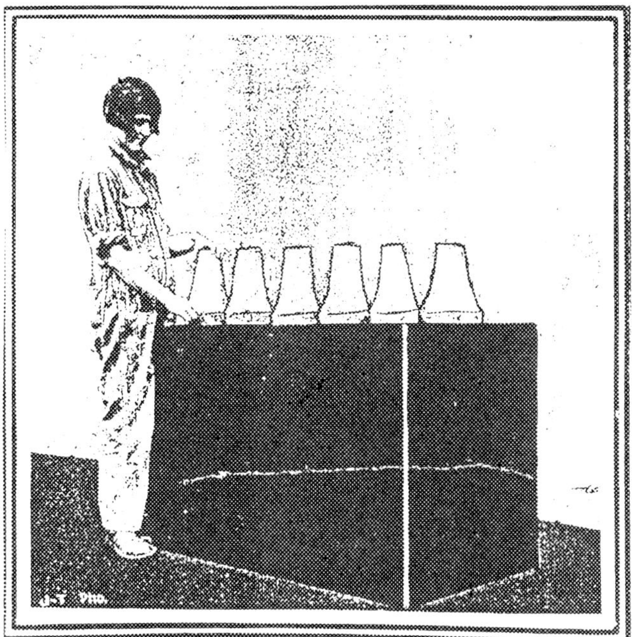

Down in staid, conservative Morton, there is a little girl who works in the pottery and wears overalls. She is Miss Emily Musselman and she works in the casting department.

These newspaper photographs were found in a scrap book kept by a pottery employee in the 1930's.

The picture of the girl in the casting room was most certainly staged. The casting department was never that clean. The molds were on slatted tables and were turned to allow excess clay to drain out on the floor. Once partially dry, the clay was scooped up and recycled in the pug mill.

The boy is surrounded by bisque ware beer steins. From the appearance of his work station, he probably glazed beer steins during the entire eight hour shift that he worked.

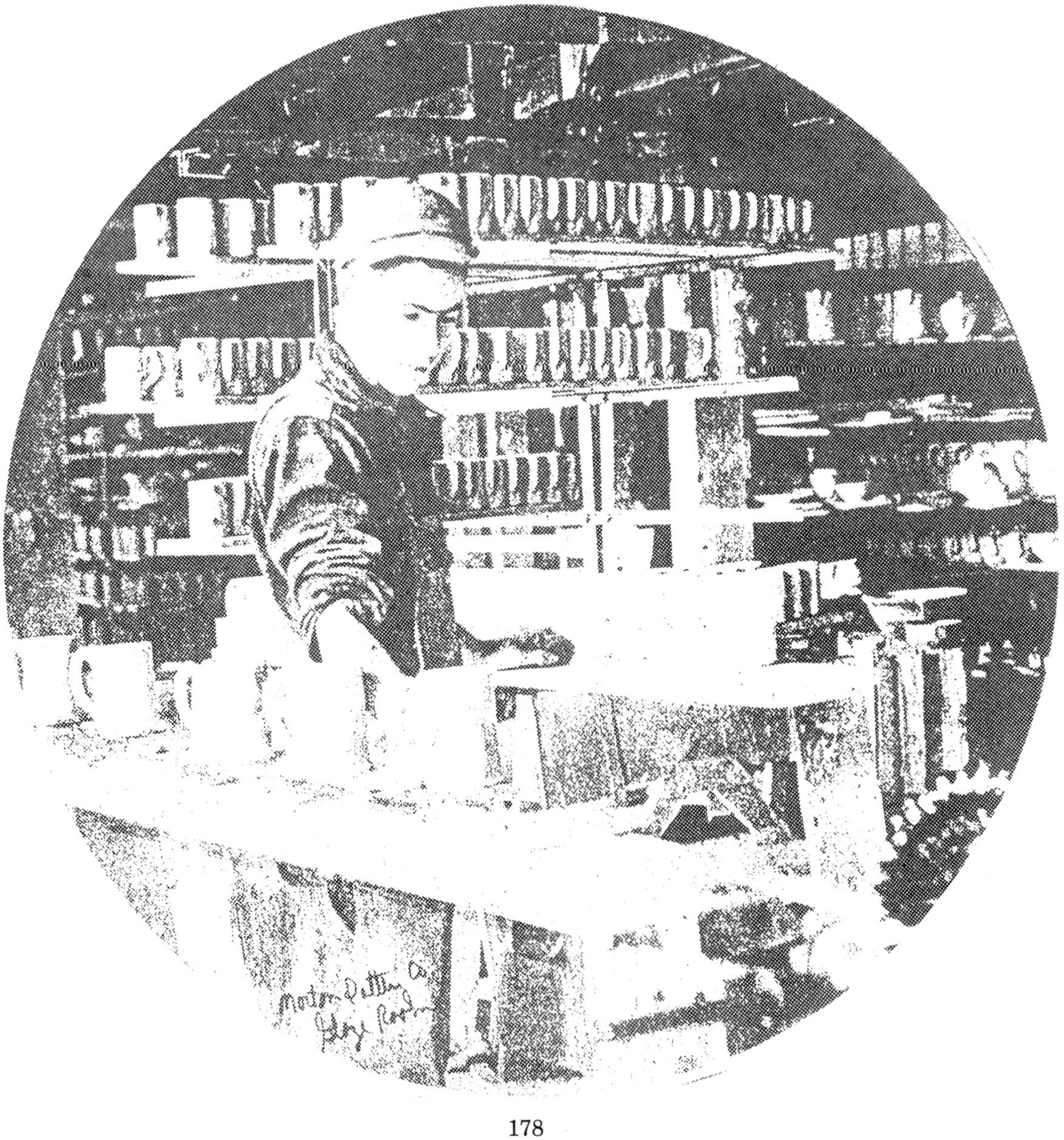

One of few political items made for a Democrat over the pottery's long period of production, was a miniature donkey made for John F. Kennedy. The donkey has "Kennedy" on one side, the other side is blank. This miniature was made for Kennedy's Presidential campaign in 1960. The reason for its creation was very personal. Gilbert Rapp, the oldest son of Samuel W. Rapp, served in the United States Naval Air Service during World War II. During training, Gilbert and Kennedy's brother, Joe Jr., trained together. They regularly flew as copilots, and were inseparable while stationed in England. They flew regular bombing missions over Germany. Gilbert was killed on March 31, 1944 while on one of those missions. Later, Kennedy was also killed while returning from a bombing mission. In memory of his brother and the men who served with him, John Kennedy wrote a collection of tributes that he called As We Remember Joe. Gilbert's family was presented an autographed copy of the limited edition book. When Kennedy got the nomination for President, there was no problem getting orders filled for his campaign mementos by Morton Pottery Company.

The period of production during the 1950's was devoted to expanded lines of novelty items. Flower containers, vases, lamps, holiday items, doll house accessories, planters, and bisque figures that held water and grew grass for hair and other ornamentation were sold across the entire United States, Canada, Mexico, and Cuba. Many of the novelty items were sold by the large mail order companies, by florists, and by five and dime or dollar store retailers. Variety stores and gift shops were also good customers. To further saturate the market, salesmen went door to door in smaller communities. The salesmen also contracted to place the novelties in grocery stores and pharmacies in those small localities. Because of that extensive sales program, the more common examples of Morton Pottery Company products can readily be found at flea markets, antique malls and shops, consignment shops, and yard sales in nearly every part of the United States.

In the summer of 1955, Walt Disney's Davy Crockett was one of the top TV mini series. The title song topped the "Hit Parade" for eight straight weeks. While that program had America in its grips, the pottery moved to take advantage of the frenzie. Two lamps and a planter were designed for production. One lamp was the adult frontiersman standing near a tree trunk with a bear sitting, cross legged on the other side. The second lamp has the same tree trunk and bear, but the adult Davy has been replaced by a child depicting Crockett at age three, when he supposedly hunted down and shot a bear. That design was altered to create the planter. Instead of the tree trunk, a hollow log was designed for the plants.

At the peak of production, three hundred molds for the adult figural lamp were made, and one hundred fifty for each of the junior items. Those molds were filled with slip clay several times each day. It only took a few hours for the clay to set up so the item could be removed from the molds and trimmed. The adult lamp bases were spray painted with two underglaze colors, brown and green. Davy's eyes, gun, and shoes were hand painted black underglaze. After the lamps were decorated, they were dipped in transparent glaze and sent off to be fired in the kiln. The firing process took twenty-four hours at 2,030 F. For the younger Davy, the brown and green glaze was used for the tree and the bear, but the boy's buckskins and coonskin cap were spray painted with a medium gray glaze. The pottery turned out about 5000 of those novelties each week. The lamp bases were packed a dozen per carton and were shipped to Chicago and New York City where fixtures were installed, and shades added. The adult form was the main item in the line. Production records from that period of time have been destroyed, but newspaper accounts indicate that during June, 15,000 of the adult lamps were made and that 5000 of the child were done. All Davy Crockett items are scarce today.

In 1956, a wing was added to the pottery to house a new ceramic tile division. Created to produce colorful tile and bathroom fixtures, that operation was developed by third generation brothers and cousins of the Rapp clan. Known as the Morton Ceramic Tile Company, a subsidiary of Morton Pottery Company, the business was selling to dealers in twelve mid-western states at the end of its first year of production. The four and one fourth inch tile squares were sold under the name "Mor-Tile". They were available in twelve colors originally. As demand grew, new colors were added to the line. In addition to the tile, several types of trim sections for finishing corners and edges were produced. Accessories such as soap dishes, towel posts, paper dispensers, tooth brush holders, and clothes hooks could be ordered in the same colors as the tile.

Much of the tile operation was automated, a technique that was relatively new at the pottery. The clay preparation was known as the "stiff mud" process. The clay was mixed and rolled before being placed in a pug mill where it was kneaded and rolled again to remove entrapped air. From the pug mill dry rolls or chunks of stiff clay were conveyed to the tile press. There large steel dies came together to form the tile. Then the tiles were released from the press. They were pushed onto another conveyor system that carried each tile through a trimming and brushing station. The tiles were then ready to be glazed. The glaze was applied by means of automatic spray guns that coated the surface of the tiles as they passed through the spray booth on a conveyor chain. Once glazed, the tiles continued on the chain to a production line where they were hand placed in setters and were put on kiln cars that were pushed through the kiln by means of a hydraulic pusher. The tile spent fifteen hours in a continuous circular kiln that was fired at an average temperature of 1900 F. Eighty-five percent of the tile emerged from the kiln as first grade quality. Ten percent was packed and sold as seconds. The remaining five percent was destroyed.

By the summer of 1966, the highly automated ceramic tile facet of the pottery's output began to feel the keen competition of Japanese tile manufacturers. Joining other American tile makers, the pottery accused the Japanese of attempting to take over the American market by illegal means. It was pointed out that Japan was involved in switch trading, a practice of purchasing ceramic tile products in Canada with American currency, then selling them in Japan at heavily inflated prices. The ceramic company struggled through the mid 1960's but was never able to match Japanese prices. The company showed significant losses in each of its annual reports.

During that same time period, the beer stein, novelty, and artware lines of Morton Pottery Company enjoyed expanded production, but Japanese competition began to impact on its profits. A new sales manager was hired with the hope that he could turn the pottery around. Edward S. Nielsen, hired for that position, had previously worked for Haeger Potteries as a sales and merchandising manager. Nielsen was also experienced in advertising. He came to Morton from an advertising agency in Chicago. The pottery did produce new lines under Nielsen's guidance, but they were not spectacular. Consisting mostly of ashtrays, lighters, and metal handled serving dishes, the new line was not popular and did little to turn the pottery around.

In addition to the traumas of foreign competition, dwindling sales, and profit losses, the pottery was faced with a series of other problems. The United Brick and Clay Workers of America tried to unionize the pottery in 1961. That action brought on some caustic moments between the management of the pottery and the laborers. Eventually the conflict was resolved when the pottery workers voted on the issue. Seventy-two workers voted against the union, fifty-seven voted favorably. The pottery was never unionized, but friction continued thereafter.

Shortly after the union problems were resolved, another fire broke out. The motor of a second floor exhaust fan shorted out in a paint spraying room causing that fire. Heat from the blaze triggered the automatic sprinkler system to activate, thus averting a major fire. The flames went through the exhaust vent and ignited a portion of the roof and was contained to that area. The fire was quickly brought under control by the firemen and its damage was minimal. Some merchandise stored on the first floor under the paint room was damaged, but final estimates placed the loss at only a few hundred dollars. That fire seemed to be the prelude to other problems that would eventually cause the Rapps to sell the pottery they had started forty years before.

One last hope for survival came in 1967, when the pottery entered into an agreement with Sears, Roebuck, and Company to produce a line of reproductions of pottery designs selected by Vincent Price who was art consultant for Sears at that time. In addition to the pottery, Price chose furniture, fabrics, wall coverings, draperies, baskets, tinware, and glass to be reproduced from early American designs. The promotional campaign was launched as "The Sears Roebuck Vincent Price National Treasures Collection." Those items had a special logo placed on the back (see marks). The collection first appeared in the Sears and Roebuck spring and summer catalog in 1967. It was carried again in the 1968 catalogs, but was not continued beyond 1968.

At the time Sears began its promotion of early American reproductions, Danish Modern hit the consumer market. It took a commanding lead in the public's demand for sleek, cold, uncluttered, smooth lined features that were more compatible with the chaotic sixties than was Sear's offerings from past American history. The Vincent Price National Treasures Collection was about twenty years ahead of its time. By the late 1980's, the early American country look came on strong, but in the sixties Danish Modern forced the unsuccessful collection off the market. The sales that the pottery had hoped would turn it around came to a halt. For a short time, the reproductions continued to be manufactured and sold at the pottery after they were discontinued by Sears Roebuck and Company, but Sears took legal action to stop the production. The items had been contracted as exclusive reproductions for the Sears National Treasures Collection. Once again, the pottery had struck out.

Family misfortunes added to the pressures of the last few years of declining sales. Nathan Rapp, the vice-president, designer, and mold maker, died in late January, 1969. Within a month, his sister, Naomi expired. She had been a decorator for twenty-eight years. She did much of the special order decorating during those years. The Rapps saw no promising future for the pottery, so they decided to sell while there was a marketable interest in the business.

The sale was quickly accomplished. Local and area newspapers reported the sale on May 15, 1969. The pottery was purchased by Ronald D. Cowan and William R. York. The new owners continued to call their business the Morton Pottery Company. Neither of the buyers had any previous pottery experience. Cowan had been a buyer for Sears Roebuck at Downers Grove, Illinois when the sale was finalized. York had his own management consultant business in St. Louis, Missouri. Plans were to continue the operation along the lines that had been developed by the Rapps. Cowan became president of the pottery. York was in charge of sales and marketing. Henry Rapp Jr., a third generation Rapp, was in charge of plant operations.

Extensive marketing research was conducted to guide immediate and long range planning. There was an air of excitement as the new business moved forward, but it met the same problems that had befallen the Rapps. Few new items were added to the line of products. Tile sales continued to decline, and artware production was fundamentally limited to ashtrays that were in overabundance. Competition intensified. The pottery struggled in its attempt to expand its profits.

In January, 1971, after only nineteen and one half months of operation, it was apparent that Morton Pottery Company was not going to pull out of its slump. On January 21, voluntary bankruptcy papers were filed. Liability and asset schedules were filed on February 8th, showing total assets of $291,851. Liabilities were listed at $476,348. In addition, there was $164,928 worth of secured claims against the business. The pottery was allowed to continue operation on a limited basis while the court appointed a receiver, whose task was to obtain a buyer for the pottery. During February, prospective buyers from New York, Illinois, and Wisconsin toured the plant several times, but the pottery was not sold. On the first of March, the federal bankruptcy referee, Judge Stephen J. Covey, ruled that unless a buyer was found within seven days, the pottery would be liquidated at auction. No buyer was found. Liquidation proceedings began on March 8. The bankruptcy auction was scheduled to be held at 10 a.m. on March 24 at the pottery site.

Under the receivership, the pottery was appraised at $254,705. The figure included real estate, machinery, office equipment, and inventories. At the auction, conducted by the U.S. District Court, the pottery sold for $155,000. Included in the purchase was all of the real estate, personal property, and other equipment necessary to operate the business. The inventory was excluded from the purchase and was auctioned later in the day.

The buyers of the pottery were A.K. Ferrara and R.J. Meyers from Addison, Illinois. Ferrara was president of UltraMATIC Equipment Company, a subsidiary of AKF Industries. Meyers was UltraMATIC's national sales manager. After the sale, the pair stated that they intended to continue the operation of the pottery as another subsidiary of AKF Industries. It would continue to produce pottery along much the same lines as in the past but with the introduction of two new products, cookie jars and inserts for Rival crock pots. Ferrara and Meyers continued to use the name Morton Pottery Company for their subsidiary.

Rival Manufacturing Corporation, of Kansas City, Missouri, soon became the pottery's largest customer. Contracting for seventy percent of the production at Morton, Rival had found an ideal source for producing inserts for their crock pot cookers. With so great an emphasis on Rival's needs, few cookie jars were ever put into production. In fact, the art pottery and novelty production was phased out as the company concentrated on the manufacture of the Rival components.

In October, 1972, a deal was made between AKF Industries and Rival. The pottery was sold again. The deed, filed with the county recorder, indicated that the sale price was $210,000. The plant became the Morton Pottery Division of Rival Manufacturing Company when the sale was finalized on November 3. The pottery continued to make crock pot inserts. In addition, the plant began to manufacture inserts for Rival's fast cooker, the crock plate. During the next four years there was a pronounced increase in the amount of inserts produced by Rival. Large surpluses accumulated.

The final phase of pottery operation at Morton was directed by Lincoln Stoneware Company of Wellsville, Ohio. In January, 1976, Rival leased the plant to Lincoln Stoneware for the sole purpose of producing ceramic components for Rival cookware. A problem began when Rival changed from non-removable components to removable ones. Another pottery, Cardinal Stoneware, in Wellsville was also producing components. Cardinal Stoneware and Lincoln Stoneware shared the same board of directors, so when orders to Lincoln Stoneware began to wane, it was decided that one plant could fill the orders, and that it would be Cardinal Stoneware.

The morning of September 8, 1976, Lincoln Stoneware employees at Morton, were gathered for a meeting at 10:30 a.m. They were told that the pottery was closing permanently at 3:30 that afternoon. The reason given was that there was no longer a demand for the various components by Rival. The pottery was overstocked, so there was no need for the business to remain open. That notice was short and final. The pottery did close that afternoon, never to reopen again. Ninety-nine years of pottery production in Morton, Illinois had come to an end.

The building sat idle from that September afternoon until it was purchased by the Morton Public Library board of trustees in January, 1979. During its idleness, the building fell into disrepair. Soon after the purchase, the building was torn down in the interest of safety.

Today, a new modern library has been built on the land that was once home to the Morton Pottery Company. There is no visage of the pottery that was one of Morton's early commercial success stories. The library has a collection of early photographs depicting Morton's past that includes views of all of the potteries. There is also a collection of pottery on display in the adult reading area. That collection includes examples from all of the potteries that operated in Morton from 1877 until 1976, ninety-nine years!

CHAPTER 12

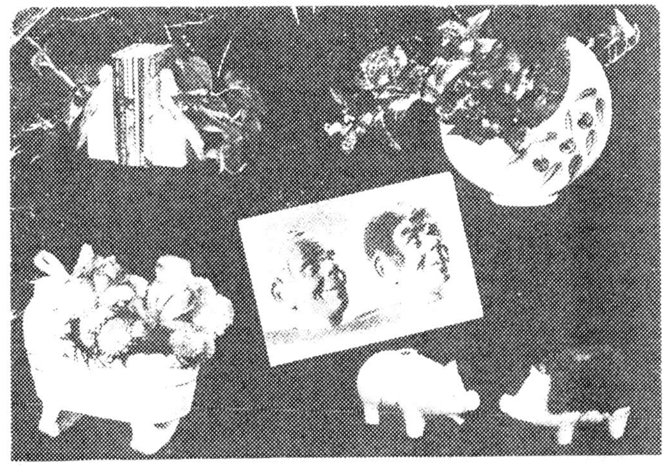

grownups, children, shut-ins, EVERYONE will like these growing gifts!

They're bald as an egg when they come to you. Just fill them with water and plant the grass seed (supplied along with full directions). Then watch them grow! Porky Pig sprouts a grassy green coat—Sunny Jim sports a bushy green head of hair and thick eyebrows—your Evergreen Tree comes out with a full set of thick grass "leaves."
The grass grows for months and you can plant it over and over. All three figures are made of durable pottery. They're ideal gifts—as table decorations, house plants, for any occasion.

ARTCRAFT POTTERY

for your home

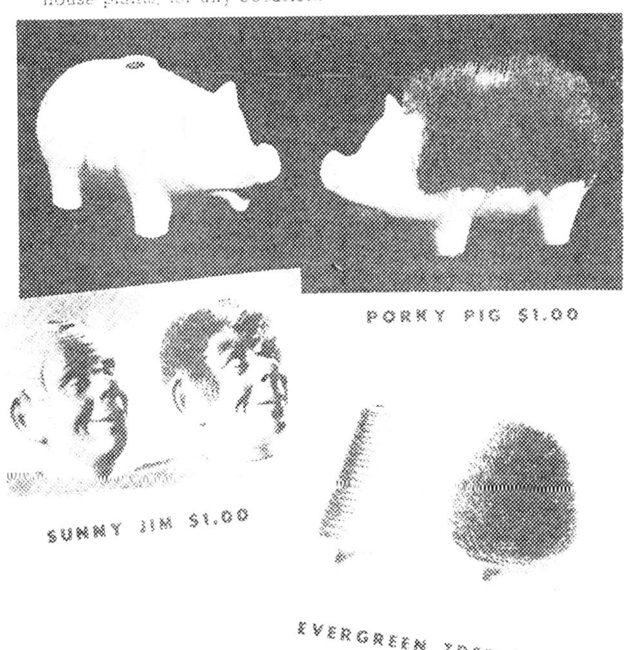

ARTCRAFT

MORTON, ILLINOIS

Send cash, check or money order.
We pay delivery charges.

The front cover of the Rapp Artcraft Pottery catalog pictures all of the pieces listed therein. The back lists thc grass growers.

Brochure - Value Range: $20-25 complete with the order form

Value Ranges for Back Cover: Pig $14-18
Sunny Jim $18-22
Evergreen tree $10-15

let these liven up your room!

PARROT BOOKENDS

Perched jauntily on your mantel, shelf or table, these bright-feathered parrots are ideal bookends—or make lovely decorations by themselves. They add a spot of color to any room—and with that perky look on their faces, you can almost imagine them talking back to you, bright and sassy. There's a hole in their backs so you can put in cut flowers. Each parrot is 6½" high, 4½" long. $1.50 per pair. Flowers not included.

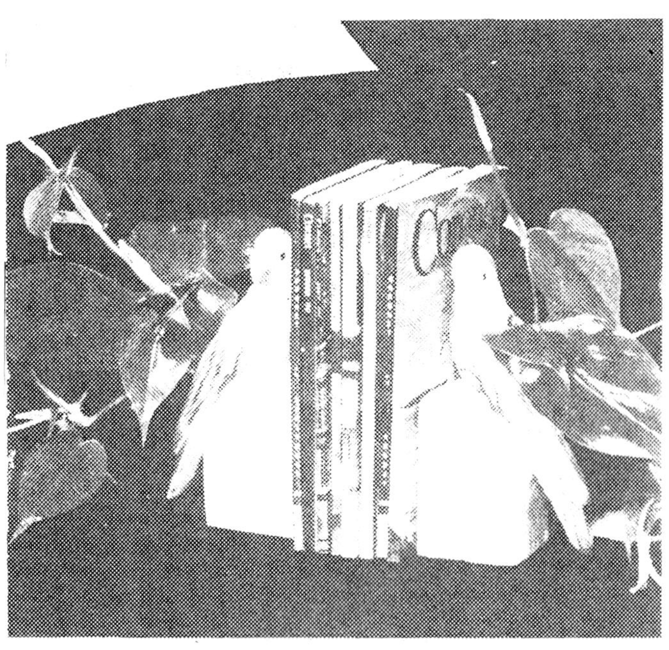

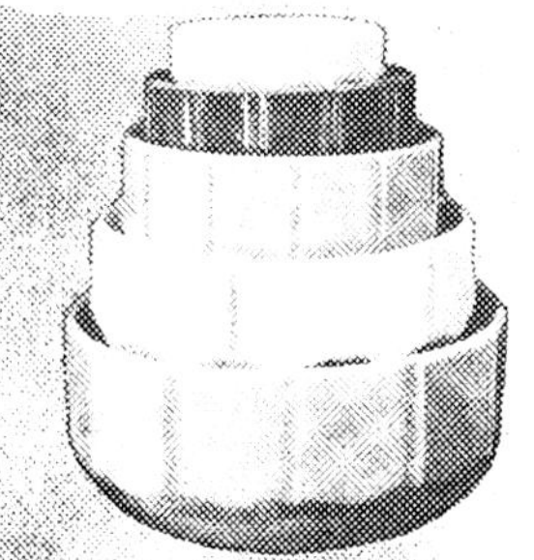

brighten your kitchen..

OLD ENGLISH STYLE

Five sturdy pottery bowls that "nest" perfectly for storage in cupboard or shelf. Ideal for baking, mixing, serving, storing left-overs, for all-round kitchen use. Ovenproof, stand any heat. Top to bottom: yellow, red, green, white, blue. Diameters 4", 5", 6", 7", 8". Get two sets—one for yourself, one for a gift. $2.00 per set.

a novel storage place...

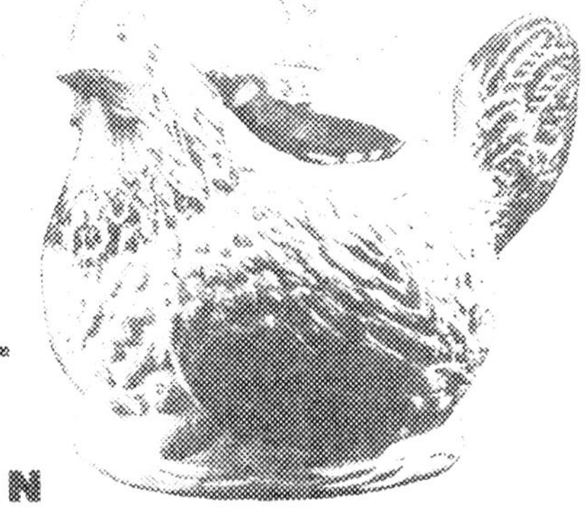

CHICKEN

Throw away that old chipped jar you're using—and put this attractive new Chicken Cookie Jar in your kitchen. Just the thing for storing cookies, sugar, receipts or any knick-knacks. Black and white, designed to true likeness of a chicken. Baby chick sits on its mother's back, making a clever handle for the lid. Lift it up and there's a roomy storage place inside. 8½" high, 6½" wide, 10" long. $2.50

Value Range: $45-55

Value Range: Book Ends $25-35
Cookie Jar $75-125

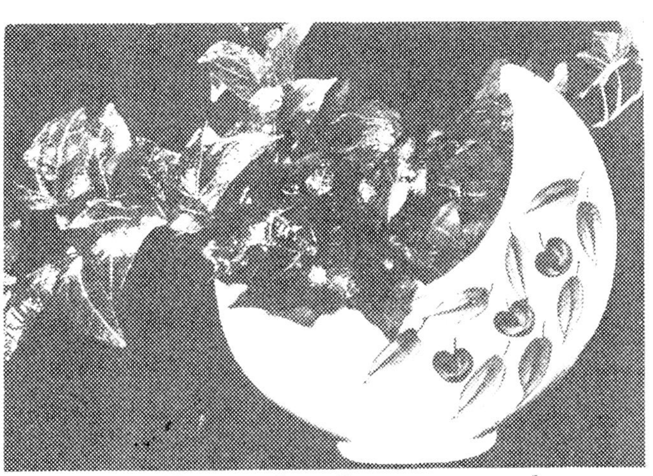

put flower freshness anywhere

MOON

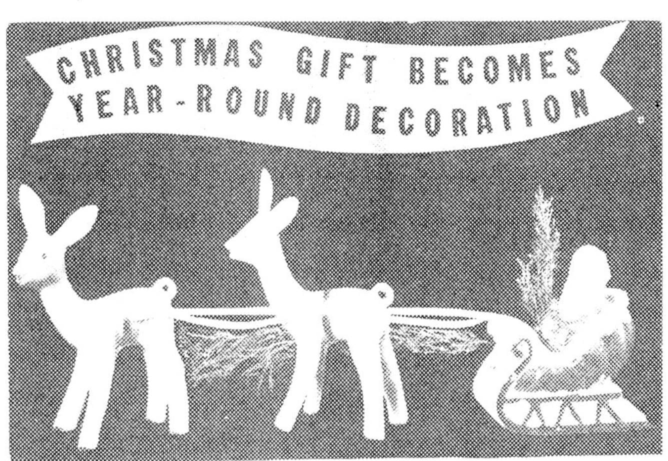

AND REINDEER

This gracefully curved pottery bowl makes a perfect decoration for living room, porch, sun parlor, hall, or any spot in your home. You can place it on a table or suspend it from the ceiling. It has holes in each tip of the crescent for easy hanging. Though it's shown here with ivy arrangement, it beautifully sets off any type of plant. Hand painted with green and red leaves. 7½" high, 8" long. $1.60. Flowers not included.

Set them under a Christmas tree, and jolly Santa is in his glory—sitting in his sleigh pulled by two tiny reindeer. Comes the end of the holiday season, and you send Santa and his sleigh into hiding—leaving two graceful fauns to set off your coffee table, book shelf or mantel. Sleigh is red, black and white. Deer are a natural faun color. Ribbon enclosed for harness. Deer are 6½" high, 5½" long. Set is $6.00.

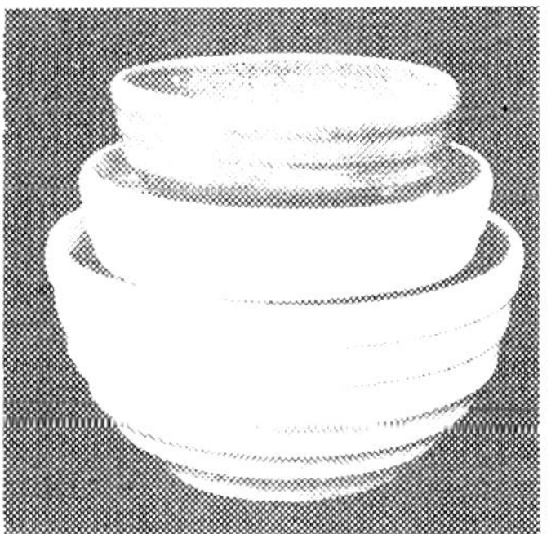

beautiful-but ever so practical!

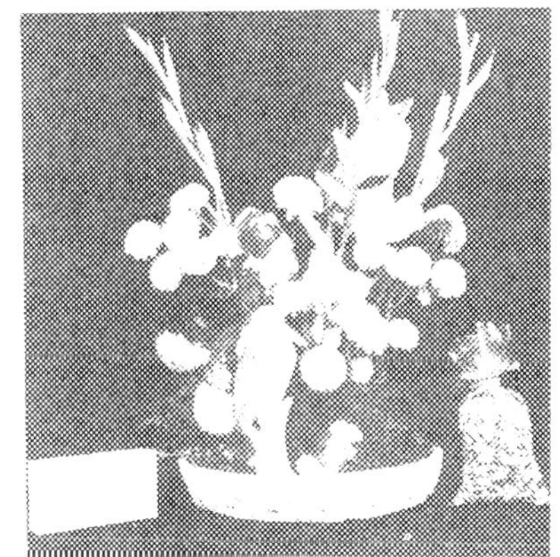

lends cheerful note indoors or out

Mixing bowl SET

Ever had a mixing bowl slip from your hand and crash on the floor? Not with this new Mixing Bowl Set. Each handsome pottery piece has neatly ridged sidewalls that give your fingers a good grasp for sure, easy handling. Each big, roomy bowl has smooth, sleek lines. Handsome to look at, practical to use. Top to bottom: red, white and blue. Diameters 7, 8, [illegible]. $2.00 for set.

Flower bowl ENSEMBLE

Cut flowers [illegible] fresh and lovely in this handsome Bowl Ensemble. Make up any type of flower arrangement and [illegible] stands [illegible] over it. Makes an eye-appealing display on porch, lawn table, [illegible] coffee table, bureau. White with [illegible]. You get [illegible] flowers. $2.[illegible] Flowers not included.

Value Range: Moon basket $18-20
Nested bowls $35-40

Value Range: Deer Santa (rare) $40-50
Deer $12-14
Sleigh (no Santa) $15-20
Flower bowl set $25-30

PLEASE THE PROUD PARENTS

when Baby comes!

Show them you're a real friend of the family—by giving a gift for baby! These original pottery pieces will long be cherished. Your choice of pink for a girl, blue for a boy.

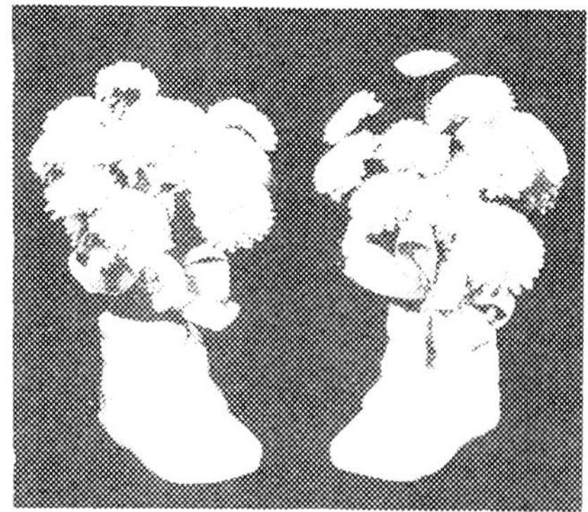

bye, bye, baby!

Modeled after the real button-down shoes that baby wears. In pink or blue. 2½" high, 4" long. $1.00 per pair. Flowers not included.

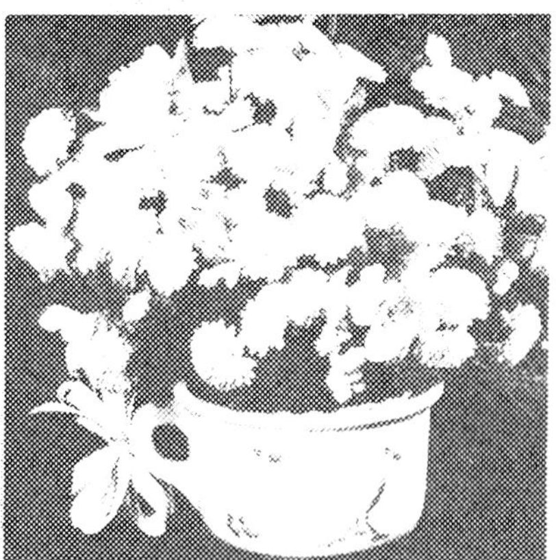

time for a change?

Lovable animal figures in blue, yellow, red. This real Pottee in pink or blue. 6" diameter, 3" high. $2.00. Flowers not included.

suppertime...

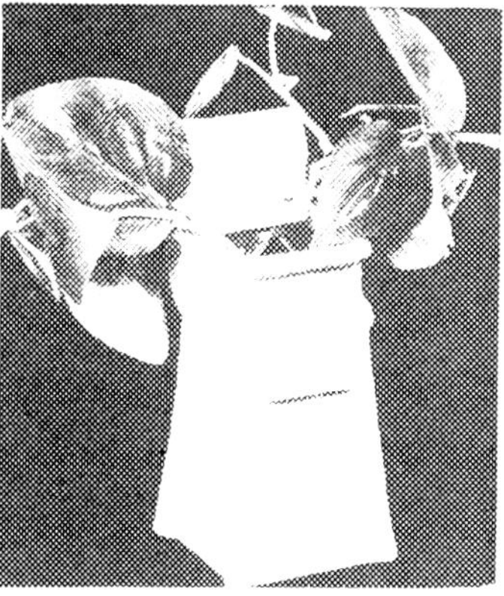

Won't quite hold baby — but it's perfect for flower arrangements. White, with pink or blue back rest. 7½" high. $1.50. Flowers not included.

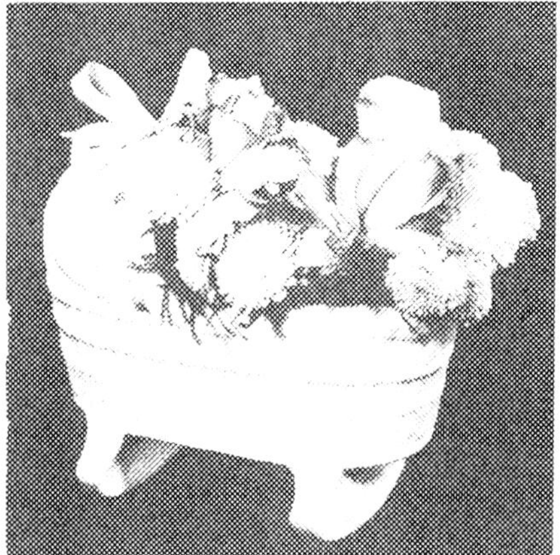

shhh! baby's asleep!

Looks just like a miniature wicker cradle. Even rocks! In pink or blue. 6" high, 8" long. $1.50. Flowers not included.

Value Range: Baby shoes $8-10
Highchair $10-$12

Value Range: Pottee $16-18
Cradle $12-14

Housewives' Delight

NEW SELF-WATERING

No need to stand "water guard" over your prize flower any more! When it grows in this amazing new flower pot you can even go away and leave it alone for days—and it will water itself while you're gone! Just put water in the base of the saucer. Through a clever wick arrangement, water is fed into the soil—in just the right amount. Always the right moisture for a growing plant. Never too damp or too dry! Comes in one sturdy pottery piece—in beautiful green or yellow. 4-inch diameter is $1.00 6-inch diameter is $1.50 Flower not included

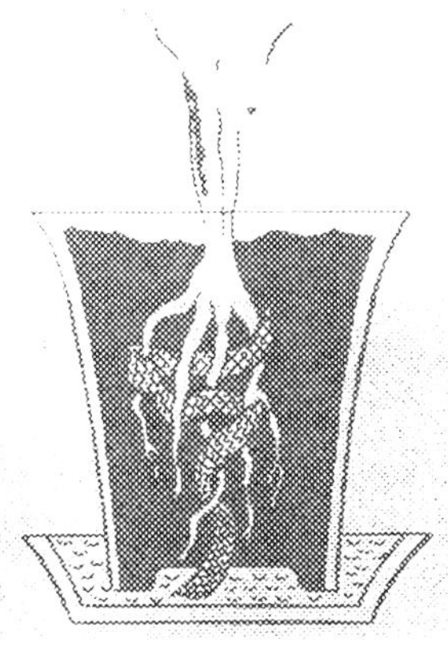

Here's how it works: Just pack soil around the wick and put in your plant. Water in base of saucer is drawn up through wick by capillary action and absorbed into soil—in the amount needed by the plant.

Spare the Table - Save the Cream

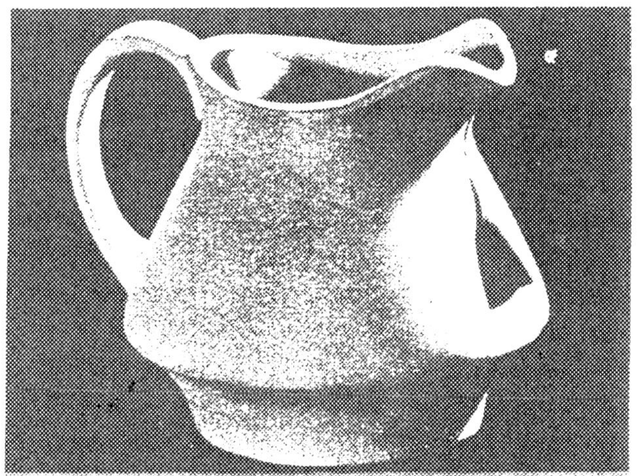

with the NEVER-DRIP *Pitcher*

Where is the housewife who hasn't fussed about those messy drippings of cream, syrup, honey, or gravy that always seem to dribble off the pitcher and wind up on the tablecloth? Here's the answer—the new Never-Drip Pitcher. This smart little pottery piece looks just like any other pitcher until you look at it head-on. Then you notice the little "pocket" down near the base, in front, and a little groove leading into it from the lip above. Drops and driblets slide down the groove into the pocket . . . never on the table. Holds one pint. Green, blue, or yellow. $1.00

EYE-CATCHER OVEN *Incense burner*

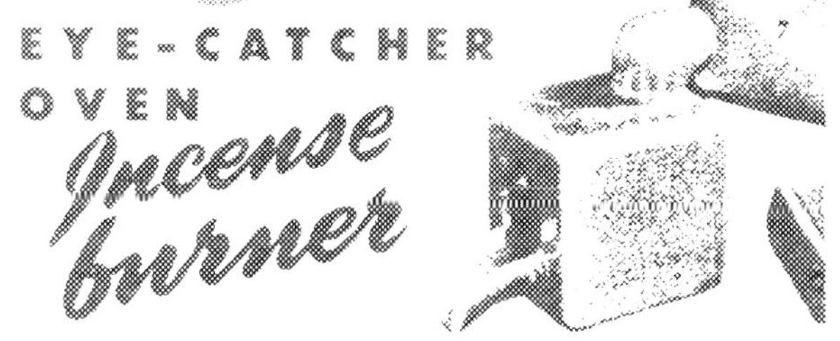

You'll get many comments from friends and neighbors when you set this droll little piece out on your table or buffet. Incense burns inside—sends its fragant aroma through the room—does away with undesirable odors. The lip sticking out there also makes a handy cigarette holder. Put the burning end of a cigaret inside the box and the smoke comes curling out the open pipe-head on top. Slight projections at the corners raise it off the table to prevent heat from scorching table. Rich maroon color. $1.00

This insert was not part of the original catalog. It was produced later, and the three items were added to the back side of the order blank.

Value Range: $12-15

Value Range: Pitcher $20-30
Incense burner $10-12

Rapp ARTCRAFT
Morton, Illinois

Please send me the following pieces:

Name and Price	Quant.	Amt. Enc.
1. Parrot Bookends @ 1.50 a pair	______	______
2. Nappie Set @ 2.00	______	______
3. Chicken Cookie Jar @ 2.50	______	______
4. Moon Hanging Basket @ 1.50	______	______
5. Mixing Bowl Set @ 2.00	______	______
6. Santa Claus and Reindeer @ 5.00	______	______
7. Flower Bowl Ensemble @ 2.50	______	______
8. Baby Shoes @ 1.00 a pair	______	______
9. Baby Highchair @ 1.50	______	______
10. Baby Pottee @ 2.00	______	______
11. Baby Cradle @ 1.50	______	______
12. Porky Pig @ 1.00	______	______
13. Sunny Jim @ 1.00	______	______
14. Evergreen Tree @ 1.00	______	______
TOTAL AMOUNT ENCLOSED		______

Send cash, check or money order. We pay delivery charge.

Name______________________________

Address____________________________

City______________State______________

(Front)

Name and Price	Quant.	Amt. Enc.
15. Self-Watering Flower Pot		
4" @ 1.00	______	______
6" @ 1.50	______	______
16. Never-Drip Pitcher @ 1.00	______	______
17. Oven Incense Burner @ 1.00	______	______

Tell your friends about Rapp Artcraft pottery . . . let them order from your booklet!

(Back)

This order form was separate from the catalog so it could easily be used to order and keep the catalog intact. When the insert was printed to list the flower pot, pitcher, and incense burner, those items were added to the back of the order form.

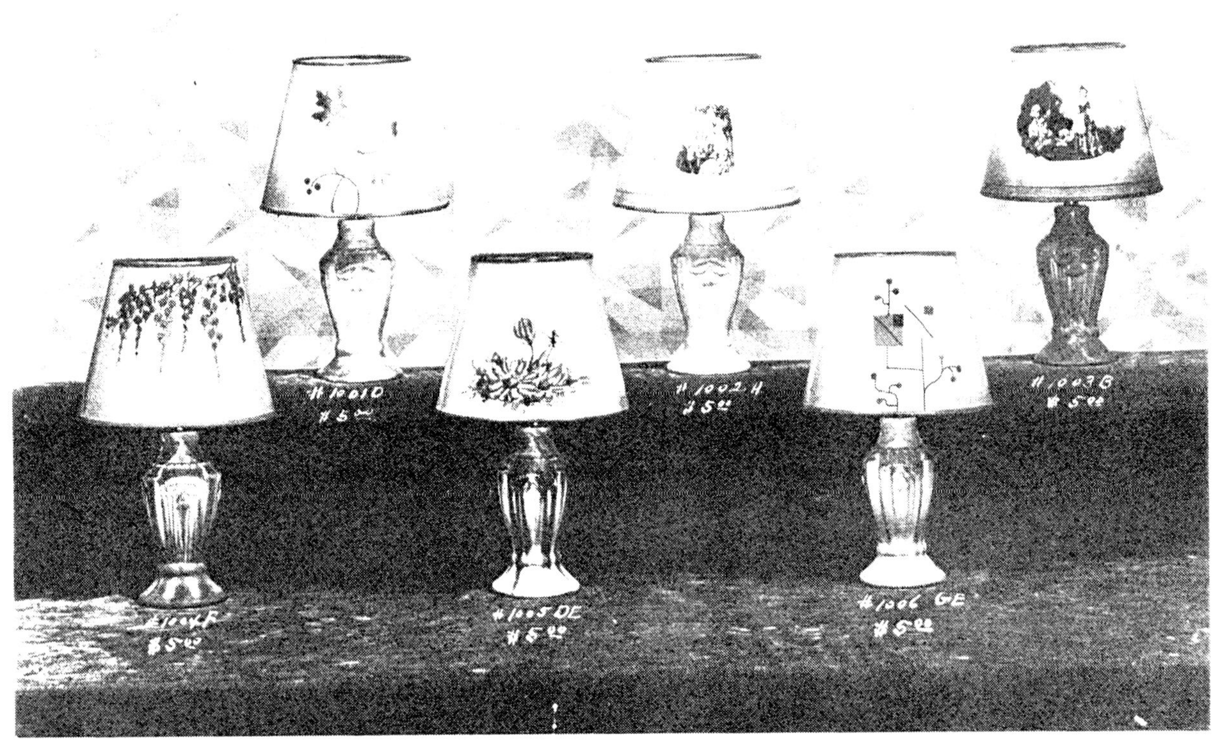

In January, 1932, the Cliftwood Potteries, Inc. opened the Cliftwood Studio on South Main Street in Morton. The purpose of the studio was to make lamp shades and decorate them to compliment the lamp bases being made at the pottery. Maude Downes, a Chicago artist, coordinated the operation that employed two other artists, Audrey York from Texas, and Richard Bettine from Chicago. Local women were employed to make the parchament shades. The studio met with instant success and was soon supplying decorated shades to Morton Pottery Company as well. The shades on these lamps are fine examples of the studio's work. Decorated shades of this type are seldom found today.

The lamps shown here are unusual examples of Morton Pottery Company wares. The pottery seldom used flowing glaze techniques. The 1000 line was ordinarily made in solid pastel colors.

Value Range: $25-45

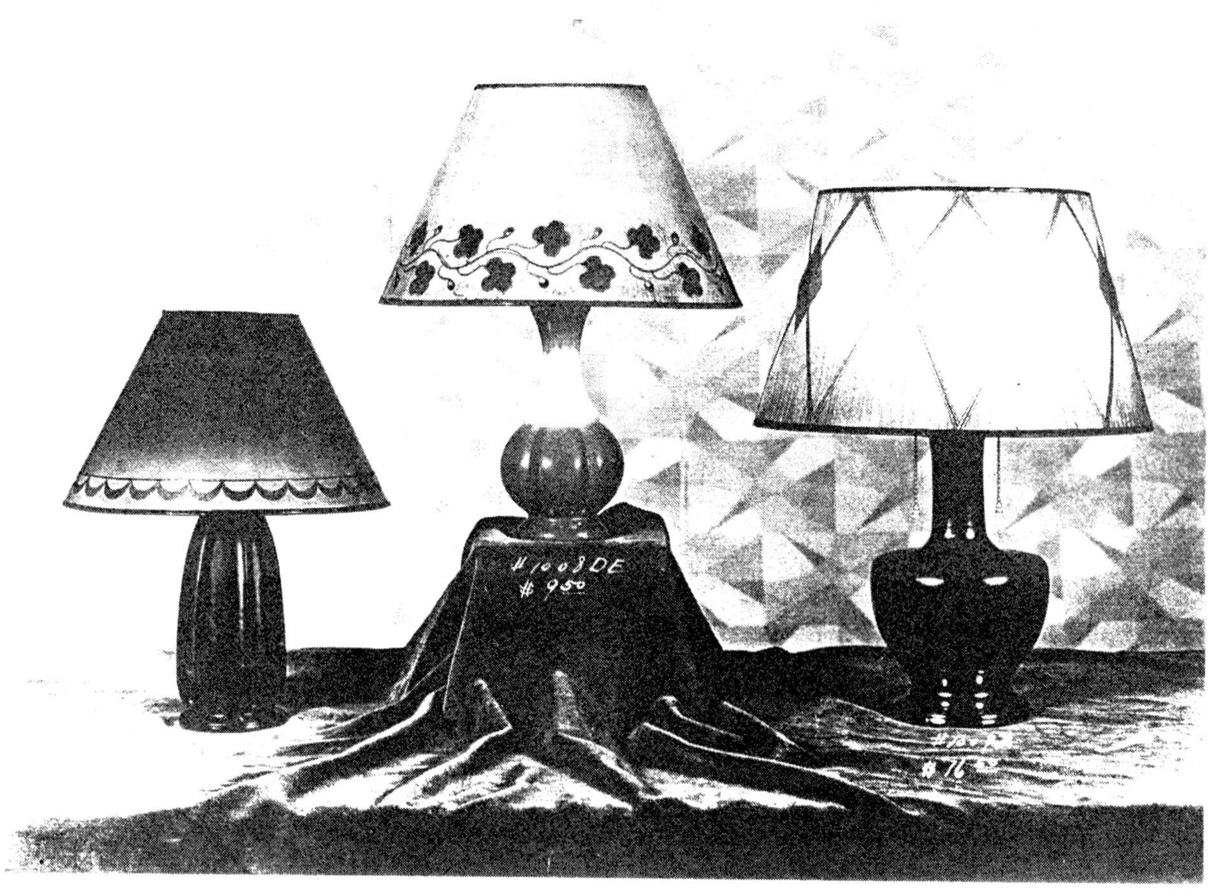

This is a studio photograph made for salesmen to include in their sales catalogs. Values are for the lamp base only. Add 100% for lamps with a shade in good condition.

Value Ranges: 1007C $30-40
1008DE $20-40
1009A $40-50

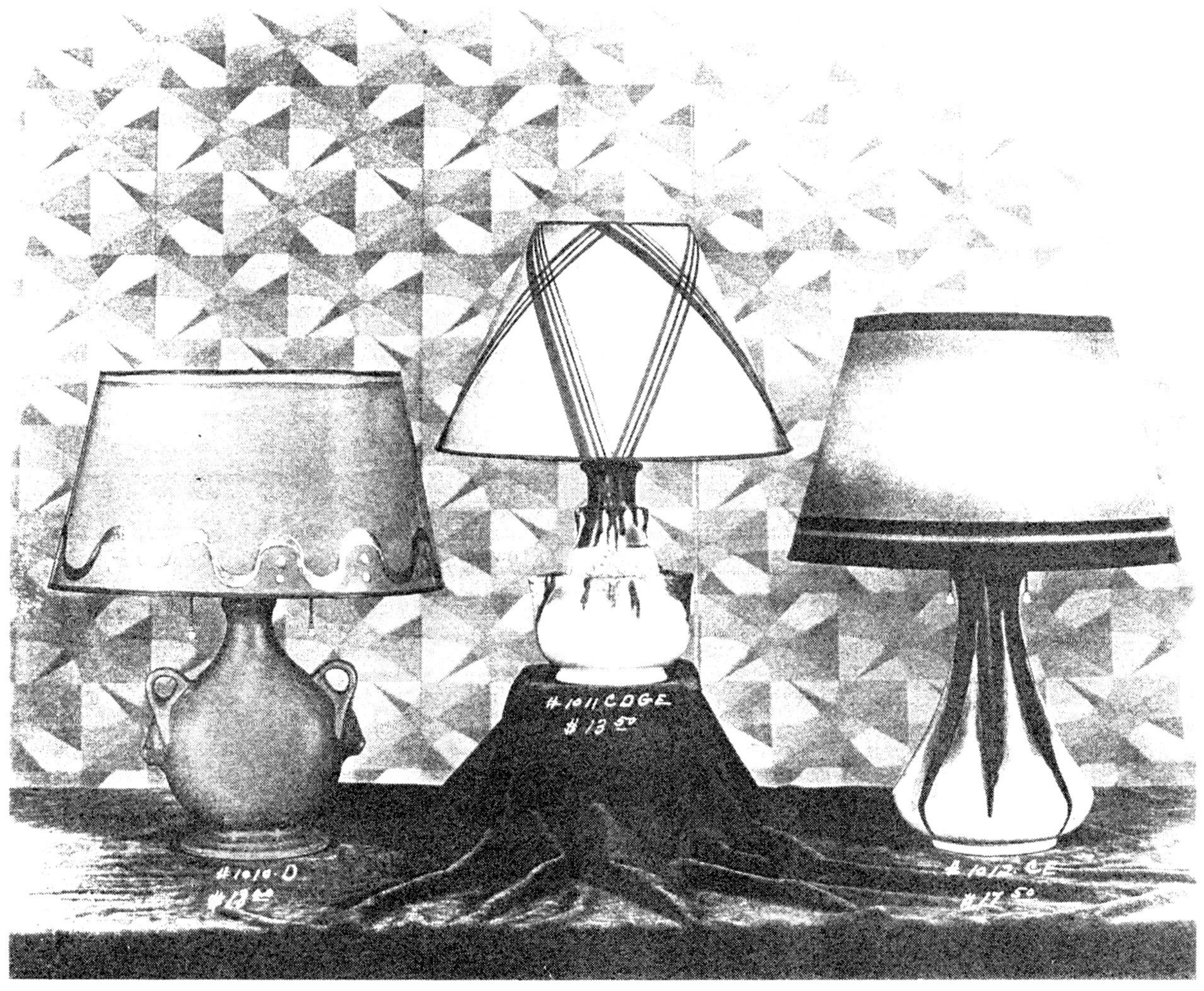

Here is another studio photograph made for salesmen to include in their sales catalogs. Values are for the lamp base only. Add 100% for lamps with a shade in good condition.

Value Ranges: 1010D $50-60
1011 CDGE $30-40
1012CE $50-60

MAILERS

Value Range: Nightingale Lamp – **Junior $6-10**
Senior $10-15
Electric $20-25
Add 50% for cobalt blue

This mailer was sent to hospitals, colleges, and universities that had nursing schools. These are sometimes found with the school's logo. The lamps were normally glazed white, but the junior size has been found in cobalt blue. The nurse's prayer is printed on the back of the mailer. (Two views shown)

THE NIGHTINGALE LAMP

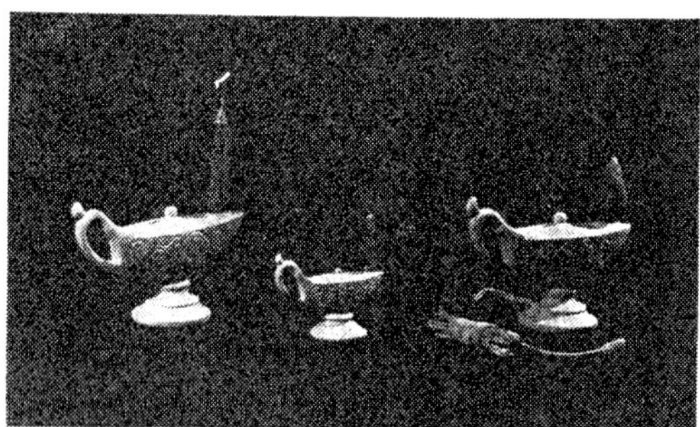

Senior Junior Electric

PRICES –
F.O.B. - MORTON, ILL.
JUNIOR
4½" long x 3" high
60¢ each $6.00 doz.
SENIOR
8" long x 4½" high
$1.00 each $9.00 doz.
ELECTRIC
8" long x 4¾" high
$2.75 each
Candles included at prices quoted

RAPP ART CRAFTS
Morton, Illinois

A NURSE'S PRAYER

I pray that I will ever be . . . A good and faithful nurse . . . And help each patient to get well . . . Or keep from growing worse . . . To aid the doctor and obey . . . The orders I receive . . . And always be available . . . And willing to relieve . . . And when my country calls me in . . . The hour of a war . . . I pray that I will be prepared . . . To serve on sea or shore . . . To heal the sick and wounded and . . . Attend the lame and blind . . . And comfort those whose nerves are frayed . . . Or who are ill of mind . . . I ask for strength and courage and . . . That I may never fail . . . To honor God, my uniform . . . and Florence Nightingale.

James J. Metcalfe
Author

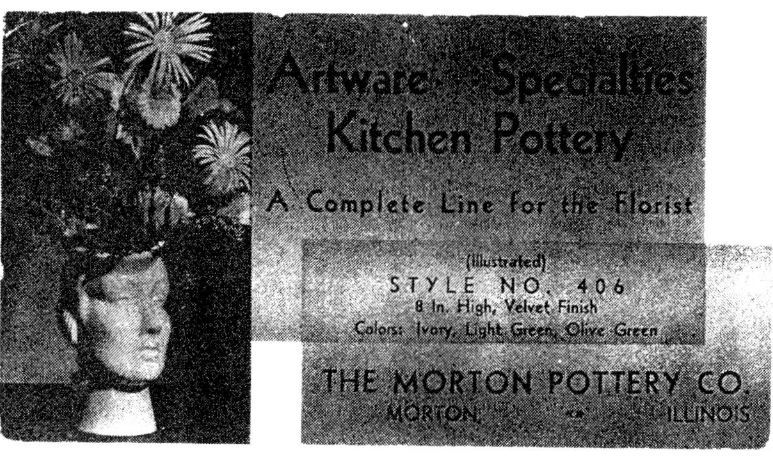

Artware . . . Specialties Kitchen Pottery advertising card

Value Range: Head vase $40-50

. . . Here They Are!! . . .

"SCOTTIES" SUGAR and CREAMER

The Newest Creation!

They Appeal to Everyone!
Suggest them as PREMIUMS,
BRIDGE PRIZES, etc.

Burned in beautiful, assorted colors.

Capacity 6 oz.

Packed 1 doz. sets in carton.

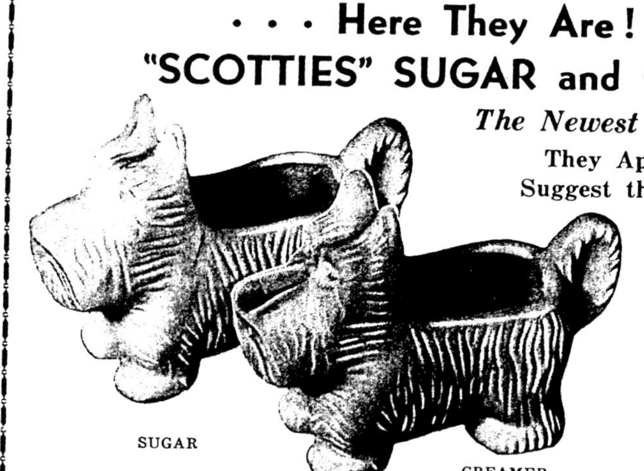

SUGAR CREAMER

Morton Pottery Co.
Morton, Illinois

Scotty dog sugar and creamer. These were copied from give-away glass sets packaged in cereal boxes.

Value Range:
$25-30 set

Globe teapot. This teapot is the same "New" globe teapot made by Morton Earthenware Company from 1915-1917.

Value Range:
48S - Black $22, Blue $30 & Woodland $50

42S - Black $25, Blue $35 & Woodland $60

36S - Black $28, Blue $40 & Woodland $60

30S - Black $32. Blue $45 & Woodland $65

24S - Black $34, Blue $50 & Woodland $70

Morton Tea Pots

Colors: Jet Black - Pilgrim Blue
Woodland Mottled

Size	Ounce Capacity	Prices - Net No Discount
48's	24	$3.00 per dozen
42's	30	3.30 per dozen
36's	40	3.60 per dozen
30's	50	4.80 per dozen
24's	64	6.00 per dozen

6% added for Packing Charge
Prices F.O.B. Morton, Ill
Terms: 1% 10 days Cash, 30 days N

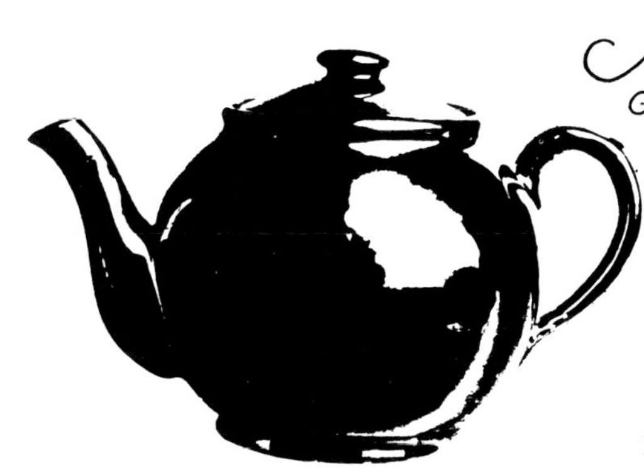

Light Weight - Glossy
Well Fired - New Shades

The Morton Pottery Co.
Morton - Illinois

• • Fancy Pottery Flower Vases • •

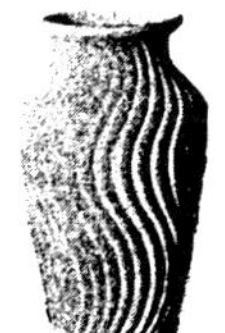
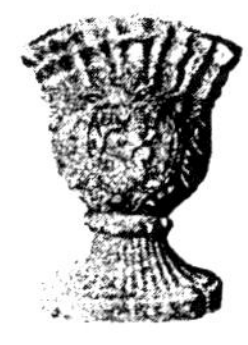
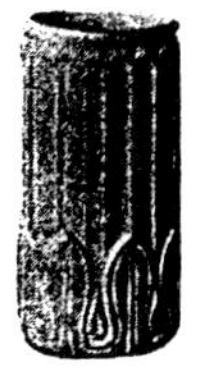
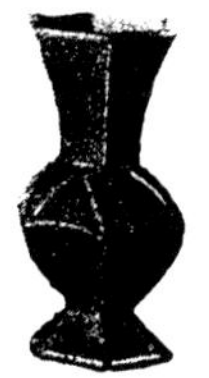

F227 F228 F230 F229 F206

EXCLUSIVE AND ATTRACTIVE DESIGNS

POPULAR HEIGHT—EIGHT INCHES

COLORS—*Ivory, Green, White, Blue, and Black*

PRICED TO *sell* AT POPULAR PRICES

MORTON POTTERY COMPANY

MORTON ILLINOIS

Value Range:

F227 - $10-12

F228 - $10-12

F230 - $15-18

F229 - $12-14

F206 - $12-14

MAILERS

These are examples of envelope stuffers that were frequently used by the pottery for advertising purposes. They were not only cheaper than newspaper and magazine advertising, but were capable of covering a much wider market. Remember, first class postage was only three cents until 1958.

This BARREL DESIGN Pitcher and Mugs to match make a very attractive set. Fired to a high temperature—that natural taste is retained. Burned with a beautiful Rockingham Brown Glaze. Pitcher capacity 90 oz. Packed one set per carton.

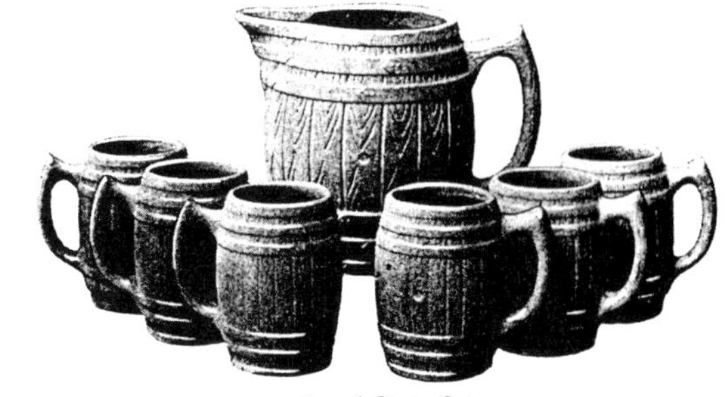

Barrel Stein Set

The Morton Pottery Co.

MORTON, ILL.

Value Range: Barrel Pitcher $35-45
16 oz. Stein $10-12

This attractive DANCERS DESIGN Pitcher and Mugs to match are very popular and an exceptional good item with us. Fired to a high temperature — that natural taste is retained. Burned with a beautiful Rockingham Brown Glaze. Pitcher capacity 80. oz. Packed one set per carton.

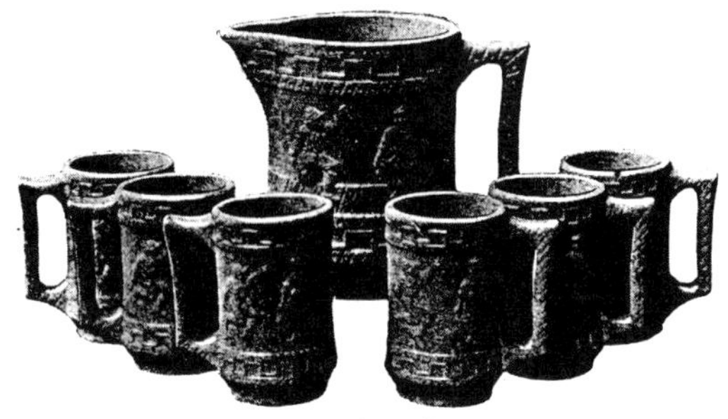

Dancers Stein Set

The Morton Pottery Co.

MORTON, ILL.

Value Range: Dancers Pitcher $50-60

15 oz. Stein $16-18

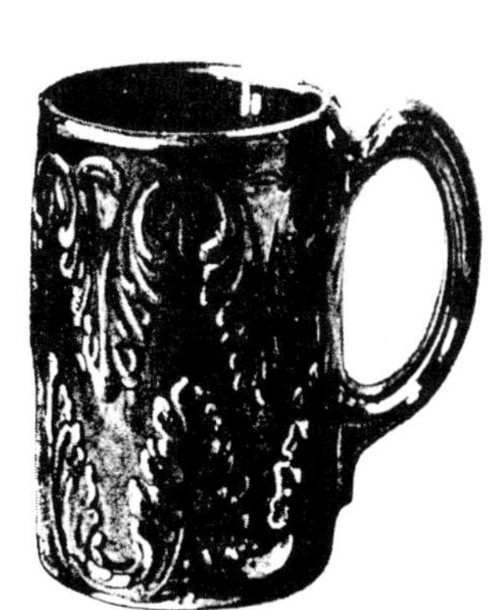

No. 21
Leaf Design

This very attractive Rockingham Brown LEAF DESIGN Mug will help stimulate sales on Malt, Coffee, Beverages, etc. Fired to a high temperature — that natural taste is retained. Capacity 14 oz. Packed one dozen in a carton.

The Morton Pottery Company

Morton, Ill.

Value Range: 16 oz. Leaf Stein $15-17

MAP "SAVINGS IN FREIGHT COST"

This handbill was widely used by the pottery in the 1920's and 1930's. It could be folded and stuffed into envelopes with invoices or other information sent from the business office.

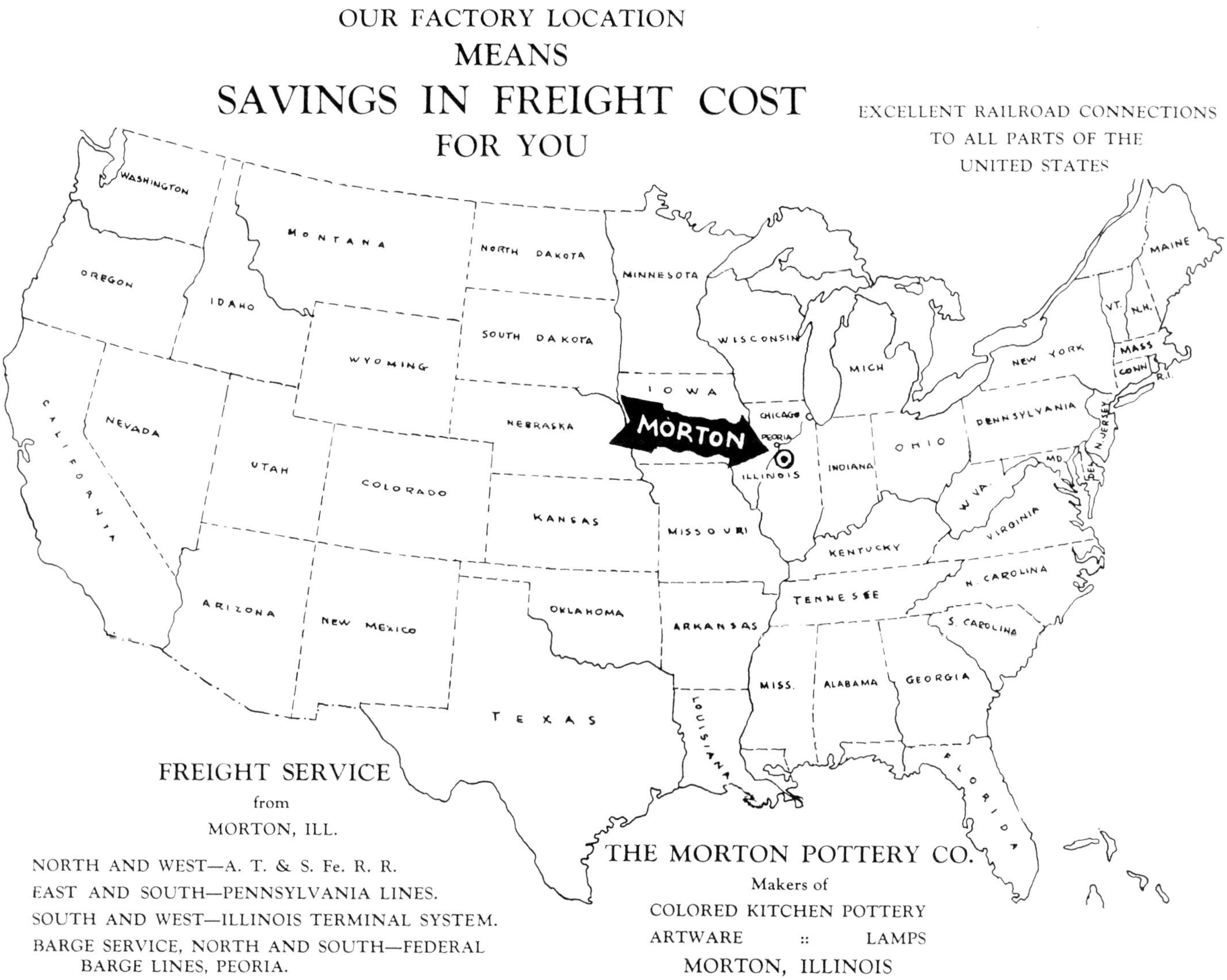

OUR FACTORY LOCATION
MEANS
SAVINGS IN FREIGHT COST
FOR YOU

EXCELLENT RAILROAD CONNECTIONS
TO ALL PARTS OF THE
UNITED STATES

MORTON

FREIGHT SERVICE
from
MORTON, ILL.

NORTH AND WEST—A. T. & S. Fe. R. R.
EAST AND SOUTH—PENNSYLVANIA LINES.
SOUTH AND WEST—ILLINOIS TERMINAL SYSTEM.
BARGE SERVICE, NORTH AND SOUTH—FEDERAL BARGE LINES, PEORIA.

THE MORTON POTTERY CO.
Makers of
COLORED KITCHEN POTTERY
ARTWARE :: LAMPS
MORTON, ILLINOIS

FLOWER HOLDERS AND BOOK ENDS

Few head vases were made by Morton Pottery Company. The baby items and the colonial ladies were popular lines. The lady with the oversize basket, No. 371, is very similar to one done by Brush McCoy Pottery. The Brush lady has a smaller basket, and it is square rather than round. In 1939, the bookends sold to retailers for 46¢ per dozen net.

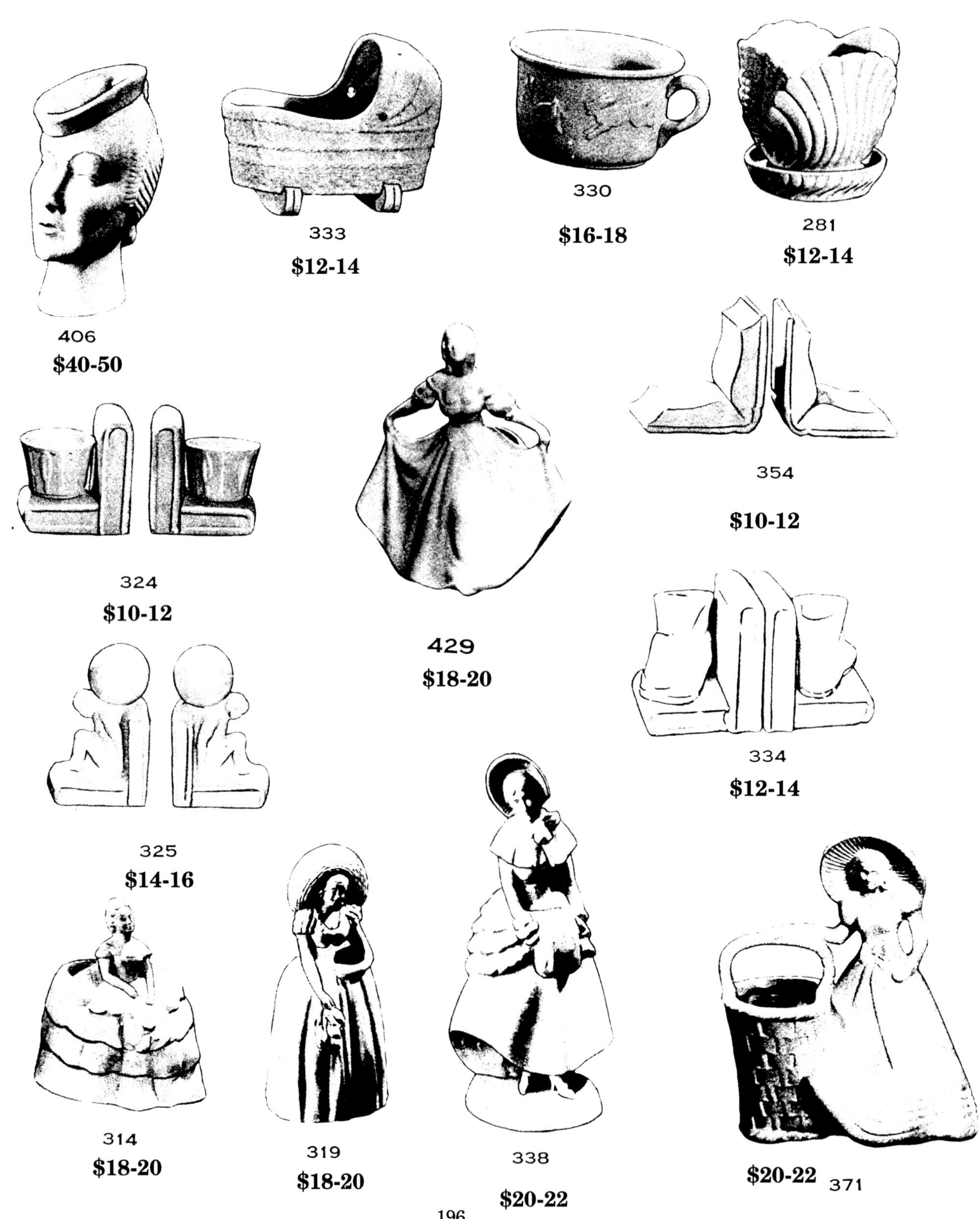

406
$40-50

333
$12-14

330
$16-18

281
$12-14

324
$10-12

429
$18-20

354
$10-12

325
$14-16

334
$12-14

314
$18-20

319
$18-20

338
$20-22

371
$20-22

HOLIDAY NOVELTIES

Except for the white sleigh, all items on this sales page were sprayed with red automobile lacquer and baked at a low temperature in the kiln.

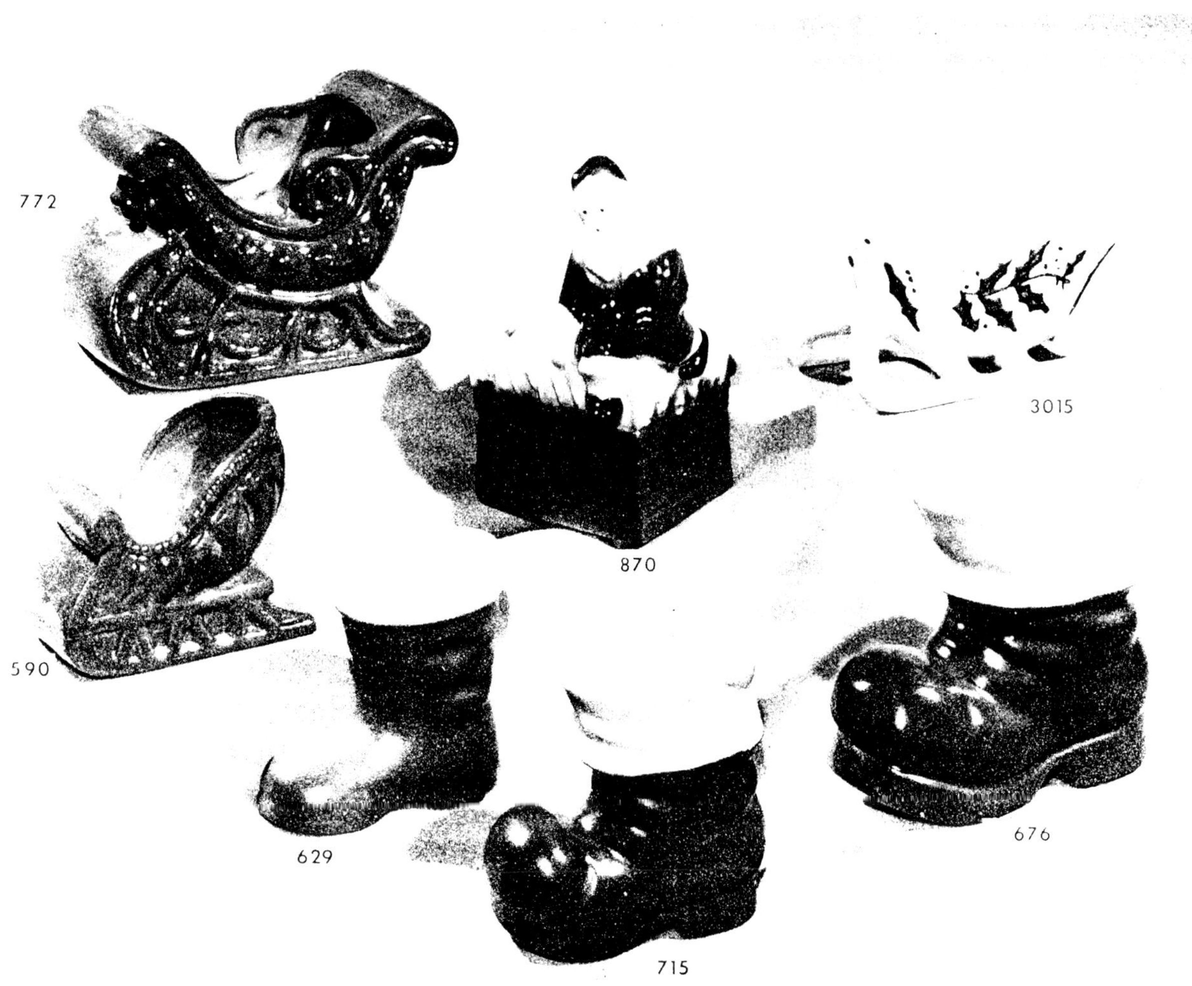

Value Range:

772	**Sleigh**	**$25-30**
870	**Santa**	**$20-25**
3015	**Sleigh**	**$18-24**
590	**Sleigh**	**$15-20**
629	**Boot**	**$10-12**
715	**Boot**	**$16-18**
676	**Boot**	**$20-22**

HOLIDAY NOVELTIES

Holiday novelties were in great demand from the early 1930's through the 1950's. Often contracted for a year or two in advance, the pottery supplied such well known chains as F. W. Woolworth, S. S. Kresge, W. T. Grant, S. H. Kress, and J. J. Newberry. The small turkey was packed two dozen per carton and was sold to those retailers for $1.92 per dozen. The large hearts were $1.80 per dozen. They were sprayed with automobile lacquer then baked because the pottery could not develop a bright red glaze.

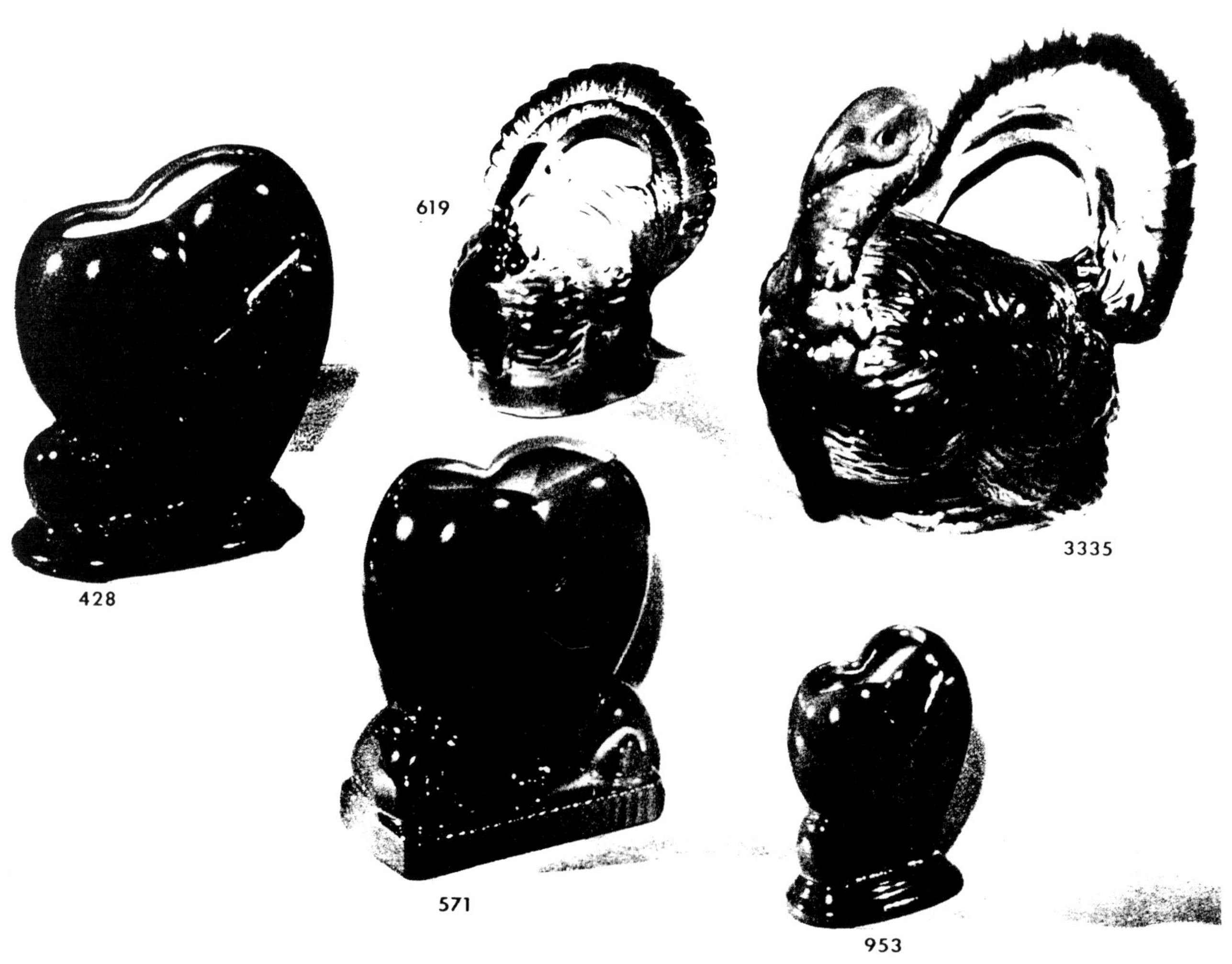

Value Range: 428 Heart $5-10
571 Heart $5-10
953 Heart $3-5
619 Turkey $12-14
3335 Turkey $35-45

(Lids were made for this planter to convert it to a cookie jar.)

MOTHER EARTH FRUIT AND VEGETABLE PLANT GROWERS

Most of these novelty planters were glazed inside and put through a high temperature firing. The bisque forms were then hand painted in natural colors. The cold paint used for decoration has deteriorated from use over the years. The planters are usually found with chipped paint, or even void of paint. Housewives used these planters on window sills for growing herbs. The value ranges are for mint or near mint condition. The letters preceding the values are C, common; E, elusive; S, scarce; and R, rare.

Value Ranges:

No. 439	Pineapple	R	$8-10
No. 390	Sweet Potato	S	$6-8
No. 437	Tomato	R	$8-10
No. 391	Egg Plant	S	$6-8
No. 392	Acorn Squash	C	$3-5
No. 395	Cucumber	S	$6-8
No. 399	Carrot	C	$3-5
No. 440	Red Cabbage	E	$4-6
No. 389	Apple	S	$6-8
No. 438	Plum	R	$8-10
No. 436	Orange	R	$8-10
No. 394	Green Pepper	E	$4-6
No. 397	Pumpkin	C	$3-5
No. 441	Banana	R	$8-10
No. 396	Summer Squash	C	$3-5
No. 398	Green Cabbage	E	$4-6
No. 393	Red Pepper	E	$4-6

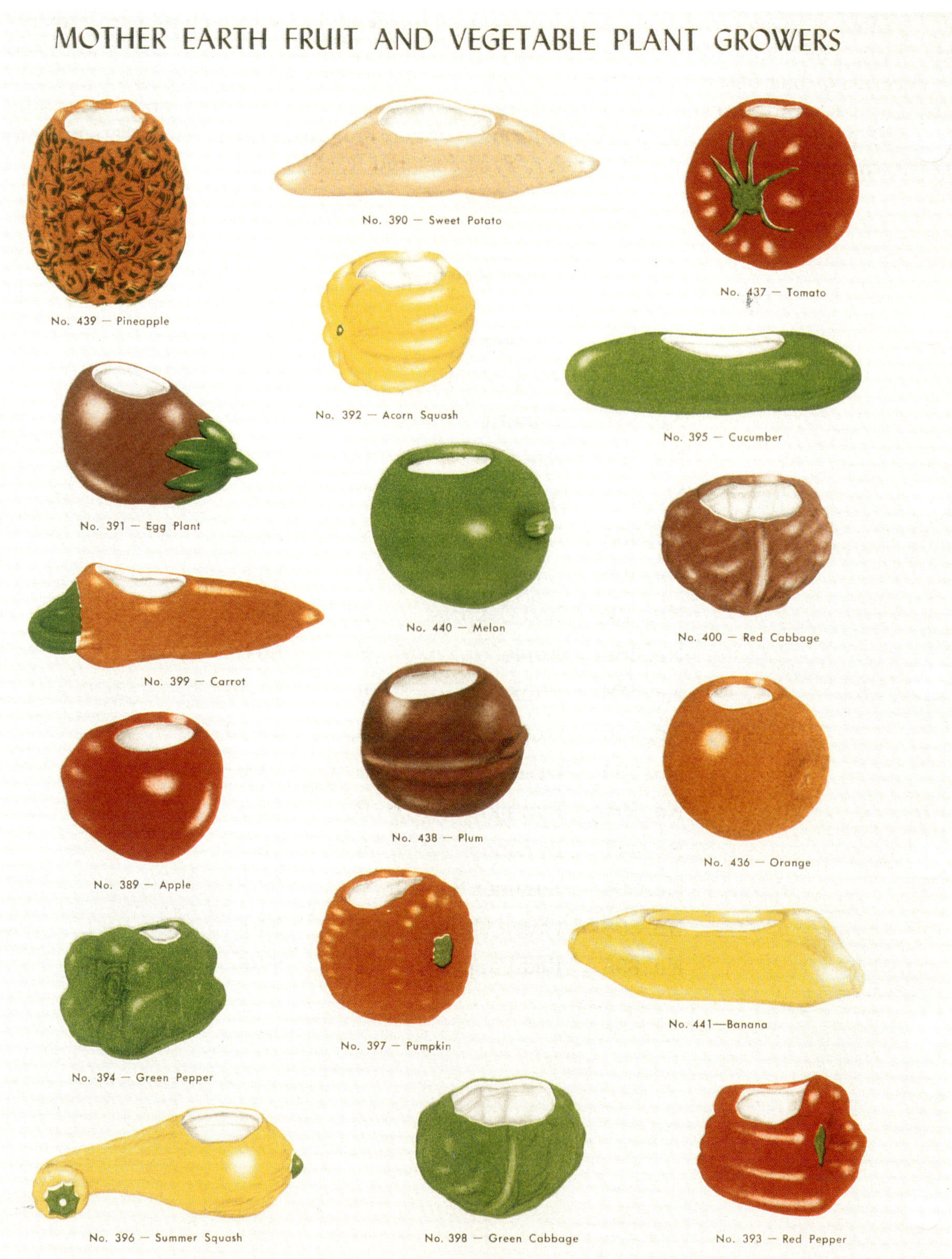
MOTHER EARTH FRUIT AND VEGETABLE PLANT GROWERS
No. 390 — Sweet Potato
No. 437 — Tomato
No. 439 — Pineapple
No. 392 — Acorn Squash
No. 395 — Cucumber
No. 391 — Egg Plant
No. 440 — Melon
No. 400 — Red Cabbage
No. 399 — Carrot
No. 438 — Plum
No. 436 — Orange
No. 389 — Apple
No. 441—Banana
No. 397 — Pumpkin
No. 394 — Green Pepper
No. 396 — Summer Squash
No. 398 — Green Cabbage
No. 393 — Red Pepper
THE MORTON POTTERY COMPANY · MORTON, ILLINOIS

NOVELTY PLANTERS

Value Ranges

No. 767	Twin Lily	$18-20
No. 881	Old Kitchen Stove	$10-12
No. 879	Large Cat	$12-14
No. 943	Old Shoe House	$14-16
No. 875	Three Pits	$10-12
No. 619	Turkey	$12-14
No. 932	Bear and Cradle	$18-22
No. 737	Pagoda Bowl	$8-10
No. 756	Bulb Bowl	$8-10
No. 775	Bulb Bowl	$8-10
No. 757	4" African Violet Pot	$8-10
No. 758	5" African Violet Pot	$10-12
No. 759	6" African Violet Pot	$12-14
No. 558	4 1/2" Art Pottery Pot	$8-12
No. 251	5 1/2" Art Pottery Pot	$12-14
No. 916	4 1/2" x 6" Ashtray	$3-5
No. 964	7 1/2" Dia. Ashtray	$6-8
No. 965	7 5/8" Square Ashtray	$4-6

NOVELTY PLANTERS

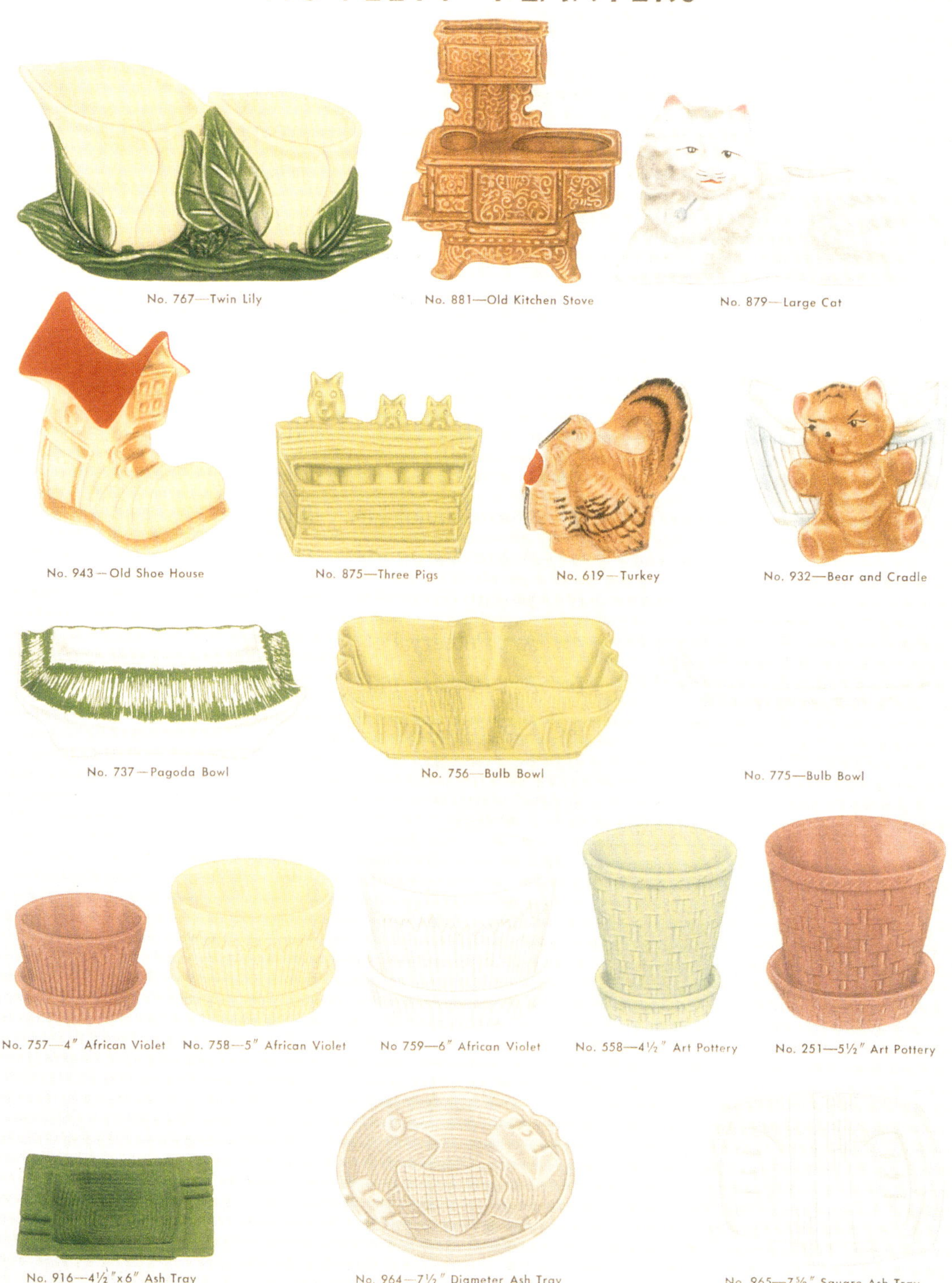

THE MORTON POTTERY COMPANY · MORTON, ILLINOIS

NOVELTY PLANTERS

These planters were supplied to 5¢ & 10¢ chain stores during the 1940's when similar novelties were no longer being shipped from Japan because of the war. They were also popular with florist shops and floral supply houses. All of these planters were made in solid pastel colors except the panda. It was always made in black and white.

Value Ranges:

No. 387	Rooster	$5-8
No. 409	Duck	$5-8
No. 388	Dog	$5-8
No. 418	Lamb	$5-8
No. 386	Bull Dog	$5-8
No. 426	Elephant	$5-8
No. 368	Camel	$5-8
No. 415	Circus Horse	$10-12
No. 417	Horse	$8-10
No. 351	Fawn	$10-12
No. 416	Love Birds	$12-14
No. 377	Fawn	$10-12
No. 430	Wheel Barrow	$5-8
No. 419	Cow	$10-12
No. 329	Gnome	$10-12
No. 316	Panda	$12-14
No. 411	Baby Buggy	$8-10
No. 410	Double Cactus	$10-12
No. 421	Boots	$8-10
No. 308	Wooden Shoe	$5-8

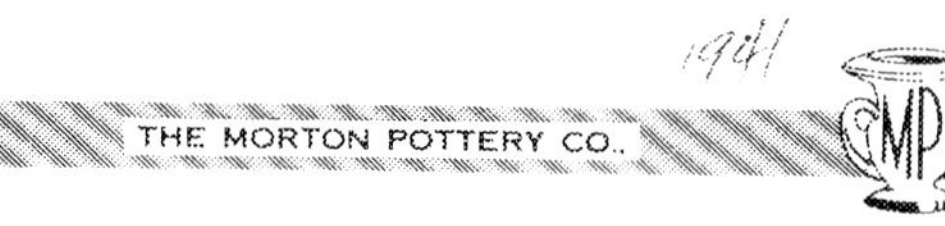

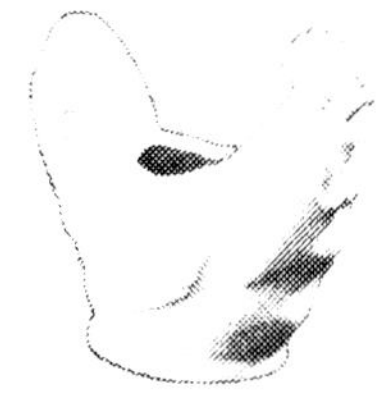

387 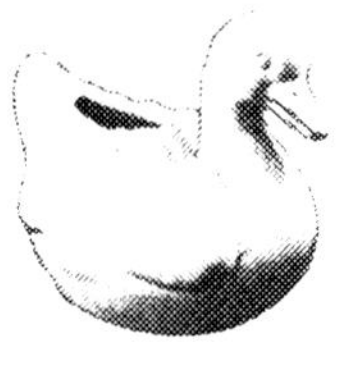 409 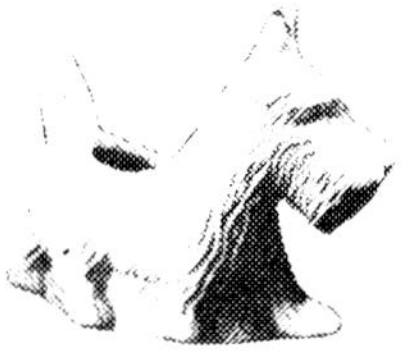 388 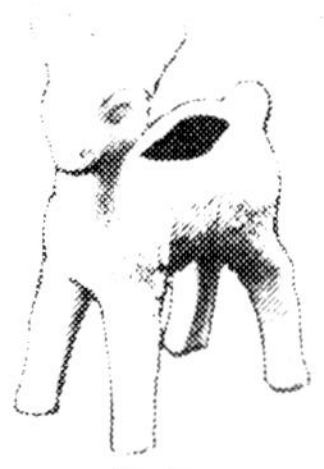 418

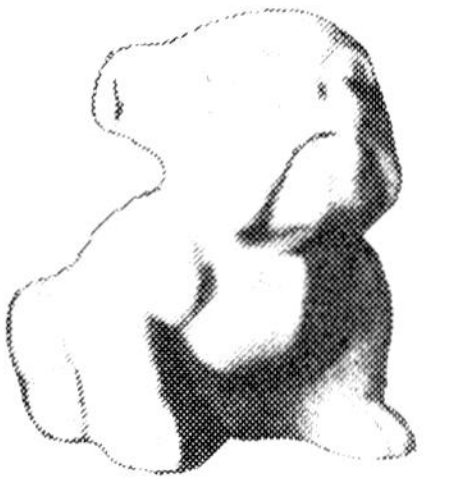

386 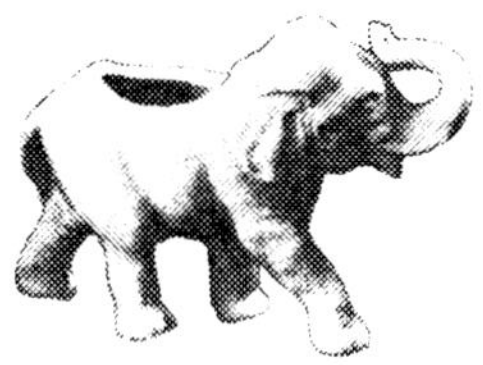 426 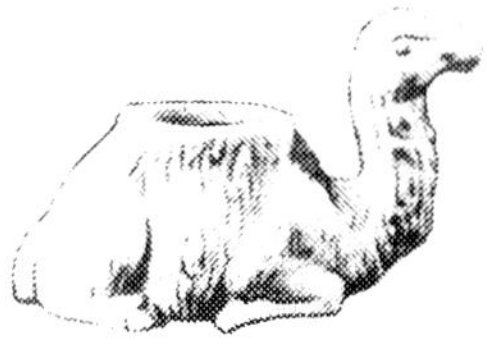 368 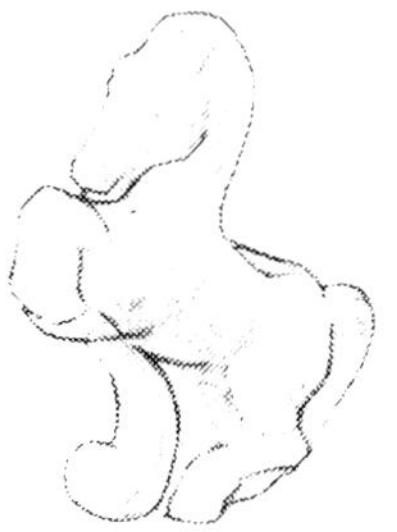 415

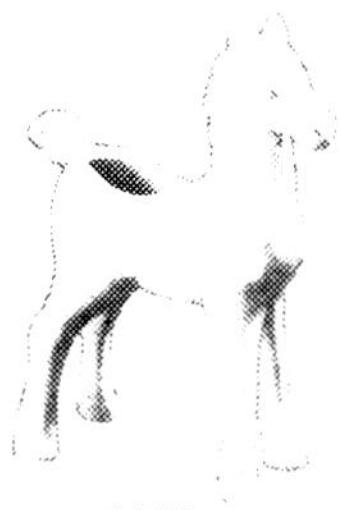

417 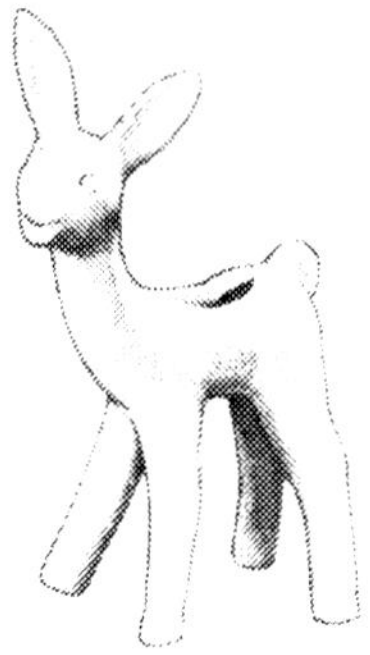 351 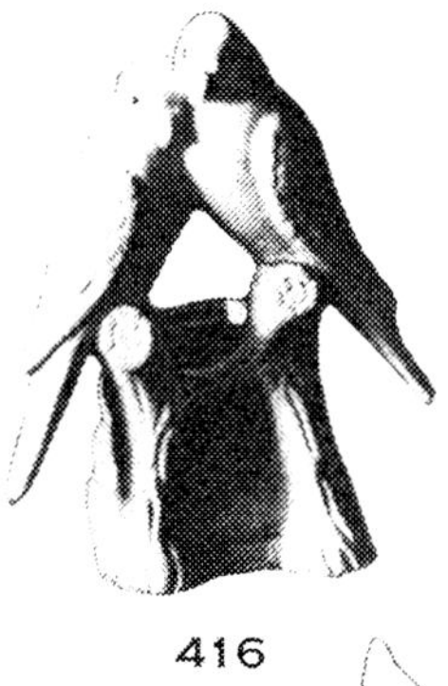 416 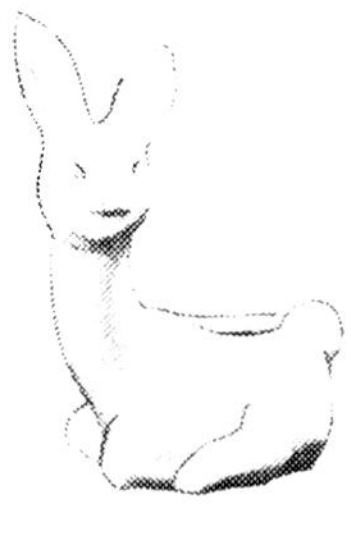 377

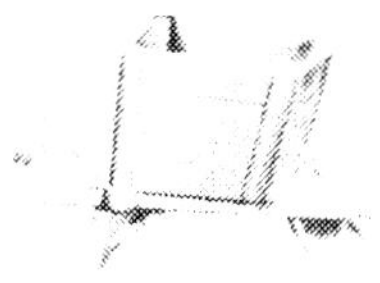

430 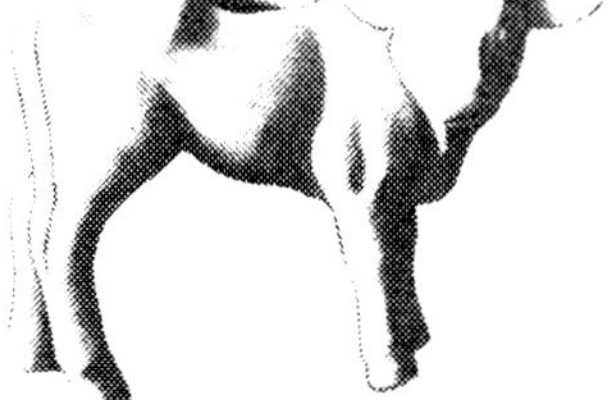 419 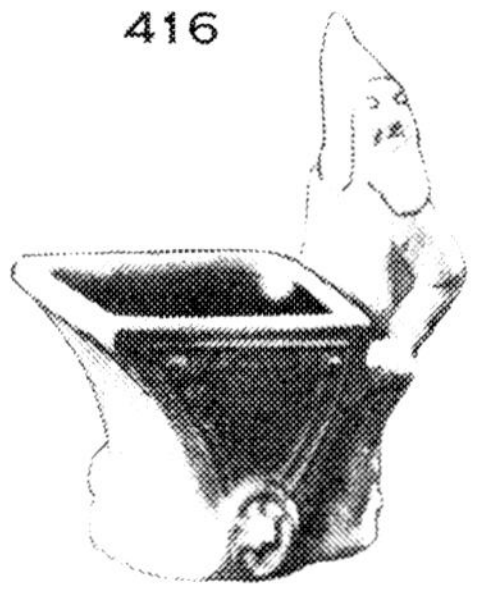 329 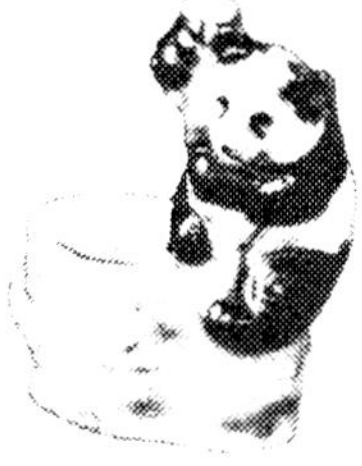 316

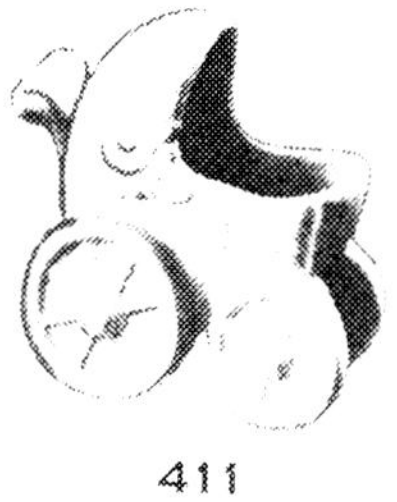

411 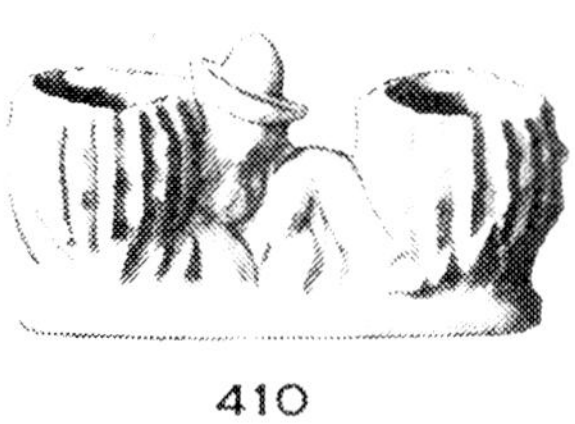 410 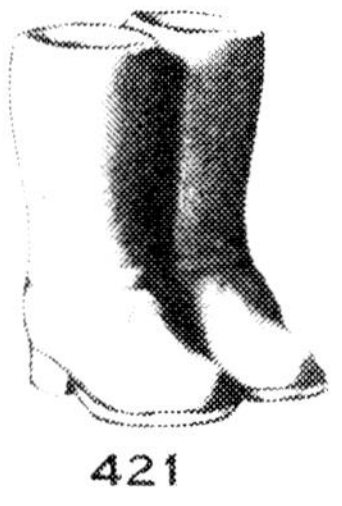 421 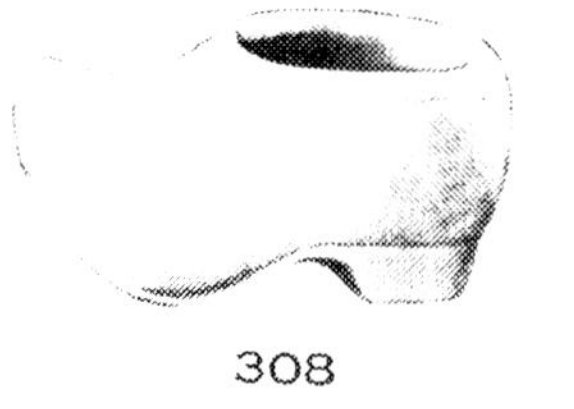 308

NOVELTY PLANT HOLDERS

The birds are the multi color yellow, blue, burgundy, and turquoise glaze style called "majolica." The colors were hand brushed after the planter had been dipped in white glaze.

The cactus planter was spray glazed. The figure's hat was always cold painted.

All of the sun bonnet girls were dip glazed in white and fired. After firing, they were hand decorated with cold paint and refired at low heat to temper the paint.

Value Ranges:

No. 416	Love Bird Planter	$12-14
No. 410	Cactus	$10-12
No. 443	Love Bird Wall Pocket Some of these had the nest closed and the back open with a nail hole in the bottom to serve as a string holder. Add 100% for the string holder.	$18-20
No. 445	Sun Bonnet Girls	$18-20

NOVELTY PLANT HOLDERS

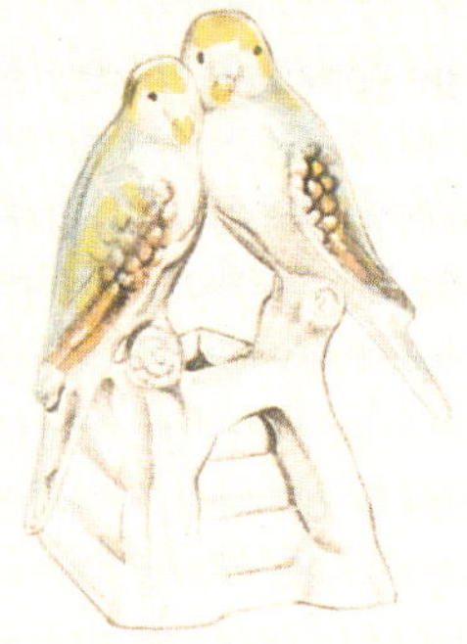

No. 416 Love Bird Planter

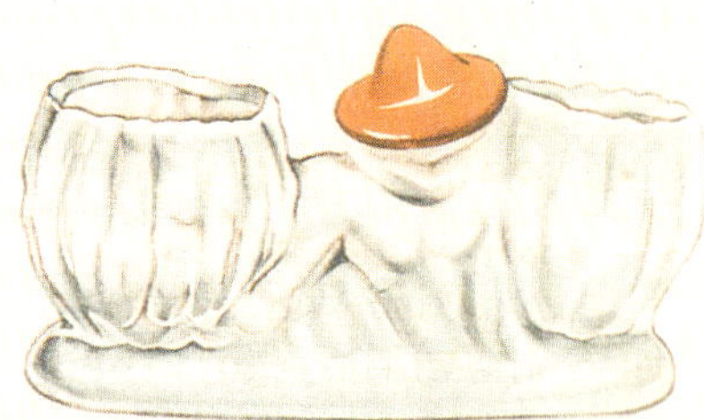

No. 410 Cactus

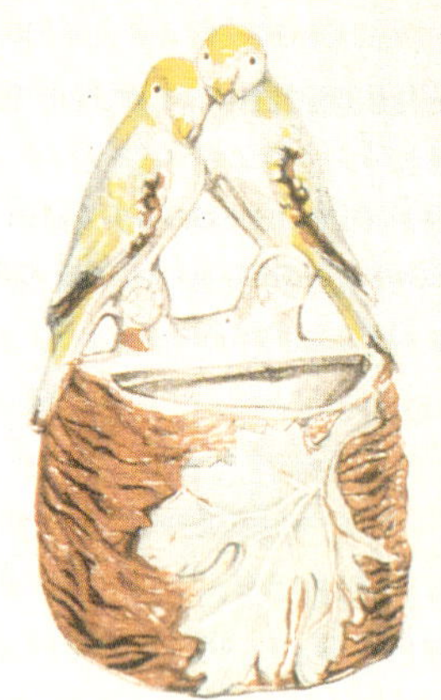

No. 443 Love Bird Wall Pocket

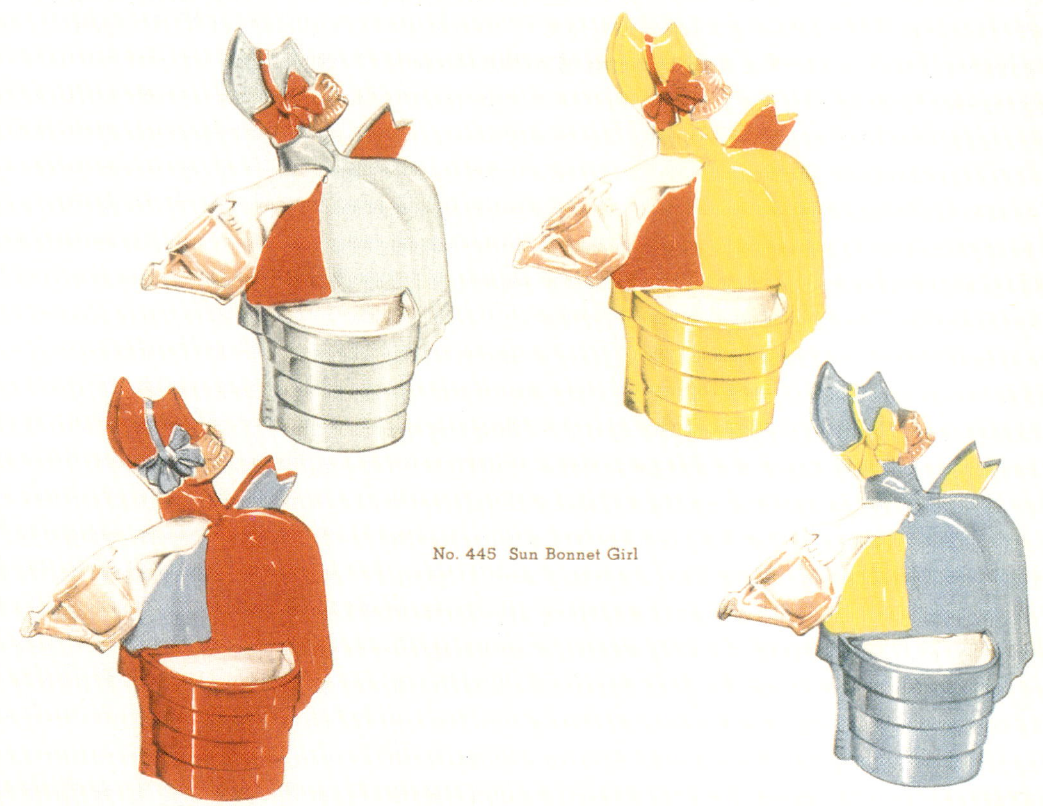

No. 445 Sun Bonnet Girl

THE MORTON POTTERY CO., MORTON, ILL., U. S. A.

NOVELTY PLANT HOLDERS

Value Ranges:

No. 619	Turkey	$12-14
No. 629	Boot	$10-12
No. 590	Sleigh	$15-20
No. 645	Fawn (Figurine)	$12-14

Novelty PLANT HOLDERS

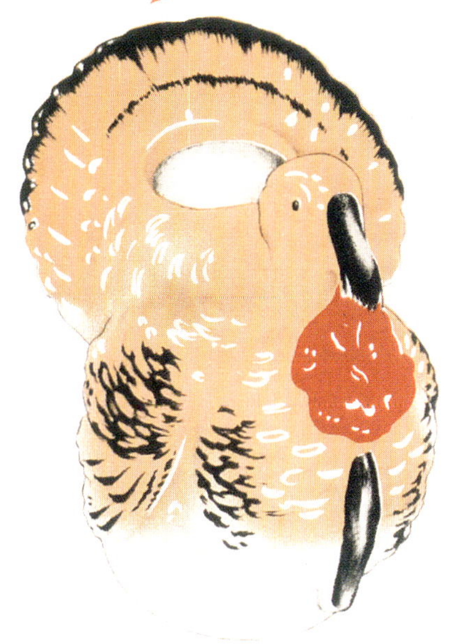

NO. 619 TURKEY

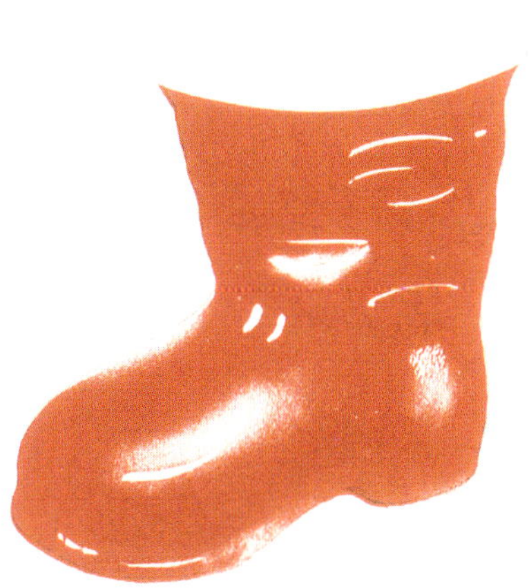

NO. 629 SANTA BOOT

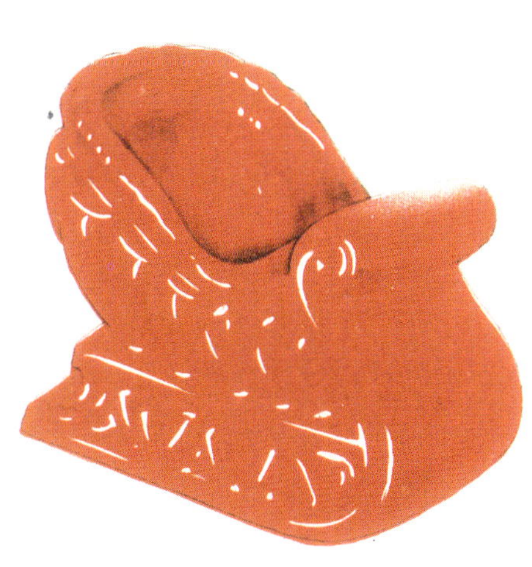

NO. 590 SLEIGH

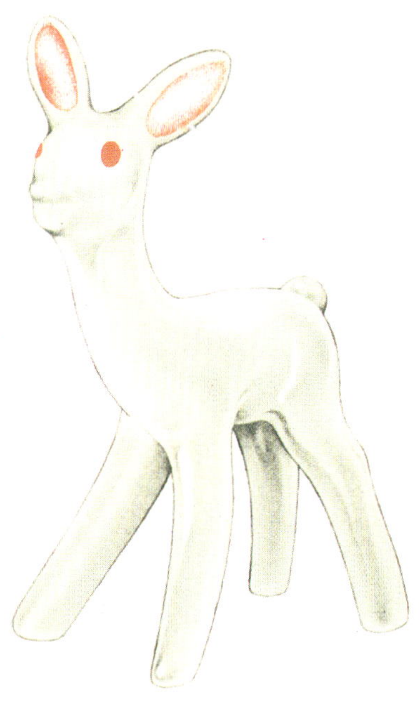

NO. 645 FAWN [Figurine]

THE MORTON POTTERY CO., MORTON, ILLINOIS, U.S.A.

NOVELTY SPOON HOLDERS

Value Ranges:

No. 808	Skillet	$9-12	No. 804	Pansy	$7-10
No. 810	Rose	$7-10	No. 833	Twin Pear	$9-12
No. 809	Fish	$6-9	Add 25% if these are found marked "Morton USA"		

NOVELTY SPOON HOLDERS

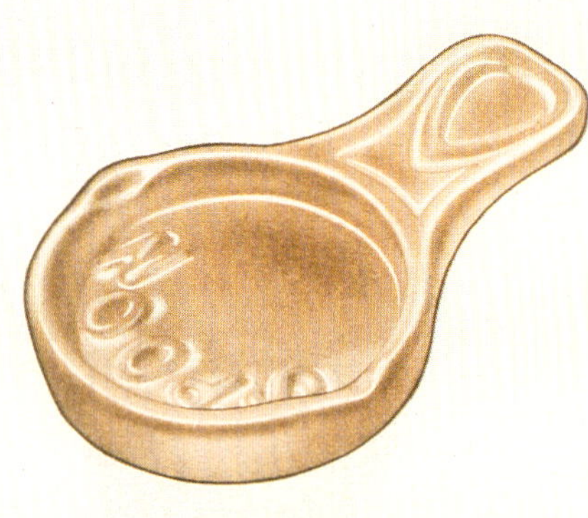

NO. 808 SKILLET

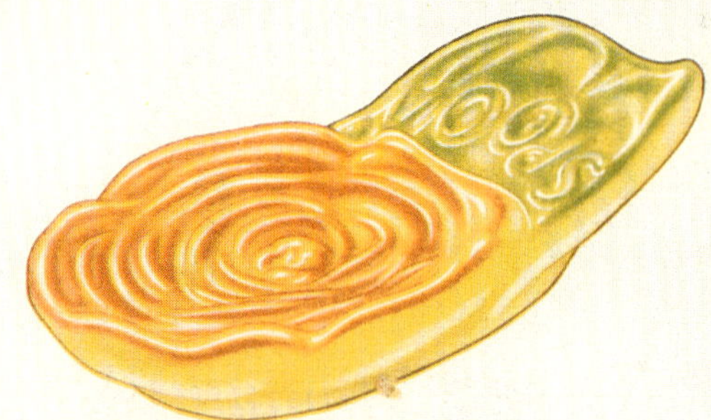

NO. 810 ROSE

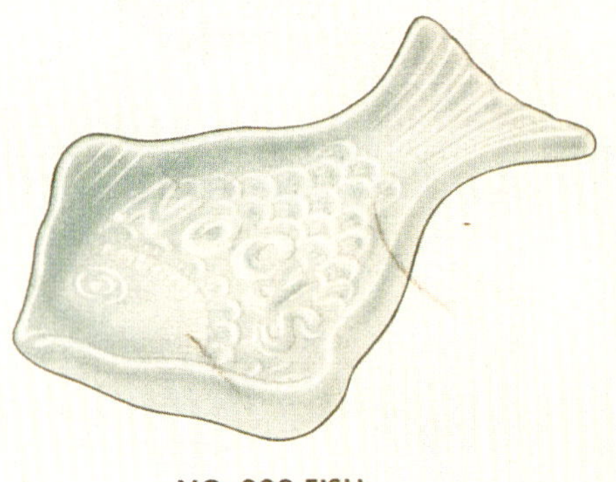

NO. 809 FISH

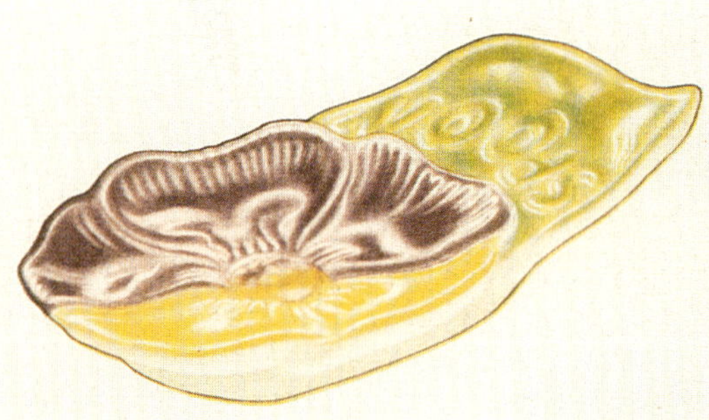

NO. 804 PANSY

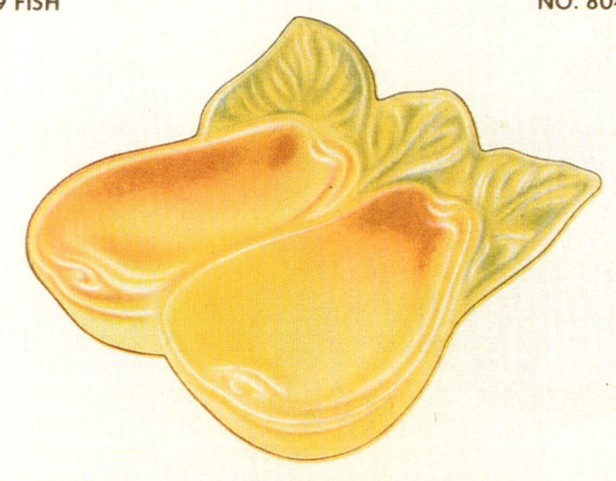

NO. 833 TWIN PEARS

THE MORTON POTTERY CO. MORTON, ILL. U.S.A.

PITCHER AND BOWL SETS

Several potteries in Ohio and Arkansas made pitcher and bowl sets similar to these. The style of handle, and the placement of the grape clusters will differ from company to company. These sets were two separate pieces. The two larger sets were often fused during kiln firing, then drilled so they could be made into lamps.

Value Ranges: 3426 Pitcher and Bowl set $20-25
Lamp $40-50

3338 Pitcher and Bowl set $15-20
Lamp $30-40

3006 Pitcher and Bowl set $10-15

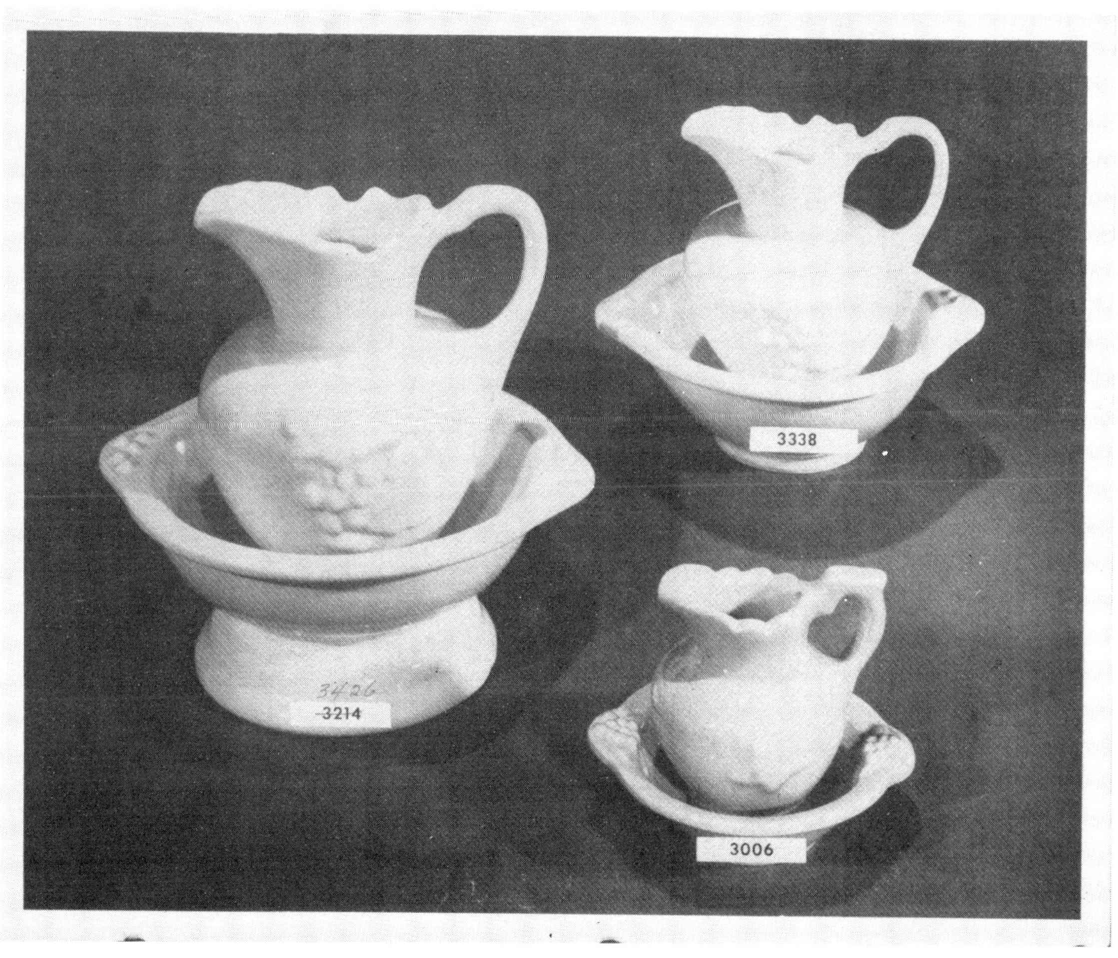

VASES

These smaller vases are on a price list dated January 30, 1939. They were also available in the assorted colors of green, ivory, yellow, white, and burgundy. The six inch vases sold for 90¢ per dozen.

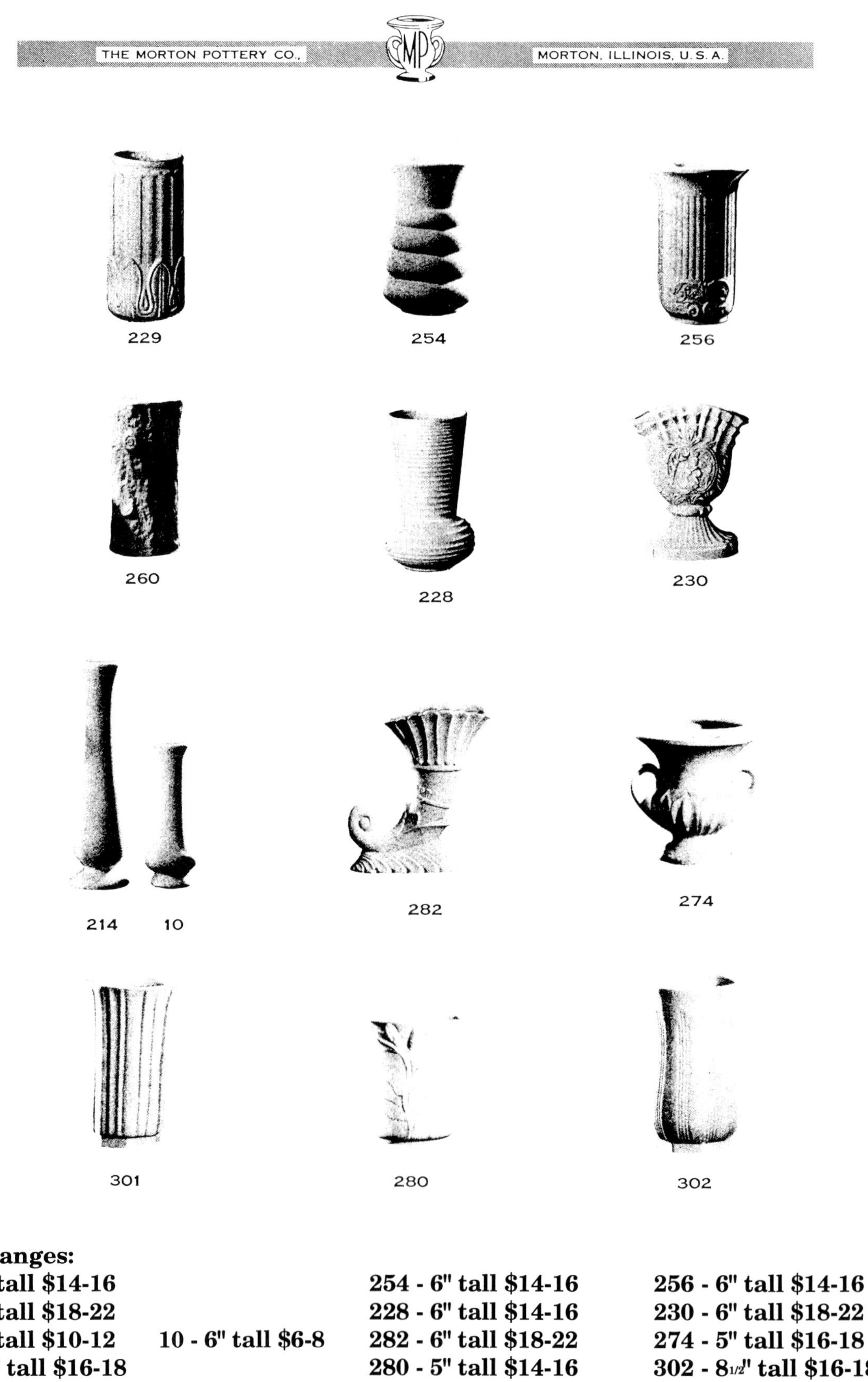

Value Ranges:

229 - 6" tall $14-16
260 - 6" tall $18-22
214 - 9" tall $10-12 **10 - 6" tall $6-8**
301 - 8½" tall $16-18
254 - 6" tall $14-16
228 - 6" tall $14-16
282 - 6" tall $18-22
280 - 5" tall $14-16
256 - 6" tall $14-16
230 - 6" tall $18-22
274 - 5" tall $16-18
302 - 8½" tall $16-18

VASES

These vases were found on a pottery price list dated January 30, 1939. They were available in assorted colors of blue, green, ivory, yellow, white, and burgundy. The eight inch vases were $2.00 per dozen except No. 283. It was $4.50 per dozen. Nine inch vases were $4.80 per dozen, and ten inch vases were $6.00 per dozen. Those prices average out at just over 36¢ per vase.

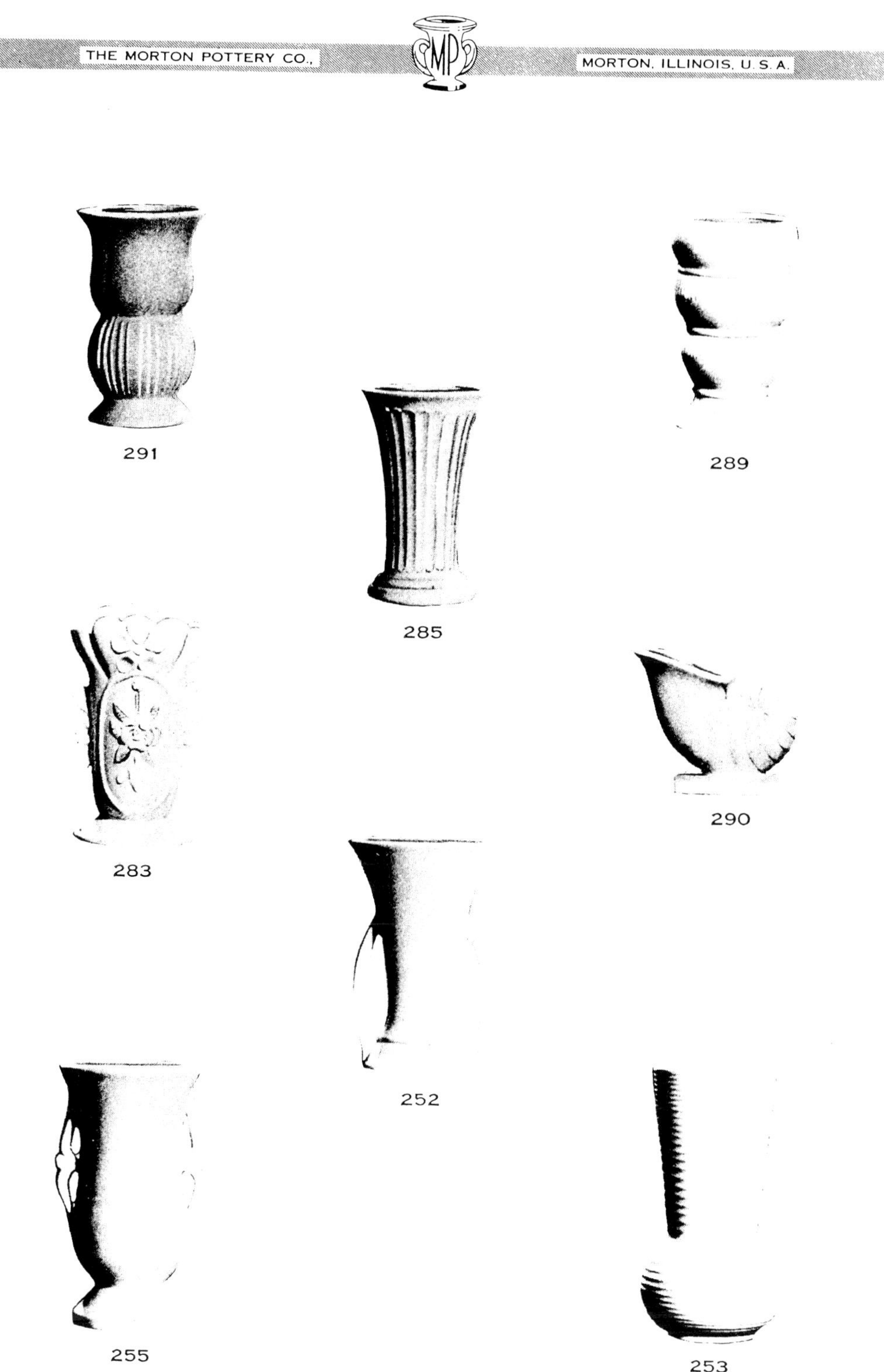

Value Ranges:

291 - 8" tall $16-18
283 - 8" tall $20-22
255 - 10" tall $22-24

285 - 8" tall $16-18
252 - 9" tall $18-20

289 - 8" tall $16-18
290 - 5" tall $14-16
253 - 10" tall $22-24

PILGRIM BLUE POTTERY

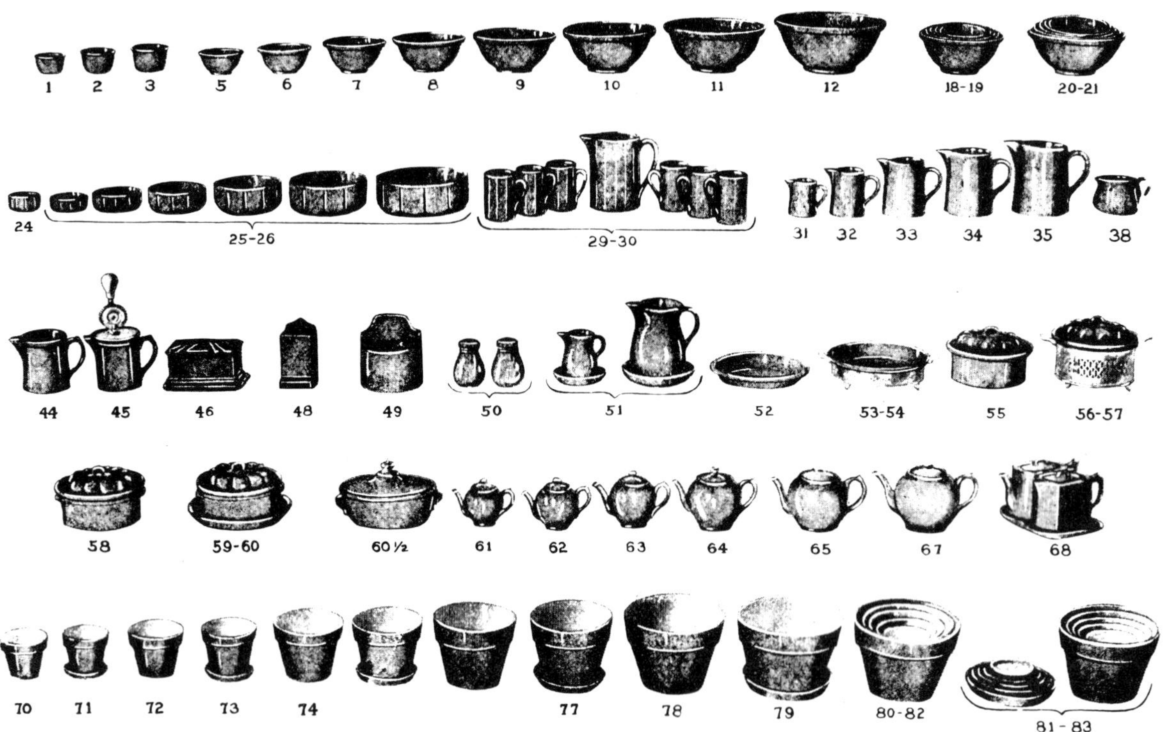

Item No.	Description	How Packed	Weight Carton	Price
1B	48's Custards	36 to carton	15 lbs.	$1.50 Dz.
2B	30's Custards	36 to carton	20 lbs.	1.80 Dz.
3B	24's Custards	36 to carton	25 lbs.	2.40 Dz.
5B	5" Mixing Bowls	12 to carton	10 lbs.	1.80 Dz.
6B	6" Mixing Bowls	12 to carton	14 lbs.	2.40 Dz.
7B	7" Mixing Bowls	12 to carton	18 lbs.	3.00 Dz.
8B	8" Mixing Bowls	12 to carton	20 lbs.	4.80 Dz.
9B	9" Mixing Bowls	12 to carton	30 lbs.	6.00 Dz.
10B	10" Mixing Bowls	12 to carton	40 lbs.	7.20 Dz.
11B	11" Mixing Bowls	6 to carton	23 lbs.	9.85 Dz.
12B	12" Mixing Bowls	6 to carton	30 lbs.	14.80 Dz.
18B	5, 6, 7, 8, 9 Bowl Nest	6 to carton	40 lbs.	1.50 Ea.
19B	5, 6, 7, 8, 9 Bowl Nest	1 to carton	8½ lbs.	1.65 Ea.
20B	6, 7, 8, 9, 10 Bowl Nest	6 to carton	60 lbs.	1.75 Ea.
21B	6, 7, 8, 9, 10 Bowl Nest	1 to carton	10 lbs.	1.87 Ea.
25B	4, 5, 6, 7, 8, 9 Baking Nappy Nest	4 to carton	45 lbs.	1.75 Ea.
26B	4, 5, 6, 7, 8, 9 Baking Nappy Nest	1 to carton	11 lbs.	1.87 Ea.
29B	Colonial Beverage Mugs	24 to carton	27 lbs.	3.00 Dz.
30B	Colonial Beverage Set	1 to carton	12 lbs.	2.50 Ea.
31B	42's Pitcher	12 to carton	10 lbs.	4.20 Dz.
32B	36's Pitcher	12 to carton	22 lbs.	6.00 Dz.
33B	30's Pitcher	12 to carton	25 lbs.	9.00 Dz.
34B	24's Pitcher	6 to carton	15 lbs.	12.00 Dz.
35B	12's Pitcher	6 to carton	36 lbs.	15.00 Dz.
38B	Ice Box Jug	12 to carton	16 lbs.	6.00 Dz.
44B	Beater Bowl Pitcher	12 to carton	22 lbs.	9.00 Dz.
45B	Beater Bowl Set	12 to carton	30 lbs.	12.00 Dz.
46B	1 Lb. Butter Box	12 to carton	35 lbs.	18.00 Dz.
48B	Match Box	12 to carton	17 lbs.	9.00 Dz.
49B	Salt Box	12 to carton	35 lbs.	12.00 Dz.
50B	Salt and Pepper Shakers	12 Pr. to carton	14 lbs.	1.00 Pr.
51B	Waffle Set	1 to carton	7 lbs.	2.00 Ea.
52B	Pie Plate Only	12 to carton	25 lbs.	.75 Ea.
53B	Pie Plate and Frame	12 to carton	16 lbs.	1.25 Ea.
54B	Pie Plate and Frame	1 to carton	4½ lbs.	1.46 Ea.
55B	Casserole only	6 to carton	25 lbs.	1.00 Ea.

Item No.	Description	How Packed	Weight Carton	Price
56B	Casserole and Frame	6 to carton	25 lbs.	1.75 Ea.
57B	Casserole and Frame	1 to carton	5½ lbs.	1.90 Ea.
58B	Casserole with handle	6 to carton	25 lbs.	1.00 Ea.
59B	Combination Casserole with handle and Pie Plate	6 to carton	40 lbs.	1.75 Ea.
60B	Combination Casserole with handle	1 to carton	7 lbs.	1.90 Ea.
60½B	Oval Vegetable Baking Dish	6 to carton	35 lbs.	2.00 Ea.
61B	60's Tea Pot, 1 Cup	12 to carton	9 lbs.	3.60 Dz.
62B	54's Tea Pot, 2 Cup	12 to carton	16 lbs.	3.60 Dz.
63B	48's Tea Pot, 3 Cup	12 to carton	18 lbs.	5.40 Dz.
64B	36's Tea Pot, 4 Cup	12 to carton	20 lbs.	7.20 Dz.
65B	30's Tea Pot, 5 Cup	12 to carton	32 lbs.	9.00 Dz.
67B	18's Tea Pot, 7 Cup	6 to carton	20 lbs.	12.60 Dz.
68B	Tea Set	1 to carton	7 lbs.	2.50 Ea.
70B	4" Flower Pot	12 to carton	7 lbs.	1.50 Dz.
71B	4" Flower Pot and Saucer	12 to carton	11 lbs.	3.00 Dz.
72B	5" Flower Pot	12 to carton	11 lbs.	2.40 Dz.
73B	5" Flower Pot and Saucer	12 to carton	17 lbs.	[illegible] Dz.
74B	6" Flower Pot	12 to carton	22 lbs.	[illegible]0 Dz.
75B	6" Flower Pot and Saucer	12 to carton	30 lbs.	7.20 Dz.
76B	7" Flower Pot	12 to carton	35 lbs.	5.10 Dz.
77B	7" Flower Pot and Saucer	12 to carton	45 lbs.	10.20 Dz.
78B	8" Flower Pot	12 to carton	42 lbs.	7.50 Dz.
79B	8" Flower Pot and Saucer	12 to carton	56 lbs.	15.00 Dz.
80B	4, 5, 6, 7, 8 Flower Pot	6 to carton	50 lbs.	~~3.85~~ Ea.
81B	4, 5, 6, 7, 8 Flower Pot and Saucers	6 to carton	60 lbs.	3.00 Ea.
82B	4, 5, 6, 7, 8 Flower Pot	1 to carton	10 lbs.	~~1.48~~ Ea.
83B	4, 5, 6, 7, 8 Flower Pot and Saucers	1 to carton	13 lbs.	~~1.50~~ Ea.

Prices F. O. B. Morton, Ill. Terms: 1% Discount for Cash in 10 Days; 30 Days Net.

THE MORTON POTTERY COMPANY

MORTON, ILLINOIS

PILGRIM BLUE POTTERY

Value Ranges:

FIRST ROW

No. 1 - $6-8
No. 2 - $8-10
No. 3 - $10-12
No. 5 - $10-12
No. 6 - $12-14
No. 7 - $14-16
No. 8 - $16-18
No. 9 - $18-22
No. 10 - $24-26
No. 11 - $28-32
No. 12 - $40-42
No. 18-19 - $60-80 set
No. 20-21 - $80-100 set

SECOND ROW

No. 24 - $8-10
No. 25-26 - $100-125 set
No. 29-30 - $100-125
No. 31 - $16-20
No. 32 - $20-24
No. 33 - $24-30
No. 34 - $30-34
No. 35 - $34-40
No. 38 - $25-30

THIRD ROW

No. 44 - $25-30
No. 45 - $35-45
No. 46 - $40-50
No. 46 - $40-50
No. 48 - $40-50
No. 49 - $50-60
No. 50 - $30-40 set
No. 51 - $75-150 set
No. 52 - $35-45
No. 53-54 - $45-50
No. 55 - $35-40
No. 56-57 - $45-50

FOURTH ROW

No. 58 - $40-45
No. 59-60 - $75-80
No. 60½ - ND
No. 61 - $20-40
No. 62 - $24-26
No. 63 - $26-28
No. 64 - $28-30
No. 65 - $30-35
No. 67 - $35-40
No. 68 - $65-75

FIFTH ROW

No. 70-72-74 - $8-10 each
No. 71-73-75 - $12-14 each
No. 76 - $18-20
No. 77 - $22-24
No. 78 - $20-22
No. 79 - $24-26
80-82 - ND
No. 81-83 - ND

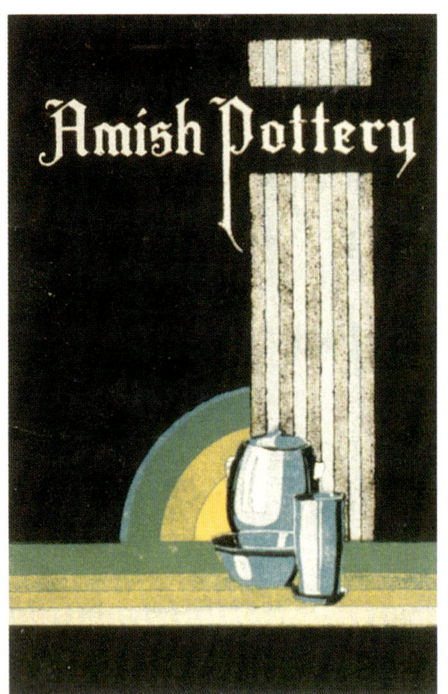

CATALOGUE

.... OF ....

AMISH POTTERY

(PANTRY WARE)

THE MORTON POTTERY CO.

MORTON, ILLINOIS

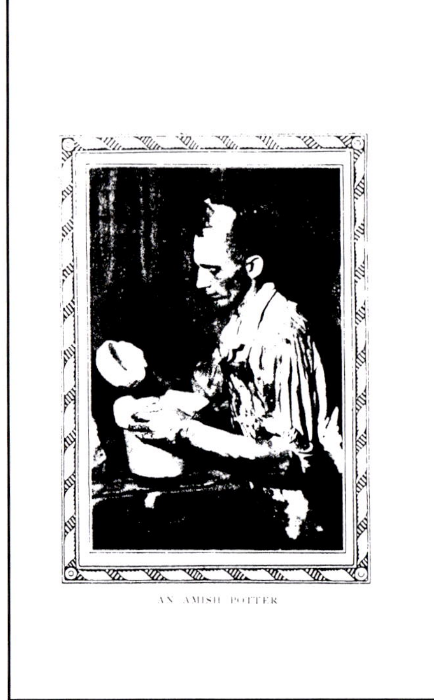

AN AMISH POTTER

AMISH POTTERY

THE Black Forest, home of the cuckoo clock, gaily painted houses, and colorful clothing, is perhaps the most beautiful, and varied of the wooded districts of Germany. It abounds with dense, pine-covered hills and valleys, miniature mountains and swiftly flowing streams. In spite of their love of color, the people of the Black Forest seem to have inherited from their gloomy, cathedral-like environment a nature somewhat sombre and deeply religious.

Years ago, many of these people in the northern part, where only the Rhine separates it from the Swiss Jura, became dissatisfied with the German Lutheran church, and formed a branch of their own, now known as the Amish Church. The creed of this church demanded a sterner code of living, strict adherence to the laws of the church, and the adoption of severe, black garments. Flat, black felt hats were adopted by the men, and a black, flat straw hat, or black poke bonnet, depending upon the season, by the women. The men wore beards, but were forbidden to wear mustaches, and the women wore their hair in long, flat, peculiar knots, low on the back of their heads, and held in place by very coarse nets of string.

The simplicity of this form of religion found great favor in the hearts of the peasants, and it soon spread to other parts of Germany and Switzerland. In order to practice their religion with greater freedom, these kindly Amish, as they have come to be called, started to emigrate to America, about sixty years ago, just as the Pilgrims had sought religious freedom many years before. Being mostly farmers it was natural for them to seek what was then the best farming section in this country, and they began to settle in central Illinois gradually buying land around Morton, until it is at this time the largest Amish settlement in Illinois and the real head of the Amish Church.

It was the aim of the founders of this community to make it self-sustaining, and as it grew, there was felt a need of field tile makers, as a great part of this land needed draining, and no drain tile could be bought within many miles. In answer to their call came the Rapp family from Nuremberg, with six stalwart sons. For centuries Nuremberg had been the seat of the tile industry in Germany. Cooking ware, tile stoves, and many other types of pottery are still made in this district in great quantities. Years of practice and experimenting have taught the people of Nuremberg how to make pottery which would withstand the intense heat of baking and cooking; how to instill permanent and wonderful coloring in their handiwork; and how to make useful and ornamental pottery.

As quickly as possible this family built some kilns in Morton and started producing drain tile. As their supply met the demand, it was natural for them to work into brick making. From this point it is very easy to see how these kilns would be converted into stoneware and pottery kilns. A community of this size demanded a great deal of kitchenware, and these German and Swiss housewives naturally wanted a type of ware with which they were familiar.

So changing conditions brought about the making of pottery in the old Rapp kilns, instead of brick and stoneware, and today the pottery made by the descendants of these same Amish is sold all over the United States. This pottery is known for its perfection of line and beauty of color. Visit the Morton Pottery today and you will find a son of Andrew Rapp directing various members of the family in the production of Amish pottery, using the same designs and colors that were used many years ago for the pottery baked in the little kilns, in the kitchens of their homes in the Black Forest of Germany.

The Amish Pottery Line

On the following pages is shown our entire line of new Amish Pottery, together with prices, sizes and weights.

Any of the pieces illustrated can be had in the highly popular blue, green or yellow that we feature.

The pleasing shapes and useful items make Amish Pottery highly popular with e v e r y o n e. Look through this catalog and if you find some items illustrated that you do not have in stock, order at once, so that you can keep your stock complete.

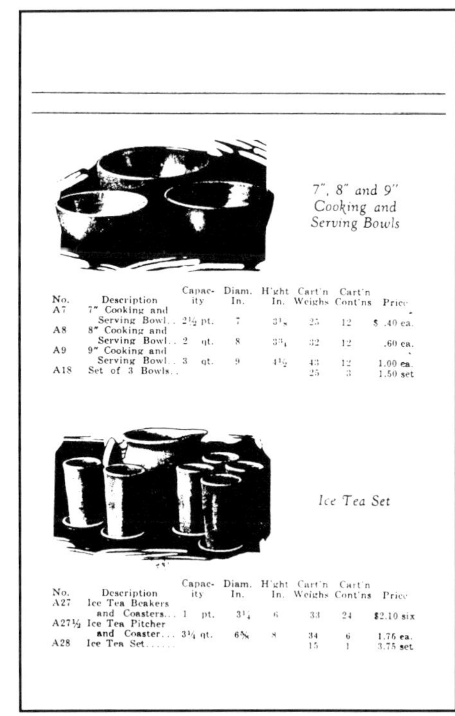

7", 8" and 9" Cooking and Serving Bowls

No.	Description	Capacity	Diam. In.	H'ght In.	Cart'n Weighs	Cart'n Cont'ns	Price
A7	7" Cooking and Serving Bowl..	2½ pt.	7	3⅛	25	12	$ .40 ea.
A8	8" Cooking and Serving Bowl..	2 qt.	8	3¾	32	12	.60 ea.
A9	9" Cooking and Serving Bowl..	3 qt.	9	4½	43	12	1.00 ea.
A18	Set of 3 Bowls..				25	3	1.50 set

Ice Tea Set

No.	Description	Capacity	Diam. In.	H'ght In.	Cart'n Weighs	Cart'n Cont'ns	Price
A27	Ice Tea Beakers and Coasters...	1 pt.	3¼	6	33	24	$2.10 six
A27½	Ice Tea Pitcher and Coaster...	3¼ qt.	6⅝	8	34	6	1.76 ea.
A28	Ice Tea Set......				15	1	3.75 set

No. A7 - $25-70 **No. A8 - $30-80**
No. A9 - $35-90 **No. A18 - $90-140**

No. A27 Beaker $15-50 Coaster $5-20
No. A27½ Pitcher $50-105 Coaster $15-50
No. 28 - $185-575

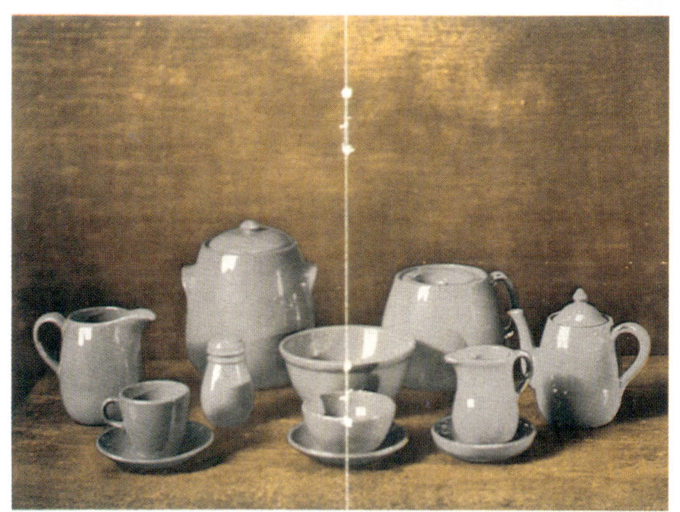

Value Ranges are not given for these items because they are found on other catalog pages.

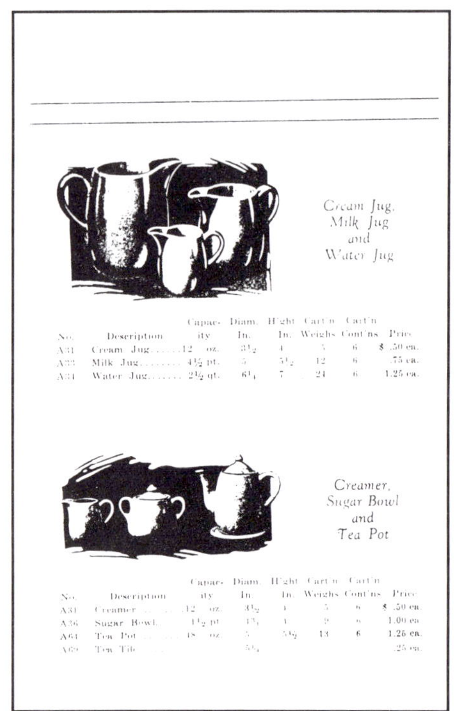

Cream Jug, Milk Jug and Water Jug

No.	Description	Capacity	Diam. In.	H'ght In.	Cart'n Weighs	Cart'n Cont'ns	Price
A31	Cream Jug......	12 oz.	3½	4	5	6	$ .50 ea.
A33	Milk Jug........	4½ pt.	5	5½	12	6	.75 ea.
A34	Water Jug......	2½ qt.	6¼	7	24	6	1.25 ea.

Creamer, Sugar Bowl and Tea Pot

No.	Description	Capacity	Diam. In.	H'ght In.	Cart'n Weighs	Cart'n Cont'ns	Price
A31	Creamer	12 oz.	3½	4	5	6	$ .50 ea.
A36	Sugar Bowl.....	1½ pt.	4¾	4	9	6	1.00 ea.
A64	Tea Pot	48 oz.	5	5½	13	6	1.25 ea.
A69	Tea Tile		5¾				.25 ea.

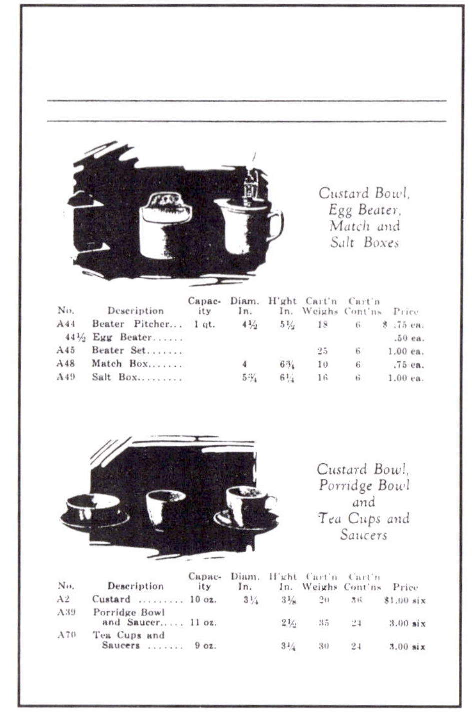

Custard Bowl, Egg Beater, Match and Salt Boxes

No.	Description	Capacity	Diam. In.	H'ght In.	Cart'n Weighs	Cart'n Cont'ns	Price
A44	Beater Pitcher...	1 qt.	4½	5½	18	6	$ .75 ea.
44½	Egg Beater......						.50 ea.
A45	Beater Set.......				25	6	1.00 ea.
A48	Match Box.......		4	6¾	10	6	.75 ea.
A49	Salt Box.........		5¾	6¼	16	6	1.00 ea.

Custard Bowl, Porridge Bowl and Tea Cups and Saucers

No.	Description	Capacity	Diam. In.	H'ght In.	Cart'n Weighs	Cart'n Cont'ns	Price
A2	Custard	10 oz.	3¼	3⅛	20	36	$1.00 six
A39	Porridge Bowl and Saucer.....	11 oz.		2½	35	24	3.00 six
A70	Tea Cups and Saucers	9 oz.		3¼	30	24	3.00 six

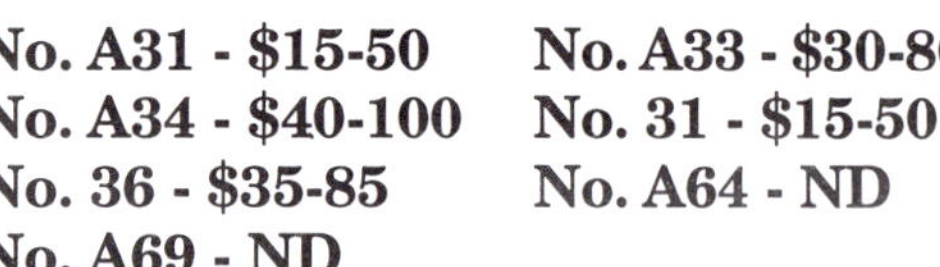

No. A31 - $15-50
No. A33 - $30-80
No. A34 - $40-100
No. 31 - $15-50
No. 36 - $35-85
No. A64 - ND
No. A69 - ND

No. A44 - $30-50
No. 44½ - $10-12
No. A45 - $40-62
No. A48 - $40-100
No. A49 - $50-105
No. A2 - $15-50
No. A39 - $25-90
No. A70 - ND

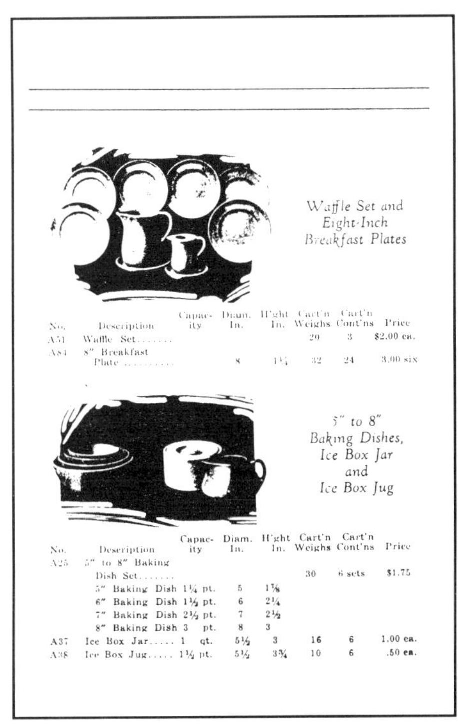

Waffle Set and Eight-Inch Breakfast Plates

No.	Description	Capacity	Diam. In.	H'ght In.	Cart'n Weighs	Cart'n Cont'ns	Price
A51	Waffle Set.......				20	3	$2.00 ea.
A84	8" Breakfast Plate..........		8	1¼	32	24	3.00 six

5" to 8" Baking Dishes, Ice Box Jar and Ice Box Jug

No.	Description	Capacity	Diam. In.	H'ght In.	Cart'n Weighs	Cart'n Cont'ns	Price
A25	5" to 8" Baking Dish Set.......				30	6 sets	$1.75
	5" Baking Dish	1¼ pt.	5	1⅞			
	6" Baking Dish	1½ pt.	6	2¼			
	7" Baking Dish	2½ pt.	7	2½			
	8" Baking Dish	3 pt.	8	3			
A37	Ice Box Jar.....	1 qt.	5½	3	16	6	1.00 ea.
A38	Ice Box Jug.....	1½ pt.	5½	3¾	10	6	.50 ea.

No. A51 - $75-220 **No. A84 - ND**
No. A25 set - $90-260
5" - $15-50 **6" - $20-60**
7" - $25-70 **8" - $30-80**
No. A37 - $45-85 **No. A38 - $30-80**

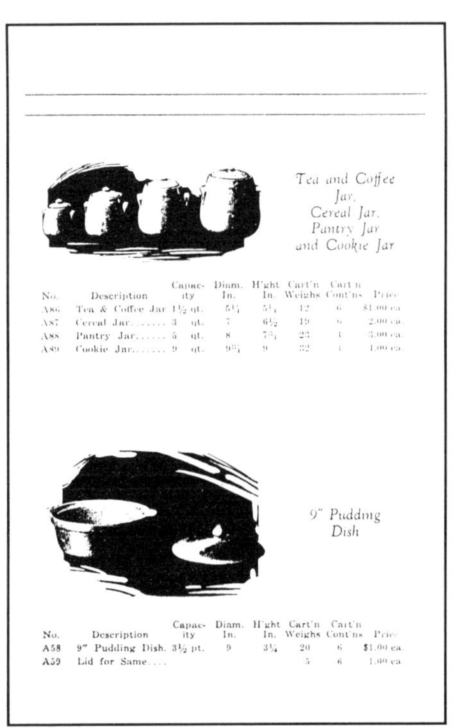

Tea and Coffee Jar, Cereal Jar, Pantry Jar and Cookie Jar

No.	Description	Capacity	Diam. In.	H'ght In.	Cart'n Weighs	Cart'n Cont'ns	Price
A86	Tea & Coffee Jar	1½ qt.	5¼	5¼	12	6	$1.00 ea.
A87	Cereal Jar.......	3 qt.	7	6½	19	6	2.00 ea.
A88	Pantry Jar......	5 qt.	8	7¾	23	4	3.00 ea.
A89	Cookie Jar.......	9 qt.	9¾	9	32	4	4.00 ea.

9" Pudding Dish

No.	Description	Capacity	Diam. In.	H'ght In.	Cart'n Weighs	Cart'n Cont'ns	Price
A58	9" Pudding Dish.	3½ pt.	9	3¼	20	6	$1.00 ea.
A59	Lid for Same....				5	6	1.00 ea.

No. A86 - $35-90 **No. A87 - $45-100**
No. A88 - $55-110 **No. A89 - $65-120**
No. A58 - $35-85 **No. A59 - ND**

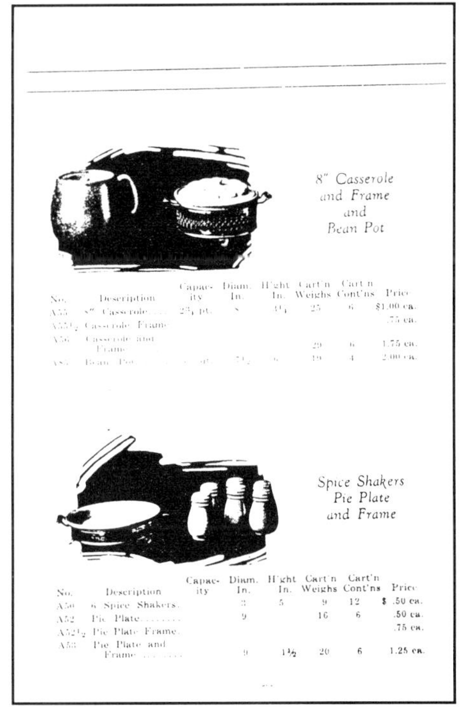

8" Casserole and Frame and Bean Pot

No.	Description	Capacity	Diam. In.	H'ght In.	Cart'n Weighs	Cart'n Cont'ns	Price
A55	8" Casserole.....	2¾ pt.	8	3¼	25	6	$1.00 ea.
A55½	Casserole Frame						.75 ea.
A56	Casserole and Frame				29	6	1.75 ea.
A85	Bean Pot	[illegible]	7½	6	19	4	2.00 ea.

Spice Shakers Pie Plate and Frame

No.	Description	Capacity	Diam. In.	H'ght In.	Cart'n Weighs	Cart'n Cont'ns	Price
A50	6 Spice Shakers.		3	5	9	12	$ .50 ea.
A52	Pie Plate.........		9		16	6	.50 ea.
A52½	Pie Plate Frame.						.75 ea.
A53	Pie Plate and Frame		9	1½	20	6	1.25 ea.

No. A55 - $30-80 **No. A55½ - $10-12**
No. A56 - $40-92 **No. A85 - $45-100**
No. A50 - $15-50ea **No. A52 - $25-75**
No. A52½ - $10-12 **No. A53 - $35-87**

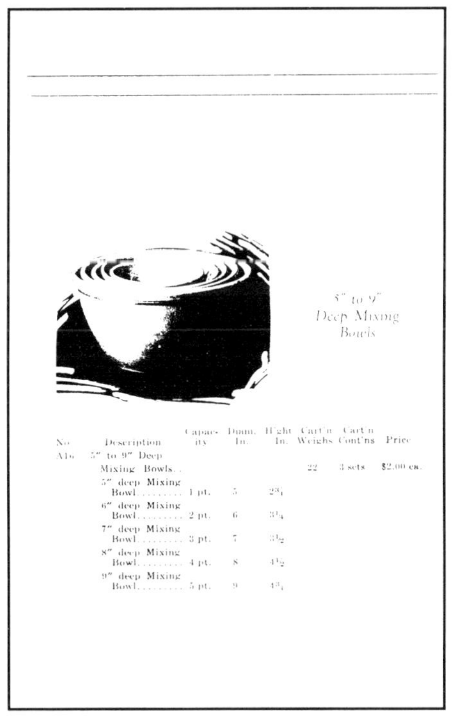

5" to 9" Deep Mixing Bowls

No.	Description	Capacity	Diam. In.	H'ght In.	Cart'n Weighs	Cart'n Cont'ns	Price
A16	5" to 9" Deep Mixing Bowls..				22	3 sets	$2.00 ea.
	5" deep Mixing Bowl..........	1 pt.	5	2¾			
	6" deep Mixing Bowl..........	2 pt.	6	3¼			
	7" deep Mixing Bowl..........	3 pt.	7	3½			
	8" deep Mixing Bowl..........	4 pt.	8	4½			
	9" deep Mixing Bowl..........	5 pt.	9	4¾			

No. 16 set $130-360 **5" - $15-50**
6" - $20-60 **7" - $25-70**
8" - $30-80 **9" - $40-100**

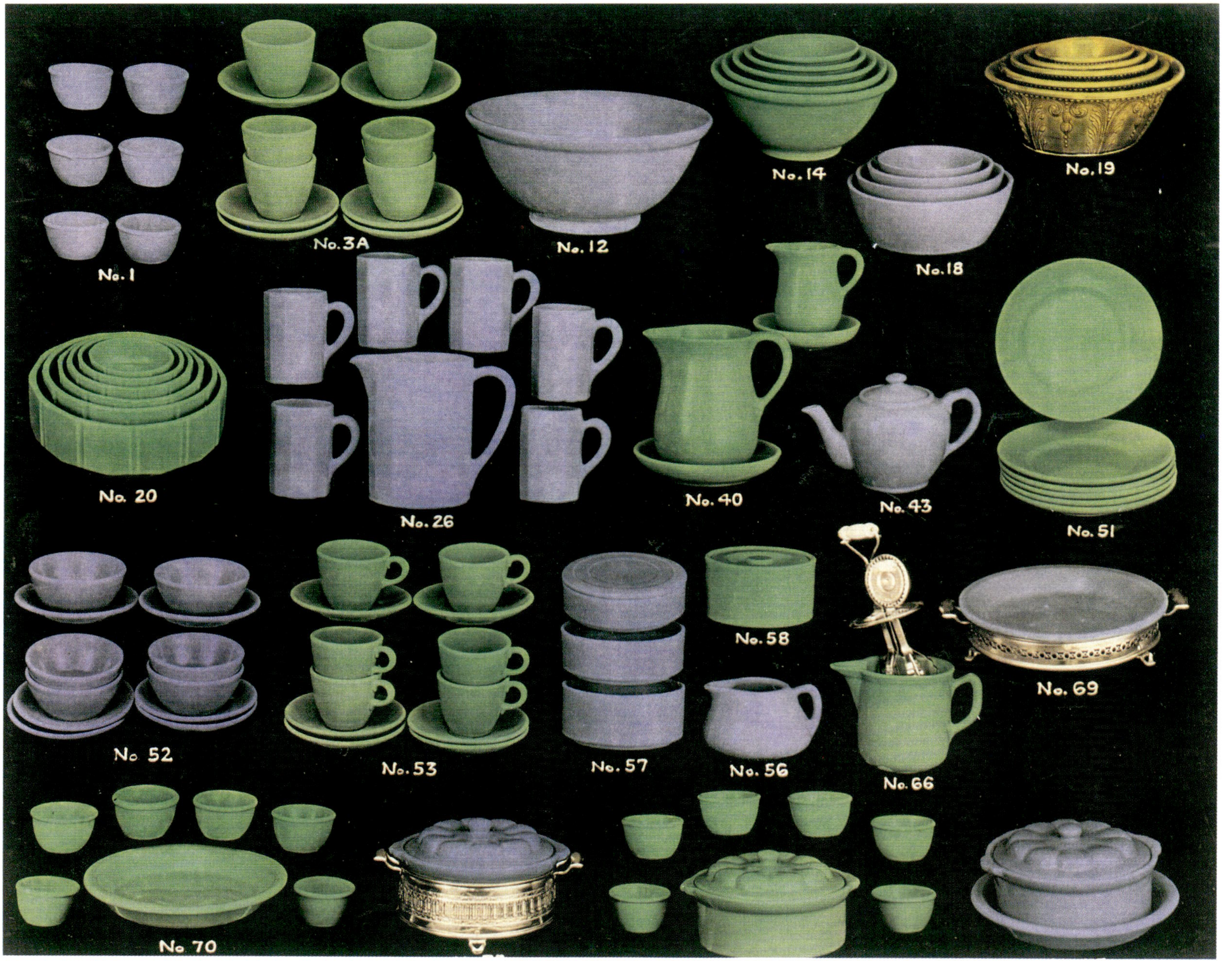
No.1
No.3A
No.12
No.14
No.19
No.18
No. 20
No.26
No.40
No.43
No.51
No 52
No.53
No.57
No.58
No.56
No.66
No.69
No 70

AMISH POTTERY
(PANTRY WARE)

In the value ranges for this page of Amish pottery, the low end should be for green, the high end for blue.

No. 1 5oz. Custard Cup – **$12-14**

No. 3A 10oz. Custard Cup and Saucer – **$15-20**

No. 12 12" Mixing Bowl – **$40-50**

No. 14 5" to 9" nested, Deep Mixing Bowls – **$90-110**

No. 18 5" to 8" nested, Deep Baking Dishes – **$125-150**

No. 19 4 1/2" to 8 1/2" embossed making dishes (Woodland Glaze) – **$125-150**

No. 20 4" to 9" Baking Nappy set – **$75-100**

No. 26 Colonial Beverage set – **$100-125**

No. 40 Four Piece Waffle set – **$75-150**

No. 43 30oz. Ball Tea Pot (5 cups) – **$45-65**

No. 51 8" Dinner Plates – **ND**

No. 52 Porridge Bowl and Saucer – **$40-50**

No. 53 Tea Cup and Saucer – **ND**

No. 56 1 1/2 pint Ice Box Jar – **$40-60**

No. 57 Refrigerator set – **ND**

No. 58 1 1/2 pint Ice Box Jar – **$45-60**

No. 66 2 pint Beater set – **$40-50**

No. 69 9" Pie Plate and Frame – **$45-55**

No. 70 9" Pie Plate with six 5oz. Custard Cups – **$90-100**

No. 73 3 quart Casserole and Frame – **$50-65**

No. 74 8" Casserole with six 5oz. Custard Cups – **$90-100**

No. 75 8" Casserole with 9" Pie Plate – **$85-95**

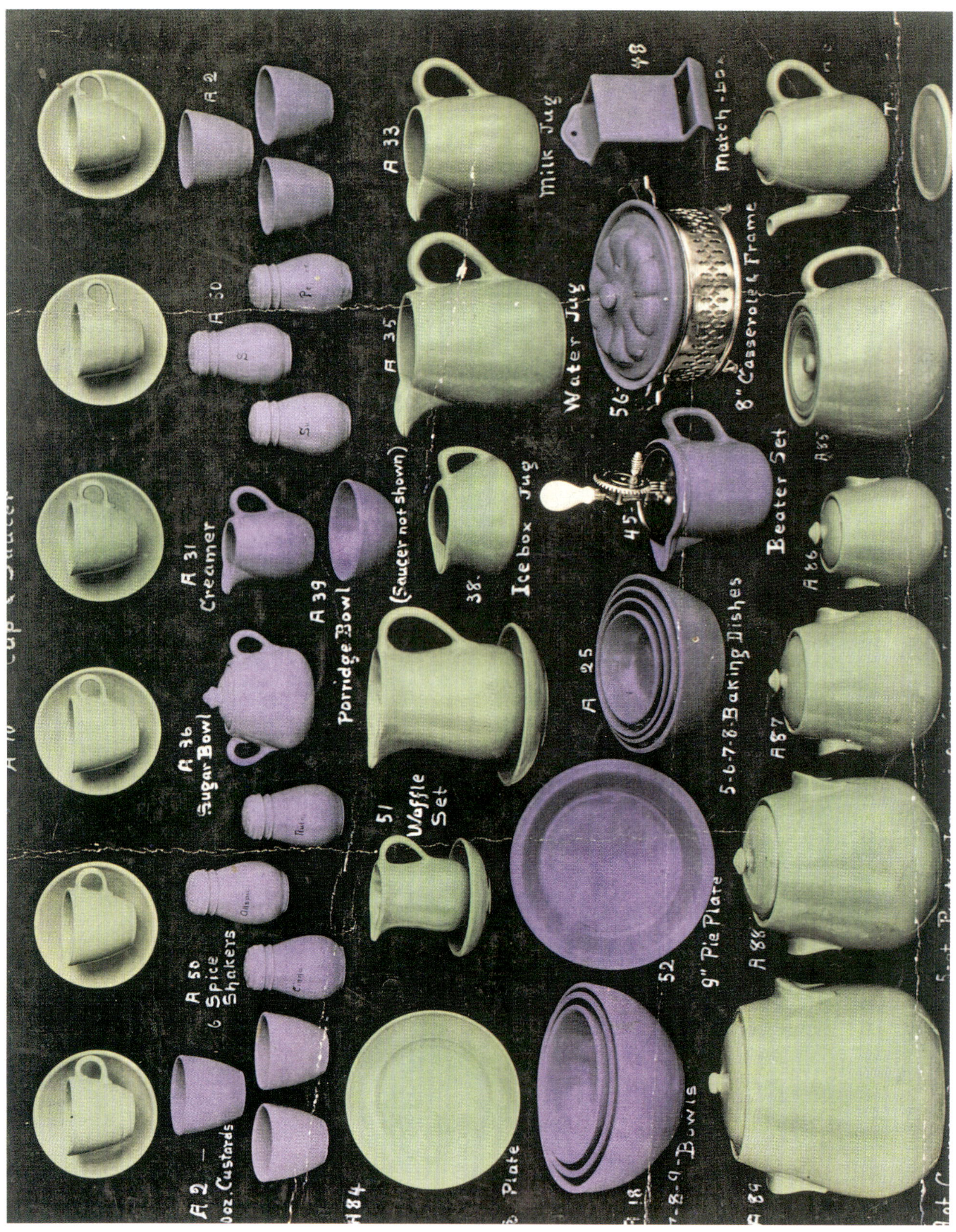
Cup & Saucer
A 2
oz. Custards
A 50
6 Spice
Shakers
A 36
Sugar Bowl
A 31
Creamer
A 50
A 2
Plate
51
Waffle
Set
A 39
Porridge Bowl
(Saucer not shown)
38.
A 35
A 33
Ice box Jug
Water Jug
Milk Jug
52
9" Pie Plate
A 25
5-6-7-8-Baking Dishes
45-
56-
48
8" Casserole & Frame
Beater Set
A 88
A 87
A 86

AMISH POTTERY
(PANTRY WARE)

In the value ranges for this page of Amish pottery, the low end should be for green, the high end for blue.

No. A70 Cup and Saucer – **ND**

A2 Custard Cup – **$15-20**

A50 Spice Shakers – **$25-35**

A36 Sugar Bowl – **$45-55**

A31 Creamer – **$25-35**

A39 Porridge Bowl – **$25-35**

A84 8" Plate – **ND**

No. 51 Waffle set – **$75-150**

No. 38 Ice Box Jug – **$30-40**

A35 Water Jug – **$40-50**

A33 Milk Jug – **$30-40**

A18 Nested Bowls – **$100-110**

No. 52 Pie Plate – **$35-45**

A25 Nested Baking Dishes – **$100-110**

No. 45 Beater set – **$45-50**

No. 56 8" Casserole and Frame – **$50-65**

No. 48 Match Box – **$50-60**

A89 9 quart Cookie Jar – **$65-75**

A88 5 quart Pantry Jar – **$55-65**

A87 3 quart Cereal Jar – **$45-55**

A86 1 1/2 quart Tea/Coffee Jar – **$35-45**

A85 3 quart Bean Pot – **$45-55**

A84 Tea Pot – **ND**

A69 Tea Tile – **ND**

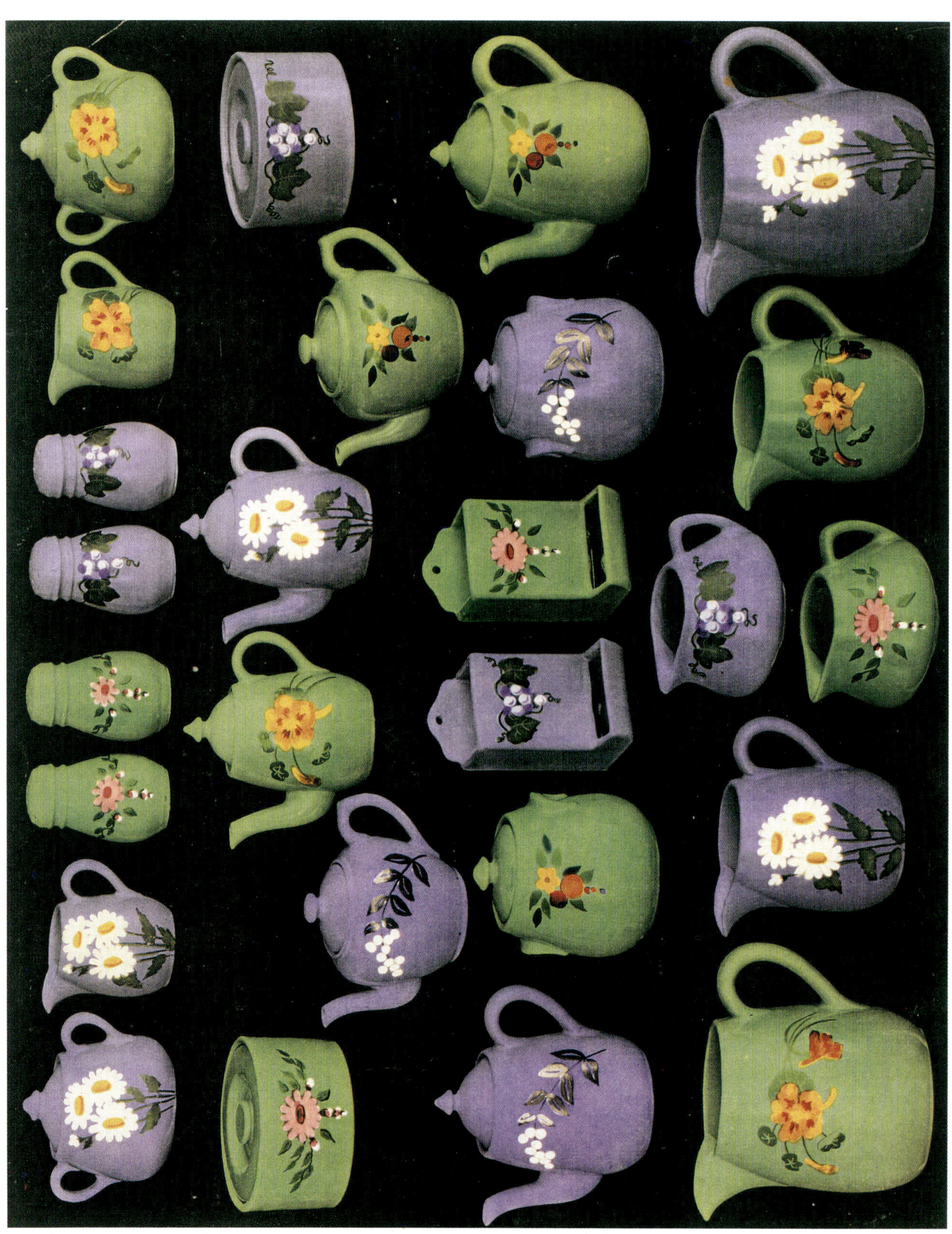

DECORATED AMISH POTTERY
(PANTRY WARE)

The flowers, fruits, and berries were hand painted cold paint over glazed items rather than underglazed decorations. Helen Hilliard of Peoria, Illinois was in charge of the decorating department when this work was done. Because of age and hard use, the paint is often flaked or chipped when found. The value ranges are for mint or near mint condition.

Top Row: Sugar Blue – **$55-65**
Green – **$45-55**
Creamer Blue – **$35-45**
Green – **$25-35**
Shakers Blue – **$35-45**
Green – **$25-35**

Second Row: Ice box Jar Blue – **$65-75**
Green – **$45-65**
Ball Tea Pot Blue – **$55-75**
Green – **$45-55**

Third Row: 48oz. New design Tea Pot – **ND**
3 quart Cereal Jar Blue – **$65-75**
Green – **$55-65**
Match Box Blue – **$60-70**
Green – **$50-60**

Bottom Row: 2 1/2 quart Water Pitcher Blue – **$60-70**
Green – **$50-60**
4 1/2 pint Milk Jug Blue – **$50-60**
Green – **$40-50**
1 1/2 pint Ice Box Jug Blue – **$50-60**
Green – **$40-50**

CHAPTER 14
MORTON POTTERY COMPANY

ANIMALS

Animals were used for many purposes at the pottery. Figurines, planters, banks, and lamps were most commonly created. Many miniatures were also done.

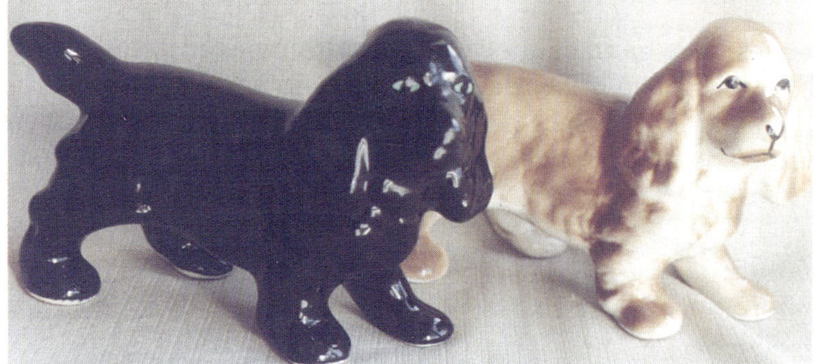

The cocker spaniels are 6" long and 4" tall. They were also done by the Midwest Pottery. It is nearly impossible to distinguish the manufacturer of the spaniels unless they are examined side by side.

Value Range: $18-20
Add 25% for black

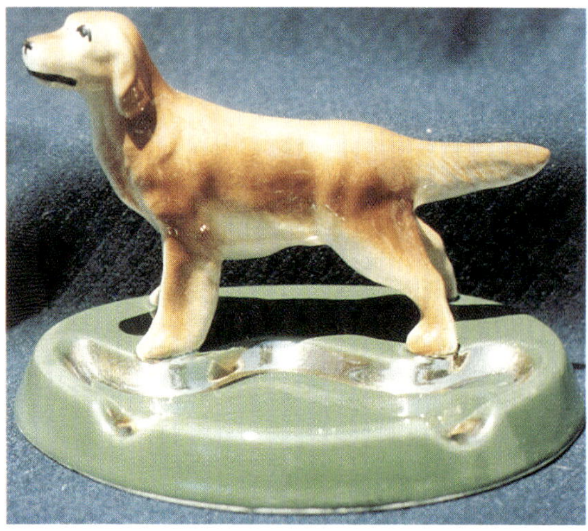

The pointer was favored by hunters. Other game dogs were used for the ashtrays.

Value Range: $10-14

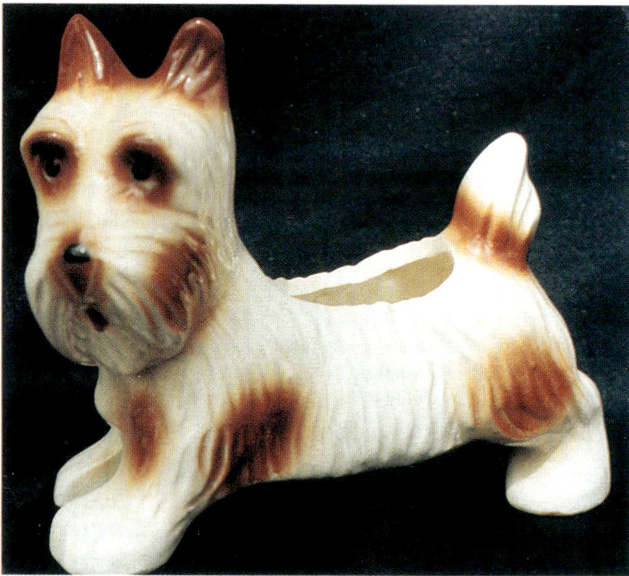

The Scottish terrier planter was popular in the 1930's. It was probably inspired by Franklin D. Roosevelt's "little dog, Falla". This dog can also be found with the back closed and a slit to transform it into a bank.

Value Range: $8-12 ***Add 50% for a bank***

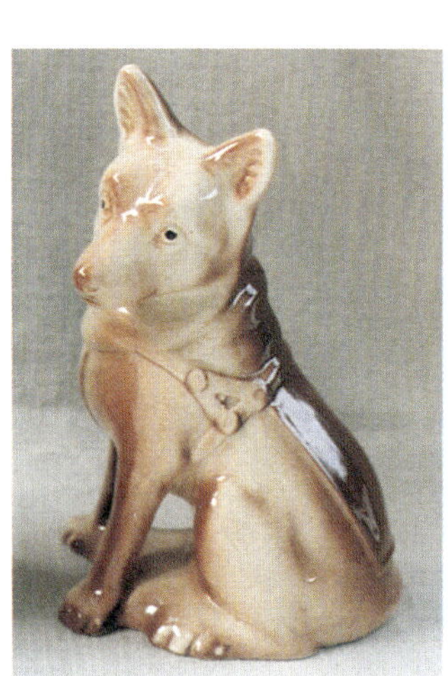

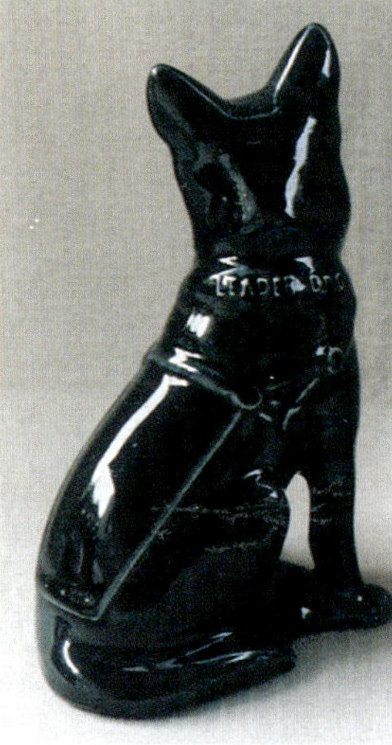

The seeing eye dog was made in black and brown. The back of the collar has "Leader Dog" on it. Front and back views are shown to illustrate the detail of the harness.

Value Range: $18-20

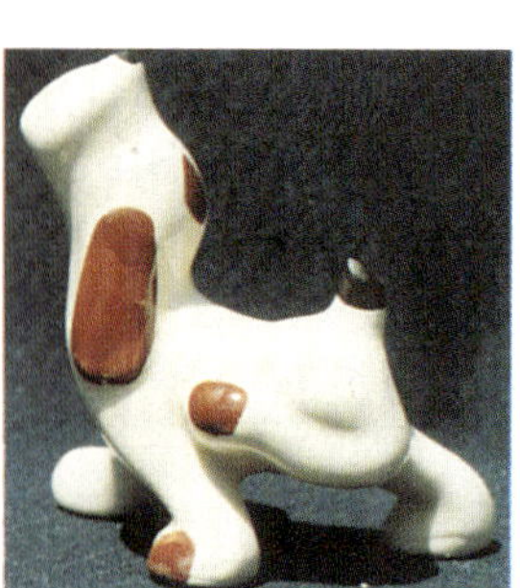

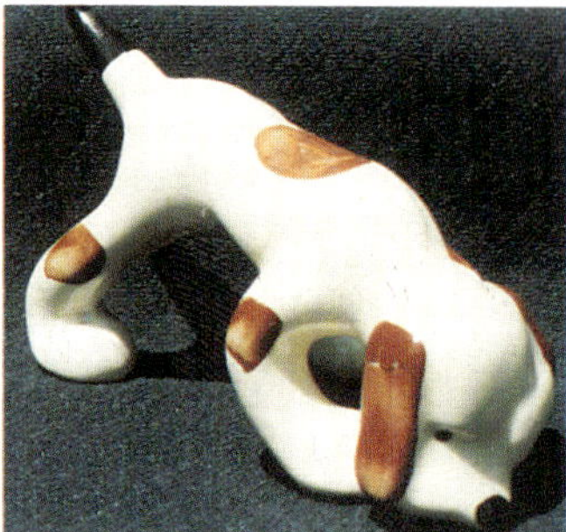

These two dogs were pictured in a 1939 sales leaflet sent out by the pottery. The dog scratching is #583. The dog with his paw over his eye is #576. These dogs were referred to as "hillbilly hounds" on order forms sent to S.S. Kresge Company in 1943.

Value Range: #583 $10-14 #576 $10-14

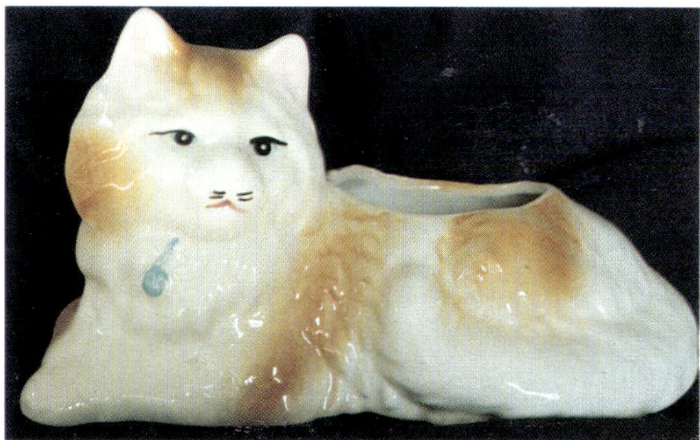

Cat planter. This cat has a hand painted underglaze face and bell. The yellow stripes and pink ears are spray glazed. The planter is 9" long and 51/2" tall.

Value Range: $12-14

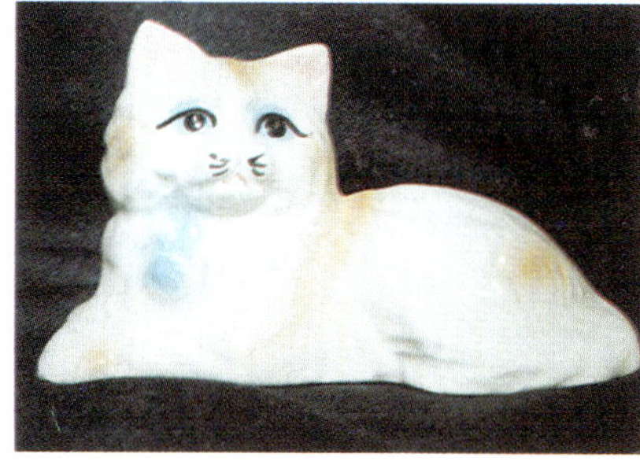

The smaller cats were made as planters, figurines, and banks. The slit for the bank was made in the back of the cat's head. This cat is 6" long and 31/2" tall.

Value Range: Planter $10-12
Figurine $12-14
Bank $18-20

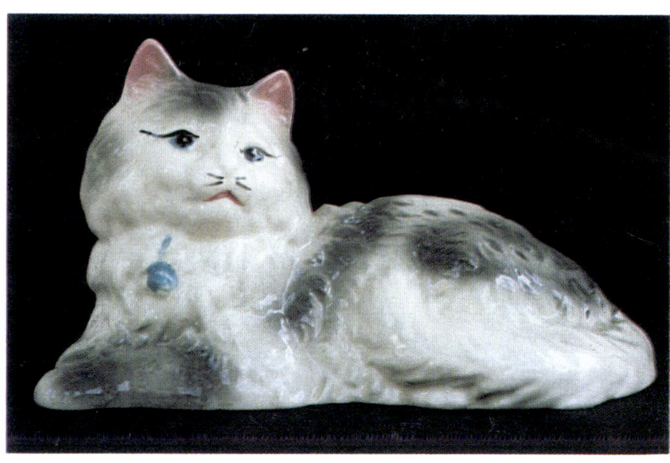

Cat figurine. This cat has hand painted, underglaze face and bell. The grey spots and pink ears are spray glazed. The cat is 9" long and 51/2" tall.

Value Range: $16-18

The white cat with pink ears was made with the two playful kittens. She can be found with a cold painted bow at her neck. These cats are more common than the decorated ones. The kittens were never decorated to match the cats above. They have only been found in white.

Value Range:
Large Cat Figurine $14-16
Large Cat Planter $10-12
Small Cat Pouncing $8-10
Small Cat Sitting $8-10

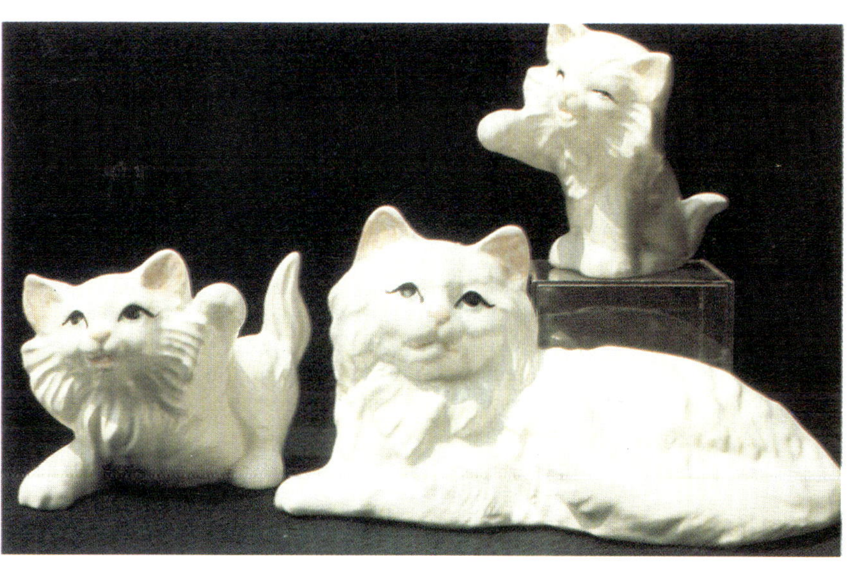

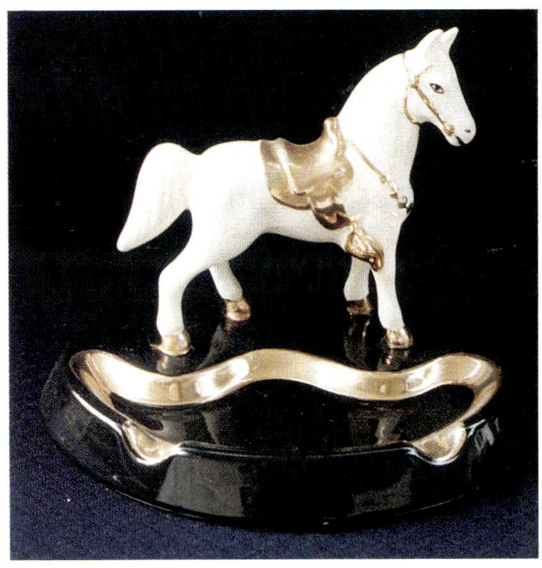

The horse ashtray is special decorated in 14K gold. The horse was more commonly spray glazed in brown, grey, or black, or left white. On a price quotation dated 1953, the spray glazing technique was described as "misted."

Value Range: $10-14
Add 25% for gold decoration

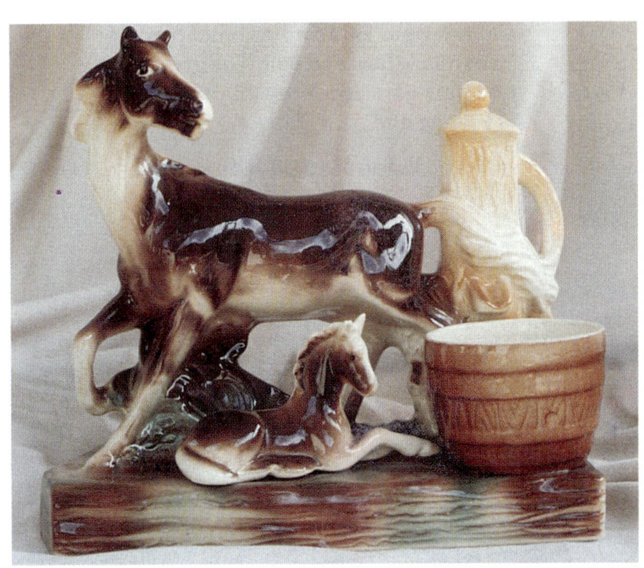

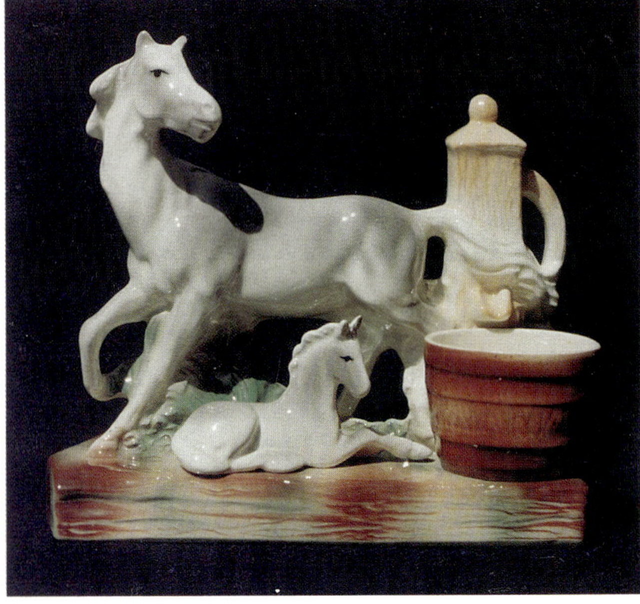

The horse and colt with wooden pump and half barrel water trough is scarce. The colt and barrel were separate molds and were placed on the base to be fused when kiln fired. The planters were converted into lamps by placing a metal tube behind the pump to allow for wiring the lamp. Lamps are rare. The two photographs are used to show a contrast in decoration.

Value Range: Planter $30-40
Add 100% for Lamps

BANKS

Banks were often made by adapting planters to serve that purpose.

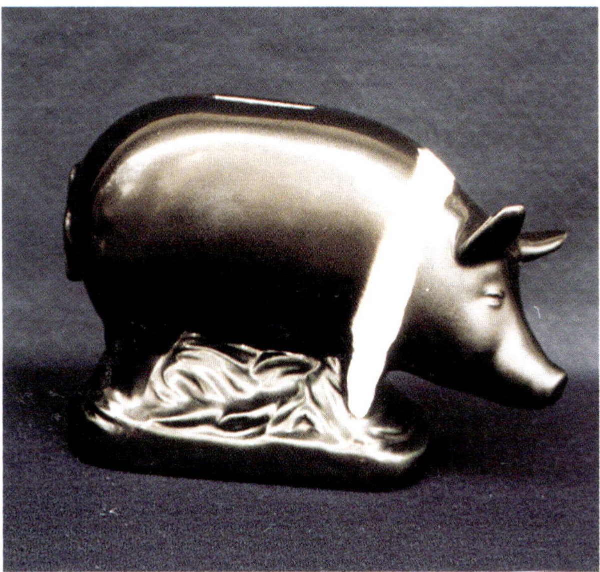

The mold for the pig bank was originally a figurine/planter designed at the American Art Pottery. At that pottery's liquidation sale, Morton Pottery Company bought those molds and converted the pig to a bank. This pig does not have the green base that was always done on the American Art pigs. The bank is 5" tall and 71/2" long.

Value Range: $40-45

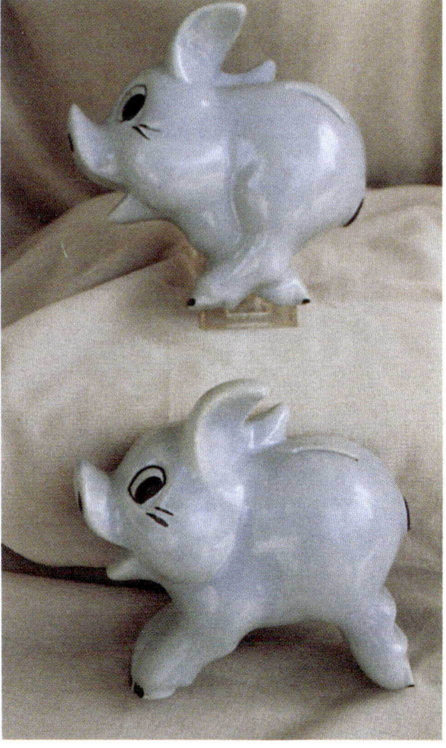

The pig wall hangers are #672, "Skedoodle," at the top, and #671, "Skedaddle," at the bottom. Though common as planters, these wall hangers are scarce as banks.

Value Range: #672 $24-26
#671 $22-24

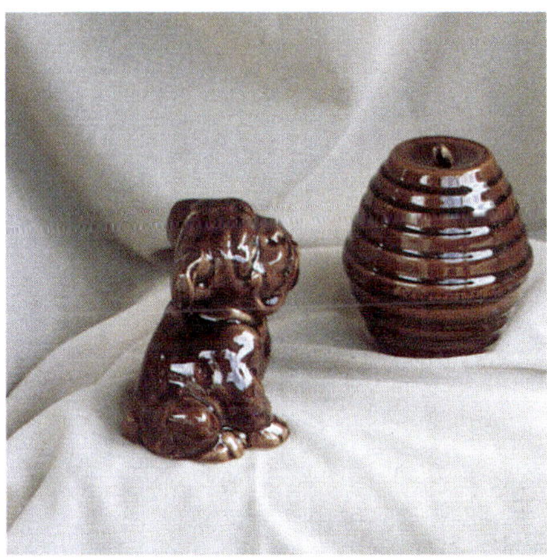

The bull dog has the slot in the back of his head for coins. It was made in all colors available.

Value Range: $14-16

The beehive is a whimsey. Made from two custard cups, it has the names of the two girls who made it and is dated September 1949. This is one of two known to have been made. There could be others.

Value Range: ND

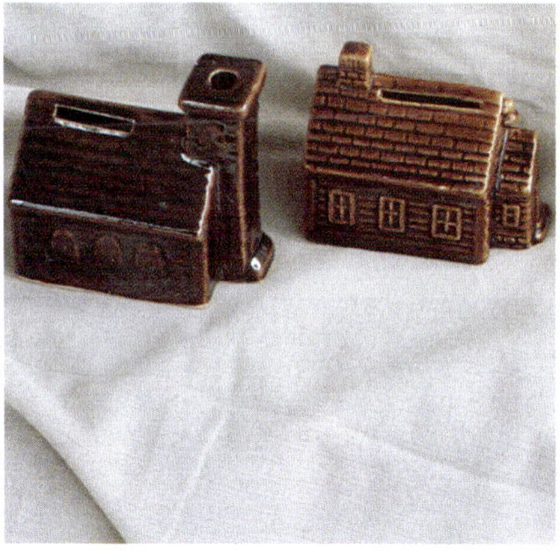

Church banks were used by Sunday school classes primarily for birthday pennies. Some churches gave banks to children to fill at home. A special "bank breaking" service was held periodically when the banks were brought to church, broken with a hammer, and the coins counted. Church banks are scarce.

Value Range: $18-22

The acorn bank was carried over from the earlier Morton Pottery Works. Instead of the dark earth tone colors, the reissues were in a variety of pastel colors. Some were special decorated upon request.

Value Range: $16-18
Add 25% for special decoration

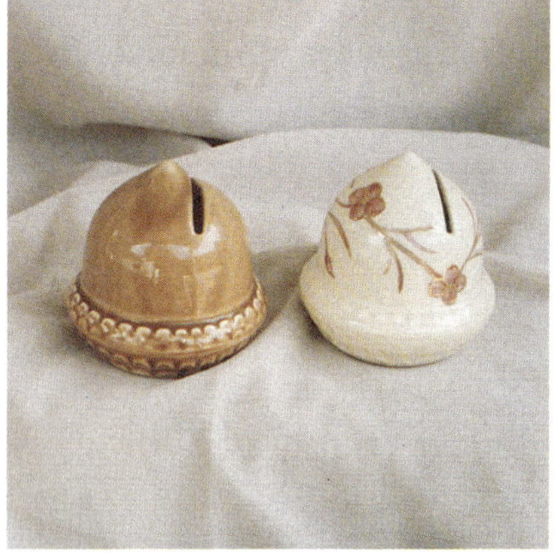

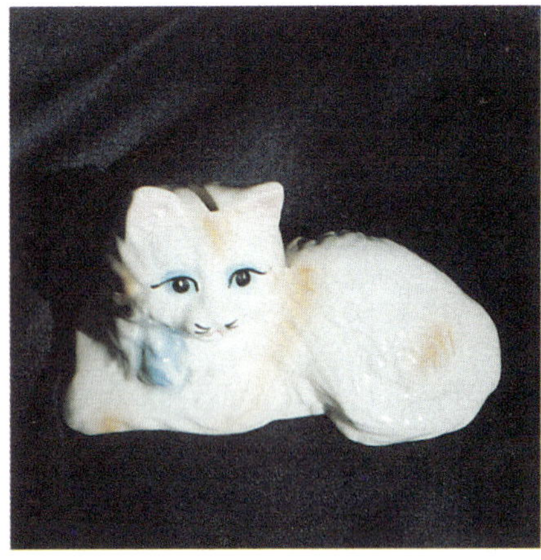

Kitten banks were white, yellow striped, or grey spotted with bows in various colors.

Value Range: $18-20

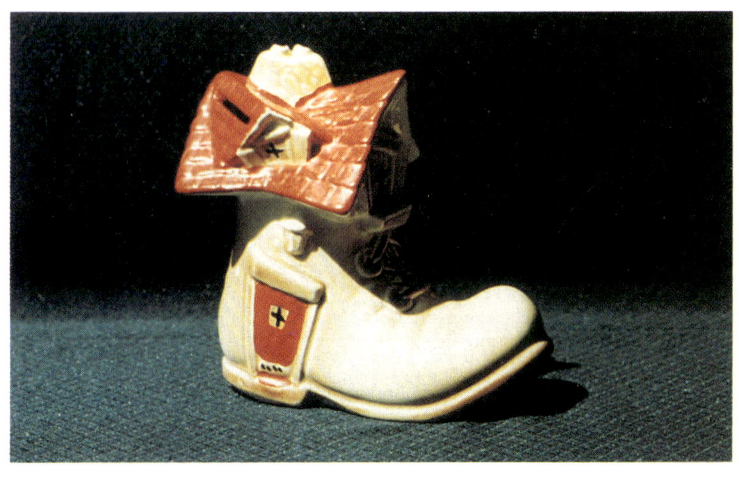

The home of "the old woman who lived in a shoe" was usually a planter. The roof may be either red or green. For a short time it was made as a child's lamp with a night light inside (see lamps). The bank is scarce.

Value Range: $25-35

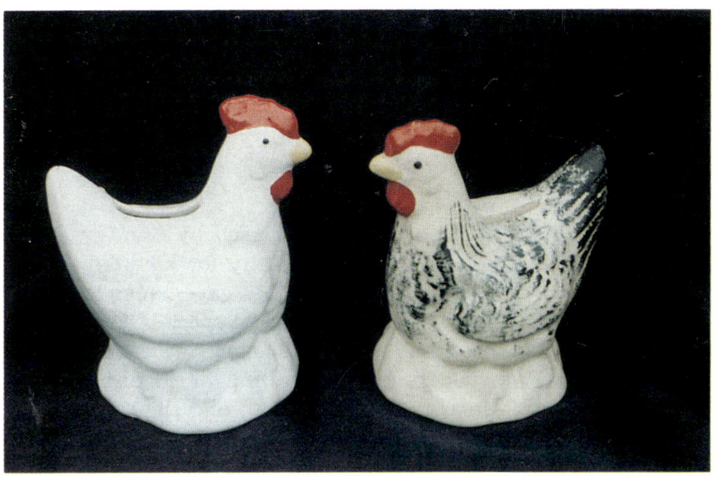

The hens were originally planters. They also served as the sugar to the rooster creamer. Banks are scarce.

Value Range: $20-25

BIRDS

Our fine feathered friends flew out of the pottery in unimaginable numbers over its forty-seven years of production. The majority of them were planters, but figurines and utility items were also made.

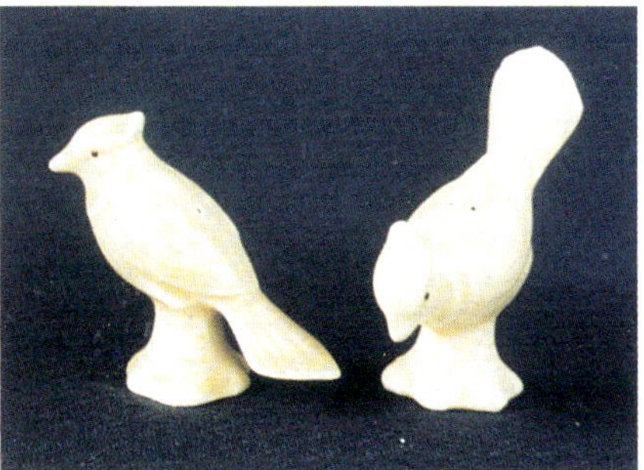

The miniature jays were made into salt and pepper shakers. They are 21/2" tall.

Value Range: $7-10

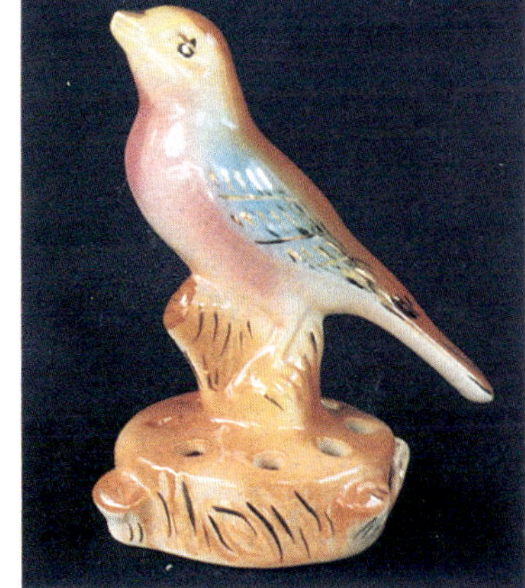

This bird flower frog was spray glazed in four colors and has been decorated with 14K gold. It was also made in solid pastel colors.

Value Range:
Solid Colors $10-12
Multi Color $18-20
Add 25% for gold decorated

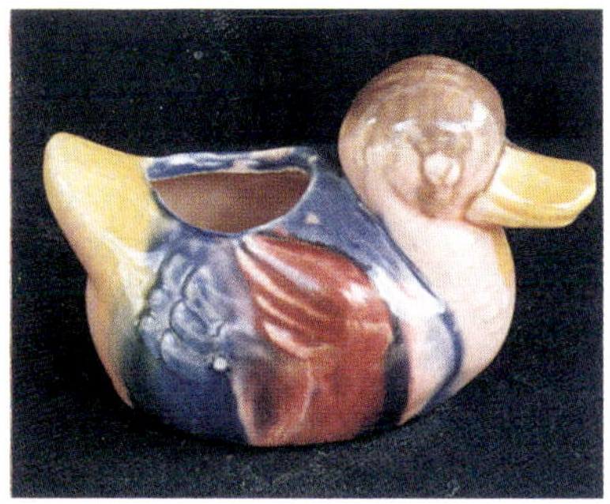

The duck is a glaze test piece used to sample new glaze colors. It has the ceramic engineer's name on the bottom. The planter was made in solid colors.

Value Range: Test Piece – ND Colors $5-8

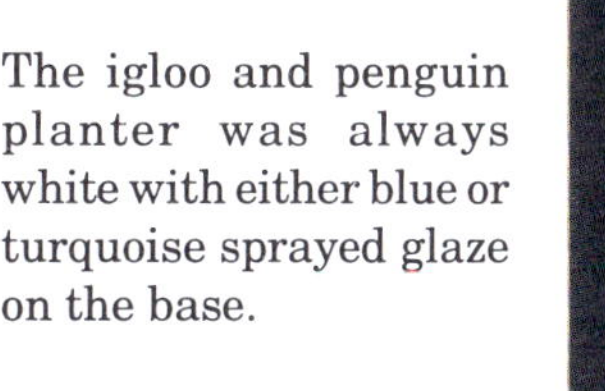

The igloo and penguin planter was always white with either blue or turquoise sprayed glaze on the base.

Value Range: $8-10

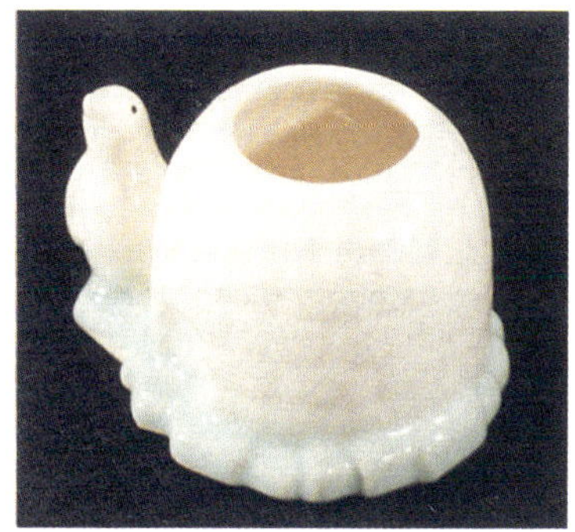

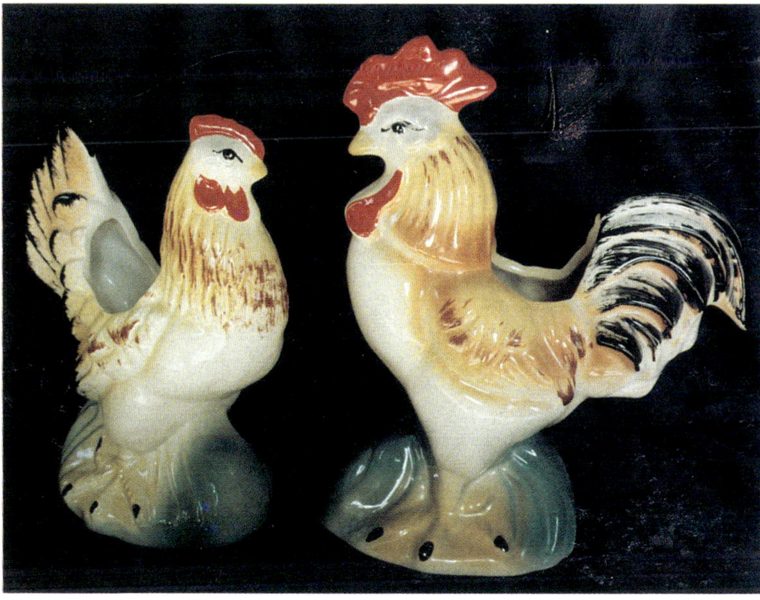

The hen and rooster planters were also made with a flat side so they could be used as wall pockets. They are a good example of spray glazing, underglaze brushing, and cold painting. They will also be found in orchid and black

Value Range: $30-35

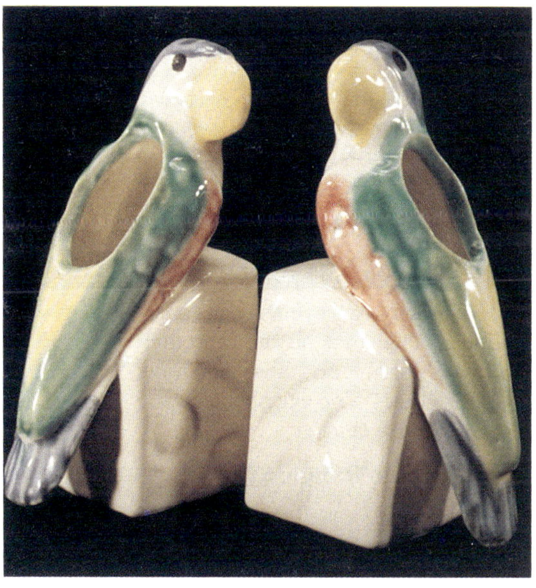

The parrot planter bookends are spray glazed with rose, yellow, green, and blue over white. The pottery called this technique majolica glaze. It was widely used for planters and wall pockets at the pottery. **Value Range: $25-35**

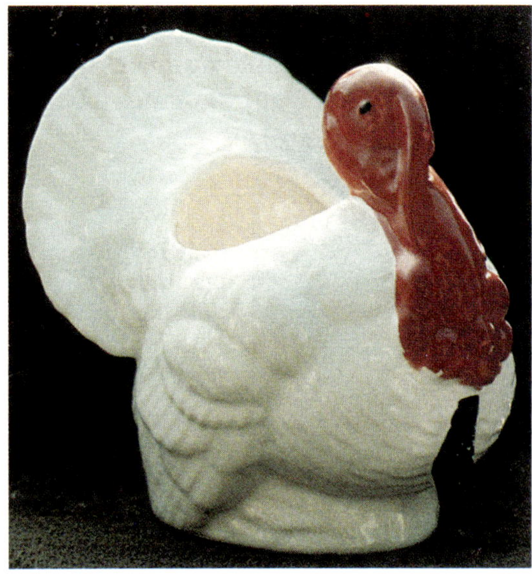

The white turkey planter was not a standard item at the pottery. It was made for a local turkey farm to be given as premiums at holiday time. The planter was usually spray glazed brown with black underglaze brushing. The head is cold painted.

Value Range: White $45-50 Brown $35-40

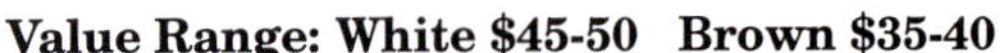

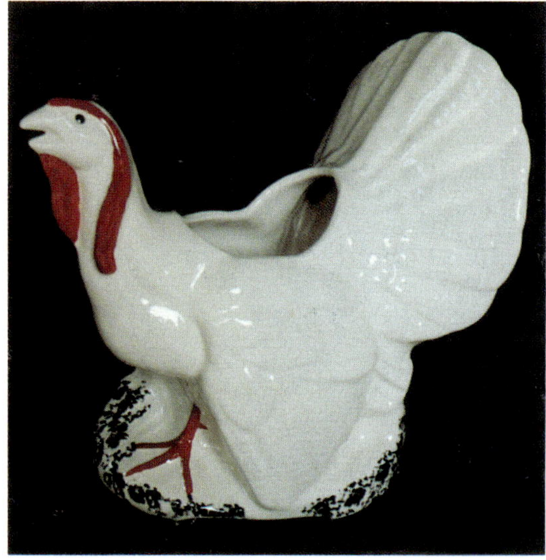

This white turkey planter has black glaze around base that was applied by sponge. The wattle and legs are cold painted. This planter has not been found in brown glaze.

Value Range: $40-45

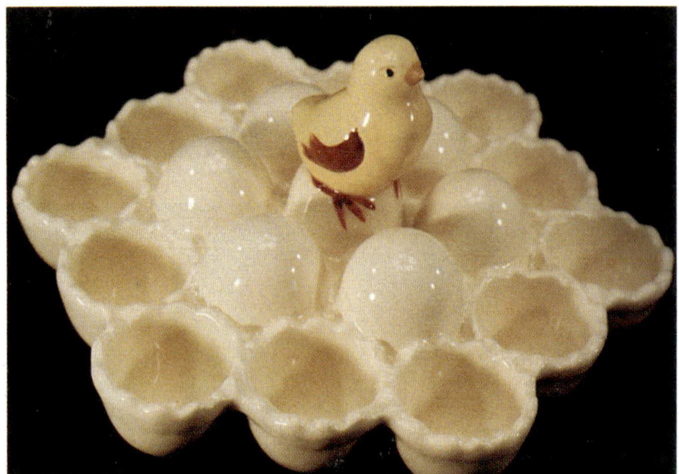

The boiled egg tray has been reproduced. The chick on the reproduction is leaner and does not have painted feet. The egg shells on the original are thicker.

Value Range: $25-30

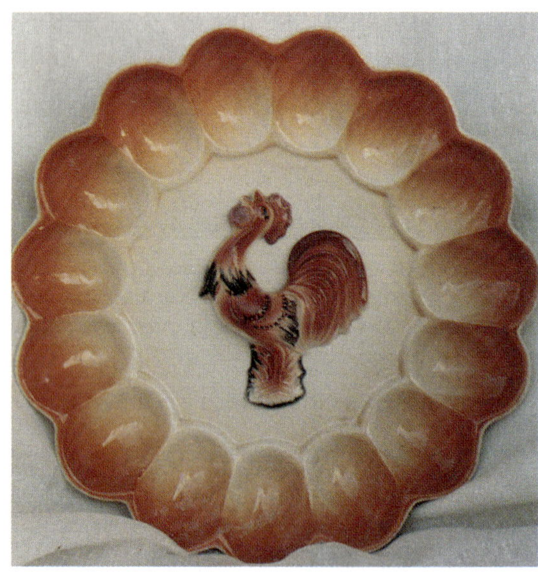

The deviled egg tray is an example of spray glazing and underglaze hand painting. **Value Range: $30-35**

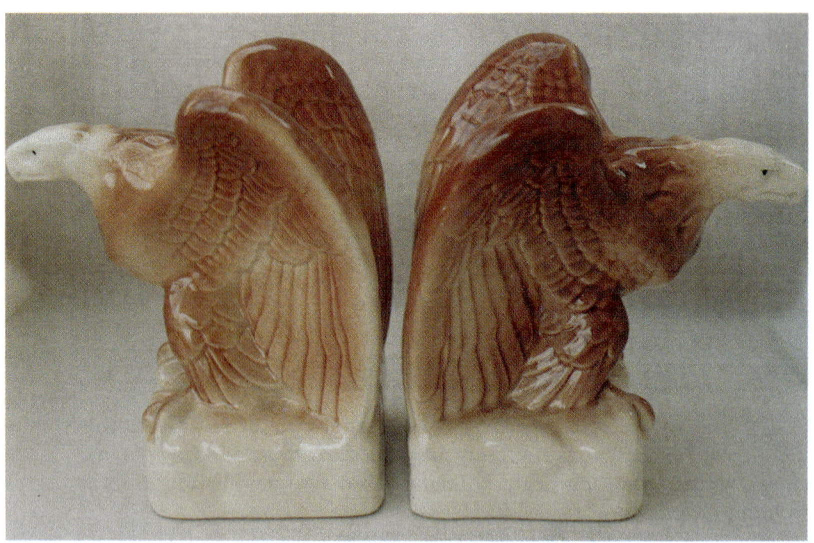

The eagle bookends are hollow with large holes in the base. They were intended to be filled with sand to add weight. The holes were then covered with cardboard and felt. They are 6" tall with the base 3 3/4" x 3 1/4".

Value Range: $30-40

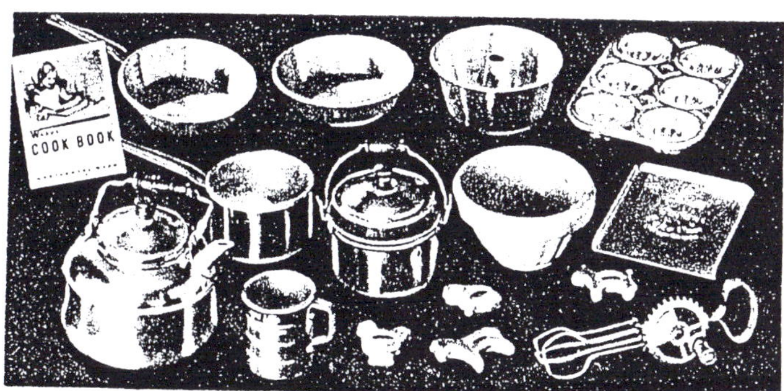

Finer 17-Pc. Aluminum Bake Set **79c**

Finer than the Set at the left because most of the pieces are shiny aluminum. Yellow glazed pottery mixing bowl 3½ in. in diameter and about 2 in. high, heavy enough to use with the 5½-inch egg beater. Aluminum pieces are: large teakettle, 6-hole muffin pan, cookie sheet, tube cake pan just right for making angel food cakes, Red handled sauce pan, pie tin, Red handled skillet, measuring cup with Red metal handle, pot with wire bail and Red wood handle, cover for the pot, 4 cookie cutters. And an 8-page Ward Cook Book with about 20 recipes written by an expert who knows just what kind of cooking little girls can do best. All in attractive box.

48 T 346—Shipping weight 2 pounds............................79c

This ad is from a 1938 Montgomery Ward Christmas catalog. The bake set contains a mixing bowl made at the pottery. It was identified as "yellow glazed pottery."

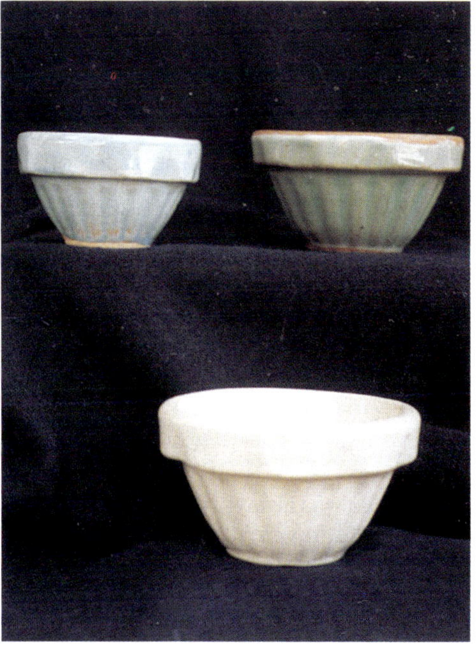

At least four different size toy mixing bowls were made at the pottery. In this group, the smallest is 1 1/2" tall, 2 3/4" diameter. The medium bowl is 2" tall, 3" diameter. The larger one is 2 1/4" tall, 3 1/2" diameter.

Value Range: $35-45

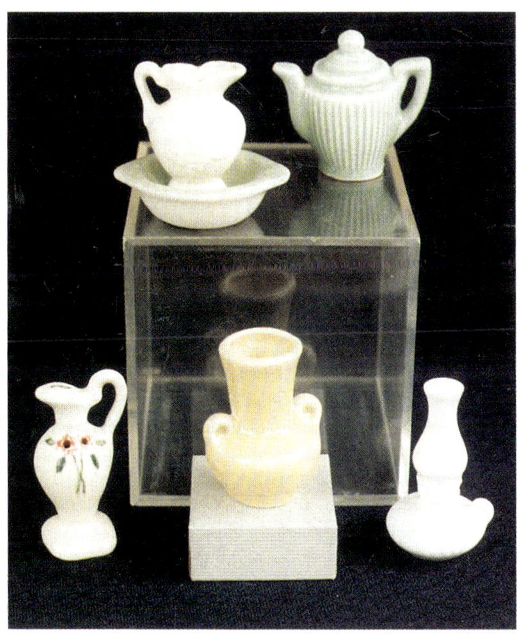

Doll house accessories are scarce. They range in height from 2" to 2 1/4".

Value Range:
Tea Pot $8-10 Bwer $6-8
Vase $6-8 Lamp $6-8

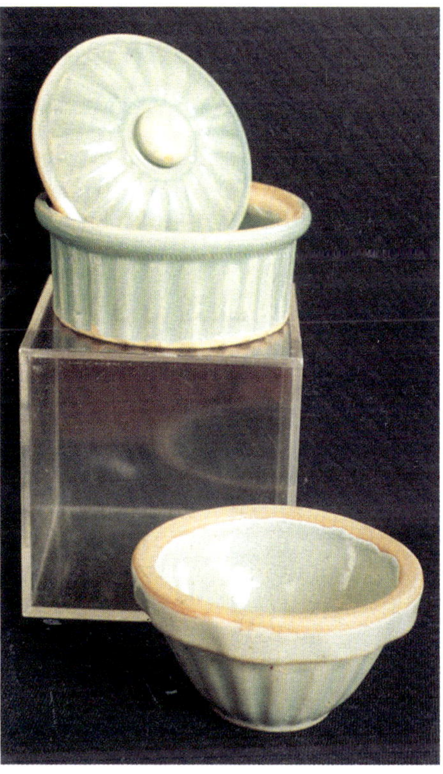

The casserole is 2" tall with a 3 3/4" dia.
Value Range: $50-55

The bowl is 2 1/2" tall with a diameter of 3 3/4". The edge is called a knife edge. It was left unglazed on regular bowls for the purpose of sharpening knives.
Value Range: $40-45

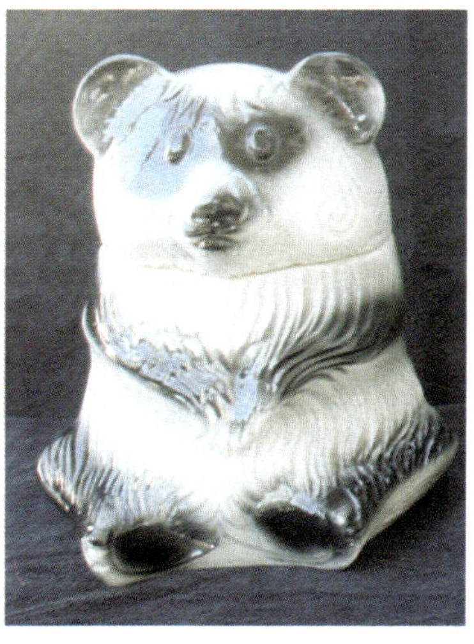

The panda was always spray decorated in this manner. It has an in mold mark, AKF in a C, on its back near the tail. It was produced from the spring of 1971 through the fall of 1972.

Value Range: $40-45

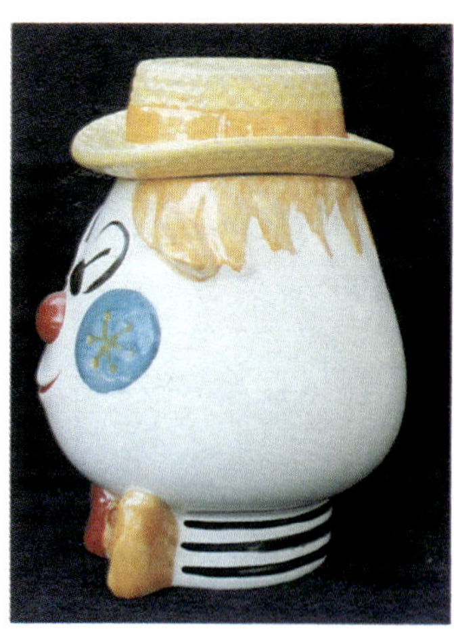

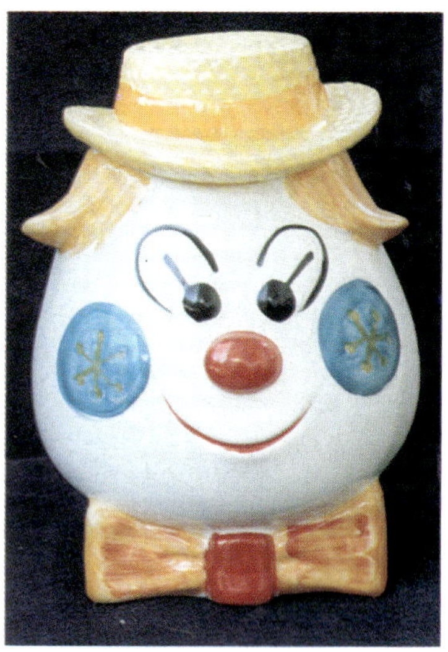

The clown has only two glaze colors, white and yellow. All other colors are cold painted. The handpainting was time consuming and costly. This jar was in limited production. The side view shows his fancy collar and ragged hair line.

Value Range: $35-45

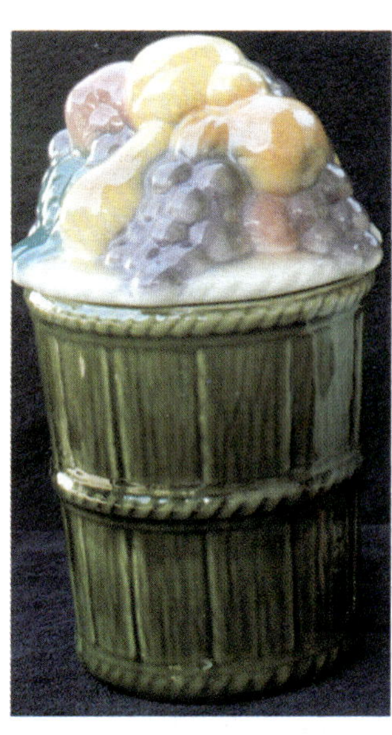

(left) The fruit basket cookie jar was made in brown as well as forest green. The fruit cluster lid is similar to Shawnee fruit lids. Some baskets are marked with the line number, 3720, under USA in a divided rectangle.

Value Range: $30-35

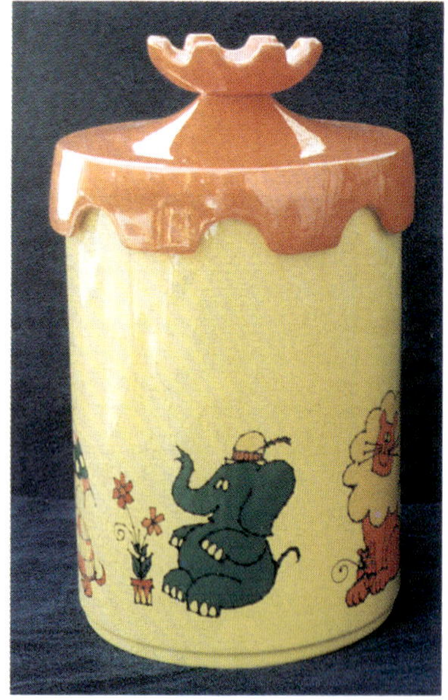

(right) The cylindrical jar is the only known jar to ever have been decorated with decals. The lid is reminiscent of the circus. The animals encircling the jar are an elephant, a turtle, a bear with fishing rod, a hippopotamus, and a lion with a mouse on his foot.

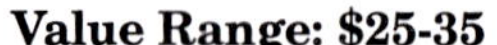

Value Range: $25-35

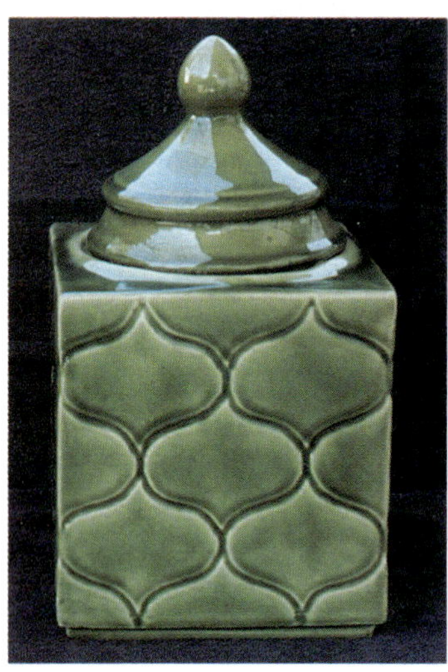

The harlequin jar was done in a variety of colors. Some have contrasting colors alternating on the design. A smaller jar of this style was also made. If marked, they will have a divided rectangle with MORTON on top and the line number, 05026, on the bottom. Some were sold to beauty supply wholesalers. Those are usually marked Lincoln Beauty Ware, made in USA.

Value Range: Large $20-25
Small $15-20

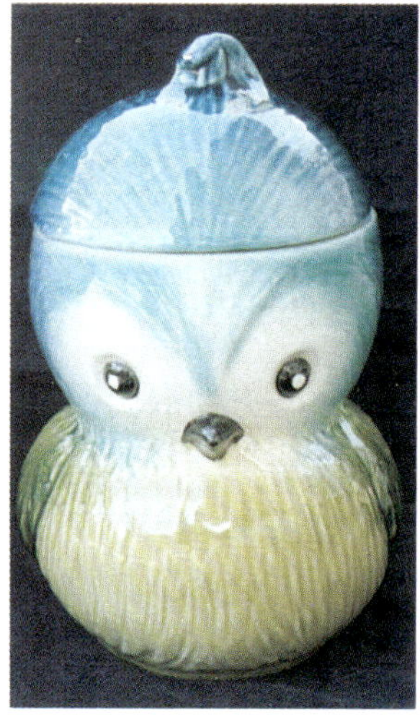

The blue bird is contemporary with the panda. It is spray glazed with the eyes and beak hand painted underglaze. It is not marked.

Value Range
$35-40

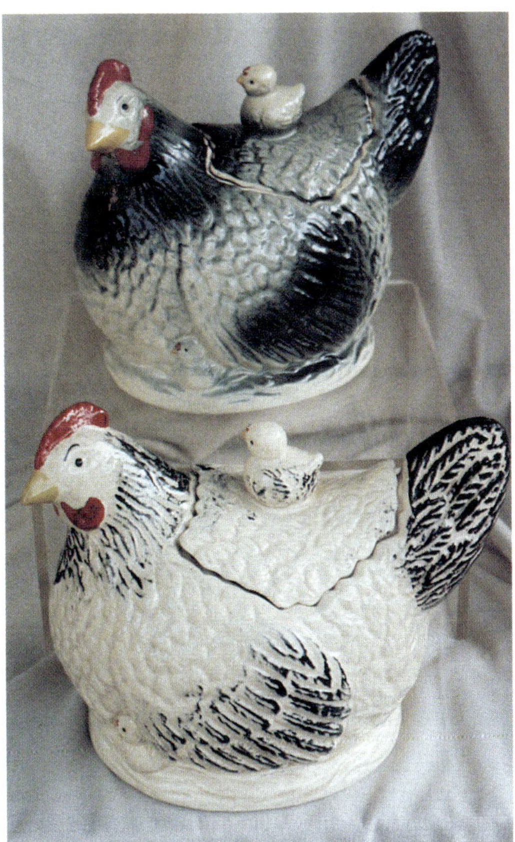

The hen cookie jar has three small chicks, one on the back for a finial, and one tucked uder each wing. The white hen with black brushed decoration is common. The air brushed grey and black jar is scarce. Hens could be special ordered in any color to match one's kitchen decor.

Value Range: White $75-100
Grey $100-125 Colors – ND

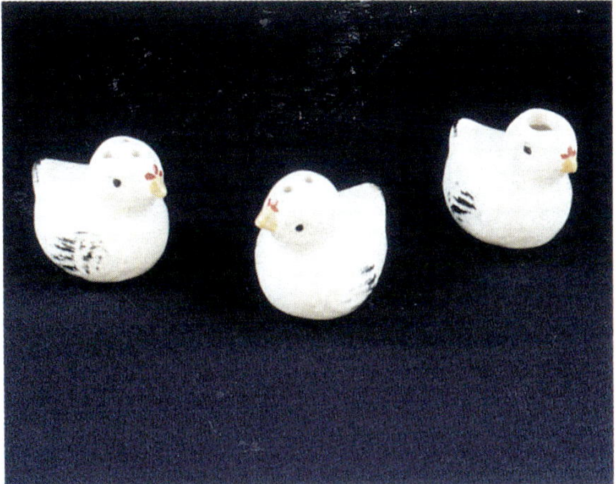

For a short period of time three additional chicks were packaged with the cookie jar. They are tiny salt and pepper shakers and a toothpick holder fashioned from the chick finial. These are extremely rare.

Value Range: ND

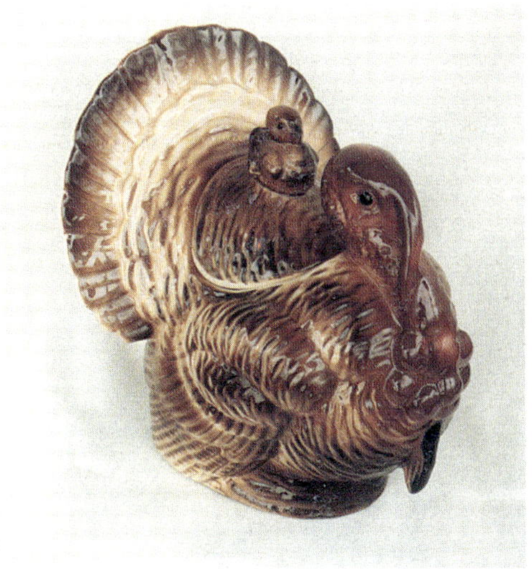

The turkey cookie jar, contemporary with the hen, was produced for a shorter period of time and is more difficult to find.

Value Range: $100-125

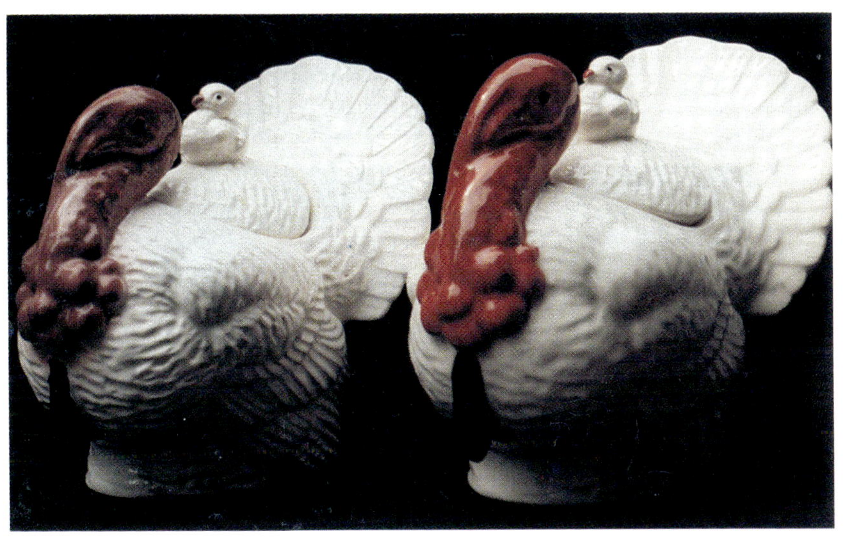

The turkey cookie jar on the right is from an old mold. Note the smoothness of the feathers. It has a cold painted head. The jar on the left is from a new mold. The detail is much sharper. Its head is glazed in burgundy red.

Value Range: $125-150

HOLIDAY NOVELTIES

CHRISTMAS

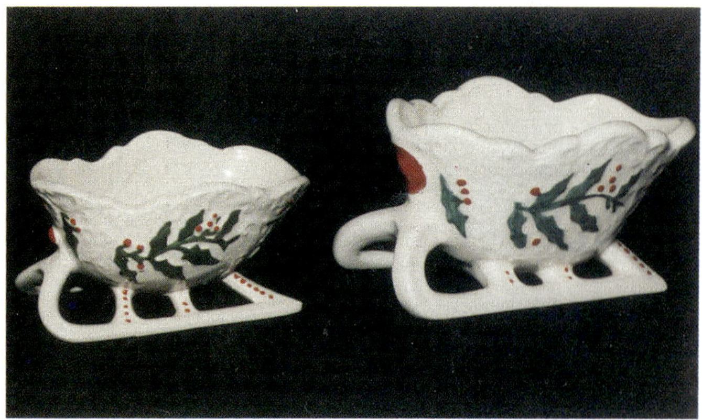

The holly leaves and berries on the white sleighs were always embossed and hand decorated in red and green cold paint. The small size is rare.

Value Range: Small $20-25 Large $18-24

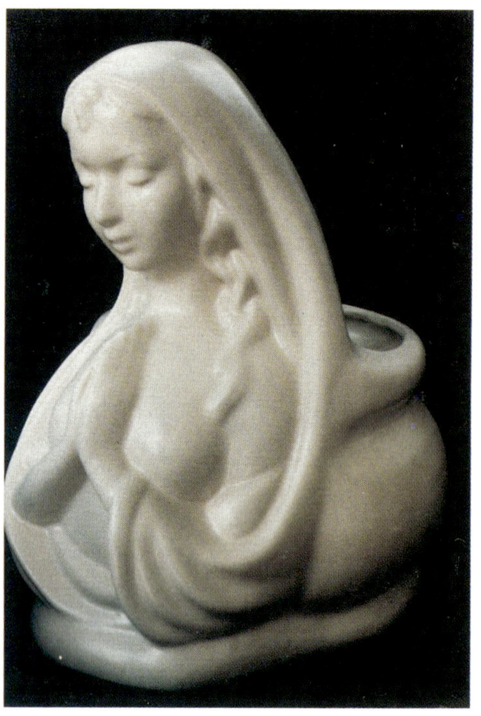

The Madonna planter was designed by Royal Hickman who also designed for Haeger Pottery. It was usually done in matte white glaze.

Value Range: $35-40

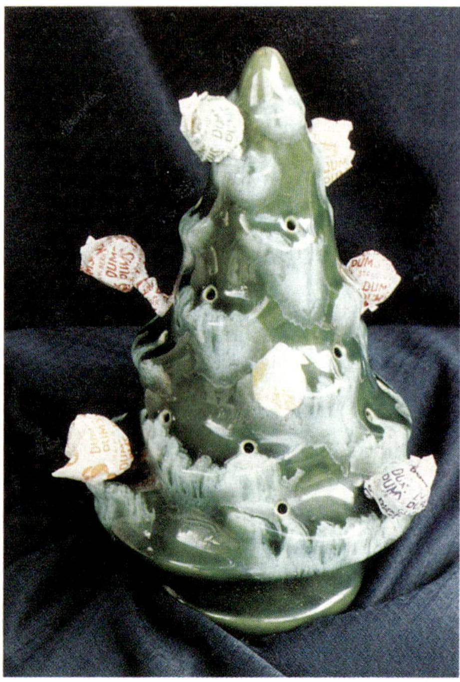

The lollypop tree is 9 1/4" tall. It was glazed green with white air brushed accents. The tree was also done in bisque and spray painted with a flat green enamel.

Value Range: $25-30

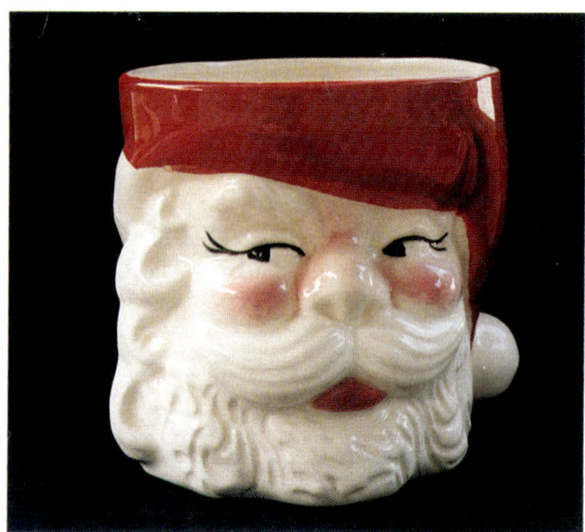

The punch bowl is rare. It has a capacity of 16 cups.

Value Range: ND

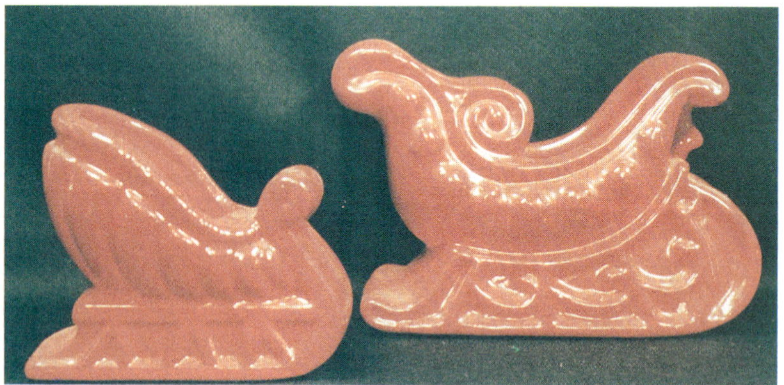

The red sleighs were either cold painted, or spray painted with red automobile lacquer.

Value Range: Small $15-20
Large $25-30

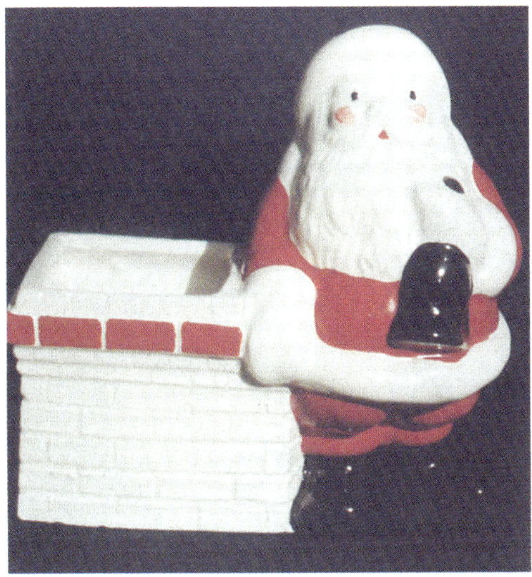

The white chimney Santa planter was hand painted with red cold paint.

Value Range: $15-18

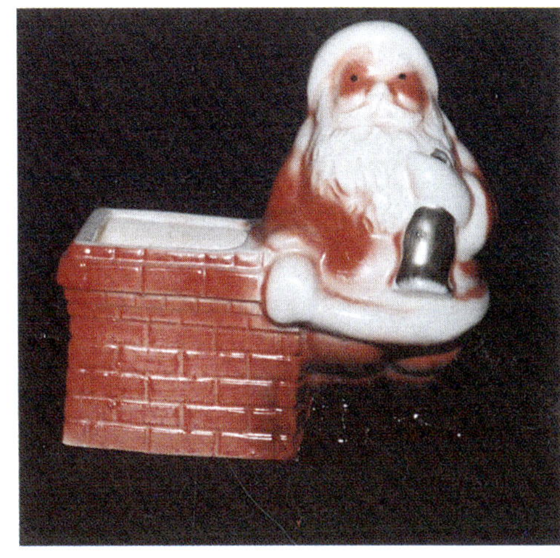

The red chimney Santa is spray painted with red lacquer. His bell is 14K gold.

Value Range: $20-22

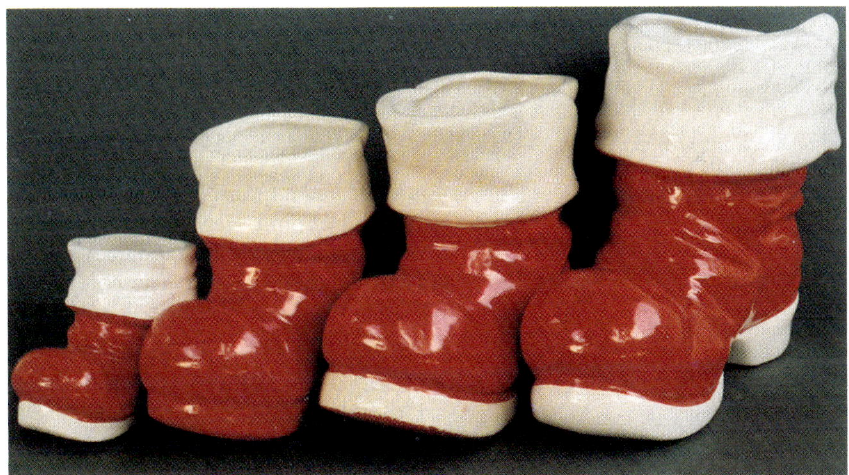

Boots are the most common Christmas item made at Morton Pottery Company. They make ideal candy containers.

Value Range: $6-22

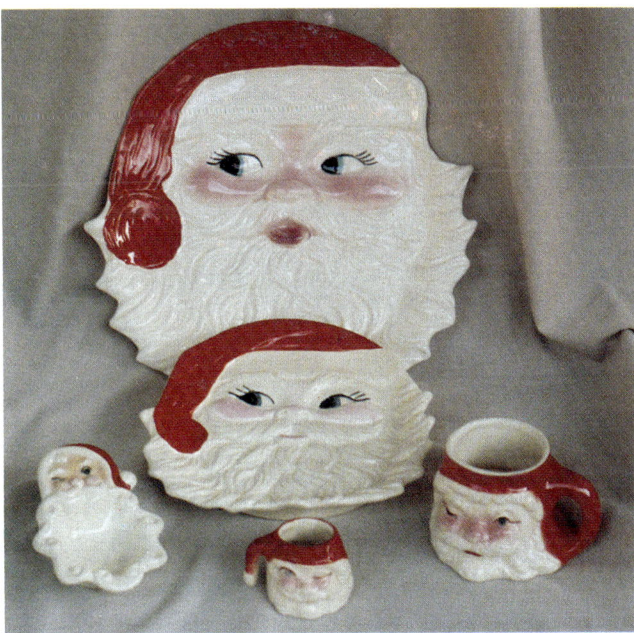

All items pictured have been hand painted with red cold paint. The faces arc a combination of spray glazing and hand painted underglaze.

Value Ranges: Large Santa Plate $40-45
Small Santa Plate $30-35 Ashtray $12-14
Nut Cup $10-12 Mug $15-18

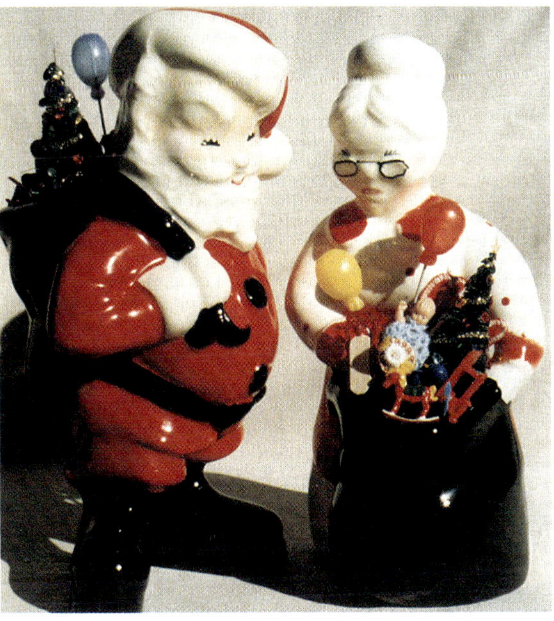

Mr. and Mrs. Santa were made as planter/vases. They are hand painted with red and black enamel. He has thick sole boots and is 91/2" tall. She wears a red apron and polka dot dress. She is also 91/2" tall.

Value Range: Santa $30-35 Mrs. Santa $25-30

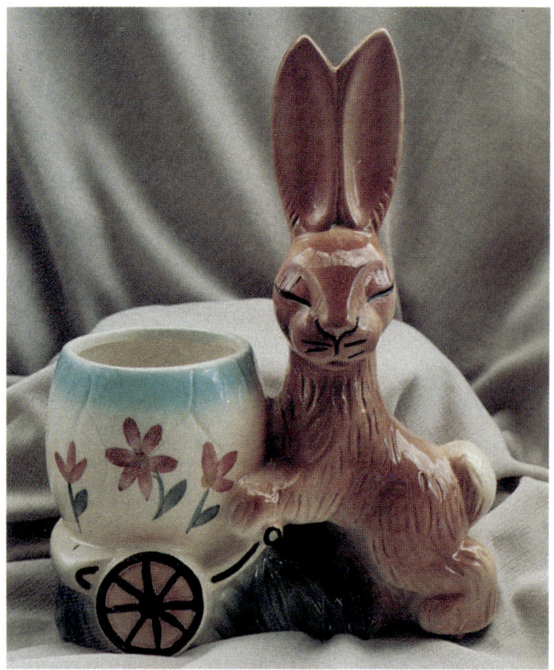

This planter encompasses both spray glaze and hand painted under glaze techniques. The rabbit is 93/4" tall.

Value Range: $18-24

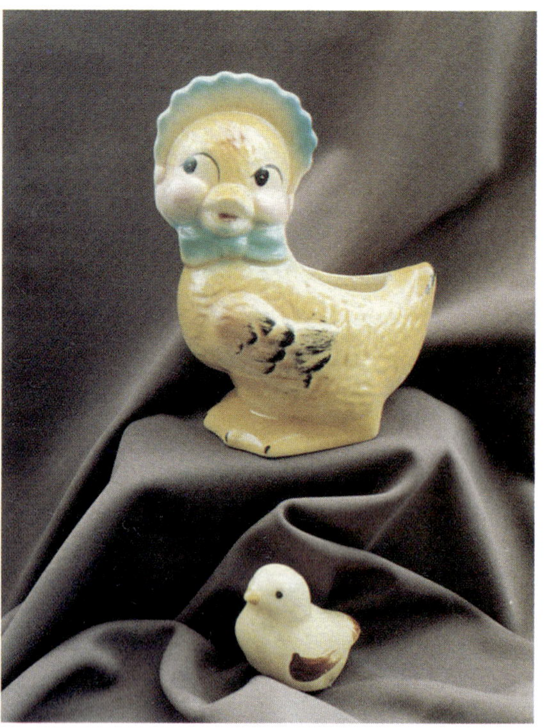

The hen planter has a quizzical look. Her bonnet can be either blue or pink. Her wings are done in a dry brush technique that was frequently used at the pottery to heighten details. The chick is the finial from a deviled egg plate. It is sometimes found as a shaker.

Value Range: Hen $15-18 Chick $3-5
Chick as shakers $8-10 pair

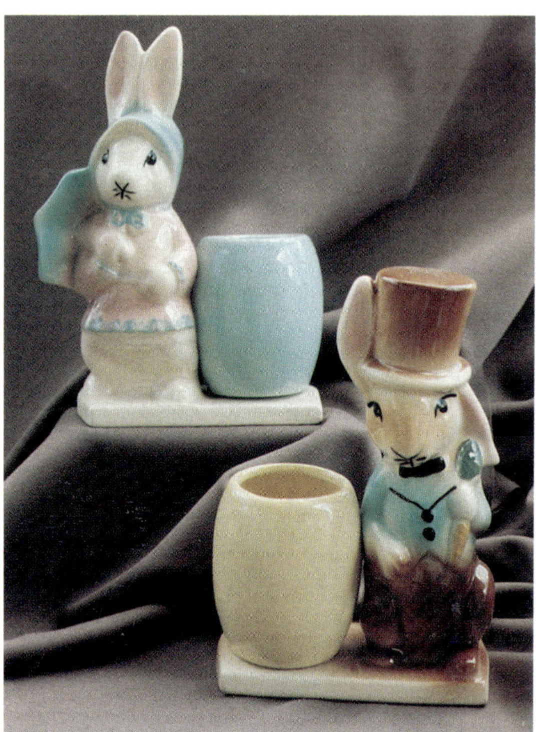

The male and female Easter bunnies were popular Easter items. This pair is spray glazed with limited hand decoration. They have jars instead of eggs for planters. The rabbits are 91/2" tall.

Value Range: $30-35 pair

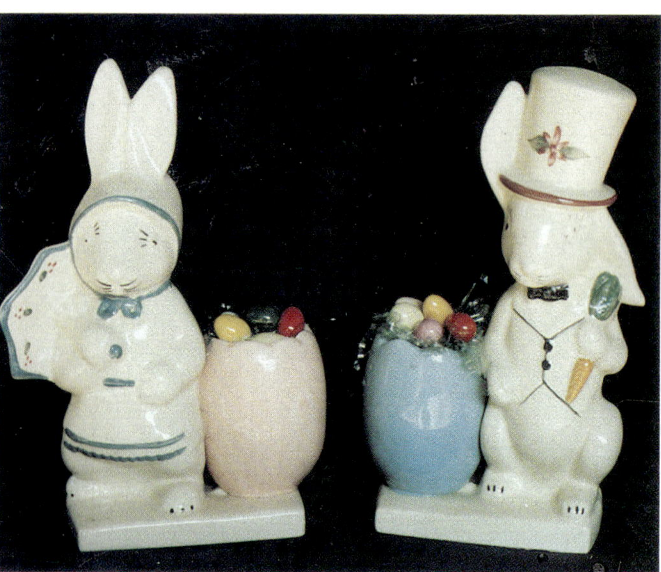

The larger rabbits were hand painted underglaze then dipped in transparent glaze to enhance the white clay. The rabbits are 10" tall.

Value Range: $35-40 pair

Note: The small eggs are not Morton Pottery Company. They are being made currently by a local ceramic shop that uses the name "Morton Pottery."

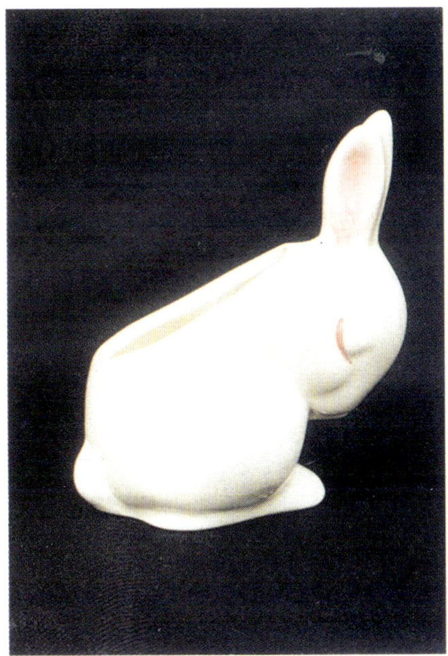

This bunny planter, #530 is 5" tall. It was also made in solid pastel colors.

Value Range: $8-10

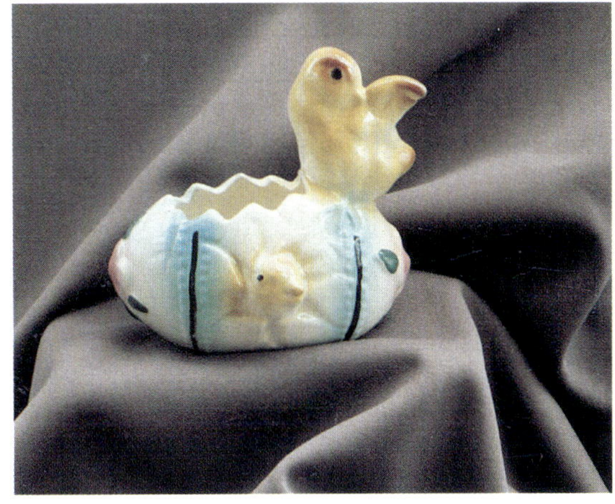

The chick on egg planter is 41/2" tall. It is spray glazed with limited hand painting.

Value Range: $10-12

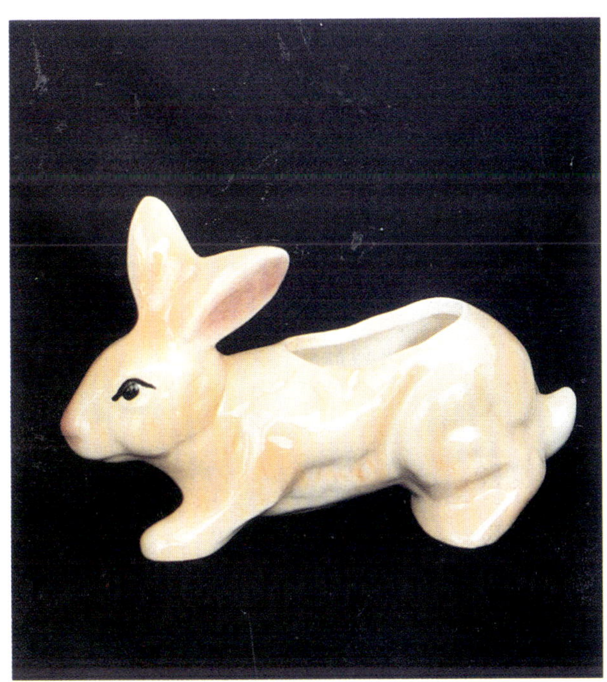

The creeping rabbit is 71/2" long and 41/2" tall. In addition to the light brown, it was made in white, dark brown, and medium grey.

Value Range: $12-16

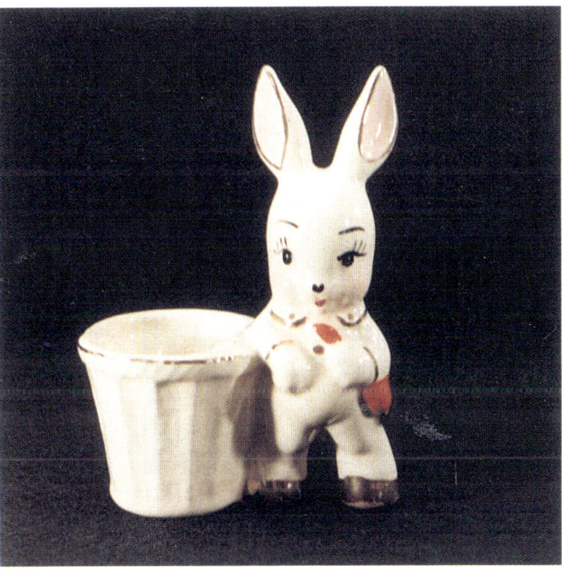

This bunny with a carrot and leaning on a woven basket is #435. He is generally found in solid pastel colors. This one is gold decorated with hand painted features. He is 53/4" tall.

Value Range: $18-20
Add 25% for special decoration

FLOWER HOLDERS AND VASES

The florist house, J.C. Nielsen Company in Chicago was one of the pottery's most extensive buyers. The Nielsen News was a trade paper sent out bimonthly by the company. A copy dated February-March 1941, offered twenty-five different Morton Pottery Company vases, bowls, and planters to its customers.

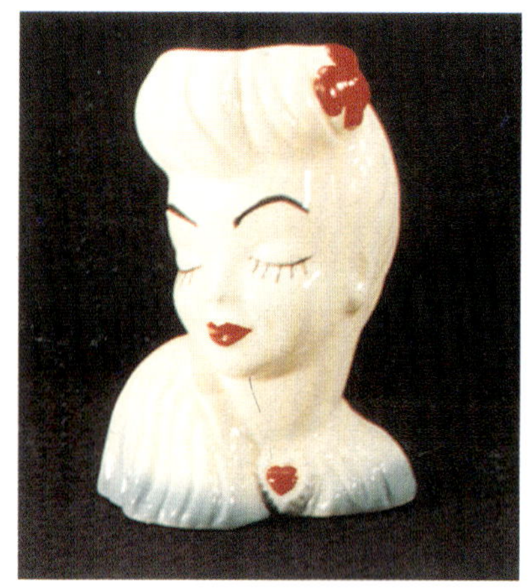

This head vase was always referred to as Betty Grable by the employees in the 1940's. Only a faint hint of color was used at the edge of the collar. All features were cold painted. Some heads were done with yellow hair.

Value Range: $20-30

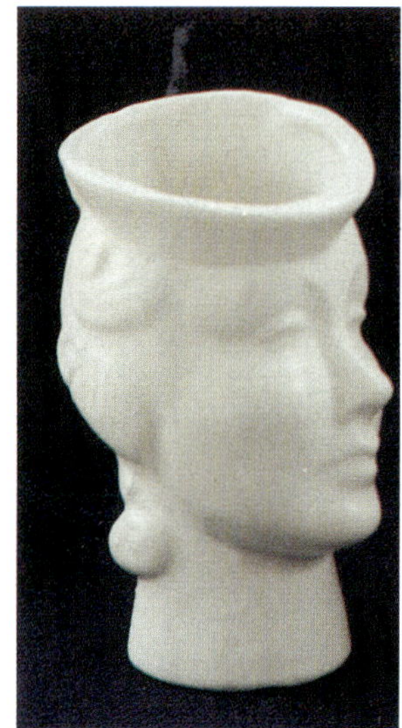

This head vase has a pillbox hat and a hair style that was popular during the 1940's. She is glazed matte white, and is very elusive.

Value Range: $35-45

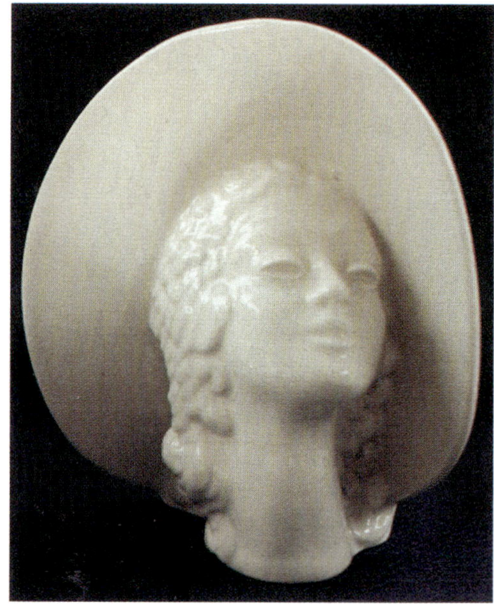

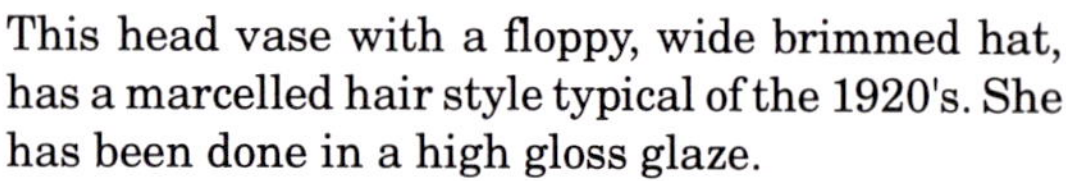

This head vase with a floppy, wide brimmed hat, has a marcelled hair style typical of the 1920's. She has been done in a high gloss glaze.

Value Range: $40-50

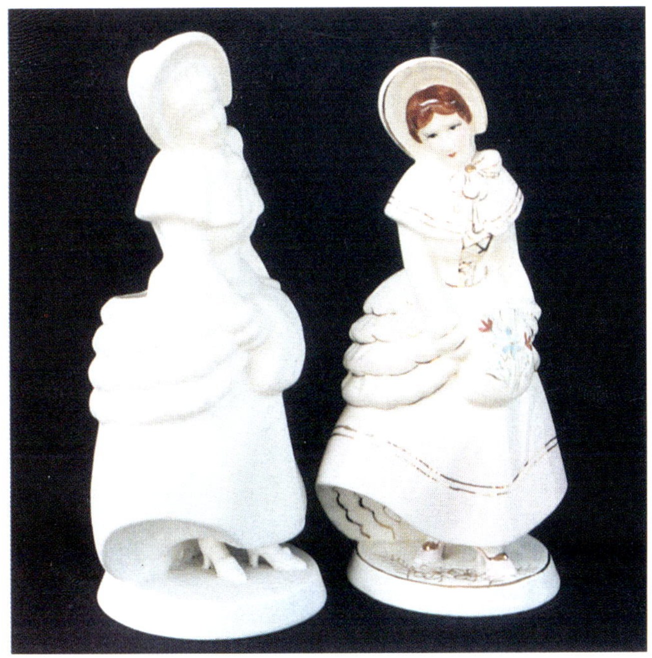

The colonial lady vase is #338. She was usually glazed in matte white or matte turquoise. High gloss colors were available in blue, yellow, pink, and green. The figurine is an adaptation of the #338 vase. It is a fine example of special decorated ware.

Value Range: Planter/vase $20-22
Figurine $25-35

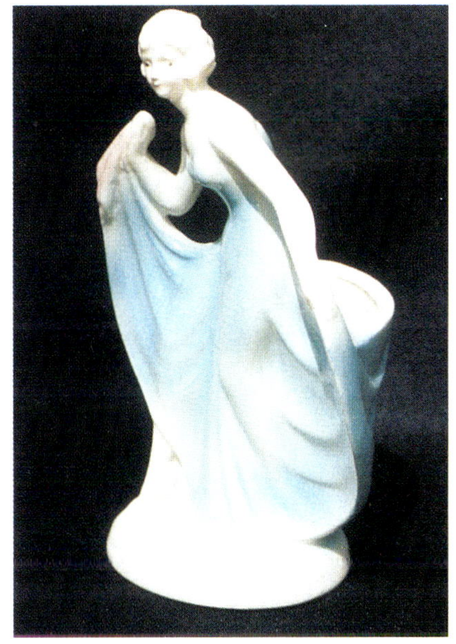

The deco lady with handkerchief and flowing dress was copied from a figurine that was made by the Midwest Pottery. Blue and orchid were the most common colors for her dress.

Value Range: $18-22

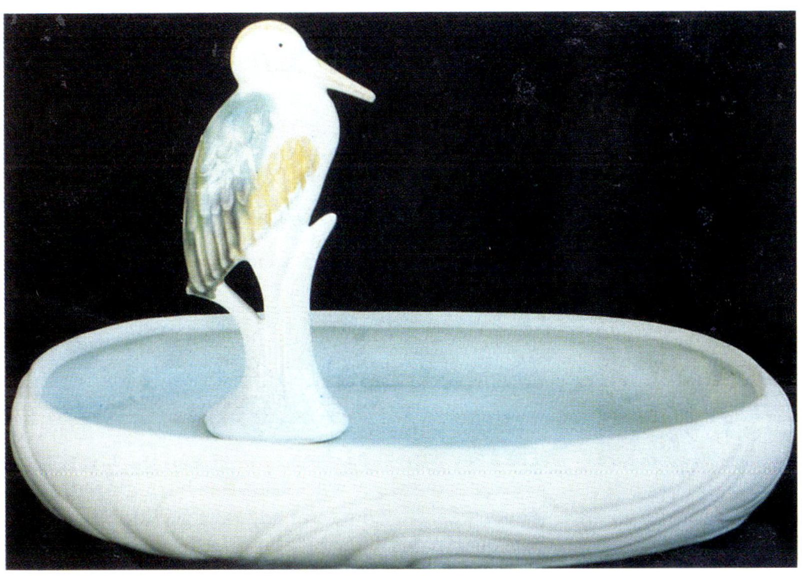

The oval flower bowl has a molded design of cattails and leaves around the outside. It was always glazed matte white with matte turquoise interior. The stork figurine is in the multi color majolica glaze. A variety of figurines was available to be used with the bowl. This set was in the Sears and Roebuck Christmas catalog in 1943, and was priced at $2.29 for the set.

Value Range: Bowl $10-15
Stork $12-14

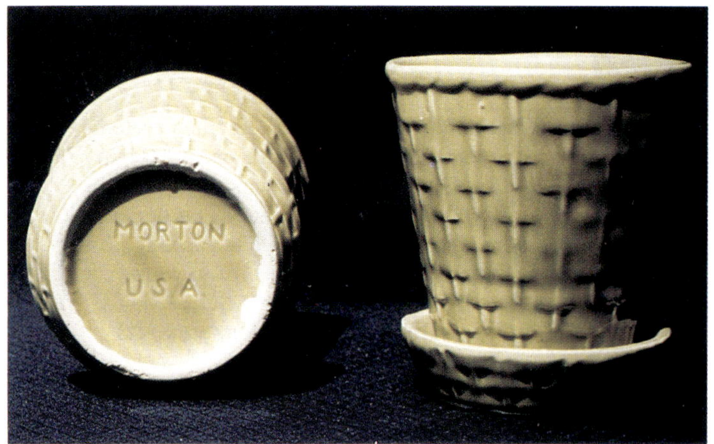

The basket weave flower pot with attached underplate was a standard line produced nearly as long as the pottery was in business. Not all pots are marked. They were made in every glaze color ever developed by Morton Pottery Company. **Value Range: $10-12**

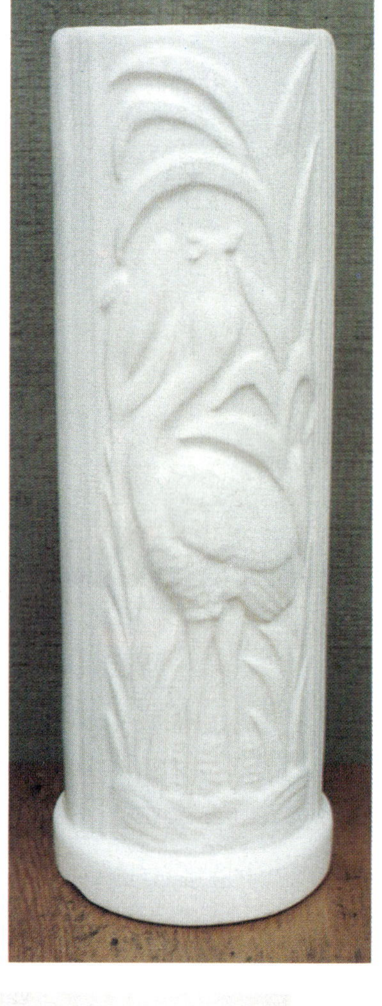

The crane vase is 121/2" tall. The back of the vase is designed to resemble a bamboo cane. The embossed crane and wetland plants are realistically executed. This vase was made in pastel colors as well as white.

Value Range: $25-35

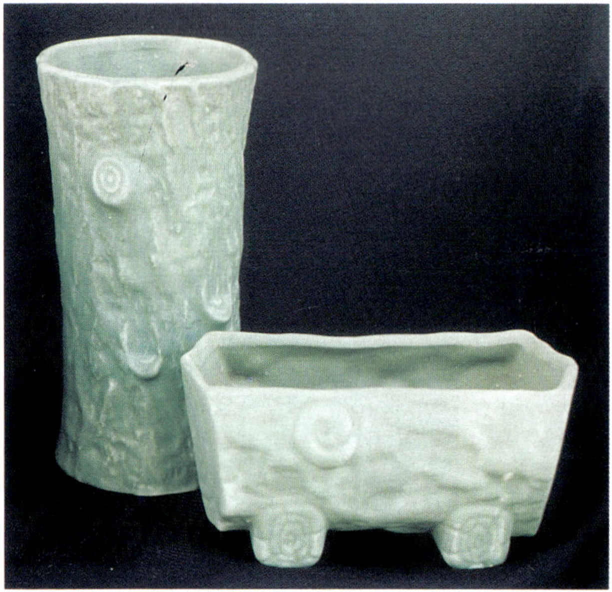

The log vase, #260, and the flower bowl, #262, are a soft matte green. They were also done in the woodland glaze.
Value Range: Vase $18-22 Bowl $16-18
Add 50% for woodland glaze

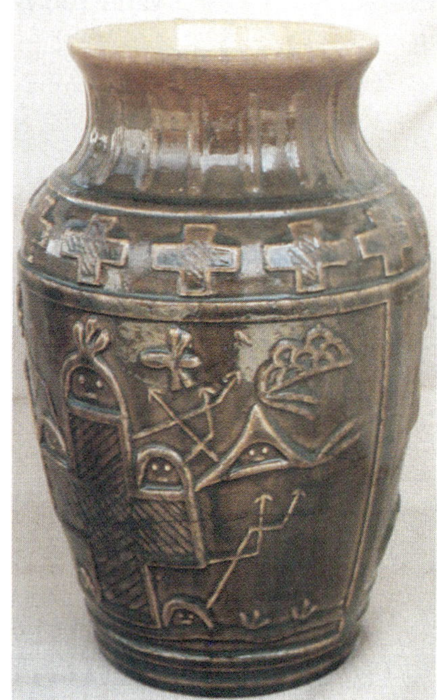

The vase with the Greek crosses and the hieroglyphic pictographs is yellow ware that has been glazed with a thin green wash to allow the edges of the embossed design to be exaggerated. The vase has also been found glazed black. This vase is rare. **Value Range: $40-50**

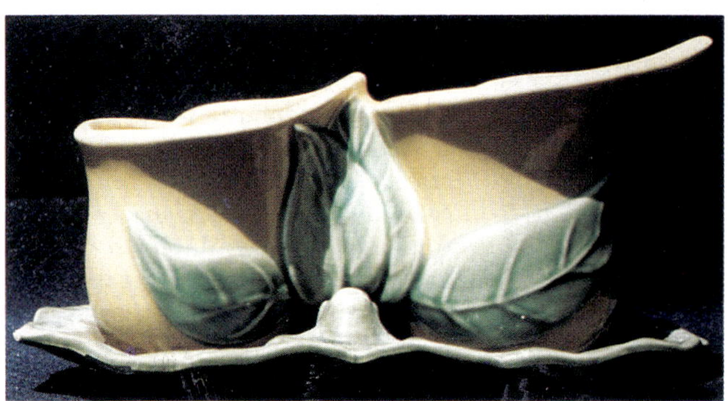

The calla lily planter was always marked "Morton USA." It was glazed in both yellow and white. It has a frog head between the lilies at the base of the leaves.
Value Range: $18-20

FUNCTIONAL ITEMS

Mortonites were noted for their meticulous cleanliness. It was only natural, in a town where laundry water was recycled for use in scrubbing porches each week, that the pottery would design and produce items to help eliminate untidy conditions.

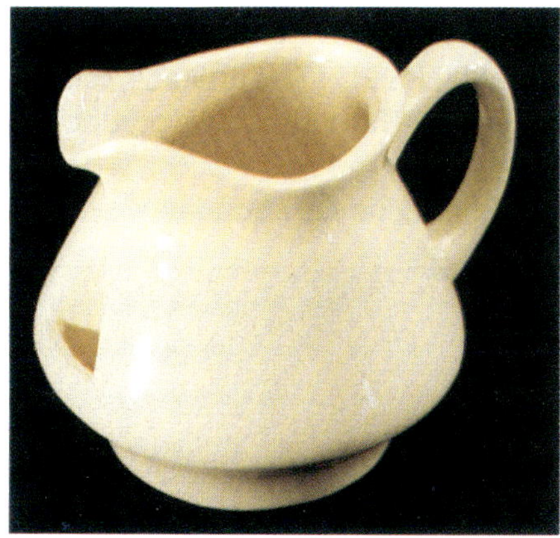

The "no-spot" pitcher was designed by Dr. R. F. Daniel, a retired dentist. A small groove runs from the lip to an open cavity at the widened portion of the base. Its purpose was to keep drippings from running down onto the tablecloth. The pitchers were designed in pint and quart sizes, but only the pint size was manufactured.

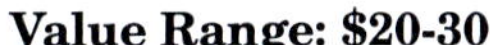

Value Range: $20-30

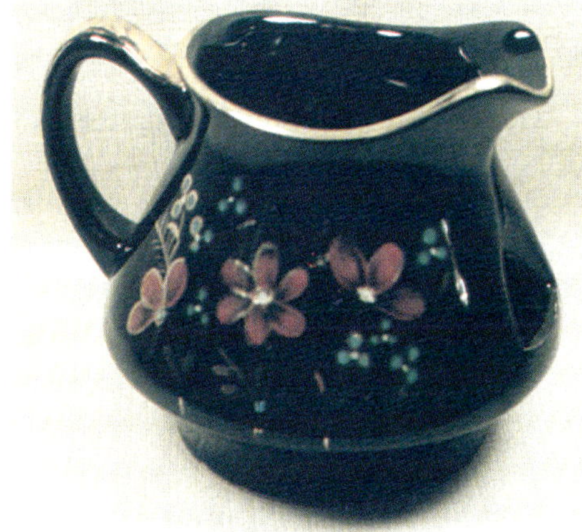

The "no-spot" pitcher was seldom special decorated. Examples of this type are scarce.

Value Range: $40-50

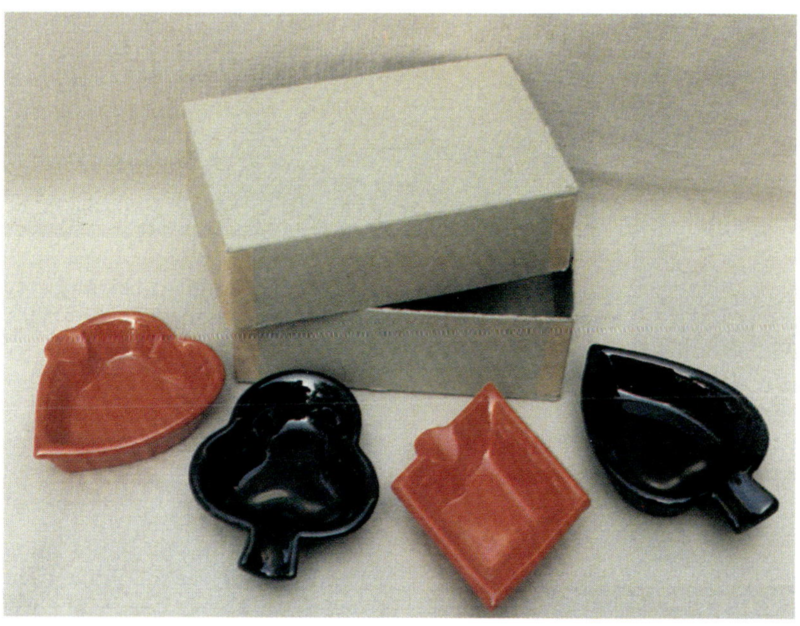

The ashtrays were made to use on game tables to keep the table tidy. The ashtrays were often used as prizes by bridge clubs. They are not often found with the original box.

Value Range: $25-30
Add 10% in original box.

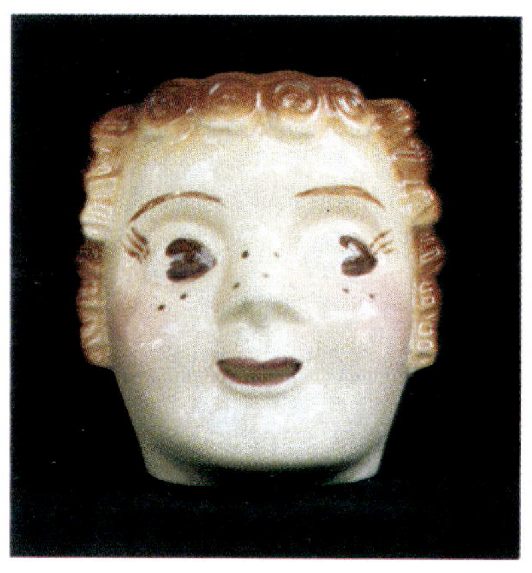

This scouring pad holder was designed to set on the kitchen sink to keep it tidy. The mouth is open so accumulated water could be poured out. Some identify this head as a string holder, but that was not its original intent. Many Mortonites recall receiving this novelty as a bridal shower gift in the 1940's.

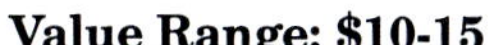

Value Range: $10-15

GRASS GROWERS

Grass growers are hollow bisque figures that can be planted with seed and filled with water. The water percolates through the figure, supplying just enough moisture to allow the seeds to sprout and grow.

In 1933, grass growers were sold to retailers for $1.14 a dozen. Their popularity swept the United States during the Great Depression because they were affordable.

The figures were packed two dozen of one design to a carton. A packet of seeds, with instructions, was supplied with each figure.

In December, 1933, a Santa Fe box car was loaded with 38,000 Paddy O'Hair heads, consigned to F. W. Woolworth Company's Manhattan district stores. In January, 1934, the pottery was producing 4,000 Jiggs head a day.

Grass growers were made until the early 1970's. There should be an abundance of them just waiting to be found.

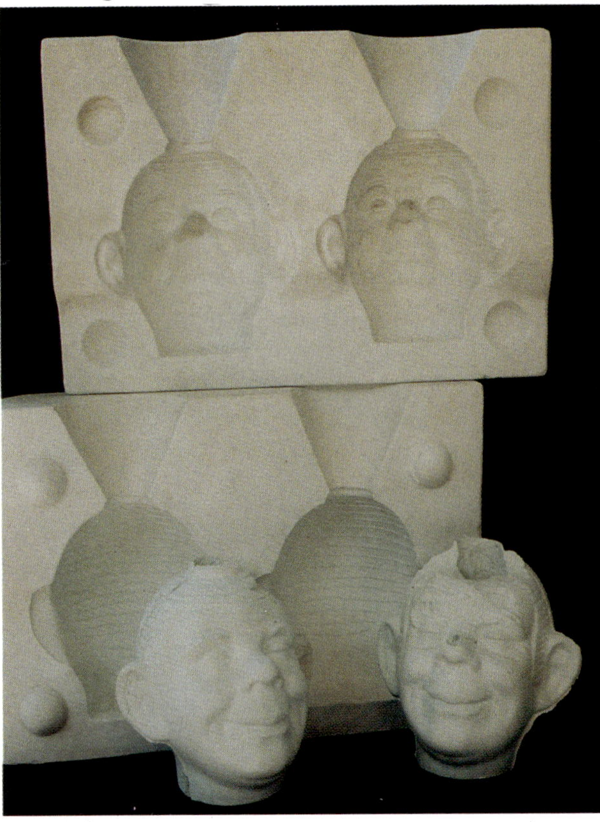

Here is the master mold with plaster casts used to create molds for Jolly Jim who had been named Paddy O'Hair when the novelty was first made. He was also called Sunny Jim in some advertising. This master mold is dated 1-11-72, and is initialed R. J.

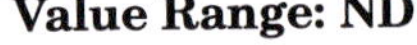

Value Range: ND

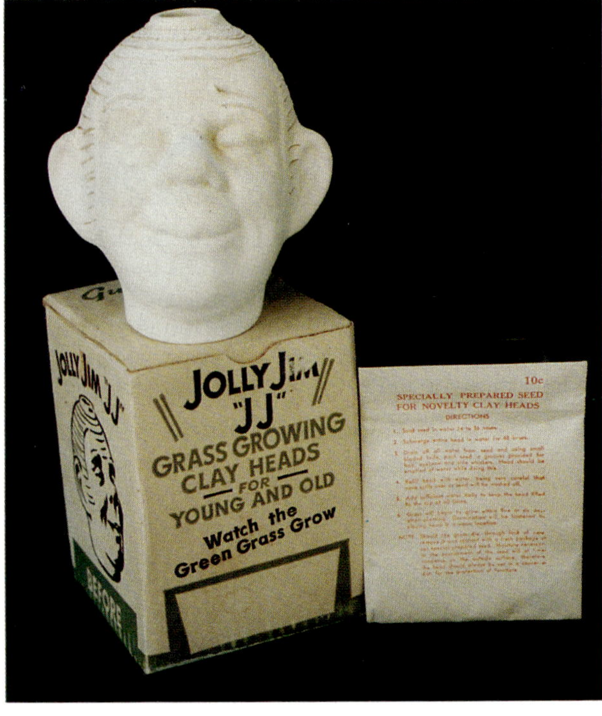

To find a grass grower with the original box and seed packet is most difficult. This one was made in the 1950's.

Value Range: Head $18-22
Add 50% for head with box and seed.

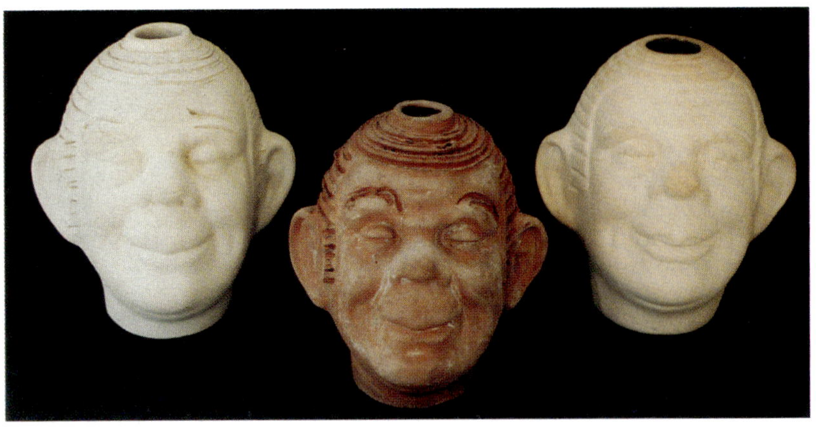

Jolly Jim is on the left. In the center is Paddy O'Hair, cast in tile clay. The grooves on these heads are not molded, but scratched into the greenware with a nail. The head on the right is a reproduction. It was made by Paddy Novelty Company, Goliad, Texas. The grooves are molded rather than scratched. It is made of very thin clay, and has a hole in the bottom. It cannot be used to grow grass.

Value Range: Jolly Jim $18-22
Paddy O'Hair $24-26
Reproduction – ND

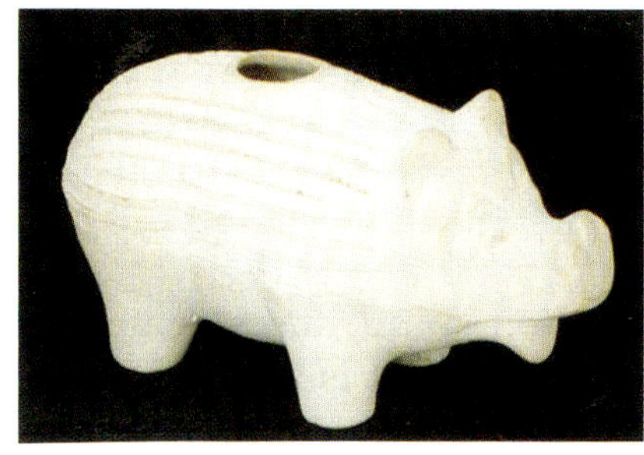

Advertised as "porky pig" long before the animated cartoon character was created, this figure is 7 1/2" long and 3 3/4" tall.

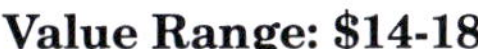

Value Range: $14-18

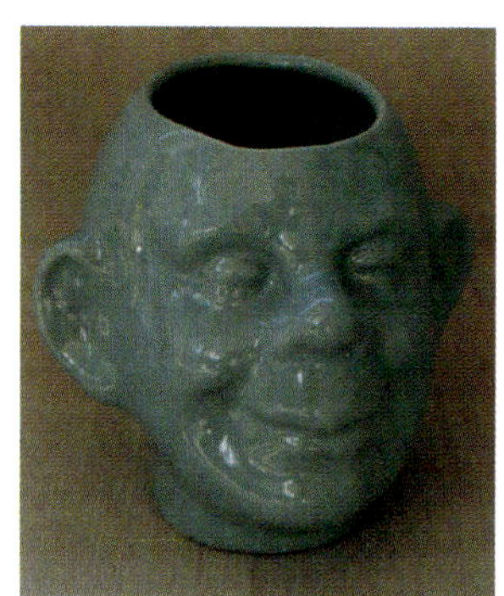

This is a whimsey done by an employee at the pottery and sneaked through the kiln. It may well be one of a kind. Pencil holders were never made from the grass growers.

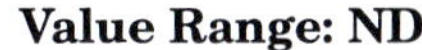

Value Range: ND

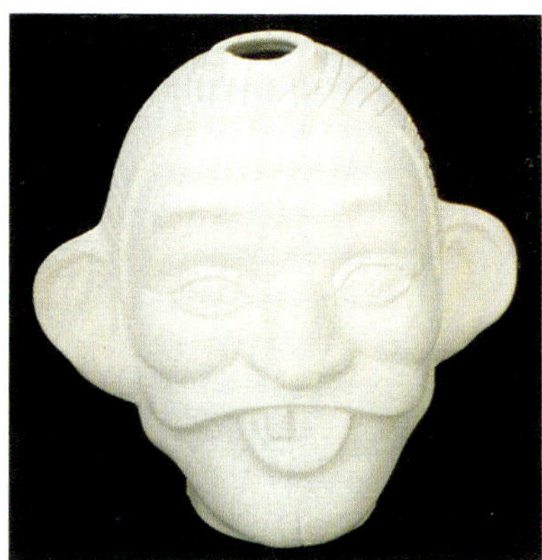

"Jake" was No. 777 on a 1951 S.S. Kresge Company order form. He is 5" tall. New heads were made from old molds in the 1980's. They are light weight, and very smooth bisque.

Value Range: $20-24

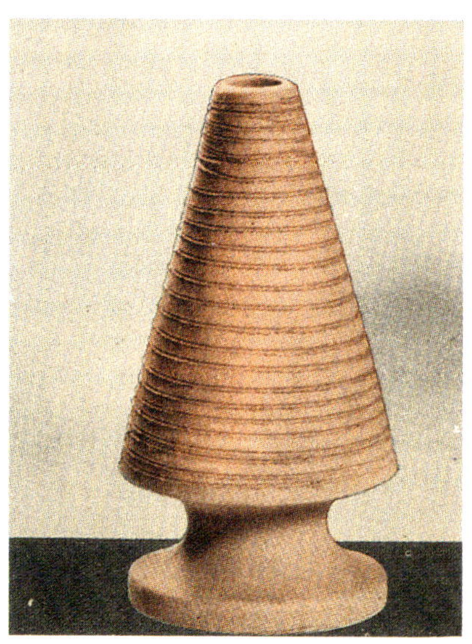

The evergreen tree, the least popular of the grass growers, is elusive. It measures 6" tall.

Value Range: $10-15

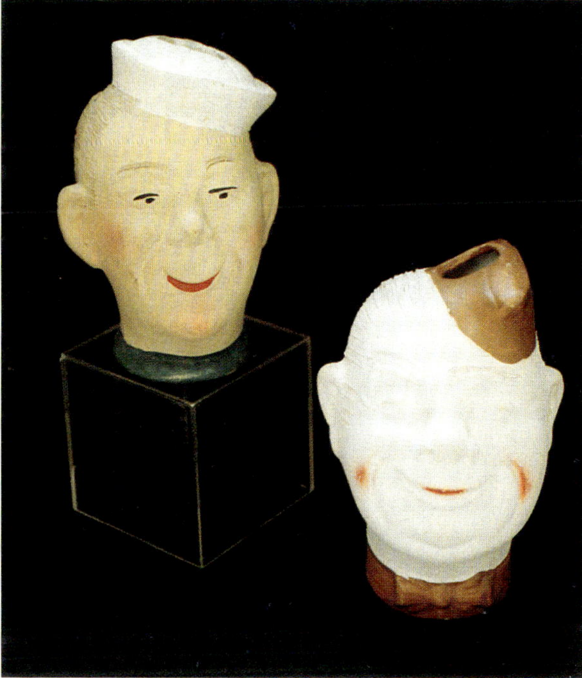

These heads were made during World War II, from 1941 to 1945. "Hi Buddy" is found on the back of the soldier's collar. The sailor is 6 1/4" tall, the soldier is 6 3/4".

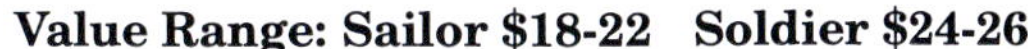

Value Range: Sailor $18-22 Soldier $24-26

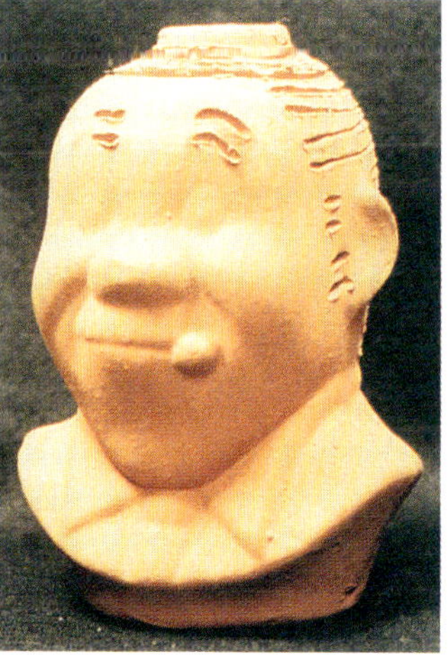

Jiggs was usually made from tile clay, but he has been found in white. Because "Maggie and Jiggs" was a copyrighted comic strip, the Rapps had to get permission from King Features before this figure could be put into production. This is an exact likeness of Jiggs. It is 5" tall.

Value Range: $25-30

GRASS GROWERS

The Santa Fe Railroad built a siding parallel to their main line so car could be pulled up to the shipping department to be loaded. The loading dock is visible just behind the box car.

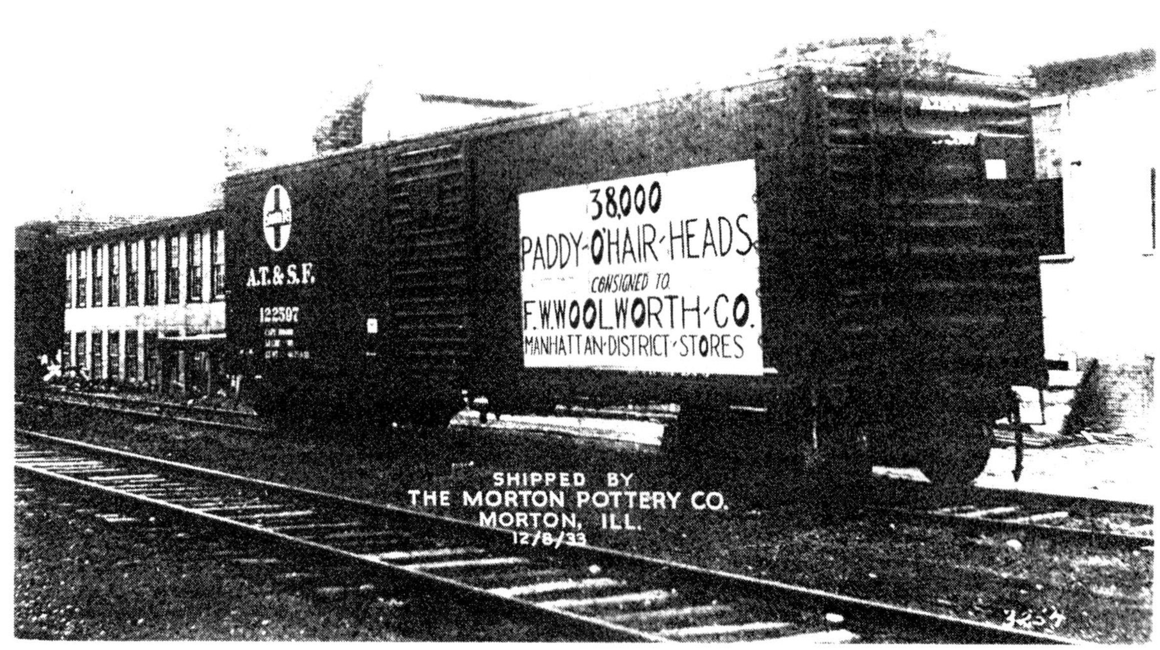

GRASS GROWERS

This is the front window of S. S. Kresge's, Peoria, Illinois store. It served as a model for other Kresge 5¢ and 10¢ stores.

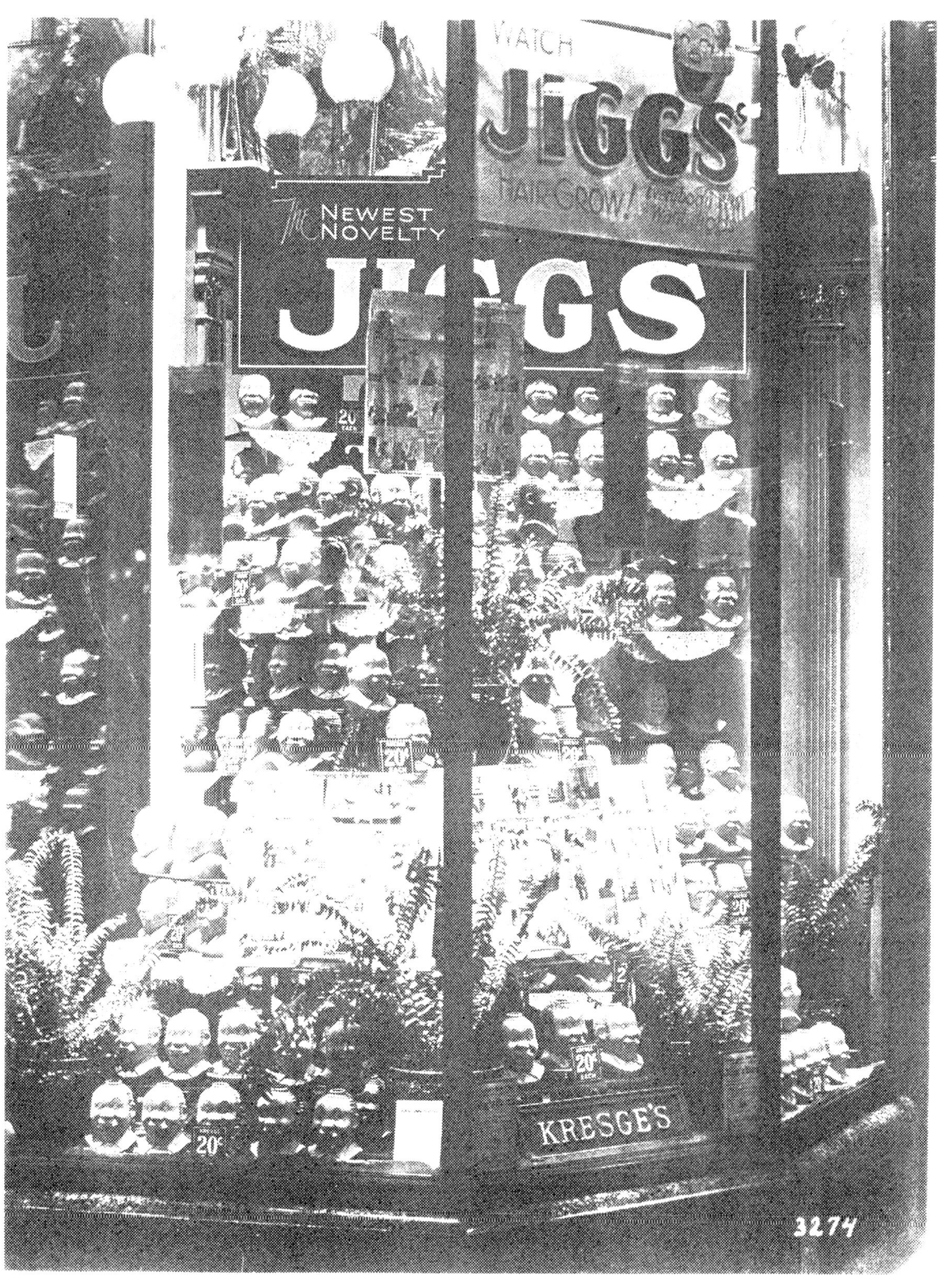

GRASS GROWERS

This letter, from T. K. Kirkpatrick, was sent to other Kresge stores to help in the promotion of the grass growing heads. Kirkpatrick was the buyer for Kresge at the general offices in Detroit, Michigan.

GENERAL LETTER
ALL 5 AND 10¢ STORES
BOCK 10. T. K. K.

Detroit, Michigan,
January 29, 1934.

GRASS HEADS

We just received the following letter from store #138, Peoria, Ill.:-

"Dear Mr. Kirkpatrick:

We put the "Jiggs" Grass Heads, received from Morton Pottery Co., on sale today for the first time. We sold 28–1/3 dozen or $68.00 selling value. We also sold 5 dozen small pottery saucers at 5¢ each to put under these Heads. Morton charges us 30¢ a dozen for them. A great many can be sold by suggesting.

We put in a full window Friday night and had a full counter end out with good signs and a few "Jiggs" with grass growing on the heads. We also had a nice write-up in one of our papers. We are attaching a copy for your inspection. The Peoria Star also has a "Jiggs"–displayed in their window with a sign reading "Jiggs, Comic Page Character in the Star".

It may be possible for the managers in the cities where the newspapers run the "Jiggs" comic strip to get similar publicity.

$68.00 in sales today from this one new item surely paid us for our efforts, 47% gross.

Yours very truly,

(signed) H.L. Newton"

We have suggested to one or two stores a demonstration on this item as follows. Cover the end of a counter with grass rugs. Also have the girl who is to demonstrate made a grass wig from a portion of one of these rugs. Have several heads planted and growing. The girl can explain to her patrons relative to filling the head, soaking the seed, etc. She can also actually apply the seed while customers look on. Try to tie up your local newspaper with your demonstration. This item should sell well up into the Spring.

Please accept this as a call for orders on Grass Heads if you do not have on hand or on order. Rush.

GRASS GROWERS

This letter was sent to Mr. Rapp with the letter sent to the other Kresge stores. It was Kirkpatrick's method of alerting the pottery to be ready for an onslaught of orders.

OFFICE OF
T. K. KIRKPATRICK

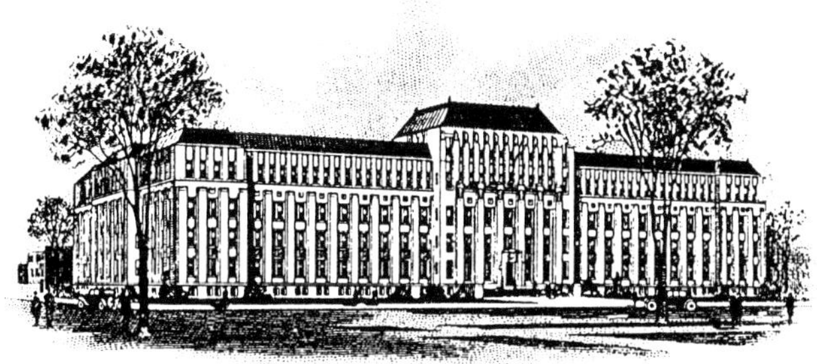

S. S. KRESGE COMPANY

GENERAL OFFICES

DETROIT, MICHIGAN

January 29, 1934.

Morton Pottery Co.

Morton, Ill.

Attention: Mr. S. Rapp.

Dear Mr. Rapp:

We are attaching copy of letter which we today circulated to all our stores and in which we gave your "Jiggs" Grass Heads an extra push.

We trust that you have sufficient stock on hand to fill all orders promptly as you will undoubtedly receive quite a number of them within the next few days.

Yours very truly,

S. S. KRESGE COMPANY

T. K. KIRKPATRICK

Buyer

D.

KITCHENWARE

Kitchenware production was carried over to the Morton Pottery Company from the Morton Earthenware Company that the Rapp brothers had operated from 1915 to 1917. Many of the molds had been preserved. They were put to use as this new pottery started operations in 1923. Yellow Ware soon gave way to colorful kitchenware. In 1929, Morton Pottery Company was the only pottery in America making colored kitchenware. An example was placed in the Metropolitan Museum in New York City to show the modern trend toward color in ordinary utility items.

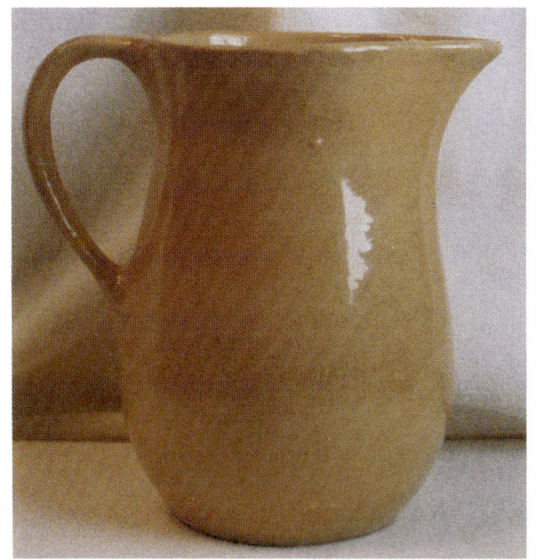

The milk pitcher was also used as a batter pitcher. An underplate was made for this item.

Value Range: Pitcher $40-100
Under Plate $10-40

The beater bowl jar predates the beater bowl pitchers. The white bands are colored slip applied with a pastry tube using the potter's wheel. Brown slip was also used for the lining.

Value Range: $50-90

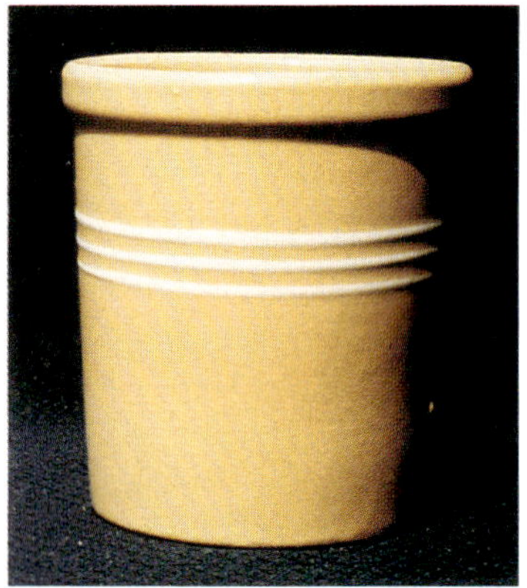

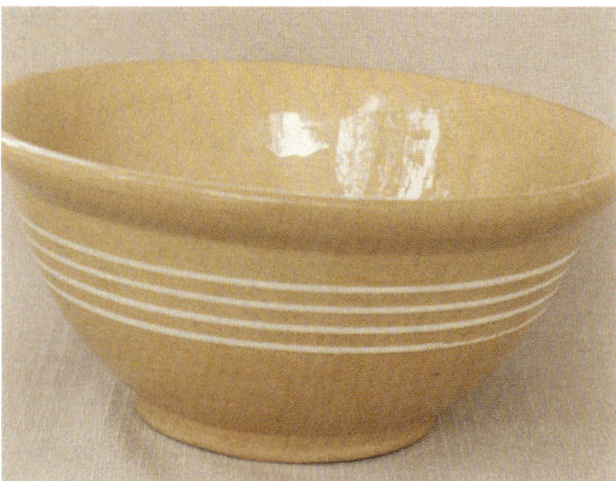

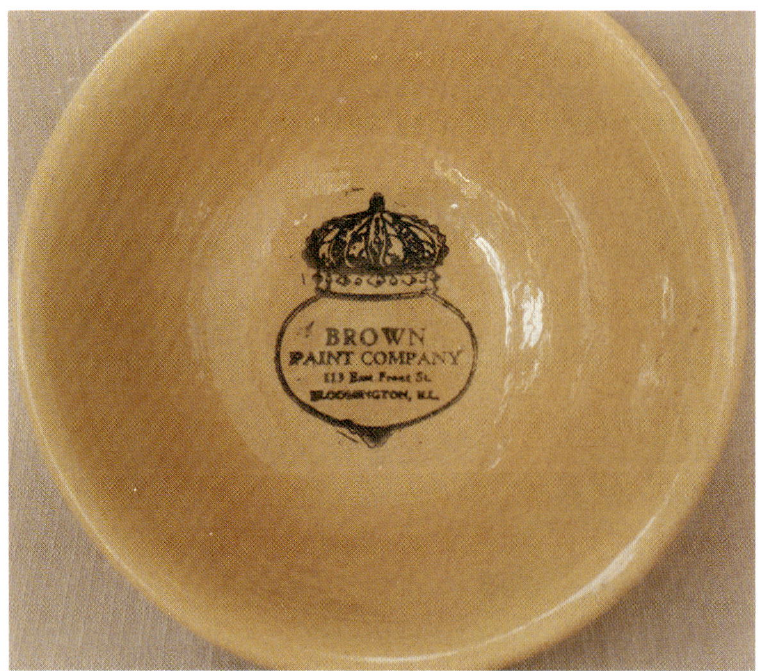

(Pictured above) This yellow ware bowl was called a shoulder bowl on price lists in 1929. It was made in 5", 6", 7", 8" and 9" diameters. A few were made as advertising give-aways. A decal logo (shown at the left) was placed in the bottom of this one under the glaze.

Value Range: $20-100
Add 25% for advertising

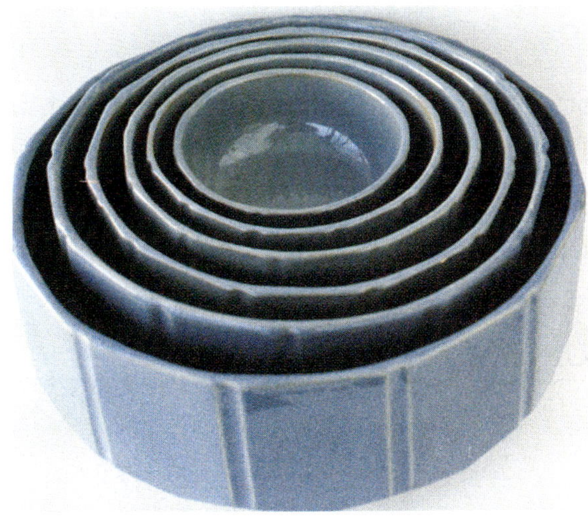

This nested nappy set was part of the Pilgrim Pottery line produced in 1926. The color was listed as Pilgrim blue.

Value Range: $100-125

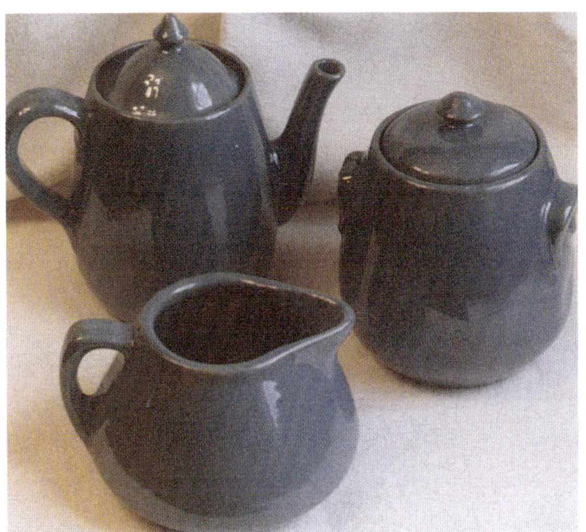

The tea set was part of the Amish Pottery (pantry ware) line produced in 1929. It was also available in yellow and green.

Value Range: Tea Pot $40-60
Sugar $35-85 Creamer $15-50

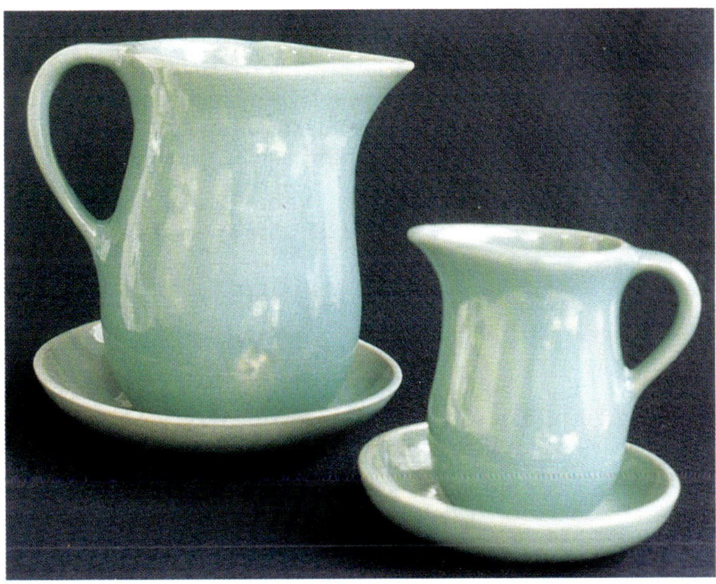

The waffle set is rare. It is usually put together one piece at a time. It was also available in yellow and blue.

Value Range:
Batter Jug $40-100
Coaster $10-40
Syrup Jug $20-60
Coaster $5-20

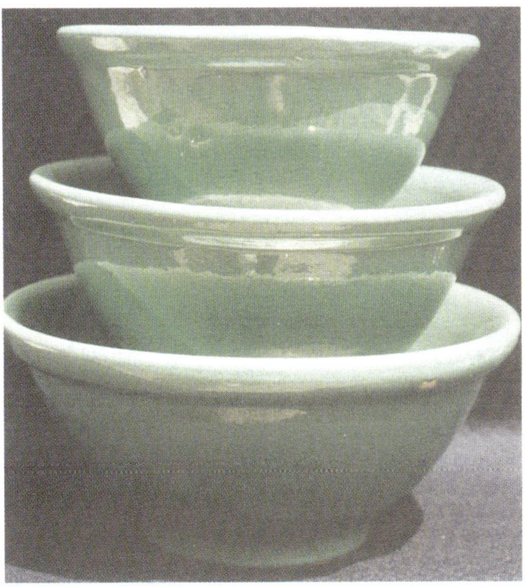

Amish Pottery (pantry ware) bowls are common. Known as shoulder bowls, this nested set was a good seller over many years.

Value Range: Small $20-60
Medium $25-70 Large $30-80

LAMPS

Lamps were a standard line at Morton Pottery Company from the early 1940's until the Rapps sold in 1969. Completely wired lamps were on display in the sales room. Lamp bases were made for Lamp-O-Lite, Le Mar Imperial, and Marshall Potteries, all located in Chicago. Lamp bases were also shipped to the Burkhart Company at Yonkers, New York. Those jobbers contracted for the bases, then assembled and sold the lamps with their own company identities.

CHILDREN'S FIGURAL LAMPS

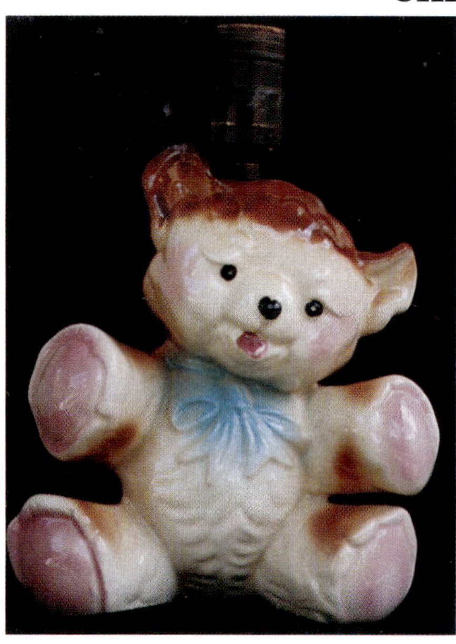

This teddy bear lamp can be found in a variety of color combinations. Its heart shape nose is an identifying mark.

Value Range: $20-25

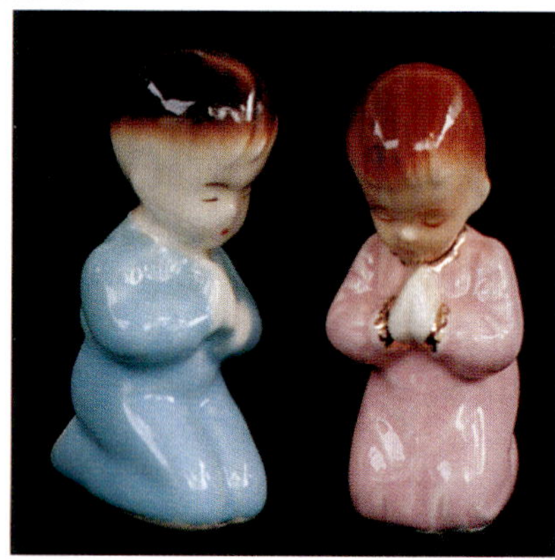

The praying boy and girl in sleepers were sold as individual figurines, but were adapted to many other uses. She has been gold decorated.

Value Range: $8-10
Add 25% for special decoration

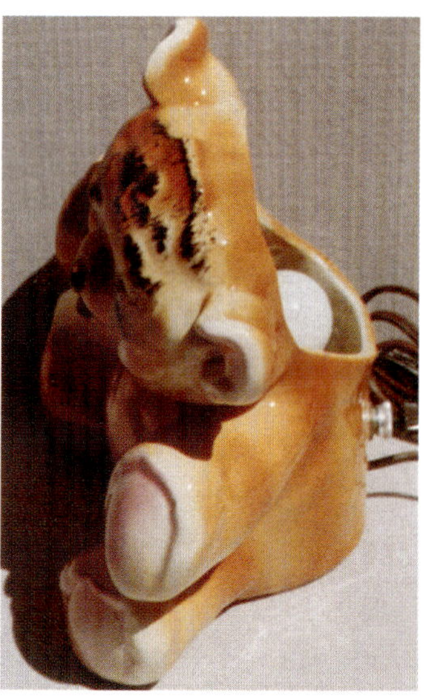

The teddy bear night light is rare. It was made from a planter that was drilled in the back for the switch and the cord.

Value Range: $25-35

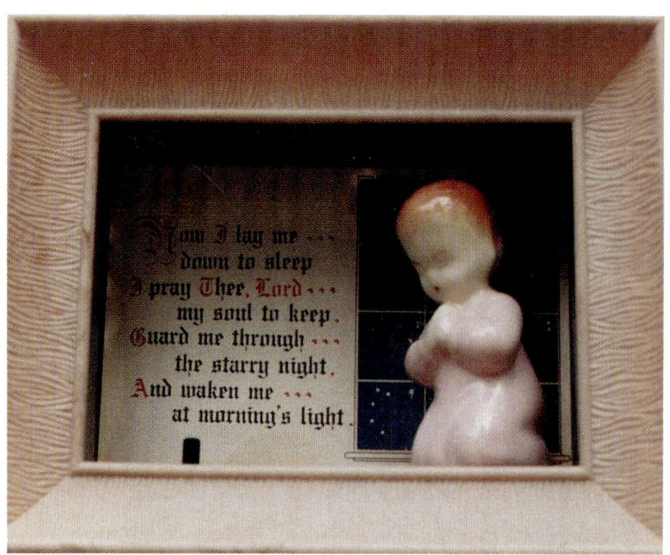

The night light is framed in pink plastic with the light in the bottom to illuminate the prayer (note switch). The night light was also made with a blue frame.

This bear was made in both pink and blue. The tree trunk is very similar to those used for the Davy Crockett lamps.

Value Range: $25-30

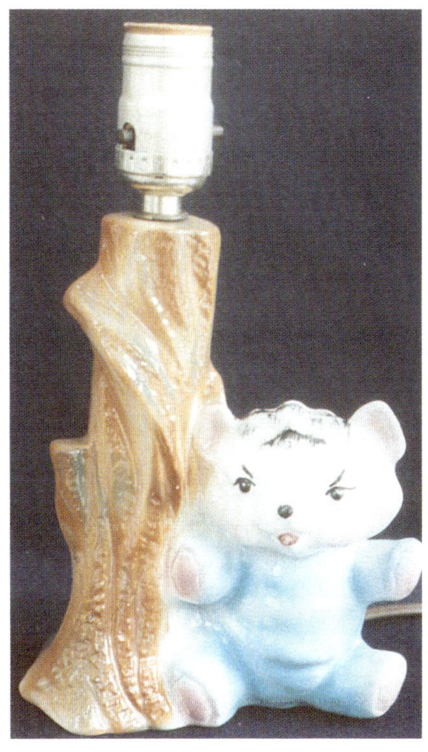

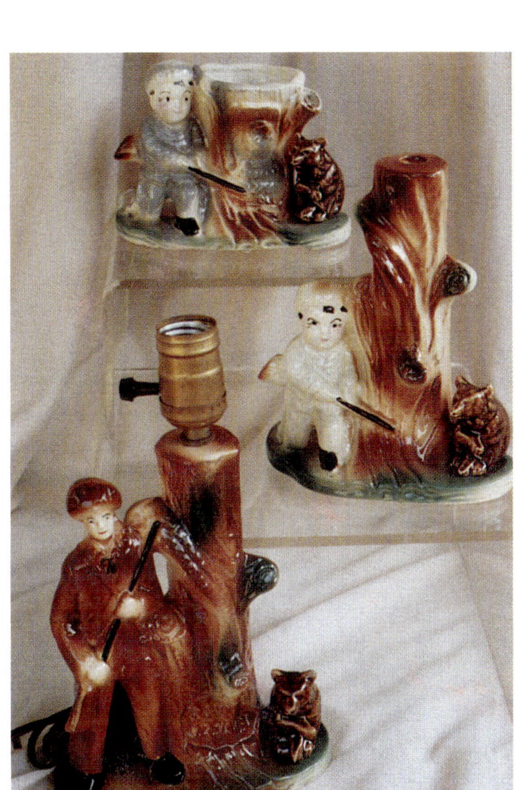

Davy Crockett lamps were made in the mid 1950's when Walt Disney's TV program was popular. The planter was a companion piece. It always depicted Crockett as a child rather than an adult.

Value Range: Planter $30-35
Young Davy Lamp $75-100
Adult Davy Lamp $50-75

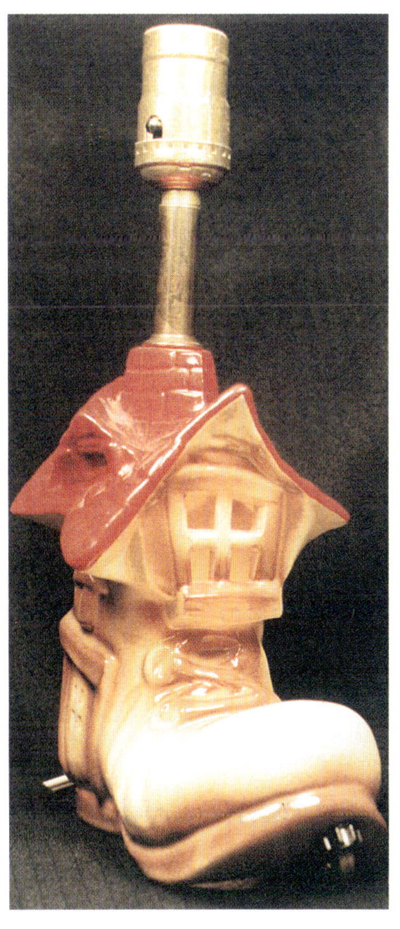

This is the "Old Woman who lived in a shoe" house. The window is open so it can be used as a night light. The lamp can also be found with a green roof.

Value Range: $25-30

LAMPS WITH PLANTER BASES

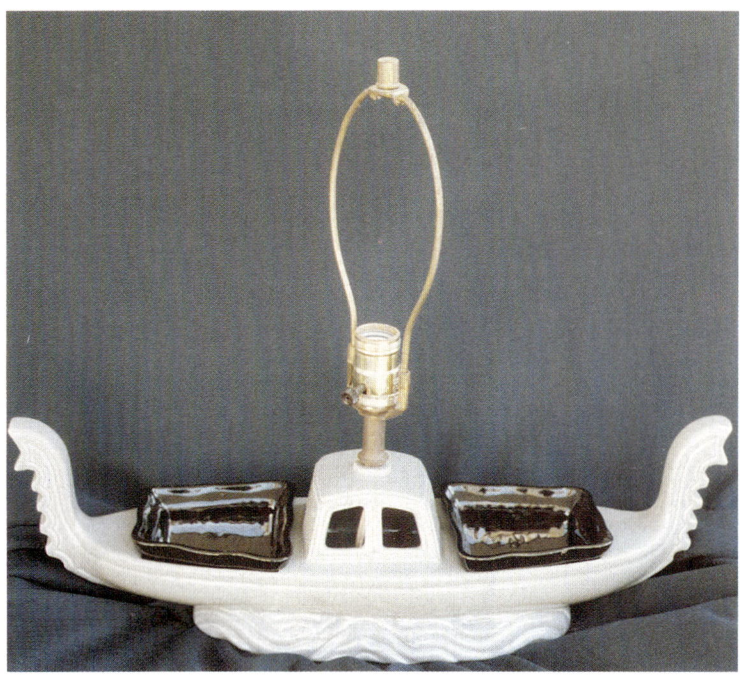

The planters on the gondola lamp are removeable. The open windows allow the light from a small bulb to act as a night light or a TV lamp.

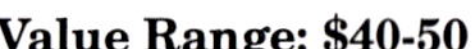

Value Range: $40-50

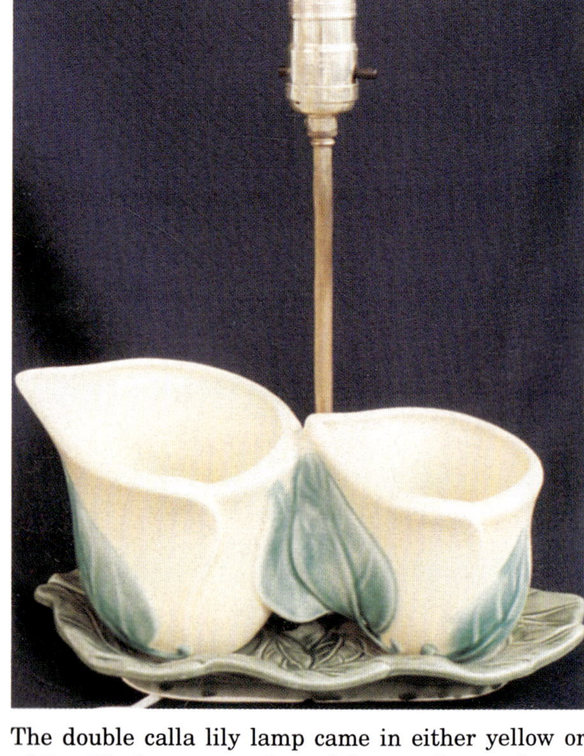

The double calla lily lamp came in either yellow or white. The lamp was adapted from a planter. It was always marked "Morton USA" on the bottom.

Value Range: Planter $18-20 Lamp $30-35

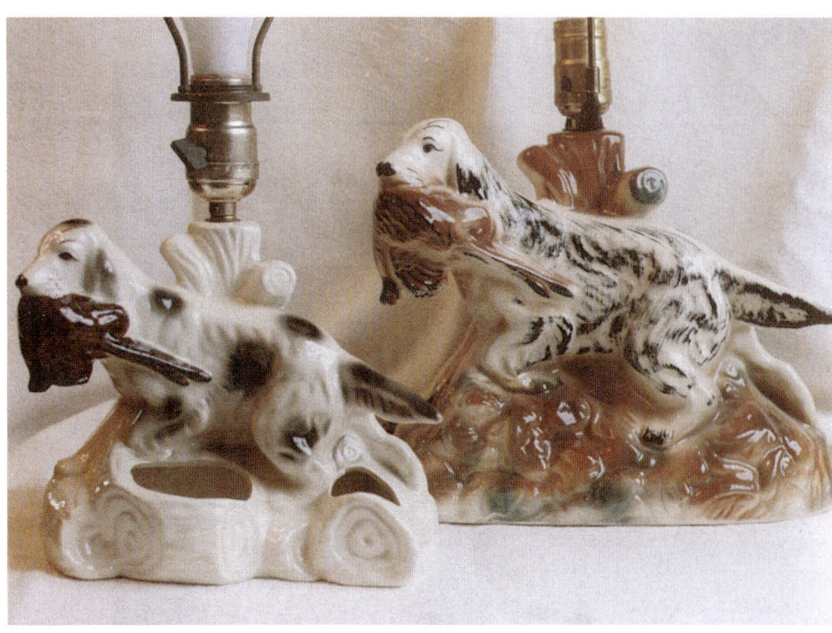

The Irish setter lamp has a low watt bulb behind so it can be used as a TV lamp. The smaller lamp also came in solid brown. The larger lamps will sometimes be found with planter openings on the front of the base.

Value Range: Small $45-55 Large $55-70

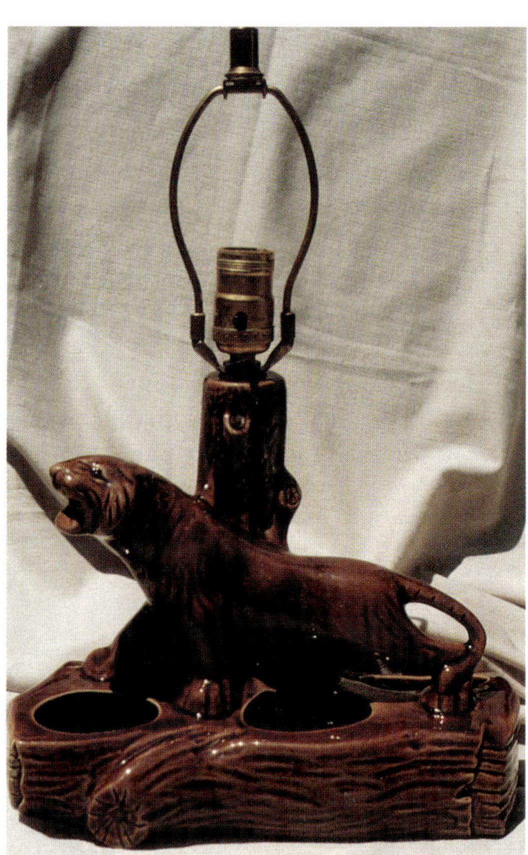

The lioness is not a TV lamp. However, she was made as a TV lamp by removing the tree trunk and closing up the planter openings.

Value Range: Planter $30-35 TV Lamp $35-45

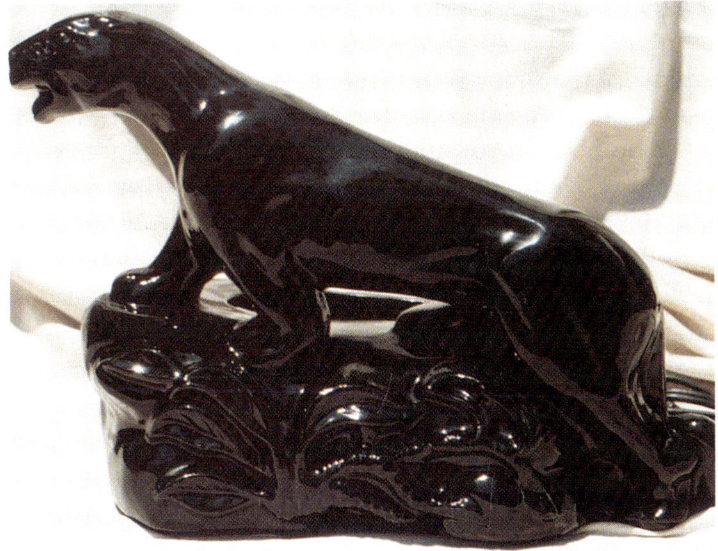

The light is behind the base of this black panther lamp, giving it a silhouette effect.

Value Range: $35-45

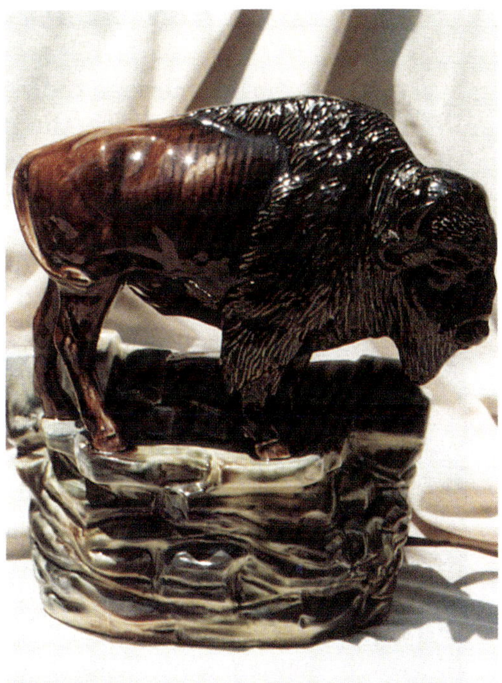

The buffalo lamp is rare. There are openings on the top of the rock allowing the animal to be highlighted.

Value Range: $75-100

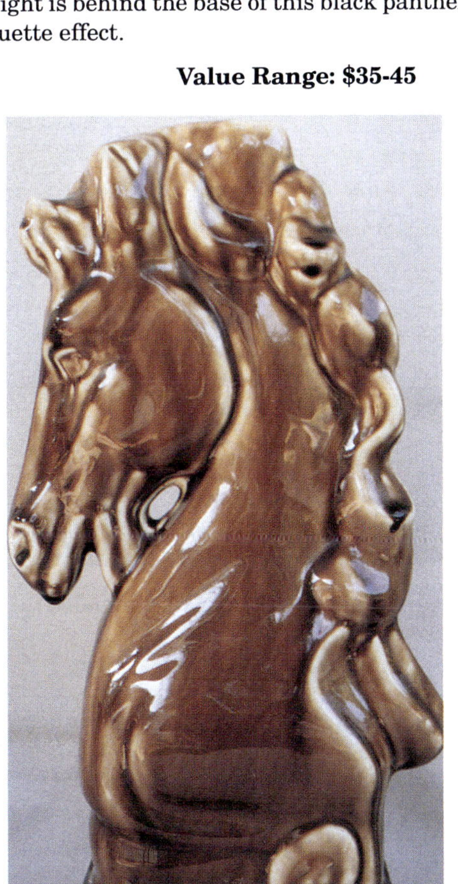

The horse head lamp is 28" tall. The back side is open to allow for the light fixture. This lamp was also three dimensional with a metal rod extended above the head to accomodate the light fixture and a large shade.

Value Range: TV Lamp $35-45
Lamp $50-60

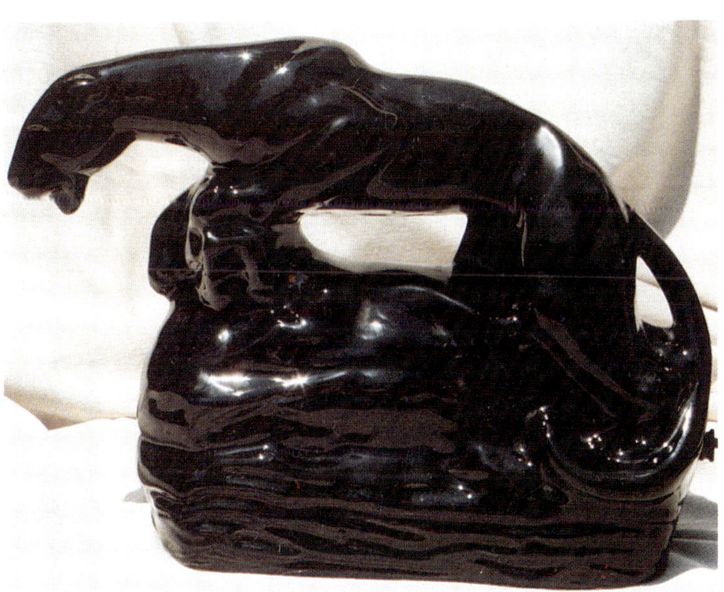

The light is placed inside the planter seen behind the panther.

Value Range: $35-45

VINCENT PRICE
SEARS NATIONAL TREASURES COLLECTION

These early American reproductions were made for Sears Roebuck and Company in 1967 and 1968. Vincent Price, the Hollywood actor, was art director for Sears at that time. He chose the items to be reproduced, thus the name of the promotion. Having been made for such a short period of time, this pottery is scarce. Demand for it has driven prices upward.

These are reproductions of old spongeware items. They were dip glazed in a light grey glaze, then the blue was hand sponged onto the form. It was mistakenly identified as spatterware in the 1967 Sears and Roebuck catalog.

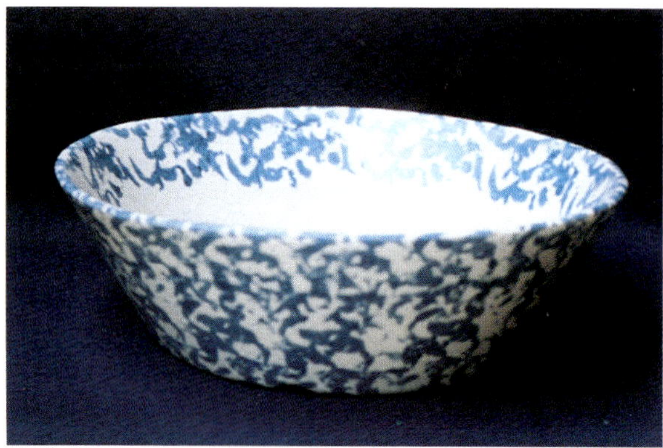

This plain nappy was reproduced from the 8" nappy made at the old Morton Pottery Works in the late 1800's.

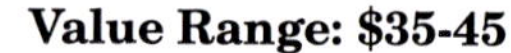

Value Range: $35-45

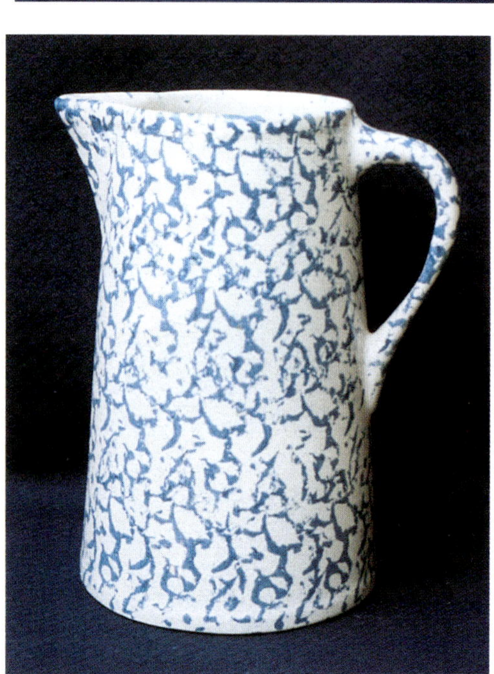

The tankard pitcher is 9" tall, and has a capacity of 21/2 quarts.

Value Range: $55-75

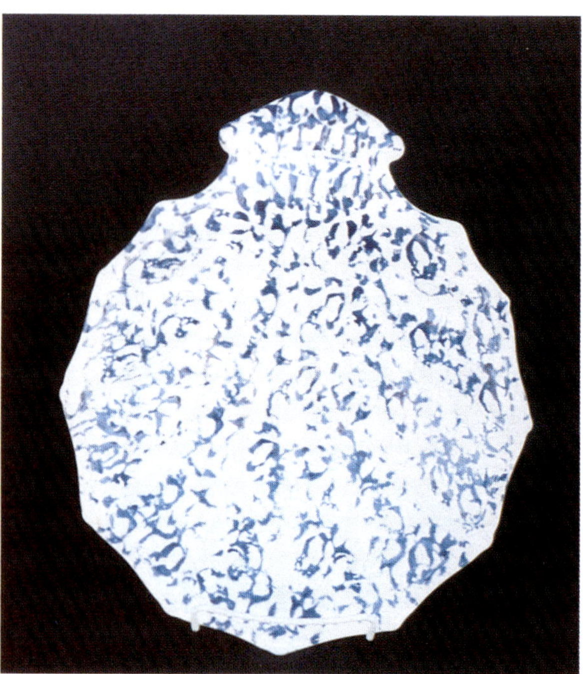

The exaggerated scallop shell bowl was intended to be used as a baker.

Value Range: $35-45

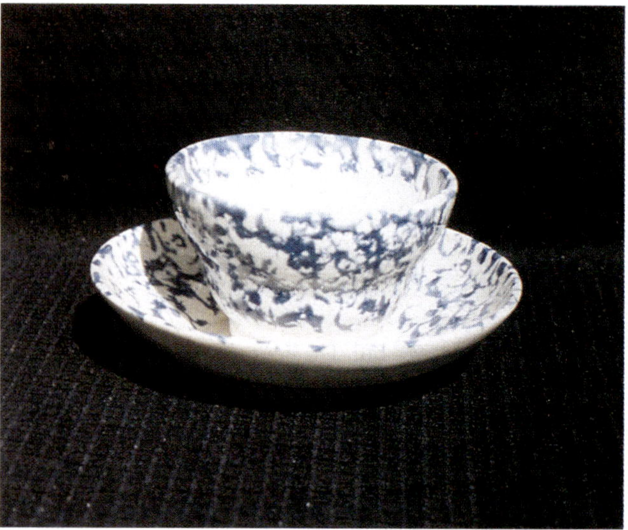

This is a French onion soup cup with liner. The cup is seldom found with the under plate.

Value Range: $25-35

These are reproductions of old spatterware and yellow ware items. They were dipped in a wheat color glaze, then they were hand spattered with a paint brush to obtain the stippled effect. It was meant to imitate the old Rockingham glaze.

PHOTO #117: The original of this rectangular vegetable bowl was made at Bennington, Vermont in the late 1840's. The Turk mold, a two quart mold for baking, was copied from Morton Pottery Works.

Value Range: Vegetable Bowl $45-55   Turk Mold $40-50

PHOTO #118: The heart mold has a cluster of dogwood in the bottom. It was done as a yellow ware reproduction. The potato masher and meat tenderizer are solid. The handles are glued into a half inch depression. They were advertised by Sears as "heavy ironstone, glazed white."

Value Range: Heart Mold $40-50   Potato Masher $35-45   Meat Tenderizer $35-45

PHOTO #119: Spice jars were sold in sets of six. The soap dish was taken from the MORE-TILE line of bathroom accessories and given the Rockingham treatment. **Value Range: Spice Jar $5-10   Soap Dish $14-18**

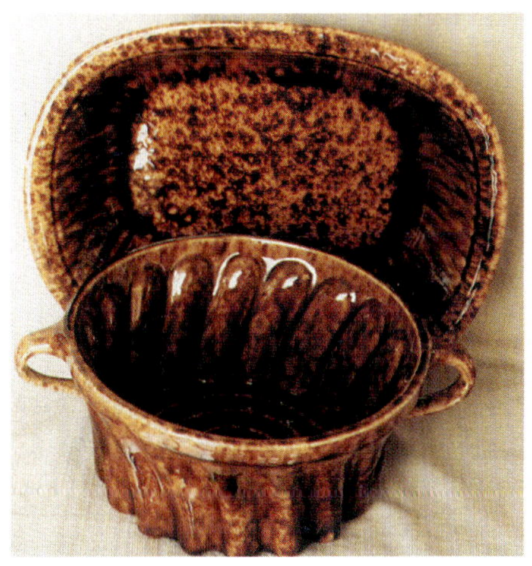

Photo #117

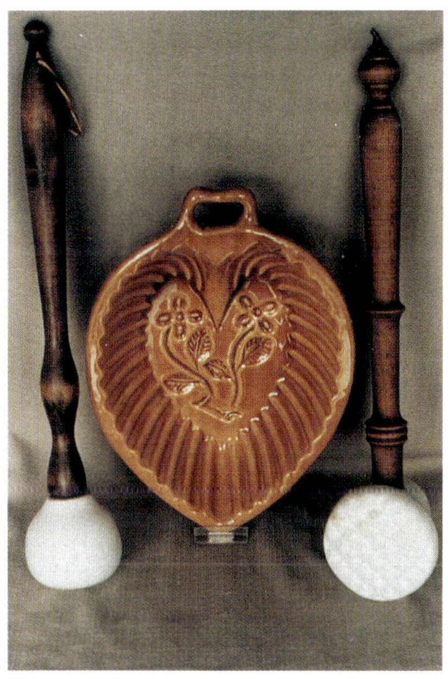

Photo #118

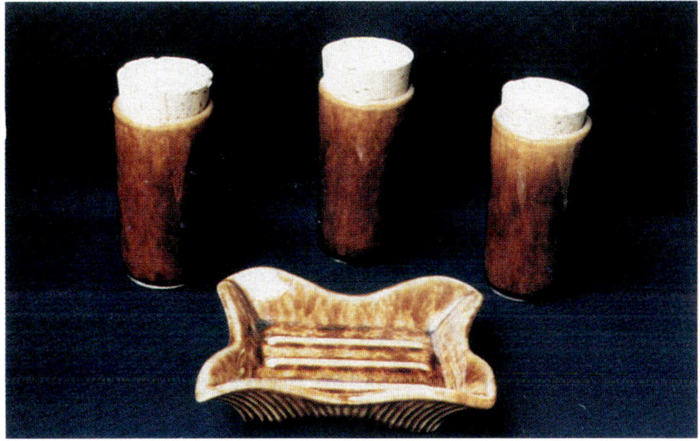

Photo #119

NOVELTIES

The broadside and photograph were used by C. A. Basset & Son, a Peoria, Illinois paint store, as promotional advertising. The sixteen hundred block of North Sheridan Road no longer exists. It was removed to make way for Interstate 74, and is now merely an overpass. All items were left in the bisque form so they could be decorated by dipping them into water on which water spar enamel was floated. The small vases were glazed inside so they could safely hold water for small bouquets. The small vases are 3" tall. The bud vase, in the center, is 5¾" tall.

Value Range: Lamp and shade – ND
Vases $3-8

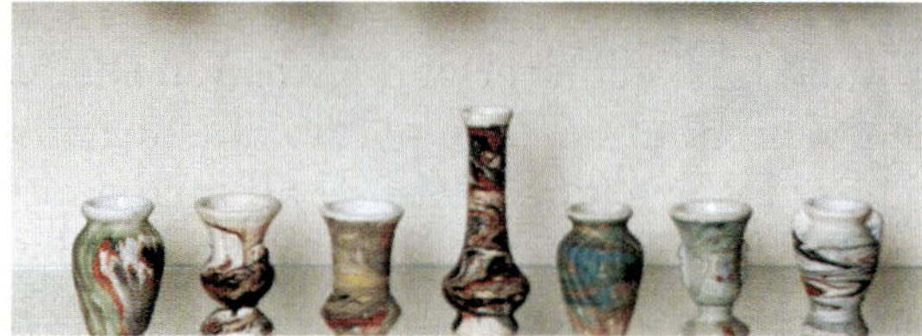

Photo #120

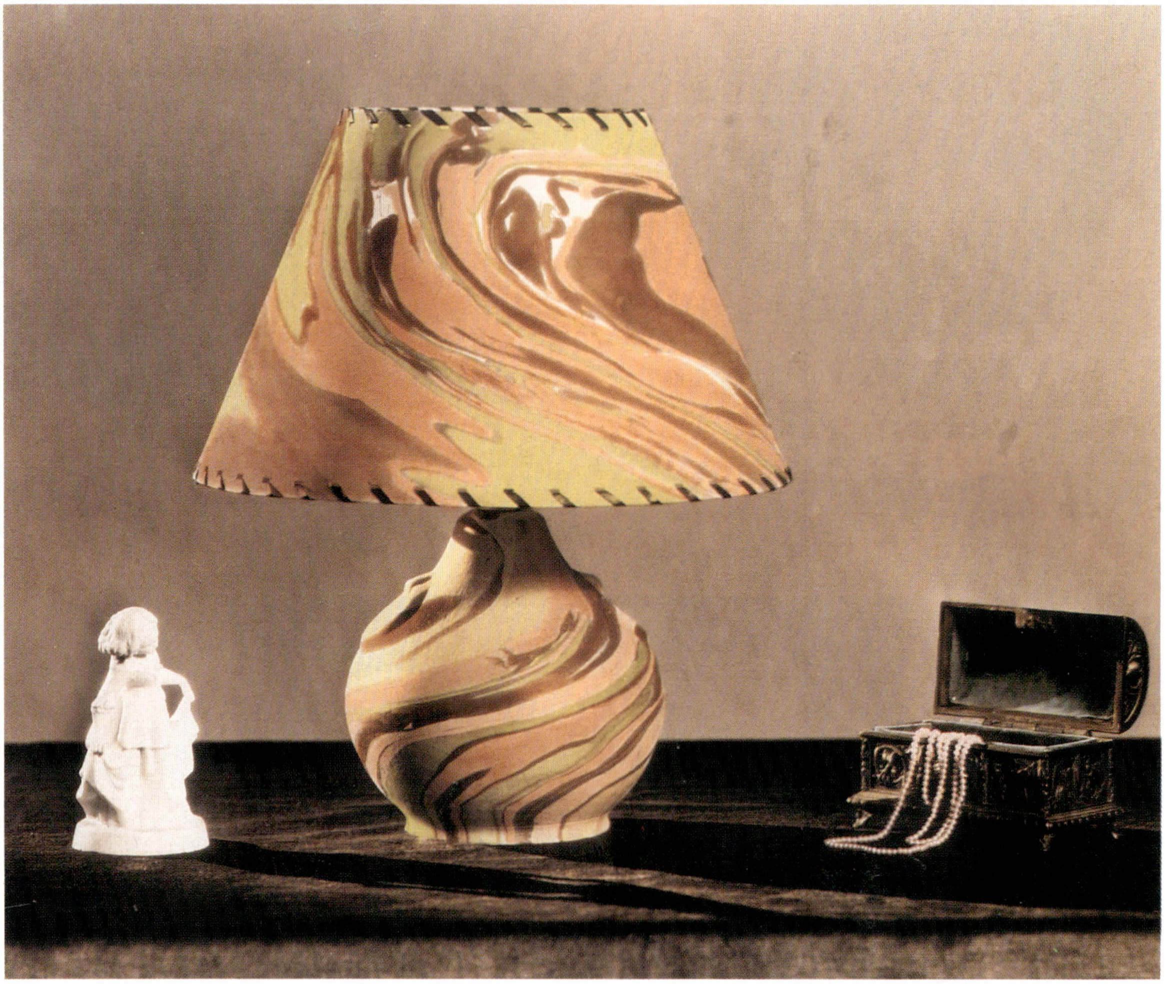

Photo #121

PIE VENTS

Two of the pie vents produced by Morton Pottery Company, the bird and the duckling, are being reproduced. They are shown here with the originals for close comparison. No reproduction of the rooster is known at this time.

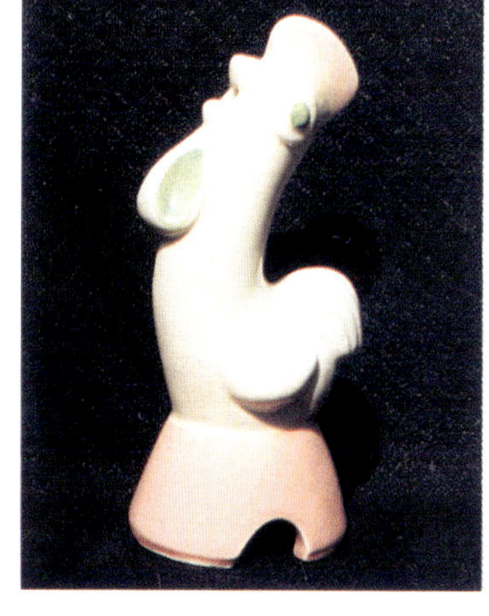

The rooster is 5 1/4" tall. It is considered rare.

Value Range: ND

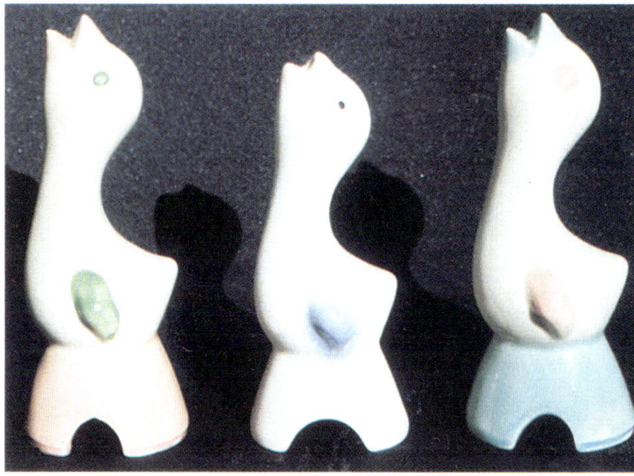

Morton's original ducklings had the base and beak glazed in the same color with a contrast color for the eyes and wings. It is 5 1/2" tall. The reproduction is 5" tall. The base is not colored. The size of the eyes and the weight are two ways to distinguish the reproduction from the original.

Value Range: Original $30-40
Reproduction – ND

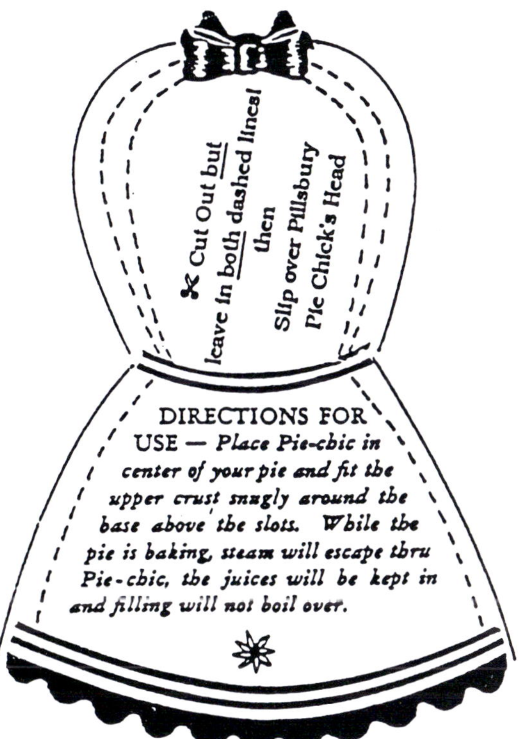

Trim around each scallop.

(Pictured at right) This paper apron was sometimes packaged with the pie duckling, also known as the "Pillsbury Chick." Not only did it provide instructions for using the pie vent, it was a clever accessory when trimmed, according to instructions, and slipped over the duckling's head.

Value Range: ND

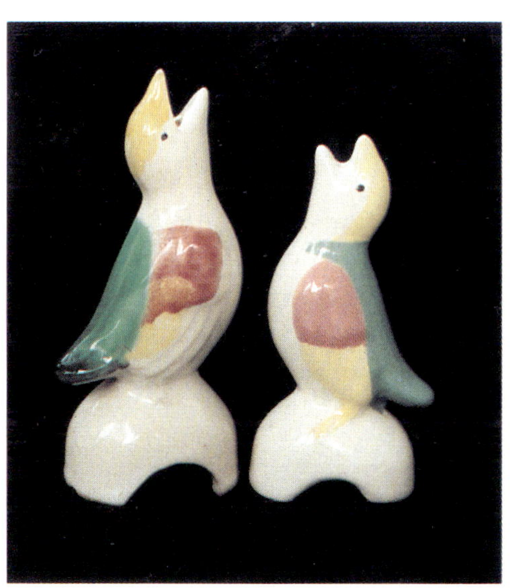

The original bird is on the left. It is 5" tall and has been spray glazed. The reproduction is 4 1/4" tall and has been hand painted by brush rather than spray glazed. Four significant differences help to identify the reproduction: the partial neck band, the painted legs on the base, it is lighter weight, and an incised mark inside the base, E and V, at opposite ends.

Value Range: Original $25-35
Reproduction – ND

POLITICAL MEMORABILIA

The Rapp's political orientation was traditionally Republican but they did produce some political items for Democrats. Miniature beer steins were made for the 1932 campaign of Franklin D. Roosevelt. The pottery stood to make substantial financial gains if FDR's promise to repeal prohibition should come about.

In 1960, the pottery made giveaway donkeys for John F. Kennedy. During World War II, S. W. Rapp's son served in the same air force squadron that Kennedy's brother, Joe Jr., was in. Both of them died serving their country.

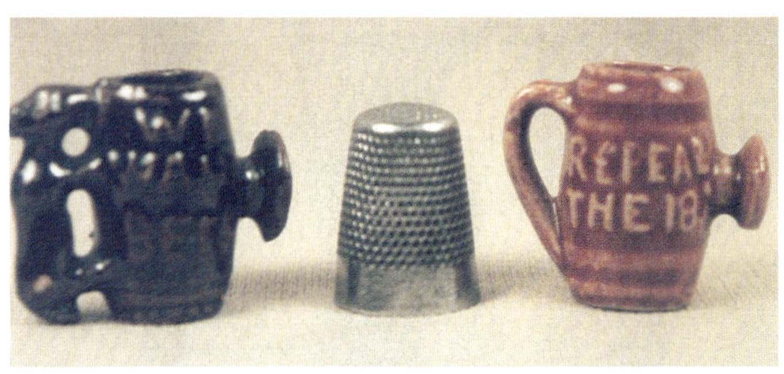

These miniature beer steins were made for the first presidential campaign of Franklin D. Roosevelt. They were intended to be worn in the button hole on a man's coat lapel. Both steins are extremely rare. They are shown with the thimble for size comparison.

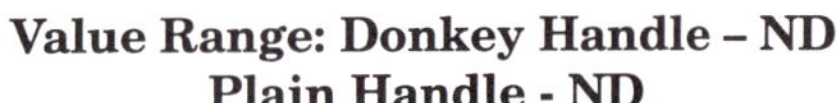

Value Range: Donkey Handle – ND
Plain Handle - ND

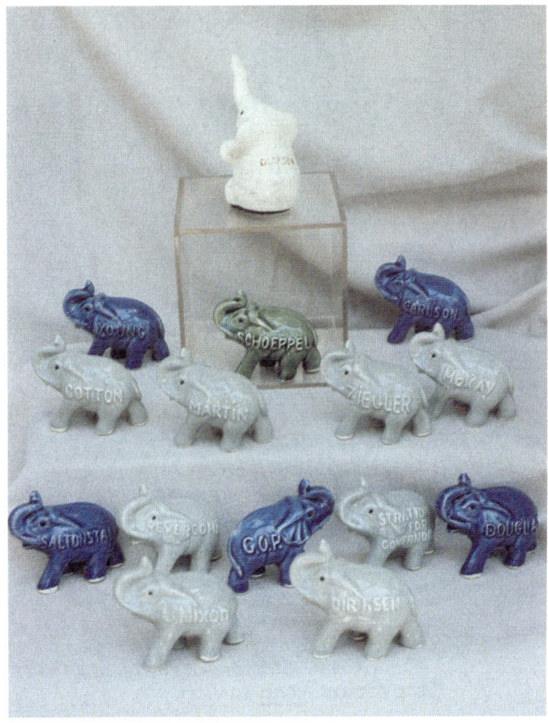

The GOP elephant giveaways always had the candidate's name embossed on one side, and GOP on the opposite side. Thousands were made so it is difficult to understand why they are so elusive.

Value Range: $15-20
Ring Holder $20-25

This set of salt and pepper shakers was used to design the political giveaways. The elephant was not altered, but the donkey had its body elongated to accommodate politicians' names.

Value Range: $20-30

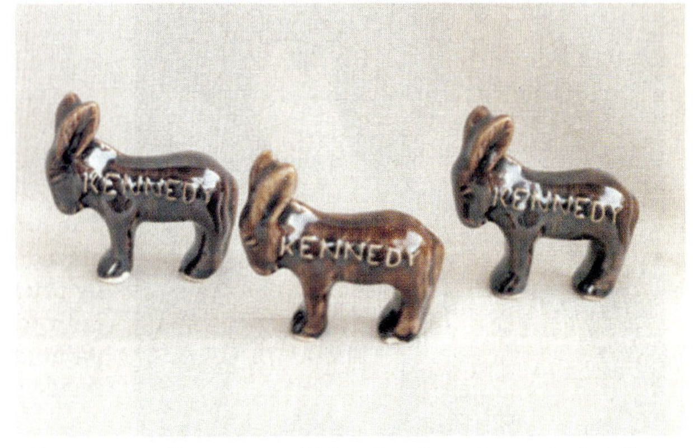

The Kennedy donkey was made only during the 1960 presidentail campaign. It is plain on the opposite side. It can be found in either brown or grey glaze. A second donkey has recently surfaced with Tawes on one side and Victory on the reverse side. Tawes was Governor of Maryland in the 1960's. The Tawes donkey was also made in brown and grey glaze.

Value Range: Kennedy $30-35 Tawes $20-25

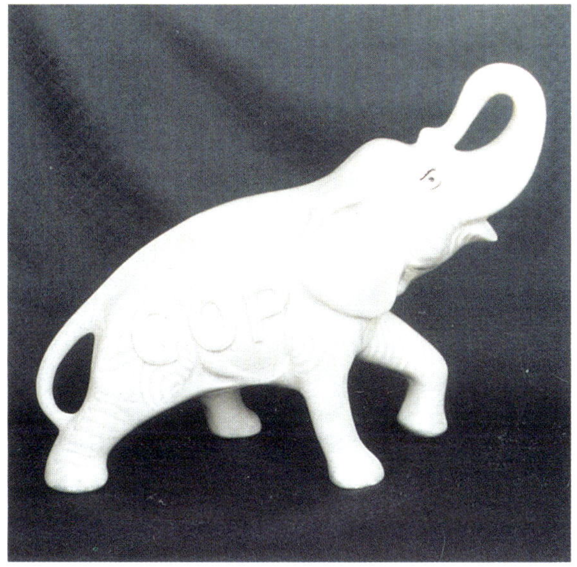

This GOP elephant was frequently given to friends and political cronies by the Rapps. The letters were sometimes cold painted in a bright blue color.

Value Range: $20-30

Senator Everett M. Dirksen from Pekin, Illinois started the use of the ashtray for a political giveaway. He ordered 2500 in 1944 when he ran for Congress from the Illinois 18th District. The Nixon ashtray was made for his first campaign for President in 1968.

Value Range:
Dirksen $15-20
Nixon $20-25

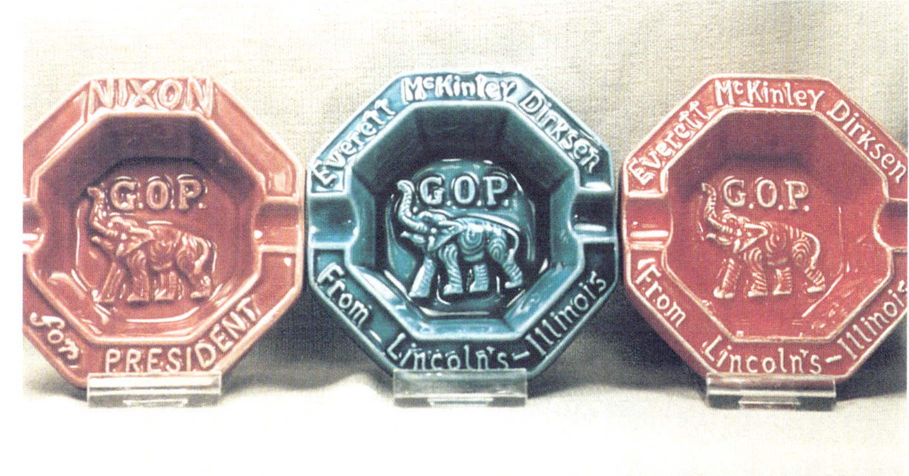

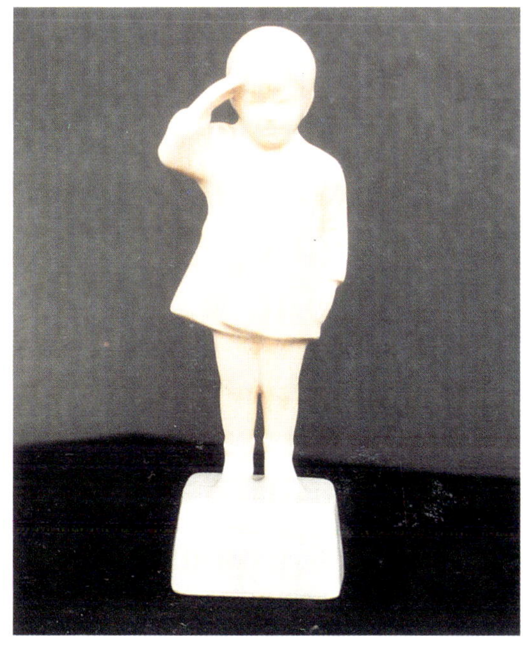

The statuette of John Kennedy Jr. was designed from an Associated Press photograph taken at his father's funeral. Because that photograph was copyrighted, the pottery was forced to stop production. A few were decorated with brown hair, blue coat, and blue sox. "John John" statuettes are rare.

Value Range: $30-35

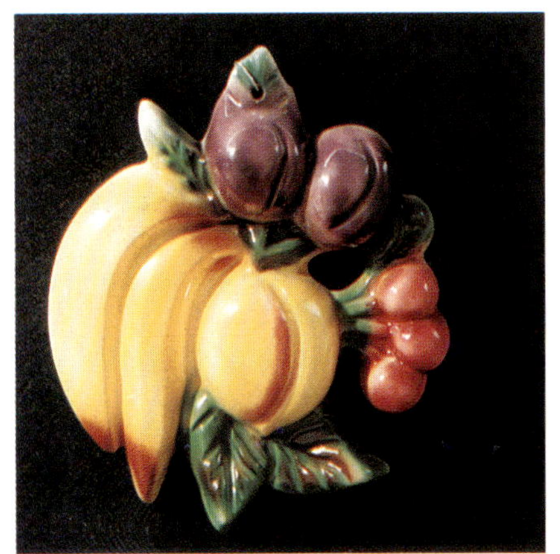

Fruit cluster
Value Range: $18-20

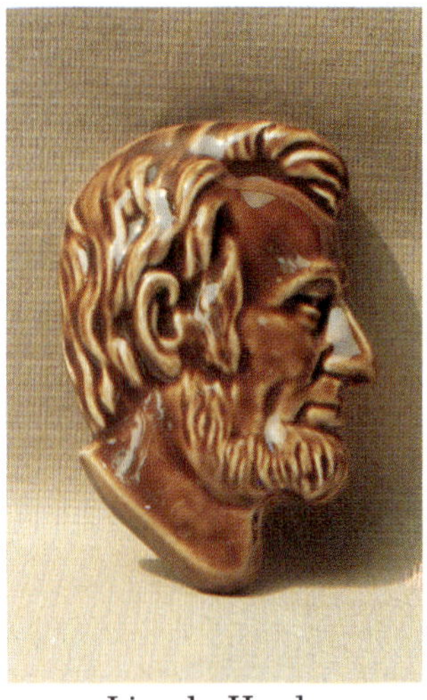

Lincoln Head
Value Range: $20-24

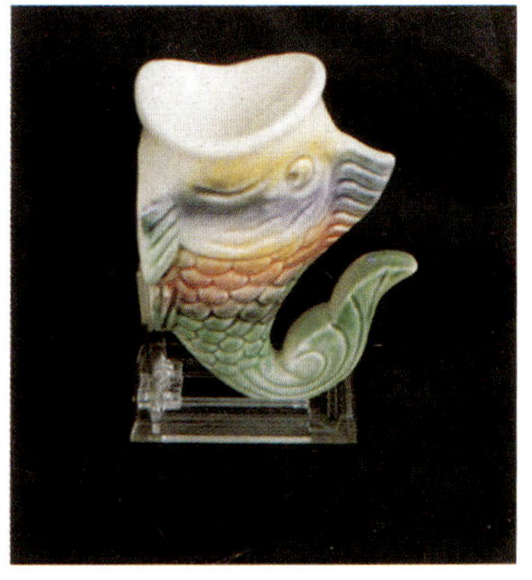

The fish can be used as a jewelry holder. The tail holds a watch or bracelets, and rings are placed in the mouth.

Value Range: $14-18

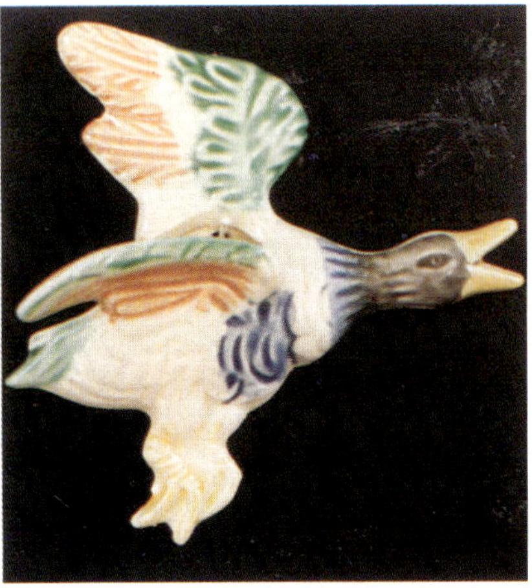

The duck was occasionally done as a wall pocket. It has been copied by the Japanese. The copy is much lighter in weight.

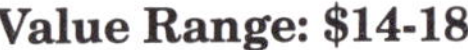

Value Range: $14-18

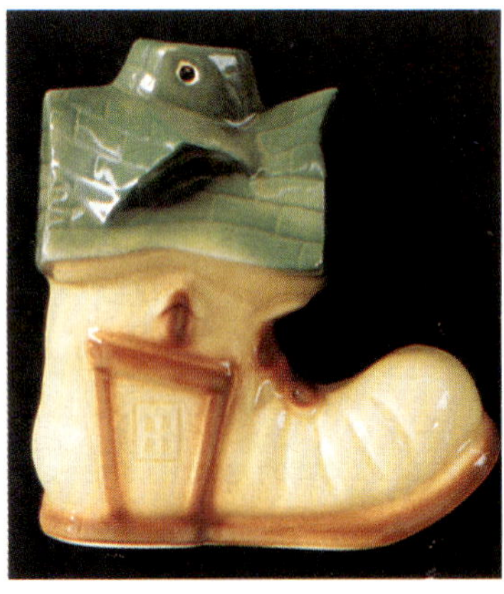

The shoe house was made to complement the lamps, planters, and banks.

Value Range: $16-20

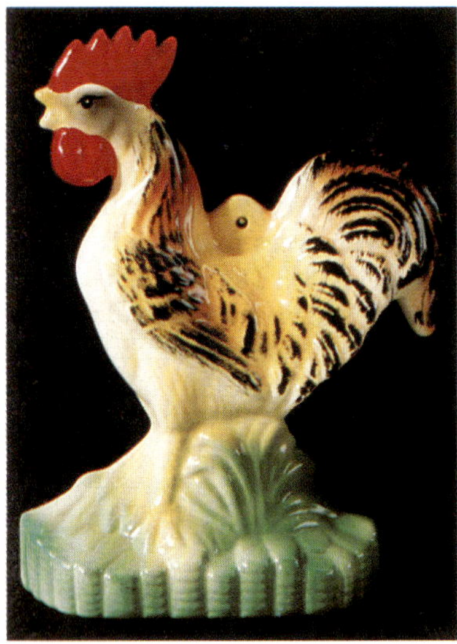

Rooster
Value Range: $18-22

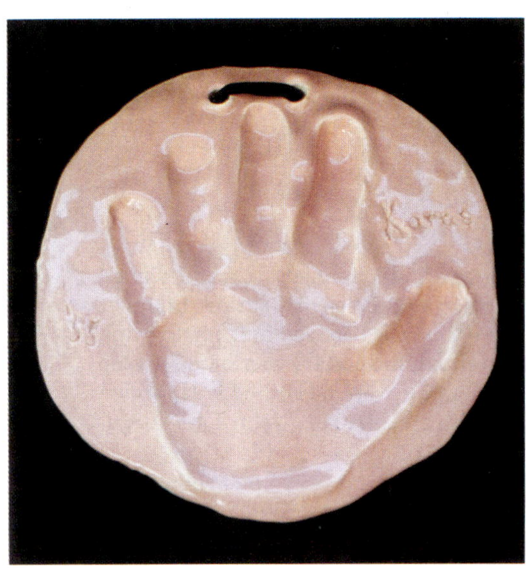

The hand print is our son's. It was made when he was in first grade in 1955. Morton Pottery Company provided the clay so students could make the plaques for Christmas gifts in their classroom. Upon completion, the plaques were taken to the pottery where they were glazed and fired as a courtesy to the teacher and her students.

Value Range: ND

WESTERN AMERICANA

The items shown here were produced during the 1930's and 1940's. Most of them range from scarce to rare. The Mexican taking a siesta between the cacti is common. The open top covered wagons are found occasionally, but should not be considered common. The covered wagons with both ends open, the team of oxen, and the small covered wagon with "49" are rare. The small "49" wagon was only made in 1949 to commemorate the hundredth anniversary of the California gold rush. It is easily found without the date. The cowboy is not scarce, but he is elusive.

PHOTO #140: The ox team is 2 3/4" tall x 5" long x 3 1/2" wide. The open top wagon is 6 3/4" x 8" long x 3 1/2" wide.

Value Range: Ox Team $30-35
Wagon $15-20

PHOTO #141: The Wiedman wagon is smaller. It was made as an advertising giveaway. The wagon is 5" tall x 61/4" long x 3" wide.

Value Range: Ox Team $30-35
Wagon, Plain $10-15
Add 50% for advertising

PHOTO #142: The wagon with both ends open is rare. It is 6 3/4" tall x 8" long x 3 1/2" wide.

Value Range: Ox Team $30-35
Wagon $30-40

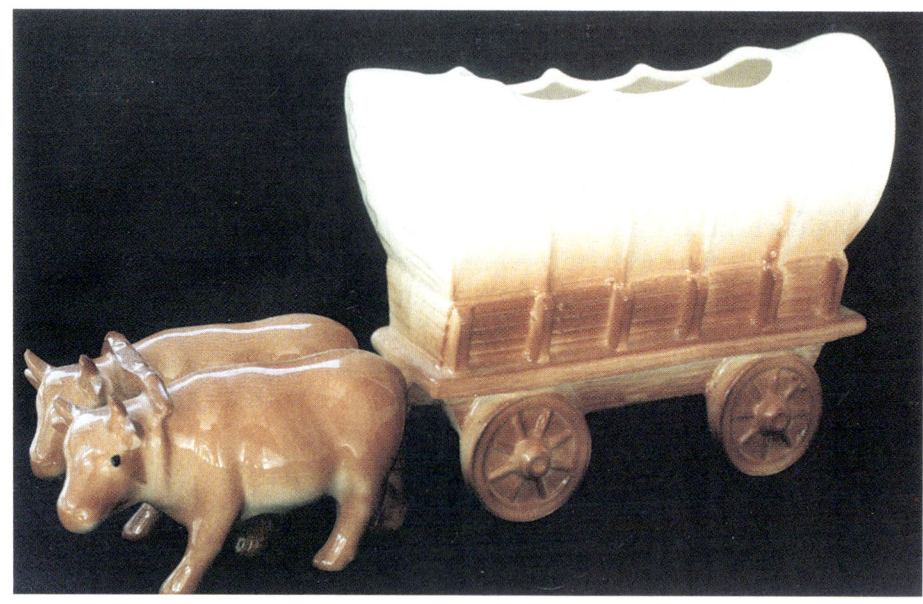

Photo #140

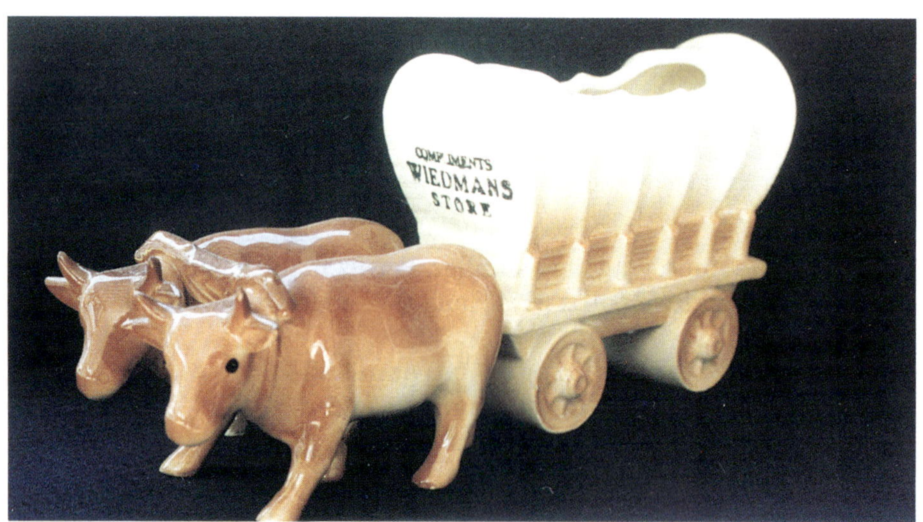

Photo #141

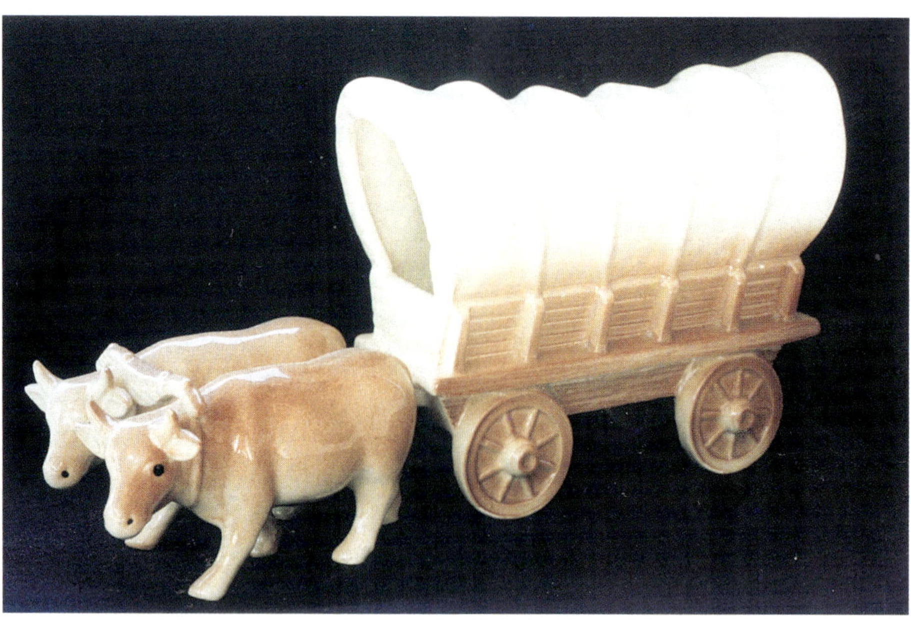

Photo #142

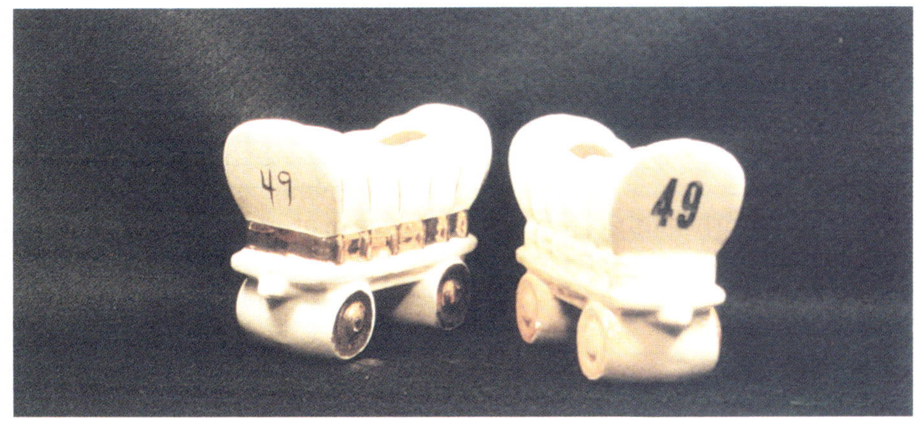

The "49" covered wagon is 3" tall x 4" long x 1 3/4" wide. There is no ox team for this size wagon.

**Value Range:
Date, ink stamp
$10-12**

**Date, gold decor
$15-18**

Not Dated $6-8

The cowboy is 6 3/4" tall. The cactus behind him is a planter.

Value Range: $12-15

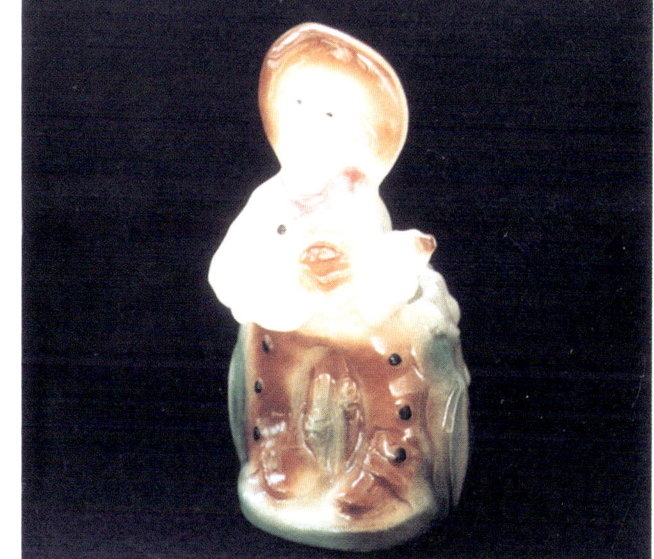

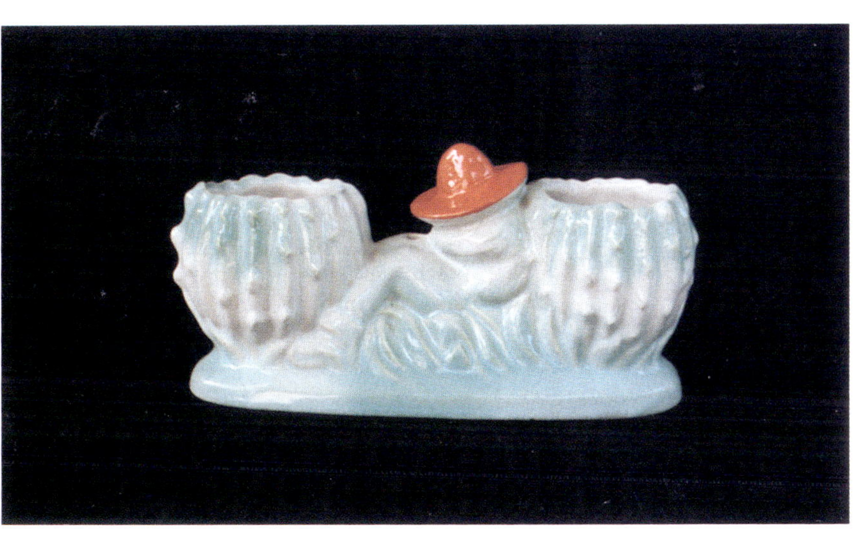

The double cactus planter with a Mexican figure in siesta is spray glazed with a cold painted sombrero. There is a smaller version of this planter with only one cactus plant.

**Value Range: Double Cactus $10-12
Single Cactus $8-10**

WOODLAND POTTERY

Woodland pottery is a beautiful blending of the forest shades of green, brown, and yellow. This line got its name from the style of glazing that it underwent. Golden ocher clay bisque items were brush spattered with brown and forest green glaze then dipped in transparent glaze. When fired, the finished ware had an amazing resemblance to the forest floor with streams of sunlight beaming through the trees. Color saturations differ because of heavy or light spattering by the decorators. No two pieces have ever been found that are identical. This spatterware should not be confused with spongeware.

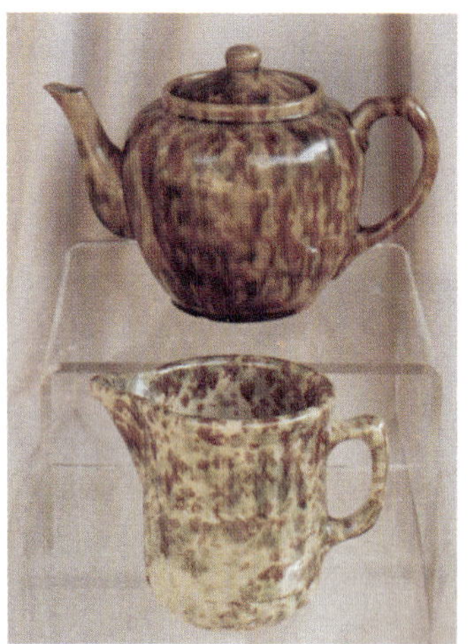

The globe teapot is #270. It has a capacity of 5 cups. The milk jug often has a panel with advertising on its side.

Value Range: Teapot $55-65 Milk Jug $40-50
Add 25% with advertising

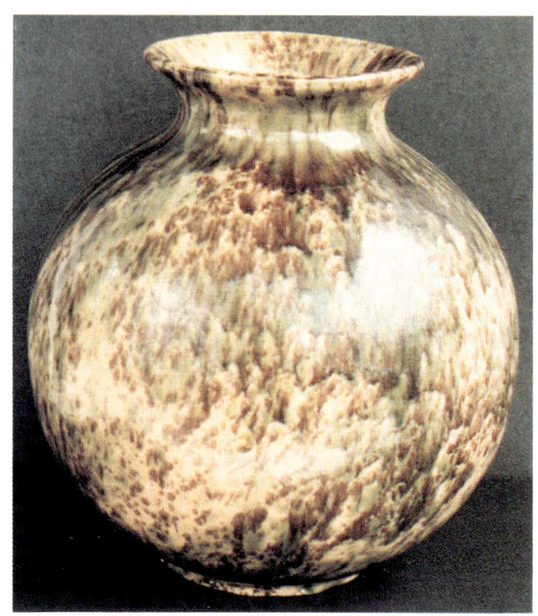

The bulbous vase is 10 1/2" tall. It has a middle circumference of 32", and a top diameter of 5 1/2". The vases were difficult to fire. They often exploded in the kiln.

Value Range: $200-225

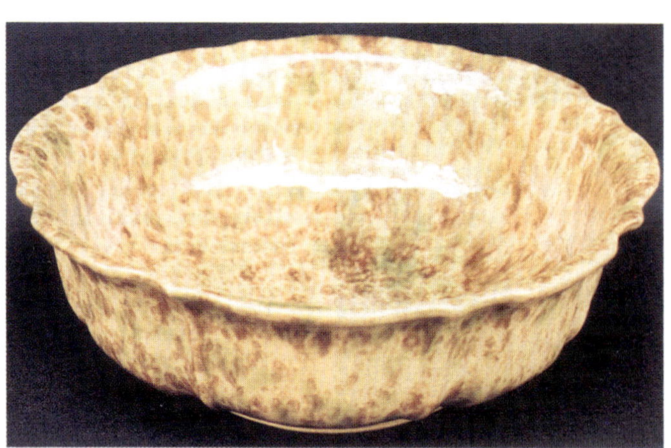

This flared, fluted, irregular scalloped edge bowl is a departure from the simplicity of the Pilgrim line that was first used for spatterware. It has a 10" diameter. This unusual shape is rare.

Value Range: $100-125

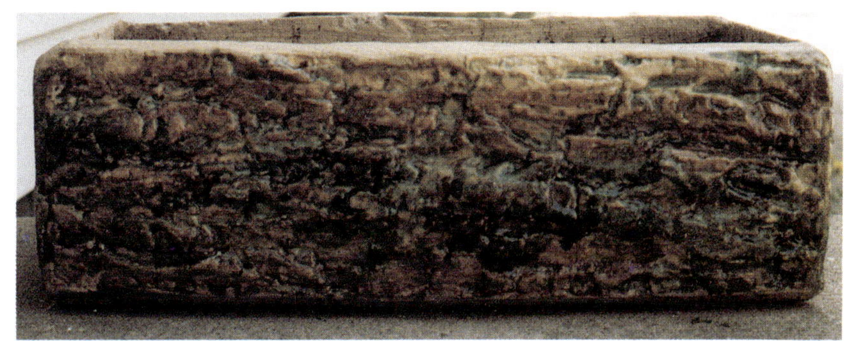

The flower box measures 42" x 14" x 12". This box is heavy and bulky. With such a large open area at the top, the sides frequently buckled during firing. For those reasons, few were made.

Value Range: ND

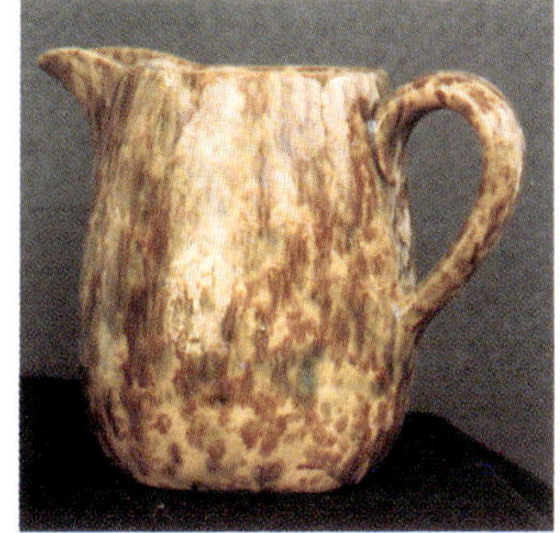

This water pitcher has a 2 1/2 quart capacity. It was also made with an ice lip. That style is scarce.

Value Range: $80-120

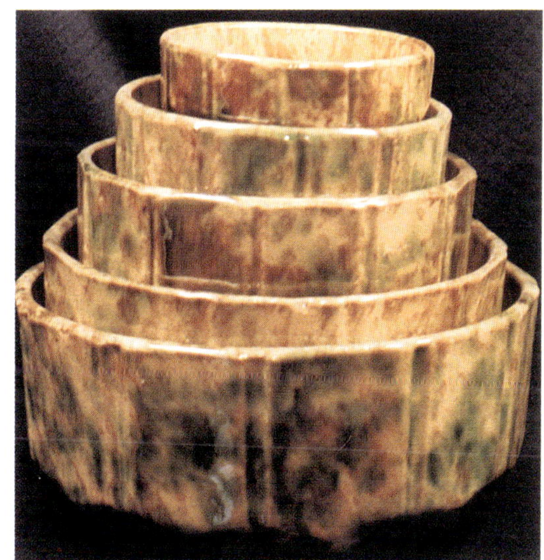

This nested set of nappies was originally in the Pilgrim pottery line. It is unusual to find it in the Woodland glaze.

Value Range: $175-200

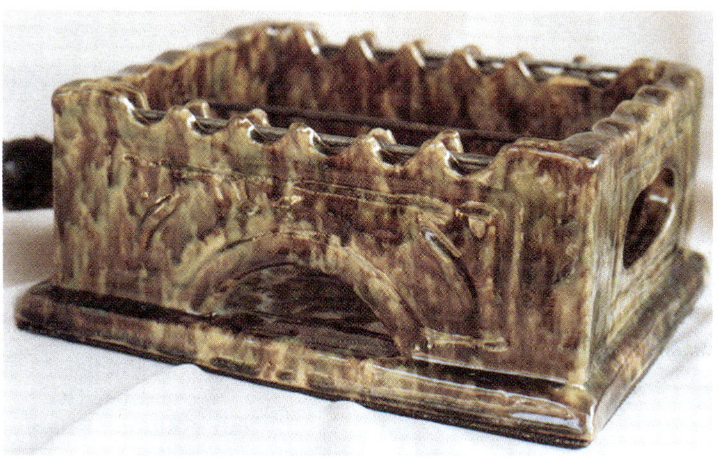

This is a weiner warmer. It measures 3 3/4" x 8 3/4" x 7". This item was made for The Jiffy Products Company, Peoria, Illinois and was sold to diners to be used behind lunch counters for quick retrieval of warm hotdogs. Factory workers referred to it as a "weiner electrocuter."

Value Range: $100-125

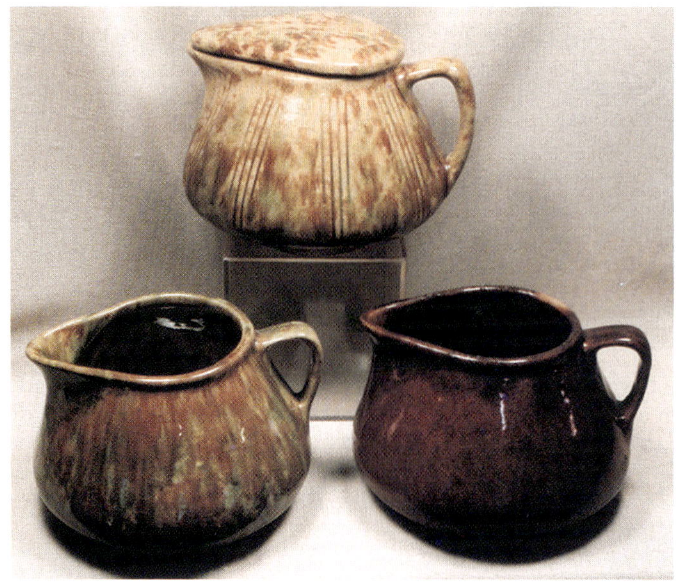

Coffee server, 8 cup capacity.
Value Range: $90-110

Pie Plate, 10" diameter.
Value Range: $100-120

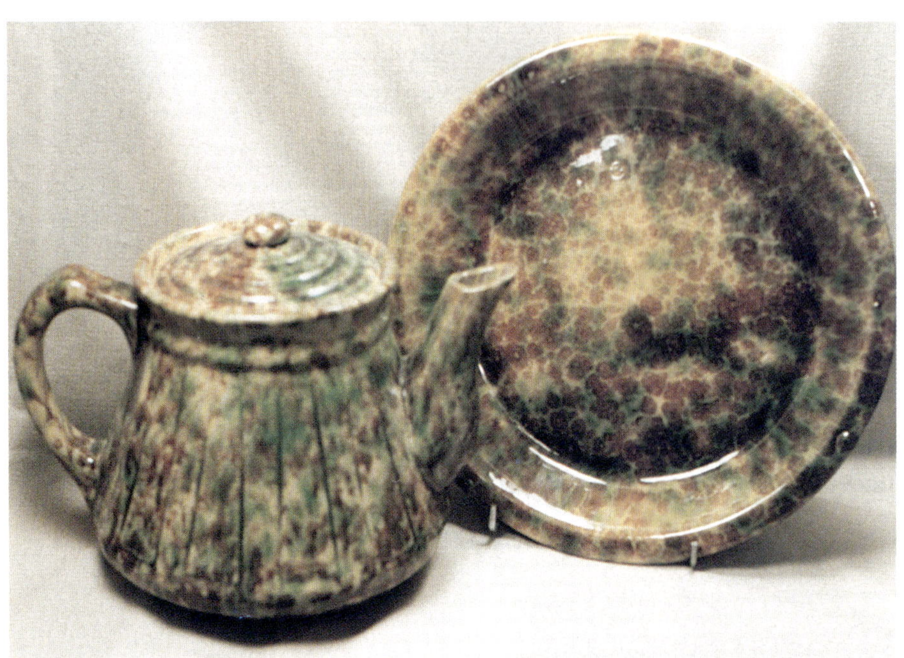

These are variations of the 11/2 pint Pilgrim Ware ice box jug. The jug with the lid is extremely rare. The graffito design was done with a four tined fork.

Value Range:
With lide $75-100
Woodland $40-50
Brown $25-35

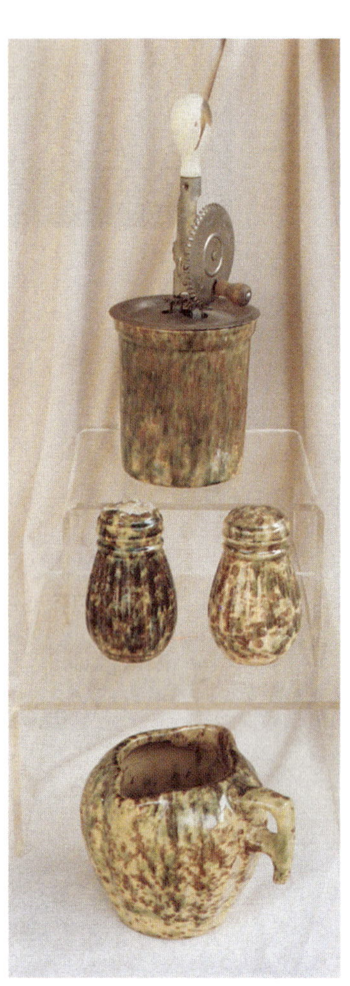

Beater jar, 51/2" tall, 41/2" dia.
Value Range: $80-90

Shakers, 5" tall.
Value Range: $60-70 pair

Double Spout Pitcher, 5" tall, 4 cup capacity.
Value Range: $70-80

Covered grease jar, 5" tall, 3" diameter.
Value Range: $30-40

Covered ringed bowl, 33/4" tall, 61/2" diameter. The bowl is common, the lid is rare.
Value Range: Bowl $25-30
Bowl with lid $60-70

Covered Casserole, 33/4" tall, 61/2" diameter.
Value Range: $60-70

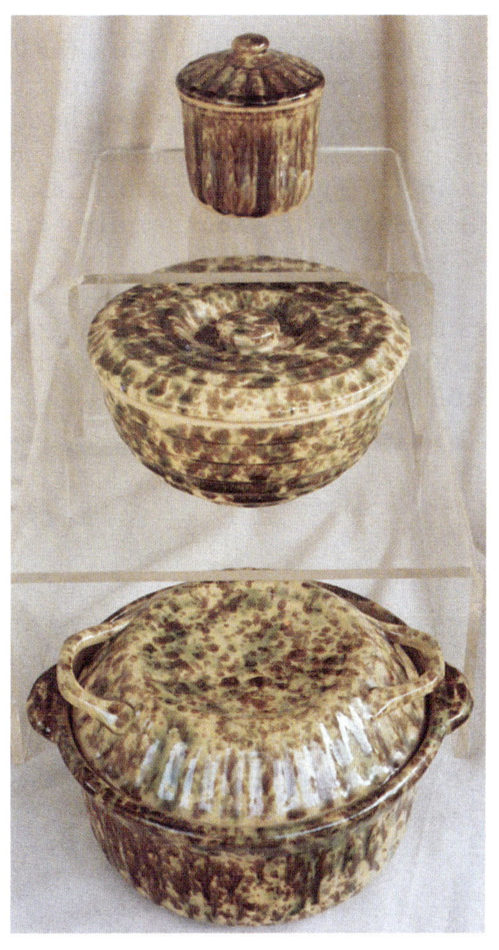

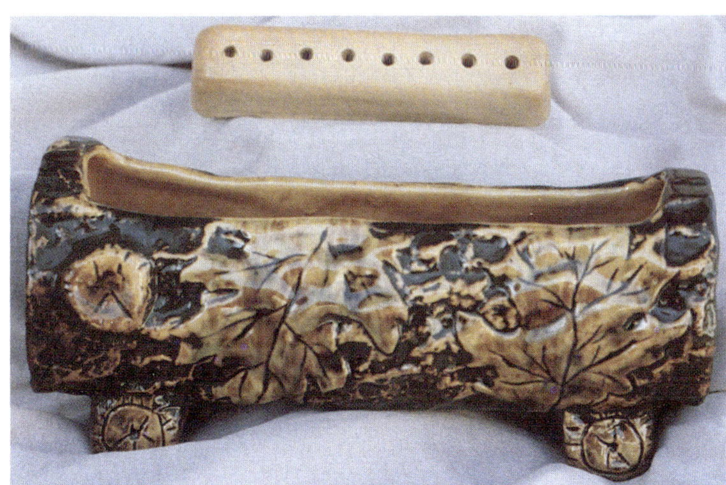

This log shape flower bowl has an oak leaf decoration. The bowl is 41/2" tall x 10" long x 33/4" wide. The removable flower holder is 1" x 61/2" x 11/2". The insert is seldom found with the bowl.

Value Range: Bowl $40-50
Bowl and insert $60-70

WOODLAND POTTERY VARIATIONS

Near the end of the 1930's, the local clay that fired out in the golden ocher color, was depleted. After 1940, clay was shipped in from South Carolina and Indiana. The new clay fired out white instead of yellow. The same brown and green glazes were used to spatter the ware, but the finished products were not the quality of the pre-1940's. The end result was a very anemic spatterware. Some collectors prefer the white based ware rather than the earlier yellow ware examples. They are somewhat more elusive.

Two new glazes were developed to spatter on the later ware, a bright blue and a medium burgundy red. The result was a pleasing red, white, and blue effect. That glaze style was used for only a short period of time and is more scarce than the brown and green spatter ware.

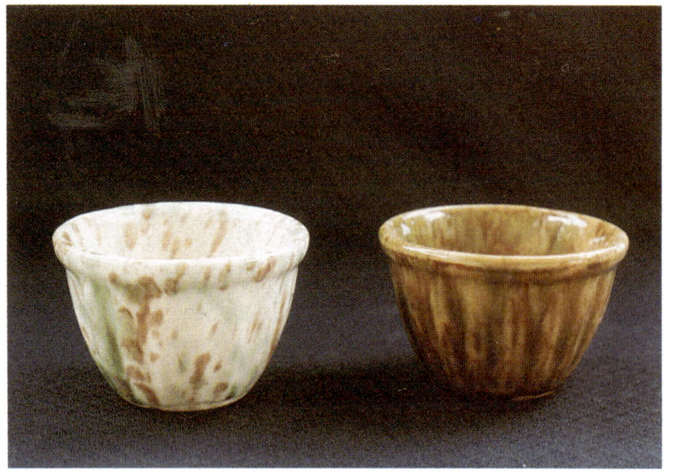

The custard cup on the left is the anemic example. Subdued shades of brown and green were often used to give these wares an even more anemic appearance.

Value Range: White $10-15
Yellow $20-30

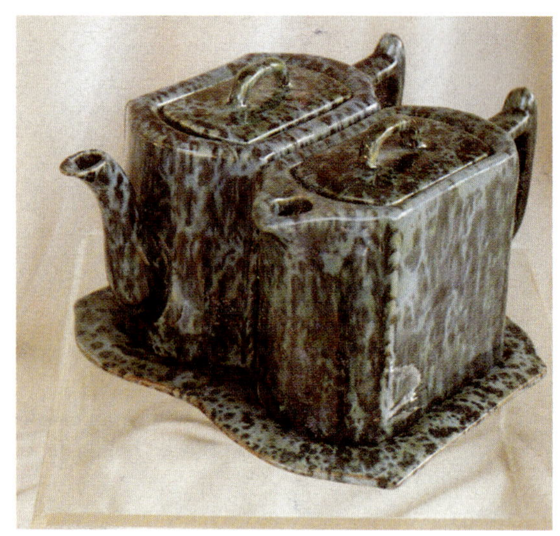

The twin tea set is from the Pilgrim Pottery line that was introduced in 1926. This set was glazed in the Pilgrim blue color then spattered with darker blue and green. Only a few examples of this glaze style have surfaced.

Value Range: $120-150

The law of supply and demand has driven the prices of red, white, and blue spatter ware completely out of the reasonable current market. Because it was not a good seller in the pottery sales room, and because few orders were received by the salesmen, this color line of spatter ware was removed from production after only a short trial period.

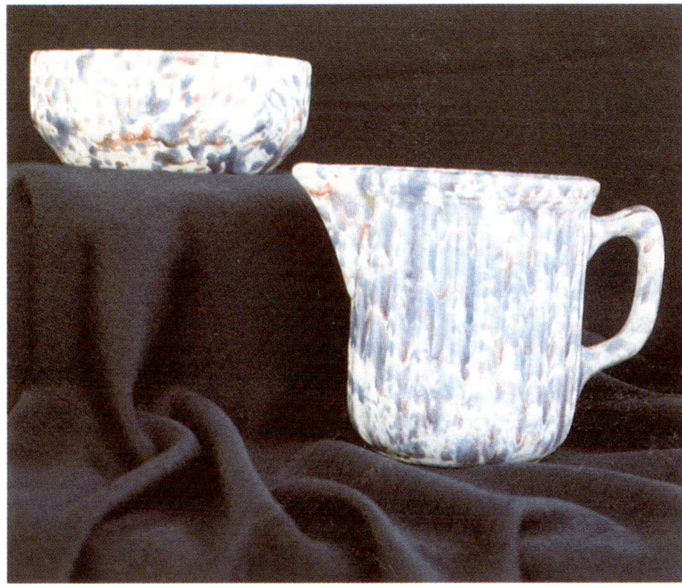

Paneled nappy, 5" diameter.
Value Range: $30-50

Milk Pitcher, 4 1/2" tall.
Value Range: $50-75

The nested bowl set #600 was produced over a long period of time, but only for a short time in the red, white, and blue spatter glaze.

Value Range: $125-150

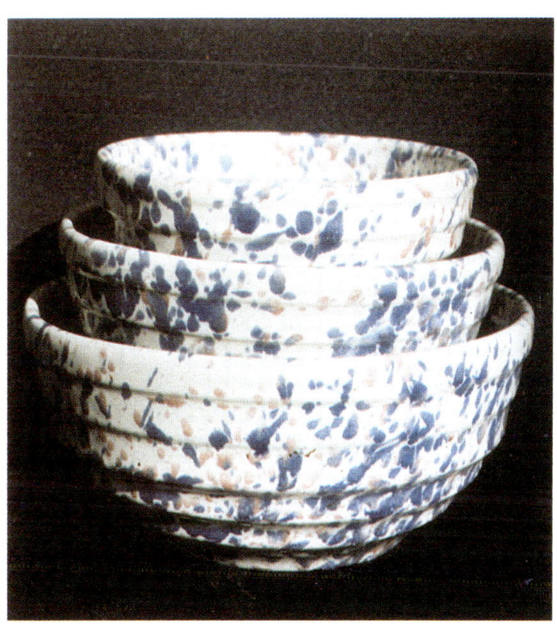

Photo #161

UNCLASSIFIED MISCELLANEOUS

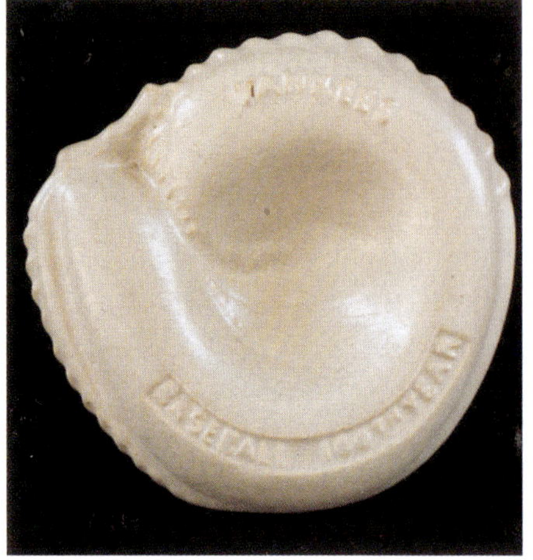

Catcher's mitt pin trays were made for professional baseball's hundredth anniversary in 1969. Mitts were made for each of the twenty-four teams in the two major leagues.

Value Range: $20-25

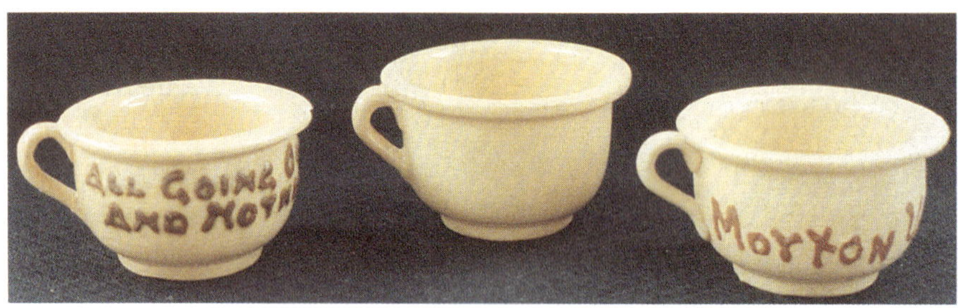

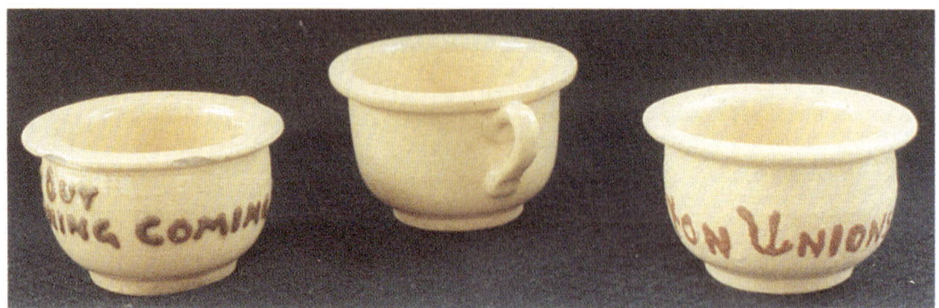

The yellow ware miniature potty in the center was a standard item at the pottery. Those on each side, with graffiti, were made by pottery executives in 1961 and given to employees in an effort to discourage them from unionizing. One has "all going out – nothing coming in," the other has "Morton Unions."

Value Range: Standard potty $25-35
Graffiti potty – ND

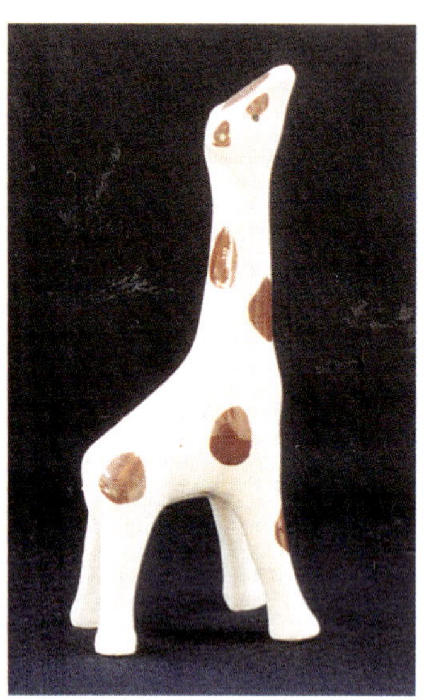

The miniature giraffe is 51/2" tall. It was not a part of the line of miniatures made at the pottery.

Value Range: $8-12

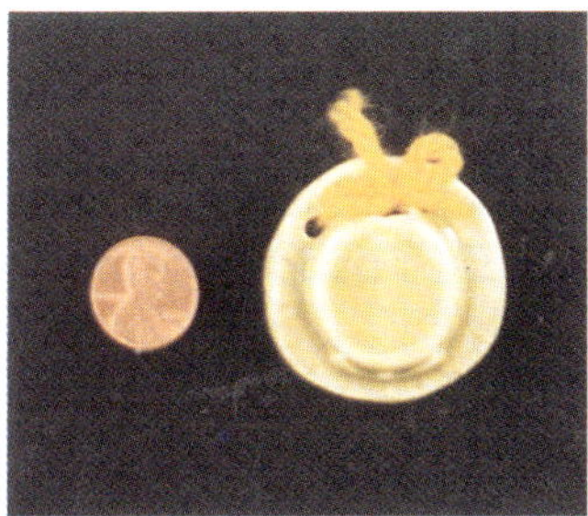

The hat is a lady's lapel vase shown with a penny to accurately establish its size. Only a few of these were made.

Value Range: $10-12

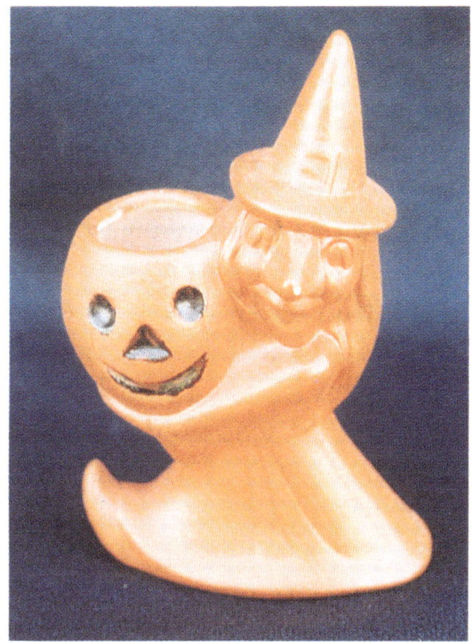

The witch with the jack-o-lantern has been copied by the Japanese and made in plastic. The plastic faces are sharply different from this one. Intended as a candy container, the figure is 3 1/2" tall. It is very rare.

Value Range: ND

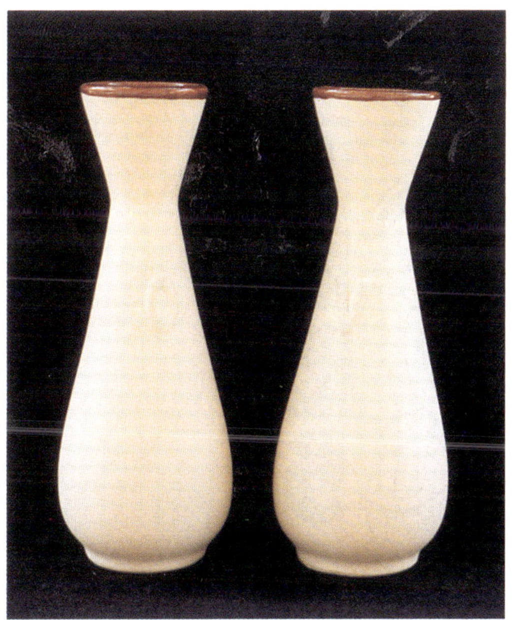

The oil and vinegar bottles were made after Rival Manufacturing Company acquired the pottery. They have bisque exteriors and are glazed inside to complement the crock pot inserts.

Value Range: $5-10 each

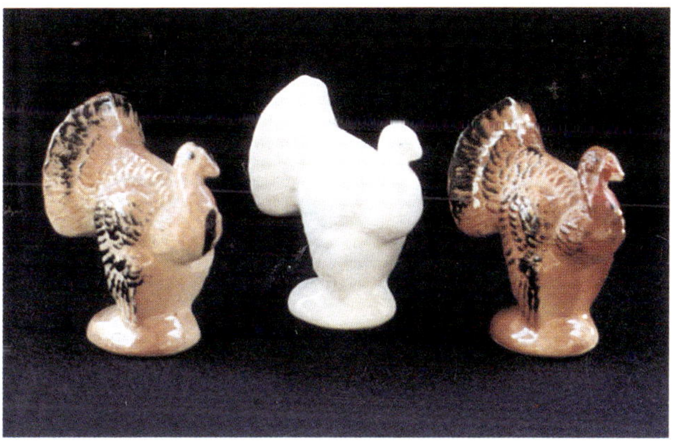

The miniature turkey was usually produced at Thanksgiving time. They were advertised as "ideal for table favors" during the holiday.

Value Range: Standard $8-10
White $14-16
Special decorated $10-12

Epilogue

Today, there is no visual evidence that any pottery ever existed in Morton. The only vestige of Morton's potteries is the name borne by the local high school athletic teams. They are known as the "Morton Potters." Their logo is an athlete whose head is a two handled vase. It is a constant reminder of Morton's rich heritage of pottery manufacturing for ninety-nine years.

The location where Morton Pottery Works, Morton Earthenware Company, Cliftwood Art Potteries, and Midwest Potteries operated is now a lumber yard and building supply store. The clay pits have been filled in and homes have been built there. A new, modern library has been built on the land that was home to the Morton Pottery Company. The two buildings that housed the American Art Potteries are still intact, but they have been altered and are not easily identified as the pottery buildings.

A ceramic shop, named Morton Pottery, operates in Morton currently, but it should not be considered an extension of the Rapp family's history. The owner did work at the Morton Pottery Company, and still has a few molds purchased at the bankruptcy auction in 1972. A variety of items is made there. However, emphasis is placed on the production of pumpkin novelties to promote Morton's claim to being the pumpkin capital of the world.

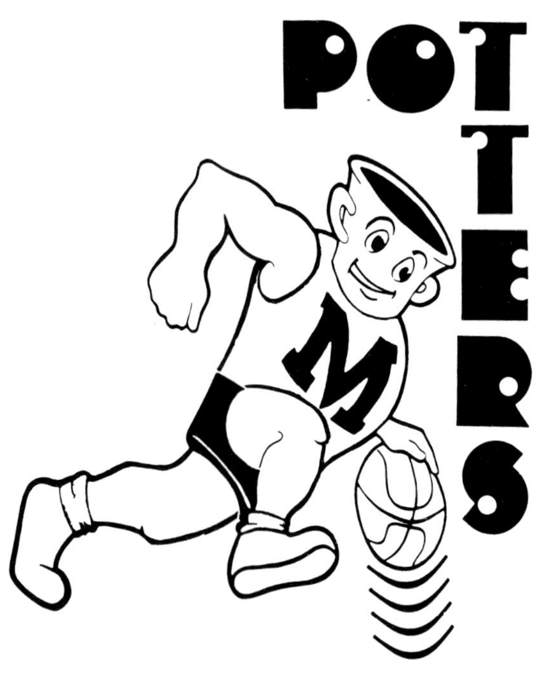